Gregory of Nazianzus on the Trinity and the Knowledge of God

OXFORD STUDIES IN HISTORICAL THEOLOGY

Series Editor
David C. Steinmetz, Duke University

Editorial Board
Irena Backus, Université de Genève
Robert C. Gregg, Stanford University
George M. Marsden, University of Notre Dame
Wayne A. Meeks, Yale University
Gerhard Sauter, Rheinische Friedrich-Wilhelms-Universität Bonn
Susan E. Schreiner, University of Chicago
John Van Engen, University of Notre Dame
Geoffrey Wainwright, Duke University
Robert L. Wilken, University of Virginia

EMPIRE OF SOULS
Robert Bellarmine and the Christian Commonwealth
Stefania Tutino

MARTIN BUCER'S DOCTRINE OF JUSTIFICATION
Reformation Theology and Early Modern Irenicism
Brian Lugioyo

CHRISTIAN GRACE AND PAGAN VIRTUE
The Theological Foundation of Ambrose's Ethics
J. Warren Smith

KARLSTADT AND THE ORIGINS OF THE EUCHARISTIC CONTROVERSY
A Study in the Circulation of Ideas
Amy Nelson Burnett

READING AUGUSTINE IN THE REFORMATION
The Flexibility of Intellectual Authority in Europe, 1500–1620
Arnoud S. Q. Visser

SHAPERS OF ENGLISH CALVINISM, 1660–1714
Variety, Persistence, and Transformation
Dewey D. Wallace, Jr.

THE BIBLICAL INTERPRETATION OF WILLIAM OF ALTON
Timothy Bellamah, OP

MIRACLES AND THE PROTESTANT IMAGINATION
The Evangelical Wonder Book in Reformation Germany
Philip M. Soergel

THE REFORMATION OF SUFFERING
Pastoral Theology and Lay Piety in Late Medieval and Early Modern Germany
Ronald K. Rittgers

CHRIST MEETS ME EVERYWHERE
Augustine's Early Figurative Exegesis
Michael Cameron

GOING DUTCH IN THE MODERN AGE
Abraham Kuyper's Struggle for a Free Church in the Netherlands
John H. Wood

CALVIN'S COMPANY OF PASTORS
Pastoral Care and Emerging Reformed Church, 1563–1609
Scott M. Manetsch

Gregory of Nazianzus on the Trinity and the Knowledge of God

In Your Light We Shall See Light

Christopher A. Beeley

OXFORD
UNIVERSITY PRESS

Oxford University Press, Inc., publishes works that further
Oxford University's objective of excellence
in research, scholarship, and education.

Oxford New York
Auckland Cape Town Dar es Salaam Hong Kong Karachi
Kuala Lumpur Madrid Melbourne Mexico City Nairobi
New Delhi Shanghai Taipei Toronto

With offices in
Argentina Austria Brazil Chile Czech Republic France Greece
Guatemala Hungary Italy Japan Poland Portugal Singapore
South Korea Switzerland Thailand Turkey Ukraine Vietnam

Copyright © 2008 by Christopher A. Beeley

Published by Oxford University Press, Inc.
198 Madison Avenue, New York, New York 10016

www.oup.com

First published as an Oxford University Press paperback, 2013.

Oxford is a registered trademark of Oxford University Press

All rights reserved. No part of this publication may be reproduced,
stored in a retrieval system, or transmitted, in any form or by any means,
electronic, mechanical, photocopying, recording, or otherwise,
without the prior permission of Oxford University Press.

Library of Congress Cataloging-in-Publication Data
Beeley, Christopher A.
Gregory of Nazianzus on the Trinity and the knowledge of God:
in your light we shall see light / Christopher A. Beeley.
   p. cm.—(Oxford studies in historical theology)
Includes bibliographical references and index.
ISBN 978-0-19-531397-0; 978-0-19-994887-1 (pbk.)
1. Gregory, of Nazianzus, Saint. 2. Trinity. 3. God
(Christianity)—Knowableness. I. Title
BR65.G66B44 2007
231'.044092—dc 22   2006030313

9 8 7 6 5 4 3 2 1

Printed in the United States of America
on acid-free paper

For Shannon

Πάντως δὲ καθάρθητε καὶ καθαίρεσθε, ὡς οὐδενὶ τοσοῦτον χαίρει Θεὸς ὅσον ἀνθρώπου διορθώσει καὶ σωτηρίᾳ, ὑπὲρ οὗ λόγος ἅπας καὶ ἅπαν μυστήριον· ἵνα γένησθε ὡς φωστῆρες ἐν κόσμῳ.

Above all, be purified and you shall be pure; for God rejoices in nothing so much as the correction and salvation of human beings, which is the purpose of every doctrine and every mystery. In this way you will become "like lights to the world" (Phil 2.15).
—St. Gregory of Nazianzus, *Oration* 39

[Ἡ Τρίας] ἣν δὴ μόνην εὐσέβειαν ἐγὼ καλῶ καὶ δόξαν σωτήριον.

I consider the Trinity the only true devotion and saving doctrine.
—*Oration* 43

Preface

This book is a study of the greatest theologian of the Christian fourth century and the subject he held most dear: St. Gregory of Nazianzus on the Holy Trinity. A man of exceptional learning and intellectual talent, Gregory Nazianzen (329–390) pioneered several new forms of Greek literature; he preserved numerous lines of classical poetry and composed thousands of his own; and he later became the chief model of Byzantine homiletical and prose style. Yet his greatest devotion in all of life was the doctrine and the worship of the Trinity. It was Gregory, more than anyone before him, who made the Trinity the centerpiece and the cardinal doctrine of orthodox Christianity. In recognition of his magisterial achievement, the Council of Chalcedon in 451 deemed him "the Theologian," a title that he shares only with St. John the Divine and the Byzantine monk St. Simeon the New Theologian, who was being compared to Gregory. In due time, Gregory the Theologian came to be regarded as one of the three "universal teachers" of Eastern Orthodoxy, together with St. Basil the Great, who was renowned for his monastic legislation, and the golden-mouthed preacher St. John Chrysostom. Gregory's immense impact on Christian tradition can be seen from the fact that his work is the most widely published in the Greek manuscript tradition, second only to the Bible.[1]

---

1. Noret, "Grégoire de Nazianze, l'auteur le plus cité après la Bible."

Since the late-nineteenth century Gregory of Nazianzus has been somewhat artificially grouped together with Basil and Gregory of Nyssa as the three "Cappadocian fathers,"[2] a designation that has tended to overstate their similarities and to obscure the sometimes painful differences that arose among them. One of the great lacunae of recent patristic scholarship has been the relative neglect of Gregory's work in comparison with the other two Cappadocians'; Basil's ecclesiastical labors and Gregory of Nyssa's philosophical mysticism seem to have appealed more to twentieth-century minds than Gregory Nazianzen's more properly theological achievement.[3] In the last forty years Gregory has been the subject of an increasing number of studies on biographical, literary, ascetical, and theological topics.[4] Thanks in large part to the critical editing of his orations and poems, which began in the late 1970s and continues still,[5] a new phase of Gregorian research emerged in the 1990s that included an extensive new biography and a full commentary on the *Theological Orations*.[6] Meanwhile, the central focus of Gregory's theological endeavors—the doctrine of the Trinity—has yet to be thoroughly examined.[7]

For Gregory Nazianzen, the doctrine of the Trinity is not a quasi-mathematical problem about how three things can be one, nor the abstract logic of the Christian God, as it is often imagined in modern theology and popular culture. Rather, it represents the fundamental origin and goal of the Christian life,[8] and it involves a whole nexus of concerns that range from biblical interpretation and epistemology to the practicalities of Christian worship, asceticism, and pastoral ministry. Gregory's doctrine is what a modern might call both theological and spiritual at the same time, integrating in a seamless fabric what have more recently been distinguished as dogmatic and ascetical theology. In other words, Gregory's doctrine of the Trinity is at every point soteriological; it represents and seeks to promote salvation and life in

---

2. Particularly in Weiss, *Die grossen Kappadocier* (1872); Böhringer, *Drei Kappadozier* (1875); and Holl, *Amphilochius von Ikonium in seinem Verhältnis zu den grossen Kappadoziern* (1904).

3. See Louth, "The Cappadocians," p. 297.

4. For example, Bernardi, *La prédication*; Spidlík, *Grégoire de Nazianze*; Ruether, *Gregory of Nazianzus*; Norris, "Gregory Nazianzen's Doctrine of Jesus Christ"; Althaus, *Die Heilslehre*; Gregg, *Consolation Philosophy*; Winslow, *Dynamics of Salvation*; and Ellverson, *Dual Nature of Man*.

5. The letters were edited by Gallay in the 1960s.

6. McGuckin, *St. Gregory*; Norris, *Faith Gives Fullness*. See also Moreschini, *Filosofia e letteratura*; Trisoglio, *Gregorio di Nazianzo*; and the articles in the bibliography by Elm, Harrison, McGuckin, McLynn, and Norris.

7. As noted recently by Markschies, "Gibt es eine einheitliche 'kappadozische Trinitätstheologie'?" p. 210n60; see also Ayres, *Nicaea*, p. 244n2.

8. A point made years ago by Rowan Greer in his study of Irenaeus, Gregory of Nyssa, and Augustine, *Broken Lights and Mended Lives: Theology and Common Life in the Early Church*.

Christ. Accordingly, this book offers a comprehensive analysis of Gregory's Trinitarian doctrine as it is situated within his theological and practical vision of the Christian life. Beginning with the spiritual dialectic of purification and illumination, it examines Gregory's doctrine of Christ, the Holy Spirit, the Trinity, and pastoral ministry as part of a unified vision of Christian existence.

One of the most distinctive aspects of Gregory's work is its highly rhetorical and contextualized literary form. We will therefore give special attention to the historical situation and rhetorical stance of his texts, beginning with an introductory overview of his life, contexts, and theological endeavors. The main chapters of the book will then seek to expose Gregory's doctrine as clearly as possible in its fine detail and synthetic interconnections, and to correct several points of misinterpretation in current scholarship. In the course of the argument selective references are made to other theologians in order to highlight particular aspects of Gregory's work: above all to his great teacher, Origen. The conclusion will then offer a detailed account of Gregory's relationship to his predecessors and contemporaries and his seminal role in subsequent Christian tradition.

Unique among modern studies, this book interprets Gregory's doctrine on the basis of his entire corpus of orations, poems, and letters, rather than focusing primarily on the famous *Theological Orations* and Christological epistles, which have too easily been misunderstood when read in isolation from other texts. Gregory is a highly poetic writer who delights in expressing sophisticated theological ideas in terse, pithy phrases. It will therefore be important to make extensive direct quotations from his texts. Not only will this afford us the opportunity to hear from Gregory himself, but it will provide a chance to offer fresh translations of certain passages, which in several cases affect their interpretation significantly.

At this point a brief disclaimer on certain words and phrases is in order, to prevent the reader from being misled by the unique biases of recent scholarly debate. The adjective "Trinitarian"—as in "Trinitarian doctrine" or "Trinitarian theology"—is not meant to indicate any particular model, theory, or structure of the Trinity. It simply means something that pertains to the Trinity. The terms "Nicene" and "pro-Nicene" are used mainly to refer to figures and doctrines that are associated with the Creed and Council of Nicaea, rather than in a technical, doctrinal sense, in which case the term "Trinitarian" is normally used instead.[9] Finally, the term "experience" refers to the lived quality or the existential dimension of a thing—something that happens to one

---

9. A detailed explanation of this choice is given at p. 10n27.

or something that one undergoes; it often translates πάθος or πάσχειν in Gregory's texts. It is not meant to suggest a vague, generic feeling or attitude divorced from knowledge, language, or theology, as it has come to mean for many in the West since the Romantic period. As I will argue at length, Gregory's doctrine does not recognize the sort of division between knowledge and experience, theory and practice, or theology and spirituality to which many moderns are so accustomed.

It is my pleasure to record my gratitude to a number of people who have contributed to this book over the years. I am especially grateful to my friend, colleague, and former teacher Professor Brian Daley, SJ, of the University of Notre Dame, who directed the dissertation from which this book arose. I have benefited greatly from his enthusiastic support of the project since its inception, our ongoing collaboration on Gregory in recent years, and his sharing with me his own translations and introduction to Gregory's work while they were still in manuscript. I owe my heartfelt thanks to several other "Gregorians" who took a special interest in this book, each of whom read the full manuscript and offered encouragement and criticism at many points: John McGuckin, who also provided me with a copy of his biography of Gregory before it went to press; Frederick Norris, who shared some of his unpublished work on Gregory as well; and Susanna Elm and Verna Harrison, who were especially enthusiastic in the final hours. I also wish to express my thanks to my former teacher and predecessor at Yale, Rowan Greer, who first read my musings on Gregory's doctrine of the Trinity when I was a student at Yale Divinity School, and who graciously commented on the manuscript many years later. I am grateful to my other friends and colleagues who offered comments at various stages: Sarah Coakley, John Hare, David Kelsey, Andrew Louth, and Miroslav Volf. Thanks also to Martha Vinson, who shared with me a copy of her English translation of Gregory's orations before it was published in the Fathers of the Church series, and to those who participated in the workshop on Gregory's theology at the 2007 Oxford Patristics Conference. Though we do not agree on all points, I have learned a great deal from my generous colleagues, and I claim all responsibility for the book's shortcomings.

I am also grateful to Yale Divinity School students Frank Curry, Matthew Benton, Timothy Boerger, Veronica Tierney, and Anthony Sciubba for their diligent research assistance; to the librarians of the Yale Divinity Library, the Hesburgh Library at the University of Notre Dame, and the Leyburn Library at Washington and Lee University; and to Stacey Maples of the Yale University Map Collection for drawing the two maps. Thanks also to Cynthia Read and Gwen Colvin, my editors at Oxford University Press, who have been a great help in seeeing the book to publication. This book was published with the assistance of a grant from the Frederick W. Hilles Publication Fund of Yale University and a faculty research grant from Dean Harold Attridge of the Yale Divinity School. I also wish to acknowledge my gratitude to my parents, Robert A. Beeley and Susan Floyd Beeley, for their generous support of my graduate theological training.

My deepest thanks, finally, go to my wife, Shannon Murphy Beeley. For her unflagging support, affection, and good humor over years that this book came into being, I am grateful beyond measure. This book is dedicated to her.

Contents

Abbreviations, xv

Maps, xvii

Introduction: Gregory's Life and Work, 3

    329–359: Childhood and Education, 5
    359–375: Ministry in Cappadocia, 10
    Excursus: The Fourth-Century Doctrinal
       Controversies, 16
    379–381: Ministry in Constantinople, 34
    381–390: Final Years in Cappadocia, 54

1. God and the Theologian, 63

    The Purification of the Theologian, 65
    Illumination: The Knowledge of the Incomprehensible
       God, 90
    Conclusion, 110

2. Jesus Christ, the Son of God, 115

    Christology and Divinization, 116
    The Identity of Christ, 122
    The Unity of Christ, 128
    Christological Spirituality, 143

3. The Holy Spirit, 153

    The Development of Gregory's Pneumatology: 372–380, 156
    Τάξις Θεολογίας: The Witness of Scripture and the Order of Theology, 169
    "A Truly Golden and Saving Chain": The Direct Proof of the Spirit's Divinity, 174
    Spiritual Exegesis and the Rhetoric of Piety, 180

4. The Trinity, 187

    Theology of the Divine Economy, 194
    The Monarchy of God the Father, 201
    Conceiving of the Trinity, 217
    Participation in the Trinity, 228

5. Pastoral Ministry, 235

    The Art of Arts and the Science of Sciences, 241
    Pastoral Experience and Priestly Virtue, 247
    Excursus: On the Love of the Poor, 254
    The Training of Holy Scripture, 258
    The Administration of the Holy Trinity, 263

Conclusion: Gregory among the Fathers, 271

    Origen, 271
    Gregory Thaumaturgus, 274
    Athanasius and Didymus, 277
    Apollinarius, 285
    Basil of Caesarea, 292
    Gregory of Nyssa, 303
    The Homoiousians and Eastern Theological Tradition, 309
    Damasus and the West, 317
    Gregory the Theologian, 319

Bibliography, 325

Index of Theological Topics in Gregory's Works, 355

Index of Citations to the Works of Gregory Nazianzen, 361

General Index, 375

Index to Biblical Citations, 397

Abbreviations

Gregory's orations are cited in notes and parenthetical references by oration and section number (e.g., 31.3); his letters and poems are indicated by the prefix *Ep.* or *Carm.* (e.g., *Ep.* 101.4; *Carm.* 1.1.2.57–63). The poem *De vita sua* (*Carm.* 2.1.11) is abbreviated *DVS*. One of the greatest obstacles to the study of Gregory's theology is the unsystematic nature of his literary corpus. In order to foster greater research, an index is proved which lists key texts according to theological topic, in addition to a serial index of passages from Gregory's work and a general index to the book.

For abbreviations to ancient sources, see the bibliography.

ACW   *Ancient Christian Writers* (Westminster, Md., and New York: Newman, 1946–).
ANF   *The Ante-Nicene Fathers: The Writings of the Fathers Down to A.D. 325.* (Edinburgh: 1864; repr., Peabody, Mass.: Hendrickson, 1995).
CSEL *Corpus Scriptorum Ecclesiasticorum Latinorum* (Vienna: C. Gerodi, etc., 1866–).
ET   English translation
FC   *The Fathers of the Church* (New York: Fathers of the Church; Washington, D.C.: Catholic University of America Press, 1947–).
GCS   *Die griechischen christlichen Schriftsteller der ersten drei Jahrhunderte* (Leipzig, J. C. Hinrichs, 1897–).

Lampe   *A Patristic Greek Lexicon.* Ed. G. W. H. Lampe (Oxford: Clarendon, 1961).

LCL   *Loeb Classical Library* (London: Heinemann; Cambridge, Mass.: Harvard University Press, 1912–).

LSJ   *A Greek-English Lexicon.* Comp. Henry George Liddell, Robert Scott, and Henry Stuart Jones, with Roderick McKenzie (9th ed.; Oxford: Clarendon, 1940).

NPNF   *A Select Library of Nicene and Post-Nicene Fathers of the Christian Church* (Series 1–2; Edinburgh: 1886– ; repr., Peabody, Mass.: Hendrickson, 1995).

PG   *Patrologiae Cursus Completus Series Graeca.* Ed. J. P. Migne (161 vols.; Paris: 1857–1912).

SC   *Sources Chrétiennes* (Paris: Cerf, 1941–).

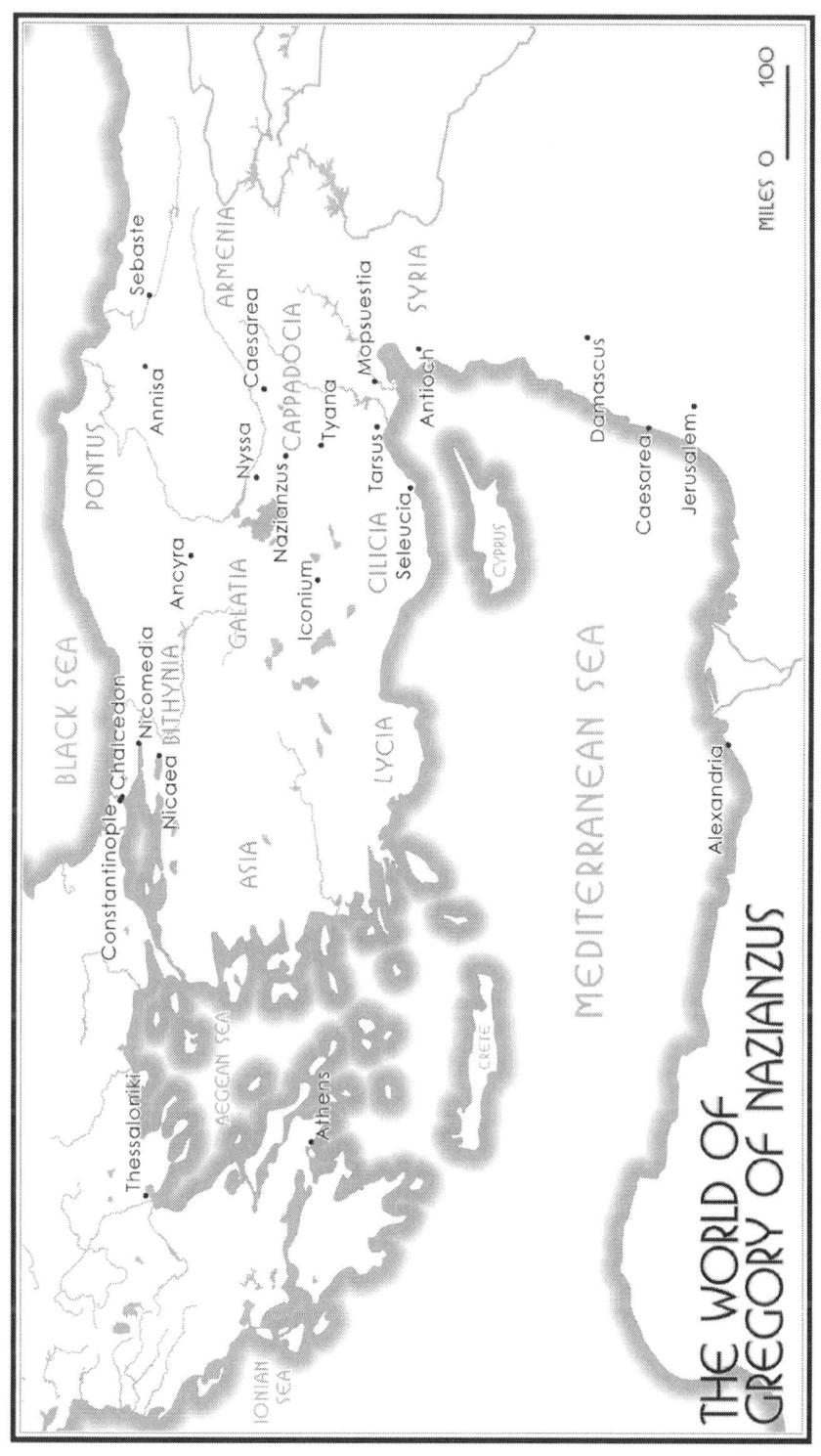

MAP 1. The World of Gregory of Nazianzus (Cartography by Stacey Maples of the Yale University Map Collection).

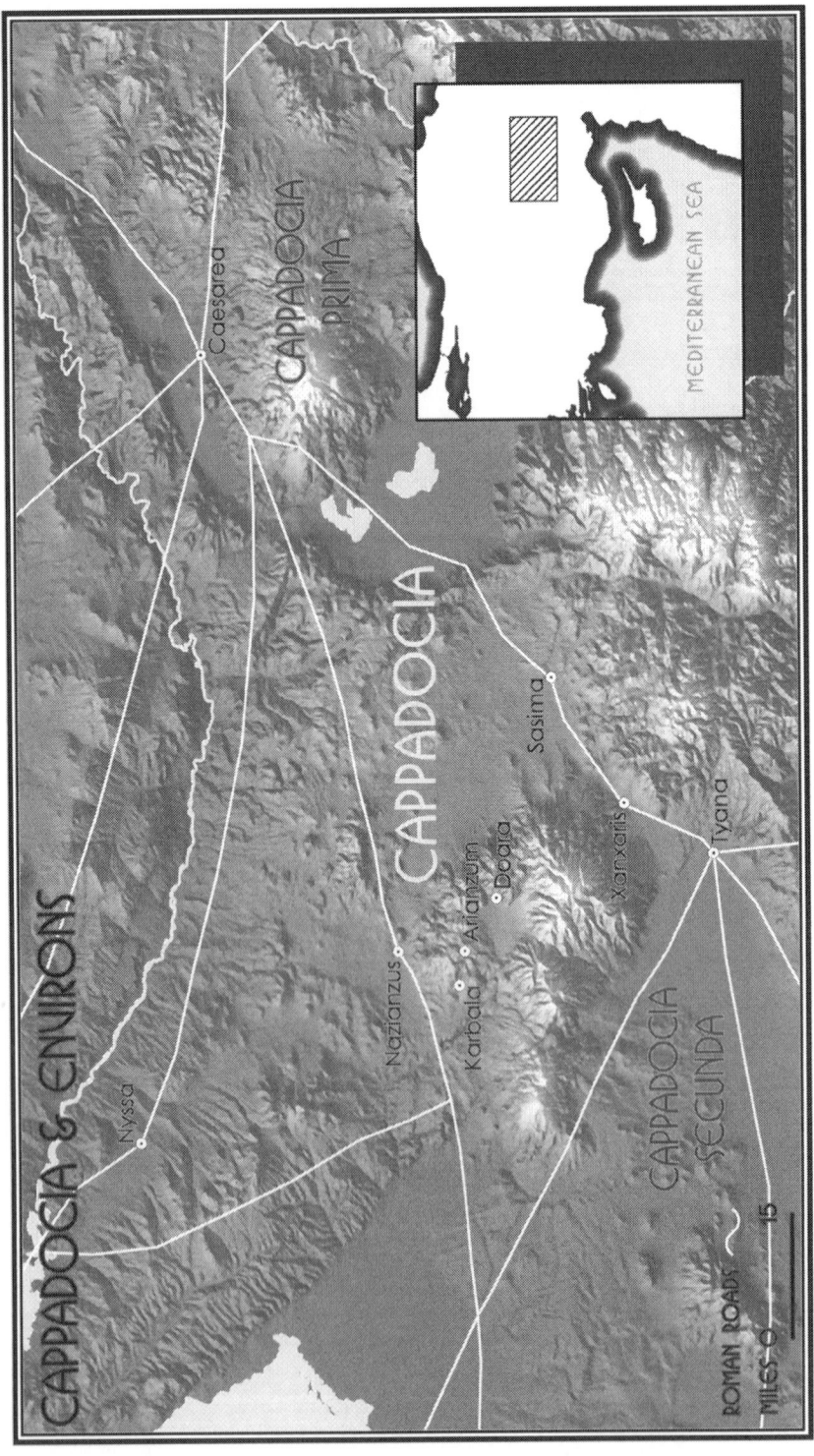

MAP 2. Cappadocia and Environs (Cartography by Stacey Maples of the Yale University Map Collection).

Gregory of Nazianzus on the Trinity and the Knowledge of God

Introduction

Gregory's Life and Work

The work of Gregory Nazianzen has long inspired Christian worshippers, pastors, and theologians. From his orthodox doctrine of the Trinity and the person of Christ to his seminal teaching on the practices of asceticism and pastoral care, Gregory quickly became one of the most formative writers in the history of the Church. Yet, paradoxically, modern interpreters have often neglected to study his work to any great extent, in comparison with that of other figures who have seemed more accessible. Both phenomena can be largely explained by the nonsystematic and rhetorical character of his literary corpus and the refinement of his Greek style. Most early Christian literature is nonsystematic in literary form (though not in theological ideas), consisting of homilies, letters, and apologetic or polemical treatises, which reflect specific social situations. This is especially true of Gregory Nazianzen: among the great patristic writers, Gregory's corpus stands out as being almost entirely occasional. While they are organized on a pattern that loosely follows Origen's *On First Principles,* Gregory's famous *Theological Orations* (Ors. 27–31) are essentially a point-by-point response to objections that have been raised to his doctrine, and they are presented in a highly rhetorical fashion rather than as a detached, positive exposition. His series of seven dogmatic poems known as the *Poemata Arcana* (*Carm.* 1.1.1–5, 7–9) also mirrors Origen's plan,[1] yet it, too, speaks directly to the theological issues of the day. Although he is remarkably comprehensive and consistent as a theologian, Gregory preferred to approach his craft from a literary and rhetorical perspective—as a great orator and a man of letters—rather than as a philosopher writing systematic treatises. He produced no full-scale systematic work like *On First Principles*, which he knew well, but chose instead to assemble a corpus that represents a wide variety of Greek literary forms, including several of his own invention, in order to provide an exemplary body of Christian literature for clergy, laity, and young students at a time when the Church was trying to make inroads in a society still defined by ancient Greek culture. Gregory assembled a collection of forty-four orations, which combine biblical proclamation and traditional Christian doctrine with the best of Greek philosophical rhetoric, including sermons for major feasts of the Church, panegyrics on notable Christian leaders, funeral orations for friends and relatives, polemical invectives, and doctrinal disputations. He published a set of 249 letters on various subjects in a range of styles, and he left some 17,000 lines of poetry, comprising Homeric hymns, narratives of his own life (including the first extant autobiography in poetic form), didactic expositions, prayers, epitaphs, and intimate reflections on the sorrows and follies of life.[2] Gregory's doctrine of the Trinity is thus embedded in a complex body of work that requires some orientation if one is going to navigate it with much success. The purpose of this introduction is to set Gregory's corpus within the context of his life and labors, highlighting those works and events that are most germane to the study of his Trinitarian doctrine.[3]

Gregory emerged from a rustic, provincial network of Christian landholders in the Roman province of Cappadocia to become the leading theologian of his day and the chief ecclesiastical leader of the Eastern Church. His life roughly corresponds with the crucial period of Church history in which the orthodox doctrine of the Trinity was articulated in its classical form, from the Council of Nicaea in 325 to the Council of Constantinople in 381 and the following decade, in which a series of imperial decrees made pro-Nicene

---

1. On the structure and purpose of the *Poemata Arcana*, see Daley, "Systematic Theology in Homeric Dress." See also the introduction and commentary by Moreschini and Sykes, *St. Gregory of Nazianzus, Poemata Arcana*.

2. The nineteenth-century Benedictine editor Caillau organized Gregory's poems by category, including those on theology (*Carm.* 1.1) and Christian morals (1.2), poems on Gregory himself (2.1), and those addressed to others (2.2).

3. The standard biography is now McGuckin, *St. Gregory*. Still useful are Gallay, *La vie*; Bernardi, *La prédication*. See also Norris, *Faith Gives Fullness*, pp. 1–12; Gómez-Villegas, *Gregorio de Nazianzo*; and the introduction to Daley, *Gregory of Nazianzus*, pp. 1–60. I generally follow McGuckin's revised chronology.

Christianity the official religion of the state. Gregory's life can be conveniently divided into four major periods:

329–359   Childhood in Nazianzus and education abroad (through age 30)
359–379   Priestly and episcopal ministry in Nazianzus, followed by a four-year retreat in Seleucia (age 30 to 50)
379–381   Episcopal ministry in Constantinople; metropolitan bishop and president of the Council of Constantinople in 381 (age 50 to 52)
381–390   Retirement; ecclesiastical and literary activities in Nazianzus (age 52 to 61)

329–359: Childhood and Education

Gregory was born around the year 329 as the oldest son and middle child of a landed Christian family.[4] The family estate of Karbala, near the village of Arianzus, stood ten miles from the larger town of Nazianzus, where Gregory's father (also Gregory) had recently been consecrated bishop. Although Cappadocia was a fairly remote province—residents of Constantinople would later make fun of Gregory's country accent—Nazianzus lay on the major road connecting the capital with the emperor's eastern headquarters at Antioch in Syria, keeping it well connected with the affairs of the wider world (though only through the late 370s).[5] Exceptionally bright, with extraordinary gifts for language, literature, and communication, Gregory was raised as a serious Christian and provided with the best education that his parents could afford.[6] His mother, Nonna, came from an established Christian family that identified itself with the old Cappadocian tradition established by Origen's disciple Gregory Thaumaturgus (the "Wonder Worker"). According to Gregory, Nonna provided the theological backbone of the household; in his funeral oration for his father, Gregory calls her the spiritual leader (ἀρχηγός) of the family and highly extols her Christian virtue (18.6–7). Nonna was responsible

---

4. On the scholarly debate surrounding the date of Gregory's birth, see Norris, *Faith Gives Fullness*, p. 1; Hanson, *Search for the Christian Doctrine of God*, p. 701. Proposals range from 325 to 330, though the general consensus is now that Gregory was born in 329 or 330. See Gallay, *La vie*, pp. 25–27.
5. After Valens' tour in 378, no emperor visited Cappadocia until Heraclius in the seventh century. Van Dam, *Kingdom of Snow*, pp. 154–155.
6. Much of the basic family narrative can be found in *Or.* 18.5–43.

for converting Gregory the Elder from what appears to have been a Jewish-Christian sect called the *Hypsistarii* (18.5) to orthodox Christianity (7.4; 18.11). It was Nonna, "the very mouthpiece of truth" (*DVS* 64), who oversaw Gregory's Christian formation, and who likely gave him an early sense of the orthodoxy to which he would devote the rest of his life. Gregory speaks of having been raised among people of virtue, ardently studying the Scriptures and striving for spiritual maturity (*DVS* 95–100). As he later recounts it (*DVS* 68–92; *Or.* 18.11), one of the most significant events of his early life was Nonna's dedication of him to God. Fearing that she would bear no male children, Nonna promised God that if she bore a son she would return the gift she had received. God then granted Nonna a dream of Gregory's appearance and the name he was to have. When Gregory was born Nonna dedicated him to God as she had promised, "like a second Samuel."

If Nonna was responsible for Gregory's early faith, it was his father who played the greatest role in the external affairs of his life. Gregory the Elder (ca. 275–374) was bishop of Nazianzus for forty-five years, from 329 to 374, spanning three-quarters of his son's life. While the elder Gregory was a caring and diligent pastor, he was not particularly gifted as a theologian. In 360 or 361 he unwittingly signed the homoian creed of Constantinople, which led to a schism in the local church.[7] Recognizing that he needed the support of his more intellectually gifted son—and probably also thinking it was time for him to put his expensive education to some use—Gregory the Elder ordained Gregory a priest against his will at the Epiphany liturgy of 362. He subsequently conspired with Basil in Gregory's unhappy consecration as bishop of Sasima. Gregory therefore had mixed feelings about his father's authority, even though he knew that he was the more gifted theologian.

Gregory's older sister, Gorgonia (ca. 326–369/70), showed herself to be a strong woman like her mother, excelling in ascetical practice and generosity to the poor, and likewise having a converting effect on her husband, Alypius. Gregory's younger brother, Caesarius (ca. 331/32–368), accompanied him for the first half of Gregory's education and later pursued a career in medicine. He was for a time court physician to Emperor Julian in Constantinople, and died prematurely in the plague that followed an earthquake in Bythinia. Caesarius was the worldly-wise brother who gave the more introverted Gregory an extra sense of confidence, and his death came as a very hard blow. Gregory delivered funeral

---

7. For a detailed account of the doctrinal controversies surrounding Gregory's career, see the excursus below, pp. 16–34.

orations for each of his siblings (*Or.* 7 on Caesarius; *Or.* 8 on Gorgonia).[8] His oration for Gorgonia is the earliest extant piece of Christian hagiography for a woman;[9] it presents her as nothing less than a Christian holy woman, analogous in many ways to Basil and Gregory of Nyssa's sister Macrina, which was an unusual description at this time for a married woman.

Gregory and Nonna saw to it that their sons received an excellent education. When Gregory was about thirteen, he and Caesarius studied with the local grammaticus in Nazianzus (7.6), followed by a brief period under the tutelage of their uncle Amphilochius in Iconium. In his uncle's house Gregory probably met his cousin Theodosia, who later sponsored his ministry in Constantinople, as well as his cousin and future episcopal colleague, Amphilochius the Younger (bishop of Iconium 373–395). Around 345 the two brothers moved to the capital city of Caesarea, where they studied in the school of grammar and rhetoric. It was most likely at this time, around the age of sixteen, that Gregory first met Basil (43.13–14). Two years later, in 347, Gregory then began a long period of study abroad, beginning in Caesarea in Palestine, the location of Origen's school and library. In this great center of Christian learning, Gregory may have first become acquainted with the theological and ecclesiastical conflict that was beginning to engulf the international Church. Here, too, he would have come into contact with the legacy of Origen, if he had not already encountered it at home. From Origen Gregory learned the rudiments and the great heights of Christian theology, and he found in Origen a clear model of the spiritual and intellectual dimensions of his own life. Like Origen, Gregory valued above all things a life devoted to study, prayer, and Christian asceticism, or "philosophy"; he, too, labored to feed the Church with his teaching from this spiritual center; he sought to bring the best of pagan Greek letters to the service of Christianity; and his work conveys a mystical spirit remarkably similar to his master's.[10] In Caesarea, Gregory continued his literary and rhetorical study under the rhetorician Thespesius (7.6).[11] We may assume that, as a Second Sophistic rhetorician, Thespesius taught Gregory a combination of philosophy, literature, literary criticism, and the art of persuasion. In all

---

8. See also *Ep.* 30 and *Epit.* 6, 10, and 19 on Caesarius.

9. See Elm, "Gregory's Women." Precedents can be found in the early martyr literature, e.g., the *Martyrdom of Perpetua and Felicitas*.

10. On Origen's influence on Gregory, see Moreschini, "Influenze di Origene"; *Filosofia e letteratura*, p. 309; and Trigg, "Knowing God." Specific points of influence will be noted throughout the book; see also the summary assessment in the conclusion.

11. See also *Carm.* 2.1.1; Jerome, *Vir. illus.* 113.14.

likelihood, it was Thespesius who first introduced Gregory to the philosophical form of rhetoric that he would practice throughout his career.[12] Decades later, Gregory writes of a "passionate love of letters" that overcame him as a youth (*DVS* 112–113)—a love that he would retain until his death.

Gregory spent the following year in Alexandria. During his visit the renowned Origenist Didymus the Blind may have been head of the city's famous catechetical school. Yet, while there are some similarities between their work, there is no indication that Gregory was influenced by Didymus, or even that he knew him.[13] Although Athanasius was in residence during Gregory's stay, he does not appear to have directly influenced Gregory's work either. It is often assumed that the Cappadocians read Athanasius' work and essentially picked up where he left off, bearing his theological mantle in the latter part of the fourth century. However, scholars have more recently observed that the issue is more complicated and difficult to determine with any accuracy.[14] The panegyric that Gregory delivered in memory of Athanasius over thirty years later indicates that he neither knew Athanasius personally nor was acquainted with his works (*Or.* 21).[15] From Alexandria Gregory finally traveled to Athens, where he spent a full decade—the better part of his twenties—studying advanced rhetoric and literature. It was a time that he later described with great nostalgia: "The fame that goes with letters was the only thing that absorbed me. East and West combined to procure me that, and Athens, the glory of Greece" (*Carm.* 2.1.1.96–97).

The second most formative event in Gregory's early life, after having been dedicated by his mother, occurred while he was sailing from Alexandria to Athens in November 348.[16] In a violent storm near Cyprus, the ship was badly tossed and nearly collided with another vessel. The prospect of imminent death reminded him that he had not yet been baptized, and he feared that he might never be cleansed by "those purifying waters by which we are made divine" (*DVS* 164). Gregory writes that he tore his clothes, prostrated himself, and prayed to Christ that if he would deliver him, he would live for Christ from then on (*DVS* 198). The storm subsided, and when Gregory arrived in Athens he made a profound commitment of himself to Christ. In his poems Gregory describes a dream in which he is granted a vision of the light of the Trinity,

---

12. On which see Norris, *Faith Gives Fullness*, pp. 17–39 and passim.
13. On Gregory's relationship to Didymus, see the conclusion.
14. E.g., Hanson, *Search for the Christian Doctrine of God*, pp. 678–679.
15. See this book's conclusion for a fuller assessment of Gregory's relationship to Athanasius.
16. Gregory's three accounts of the incident are in *DVS* 121–209; *De rebus suis* 2.1.1.307–321; *Or.* 18.31.

while accompanied by the figures of Wisdom and Chastity.[17] The vision gave him "a divine and burning love for the life of wisdom" which would lead him "up on high, transfigured in light, ... to stand in the radiance of the Immortal Trinity."[18] As a result of this vision, he says, "I died to the world and the world to me."[19] These narrations seem to provide a formal account of his choice of profession, as an educated, young Roman would have learned to do: so Gregory commits himself to a life of Christian philosophy. Judging from his report of the event in his funeral oration for his father (18.31)[20] and from the ascetical practice that he undertook at this time, the vision suggests that Gregory was baptized upon his arrival in Athens.[21] Gregory's account thus speaks of the commitment to ascetical practice that baptism had come to involve for serious-minded Christians in the late fourth century.[22]

Having thus recommitted himself to Christ, Gregory began his studies in Athens together with Basil, who had traveled there from Byzantium (43.14). Together they shared this new life of Christian discipleship, while they also trained as professional orators, and so enjoyed the happiest time of their friendship. Gregory later writes that they were "brought together by God and a desire for higher things," as they "shared all things in common, and one soul united our two separate bodies" (*DVS* 229–232). However, to Gregory's surprise and great disappointment, Basil unexpectedly left Athens around 356 and returned home to Caesarea. Gregory continued his studies in philosophical rhetoric until 358 with the pagan Himerius and the Christian Prohaeresius, who also taught the emperor Julian.[23] By the end of his stay, Gregory had distinguished himself to such an extent that he was offered one of the three funded positions in Athens as a teacher of rhetoric.[24]

---

17. *Carm.* 2.1.1.195–212 *De rebus suis*; 2.1.45. 191–269 *Carmen lugubre*.
18. *Carm.* 2.1.45. 261–262.
19. *Carm.* 2.1.1.202.
20. "We became an offering to God on account of that danger [the storm], because we had promised ourselves to God if we were saved, and when we had been saved, we gave ourselves to him."
21. Benoît, *Saint Grégoire*, pp. 47–48; Baronius, *Dissertationes theologicae*, t. 15, p. 376; and McGuckin, *St. Gregory*, p. 55 and n88. Gregory's seventh-century biographer, Gregory the Presbyter (*V. Greg. Naz.*;*PG* 35.257), dates Gregory's baptism to his return to Cappadocia in 358, based on little evidence. This dating has since been followed by Clémencet (*PG* 35.173A), Tillemont (*Mémoires*), Gallay (*La vie*, p. 67 and n3), Hanson (*Search for the Christian Doctrine of God*, p. 701), and Meehan (*FC* 75, p. 35n24). However, the reference in *De vita sua* to "preliminary initiations to greater mysteries" (*DVS* 276) at that time, which has been taken to refer to Gregory's delay of his baptism until his return to Cappadocia, is better understood as referring to Gregory's lingering decision about whether to adopt the active or the contemplative form of life, and whether to abandon the public practice of rhetoric. The lines that follow report that he decided on a middle way, combining the two (*DVS* 300–311).
22. McGuckin, *St. Gregory*, p. 75.
23. Socrates, *HE* 4.26; Sozomen, *HE* 6.17.
24. See Libanius, *Or.* 1.24–25; 2.14; Norris, *Faith Gives Fullness*, p. 5n29.

359–375: Ministry in Cappadocia

Gregory returned to Cappadocia in 358 or 359 at the age of thirty (*DVS* 239). He taught rhetoric in Nazianzus for a short time, possibly to fulfill local, familial obligations,[25] and he made several visits to see Basil in Pontus, where the two men continued their monastic practice of study and prayer.[26] During the first years of his return to Cappadocia, Gregory's formation in strongly Trinitarian,[27] Origenist Christianity seems to have been largely completed, at least in its basic outline. Sometime between 358 and 362 he and Basil compiled an anthology of Origen's writings on biblical exegesis and the freedom of the will known as the *Philocalia*, a work that remains our only source for the Greek text of certain passages in *On First Principles* books 3 and 4, several homilies and commentaries, and selections from *Against Celsus*. It is unclear exactly how the two men influenced each other at this point, but Basil's early major work, *Against Eunomius*, written probably in 363 in response to Eunomius' *Apology* of 360–361, certainly reflects their common labors.[28] In this work Basil defends the proclamation of the full divinity of Christ against Eunomius in a way that

---

25. On the motivations of Gregory's teaching of rhetoric in Nazianzus, see McLynn, "Among the Hellenists."

26. The name "Annisa" ("Annesi" or "Annesa") for Basil's family's estate in Pontus, based on a singular reference in Basil's *Ep.* 3, is uncertain and may possibly refer to a Cappadocian locale. See Huxley, "Saint Basil the Great and Anisa"; Rousseau, *Basil*, p. 62n7, with additional bibliography. In the absence of further information, I have accepted the conventional name; see this book's map section.

27. I use the term "Trinitarian" or "strongly Trinitarian" to refer to the confession of the full divinity of the Son and the Holy Spirit and the unity and shared Divinity, or divine being, of the Trinity, which is articulated in various ways by theologians of different regional traditions. I use "Nicene" or "pro-Nicene" not as a normative doctrinal term, as do Hanson (*Search for the Christian Doctrine of God*), Behr (*Nicene Faith*), and Ayres (*Nicaea*), but to refer to the explicit adherence to the doctrine or Creed of the Council of Nicaea as a universal conciliar standard of the faith. I do not adopt the definition of pro-Nicene doctrine found in Ayres' *Nicaea* (see esp. pp. 236–240), because it is overly technical in a way that distorts many of the theologians it aims to describe. Ayres' second defining point, that "the eternal generation of the Son occurs within the unitary and incomprehensible divine being," is esp. un-Gregorian. It is important to differentiate "Trinitarian" from "pro-Nicene" because (a) at this point Gregory and other Asian theologians do not identify themselves with Nicaea with any consistency or determinative theological sense; (b) when he does cast in his lot with the wider pro-Nicene movement, Gregory's doctrine retains the defining character of the Asian theological tradition (later called homoiousian, distinct from homoian and heterousian doctrine), which has strong roots in the earlier Eusebian tradition that famously *opposed* Nicaea; (c) Gregory identifies himself with Nicaea loosely and without anything near the frequency, consistency, or determinative level of definition that we find in, e.g., Athanasius or Damasus; and therefore (d) the distinctive terminology and phrasing of Nicaea—that the Son is "of one being with the Father" (ὁμοούσιος τῷ Πατρί) and is begotten "from the being of the Father" (ἐκ τῆς οὐσίας τοῦ Πατρός)—is of limited value in understanding Gregory's doctrine.

28. The prevalent view that Basil is the major source for Gregory's work—see, e.g., Markschies, "Gibt es eine einheitliche 'kappadozische Trinitätstheologie'?" p. 210, following Holl, *Amphilochius*, pp. 158–159—must be thoroughly reconsidered.

resembles Gregory's work up to a point. In particular, Basil addresses the nature of theological language and the identities of the Father, Son, and Holy Spirit.[29]

Several events occurred in the first years of Gregory's adulthood in Cappadocia that dramatically altered the course of his life. Under the sponsorship of Emperor Constantius, a synod in Constantinople in 360 promulgated an anti-Nicene, homoian doctrine of Christ—one opposed to the faith of Gregory's upbringing and of his father's church in Nazianzus—as the official creed of the empire. In the same year the heterousian theologian Eunomius was consecrated bishop of Cyzicus, and by 361 he produced his *Apology* defending a radically subordinationist doctrine, such as he had presented to the synod of 360. To make matters worse, by the spring of 361 Gregory's father inadvertently signed the homoian creed of Constantinople, causing a number of local monks to withdraw from communion with him and thus placing the local church in schism. On November 3, 361, Constantius then died, and his successor, the Emperor Julian, immediately began a systematic effort to obstruct the Christian Church and restore the ancient Greek cults. Needless to say, these developments dealt a severe blow to the nascent pro-Nicene movement, with which Gregory and many other Christians in Asia Minor had recently begun to align themselves.

The event that brought them all home to Gregory occurred when his father forcibly ordained him a priest at Epiphany 362, to secure his assistance with the fractured local church. Gregory later describes his ordination as "a terrible shock" and "tyrannical behavior" at the hands of his father (*DVS* 337, 345), and it has long been the accepted view that he despised the public service of ordained ministry because it deprived him of the contemplative solitude that he so enjoyed. Yet Gregory's protestations that he never desired the authority imposed on him all appear in heavily apologetic works that seek to defend that same authority when it was being questioned after 381; such complaints, moreover, are a standard tactic of Hellenistic political rhetoric intended for this very purpose. Apart from these remarks, it is plain that he cared deeply about the direction and leadership of the Church, and he made numerous sacrifices over the course of his career to make his influence felt. For the time being, he returned to Pontus for a further period of study and prayer with Basil. The two men reflected on the troubled state of the Church and on their own sense of responsibility, as highly trained, young Christian intellectuals, to take part in its leadership. During this time (if not earlier) Gregory fashioned his characteristic ascetical theory of an

---

29. See this book's conclusion for an examination of the relationship between Gregory's and Basil's work.

ideal "middle path" that combines quiet study and public service to others.[30] When he returned to Nazianzus at Easter 362, he came with both a renewed sense of personal commitment to the priesthood and a carefully considered understanding of the nature of Christian leadership. (Basil's turn would come soon enough; he was ordained a priest in Caesarea by Bishop Eusebius the following year, and by 370 he was bishop of the city.) As he took up his new pastoral responsibilities, Gregory devoted his first three published orations to explaining his flight and return, reflecting on the nature of priestly ministry, mending the local schism, and preparing for the assault on the Church that the emperor had set in motion.[31] Gregory's *Oration* 2 is an extensive study of the nature of the priesthood, the first of its kind in extant Christian literature, and the major source of later patristic treatises on the ministry; we will consider it in detail in chapter 5. In an effort at damage control, Gregory appeals to the local monks, in *Oration* 3, to renounce their differences, return to his father's flock, and leave it to Gregory to craft a theological resolution (3.7). This oration marks the first of several instances in which Gregory indicates his awareness that his theological capabilities exceed those of his father. Thus, despite the conventional view of his ecclesiastical ambivalence, Gregory began his priestly ministry determined to renew the leadership of the Church, and particularly the central place that a fulsome doctrine of the Trinity must hold in it.

Gregory's strong sense of his own theological and ecclesiastical leadership can be seen in the events of the next two years. In the midsummer of 362 Julian formally banned Christians from teaching rhetoric and Greek literature in the empire,[32] and Gregory immediately launched a counterattack. He wrote to his brother, asking him to resign as court physician on account of the scandal that his association with Julian was causing in the church of Nazianzus (*Ep.* 7), and in 362–363 he wrote two long invectives *Against Julian* (*Ors.* 4–5), which he signed in his own name and Basil's.[33] In these long orations, which he prob-

---

30. On Gregory's combination of monastic retreat and public service to the Church, see Gautier, *La retraite*; McLynn, "Self-Made Holy Man," p. 464; and below, pp. 74–75, 159.

31. In the winter of 361–362, Julian sent his uncle to restore the pagan cults in Antioch. On the way, he may have provoked a local Cappadocian reaction, including the destruction of a temple to Fortune in Caesarea. See Gregory's *Or.* 2.87 ("I do not fear the war that is coming from the outside, nor that fulfillment of evil, the beast that is rising up now against the churches"); 4.92; Van Dam, *Kingdom of Snow*, p. 190.

32. See *C. Th.* 13.3.5, which is sometimes credited with this enactment, although it does not actually mention Christians and indeed bears a different context. However, Ammianus Marcellinus clearly criticizes Julian for having prohibited Christian teachers by the time of his early residence in Antioch, which began in July 362 (*Amm. Marc.* 22.10.7). Julian's *Ep.* 36, which does mention the proscription, may reflect the text of a lost edict decreed not long after June 17. In any event, the legislation was clearly enacted in some form. See Friend, *Rise of Christianity*, p. 612n58; Matthews, *Laying Down the Law*, pp. 274–275.

33. "Basil and Gregory send these words to you" (*Or.* 5.39).

ably never delivered orally, Gregory gives an account of the fate of orthodox Christianity since Constantine, and he defends the place of Christians in Greek society and culture. In particular he argues for the superiority of Christianity to Greek religion and philosophy, and he characterizes the Church as the community that supremely exemplifies the social virtue of *philanthropia*.[34] In an oration to the Nazianzen church in late 362 (*Or.* 15), Gregory urged his congregation to prepare for greater persecution under Julian. Concerned to strengthen the Church throughout the region, Gregory wrote to Basil and encouraged him to join the Caesarean clergy under the new metropolitan, Eusebius (*Ep.* 8.4). Later in the year Gregory then traveled to Caesarea to recommend Basil to Eusebius in person, and to seek Basil's support for his efforts to repair the continuing schism in Nazianzus. On his return home Gregory appears to have accomplished this reconciliation in his *Oration 6*, the *First Oration on Peace*, which reflects an even higher degree of theological brokering than before, and contains a brief but important passage on the Trinity (6.22). In 363, Gregory also wrote to Basil's younger brother Gregory of Nyssa, on the urging of their older sister Macrina, to persuade him to abandon his career as a professional rhetor and to devote himself instead to the service of the Church as a priest (*Ep.* 11). In this series of gestures toward his friends and family we can see already the extent of Gregory's commitment to the Church's leadership.

Circumstances again shifted when Julian suddenly died in 363. He was succeeded briefly by the Nicene emperor Jovian, who reigned for only a year, followed by the long reign of the homoian Valens, who became augustus of the Eastern empire in 364. Gregory's instrumental role in the Caesarean church continued for several years. In 365 Eusebius invited him to a theological debate with Valens' imperial retinue, which traveled to the area to examine the confession of the Cappadocian church. Gregory used the occasion to secure Basil's reinstatement in the Caesarean clergy, after a rift had developed between him and Eusebius (*Ep.* 16–19; *Or.* 43.31). Together Gregory and Basil worsted Valens and his court rhetors in theological debate (43.32)—a performance they would repeat in 372, when Basil was bishop.[35] In the wake of a Cappadocian famine in the late 360s, Gregory played a key part in a social project of lasting significance: the development of a hospice and medical facility for the destitute poor on Basil's family's estate outside Caesarea. In addition to apartments for the bishop

---

34. On the history and nature of Greek and Christian philanthropy, see Daley, "Building a New City."
35. It was with reference to this second debate that Gregory immortalized (and possibly invented to some extent) Basil's legendary display of episcopal *parrhesia* before Valens' deputy Modestus (*Or.* 43.49–50).

and travelers, the πτωχοτροφεῖον, as Basil called it,[36] was a place to feed and care for the poor and where the sick could receive medical attention. Gregory delivered *Oration 14 On the Love of the Poor*—one of several sermons on the subject by the Cappadocians—possibly in multiple locations for the purpose of raising money for the project. In this powerfull address he outlines a new program of Christian philanthropy toward the sick and the poor, giving us a concrete view of how Gregory understands the basic ministry of all Christians; we will examine it thoroughly in chapter 5. The Construction of the new facility was finally completed during Basil's episcopate, after he and Gregory had become estranged, and it eventually became large enough to be called the "new city" (43.63) and to redefine the city limits of Caesarea.[37] Thanks in part to his flattering remarks about Basil's work (43.63), Gregory's role in the project has typically been underestimated; it became known to posterity simply as the "Basiliad."[38]

Between 368 and 370 Gregory suffered a series of family deaths which affected him deeply: those of his brother, Caesarius; his cousin Euphemius; his sister, Gorgonia; and her husband, Alypius. Perhaps even greater than these losses, however, was the rupture of his long friendship and collaboration with Basil. In 370 Basil's aggressive campaign for the see of Caesarea drove the first serious wedge into the relationship; and it is not out of the question that Gregory himself may have wanted the post. But the final blow came in 372. When Valens divided Cappadocia into two administrative dioceses and Anthimus arranged for himself to be made bishop of Tyana and metropolitan of Cappadocia Secunda,[39] Basil conspired with Gregory the Elder to appoint Gregory as bishop of the dismal crossroads of Sasima in order to expand Basil's power base. Gregory may have initially accepted the appointment with the expectation of being coadjutor and an episcopal orator with Basil in Caesarea.[40] In any event, when he realized that Basil actually meant for him to take up residence in Sasima, the imperiousness with which Basil exercised his episcopal authority severed the relationship beyond repair. Gregory was consecrated in the church of Nazianzus by the end of the year. Although it has been overlooked in most modern historiography, the falling-out between Gregory and Basil—even while they continued to cooperate to some degree in the

---

36. Basil, *Ep.* 176.
37. Holman, *The Hungry Are Dying*, pp. 74–75.
38. Sozomen, *HE* 6.34.
39. Anthimus' theological position in terms of the wider debate is unclear, a fact which helps to illustrate how fluid the public theological categories were, and to underscore their often limited usefulness in identifying actual theological positions.
40. McGuckin, *St. Gregory*, p. 191.

interest of the orthodox faith—played itself out in significant ways in the theological developments of the next decade.[41]

Once again, Gregory's move into a leadership position in less than ideal circumstances proved to have extraordinarily fruitful results. It appears that he never took up his see in Sasima, but instead joined his father as bishop coadjutor in Nazianzus. In his first episcopal sermons of 372 and early 373 Gregory again reflects on the nature of his profession, and he boldly announces his Trinitarian doctrinal program (Ors. 9–12). Overpowered yet again, Gregory dedicates himself to a middle course between monastic communion with the divine light and the publication of that light to others as a bishop of the Church—a form of life which he says combines his desire for solitude and the leading of the Holy Spirit—since "the reformation of a whole church is preferable to the progress of a single soul" (12.4). He describes his new episcopate primarily in terms of the work of the Holy Spirit, in contrast with the all-too-worldly ministries of some bishops he knows (probably referring to Basil; 12.1–3). At this point Gregory defines his theological position chiefly against "those who fight against the Spirit," even if they confess the deity of the Son (11.6);[42] at the moment this includes Basil, who refuses to join him in the full confession of the Spirit's divinity. Later in 373 Gregory preached at the consecration of Eulalius, the new bishop of Doara in Cappadocia Secunda (Or. 13), a gesture that shows him exercising his episcopal authority apart from Basil's canonical jurisdiction. Gregory gives an indication of his theological agenda as he commissions Eulalius with a moderate Trinitarian statement: "Teach the worship of God the Father, God the Son, and God the Holy Spirit in three *hypostases* and in one glory and splendor" (13.4).[43] Some of the monks in attendance, who preferred Gregory's full doctrine of the Trinity, criticized Basil's economy of words on the question of the Spirit's divinity, which again prompted Gregory to exhort Basil to make the full confession (Ep. 58).[44] Basil responded angrily and refused to do so.[45]

The next two years were a time of further sorrow for Gregory. Late in 373 he faced a severe pastoral crisis when Cappadocia suffered both famine and

---

41. For helpful reconstruction of the separation between Gregory and Basil, see McGuckin, *St. Gregory*, pp. 167–198.

42. οἱ πολεμίοι τοῦ Πνεύματος. On the newly emergent group of "Spirit-Fighters," see below, p.29.

43. Or "Teach the worship of the Father as God, the Son as God, the Holy Spirit as God...." Δίδασκε προσκυνεῖν Θεὸν τὸν Πατέρα, Θεὸν τὸν Υἱόν, Θεὸν τὸ Πνεῦμα τὸ ἅγιον, ἐν τρισίν ὑποστάσεσιν, ἐν μιᾷ δόξῃ τε καὶ λαμπρότητι. It is a strong confession in that it calls the Spirit "God," but also moderate in speaking of the divine unity in terms of glory and splendor, rather than essence.

44. This letter has often been read as indicating Gregory's support of Basil's "economy"; however, Gregory's apparent praise is in fact a sharp, sarcastic criticism. See further discussion in chap. 3.

45. Basil, Ep. 71.

financial ruin. With his father weary from the destruction, Gregory took over the church and did his best to address the needs of the community (*Ors.* 16–17).[46] At this time he wrote his long *Poem of Lament* (*Carmen lugubre*) over the sin and suffering of his own life.[47] After forty-seven years of pastoral ministry, Gregory the Elder finally died at the age of 100. In his funeral oration Gregory sincerely eulogizes his father, commending his earnest care for God's Church, yet he also reproves him—as well as Basil, who had traveled there for the occasion—for conspiring in his consecration to the see of Sasima (18.35, 37). This piece also contains Gregory's first extant reference to the Council of Nicaea (18.12). Gregory's mother died shortly thereafter; in lieu of a funeral oration he composed thirty-six epitaphs for her.[48] Combined with the other strains of this time, the deaths of his remaining family members left Gregory in a state of depressed ill health. He left the church in the hands of his presbyters, removed himself to Arianzus, and finally left the area entirely for a long period of retreat in Seleucia on the coast of the Mediterranean.

Excursus: The Fourth-Century Doctrinal Controversies

At the midpoint of his career—after thirteen years of work in Nazianzus and with eleven years to come in Constantinople and Cappadocia—Gregory spent about four years in Seleucia, probably at St. Thekla's Monastery. Our sources of information for this period are scarce, but given his scholarly disposition and his professed mixed style of monasticism, as well as the greater theological focus of his later work, we can be fairly certain that Gregory spent a good deal of his time in further theological study. By habit, he would have continued to steep himself in the Bible and Origen. In his work thus far Gregory has shown himself to be informed to some extent of the tensions between the current homoian ascendancy and the fully Trinitarian doctrine professed by himself and his associates. Gregory may therefore have continued his theological development with some awareness of these wider issues, stimulated by whatever correspondence he may have had with like-minded theologians in the vicinity of nearby Antioch. It will be helpful at this point, as we observe Gregory's period of retreat, to highlight the key doctrinal debates and ecclesiastical issues of the mid-fourth century, which would soon involve Gregory himself in a central way.

---

46. For a perceptive analysis of the civic crisis and Gregory's response in *Or.* 16, see Holman, *The Hungry Are Dying*, pp. 169–177.

47. *Carm.* 2.1.45 *De animae suae calamitatibus carmen lugubre.*

48. *Carm.* 2.2.66–102.

When Gregory began his ecclesiastical career in the early 360s, the Trinitarian faith of his upbringing was out of step with the official imperial doctrine. Since his accession as sole emperor in 351, Constantius had aggressively promoted the ecclesiastical unity of the empire on the basis of a particular, narrow-minded version the old "Eusebian" theology.[49] Around the time of the Council of Nicaea in 325, a group of theologians led by Eusebius of Caesarea, Eusebius of Nicomedia, and Asterius the Sophist emphasized the distinct, heavenly existence of the Son and Word of God as the mediator and revealer of the knowledge of the transcendent God, against what they perceived to be the new doctrine being advanced at Nicaea. They argued that the Father, Son, and Holy Spirit are three "substances" or "subsistent things" (οὐσίαι or ὑποστάσεις), and they identified Christ primarily as the "image" of God the Father; only by means of the real existence of the Son as the image of God, they believed, could people know and participate in the transcendent God. The Eusebians came to define their doctrine chiefly in contrast with that of Marcellus of Ancyra, who had been active in Asia Minor and Constantinople since at least 314, and later with that of Alexander of Alexandria, the Council of Nicaea, and Athanasius, on the grounds that this latter group denied the Son's distinct being or subsistence.

Marcellus in turn argued against the Eusebians that the Word is not a distinct substance or subsisting thing, but is the creative energy of God the Father, internal to the Father's being, which comes forth from the Father for the purposes of creation (and therefore does not eternally exist as such).[50] The term "Son," however, applies only to the incarnate Christ, who is distinct from the Father only in his enfleshed, human form; as God, Christ has the same being as the Father. For this reason Marcellus was a keen supporter of the Nicene phrases that the Son is "of the same being with the Father" (ὁμοούσιος τῷ Παρτί) and was begotten "out of the being of the Father" (ἐκ τῆς οὐσίας τοῦ Πατρός). On the basis of 1 Corinthians 15.24–28, Marcellus held that at the end time the Son will be entirely subsumed into the Father, so that "God will be all in all."

According to Eusebius of Caesarea, who developed the "Eusebian" position most fully in his *Against Marcellus* and *Ecclesiastical Theology*, Marcellus'

---

49. The collective term, originally used by Alexander of Alexandria to describe those who supported Eusebius of Nicomedia, can now be used to designate those who found common cause with him or with Eusebius of Caesarea against Alexander and later Marcellus. See Lienhard, *Contra Marcellum*, pp. 34–35. The extensive work of Eusebius of Caesarea in the late 330s played a large role in defining Eastern anti-Nicene doctrine of the mid-fourth century.

50. Chiefly in his *Against Asterius*. On the work of Marcellus, see Lienhard, *Contra Marcellum*; Parvis, *Marcellus of Ancyra*; and Vinzent, *Pseudo-Athanasius, Contra Arianos IV*.

denial that the being of the Son is permanently distinct from the Father's represented, for all intents and purposes, the legendary "Sabellianism" of Paul of Samosata, who had been condemned at synods in Antioch in 264 and 268 for denying the permanent distinctions within the Trinity as well as the preexistence of Christ as a divine figure. Eusebius also accused Marcellus, like Paul, of holding an adoptionist Christology. In reply, Eusebius taught that the Word of God took the place of Jesus' human soul in the incarnation, which rules out both adoptionism and what he believed was Marcellus' implicit doctrine that there are two sons in Christ. The Eusebians supported Arius from the outbreak of the controversy over his teaching in the 320s until his death in 336.

Thanks in part to the influence of Marcellus at court, Alexander of Alexandria and his successor Athanasius managed to secure an ambiguous victory over Arius and the Eusebians at the Council of Nicaea in 325, which officially lasted through the reign of Constantine, until 337. In the 340s, when the empire was ruled jointly by Constantine's sons, Constans in the West and Constantius in the East, the Eusebians gained control of the Church in the East and secured the deposition of Marcellus and Athanasius, who then fled to Rome, where they received the support of Bishop Julius and collaborated with one another. While gathered in Antioch for the dedication of a new church erected by Emperor Constantius, a group of ninety bishops held an important meeting, most likely under the leadership of Eusebius of Constantinople (formerly of Nicomedia) and Acacius of Palestinian Caesarea, successor to the other Eusebius; also present were George of Laodicea, Dianius of Cappadocian Caesarea, probably Basil of Ancyra, and possibly the emperor himself. The "Dedication Council" of 341 produced a set of doctrinal statements that were foundational for the conciliar work of the next two decades, and which show a surprising (though not complete) balance in light of the fragmentation to come. The bishops signal a positive regard for Nicaea and seek to distance themselves from the legacy of Arius,[51] yet they also reassert an anti-Sabellian doctrine, which they saw as a necessary corrective to the modalist tendencies of Nicaea.[52] The council's second statement, the so-called Dedication Creed, reiterates the distinct existence of three *hypostases* within the Trinity; it specifies that Christ is the "exact image" (ἀπαράλλακτος εἰκών) of the Divinity, being, power, will, and glory of the Father; and it asserts Christ's distinctiveness among the things created or made by God—yet it also denies that the Father

---

51. In the council's first canon (Mansi 2.1308c) and first doctrinal statement (Hahn sec. 153), respectively.
52. In the council's second statement, the "Dedication Creed" (Hahn sec. 154).

precedes the Son in any temporal sense, as Arius held. This statement is strongly Origenist in character,[53] and it seems to have been intended as an improvement on Nicaea.[54] The fourth statement associated with this council, but which was drafted months later probably by a different group in Antioch,[55] is even more innocuous and reconciling: it omits the language of *ousia* altogether, echoes the Nicene canon against the Arian doctrine of the Son's creation *ex nihilo,* and is less anti-Sabellian than the Dedication Creed (except for one statement against Marcellus); it became the basis for several creeds in the next fifteen years. A further attempt at reconciliation was made at the Council of Serdica in 343, but the Eastern and Western delegations failed to meet together. The so-called Macrostich (long-lined) Creed of Antioch, in 344, reiterated the fourth creed of 341 against Marcellus and his follower Photinus. Although it avoids certain contentious phrases, it continues to stress that the Father somehow precedes the Son (though not by a chronological interval) and that the Son is generated only by the will of the Father, not as a necessary generation by or out of the Father's essence, as they took Nicaea to mean. Meanwhile, Athanasius was writing against the "Eusebians" in 339, and around 340 he began his three *Orations Against the Arians*. By 345 he had broken his association with Marcellus, and in the following year a council in Milan signaled the same rejection by its condemnation of Photinus.

Now sole emperor, Constantius endeavored in the 350s to have the condemnation of Athanasius ratified throughout the East, with the help of bishops such as Acacius of Caesarea and Eudoxius of Antioch. At the same time Athanasius began to identify Nicaea as an important marker of orthodoxy, as demonstrated in his treatise *On the Decrees of Nicaea* from 352. While Athanasius was crafting alliances under the banner of Nicaea, through a series of councils the former Eusebian doctrine was consolidated into a fragile consensus that came to define itself against the doctrine of Nicaea. The most significant council since Antioch 341 was the Council of Sirmium in 351, which again condemned Marcellus, Photinus, and Athanasius. Repeating the pluralist doctrine of Antioch 341, Sirmium 351 further signaled a reluctance to use the language of substance or being (οὐσία) with respect to the Son at all,[56] which may be a reference to Nicaea. Over the next decade Constantius exerted

---

53. As noted by Schwartz, *Gesammelte Schriften* 3.10, pp. 311–312.
54. Hanson argues that it was meant as a replacement (*Search for the Christian Doctrine of God*, p. 290), but Ayres rightly points out that Nicaea itself does not yet have such normative status (*Nicaea*, pp. 119–120).
55. Hahn sec. 156.
56. By anathematizing those who claim that the being of God is extended or contracted, or who say that the being of God is extended to the Son (anathemas 6–7; Hahn §160).

significant imperial pressure to enforce the decrees of Sirmium 351, on pain of exile for nonsignatories. The Council of Sirmium in 357 marked the first explicit refutation of Nicaea—earning it the title the "Blasphemy of Sirmium" among pro-Nicenes—and it formally prohibited the use of all *ousia* language with reference to God (οὐσία, ὁμοούσιος, or ὁμοιούσιος). By the late 350s, the legacy of the Eusebian theology thus came to be defined by a repudiation of Nicaea and opposition to the language of being in reference to God. At a meeting in Sirmium in 358, Constantius commissioned a new statement of faith to be written in preparation for a joint council that he intended to sponsor the following year. The so-called Dated Creed, which was promulgated on May 22, 359, declared that the Son is "like the Father in all things, as the Holy Scriptures say and teach," and it prohibits the use of the term *ousia* because it is not found in Scripture and is therefore confusing to the people.[57] On account of this preference for saying that the Son is "like" (ὅμοιος) the Father, this doctrinal position has since come to be known as "homoian." In order to ratify the doctrine presented in the Dated Creed, Constantius sponsored the twin councils of Ariminum and Seleucia, held in 359, which he seems to have envisioned as another general council of the Church, much as Nicaea was coming to be seen by this time. The Dated Creed represented an uneasy consensus in the first place, and accord at Ariminum and Seleucia proved even harder to achieve. The assembled bishops at both councils opposed the new program and the strong subordination of the Son to the Father that it plainly indicated, but they were eventually pressured into subscribing to it. The majority at Ariminum declared its allegiance to Nicaea over the proposed Dated Creed; those at Seleucia likewise opposed the Dated Creed in favor of the Dedication Creed of 341; they rejected the proposal to discipline bishops such as Cyril of Jerusalem who were closer to the Athanasian-Nicene position; and they deposed several homoian bishops. However, the minority at Ariminum managed to gain the emperor's approval, supporting the Dated Creed minus the phrase "in all things" (thus further reducing the degree of likeness between the Father and the Son) and reiterating the prohibition of *ousia* language and the similar description of the Father, Son, and Holy Spirit as "one *hypostasis*"; the deposed minority at Seleucia likewise appealed their case to Constantius. The situation thus remained unresolved, and the debates moved to Constantinople.

Two developments in the late 350s significantly weakened Constantius' already fragile homoian policy. Certain homoian theologians began to argue

---

57. Hahn §163, from Athanasius, *Syn.* 8.

even more strongly for the Son's subordination to the Father, emphasizing the differences between them and going so far as to say that the Son is unlike the Father according to essence—thus warranting the name Heterousians ("unlike in essence").[58] The first Heterousian of note was Aetius, who had a reputation for being a strong subordinationist even among the Eusebian supporters of Arius, with whom he studied in the 320s. Aetius' secretary, Eunomius, became the most well-known proponent of the heterousian doctrine, earning him rebuttals from Nicene theologians for generations to come; other Heterousians included Eudoxius of Antioch and Acacius of Caesarea, Eusebius' successor.[59] During his two years as Nicene bishop of Constantinople Gregory identifies Eunomius as his major theological opponent and the one whose extreme views represent the logical end of all those who deny the full confession of the Trinity. What inspired the heterousian doctrine is unclear; it may be a reaction to Athanasius' increasing appeal to Nicaea and/or simply the result of a process of reflection on the fact that God the Father is unbegotten, or on his "unbegottenness" (ἀγεννησία), which became their central theological category.[60]

The emergence of this more extreme, heterousian position within homoian groups quickly attracted the attention of moderate Eusebians such as Basil of Ancyra and George of Laodicea. Although he had long been aligned with the Eusebian orthodoxy, as the episcopal replacement for the arch-Nicene Marcellus in 336, Basil's own doctrinal position proved in the intervening years to be far more comprehensive than Constantius' narrow homoian program. He had signed the Macrostich Creed of 344 and probably participated in the Dedication Council of 341.[61] In 358 he sought to address the heterousian situation at a council convened in Ancyra for the dedication of a new church. George wrote to the council in advance to express his concern for those in the Antiochene vicinity who had been excommunicated by the new, heterousian bishop, Eudoxius—a situation that he called "the shipwreck of Aetius."[62] Along with Basil, Eustathius of Sebaste and Macedonius of Constantinople were present, and George of Laodicea later signed the council's statement.

---

58. The term "Anomoian," used by their opponents, is misleading, since they do not claim that the Son is unlike the Father in all respects.

59. I will address the doctrine of Eunomius more directly in the chapters that follow. Good summaries of heterousian doctrine can be found in Michel René Barnes, *Power of God*, chap. 5; Vaggione, *Eunomius of Cyzicus*, chap. 5; Behr, *Nicene Faith*, pp. 267–282; and Ayres, *Nicaea*, pp. 144–149.

60. For the former suggestion, see Behr, *Nicene Faith*, p. 87; for the latter, Ayres, *Nicaea*, p. 147.

61. Hanson, *Search for the Christian Doctrine of God*, p. 349.

62. Sozomen, *HE* 4.13.

Basil's council continued to reflect the traditional Eusebian concern to uphold the distinctness of the three persons, and even endorsed the anti-Marcellan councils of Constantinople 336, Antioch 341, Serdica 343, and Sirmium 351. Yet, in reaction to the Heterousians, the signatories made the important argument that the concepts of Creator and creature must be sharply distinguished from the concepts of Father and Son—a point that Athanasius had been arguing against the Eusebians since the 330s. In contrast with the Creator-creature distinction, the Father-Son relationship, they argued, involves the Son's being "like in essence" (ὅμοιος κατ' οὐσίαν) to the Father,[63] a phrase that has since earned its proponents the title Homoiousians.[64] While they continued to reject the Nicene term ὁμοούσιος, because they felt that it compromised the distinctness of the three persons in a modalist direction, the so-called Homoiousians came to have even more in common with the position of Athanasius—who also meant to preserve the distinctness of the three persons and had broken ranks with Marcellus over this very point[65]—than they did with Constantius' homoian doctrine and the new party of Heterousians. This similarity between the Asian Homoiousians and Athanasius is probably not so much a case of direct influence or rapprochement as an indication of distinct, regional groups and traditions expressing a similar faith in somewhat different terms.

The emperor temporarily accepted the Council of Ancyra's statement as a new compromise position, until the Dated Creed and the councils of Ariminum and Seleucia in 359, and he sent the Heterousians Aetius, Eunomius, and Eudoxius into exile. When Basil signed the Dated Creed of 359, which states that the Son is "like the Father in all things according to the Scriptures," he added the qualification that this includes the Son's being like the Father in being as well.[66] In order to clarify that Basil had not renounced his views in signing the Dated Creed, George of Laodicea (or possibly George and Basil

---

63. Epiphanius, *Panar.* 73.4.2.

64. Although the term ὁμοιούσιος does not appear in Basil of Ancyra's writings, it is descriptive nevertheless as a shorthand for ὅμοιος κατ' οὐσίαν. The term "semi-Arian," coined by Epiphanius for the group (*Panar.* 73), is grossly misleading. Even the mainstream Eusebians had long ago distanced themselves from Arius in sincere and specific ways, and Homoiousians such as Basil were now moving even closer to the homoousian doctrine, as Athanasius was soon to recognize.

65. Although Athanasius favorably commented on Basil of Ancyra's doctrine (*Syn.* 41, around 360 or 361), his assessment is not entirely accurate (Simonetti, *Studi*, p. 179n94; Hanson, *Search for the Christian Doctrine of God*, p. 244n32), and in any event we should not assume a working relationship between Athanasius and the Homoiousians at this point—certainly not before the Council of Alexandria in 362, where Athanasius secures the acknowledgment of certain homoiousian representatives that they in fact agree on several fundamental points.

66. "Not only according to will, but according to *hypostasis* and according to existence (ὕπαρξις) and according to being (τὸ εἶναι)." Epiphanius, *Panar.* 73.22.7.

together) wrote a letter that further emphasizes that the Son is like the Father in being, and which characterizes the Heterousians as the logical consequence of the homoian position.[67] The letter argues that the concept of *ousia* is implied in the Scriptures, even if it is not explicitly stated, and that the term "Father," which indicates the generation of the Son, is a more definitive term for God than "Unbegotten," which simply states that God has no source. It also attempts to clarify the controversial terminology of three *hypostases* that was used by Origen and in the original Eusebian doctrine. It explains that the Easterners speak of *hypostases* "in order to acknowledge the subsisting, existing properties of the persons,"[68] but that they anathematize anyone who claims that the three *hypostases* are three first principles (ἀρχαί) or three gods. Instead, "they confess that there is one Divinity, which encompasses all things through the Son in the Holy Spirit; [but] while they confess one Divinity, one kingdom, and one first principle, they also piously acknowledge the persons in the properties of the *hypostases*."[69] This letter is a major witness to the sort of strongly Trinitarian position that was emerging at this time in Asia Minor, and which later associated itself with Nicaea, as Athanasius had done; we will comment on Gregory's relationship to this group and its doctrine in this book's conclusion. While it brought theologians like Basil, George, and Eustathius to a new point of conceptual clarity, the emergence of the Heterousians and the Homoiousians from within the broad homoian movement also set up a tension that was left unresolved at the beginning of the 360s—a tension which determined much of the shape of Gregory's work.

With all of these forces in play, the fragmented discussions of Ariminum-Seleucia moved to Constantinople in 360, where the Heterousians held sway for a short time. The city prefect arranged a debate between Aetius and Gregory's friend Basil, the future bishop of Caesarea, who accompanied Basil of Ancyra and Eustathius of Sebaste to the capital; however, when Basil saw that his own party was outnumbered, he withdrew. Basil of Ancyra appears to have debated Aetius instead, and lost.[70] When further discussions produced no clear result, a local council was summoned under the leadership of the Heterousian Acacius of Caesarea in order to ratify the homoian agenda of Ariminum-Seleucia. The Synod of Constantinople in 360 appointed the heterousian Eudoxius as bishop of Constantinople and Eunomius as bishop of Cyzicus, and

---

67. Epiphanius, *Panar.* 73.2.1–11.11.
68. ἵνα τὰς ἰδιότητας τῶν προσώπων ὑφεστώσας καὶ ὑπαρχούσας γνωρίσωσιν. Epiphanius, *Panar.* 73.16.1.
69. Epiphanius, *Panar.* 73.16.3–4.
70. See Philostorgius, *HE* 4.12.

deposed a number of Homoiousians, including Basil of Ancyra, Macedonius of Constantinople, Eustathius of Sebaste, Melitius of Antioch, Eleusis of Cyzicus, and Cyril of Jerusalem. Basing itself on the statement of Ariminum (which had been issued at Niké when the minority group moved there), the synod issued a statement of faith that became the officially sanctioned creed of the Eastern empire for over twenty years and thus represented the final victory of Constantius' homoian program. The creed stated that the Son is "like the Father according to the Scriptures" (not "in all things") and prohibited all use of the terms *ousia* and *hypostasis*. During the proceedings Eunomius seems to have given an oral defense of his position, which he later edited and published as his *Apology*. Despite the bland and compromising appearance of its language, the Synod of Constantinople 360 represented the victory of an aggressive homoian program, giving a clear place for the Heterousians while banishing the Homoiousians from ecclesiastical leadership.

The homoian settlement at Constantinople met with widespread resistance. After watching the developments of the 350s, Athanasius and the Homoiousians in Asia had both come to recognize that the homoian program represented a deeply subordinationist Christology, and as a result more bishops began to turn toward Nicaea as a more credible standard of the faith.[71] Between 359 and 361 Athanasius wrote the treatise *On the Councils of Ariminum and Seleucia*, the first two-thirds of which argues that the councils of Ariminum and Seleucia were the culmination of theological developments that began with Arius, and the remainder of which seeks to find common ground with the Homoiousians, to the limited extent that Athanasius knows their work. He suggests that the Nicene phrase "from the essence of the Father" best expresses the distinctiveness of the Son's relationship to the Father, in contrast with the relationship of all creatures to their Creator, appealing to the same distinction that the Homoiousians had addressed in 358. For Athanasius, this phrase indicates that the Son does not come from any *hypostasis* other than the Father, that he is not a creature or work of God, but the Father's own genuine and natural offspring, eternally with the Father as his Word and Wisdom. Furthermore, Athanasius contends, the Homoiousians should recognize that the second Nicene term, that the Son is "of the same essence (*homoousios*) with the Father," is the necessary corollary of the idea that the Son is "from the essence of the Father." The homoiousian phrase "like (*homoios*) the Father in

---

[71]. Lewis Ayres has ably shown that one of the products of the 350s, for both Athanasius and the Homoians, was to develop the very idea of a universal creedal standard, which had not existed before. See *Nicaea*, chap. 6 and passim.

essence" can therefore admit an orthodox sense if it is used to mean "from the essence of the Father," in which case it really means "of the same essence as the Father," but apart from these qualifications it is not orthodox. Despite Athanasius' insistence, though, Asian theologians such as Basil of Ancyra—and in the next decade Basil of Caesarea and Gregory Nazianzen as well—continue to approach the task of articulating a strong Trinitarian faith, which includes adherence to Nicaea, in different terms. While they, too, will eventually come to see the usefulness of the Nicene term *homoousios,* they do not adopt the phrase "from the essence of the Father," nor Athanasius' distinctive conceptuality of the Son's being "internal" to the being of the Father. Despite the conventional textbook story, Athanasius is not the great unifying force of Nicene doctrine in the 350s and 360s, and we are in fact dealing with fairly independent traditions that approach the matter in noticeably different ways.

Just as the final homoian settlement was coming to a head, in 358 or 359, Gregory returned home from Athens. He then began his ecclesiastical career in the immediate aftermath of the council of 360 and was ordained by his father specifically to help him deal with local disputes over the new homoian creed. Theological developments from 360 to 380 are less clear than those which we have just examined, and so we must be wary of too quickly identifying Gregory with idealized positions. On the death of Constantius in 361, Trinitarian theologians were free to gather new momentum. Not only did the homoian campaign of Constantius come to an end, but his anti-Christian successor, Julian (r. 361–363), recalled all exiled bishops in order to foment dissent among the various parties, thus allowing pro-Nicenes and other Trinitarians to reorganize. However, after the very brief reign of the pro-Nicene emperor Jovian, the homoian cause was reestablished with vigor by his successor, Valens (emperor of the East; r. 364–378).[72] Valens upheld the homoian creed of 360 and generally promoted homoian theology,[73] though he did so in a pragmatic way that could find a use for Nicenes such as Athanasius, whom he recalled from exile during a rebellion in 365–366, and Basil of Caesarea. At the same time that Valens was pressuring the Nicenes in Cappadocia to subscribe to the homoian doctrine during his trip there in 372, Basil did not refrain from giving him communion, and Valens put Basil in charge of restructuring the church in Armenia. Yet despite these working arrangements, the potential for effective ecclesiastical resistance against the homoian ascendancy was strictly limited. Meanwhile, the

---

72. Valentinian, emperor of the West from 364 to 375, was more supportive of Nicenes.

73. In his religious policy, Valens appears to have been heavily influenced by his Eastern prefect, Modestus. Van Dam, *Kingdom of Snow,* pp. 136–137.

arch-heterousian Eunomius became even more unpopular with other Homoians, incurring the disfavor of Eudoxius of Constantinople and his successor, Demophilus, as well as Dorotheus, Euzoius' successor in Antioch; as a result Valens banished him to the island of Naxos. Although the scope of their influence was limited, certain Trinitarian theologians—mainly the loosely defined group we have termed Homoiousians—continued to organize themselves in the 360s and 370s, becoming increasingly opposed to the Homoians, and, by the mid-370s, adhering even more closely to Nicaea.

During this time Athanasius continued to labor for the consolidation of the Nicene position in his areas of influence. In 362 he held an important synod in Alexandria, which sought to bring together, under broad, Nicene terms, a variety of theologians who were disaffected by the homoian establishment. The synod's *Catholic Epistle* broadly defines the conditions for re-establishing communion among Nicenes as the confession that the Son and Holy Spirit are not creatures, that "the Trinity is of one essence" (ὁμοούσιος ἡ Τρίας), and that true God became human from Mary. The synod's second and more important document, the *Tome to the Antiochenes,* seeks to reconcile divisions among two rival Nicene groups in Antioch: the old Eustathians, who were now led by Paulinus, and the larger group led by the homoiousian bishop Melitius, which was now gathered in the old church. The *Tome* recommends accepting into communion all who are willing to anathematize the Arian heresy and those who say that the Holy Spirit is a creature and separate from the essence of Christ, and to confess the faith of Nicaea.[74] Athanasius goes on to explain that he has examined the varying doctrines of each group and found that they do not disagree with the Nicene faith. The Melitians, who confess three hypostases in the traditional Eusebian fashion, simply mean to acknowledge that the Father, Son, and Holy Spirit truly exist and subsist (ὄν καὶ ὑφεστώς). They neither divide the three *hypostases* from one another, in the way that creatures are divided, nor consider there to be three sources or first priniciples (ἀρχαί) within the Trinity, but they acknowledge only one Divinity and ἀρχή, and they agree that the Son is consubstantial with the Father.[75] Likewise, in confessing only one *hypostasis,* the Paulinians are not saying that the Son and the Spirit do not properly exist (ἀνούσιος, ἀνυπόστατος). Rather, they are using the terms *hypostasis* and *ousia* as synonyms, so as to maintain that there is only one Divinity or divine nature, because the Son is "from the essence of the Father," as Nicaea states. Both sides agreed to anathematize

74. *Tom.* 3–4.
75. *Tom.* 5.

Arius, Sabellius, and Paul of Samosata and to recognize Nicaea as the best available creedal standard.[76] Athanasius goes on to say that both sides have agreed to several further points of Christology: that in Christ the Word does not dwell as in a prophet, but was himself made flesh and became human from Mary; that Christ's body does not lack a human soul or mind;[77] and that the Son of God became also Son of man, remaining one Son and not two.[78] On the basis of these central points of Nicene doctrine, Athanasius requests that the document be read publicly, and he urges the Antiochene groups to unite in one assembly.[79] Athanasius' *Tome* is important not only because it seeks to address the division in Antioch, which was a serious detriment to the Nicene cause (and would continue to be so for decades), but also because, by way of foreshadowing, it shows how different theological traditions can be seen to agree on a common, orthodox faith identified with the Council of Nicaea.[80] Although Gregory is not a direct heir of Athanasius' work—and indeed Athanasius' proposals for the most part fell flat on arrival—Gregory will nevertheless proceed with an agenda remarkably similar to the one proposed at the synod of 362.

Gregory and his associates were powerfully affected by the nearby Antiochene schism, which was quickly becoming a matter of serious concern to catholic bishops throughout the Church.[81] Following an abortive appointment as homoian bishop of Sebaste, Melitius was elected bishop of Antioch in 360, under the sponsorship of the aggressively homoian Eudoxius of Constantinople. Before the end of the year, however, Melitius delivered a sermon before the emperor in which he betrayed homoiousian leanings, and he was deposed within a month of his appointment and sent into exile.[82] In 363 he was then recognized by Jovian as the pro-Nicene bishop of Antioch. As he became a more convinced Trinitarian, Melitius gained the support of several important bishops in Asia Minor, including Amphilochius of Iconium and the three Cappadocian fathers. Before Athanasius' *Tome* arrived from the council of 362, Lucifer of Cagliari consecrated Paulinus bishop of the Eustathian party,

---

76. *Tom.* 6.

77. This statement is not asserting the presence of a human mind and soul against the Apollinarians, who were able to sign the document with impunity, but repudiating the adoptionism of Marcellus and Photinus. See Spoerl, "Apollinarian Christology," p. 567n73; Behr, *Nicene Faith*, p. 98.

78. *Tom.* 7.

79. *Tom.* 9.

80. The actual agreement between such parties took much longer to achieve. See below on Melitius' excommunication of Athanasius and the work of consensus building in the 370s.

81. Some, but not all, of whom are at this point pro-Nicene.

82. He would spend virtually half of his episcopate in exile, during the years 360–362, 365–366, and 371–378.

which formally created rival Nicene factions in this major Christian see. A signatory of Nicaea, Bishop Eustathius had strongly opposed Eusebius of Caesarea and was temporarily deposed by the end of 326. The Eustathian party resisted the authority of Melitius on account of his former homoian associations and for his continued reference, in Eusebian terms, to the Father, Son, and Holy Spirit as three *hypostases*. In 363 Melitius refused communion with Athanasius, out of concern for the latter's association with Marcellus, and Athanasius in turn rejected communion with Melitius and supported Paulinus instead. In the later 360s and the 370s, however, Melitius and other Homoiousians identified themselves with Nicaea and sought communion with other Nicenes in Alexandria and Rome. Between 364 and 366 (the death of Liberius), communion had been established between Liberius of Rome, Eustathius of Sebaste, Melitius of Antioch, Silvanus of Tarsus, and Basil of Caesarea.

During the 370s Damasus of Rome and the Italian bishops began to work toward establishing communion with both Antiochene bishops, in order to resolve the schism and strengthen the cause of the Trinitarian faith. Sometime between 374 and 379 Damasus sent a letter to Melitius which offered communion with the Roman church on the basis of a brief Trinitarian statement.[83] Around the same time Damasus also wrote to Paulinus with the same purpose,[84] seeking first to establish a common doctrine, on the basis of which canonical and disciplinary order could then be reestablished between the rival Antiochene bishops. Jerome likewise sought to receive the communion of both Melitius and Paulinus. By 377 he wrote to Damasus to find out which bishop was recognized by the Roman church;[85] around the same time he signed doctrinal statements that seem to represent the views of Basil of Caesarea and Melitius;[86] and in 380 or 381 he was ordained to the presbyterate by Paulinus.[87] Yet, despite the efforts of Damasus and others, neither man could claim canonical validation or a consensus among Eastern and Western Nicenes as the rightful bishop of Antioch. At some point Melitius and Paulinus recognized one another's office and entered into an agreement whereby the survivor would become sole bishop upon the death of the other. When Apollinarius

---

83. *Ea gratia.* "The Trinity is of one strength, one majesty, one Divinity, one being, so as to be an inseparable power.... This, most beloved brothers, is our faith. Everyone who follows it is our partner.... For these we give ourselves as communion." (Field, p. 14, ll. 49–50; p. 16, ll. 69–71). See below, pp. 317–319.

84. *Per filium meum.* Sometime after 382 this text was attached as a proem to the *Tomus Damasi*, which was probably written (or at least completed) by the Roman synod of the same year. See Field, *On the Communion*, pp. 143–146, 168.

85. *Ep.* 15.2; 16.2.

86. *Ep.* 17.2–3; 18.1.

87. *Lib. Pamm.* 41. See Field, *On the Communion*, p. 144.

ordained Vitalis bishop in 376, there were then three Nicene claimants to the throne, in addition to the homoian community under Euzoius. By 381 the situation came to a head, and proved to be decisive for the course of Gregory's career and the outcome of the Council of Constantinople that year.

In the late 360s and early 370s a further theological development occurred in Asia Minor that soon involved Gregory directly. It appears that certain homoiousian theologians began to voice objections to the divinity of the Holy Spirit. These "Spirit-Fighters" (Πνευματομάχοι, Pneumatomachians),[88] or "Macedonians" as they were later called,[89] supported the confession of the divinity of the Son, but resisted the idea that the Spirit was also similar in essence, or of the same essence, with the Father, or should be called "God." They seem to have been concerned about the modalist implications of a fully Trinitarian confession like Gregory's. Why this concern applied to statements about the divinity of the Spirit but not to those about the Son remains a puzzle; Gregory and other pro-Nicenes would exploit this inconsistency in their arguments with the Pneumatomachians. A leader of this group was the Homoiousian Eustathius of Sebaste (bishop ca. 358–372/73), an ambassador to Rome who subscribed to Nicaea in 360 and joined in the confession of Basil of Ancyra and George of Laodicea mentioned above. Eustathius was initially an important mentor to Basil of Caesarea, but by 373 their relations had soured and two of Eustathius' associates had begun to criticize Basil on what appear to be accusations of Sabellianism. Basil was subsequently called to Armenia to defend his orthodoxy to Melitius of Antioch and Theodotus of Nicopolis, which he managed to do while he was reorganizing the Armenian church at Valens' request. Basil met with Eustathius, who agreed to a pro-Nicene statement; but their disagreement over the doctrine of the Holy Spirit continued. Basil's *Against Eunomius* book 3, from 363–364, presents a doctrine of the Spirit that can be seen as stronger than homoian, but not plainly homoiousian or homoousian. He later produced his major work *On the Holy Spirit* in 375 partly to

---

88. We have already noted Gregory's mention, in 372, of οἱ πολεμίοι τοῦ Πνεύματος (11.6). This is the first such reference in Asia Minor. Basil (*Spir.* 11.27; 21.52; *Ep.* 140.2; 263.3), Epiphanius (*Ancor.* 13.7; 63.6), Amphilochius (*Ep. syn.* 54), and Gregory of Nyssa (*Spir.* 3.1.89.t3; *Pent.* PG 46.700.38) each later refer to Πνευματομάχοι. Although Athanasius refers to Serapion's opponents by the same term (in verbal form, πνευματομαχεῖν, *Ep. Serap.* 1.32; 4.1), there does not appear to be any connection between the Egyptian group and the people in Constantinople and Asia Minor. Whether Basil read Athanasius' letters and borrowed the term for what he thought was a doctrinal similarity is unclear. For the verbal form, see also Basil, *Spir.* 27; Gregory of Nyssa, *Orat. Dom.* 264.25; *Steph.* 32.23; 34.10; 36.22; Didymus, *Comm. Zach.* 4.87.5; and Pseudo-Basil, *Eun* 5.2. It is possible that by 379 or 380 this group included a number of Antiochenes. On Gregory's use of the term, see p. 157n14.

89. Named, perhaps erroneously, after Macedonius, the homoiousian bishop of Constantinople who was exiled in 360. See Gregory of Nyssa, *Spir.* 3.1.89.t3; Epiphanius, *Rescr.* 4; *C. Th.* 16.5, 11–13; and Socrates, *HE* 1.8.24. Gregory Nazianzen refers to them by this name only once, at the end of his career (*Ep.* 202.5).

signal his break with Eustathius. In 376 Bishop Amphilochius presided over a council in Iconium that supported the divinity of the Spirit, largely in terms of Basil's work.[90] When Basil died on January 1, 379,[91] Gregory was left with no little remorse over the falling-out that had occurred between them. He wrote a letter of consolation to Basil's brother Gregory of Nyssa, excusing his absence from Basil's funeral on account of illness and saying that he was comforted to know that Gregory was in many ways a reflection of his late brother (*Ep.* 76).

The cause of Trinitarian theology received a problematic though welcome form of support when the homoian emperor Valens was killed at the battle of Adrianople on August 9, 378, and the Western emperor, Gratian, appointed the pro-Nicene Spanish general Theodosius as emperor and augustus of the East on January 19, 379. Theodosius fashioned himself in the image of the first Christian emperor, Constantine, which included a determination to meddle in ecclesiastical affairs, with similarly inept results.[92] At his inauguration, Theodosius was clothed with Constantine's own imperial robe, and at the anniversary celebration of the founding of Constantinople, he had the statue of Emperor Constantine processed to his box at the Hippodrome.[93] Theodosius later had the audacity to claim credit for the Nicene triumph by telling Gregory that God had given the Church of the Holy Apostles to him to hand over to Gregory, at his installation as archbishop (*DVS* 1311–1312). Much as Constantine declared Constantinople to be the "Second Rome" at its original dedication in 330, so Theodosius' council of 381 proclaimed it the "New Rome," in order to elevate the city politically and ecclesiastically.[94] Theodosius' imposition of his imperial authority in Church matters would, in Gregory's view, wreak havoc on the emerging Nicene consensus, and cause Gregory no end of troubles in the years ahead. Meanwhile, Gratian issued a decree of toleration, allowing all bishops to return to their sees and pronouncing all groups free to worship, except the Eunomians, Photinians, and Manichees.[95] Gregory's long-

---

90. The official *Synodical Letter* was written by Amphilochius. Basil is briefly acknowledged; *Ep. syn.* 219, ll. 16–17.

91. For recent discussions of the dating of Basil's death, which uphold the traditional date of January 1, 379, see Rousseau, *Basil*, pp. 360–363; T. D. Barnes, "The Collapse of the Homoeans in the East."

92. On the distinctive authority retained by the Church under Christian emperors in the fourth century, see Honoré, *Law in the Crisis of Empire*, pp. 3–6. An ambiguous dynamic of ecclesiastical power quickly arose between the newly baptized emperor Theodosius and his initiator, Bishop Acholius of Thessalonica. Later writers sought to rationalize the situation by having Theodosius examine Acholius' orthodoxy before being baptized. Socrates, *HE* 5.6; Sozomen, *HE* 7.4. Van Dam, *Kingdom of Snow*, p. 143.

93. Van Dam, *Kingdom of Snow*, p. 147n24, with bibliography.

94. The orator Themistius soon compared Theodosius with Constantine (*Or.* 18.223a–b), as did new statuary erected in the capital. Van Dam, *Kingdom of Snow*, p. 149n29.

95. As implied in *C. Th.* 16.5.5.

time supporters Melitius of Antioch and Eusebius of Samosata, as well as Gregory of Nyssa, returned from their exiles.

Heterousian theologians continued to be active during this time; sometime between late 378 and early 380 Eunomius wrote his *Apology for the Apology* in response to Basil's *Against Eunomius*, and, with two other heterousian bishops, consecrated a bishop to serve in Palestine, after which the four held a council in Antioch. The Homoiousians likewise remained active: after holding a council in 376 that endorsed the Dedication Creed of 341 and the phrase ὅμοιος κατ' οὐσίαν, they attempted to repossess some of their churches in 378–379, and, at another council in Antioch in Caria, they again rejected the term ὁμοούσιος in favor of ὅμοιος κατ' οὐσίαν. Another imperial edict on August 3, 379, declared that all illegal heresies should cease.[96]

In the autumn of 379 Melitius called a synod in Antioch to strengthen the cause of Trinitarian orthodoxy among the Eastern bishops—and probably also to signal to the new emperor, Theodosius, where he might consider taking his ecclesiastical policy.[97] Whether Theodosius supported the meeting is unclear, as is the extent to which his theological position was even known at this point. Melitius, Eusebius of Samosata, and Gregory of Nyssa were all present. The synod received a dossier of formal documents issued by Damasus and the Italian bishops through a series of councils, and it issued a confessional statement of its own. Through its reception of the Western documents, which are assembled in the imperial rescript *Codex Veronensis LX*,[98] the Antiochene synod represents a crucial point of contact between Eastern and Western bishops at a key moment in the development of a new catholic consensus, and it forms a major part of the immediate context of Gregory's work over the next two years. During the 370s there had been a fair amount of correspondence between Italian bishops and those in the East. Early in the decade Basil of Caesarea made several appeals to the bishops and Italy and Gaul for their support of the Eastern Trinitarians, and for their assistance in mending the Antiochene schism.[99] Although Basil never received the decisive intervention

---

96. *C. Th.* 16.5.5. The decree does not provide a new list of heresies.

97. Our sources for this important Eastern synod are regrettably sparse, having apparently been eclipsed in the historical record by the Council of Constantinople in 381 and its Western sequel in Aquileia in the same year. Gregory of Nyssa mentions having attended a council in Antioch before visiting Macrina on her deathbed (*V. Macr.*, p. 386). The Constantinopolitan synod of 382 mentions a meeting in Antioch prior to the ecumenical meeting in Constantinople in 381 (Theodoret, *HE* 5.9.13). See the discussion by Hanson, *Search for the Christian Doctrine of God*, p. 803; Simonetti, *La crisi Ariana*, p. 446; and the work of Field.

98. For the critical edition, along with a thorough discussion of the events surrounding the codex, see Field, *On the Communion*; still helpful is the previous edition by Eduard Schwartz.

99. See esp. *Ep.* 92, 243, 263.

that he was hoping for, a Roman synod around 371 issued a letter to the bishops of Illyrium, a fuller version of which survives in the *Codex Veronensis* as the *Confidimus quidem*, now addressed to the catholic bishops of the East altogether.[100] The letter contains a statement of catholic doctrine and communion, which it identifies with the faith of Nicaea and defines as belief "that the Father, Son, and Holy Spirit are of one Divinity, one virtue, one form, one substance." The Western letter either prompted or responded to an Antiochene synod called by Melitius in 372, which stressed its shared faith with the bishops of the Western churches and invited them to attend an Eastern synod; the signatories included Melitius, Basil, Gregory the Elder of Nazianzus, and Gregory of Nyssa.[101] Following the Eastern reception of *Confidimus quidem*, further documents that are difficult to date were then joined to the original letter,[102] which expand the doctrinal definition, adding new emphases on the divinity of the Holy Spirit against the Pneumatomachians, and on the full humanity of Christ against the Apollinarians, apparently in response to earlier initiatives by Basil.[103] In 379, Damasus sent these assembled documents, the *Exemplum* of a Roman synod of ninety-three bishops, to the synod that Melitius had called in Antioch in order to reaffirm the communion between the Eastern and Western Nicenes, and to solicit Eastern support for his own threatened position in Italy. According to the final document contained in the imperial rescript, "this [composite] exposition or letter of the Roman synod held under Pope Damasus was also transmitted to the East, in which a synod at Antioch was made with every Eastern church in harmony with the faith." The *Exemplum* was then signed by Melitius, Eusebius of Samosata, Pelagius of Laodicea, Zeno of Tyre, Eulogius of Edessa, Helladius of Caesarea (Basil's successor), Diodore of Tarsus, and 146 other bishops, whose signatures are said to be on file in the archive of the Roman church.[104] The Antiochene synod thus ratified, signed, and returned

---

100. Field, *On the Communion*, pp. 10–14.

101. Basil, *Ep.* 92.

102. *Ea gratia*, *Illut sane*, and *Non nobis*. The *Ea gratia* was originally sent to Melitius of Antioch, possibly in response to Basil's *Ep.* 243, which stressed the divinity of the Holy Spirit and the continuing distress of the Eastern churches.

103. See *Ep.* 263, from around 377, which warns of the Pneumatomachoi, Eustathius of Sebaste, and the Apollinarians, and hints that Paulinus of Antioch may be Marcellan. By the end of his labors, Basil had favorably corresponded with Acholius of Thessalonica, Ambrose of Milan, Peter of Alexandria, and Damasus of Rome, and was eventually accepted as orthodox by Athanasius before his death in 373—thus making great progress toward the East-West Nicene communion that Damasus, Melitius, and Gregory Nazianzen would seek to finalize from 379 to 381. See Field, *On the Communion*, pp. 129–130, with bibliography.

104. *Haec exposito* (Field, p. 20).

the Western documents,[105] and issued its own doctrinal *Tomus*, which is no longer extant but seems to have agreed with the Western documents to a large extent.[106] The Western bishops' reception of the *Exemplum synodi* signed by the Antiochenes also entailed their recognition of Melitius as bishop of Antioch. This important exchange of conciliar documents sought to define a common faith and communion among the Western bishops assembled at Damasus' Italian synods and the Eastern bishops represented by Melitius' synod of 379, and in turn to reinstate proper ecclesiastical order in Antioch.

As part of its doctrinal and canonical work, Melitius' synod of 379 appointed Gregory to become bishop of the orthodox community in Constantinople.[107] Gregory later tells us that he was summoned to the capital by an orthodox, though incomplete, synod of bishops (compared to Constantinople 381) and by a particular "upright person." Given the correspondence of this council with the timing of Gregory's move to the capital and the continued support offered to him by Melitius on arrival, this surely refers to the Synod of Antioch and Bishop Melitius.[108] According to Gregory's report, the council commissioned him "to defend the Word" in the capital against a new heresy being promoted by certain bishops, which he goes on to describe in terms that refer to Apollinarianism, namely the teaching that Christ lacks a human mind (*DVS* 607–631). During his time in Seleucia Gregory appears to have made his own study of the Christological debate that had been taking place in the Antiochene vicinity in the 370s between the pro-Nicene Apollinarius of Laodicea and Melitius' presbyter and chief assistant, Diodore.[109] In 378 Diodore was

---

105. The current form of the *Exemplum* shows indications of having been assembled in Antioch before being put in rescript by the imperial chancery. See Field, *On the Communion*, p. 133.

106. In the synodical letter of Constantinople 382 sent to Damasus, the Eastern bishops excuse themselves from attending a synod in Rome by directing the Westerners to consult the *Tome* of Antioch 379, as well as the fuller statement of Constantinople 381 (Theodoret, *HE* 5.9.13). Field, *On the Communion*, p. 121n13.

107. In *Or.* 43.2 Gregory notes that his work in Constantinople on behalf of true doctrine was "not without the approval of that noble champion of the truth." McGuckin suggests that Eusebius of Samosata vetted the idea with Basil on behalf of the Antiochenes (*St. Gregory*, p. 236n28). Such a communication before Basil's death on January 1, 379, assumes, of course, that Melitius and company were considering the idea of sending Gregory as their representative to the capital well before the Antiochene council actually commissioned him to do so. Given the complicated motives of Gregory's memorial oration for Basil (on which see below), we should not place too much confidence in this single passage. The reference to "an upright person" who called Gregory to Constantinople (*Carm.* 2.1.12.77–78; see n106 below) most likely refers to Melitius, but probably not Basil, and so should not be taken as a corroborating witness for 43.2.

108. *Carm.* 2.1.12.72–82. See also *DVS* 596; *Or.* 33.13: "I was invited and compelled, and have followed the scruples of my conscience and the call of the Spirit"; Socrates, *HE* 1.5.6.

109. McGuckin's speculation (*St. Gregory*, p. 226), on the basis of a veiled reference in *Carm.* 2.1.19.61–74, that Gregory encountered the Apollinarians even earlier, when they sought to take over the see of Nazianzus before he left in 375, seems to me unlikely.

appointed bishop of Tarsus, not far from Gregory's retreat in Seleucia, and it may have been he who first impressed on Gregory the problems inherent in Apollinarius' Christology. We will consider the matter in detail below, but for the moment we may note that while he did fulfill his charge to strengthen the pro-Nicene community in Constantinople, Gregory did little to oppose the Apollinarians, and in fact he advanced a strikingly different Christology from that being proposed by Diodore and his Antiochene associates. As the political winds shifted, Gregory once again found himself promoted to a new position of leadership, as pastor of the pro-Nicene community at the seat of imperial power. Thus began the briefest and yet the most productive phase of his ecclesiastical career.[110]

379–381: Ministry in Constantinople

Gregory's short tenure in Constantinople was both the most arduous and the most fruitful period of his life, and nothing short of decisive for the course of Trinitarian orthodoxy. In less than two years he consolidated and increased the pro-Nicene community in the capital, almost solely through the force of his own pastoral and theological endeavors, and independent of imperial patronage—a role that he later came to see as the crowning achievement of his career.[111] In the course of his stay, Gregory became the sole bishop of the capital see upon the arrival of Emperor Theodosius; he served as president of the Council of Constantinople in 381; and he produced twenty-two of his forty-four extant orations. He was hosted by his cousin Theodosia, who offered him the use of her villa for lodgings and as a place for his congregation to gather. Gregory dedicated part of the villa as the Church of the Resurrection, the *Anastasia*, to symbolize the resurrection of the orthodox faith that he hoped to foster there. The Constantinopolitan orations figure prominently in the rest of

---

110. Arguments that Gregory went to the capital in 378 or earlier rely on the reference to Basil's involvement in *Or.* 43.2. See Van Dam, *Kingdom of Snow*, p. 138n5, with bibliography. However, even allowing for this passage, most scholars have recognized that the cumulative evidence of Gregory's texts more strongly favors autumn 379. See McGuckin, *St. Gregory*, pp. 236–238; Daley, *Gregory of Nazianzus*, pp. 14–15.

111. After the council Gregory writes that he was never a suppliant at the imperial court, but instead advises kings like the prophet Samuel (42.19). He ignores the imperial edict of 379 (see Van Dam, *Kingdom of Snow*, pp. 141–142), and his work shows no dependence on it. Once he was installed as archbishop in the Church of the Holy Apostles, though, he naturally sought to influence Theodosius' program; see Gregory's recommendation to the emperor at 37.23, which is followed not long afterward by the issue of *Nullis haereticis* (*C. Th.* 16.5.6).

this book; here we will situate them among the surrounding events and briefly introduce their main concerns.[112]

Gregory delivered four orations before the end of 379, which illustrate his initial attempts to consolidate the faithful around a basic exposition of the faith, and to repair the divisions between rival factions. He inaugurated his preaching mission with a summary of his doctrine and his basic approach to theology (*Or.* 20).[113] Echoing passages from his earlier work, Gregory argues that Christian theology involves both a right understanding of God, Christ, and the Holy Spirit, and a corresponding state of spiritual purification and speculative reserve on the part of the theologian. The oration is composed of two parts. In the first Gregory makes use of several Old Testament figures to consider the nature of the knowledge of God, focusing especially on Moses' ascent up Mount Sinai (20.1–4). He later returns to Moses in several other works as a cardinal example of theological vision, thus providing a motif that will become highly influential in later Christian tradition. In the second, longer part of the oration, Gregory gives an important summary of Trinitarian doctrine, by which he hopes to redefine the orthodox community in the capital (20.5–12). This interrelationship between the content of theology and the state of the theological knower remains central to Gregory's work as a whole, and it lies at the heart of our concern in this book.

In *Oration* 22, the *Second Oration on Peace*,[114] Gregory addresses the division among Nicenes in Constantinople, which are largely the result of the schism in Antioch. Appealing to the precedent of biblical peacemakers (22.1–2, 8, 15–16), he issues a plea for peace among the rival parties under the aegis of a centrist Trinitarian position (22.12). Significantly, when Gregory turns to the Antiochene schism, he first points not to the dispute between the Eustathians and the Melitians over the rightful bishop of the city, but to the Christological debate between Diodore and Apollinarius (22.13).[115]

---

112. The sequence of Gregory's orations in the capital is difficult to determine; I generally follow McGuckin's revision of the earlier dating established by Sinko, Bernardi, and Gallay: autumn 379: *Ors.* 20, 22, 24 (Oct. 2), 32; after Easter 380: *Ors.* 23, 33, 21 (May 2), 34, 41 (Pentecost), 27–31 (the *Theological Orations*; July and August), 25, 26, 36, 37 (after Nov. 27, installation as bishop of Constantinople), 38 (Dec. 25); 381: *Ors.* 39 40 (Jan. 5–6), 42 (July, on resigning the Council of Constantinople). McGuckin, *St. Gregory*, pp. ix, 240n44. Gallay arranges them in the following order: *Ors.* 22, 32, 25, 41, 24, 38–40, 26, 34, 23, 20, 27–31, 37, 42 (*La vie*). See also Sinko, *De traditione orationum*; Bernardi, *La prédication*.

113. Later entitled *On Theology and the Installation of Bishops*.

114. According to McGuckin's revised dating, *Or.* 22 is now the *Second Oration on Peace* and *Or.* 23 the *Third*, the reverse of the titles given by the Benedictines and in Migne.

115. The figure of Diodore in this passage has typically gone unnoticed.

In an amusing hagiographical blunder, Gregory gives his next oration (*Or.* 24) in praise of Cyprian the martyr, probably just after the celebration of Cyprian of Antioch in early October 379. He conflates the famous North African bishop with the Antiochene bishop of the same name,[116] lauding the great "Cyprian" for his Trinitarian faith and invoking his patronage against the dissensions that threaten the contemporary Church (24.19). Gregory apologizes for having been away for the martyr's celebration (24 tit., 1), and he works hard to lobby further for peace among Trinitarian groups in the capital. The oration indicates the fragility of the pro-Nicene alliances at this point in Constantinople, in addition to providing another example of Gregory's panegyrical celebrations of local festivals. Gregory's final oration of 379 was *Oration 32 On Moderation in Debate*, delivered to a sizable congregation at the Anastasia. He laments the numerous factions in the Church, like so many Pauls, Apolloses, and Cephases (1 Cor 3.4–9, 22), and so many Christs and Holy Spirits (32.5), and he again appeals for peace and unity, both on moral grounds and on the basis of a simple Trinitarian confession (32.5, 21). Gregory also highlights his own authority as a teacher (32.12), he invokes Paul's image of a variety of members and gifts united in the one Christ (32.11–13, 15),[117] and he refers again to the figure of Moses (32.16–17).

Although we have no more orations until the following spring, the winter months of 380 brought several important events. In February, Theodosius issued *Cunctos populos* from Thessalonica: his famous decree that the official religion of the empire would be the catholic faith, as confessed by Damasus of Rome and Peter of Alexandria, which if defines as belief "in the one Divinity of the Father and of the Son and of the Holy Spirit, within an equal majesty and an orthodox Trinity."[118] In the months following Theodosius' decree, the level of conflict and threats against Gregory's community at the Anastasia seems to have escalated. Gregory celebrated his first baptisms in the city at the Easter Vigil, during which a group of vandals attacked his church, destroying the altar and hurling stones at Gregory. In his *Letter* 77 to Theodore of Tyana, who is angry over the attack, Gregory makes a case for the superiority of forgiveness and the mercy of God over justice and retaliation, arguing that it is only by mercy and kindness that they can hope to win over their opponents.[119] In the end, he was forced to appear in court, and he reproduced parts of his defense

---

116. Mossay, SC 284, pp. 21–24. On the possible date and location of the oration, see Bernardi, *La prédication*, pp. 161–164.

117. Rom 12.5–6; 1 Cor 12; and Eph 4.4, 15–16.

118. Secundum apostolicam disciplinam evangelicamque doctrinam Patris et Filii et Spiritus sancti unam deitatem sub parili maiestate et sub pia trinitate credamus. C. Th. 16.1.2.

119. See also *Carm.* 2.1.11.665 DVS; 2.1.12.103 *De seipso et de episcopis*; 2.1.15.11; 2.1.30.125; 2.1.33.12.

speech in his next two orations (*Ors.* 33 and 23). Gregory reports another incident at this time in which a poorly dressed young man who made his way to Gregory's bedside burst into tears and confessed that he had come to assassinate him. Gregory forgave him immediately, which won him even greater support around the city (*DVS* 1466–1474; *Or.* 33.5).

The next year's work—from the spring of 380 to the spring of 381—was the most concentrated period of theological productivity of Gregory's life. In a sequence of seventeen densely packed and carefully wrought orations, he strove to articulate the Christian faith with sophistication and persuasive power. This body of work represents his greatest theological effort, even as it indicates that his earlier attempt to build a consensus on the basis of simple, formulaic confessions was only a beginning. In the late spring, Gregory addressed the continuing hostility shown by anti-Nicenes against his congregation. In *Oration 33 Against the Arians and on Himself,* he answers the homoian bishop Demophilus' challenge to his episcopal authority (33.1) and gives a list of recent "Arian" crimes, including attacks on Peter of Alexandria and the murder of Gregory's mentor Eusebius of Samosata (33.1–5). For his part, Gregory claims that he has not returned violence for violence (33.6–12), and he concludes with another brief account of his doctrine, defined in conventional form against various heresies (33.16–17).

Soon afterward, in *Oration 23,* the *Third Oration on Peace,* Gregory again defends his community's response of love in the face of attacks and legal harangues (23.1–2) and issues an invitation for his opponents to "come and partake of our mysteries" (23.3). He then gives his most expansive doctrinal exposition to date, and one of the most important passages on the Trinity in his entire corpus (23.7–13); we will examine it in detail in chapter 4. As the nautical season resumed, Peter of Alexandria sent a delegation of Egyptians to strengthen Gregory's congregation—and probably also to reassert an Alexandrian influence in the capital. The group included Maximus the Cynic, a pro-Nicene theologian who was initially a great help to Gregory but ultimately became an instrumental cause of his downfall (*DVS* 810–814). In honor of the new Egyptian contingent, Gregory prepared a pair of celebratory orations. *Oration 21 In Praise of Athanasius* venerates the former bishop of Alexandria as a symbol of faithfulness and successful theological endeavor on behalf of the Nicene faith. Marking a transition in his own work, Gregory declares that he will no longer restrain himself with the abbreviated, "economic" summaries of the faith that he has given up to now, but he will teach his doctrine fully and with confidence, as Athanasius[120]

---

120. On the broad range of meaning of "economy" in Gregory's work, see chap. 4, pp. 195–196.

had done (21.34). Along with the expected praise of Athanasius' personal and pastoral virtues, Gregory gives a narrative account of the doctrinal debates in the fourth century in which Athanasius stands out as the champion of the Nicene faith, though mainly for the purpose of highlighting Gregory's own authority in the capital. (21.13–37). Delivered only seven years after Athanasius' death, Gregory's memorial address is the first piece of canonizing literature for the great Alexandrian; we will examine it more closely, to determine Gregory's actual knowledge of Athanasius, in this book's conclusion. In the second piece, *Oration 34 For the Arrival of the Egyptians*, delivered probably in mid-May, Gregory responds loyally to Peter of Alexandria's gesture of doctrinal alliance—in keeping with *Cunctos populos*, we may note—followed by another long discourse on the Trinity, with particular attention to the Holy Spirit (34.8–15).

The feast of Pentecost on June 9, 380, presented Gregory with a natural occasion to renew his treatment of the Holy Spirit, which he had begun in his first episcopal orations of 372. Although we cannot be sure, his motivation to do so may also have stemmed from increased resistance by his opponents and/or a desire further to convince the Egyptians of his orthodoxy. *Oration 41 On Pentecost* marks a second turning point in Gregory's approach, as he now addresses a point of contention within his own ranks: the divinity of the Holy Spirit. Along with more general, celebratory remarks on the character and work of the Spirit, he argues for the Spirit's divinity on the basis of a dual appeal to the redemption that the Spirit causes and the Spirit's self-revelation in the Church—both themes that he will develop at greater length very soon, and which will demand our full consideration in chapter 3. While he is certainly trying to persuade Homoians and Heterousians as well, Gregory directs his attention toward the Nicene Spirit-Fighters, presumably members of his own congregation who are "sound with respect to the Son" but who still deny the divinity of the Spirit.[121] He speaks to them as brothers, acknowledging their theological and practical virtues while seeking to persuade them gently step by step toward a full confession. Yet his conciliatory tactics do not appear to have worked; from this point onward, Gregory argues more directly and forcefully for the Trinitarian doctrine that has already become his life's work, against a range of different positions.

---

121. McGuckin suggests that Gregory may be addressing Nicene monks from Antioch who were still loyal to the legacy of Eustathius of Sebaste (*St. Gregory*, p. 273), and he speculates that the heightened Origenist theories advanced in *Or.* 41 indicate that Jerome and Evagrius Ponticus may have been among his auditors that day (p. 276n263). It is impossible to know for certain when they joined Gregory's community, but this occasion is as likely a point as any.

Gregory delivered his famous series of five *Theological Orations* (*Ors.* 27–31) at the Anastasia in July and August 380. There is some discrepancy among the more than 1,000 manuscripts as to their original sequence, particularly regarding the place of the second oration (*Or.* 28).[122] Judging from irregularities in the manuscript tradition as well as the internal argumentation of the series, Tadeusz Sinko and Jean Bernardi have argued that Gregory added or significantly altered *Oration* 28 after its original delivery in 380.[123] In any event, there is sufficient justification for preserving the conventional numbering of the set, and we will interpret them accordingly. As we noted above, the *Theological Orations* are organized roughly in accordance with the order of main topics in Origen's *On First Principles*, and in a manner similar to Basil's *Against Eunomius*, beginning with two orations on theological method and the incomprehensibility of God (27–28; cf. *Eun.* 1), followed by two orations on the divinity of the Son (29–30; cf. *Eun.* 2), and finally an oration on the divinity of the Holy Spirit (31; cf. *Eun.* 3). Although it is difficult to know for certain, Gregory's auditors may have included homoian theologians representing Demophilus, heterousian Eunomians (Gregory's primary opponents in the text), and homoiousian Spirit-Fighters, possibly under the leadership of Eustathius of Sebaste.[124] While they are reputed to be Gregory's definitive statement on the Trinity,[125] the *Theological Orations* are not so much a positive doctrinal exposition, such as he has given several times already,[126] as a carefully crafted set of responses and counterarguments to his opponents' objections, giving the impression of a momentous theological showdown. Gregory's main argument in the series is negative and defensive, seeking to answer his opponents' charges against the divinity of the Son and the Spirit, and thus a full doctrine of the Trinity. *Orations* 27–28 deal primarily with the character of theology in light of the respective natures of God and human beings; *Orations* 29–30 are a defense of the divinity of the Son against logical and biblical objections; and *Oration* 31 is a defense of the divinity of the Holy Spirit against logical and biblical objections, with summary passages on the Trinity interspersed throughout.

---

122. On the manuscript tradition, see Norris, *Faith Gives Fullness*, pp. 71–80; Lafontaine, Mossay, and Sicherl, "Vers une édition."

123. Sinko, *De traditione orationum* I, pp. 11–12, 20–21; Bernardi, *Le prédication*, pp. 183–185; and Norris, *Faith Gives Fullness*, p. 76nn386–387. See also McGuckin, *St. Gregory*, p. 278.

124. McGuckin speculates that Gregory was aided in their composition by Maximus the Cynic and possibly Jerome and Evagrius. *St. Gregory*, pp. 277–278.

125. See McGuckin, *St. Gregory*, p. 264.

126. E.g., *Ors.* 20.5–12; 23.7–37; 34.8–15.

In addition to the negative character of its argumentation, the series contains several irregularities that make it distinctive in Gregory's corpus. *Oration 28* contains a rare discussion of divine incomprehensibility;[127] there is a unique set of passages in *Oration 30* that suggest an uncharacteristically dualistic understanding of Christ;[128] and Gregory makes several unusual statements about divine causality.[129] These idiosynchrasies have often misled scholars who have interpreted the *Theological Orations* in isolation from other texts. They not only point to the unusual polemical situation in which Gregory found himself in the summer of 380, but suggest the possibility that he collaborated with colleagues such as Maximus the Cynic, Gregory of Nyssa, Jerome, or Evagrius in their composition. In light of their distinctiveness, it is noteworthy that Gregory's influence in Byzantine tradition came largely through other texts—such as the orations that were sung in the liturgy and often illuminated in manuscripts, as well as the many poetic passages that formed much of Eastern hymnody—whereas modern scholars have tended to focus almost exclusively on the *Theological Orations,* resulting in wildly different assessments of Gregory's work. Teachers and students of Gregory should therefore be advised to interpret them carefully, in consideration of their form and purpose within the contemporary debates and in concert with other texts that are often clearer and more straightforward. With these caveats in mind, we will make extensive use of the series in the chapters that follow. Coming at the end of a long and contentious summer, Gregory's landmark performance understandably left him exhausted.[130]

On the heels of this heroic endeavor, Gregory then made the single greatest mistake of his career—a debacle that led to widespread suspicion about his competence and ultimately contributed to his downfall at the Council of Constantinople.[131] As Maximus the Cynic prepared to embark for Alexandria at the end of the summer, Gregory mounted a grand farewell speech in his honor, *Oration 25 In Praise of Hero the Philosopher.* Gregory calls Maximus forward to the altar and praises him as an exemplary philosopher and "defender of the Trinity to the death" (25.2–3). After giving a description of the ideal Christian philosopher, he then commissions Maximus to teach the true faith, which he outlines in one of his most important doctrinal expositions (25.15–18). Gregory may have thought that this gesture would further strengthen the Egyptians' support of him, but once again he misplaced his trust. As with Basil, he made a

---

127. See chap. 1.
128. See chap. 2.
129. See chap. 4.
130. See Gregory's comment at the beginning of his next oration, *Or.* 25.1.
131. Gregory narrates the episode at length in *DVS* 728–1112.

serious misjudgment of character; more damningly, he showed a naive disregard for the ambiguities of his position among those who were vying for influence in the capital at the beginning of a new regime. He overlooked the poignancy with which the question of Demophilus' succession was being watched around the international Church, and he neglected to consider that the Alexandrians might have less than charitable designs on his future as the de facto Antiochene ambassador. The Egyptians, as it turned out, proved to be infinitely more trouble than they were worth. As Maximus sailed for Alexandria, possibly carrying Gregory's oration as a formal recommendation,[132] Gregory retreated to the country for a much needed rest (*Or.* 26 tit., 1, 8).[133] Bishop Peter immediately sent a party back to Constantinople to consecrate Maximus as archbishop. Maximus and his entourage proceeded to the Anastasia at early dawn, but they met with unexpected resistance from the clergy, who lived nearby, and a crowd of civil servants, Homoians, and non-Christians (*DVS* 887–902). Gregory reports that the Alexandrians then moved their service to Maximus' house, where they consecrated him as their shepherd (*DVS* 905–912). The incident severely threatened Gregory's reputation; he returned to town and quickly prepared *Oration* 26 to provide damage control. Gregory reminds his congregation of their mutual affection for each other (26.1), vilifies the Egyptian clergy (26.3), defends himself against accusations of financial impropriety (26.4–6), answers a series of personal threats that the Egyptians had made before departing (26.14–19), and gives another encomium of the ideal Christian philosopher (26.9–13). In order to vindicate himself Gregory then made the risky move of feigning his resignation, only to have the congregation plead for him to stay, lest he "throw out the Trinity" along with himself (*DVS* 1100).

In yet another ironic turn of events, at the lowest moment of his career thus far, Gregory suddenly found himself elevated to the episcopal throne at the center of the Eastern empire. On November 24, 380, Theodosius entered his capital. When presented with the emperor's new religious policy, the homoian bishop, Demophilus, chose exile rather than confession of the Nicene faith. On the following day, November 27, Theodosius installed Gregory as the new archbishop (*DVS* 1311–1312).[134] Gregory later tells the dramatic story of his procession to the Church of the Holy Apostles under a dark, overcast sky. Theodosius first had him escorted to the church through a city

---

132. So speculates McGuckin, *St. Gregory*, pp. 312–313.

133. In the title of *Or.* 26, some of the manuscripts read "on his return from the country." Mossay, SC 284, p. 224n2.

134. At this point the canonical status of Gregory's appointment is still undecided. See Gallay, *La vie*, pp. 186–188; Bernardi, *Le prédication*, pp. 191–192; and McGuckin, *St. Gregory*, pp. 326–328.

gone wild.[135] Just as they arrived, the clouds parted and the sun broke through, illuminating the whole building, while rich and poor alike cried out for their new archbishop (*DVS* 1325–1391).

In late November or early December 380, Gregory delivered his first oration before the emperor in Holy Apostles, *Oration 36 On His Own Position, Against Those Who Maintained That He Coveted the Throne of Constantinople*. After quieting the cheers of the crowd, he declares that he is not the first to preach the orthodox faith to them, but is merely the successor to Alexander (36.1–2), the archbishop under Constantine who, along with Athanasius, refused the emperor's demand to receive Arius back into communion. He then defends himself against charges that he originally came to the capital to seize the throne—an ironic accusation, considering the betrayal he had just endured at the hands of the Alexandrians—and he looks forward to his appointment's being properly ratified by the council that was already being planned (36.2, 6–9). He then gives a moderate and uncontroversial statement of his faith (36.10); he admonishes the emperor and the city to cultivate faith and virtue (36.11–12); and he encourages them not to submit to the primacy of Rome (36.12), which may be a tacit reference to Alexandria as well, given its long-standing alliance with the West. Before the end of 380 Gregory also delivered *Oration 37 On the Gospel Text "When Jesus Had Finished These Words"* (Mt 19.1–12), in which he states his views on Christian marriage and argues for a change in the divorce laws on the basis of the compassion of the Gospel as a whole (37.1). If God made human beings male and female, why, he asks, does Roman law punish adulteresses, while adulterers go unscrutinized? Obviously because the law was made by men. "I do not approve of this custom," he says (37.6). On the question of remarriage, first marriages are "according to the law"; second marriages are "according to indulgence" because of Christ's overarching compassion; third marriages are "transgressive" and should be subject to some penalty; while fourth marriages are "swinish" and downright wicked—though in any event Christ allows divorce only in cases of infidelity (37.8). This pronouncement later became the basis of Eastern canon law on divorce and remarriage.[136] Finally, showing his ascetical moderation, Gregory extols the virtues of both marriage and virginity, which are mutually dependent on each other (37.10–11), and argues for the value of spiritual chastity above all, namely orthodox faith (37.22). Gregory does not hesitate to ridicule the court eunuchs, whose muti-

---

135. Demophilus had likewise been consecrated under the protection of military guard. Socrates, *HE* 4.14–15; Sozomen, *HE* 6.13; Van Dam, *Kingdom of Snow*, p. 138n4.

136. McGuckin, *St. Gregory*, pp. 334–335.

lation he does not approve (37.16–18). This oration is Gregory's longest piece of sustained exegesis of a single biblical text, a fact that indicates just how little we can rely on formal commentary to understand his rather substantial practice of biblical interpretation.

At the feasts of Christmas and Epiphany 380–381, Gregory delivered a set of three orations that contains his most comprehensive treatment of Christian theology and spirituality. It is unclear whether he delivered *Oration* 38 at a newly established celebration of Christmas on December 25, followed by *Orations* 39 and 40 on the eve and the feast of the Epiphany twelve days later, or whether all three orations belong to the Epiphany celebration.[137] In any event, the three pieces clearly form a planned series; all three will figure heavily in the analysis that follows. As the new metropolitan bishop, Gregory offered the traditional baptismal catechesis and administered the Epiphany baptisms. Since many of the candidates that day had only recently been catechized under the homoian Demophilus, Gregory made a special effort to outline the faith in clear and comprehensive terms. *Oration* 38 *On the Theophany* commemorates Christ's birth; *Oration* 39 *On the Holy Lights* celebrates Christ's baptism and revelation to the world, which remains the primary focus of the Epiphany in the East, rather than the gifts of the Magi, as in the West; and *Oration* 40 *On Baptism* reflects extensively on the rite itself.

Four days later, on January 10, Theodosius issued the decree *Nullis haereticis*, prohibiting heretics from worshipping in church buildings or inside the walls of any town.[138] The edict specifically names only the Arians, Eunomians, and Photinians, though the list will soon expand.[139] Now that he has taken up residence in the capital, where the influence of the Antiochenes and Gregory's Nicene community was more keenly felt, Theodosius' decrees no

---

137. Near the end of *Or.* 38 Gregory writes that the celebration of Jesus' baptism (in *Ors.* 39–40) will come "very shortly" (μικρόν, 38.16), which could signify an interval of a few hours or twelve days. At the beginning of *Or.* 39 Gregory takes a moment to explain the name of the feast of Holy Lights, as if it were a new celebration (39.1), which would seem to indicate that it, and not *Or.* 38, is the first sermon of the feast. Unfortunately, there is little direct evidence for when the December 25 celebration of Christmas began in Constantinople and the East; Gregory's *Or.* 38 is often cited in this regard, which obviously begs the question. See Mossay, *Les fêtes*, pp. 21–30; "La Noël et l'Épiphanie"; Talley, *Origins of the Liturgical Year*, pp. 137–138; Roll, *Toward the Origins of Christmas*, pp. 189–195; and McGuckin, *St. Gregory*, pp. 336–340.

138. *C. Th.* 16.5.6.

139. "That person shall be accepted as a defender of the Nicene faith and as a true adherent of the catholic religion who confesses that Almighty God and Christ, the Son of God are one name, God from God, light from light; who does not violate by denial the Holy Spirit, whom we hope for and accept from the highest Author of things; who esteems, with the perception of an undefiled faith, the undivided substance of the incorruptible Trinity, which those who believe rightly call by the Greek word *ousia*." According to Socrates, Theodosius was at this point trying to win over the Macedonians (*HE* 5.8), which may explain the unspecific language regarding the divinity of the Spirit. See Behr, *Nicene Faith*, p. 119.

longer stipulate Alexandria and Rome as arbiters of the catholic faith. In order to solidify his religious policy, Theodosius then called a council of Eastern bishops in Constantinople the following summer—a meeting that later became known as the second Ecumenical Council. We possess no official records or acts of the council, and, except for a brief mention by Rufinus, no historical account before Socrates' *Ecclesiastical History*, written approximately sixty years later. Gregory's lengthy discussion of the proceedings is thus a rare contemporary source for what took place.[140] The 150 bishops who attended were primarily from Asia Minor and the areas under Melitius' influence—nearly the same group that attended the Antiochene synod of 379—which suggests that the organizers expected the council to endorse the Trinitarian doctrine of the earlier gathering,[141] and that it was clearly conceived as an Eastern synod. Theodoret dramatically portrays Melitius as the center of Theodosius' attention, seen by the emperor in a dream vision and then greeted in person with copious kisses.[142] Although it does not seem to have been conceived as a universal council like Nicaea or Ariminum-Seleucia,[143] Theodosius was nevertheless working for a religious settlement for the Eastern empire, as is apparent from the synods and legislation of the next two years. Under the presidency of Melitius, the council's agenda contained three interrelated items: confirming a bishop of Constantinople, reconciling the Pneumatomachians with the fully Trinitarian doctrine, and providing further definition of the faith. The council produced the so-called Niceno-Constantinopolitan Creed; a *Tomos* that summarized its doctrinal position at greater length,[144] which we no longer possess; and four canons. The order of events is only partially known, and must be reconstructed. The accounts of the fifth-century historians are occasionally improbable and often mutually contradictory. Yet, since it would not have served Gregory's apologetic purpose to alter the story too drastically (his audience in Constantinople would have surely known better), we can rely on his account as a fairly reliable source for the sequence of events and the basic outcome of the council, even if his interpretation of them is admittedly biased.

---

140. DVS 1506–1918; Rufinus, *HE* 2.19; Socrates, *HE* 5.8–9; Sozomen, *HE* 7.7–11; and Theodoret, *HE* 5.6–8. The most important recent studies of the council are Ritter, *Das Konzil*; Hauschild, "Das trinitarische Dogma von 381"; Simonetti, *La crisi Ariana*, pp. 527–541; Hanson, *Search for the Christian Doctrine of God*, pp. 791–820; and Staats, *Das Glaubensbekenntnis*; see also Kelly, *Early Christian Creeds*, pp. 296–367.

141. According to the historians, the emperor summoned a synod of "prelates of his own faith" (Socrates, *HE* 5.8), or "a council of orthodox bishops" (Sozomen, *HE* 7.7).

142. *HE* 5.6–7.

143. Ayres, *Nicaea*, p. 253.

144. As reported by the Synod of Constantinople in 382. Theodoret, *HE* 5.9.

The council's first task was to confirm Gregory as archbishop of Constantinople.[145] Up to this time he had been serving as acting pro-Nicene bishop, representing a broad Eastern sponsorship that included the homoiousian network of Melitius and Basil of Ancyra, with whom Gregory of Nyssa was associated, the Cappadocian group that included Amphilochius of Iconium and the late Basil, and important individuals such as Jerome—and more recently as the imperially appointed successor to Demophlius. As an indication of the Church's continuing power over its own affairs in the fourth century, despite the meddlesome designs of several emperors, everyone recognized that, whatever Theodosius may think, it fell to the council to appoint Gregory as sole bishop of what was quickly becoming a patriarchal see. The somewhat fanciful accounts of Socrates and Sozomen signal the importance of Gregory's appointment, particularly in the way that they closely associate it with the work of Melitius. According to Socrates, Gregory showed early indications of his future role by visiting the capital several times while he was still bishop of Nazianzus (i.e., in the early 370s) to strengthen the orthodox community there. He was then formally translated to Constantinople by the decision of many bishops (an echo of Melitius' synod of 379), and Melitius traveled to the capital to take part in his installation.[146] In Sozomen's account, as soon as Melitius had settled the conflict in Antioch, he made his way to Constantinople to take part in a council of bishops that was planning to translate Gregory to the capital see.[147] Together with the promulgation of a doctrinal statement, it appears that Gregory's confirmation was the council's chief item of business.[148] The bishops in turn denounced Maximus' ordination and everything done in his name.[149]

---

145. *DVS* 1513 (literally "to establish the seat of piety," i.e., the orthodox faith: ὡς πήξοντες εὐσεβῆ θρόνον); Socrates, *HE* 5.8; Sozomen, *HE* 7.7; and Theodoret, *HE* 5.6. Socrates and Sozomen place the election of Constantinople after an early attempt to reconcile the Macedonians, who subsequently departed; they also overlook Gregory's election and move straight to that of Nectarius. Theodoret reports an Egyptian move to ordain Maximus, which divides them from the rest of the council. The council sides with Gregory, who then declines the position; Nectarius is elected, and Maximus is denounced as an Apollinarian!

146. Socrates, *HE* 4.26; 5.6, 8.

147. Sozomen, *HE* 7.3, 7. Gregory's later disgrace can be seen in the fact that Socrates has Gregory resign his see before the council even started. *HE* 5.7–8.

148. Socrates (*HE* 5.8) and Sozomen (*HE* 7.7) list these two purposes first, then add the Macedonian problem as a secondary matter. Theodoret says the council was called to cure the East of Arian infection, and he concentrates first on Gregory's confirmation, ignoring the Macedonian question altogether (*HE* 5.7–8). Gregory elides the two purposes into one (*DVS* 1513; cf. 1525).

149. As enshrined in the council's fourth canon. A council held in Aquileia later the same year continued to press for Maximus' recognition as the rightful bishop. Ambrose, *Ep.* 9.13; Hanson, *Search for the Christian Doctrine of God*, p. 822n1117.

Not long after Gregory's appointment was confirmed, Melitius died (*DVS* 1578), and Gregory unexpectedly found himself both archbishop of the imperial capital and president of the most important Church council under the new regime. Most of the bishops present were from Melitius' network, though Paulinus' group was represented as well. Given the predominance of Antiochenes, it is not surprising that the schism in this major Christian center would dominate the atmosphere of the meetings. While uncertainties remain at this point,[150] Gregory's account, for all its biases, makes the most sense of what happened.[151] As he describes it in retrospect—no doubt to highlight the source of his later problems (*DVS* 1506)—the council was plagued from the very beginning by strife among the rival Antiochene factions, compounded by the competing intrigues of the wider Eastern and Western churches. Tensions between East and West had run high at several points since the rise of the Eusebian party in the East and the support of Marcellus and Athanasius by the West in the late 330s. The divisions in Antioch reinstated some of the earlier opposition, with the post-Eusebian Melitius carrying the support of most of the bishops in Constantinople and Asia Minor, and more recently Damasus of Rome, and Paulinus having the favor of Damasus as well, and especially that of Alexandria. Gregory says that he initially agreed to become archbishop because he thought he would be able to broker a peace between them (*DVS* 1525–1534)—an intention shared, as we have seen, by both Damasus' Roman synods of the late 370s and the Antiochene synod of 379. Gregory indicates that the source of the dispute at the council was neither Melitius nor Paulinus, but rather "power seekers on both sides" who added fuel to the controversy (*DVS* 1546–1547, 1566–1569). This must certainly refer to Diodore of Tarsus, Melitius' chief associate, who had overseen his community while Melitius was in exile in Armenia, and probably also to Paulinus' presbyter Flavian—both of whom continued to cause Gregory grief as events unfolded. When Melitius died, Diodore most likely became the main spokesman of the majority Antiochene faction, though he himself was unable to be a candidate for the see of Antioch, since he was already bishop of Tarsus.[152] According to the prior arrangement of Melitius and Paulinus, which Gregory suggests came at Me-

---

150. Socrates (*HE* 5.9), Sozomen (*HE* 7.11), and Theodoret (*HE* 5.23) all place Flavian's election at the end of their narratives of the council.

151. It is possible, for example, that Gregory passed over the first stage of doctrinal debate in order to emphasize the Antiochene strife as the real problem besetting the council.

152. Sozomen says that it was Diodore who sponsored Nectarius for archbishop of Constantinople when Gregory later resigned (*HE* 7.8).

litius' initiative (*DVS* 1576–1577), when one bishop died the other would occupy the throne of Antioch until he died, at which time a new bishop would be elected.[153] Equally important, Gregory recognized that the West had heretofore been absent from the council's proceedings,[154] and he knew that its wishes must be considered if a true theological consensus had any hope of being established. He therefore considered the appointment of Paulinus—the designated successor to Melitius and a bishop already in communion with Rome and Alexandria—as a crucial step toward unifying the Eastern and Western churches. Unfortunately, Paulinus' nomination proved far too contentious at the council, even for Melitius' party (despite his own wishes before his death), and so a group suggested to Gregory that a new bishop of Antioch be elected (*DVS* 1583–1588), at which point Diodore most likely nominated Flavian.[155] Gregory thought it positively scandalous that the incumbent Paulinus, whose succession of Melitius was prearranged and who had the support of the West, should be ejected from his see and replaced with a new bishop. He tried to make his case to the council, and once again he threatened to resign if his advice was not followed (*DVS* 1591–1679).[156] At this suggestion, Gregory tells us, the younger members, and eventually their elders as well, screeched in revolt, defending the prerogative of the Eastern churches to manage their own affairs, on the dubious grounds that both Christ and the sun come from the East (*DVS* 1680–1702). In the end, Gregory was overruled, and Flavian was elected bishop of Antioch. Because he was from Paulinus' party, yet now also represented the Melitians (being a friend of Diodore), it has been argued that

---

153. Hanson writes that modern historians have almost universally denied this arrangement (*Search for the Christian Doctrine of God*, p. 801 and n51). However, a number of indications—Gregory's report; the actions of the Antiochene council of 379 to enter into communion with Damasus, in which Paulinus also shared; the support of Paulinus over Flavian by the Council of Aquileia in 381, on the basis of "the pact between the parties" that the survivor should become sole bishop (Ambrose, *Extra collectionem Ep.* 6.5); and the echo of that view by the Council of Rome in 382—strongly suggest not only that such a pact had been made, but that it was taken as canonically normative by Gregory and the Westerners. See Field, *On the Communion*, pp. 166, 189. See also McGuckin, *St. Gregory*, p. 351.

154. In anticipation of the council, Damasus wrote to Acholius of Thessalonica, his informal representative, denouncing the Alexandrian claims of Maximus' episcopate and the transferrence of bishops either from active congregations or out of ambition (again against Maximus), and asking him to make sure a godly bishop is elected to the see of Constantinople. Damasus, *Ep.* 1.

155. After the fact, the Roman synod of 382 upheld the former arrangement for succession, as well as Gregory's position at the council and Damasus' earlier initiatives in establishing communion with both Paulinus and Melitius. It refused to recognize Flavian's election, addressed its *synodica* instead to Paulinus, and excommunicated Diodore and Acacius of Beroea for ordaining Flavian. Sozomen, *HE* 5.23; Field, *On the Communion*, p. 183.

156. This gesture may be a later interpolation, since it comes in the middle of disparaging remarks against bishops who trade in offices, referring probably to Gregory's successor, Nectarius.

Flavian's election kept to the spirit of the original agreement and achieved some measure of reconciliation between the rival groups.[157] Yet Gregory did not see it that way at all; indeed the Antiochenes remained divided for several more decades.

With Gregory confirmed as archbishop and the Antiochene dispute settled for the moment, the council's final item of business was to define the orthodox faith for the Eastern empire and to reconcile the Pneumatomachians to the new doctrinal program.[158] This theological work was Gregory's main concern, and for the rest of his life it remained, in his mind, the determining factor of the council. Yet surrounding the council's doctrinal deliberations lies the greatest ambiguity of all. Gregory speaks of doctrinal debates taking place after the Antiochene fiasco (*DVS* 1704–1743 and ff.), and he also seems to indicate that they had gone on in previous sessions (*DVS* 1739). However, he makes no mention of the Pneumatomachians at the council either in the *De vita sua* or in *Oration* 42,[159] except possibly in an oblique reference to the Moabites and Ammonites who were scandalously allowed to reenter the church after the Antiochene debates (*DVS* 1738–1739).[160] His intention was presumably to purge them from the record as completely as possible.[161] Socrates and Sozomen both report that as the first item of business the emperor and the bishops did their utmost to reconcile the Pneumatomachians ("Macedonians") and their leader, Bishop Eleusis, with the majority group, but that they refused and departed.[162] Yet we know that Theodosius continued his attempts to incorporate them until 384, and he would have most likely tried to convince them to rejoin the discussions if he could. It therefore appears that there were initial doctrinal conversations and a failed attempt to reconcile the Pneumatomachians early in the council, probably while Melitius was still alive,

---

157. See Hanson, *Search for the Christian Doctrine of God*, p. 810; McGuckin, *St. Gregory*, pp. 351–354. Ritter speculates that some bishops traveled immediately to Antioch and elected Flavian there (*Das Konzil*, pp. 102–103). The *Tome* of 382 says that the Syrian bishops ordained Flavian (presumably at a concurrent meeting), and that the ordination was then sanctioned by the "general council" (Theodoret, *HE* 5.9).

158. Socrates (*HE* 5.8), Sozomen (*HE* 7.7), and Theodoret (*HE* 5.7) all list this as the primary purpose of the council.

159. When Gregory refers to the arrival of the Macedonians (*DVS* 1800), he is referring to Acholius of Thessalonica, not to the Pneumatomachians.

160. The reference is made clear by comparing it with *Or.* 42.18, where Gregory refers to the Moabites and Ammonites who mischievously inquire into the generation and procession of God, in opposition to the Divinity, and therefore should not be allowed to enter the Church.

161. McGuckin, *St. Gregory*, p. 355.

162. Socrates' report is very tightly compressed, and he has Gregory's successor, Nectarius, elected before Melitius has even died (*HE* 5.8). Sozomen places the Macedonians' departure before Gregory's election—adding the strange detail that they denied the *homoousion* of the *Son*, not the Spirit (*HE* 7.7).

and that after the Antiochene dispute there were further deliberations, which the Pneumatomachians rejoined before departing for good.[163]

At the emperor's initiative, then, the council attempted to broker a settlement of the catholic faith that would represent both Trinitarians like Gregory and the bishops of Melitius' synod of 379, as well as bishops who were uncomfortable with confessing the divinity of the Holy Spirit, possibly because it smacked of modalism.[164] During the course of the deliberations, Gregory tried to persuade the bishops to accept a full doctrine of the Trinity, with the explicit declaration of the Spirit's divinity and consubstantiality with God the Father. Instead, they opposed his doctrine as an innovation (*DVS* 1760), preferring a more moderate position, as Theodosius had urged, in hopes of appealing to a greater majority, which at this point probably still included the Pneumatomachians. Even some of Gregory's close friends, he says, tried to convince him to go along with the party line—a reference possibly to Gregory of Nyssa (*DVS* 1766).[165] But in Gregory's view this proposal was deceitfully and disingenuously unorthodox (*DVS* 1750), meant to serve a dubious imperial agenda— "whatever pleased the Powerful!" (*DVS* 1709). He comments that while some actively promoted Theodosius' strategy of accommodation, many either unwillingly acquiesced to the force of authority, aided by their theological ineptitude and by the enigmatic nature of the confession (*DVS* 1750–1754), or were simply too young and inexperienced to know the difference (*DVS* 1712–1718). Gregory viewed this emerging policy of doctrinal moderation and fence-sitting as nothing short of a politically motivated betrayal of the apostolic faith, as it had been conceived already at Nicaea (*DVS* 1703–1709). Hell would freeze over before he betrayed even a small part of his salvation (*DVS* 1774–1776).

Exasperated with all this "Christ-trading" (*DVS* 1756)—and possibly just when the Pneumatomachians were readmitted (*DVS* 1737–1738)—Gregory finally stood in front of the pulpit and delivered a sardonic invitation for people to step right up and change their views again, since variety is the spice of life (*DVS* 1724–1732). At this point he had clearly lost control of the meeting.

---

163. Gregory remarks that Melitius "endured much for the sake of the Spirit, even though he was deceived at the hands of strangers" (*DVS* 1522–1523). When Gregory complains about the readmission of "the Moabites and Ammonites," his opponents assume that he had approved "these things" before—presumably referring to earlier discussions with the Pneumatomachians—and Gregory replies that someone else was in charge at that time (*DVS* 1736–1741).

164. In this regard Sozomen's report of their finally denying the consubstantiality of the Son has some plausibility. See above, n162.

165. This suggestion of McGuckin's seems entirely plausible (*St. Gregory*, p. 356). Gregory of Nyssa's close alliance with the Antiochenes and the new imperial establishment can be seen in the fact that he delivered the funeral oration for Melitius as well as for Theodosius' wife and daughter.

He soon fell ill, left the assembly, and began to move out of his lodgings (*DVS* 1745, 1777). Gregory reports that his supporters at the Anastasia again cried for him not to abandon his children, for whom he had labored so hard (*DVS* 1781–1795). Alarmed at the frayed state of the deliberations, Theodosius at this point summoned the "Egyptians and Macedonians,"[166] who represented Western interests, to bring some resolution to the council (*DVS* 1798–1802). The Egyptians arrived in mid-June and apparently tried to take charge at once, possibly even attempting to reverse the work of the previous sessions; however, they met the immediate resistance of the Eastern bishops, and another furious confrontation ensued (*DVS* 1803–1808). The Alexandrians then engaged in a bitter dispute with the Antiochenes and Constantinopolitans. Although they initially supported Gregory's ministry in the capital,[167] the Alexandrians had since tried to impose their own candidate as archbishop, and—now the decisive factor—they profoundly resented Constantinople's aspiration to be recognized as the second see of the Church after Rome.[168]

In their effort to assume control, the Egyptians questioned the legitimacy of Gregory's office on the dubious grounds that he had violated canon 15 of the Council of Nicaea, which prohibits the translation of bishops from one see to another. Gregory reports that they told him in secret not to take it personally, and that it was a tack aimed at thwarting the Antiochenes, who had appointed him. He knew very well that it was a trumped-up charge, based on a rule that had long been defunct,[169] and which did not apply to him anyway, since he had never been installed at Sasima and he was not the ordinary bishop

---

166. That is, representatives of the provinces of Macedonia, esp. Acholius of Thessalonica. This reference, along with the absence of the term in Gregory's description of the Pneumatomachians earlier in the poem (*DVS* 1180), suggests that, in 382, they are not yet known as "Macedonians."

167. See *Ors.* 21 and 34.

168. See canon 3, discussed below. The Antiochenes were seen as being allied with Constantinople in this regard, in what was becoming a grand East-West conflict. It was to have a long and equally undignified future.

169. Rufinus concurs with Gregory's judgment (*HE* 9.9); see Ritter, *Das Konzil*, p. 104n5. There are numerous examples of the uncontested translation of bishops after the Council of Nicaea. The Council of Serdica in 343 further qualifies the rule, specifically banning the "transmigration" of bishops, which it defines as a move to another see out of personal *ambitio* or *dominatio* (*Concilium Sardicense* 1; *EOM* 1.2.452–453). In the same vein, Damasus' denouncement of translations in his letter of 380 to Acholius refers only to Maximus, who sought to usurp Gregory out of obvious ambition (Damasus, *Ep.* 1), but not to Gregory himself, whom Damasus never mentions in connection with translation in any of his efforts to renew the disciplinary canons. Between 371 and 379 little attention was paid to reinstatement or enforcing the ban (see *DVS* 1800–1811); Basil even wrote to both congregations in *defense* of the translation of Bishop Euphronius from Colonia to Nicopolis in 375 (*Ep.* 227–230). Partly in response to the Antiochene schism, Damasus began to urge a greater enforcement of canonical order in conjunction with the Antiochene synod of 379. Gregory can therefore claim that he ministered in Constantinople with full knowledge and support of the Roman church, which he esteems more

of Nazianzus (*DVS* 1810–1817).[170] But this was the last straw. Gregory was now so thoroughly disgusted with the proceedings that he accepted the Egyptian intrusion as a providential opportunity to be relieved of a thankless job. It was a complex turn of events: he clearly wanted to be rid of the wretched ordeal, yet at the same time he took it as a defeat of his arduous theological labors of the last two years; and he was of course deeply embarrassed at such a public disgrace.[171] It may be that Gregory could have weathered the Egyptians' charges and remained archbishop if he had supported the election of Flavian,[172] but he could no longer bear what he saw as a fundamental compromise of the Church's faith.

Gregory later came to see the dispute over the Antiochene succession as the central and lingering plague of the council, and the main cause of its failure to promulgate the orthodox faith. When he appeared before the bishops to answer the charges brought by the Egyptians, he surprised them with a speech of resignation instead (*DVS* 1827–1855). Gregory declared his allegiance to the Trinity one last time, and he willingly accepted the role as Jonah, to be tossed overboard for the sake of the ship—though in his case the storm was not of his making—if only the bishops would unite themselves in the true faith. He then walked out of the assembly, to the shocked applause and honors of the bishops, and proceeded to ask the emperor's consent to resign (*DVS* 1879–1904).

As Gregory's replacement, the council elected the unbaptized civil servant Nectarius, probably on the recommendation of Diodore.[173] R. P. C. Hanson's comment aptly captures the situation as Gregory saw it: "It was as if the cardinals had chosen as Pope, in default of any other, the mayor of Rome.... Few people can have been less qualified for greatness suddenly thrust upon them."[174] Gregory realized all too well that the theologically uneducated but highly polished Nectarius would splendidly represent the interests of Theodosius and Diodore and be an ideal imperial bishop. The council's final doctrinal definitions most likely came after Gregory left. All three historians report

---

highly than most other sees, and that it blames his opponents—the Alexandrians and Diodore—for his undoing (*Carm.* 2.1.12.125–134). The prohibition of translations of sees in the ninth anathema of the *Tome of Damasus* dates from the final redaction of the document in 382, after the events of 381. See Scholz, *Transmigration*; Field, *On the Communion*, esp. pp. 156–163, 182–185, and app. III (on translation), and pp. 139–40, 184–185 (on the *Tomus Damasi*).

170. See also *Ep.* 87.5. In his will, which he probably wrote at the end of 381, Gregory designates himself bishop of Constantinople. In the bishops' lists of the Council of Constantinople he appears as bishop of Nazianzus. Daley, *Gregory of Nazianzus*, pp. 184–185.

171. Gregory's resentment can be seen in an earlier passage on the history of the Nicene movement, where he makes it a point to note that Arius was an Egyptian (*DVS* 576).

172. McGuckin, *St. Gregory*, p. 361.

173. Sozomen, *HE* 7.8.

174. Hanson, *Search for the Christian Doctrine of God*, p. 811.

that the council issued its doctrinal statement and canons under Nectarius' leadership,[175] and Gregory himself intimates as much (*DVS* 1749). He would certainly have learned of it in any case, and so his later impressions need not depend on his presence at the time. In its canons the council declared the faith of Nicaea still to be established and denounced all heresies, specifically the Anhomoian Eunomians, the Arian Eudoxians, the Semiarian Pneumatomachians, and the Sabellians, Marcellans, Photinians, and Apollinarians. (canon 1).[176] It also regulated the boundaries of dioceses and provincial synods, especially those of Alexandria, Antioch, and the dioceses of Asia, Pontus, and Thrace (canon 2);[177] it declared the see of Constantinople second in honor after the see of Rome, "because it is the New Rome" (canon 3); and it denounced Maximus and declared his ordination null and void (canon 4). Thus the council established Constantinople as the chief patriarchate of the Eastern church, a position that would be reiterated in canon 28 of the Council of Chalcedon in 451, although it would continue to be denied by the West.

In addition to reaffirming the Creed of Nicaea ("N"), the council also issued the famous Niceno-Constantinopolitan Creed, later found in the common eucharistic liturgies ("C").[178] Considering that the council reaffirmed N in canon 1, and that nine of the twelve variations between C and N are insignificant, C appears to be neither a replacement for N nor a revision of it, but rather the council's own statement and fuller explanation of the Nicene faith, possibly based on a local baptismal creed or that of another Eastern church—*a* Nicene creed, in other words, of which there were many in the fourth century. Among the three significant variants with N, the addition of the phrase "whose kingdom will have no end" to the article on the Son was by now a stock element aimed against Marcellus, which would elicit no objection from Gregory. More significant is the lack of the Nicene phrase that the Son is "of the substance of the Father," which may well have been omitted during negotiations with homoiousian Spirit-Fighters, if it was even there to begin with.[179] Considering the central place that this phrase holds in Athanasius' explanation and defense

---

175. Socrates, *HE* 5.8; Sozomen, *HE* 7.9; and Theodoret, *HE* 5.8. Hanson concurs as well (*Search for the Christian Doctrine of God*, p. 811).

176. The Greek text of the canons can be found in Lauchert, *Kanones*, pp. 84–85.

177. A dead letter as soon as it was legislated. Hanson, *Search for the Christian Doctrine of God*, p. 808.

178. The best treatment of the creed of Constantinople is Kelly, *Early Christian Creeds*, pp. 296–367. See also Ritter, *Das Konzil*, pp. 123–147; Simonetti, *La crisi Ariana*, pp. 538–542; and Hanson, *Search for the Christian Doctrine of God*, pp. 812–820. For the Greek text, see Dossetti, *Il símbolo*, pp. 244–250; reprinted with English translation in Kelly, *Early Christian Creeds*, pp. 297–298.

179. As May ("Die Datierung," pp. 53–54) and Ritter (*Das Konzil*, pp. 132–147) argue. Hanson, however, is skeptical (*Search for the Christian Doctrine*, p. 818; see also Sozomen, *HE* 7.7).

of the *homoousion* of the Son, its omission in C is an important marker of the continuing distinctness of Eastern confessions (even with a contingent of Alexandrians present) from the doctrinal edifice of Athanasius and those who later followed him. Yet of the greatest consequence is the long addition to the article on the Spirit: "And we believe in the Holy Spirit, the Lord and giver of life, who proceeds from the Father, who with the Father and Son is together worshipped and together glorified, who spoke through the prophets."[180] What this statement does not mention is that the Spirit is "God" (θεόν) or "of the same being with the Father" (ὁμοούσιον τῷ Πατρί), as the creed states regarding the Son. The language used seems to have been chosen originally to accommodate the Pneumatomachians, then retained to please either the emperor, in hopes of future reconciliation, or another group of bishops about whom we have little information. It closely reflects Basil's reserve on the divinity of the Spirit in the mid-370s,[181] which Gregory of Nyssa also showed, but it represents exactly what Gregory objected to, both in the 370s and at the council of 381. His comments in the *De vita sua* probably refer to C, or a draft of it: in language that suggests he is comparing the two creeds, he complains that the doctrinal work of the council was "an offspring completely unlike its parents"—i.e., the council distorted the faith of Nicaea. (*DVS* 1755).[182] It is possible that Diodore, Gregory of Nyssa, and the other bishops sincerely thought that this less offensive statement was an adequate way to confess a pro-Nicene doctrine of the Spirit, with the added benefit of ecclesiastical peacemaking,[183] but Gregory is not so sure. In his mind it would have been better to stay with the bare terms of Nicaea than to promulgate a creed which in the current debates was obviously intended to leave room for Pneumatomachian or similar views. According to the synodical letter of 382, the council also produced a longer *Tomos*,[184] but regrettably this is lost.

On July 9, 381, the council ended, and on July 30 Theodosius confirmed its conclusions in the edict *Episcopis tradi,* which named as arbiters of the catholic faith Nectarius and Timothy—representing Constantinople and Alexandria, in that order—then Pelagius of Laodicea and Diodore of Tarsus of the diocese of

---

180. Hanson points to four significant variations (*Search for the Christian Doctrine of God*, pp. 816–818, following the original analysis of Kelly). The fourth of these, the lack of any anathemas in C, is not to my mind significant, in light of the denunciation of heretics in canon 1. The third significant variant is the lack of the phrase "that is, of the substance of the Father."
181. See Basil, *Ep.* 110.2. It also reflects the earlier language of Athanasius, *Ep. Serap.* 1.31.
182. See also *DVS* 1703–1709.
183. As Anthony Meredith has argued: "Pneumatology of the Cappadocian Fathers."
184. Theodoret, *HE* 5.9.

Oriens, Amphilochius of Iconium and Optimus of Pisidian Antioch in Asia, and Helladius of Caesarea, Gregory of Nyssa, and Terennius of Scythis, as well as Marmarius of Marcianopolis in Pontus.[185] Having resigned his see, Gregory is not mentioned in this list—although neither is Damasus of Rome or Flavian of Antioch. By this time Gregory was well on his way back to his home in Cappadocia, if he was not there already.

381–390: Final Years in Cappadocia

Gregory's hard labor and ultimate defeat at the Council of Constantinople had a profoundly determinative effect on the final shape of his literary and theological work. Although he had been so frustratingly vanquished in the capital, he knew that his work on behalf of the Trinity was far from over, and he hastened home to repair the damage that had been done. While he felt that he had been personally insulted, Gregory believed that he had an even greater pastoral and theological responsibility to defend his work. In the remaining years of his life, he conducted a massive literary campaign to rehabilitate his ecclesiastical reputation and to persuade his contemporaries and his posterity of the true, saving doctrine of the Trinity. This included a whole array of autobiographical and theological poems, four more orations, and many more letters—much of which was addressed and sent directly back to Constantinople.

Soon after his return, Gregory wrote five major pieces to this end.[186] He seems to have very quickly written the long poem *De seipso et de episcopis* (*Carm.* 2.1.12), an apologetic diatribe against bad bishops, which draws from his earlier work on pastoral ministry and is prefaced by a brief account of his tenure in Constantinople.[187] He then composed the *De vita sua* (*Carm.* 2.1.11), a much more extensive account of his life, which was designed to vindicate his work in Constantinople, focusing especially on the council. An innovative piece of autobiographical literature, the poem's greater length would have taken more time, but it, too, shows signs of having been written in haste.[188] By the end of the year, he also produced *Oration 42 The Last Farewell* and *Oration 43 Funeral*

---

185. *C. Th.* 16.1.3.

186. On Gregory's early works in retirement, see McLynn, "Voice of Conscience"; Elm, "Inventing the 'Father of the Church,'" and Sykes, *Poemata Arcana*, p.66.

187. McLynn's argument that Gregory wrote this poem before Nectarius was consecrated, in order to influence the choice of his successor ("Voice of Conscience," p. 303), seems to me unlikely, given the retrospective character of the work.

188. McLynn, "Voice of Conscience," p. 299.

Oration for Basil the Great; and, by early 382, the systematic *Poemata Arcana*, modeled on the structure of Origen's *On First Principles*. In *Oration 42* Gregory records his final speech to the council, in which he provides another account of his work in Constantinople on behalf of the Trinity and gives an important summary statement of his doctrine in moderate, formulaic terms (42.14–18). Although the oration purports to be Gregory's final speech before the council, it is a considerably longer address than the one presented in the *De vita sua* (*DVS* 1827–1855). Jean Bernardi has convincingly argued that the oration was written and distributed in several stages,[189] and that in its current form Gregory describes himself as no longer holding major pastoral responsibilities or dwelling in the capital.[190] Given the common themes between the two speeches, they may both derive from the same original address, though *Oration 42* is more polished and elaborate.[191] As its title indicates, the oration is presented as a farewell address (λόγος συνακτήριος), but by section four it has become a formal defense of Gregory's work in the capital (λόγος ἀπολογήτικος). Susanna Elm has shown, moreover, that Gregory carefully presents his case in the rhetoric and legal terminology of a civil servant giving an account of himself at the end of his career, while also presenting his own certificate of discharge, such as a magistrate might receive from the emperor.[192] Thus Gregory makes his case to the bishops and the emperor in Constantinople and at the same time portrays himself as the exemplary bishop and judge, the true teacher of the faith who continues to instruct his charges from his place of retreat.

On January 1, 382, Gregory delivered his famous memorial oration in praise of Basil (*Or*. 43) to what remained of Basil's community in Caesarea on the third anniversary of his death. Basil's death had left Gregory with mixed feelings about what had been his most intimate adult relationship, an important professional collaboration, and yet his most painful personal betrayal. Moreover, Basil's successor in Caesarea, Helladius, does not appear to have held Basil in high regard.[193] Gregory therefore made use of the anniversary— his first such opportunity since returning from the capital—to celebrate the

---

189. Based on significant variations and insertions in the manuscript tradition. Bernardi, SC 384, p. 24.

190. The key phrase is Gregory's statement that he now enjoys the "freedom of obscurity" (42.22). Bernardi, SC 384, p. 14.

191. McGuckin hypothesizes that after Gregory's resignation speech in *DVS* 1827–1855, the bishops, by order of the emperor, sought to honor him by inviting him to deliver a series of orations before leaving, of which only *Or*. 42 remains (*St. Gregory*, pp. 361–362 and n268). But there is no evidence that this occurred, and it seems unlikely given the contentious state of the council.

192. The first seven sections are organized in accordance with the requirements for such an address in *C. Th.* 1.32.2, 67–68. See Elm, "Inventing the 'Father of the Church,'" pp. 9–11 and nn21, 24.

193. Van Dam, *Becoming Christian*, p. 96.

memory of his friend, and at the same time to reestablish himself among the Caesarean Christian community. As Neil McLynn has observed, Gregory narrates Basil's life and work chiefly in terms of its relation to himself.[194] He bolsters his own image by praising Basil as the ideal Christian bishop, one whose ministry is characterized by personal virtue, pastoral concern, and faithfulness to the doctrine of the Trinity. The work has long been hailed as a masterpiece of Greek rhetoric and Christian hagiography. The longest of Gregory's orations, it could hardly have been delivered in its current form,[195] and so must have been expanded later. *Oration* 43 is a major source of information on both Gregory's and Basil's lives, and a key witness to Gregory's ideal of pastoral ministry. Thanks to its monumental rhetorical success, it is also the chief reason why Basil has typically been regarded as the theological leader of the two, and why their relationship has been considered so harmonious.[196] All the same, Gregory does indicate that he was Basil's mentor and initiator in Athens (43.16–22), and he makes no mention at all of Basil's sister Macrina or of Eustathius of Sebaste, the two main influences on Basil's development besides Gregory—doubtless because of their reputation for being less than fully sympathetic with Gregory's Trinitarian program. While the piece may have initially been directed to the Caesarean community and not among the original missives sent to Constantinople, Gregory obviously intended the final version for posterity; we will examine it in detail in chapter 5. In addition to these four major pieces, Gregory also wrote and circulated many poems on the Trinity and on himself during his early retirement.[197]

At the end of his speech to the council in *Oration* 42, Gregory tells the bishops that, although he will no longer address them in person, his tongue will not cease to "fight with pen and ink" (42.26). In his late works, Gregory strenuously defends his life's work on behalf of the Trinity. As he narrates his upbringing and education, his unsought ordination and episcopal consecration, his ministry in Nazianzus and Constantinople, his auspicious installation in the Church of the Holy Apostles, and his unwanted presidency of the council—every episode proves his credentials as an inspired Christian teacher (*DVS* 51–551). He then sets his work in a larger, providential context: Although the true faith once flourished in Constantinople, it had been ravaged by heresy since the time of Arius (who, he is happy to note, came from the wicked city of

---

194. McLynn, "Gregory Nazianzen's Basil," esp. pp. 180–181.
195. Gallay estimates it would have taken two and a half hours to deliver it orally (*La vie*, p. 214).
196. See, e.g., *Or.* 43.17.
197. *Ep.* 176 indicates that Gregory's poetry was being read and responded to by both friends and opponents. McLynn, "Voice of Conscience," p. 300. See also Gregory's "Defense of His Verses" (*Carm.* 2.1.39).

Alexandria, *DVS* 574–578; *Or.* 42.3); yet God summoned Gregory to revive the parched souls of the faithful with a stream of true doctrine (*DVS* 592–599). Through his faithful teaching and pastoral care, Gregory succeeded in establishing the sound faith at the heart of the empire, "the eye of the *oikoumene*" which was to be the source of orthodoxy throughout the world (42.10). During this time the faithful came to him as the only orthodox teacher they could find (*DVS* 1140). It was nothing short of a "resurrection" of the faith that lay buried (42.6)—the very name of Gregory's congregation (42.26)—in which Gregory was the instrument of redemption. In these accounts, Gregory wants to make it clear that he reestablished the true faith independently of the Antiochenes who had invited him (*DVS* 1127–1128, a hint to Diodore and Flavian), and before the intervention of Theodosius in 380 and the council in 381 (a hint to Nectarius).[198]

Yet despite all his efforts, Gregory tells his readers, he met resistance all along the way. Not only was there initial opposition from Eunomians, Homoians, and others, and the embarrassing betrayal by Maximus, but Gregory ultimately had to contend with the enmity of those he thought loyal to the cause of the Trinity. While Gregory pursued salvation, moderation, and withdrawal for the sake of purification (*DVS* 1414, 1434, 1866–1867), he was faced with bribery at court, charges of malfeasance, and an attempt on his life (*DVS* 1424, 1441–1484). Worst of all, however, was the envy of the bishops and the lust for power at the council (*DVS* 1506–1508). He complains that his hearers want "not priests but orators, not stewards of souls but treasurers of money, not pure offerers of the sacrifice, but powerful patrons" (42.24). In short, Gregory thought the council's failure to achieve an East-West consensus over a strong pro-Nicene confession was an inexcusable and unfathomable loss (*DVS* 1560–1561, 1645–1647), and that the disputing parties were simply derelict in their duty as bishops (*DVS* 1591–1595). In the end, he could no longer bear the unholy war between East and West and the hostile rivalry of the bishops (42.20–22): he must now fight from a distance. In several of these passages, and in many of the letters written at this time, Gregory vigorously (though often anonymously) attacks particular bishops, above all his successor, Nectarius, Timothy of Alexandria, and Diodore of Tarsus.[199] Meanwhile, he claims the fruit of his labors, which is his congregation of the Anastasia and those bishops whom he led to the Trinitarian faith (42.1–2, 9, 11–12, 15, 27)—no doubt a signal to his remaining supporters to disseminate the true faith as best they can.

---

198. See also *DVS* 1854: "What tongue will defend the Trinity now? An independent and zealous one."
199. See McGuckin, "Autobiography as Apologia."

In his farewell address, Gregory gives a summary exposition of the faith (42.14–18), which he offers as a final bargaining chip that all can agree on. Once more he tries the conciliatory approach (as he had in *Or.* 41), encouraging those who are "hiding their piety" and those who are close to proclaiming it, but hesitate out of fear or cautious reserve (οἰκονομία) to come around to the true faith (42.14).[200] As in the case of Basil's "economy" or equivocation over the Spirit,[201] Gregory hardly thinks that such a position is justifiable, and he is prepared to lead the way once again in making the bold confession. For further instruction, he recommends that they refer to his earlier writings, the body of orations that he had delivered in the capital and left as a legacy (42.18). As he bids farewell to the Anastasia, the Holy Apostles, the city, and the assembled bishops, he gives them a final charge, "Approach the truth; be converted even in this last hour!" (42.27). Around the same time, on December 31, 381, Gregory executed his will at a gathering of local bishops; in it, he bequeaths most of his resources to the poor in Nazianzus.[202] In this formal and symbolically final document, he conspicuously designates himself "Gregory, bishop of the Catholic Church in Constantinople."[203] No matter how circumstances may appear, he is still the rightful shepherd of the imperial capital and the chief theologian of the Eastern Church. According to the fifth-century historians, certain emperors greatly enlarged Gregory's Church of the Anastasia, making it both beautiful and grand. Theodosius may have been the first such emperor, and Gregory's much loathed successor may have donated marble panels for the beautifications.[204]

Although the council of 381 has come to be seen as the great triumph of the Nicene faith under the Theodosian settlement, Gregory's work in this period shows just how fragile and tumultuous things really were. Gregory again took up the pastoral oversight of his father's church in Nazianzus, with the help of his presbyter Cledonius, as he continued to press for the orthodox faith in the wider Church. In the spring of 382, as the capital prepared to celebrate its first Theodosian Easter, Gregory protested the imperial settlement by observing a "silent Lent," which he then loudly advertised to the bishops and

---

200. See also *Ors.* 42.18: Gregory delivered the doctrinal summary mainly to show that they were on the same side, sharing the same doctrine; 42.25: the Trinity was their common worship and hope.

201. See *Or.* 43.68–69.

202. On the long-contested dating of Gregory's will, see Daley, *Gregory of Nazianzus*, pp. 184–186. See also Van Dam, "Self-Representation in the Will of Gregory of Nazianzus," pp. 136–137, on the hypothesis that Gregory altered it later.

203. See also Gregory's final words of farewell, in which he prays to the Trinity to preserve his flock, "for they are mine, even if I have been assigned elsewhere" (*Or.* 42.27).

204. Socrates, *HE* 5.7; Sozomen, *HE* 7.5. See Snee, "Gregory Nazianzen's Anastasia Church."

the emperor at court.²⁰⁵ He was invited to attend the council held in the summer of 382, but he was so disgusted with Church meetings that he declined to attend (*Ep.* 130–131) and instead wrote letters to Theodosian generals urging them to press for harmony in the Church (*Ep.* 132–133, 135–136). In a series of letters he also criticized the inept Nectarius and tried to provide some needed guidance from his remove in Nazianzus. Because he often levels his criticism under the veil of sarcastic praise, in keeping with the conventions of Hellenistic rhetoric, Gregory's regard for Nectarius has long been thought to be pleasant and supportive. But the letters show the true extent of his virulent feelings for his successor, who he thought was a state-sponsored affront to the Christian gospel and the antithesis of the faithful leadership that a bishop was supposed to provide.²⁰⁶

At Easter 383 Gregory delivered *Oration 45 On Holy Pascha*, which repeats verbatim several sections of *Oration* 38²⁰⁷ and contains some of the most important passages in his corpus on the identity and the saving work of Christ. In their conventional numbering, *Orations* 1 and 45 thus frame Gregory's corpus of orations with the theme of Resurrection (ἀνάστασις), again the name of his congregation in Constantinople. On the following Sunday (if not at an earlier date)²⁰⁸ he preached *Oration 44 On the New Sunday* for the feast of the Cappadocian martyr Mamas, possibly in the basilica of Caesarea. The sermon focuses on the Easter Light of the Trinity, and includes extensive moral paranesis based on the example of the local monks.

The final theological debate of Gregory's career began in the autumn of 383, when a group of Apollinarians attempted to take over his church at Nazianzus. Cledonius sent news to Gregory at the hot springs in Xanxaris, where he was recuperating from another illness, and Gregory responded with *Letter* 101, his best-known Christological treatise. In the following year he further addressed the problem in a letter to Nectarius (*Ep.* 202), followed by a second letter to Cledonius in 384 or 385 (*Ep.* 102).²⁰⁹ In subsequent theological tradition these three letters became a classic expression of Christological orthodoxy and a major influence on the terminology of the fifth- through eighth-century Christological controversies; we will consider them in detail in chapter

---

205. Through Palladius, the *magister officiorum* (*Ep.* 119). See Gallay, *Saint Grégoire de Nazianze, Lettres*, vol. 2, p. 5; McLynn, "Voice of Conscience," p. 301.
206. See McLynn, "Voice of Conscience," p. 303. See also, for a full discussion of the correspondence, McGuckin, *St. Gregory*, pp. 377–384.
207. *Or.*, 45.3–9 = 38.7–13; 45.26–27 = 38.14–15.
208. On the questionable dating of this oration, see Daley, *Gregory of Nazianzus*, pp. 154–155.
209. See also *Ep.* 115, 121, 138; *Carm.* 2.1.19.101–102.

4. In *Letter* 202 Gregory seeks Nectarius' and Theodosius' support in opposing the Apollinarians, and he mentions Theodosius' recent council with the Arians, Macedonians, and Eunomians—to which Nectarius had not invited Gregory, but instead consulted the schismatic Novatians[210]—and Theodosius' suspension of his own earlier laws that banned the Arians from assembling inside the city walls (202.4). Although these letters are almost universally regarded as anti-Apollinarian treatises,[211] they in fact declare Gregory's Christological position much more broadly, and are arguably oriented at least as strongly against Diodore as they are against Apollinarius.[212] All of these points work together to suggest that Gregory considers Diodore—probably the person most responsible for his downfall at the council, the man who recommended Nectarius as Gregory's replacement, and now an influential and well-established advisor to the emperor—an even greater threat to the faith than Diodore's Christological rival, Apollinarius, even as he still urges Nectarius and Theodosius to wake up and deal with the Apollinarians. Apollinarius was finally listed as a heretic in December 383.[213] In Gregory's view, the imperial religious settlement was not going well, and Nectarius was managing to ruin the Trinitarian consensus that he and Melitius had been laboring to renew since 379.[214]

Gregory's literary campaign occupied him for several years. By the end of 383 he was ready to retire from public life for good, so he arranged for his cousin Eulalius to be consecrated as bishop of Nazianzus. Having turned the church buildings in Nazianzus and his estate at Karbala into a monastic establishment, he permanently retired to Karbala, with his deacon Gregory and the monk Eustathius.[215] During his final years, he continued to write poems and letters and to exert his influence through his literary activity and modest socializing. Through it all, Gregory proved himself to be a master of communication and in many ways a literary pioneer. With the help of his great-nephew Nicobulus (*Ep.*

---

210. Socrates, *HE* 5.10.

211. See, e.g., the current critical edition and introduction by Gallay (*SC* 208) and the most recent English translation and introduction by Wickham (*St. Gregory of Nazianzus, On God and Christ*, pp. 149–172, which contains only *Ep.* 101–102).

212. On which see chap. 2.

213. *C. Th.* 16.5.12. Passages in *Or.* 22, from 379, and the *De vita sua*, originally written in 382, were probably added at this time or later. Apollinarius is also anathematized in the canons of the council of 381 (canon 1).

214. Gregory of Nyssa also preaches against the incompetence of Nectarius in 383 or 384; *Deit. Fil. et Spir.* (*PG* 46, 556D). See Bernardi, *Le prédication*, pp. 329–330; McLynn, "Voice of Conscience," p. 307n40.

215. Gregory had willed all of his property to "the catholic Church in Nazianzus" for the care of the poor, under the supervision of the deacon Gregory (*Test.*). McGuckin argues that a monastic community continued there for a long time after Gregory's death (*St. Gregory*, pp. 385, 394).

52–53), he became the first known Greek writer to collect and publish his own letters, together with a selection of Basil's letters to him. Gregory's epistolary and poetic activity in the 380s reflects a continuing engagement with the classical schools and the literary world of Cappadocia—arguably the greatest such involvement among the early fathers of the Church[216]—as well as a continued effort to bolster his ecclesiastical reputation through his relationship with Basil.[217] Included in the collection is a letter to Nicobulus that has become an exemplary treatise on Hellenistic epistolary theory (*Ep.* 51). During this period Gregory also edited and published his orations, either as a single set or in various combinations, with the help of Eulalius.[218] By the time of his death in 390, at the approximate age of sixty-one,[219] he had also produced some 17,000 lines of extant poetry, most of it during his retirement, which he also seems to have published in some form. Gregory's poetry served both a private function, as an ascetical exercise and a comfort in the illness of his old age, and a public purpose, in order to benefit the young by providing a new body of Christian poetry (*Carm.* 2.1.39.37–39), much as he sought to provide a corpus of essential Greek Christian sermons by publishing his orations.[220] The poems are a major source for our knowledge of Gregory's views on a number of personal, moral, and political subjects. But, like much of his work, they have often been read far too straightforwardly, to the neglect of their highly stylized literary form, which has resulted in the unlikely image of Gregory as a persistently melancholic complainer. On the contrary, as McGuckin has adeptly shown, Gregory was a consummate artist in his poetic self-portrayal and his literary jousts with his rivals, just as he was in his orations and letters. In the process, he also created several subgenres of Greek literature.[221]

In sum, Gregory produced nothing short of an all-encompassing, classical Christian *paideia*, centered around the confession of the Trinity.[222] His own

---

216. McLynn, "Among the Hellenists," pp. 218, 238.

217. The selection and structure of the collection highlight Gregory's leadership and influence in the relationship. McLynn, "Gregory Nazianzen's Basil," pp. 184–186. On Gregory's leadership in the doctrine of the Holy Spirit, which is esp. evident in the letters, see chap. 3.

218. E.g., *Or.* 13 bears the title *On the Consecration to Doara, edited by Bishop Eulalius* (PG 35.852).

219. On the date of Gregory's death, see Nautin, "La date." Hartmann, "Gregory of Nazianzus," gives ca. 326 for Gregory's date of birth, citing *DVS* 239 and 512f., as well as *Ep.* 50.8; however, the latter reference is irrelevant.

220. On the scope, purpose, and editing of Gregory's poetry, see McGuckin, "Gregory: The Rhetorician as Poet," esp. pp. 202–204.

221. Including the apologetic sermon (*Ors.* 1–3, 9, 12, on his reluctant ordination and consecration), the Christian eulogy (*Ors.* 7, 8, 18), the damning obituary (*Ors.* 4–5 against Julian), and the poetic autobiography (*Carm.* 2.1.11 *De vita sua*). See McLynn, "Voice of Conscience."

222. McGuckin, "Gregory: The Rhetorician as Poet," p. 210.

corpus is his clearest statement of the use of classical literature in the service of Christian culture, and his most resounding reply to the attempted censure of Emperor Julian. Gregory's aim as a preacher, a pastor, and a writer was both to influence the Church and empire of his own day and to bequeath to posterity a new body of Christian literature, which could be used for theological reference, grammatical exercises, and rhetorical training—much as it was during the long Byzantine era. In the end Gregory was eminently successful: he far outlasted his less gifted contemporaries and became the single most influential writer in Byzantine culture. Although he was defeated at the council, it was Gregory who ultimately wore the victor's crown (στεφηφόρος, DVS 1919–1920) as the real arbiter of the orthodox faith and the seminal teacher of the classical Christian doctrine of the Trinity.[223] This book is devoted to exploring the meaning of that doctrine as a theological and practical vision of the Christian life.

---

223. If the synodical letter of 382 is any indication, Gregory may have had some effect almost immediately. In language that reflects the Western councils of the 370s (*Ea grat.* 14.49; *Non nobis* 18.108) as well as Athanasius (*Ep. cath.* 7), it states that the council of 381 confessed the "consubstantial and coeternal Trinity" (Theodoret, HE 5.9)—more like the doctrine that Gregory *wanted* the council to confess, but which it did not.

I

God and the Theologian

Where there is purification there is illumination; and illumination is the satisfaction of desire for those who long for the greatest things, or The Greatest Thing—or That Which Surpasses All Greatness.

—*Oration* 39

Gregory of Nazianzus is best known in Christian tradition for his definitive teaching on the Holy Trinity. Yet, in a way that does not fit neatly into the divisions of modern systematic theology, his Trinitarian doctrine consists less in devising technically accurate statements about how God is both one and three, or even in the doctrine of God per se, than it does in a whole nexus of concerns that bear as much on Christian anthropology, language theory, and sacramental theology as they do on the loftier spheres of modern Christian dogma. One of the most characteristic aspects of Gregory's oeuvre and a cardinal principle of his theological system is his repeated insistence that the knowledge of God is inseparably related to the condition of the human knower—that theology both demands and causes a change in the state of the theologian, and that it involves a wide range of practical and theoretical concerns that are integral to its basic meaning. What later writers, especially in post-Reformation Western circles, have sharply distinguished as theology, Christology, and anthropology are in Gregory's work unavoidably intermingled, in both rhetorical form and dogmatic content. By sheer volume, Gregory devotes more attention to ascetical and spiritual themes than he does to Christ or the Trinity. Accordingly, scholars in the twentieth century produced more studies of Gregory's ascetical theology than of his Christology and Trinitarian doctrine combined[1]—though, in keeping with the modern, Western approach, they tend to be artificially disconnected from his broader dogmatic system. In Gregory's view, Christian theology involves and represents a dynamic, lived relationship between God and the theologian, and so it begins not with abstract information about God—as if this could ever be acquired neutrally—but with the transformation of the theologian within the horizon of God's presence and activity in the world, as it is recognized and celebrated in the life of the Church. It is a common refrain in Gregory's work that spiritual progress and right belief unavoidably go together. In other words, Gregory's doctrines of God and of the human person intrinsically involve each other; as Jean Plagnieux observes, it is impossible to separate Gregory's doctrine of God from his doctrine of the means by which God is known.[2] Gregory's doctrine of the Trinity thus includes the theologian's own situation with respect to God, and theology is a real illumination by which the theologian is initiated into the divine mystery in concrete and far-reaching ways. It is here, Gregory repeatedly insists, that we must begin.[3]

The first point of Gregory's doctrine, then—both in the argument of his major texts and in the epistemic priority of the reader—is a two-poled dialectic of purification and illumination, which constitutes the spiritual framework in which the knowledge of God takes place and the content of theology has its meaning. This dynamic runs throughout Gregory's corpus, and it becomes especially prominent in his mature work, from his arrival in Constantinople until the end of his life (379–390). It is significant that when he sets about to give a summary account of his doctrine, Gregory typically begins with the purification that is required in order to know God: in his first oration in Con-

---

1. See esp. the work of Bouyer, Ellverson, Gilbert, McGuckin, Norris, Pinault, Plagnieux, Ruether, Spidlík, and Szymusiak, in addition to the many works on Gregory's rhetorical style and poetics.

2. Plagnieux, *Saint Grégoire*, p. 109; see also Bouyer, *Spirituality*, pp. 348–350.

3. In this respect Gregory's work gives a similar sort of fundamental place to the practices, contexts, and concrete ways of learning language that Wittgenstein addresses in his mature philosophy. Among the recent theologians who have noted similar connections between traditional Christian doctrine and the work of Wittgenstein, see Rowan Williams, *On Christian Theology*, pp. 152, 201; *Why Study the Past*, pp. 90–91 and passim. See also Norris, "Theology as Grammar."

stantinople (20.1–4), the *Theological Orations* (*Ors.* 27–28), the great Epiphany cycle (38.1, 4–6),[4] and the programmatic *Poemata Arcana* (*Carm.* 1.1.1.1–5, 7–9). In the *Theological Orations,* his most famous defense of Trinitarian doctrine, Gregory begins not with ideas about God, Christ, or the Holy Spirit, but with a rhetorically charged prologue that focuses on the reader's own character and attitude toward God, in order to establish the human conditions for the possibility of knowing God. He devotes the first *Theological Oration* entirely to this subject, and at the beginning of the second he gives his most paradigmatic statement of the idea. Here Gregory dramatically portrays the relationship between God and the theologian in a first-person narration of Moses' ascent up Mount Sinai to meet with God (28.2–3)[5]—a motif that was to become enormously influential in later traditions of Christian spirituality.[6] In two distinct movements, the passage depicts the dialectic of purification and illumination in which the knowledge of God takes place. This text encapsulates much of Gregory's thinking on theological development, and so it will serve as an organizing device for the multiple texts and themes of this chapter.

The Purification of the Theologian

As a model for Christian theology, Gregory looks to the theophany of Moses at Mount Sinai, the paradigmatic biblical encounter with God before the

---

4. In *Or.* 38 the ascetical themes are intermixed with Christology, as befits a festal oration, though they are equally fundamental to the work.

5. Based on Ex 19–20 and 24. Gregory frequently refers to Moses as a paradigm of the knowledge of God and an exemplary spiritual leader; see esp. *Ors.* 2.92; 9.1; 18.14; 20.2; 32.16, 33; 28.2–3; 31.1; 37.3; 39.9; 40.45; 45.11; *Carm.* 1.1.1.11–13. On Gregory's extensive use of personal and impersonal examples (παραδείγματα), see Demoen, *Pagan and Biblical Exempla.*

6. Gregory is largely responsible for creating the image of Moses as a primary model of Christian growth and the vision of God. There are brief statements in Origen that hint at such a use of Moses. In *Comm.Jn.* 32.338–343 Origen refers to the glory that shone in Moses' face "when he was conversing with the divine nature" on Mount Sinai, to which he adds a summary comment on purification and contemplation: "The mind that has been purified and has surpassed all material things, so as to be certain of the contemplation of God, is divinized by those things that it contemplates" (trans. Trigg). Yet on the whole—in what remains of his corpus, at any rate—Origen *contrasts* the glory of Moses' face on Mount Sinai with the glory of Christ's transfiguration, following Paul's argument in 2 Cor 3 (*Hom. Ex.* 12.3; see also *Cels.* 1.19; *Hom. Num.* 22.3; *Hom. Ps.* 36.4.1). Moreschini overstates Origen's use of Moses as "il coronamento della mistica ascesa dell'anima a Dio" ("Influenze di Origene," p. 43); the episode does not figure centrally, e.g., in Origen's *Hom. Ex.* Gregory, however, makes Moses' encounter with God on Mount Sinai paradigmatic for Christians. Through Gregory of Nyssa's *Life of Moses* and the Pseudo-Dionysius' *Mystical Theology* as well—both of which follow Gregory Nazianzen's work—the motif becomes standard in Eastern and Western spirituality.

incarnation of Christ. Thus begins the knowledge of God and the transformative work of theology:

> I ascend the mountain with eagerness—or, to be honest, I am eager with hope, but at the same time I am afraid for my weakness!—to enter into the cloud and meet with God, as God commands. If anyone is an Aaron, let him go up with me and stand nearby, being willing to remain outside the cloud if necessary. If anyone is a Nadab or an Abihu or one of the Elders, let him by all means ascend; but let him stand far away, according to the worth of his purification (κάθαρσις). If any are from the multitude and unworthy of such a height of contemplation—if they are altogether impure (ἄναγνος)—let them not approach at all, for it is not safe. If anyone is purified (ἡγνισμένος), at least for the time being, let him remain below and hear only the voice and the trumpet, the bare words of piety; and let him behold the mountain smoking and lightning—at once a terror and a marvel for those not able to ascend. (28.2)

As a bishop charged with the responsibilities of teaching, liturgical celebration, and pastoral care in a time of great doctrinal controversy—though with mixed feelings about his own worthiness—Gregory thus attempts to lead his flock to the knowledge of God, to which all are called.

By portraying himself in the role of Moses, Gregory is establishing the traditional pastoral prerequisite of his own authority as an inspired and knowledgable teacher, and hence the credibility of the doctrine he plans to offer.[7] The basic point of the passage is clear: one must be purified in order to know God.[8] After registering his own uncertainty in the face of such a prospect, Gregory lists each of the characters in the Exodus story as an example of the way in which one's knowledge of God corresponds to the degree of one's purification. While all are enjoined to approach God—the Greek text consists of a long series of imperatives—each character is able to ascend only as far as his or her purification allows, including those who are just barely purified and must listen from below to "the bare words of piety." However, those

---

7. Much as Origen had also done, in the authoritative spiritual exegesis that he offers in texts like *Comm. Jn.*, which Gregory knew well (as of course Paul did before him [e.g., 2 Cor 1–3]). See Trigg, "Knowing God." In the categories of Hellenistic rhetorical theory, Gregory is establishing the *ethos* of his speech. See Norris, *Faith Gives Fullness*, p. 35.

8. The most important studies of Gregory's doctrine of purification are Gottwald, *De Gregorio Nazianzeno Platonico*; Pinault, *Le Platonisme*, pp. 113–148; Plagnieux, *Saint Grégoire*, pp. 81–113; and Moreschini, "Luce e purificazione," pp. 538–542; "Lumière et Purification," pp. 66–70; *Filosofia e letteratura*, pp. 69–81.

who are entirely impure and unworthy of this level of divine knowledge must stay away from the mountain on account of the danger that it poses to them.[9]

Yet there is also a second group of figures, whose outright opposition to the knowledge of God indicates their impurity. A whole array of biblical beasts lies in the woods, Gregory says, seeking to tear to pieces the "sound doctrine" (Ti 2.1) that he plans to offer; these he admonishes to flee from the mountain, lest the words of truth crush them like stones. This group of adversaries obviously reflects Gregory's polemical situation in Constantinople. In the figure of the foreign wolf, clever in the tricks of argumentation, it is possible to recognize the Eunomians, Gregory's paradigmatic theological opponents, while other creatures may represent homoiousian or homoian theologians in attendance at his lectures; yet he also includes other readers beyond his immediate situation.[10] In this complicated pastoral situation, Gregory illustrates the various possibilities of "contemplation and theology" in a scheme that corresponds to the degree of one's purification. The knowledge of God is thus like Moses' stone tablets, engraved on both sides, the outer part being visible to the multitude below, and the inner, hidden part visible only to those who ascend the mount of contemplation through purification.

Gregory's dramatic call for purification in *Oration* 28 recapitulates the main theme of the first *Theological Oration*. After brief introductory remarks against the Eunomians, he comes straight to the point in a famous passage:

> It is *not* for everyone, people, philosophizing about God is not for everyone. It is not something that can be bought at a cheap price or for those who crawl on the ground. What's more, it is not for every occasion or every audience or every subject, but there is a proper time and audience and subject. It is not for everyone, because it is for those who have been tested and have found a sure footing in contemplation—and, most importantly, who have been purified in soul and body, or at the very least are being purified. For it is dangerous

---

9. Here Gregory builds on Origen's basic distinction between simple faith, which is rooted in the plain meaning of Scripture, and higher stages of Christian growth, which correspond with deeper levels of biblical meaning. See, e.g., *Princ.* 4.2.1–2 on simple believers who perceive only the letter and not the spirit of Scripture.

10. On the specific references, see McGuckin, *St. Gregory*, 277; Norris, *Faith Gives Fullness*, p. 108. Alternatively, Lim argues that, contrary to the ancient testimonia and the accepted modern interpretation, Gregory is not speaking of the Eunomians in particular, but to a larger group that engages inappropriately in the public disputation of theology. See *Public Disputation*, pp. 160–162. If Gregory edited *Or.* 28, or even wrote it afresh in his retirement, as the manuscript tradition suggests, then the list of animals could also represent Pneumatomachian and other bishops whom Gregory believes betrayed the faith at the council of 381.

for someone who is not pure to lay hold of what is pure, just as it is for weak eyes to gaze at the brightness of the sun. (27.3)

While all people are called to know God, Gregory recognizes that in actual practice this knowledge can only be attained with certain accompanying conditions, as had long been observed in the Alexandrian tradition of Clement and Origen.[11] Gregory defines the parameters governing the knowledge of God using standard rhetorical categories that would be familiar to the educated members of his audience, and which express commonsense notions of religious knowledge perceptible by those of any class who are sensitive to such matters.[12] Christian theology requires the proper individual and social conditions, the most important being the purification of the theologian. The wider context of the above passage indicates that "philosophizing about God" refers both to learning about God and to the public teaching of Christian doctrine; for Gregory the requirements for both are essentially the same.[13] The knowledge of God is therefore not something that can be acquired or taught irrespective of one's moral and spiritual condition; it belongs only to those who have undergone the costly process of transformation that Gregory calls purification.

Beyond the immediate controversial context of the *Theological Orations*, the requirement of purification is a staple element of Gregory's doctrine throughout his work. In his first doctrinal summary in Constantinople he makes the point succinctly, borrowing a well-known phrase from Plato: "One must first purify oneself, and then draw near to the pure" (20.4).[14] Speaking of the knowledge of the Trinity, Gregory exhorts Maximus the Cynic, "First *become* one of the things that we have been talking about [the Father, Son, and Holy Spirit], or someone like them, and then you will come to know them to the

---

11. For example, Origen, *Princ.* 1.1.7; *Comm. Jn.* 10.40.283; *Cels.* 6.69. See Moreschini, *Filosofia e letteratura*, pp. 100–112; "Nuove Consideratione," pp. 214–218; Kovacs, "Divine Pedagogy"; and Trigg, "God's Marvelous *Oikonomia*."

12. See Aristotle, *Rhet.* 1356a; Norris, *Faith Gives Fullness*, pp. 35, 89. On this point Gregory has been rather misunderstood by modern scholars. Plagnieux takes him to be identifying the higher way of *theoria* with "the few" and the lower way of praxis with "the many" in a literal, social sense (*Saint Grégoire*, pp. 151–160). See also Lim, *Public Disputation*, pp. 158–171; Elm, "Diagnostic Gaze"; "Orthodoxy and the Philosophical Life." Yet, despite their resonance with Roman ideas about social class, Gregory uses these terms primarily in the biblical sense, where the kingdom of God is a pearl of great price and a narrow gate, in which many are called but few are chosen. While he shares many of the attitudes of the contemporary Roman aristocracy and appreciates the value of a good education and intellectual leisure for theological work, he by no means believes that only the leisured class can know God. As we will see later, what counts for adequate theological preparation is anything but the conventional social mores of the Greco-Roman elite.

13. Plagnieux, *Saint Grégoire*, p. 160, pace Winslow, *Dynamics of Salvation*, pp. 23–28. We will focus here on the former, and we will consider the work of theological teaching in chap. 5.

14. *Phaed.* 67b. Similar statements can be found in *Ors.* 2.71; 39.9; 2.2.7.221. See below on Gregory's use of Plato.

same extent that they are known by one another" (25.17).[15] Purification is therefore required of all: Gregory's congregation at the Anastasia, a pro-Nicene ally, rival theologians in Constantinople, and his chief literary opponent, Eunomius. To attempt to know God apart from this transformation represents the kind of knowledge which, according to Paul, puffs one up with pride (32.12; 1 Cor 8.1). The first approach to the knowledge of God, then, is to enter into the profound transformation that God requires and enables.[16]

For Gregory, "purification" (κάθαρσις and its cognates) means first of all a radical change in one's character and way of life. All are called, Gregory says, to the transformation that the Gospel requires—"man and woman, old and young, city dweller and rustic, private citizen and public leader, rich and poor, for the same contest calls us all. So let us change our lives" (19.6). Near the end of his career he argues that the primary way to celebrate this new life in Christ is to be constantly transformed: "Present yourself now as a new person, different in character, completely changed.... You should be in constant change, improving, ever a new creature, repenting if you should sin and pressing forward if your life is virtuous" (44.8).[17] In order to approach the knowledge of God one must become nothing less than a new creature. For a clearer definition of purification, we will do best to look at a key passage in the second Epiphany oration, *On the Holy Lights*. As he had done at the beginning of *Oration 38*, Gregory begins *Oration 39* by reemphasizing the great contrast between the Christian baptismal feast and the life it represents on one hand, and the lifestyle and ceremonies of pagan Greek culture on the other. In light of the saving grace that has been given in Jesus Christ, it must be borne in mind where Christian doctrine and life begin. The passage bears quoting in full, as we will refer to it several times in the following pages.

> The best place to begin our philosophy is where Solomon commanded us to begin, when he said, "As a beginning of wisdom, acquire wisdom for yourself!" And what does he mean in speaking of "the beginning of wisdom?" Fear (Prv 1.7). For one shouldn't begin with contemplation and then come to an end in fear—after all, a freewheeling kind of contemplation might push you over the cliff. Rather, being instructed in fear, purified, and (one might even say) lightened by it, one should then be lifted on high. Where there is fear

---

15. See also *Ors.* 23.11; 32.12.
16. On the requirement of purification, see also *Ors.* 15.1; 4.11; 6.1; 7.17; 9.1–2; 20.1–4; 32.12; 36.10; 38.7 (= 45.3); 39.8–10, 14; 45.11; *Carm.* 1.1.1.8b–15; 1.2.10.972f.
17. On the unending nature of Christian progress as applied to pastors, see *Or.* 2.14–15.

there is the keeping of the commandments; and where there is keeping of commandments there is a purification of the flesh, that cloud that covers the soul and does not allow it to see the divine light. But where there is purification there is illumination; and illumination is the satisfaction of desire for those who long for the greatest things, or The Greatest Thing—or That Which Surpasses All Greatness.

For this reason one must first purify oneself, and then approach the Pure, if we are not to undergo what Israel experienced, when it was unable to bear the glory shining in the face of Moses, and so demanded a veil. . . .

For the same Word is both fearful to those who are unworthy on account of its nature, yet on account of its loving kindness also accessible to those who are converted in the way we have described, who have driven out the unclean, material spirit from their souls, and have swept and adorned their own souls by self-examination . . . and who, besides fleeing from evil, practice virtue and make Christ to dwell within them entirely, or at least as much as possible. . . . [When we have done this] and so enlightened ourselves with the light of knowledge, then let us speak of the wisdom of God that is hidden in a mystery and enlighten others. Meanwhile, let us purify ourselves and be initiated into the Word, so that we may do as much good to ourselves as possible, forming ourselves in God's image and receiving the Word when he comes—not only receiving him, in fact, but holding onto him and revealing him to others. (39.8–10)[18]

As he completes the catechesis of the baptismal candidates and prepares a summation of Christian doctrine for wider publication, Gregory characterizes purification as a process, or sequence, of moral and spiritual growth toward God: by keeping the commandments out of the fear of God, as Solomon says, one is purified and becomes illuminated with the divine light. Purification thus consists in moral reform according to the commandments of Scripture. As he puts it in a famous passage in *Oration* 20: "Approach [God] by the way you live, for what is pure can only be acquired through purification. Do you want to become a theologian someday, to be worthy of the Divinity? Keep the commandments. Make your way forward through observing the precepts, for Christian practice (πρᾶξις) is the stepping-stone to contemplation (θεωρία)"

---

18. Trans. adapt. Daley.

(20.12). Purification is the change of one's whole conduct of life, one's praxis, which is the necessary basis and context for the deep knowledge of God that Gregory calls "contemplation."

Purification thus represents the first part of a two-part process of change that leads to illumination. As the word literally suggests, purification is the removal of unclean elements—one's sin and the unclean spirits of the world—that pollute one's life and prevent one from knowing God. In *Oration* 39 above, Gregory describes this twofold movement in terms of Jesus' story of the unclean spirit that returned to its previous owner (39.8–10; Mt 12.43–45; Lk 11.24–26). In order to know God truly, one must first drive out the unclean, worldly spirit from one's soul—referring especially to the pagan life and ritual described in the opening sections of the oration—and adorn the soul instead with virtue, by which Christ dwells within. In *Oration* 20, Gregory illustrates this dual process with a spiritual interpretation of the story of Zacchaeus (Lk 19.1–10). Just as Zacchaeus climbed the sycamore tree in order to see Jesus, we, too, must put to death "what is earthly" in us (Col 3.5) and waste "the body of our lowliness" (Phil 3.21), so that we may receive Christ and hear him say, "Today salvation [has] come to this house" (Lk 19.9). The practical disciplines of Christian ascesis help to bring about the purification of both body and soul.

The specific elements that make up the work of purification are many. In the most general sense, Christians are purified through mindfulness of God (μεμνῆσθαι θεοῦ) in constant meditation, prayer, witness, and praise (27.4),[19] and through "a contrite heart and the sacrifice of praise" (16.2).[20] Like most pastoral theologians of his time, Gregory also recommends a fuller range of practices to aid purification, acts of piety and spiritual training, or ascesis, drawn from biblical and philosophical sources, which were becoming relatively standardized through the influence of Origen and the emerging monastic movement. Once the foreign elements of pagan religion have been renounced, Gregory writes, one must "polish to beauty the theologian within, like a statue."[21] One must chip away the impurities of sin through practices like hospitality, brotherly love, conjugal affection, chastity, feeding the poor, singing psalms, nightlong vigils, penitence, fasting, prayer, meditation on death, and mastery of the passions (27.7). Likewise, as he exhorts the baptismal candidates

---

19. Quoting Ps 1.2; Jo 1.8; Pss 55(54).17(18); 34(33).1(2); and Dt 6.7. See also *Or.* 39.11: remembrance of God is the chief point of the festival; in heaven the worthy sing hymns and praises to God.
20. See Pss 50.23; 51.19.
21. Gregory borrows the image from Plotinus, *Enn.* 1.6.5–9, which refers to Plato, *Phaedr.* 111d. In addition to ascetical practices, Plotinus discusses the pagan mysteries, from which Gregory clearly wants to distance himself. See Plagnieux, *Saint Grégoire*, pp. 87–88 and n48.

to purify themselves in preparation for baptism, Gregory recommends the practices of "vigils, fasts, sleeping on the ground, prayers, tears, and almsgiving to those in need," with special emphasis on generosity and care for the poor (40.31).[22]

Gregory typically refers to this kind of disciplined Christian practice with the traditional term "philosophy."[23] Speaking of his time with Basil in Athens, he writes that "philosophy was our chief aim," as they withdrew themselves from the world and practiced a life of godly love, Christian virtue, and eschatological hope (43.19–20).[24] After leaving Athens and returning to Cappadocia, he relates that he "resolved to practice philosophy, and to seek the higher life" (7.9), which involved submitting his renowned rhetorical skills to the service of God (*DVS* 270). As he continues in the *De vita sua*, Gregory describes Christian philosophy as not merely to seem, but actually to be, a friend of God (*DVS* 321–324), to live out the Gospel in the fullest possible sense. For Gregory, as for many in the Hellenistic period, philosophy was not an exclusively mental exercise, as it is sometimes imagined in modern times. Drawing on Plato and Aristotle, Hellenistic writers of various sorts came to regard philosophy as concerning one's entire way of life, and especially what we could call intentional philosophical or religious practice. As Anne-Marie Malingrey has shown, both Jewish and Christian writers took up the language of philosophy to express their own belief systems and ways of life in the Hellenistic environment. Gregory then inherited this practice from Clement and Origen, and probably also Eusebius of Caesarea, in conjunction with his study of Scripture and the ancient Greeks.[25] Gregory's *Orations* 4–5, for example, indicate that he was acquainted with most of the Greek philosophers from the pre-Socratics to the Neoplatonists in some form, probably learning much through lectures and handbooks while studying a fair amount of Plato and Aristotle directly. Yet for all his knowledge of Greek philosophy, Gregory is concerned above all with setting the pagan and Christian philosophies in contrast with one another.

---

22. See also *Ors.* 6.6; 11.4–5; 14.37 on acts of mercy toward the poor; 40.39–40 on the purification of each of the parts and functions of the body; 43.9; 44.9; *DVS* 1218–1224, where care for the poor and hospitality to strangers are listed first.

23. On Gregory's adaptation of Hellenistic and Christian ideas of philosophy, see Malingrey, "*Philosophia*," pp. 237–262; Pinault, *Le Platonisme*; Asmus, "Gregorius von Nazianz"; Pelikan, *Christianity and Classical Culture*; Elm, "Orthodoxy and the Philosophical Life"; Gautier, *La retraite*, pt. 1; and Daley, *Gregory of Nazianzus*, pp. 34–41.

24. See also *DVS* 261.

25. The Alexandrian tradition of Clement and Origen played a formative role in introducing Gregory to the possibilities of Christian Platonism. See Pinault, *Le Platonisme*; Moreschini, "Nuove Consideratione," pp. 214–218. On Origen's critical use of Plato, see the fine study by Mark Edwards, *Origen Against Plato*.

Pagan philosophy, he says, "plays with shadows of the truth under the cloak and guise of philosophy," whereas Christian philosophy, "although it may in all appearances be lowly, is inwardly sublime and leads to God" (25.4). After severely criticizing the various Hellenistic schools, he concludes that it is the Christian, who serves the well-being of all, who is really "the lover of wisdom, as opposed to those who lack it" (25.6–7).

While Gregory occasionally speaks of philosophy as involving both practical and speculative dimensions, or practice and contemplation (e.g., 4.113), he mainly focuses on the practical discipline of conducting one's life in light of one's highest values. Gregory's philosophy is constantly defined by a Christian understanding of God and created existence, as we saw above in his reference to "philosophizing about God" (27.3); nevertheless, it typically has to do with the practices of self-mastery required to be united with God, and the practical way of life that the knowledge of God inspires.[26] His most comprehensive portrait of the Christian philosopher comes in *Orations* 25–26, which he delivered before and after the infamous Maximus affair. In the first oration, just as Maximus was preparing to leave Constantinople and return to Alexandria, Gregory portrays the Egyptian theologian as a Christian philosopher par excellence. No doubt with some hope of garnering support from the Alexandrians, Gregory lavishes praise on Maximus for his mastery of all practical and theoretical virtue: his Cynic dress; his poverty; his frank speech (παρρησία); his defense of the good; his care for the moral development of others (25.2, 7); his rejection of luxury, wealth, and power; his mastery of the passions; his detachment from matter; and his adherence to the world that abides (25.4). As a qualified Christian philosopher, Maximus also champions the truth by defending the orthodox doctrine of the Trinity (25.3) and practicing the mixed life of private solitude and public service (25.4–6). Finally, Gregory makes special reference to Maximus' suffering and exile on behalf of the Trinitarian faith and commissions him with a summary of his Trinitarian doctrine (25.13–19).

After Maximus turned on him by attempting to seize the throne of Constantinople,[27] Gregory then gives an even clearer portrait of the philosopher in *Oration* 26. The Christian philosopher, he says, can be of any social class (26.10) and makes his or her life one of virtue by practicing self-control, frank speech, almsgiving, vigils, fasting, simplicity, endurance, prayer, and nonviolence, all with the knowledge that Christ suffered worse for the salvation of the world (26.11–12). In the face of temptation such a person thus becomes a

---

26. Daley, *Gregory of Nazianzus*, p. 37.
27. On Maximus' bogus philosophy (from the clarity of hindsight), see also *DVS* 758 and 1030.

rock worthy of the Rock that Christians worship, increasing in stature through afflictions and winning glory through adversity (26.9–10). In sum,

> there is nothing more impregnable, nothing more unassailable than philosophy! Everything else collapses before the philosopher does. He is a wild ass in the desert, as Job says, unfettered and free (see Job 39.5–12).... Let me put it in a nutshell: two things are beyond our control, God and an angel—and in third place is the philosopher. He is immaterial in matter, uncircumscribed while in a body, heavenly on earth, impassible in the midst of passions, beaten in all things except his thoughts (φρόνημα), conqueror over those who think they have overpowered him, simply by being conquered. (26.13)[28]

While Gregory's ideal of the philosophical life may seem austere, we must guard against a simplistic interpretation of these passages. Gregory's own ascetical practice was in fact moderate compared to Macrina's and Basil's more aggressive experiments, the extreme component of the contemporary Cappadocian monks, or the monks of the Egyptian desert.[29] While he extols virginity, for example, he also highly lauds the goodness of conjugal affection (*Carm.* 1.2.1.189–526), and he emphasizes the value of spiritual over physical chastity (37.9–11, 17). In terms that reflect the traditional philosophical *otium* of the Greco-Roman aristocracy as well as the spirituality of Origen, Gregory champions above all the practice of biblical study and meditation.[30] His negotiation of the competing demands of contemplative solitude and ecclesiastical engagement has traditionally been interpreted as an unhappy and irresolvable tension that loomed over his life, dooming him to flounder among his contemporaries and to pale in the light of Basil's heroic churchmanship and Gregory of Nyssa's metaphysical genius.[31] However, Gregory plainly tells us that he consciously—and we may add rather successfully—chose a "middle way" between contemplative retreat and service to the Church and society,[32] arguing that the combination of a well-developed inner life and dedicated

---

28. Trans. adapt. Daley. Among the over 400 instances of φιλοσοφία and its cognates, see also *Ors.* 2.7, 103; 7.1, 15; 10.1; 27.7; 37.14; 43.2; 44.9; *Ep.* 119.

29. Bouyer, *Spirituality*, p. 342.

30. McGuckin, *St. Gregory*, pp. 28, 72, 87–99, 149, 172, 205, 335–336. See also Daley, *Gregory of Nazianzus*, p. 40.

31. The classic study is Otis' "The Throne and the Mountain." See also Winslow, *Dynamics of Salvation*.

32. See, e.g., *Ors.* 14.4; 12.4; *DVS* 300–311. On Gregory's combination of monastic retreat and priestly service, see Gautier, *La retraite*. See also Elm's convincing analysis of Gregory's public leadership in the traditional terms of Hellenistic political rhetoric: "Inventing the 'Father of the Church,'" as well as chap. 5 in this book.

service to others is the life most fitting to the Christian Gospel and the ideal form of life for bishops. Gregory's moderate, scholarly asceticism made him the chief pioneer of the urban form of Byzantine monasticism and thus equal in influence to Basil. In this regard (among others), we may note that Gregory showed himself to be a more faithful disciple of Origen than either of his Cappadocian contemporaries.[33]

It has long been recognized that the language, and to some extent the religious spirit, of Gregory's doctrine of purification evokes a long-standing philosophical tradition stemming from Plato.[34] Gregory's oft-repeated principle that one must purify oneself in order to reach God, who is pure,[35] distinctly echoes the first half of Plato's *Phaedo*.[36] Socrates' doctrine of purification in this work became widely influential in later Hellenistic traditions, and the Neoplatonist Plotinus, whom Gregory probably also read, popularized a modified Platonic doctrine of purification.[37] Scholars have been too quick to assume that such parallels indicate a predominance of Platonic doctrine over biblical Christianity in Gregory's work, based on certain modern theories about the purity and incommensurability of the two. While Plato and Plotinus certainly teach that the pure God (or the One) is known only by the pure knower, similar ideas also appear in the Bible. To name just two examples in the New Testament, the First Letter of John states that when Christ is revealed believers will be like him and "see him as he is. And all who have this hope in him purify themselves, just as he is pure" (1 Jn 3.2–3).[38] More famously, in the Sermon on the Mount in the Gospel of Matthew, Jesus declares, "Blessed are the pure in heart, for they shall see God" (Mt 5.8). Gregory indicates the biblical sense of purification in many passages. In an early episcopal oration, for example, he writes,

> Let us free ourselves [the NT text reads "Let us purify ourselves (καθαρίσωμεν)"] "from every defilement of body and spirit" (2 Cor 7.1). Let us wash and become clean (καθαροί) (Is 1.16). Let us present

---

33. See Moreschini, *Filosofia e letteratura*, pp. 111–112.

34. On Gregory's use of Platonist tradition, see esp. Dräseke, "Neuplatonisches"; Gottwald, *De Gregorio Nazianzeno Platonico*; Pinault, *Le Platonisme*; Moreschini, "Il Platonismo Cristiano"; *Filosofia e letteratura*, pp. 22–60; and Plagnieux, *Saint Grégoire*. For the broader range of classical and Hellenistic philosophy, see Pinault, *Le Platonisme*; Norris, *Faith Gives Fullness*.

35. See *Ors.* 2.39, 71; 17.12; 18.3; 20.4, 12; 27.3; 30.20; 39.9.

36. E.g., *Phaed.* 67b: "It is forbidden for one who is not pure to touch what is pure"; 69c: "The true moral ideal, whether self-control or integrity or courage, is really a kind of purgation from all these emotions, and wisdom itself is a sort of purification."

37. For example, *Enn.* 1.2.7: "all virtue is purification."

38. Or "when God is revealed" (ἐὰν φανερωθῇ).

> our very "bodies" and souls "as a living sacrifice, holy and acceptable to God, which is [our] spiritual worship" and petition (Rom 12.1). For nothing is so precious to the One who is pure (ὁ καθαρός) than purity and purification (καθαρότης καὶ κάθαρσις). (11.4)

Indeed, the language of purification and cleanliness has considerable currency in both the Septuagint and the New Testament.[39]

Several scholars have made detailed comparisons of Gregory's doctrine of purification with those of Plato and Plotinus—though without considering the biblical material—and several views have been advanced.[40] Yet, in order to interpret Gregory's work, we must attend closely to the immediate context and purpose of his doctrine, rather than merely collect verbal echoes from a variety of sources. To this end we can turn again to the Epiphany orations of January 381. As Claudio Moreschini has observed, in these stylistically beautiful and doctrinally rich sermons Gregory provides a rhetorical and artistic *logos* to communicate the Christian revelation to a culture that he believes is still largely pagan.[41] Thus each of the three sermons opens with a discussion of the wickedness of pagan rituals and behavior, and an admonition that his hearers renounce (or reaffirm their renunciation of) them and embrace instead the Christian life (38.4–5; 39.1–7; 40.3–4).[42] Significantly, the contrast is most pronounced exactly where Gregory gives his clearest statement of purification (39.8–10, quoted above). Moreover, his insistent and rather lengthy exhortation that people not delay seeking baptism, as they often did (40.11–40), further indicates that he views Constantinopolitan society as a culture which, although it may seem Christian in appearance, is still in many ways unconverted.[43] And so he describes Christ's baptism in just these terms in the opening of *On the Holy Lights*:

> Again my Jesus, and again a mystery: not deceitful or disorderly, nor belonging to Greek error or drunkenness—for so I call their solem-

---

39. Chiefly in the terms καθαρίζειν/καθαρός and ἁγνίζειν/ἁγνός (negatively, ἀκαθαρσία/ἀκάθαρτός) and, more frequently, in the related terms for holiness, ἁγιάζειν/ἅγιος. In the LXX, the idea is initially rooted in the concern for ritual purity and impurity, as codified in the Mosaic covenant, after which it is conceived in broader moral and spiritual terms. See, e.g., Gn 7.2, 8; Lv 7.19–21; 11–15; Nm 18–19; Dt 12.15, 22; 14–15; Pss 24[23].4; 51[50]; 73[72].1; Job 16.17; 33.3; Is 6.5; 35.8; and Ez 39.24. The latter sense predominates in the NT. See, e.g., Mt 23.26: "Blind Pharisee! First purify the inside of the cup, so that the outside may be pure also"; Hb 9.14: "the blood of Christ... purifies our consciences from dead works, so that we may worship the living God"; Acts 15.9; 2 Cor 7.1; and 2 Tim 2.21.
40. Most recently, Pinault, Plagnieux, Moreschini, Norris, and Sykes.
41. Moreschini, SC 358, pp. 22–23.
42. Gregory inveighs against the evils of pagan religion at great length in *Ors.* 4–5.
43. Moreschini, SC 358, p. 33. In this connection see also Gregory's discussion of penitence in *Or.* 39.17–19.

nities, and so I think will every person of sound sense—but a mystery lofty and divine, and allied to the Glory above. For the Holy Day of Lights, to which we have come and which we are celebrating today, has as its origin the baptism of my Christ, the true Light that enlightens every person who comes into the world (Jn 1.9); and it effects my purification and assists that light that we received from him in the beginning from above, but which we darkened and confused by sin. (39.1)

Gregory emphasizes that the basic purpose of the Christian mystery is the conversion of fallen humanity, which, he believes, is represented in a particularly egregious way by the lingering pagan worship and moral vices of late-fourth-century Constantinople. We may recall that Gregory witnessed with horror the banishment of Christian intellectuals from centers of learning and the restoration of the pagan cults by his former schoolmate Julian. Moreover, as Julian himself exemplified, Neoplatonist philosophers regularly participated in the cultic sacrifices to the pagan gods.[44] In telling his hearers to purify themselves, then, Gregory is first of all exhorting them to turn from the sin and darkness that are typified in pagan culture, and to be converted to the divine life that is being offered in Jesus Christ. In the first *Theological Oration* Gregory strongly argues that pagan worship of the passions and fabricated gods is inimical to Christian teaching and a perspective entirely foreign (ἀλλότριος) to the subject of Christian theology (27.6–7).

In light of this larger intention of conversion, we may note, additionally, that as a highly educated Greek Gregory is well aware that Platonic *katharsis*, in conjunction with certain Stoic and Cynic ideals, is still part of the common spiritual currency of the Constantinopolitan elite. Plagnieux observes that, in their mystical resonance even more than their vocabulary, these themes evoke the philosophy of an entire epoch, in which the philosopher communicates a spiritual life and a religious philosophy.[45] Whereas the crowd wanted mystery religions, the pagan elite used philosophy to achieve contemplation and divinization through a liberating ascesis. Although they are not his only audience, Gregory certainly means to convert his aristocratic peers, whose crucial importance in supporting the Church in the capital is not lost on him. In his doctrine of purification, as in so much of his work, Gregory brings a fundamentally biblical idea into contact with Hellenic traditions in order to communicate the

---

44. Daley, *Gregory of Nazianzus*, pp. 6–7.
45. Plagnieux, *Saint Grégoire*, pp. 90–92. For a similar approach, see also the work of Hadot.

Christian Gospel, both to convert his contemporaries and to inspire Christians toward growth in holiness, thereby crafting, as John McGuckin has argued, a Christian Hellenism for missionary purposes.[46]

Henri Pinault and Moreschini have pointed out that in most respects Gregory's use of Plato follows the precedent of the Alexandrian Christian tradition of Clement and Origen.[47] Even though he was directly acquainted with Plato, Gregory is led by the Alexandrians, above all Origen, in the adaptation of certain Platonist themes for his Christian program. Like Clement and Origen, he seeks to preserve and transform the best of Greek culture for Christian purposes, only with an even more focused intent. Louis Bouyer summarizes the phenomenon well, speaking of all three Cappadocians:

> On the one hand, they are stricter than any of their predecessors among hellenizing Christians in their fidelity to the Word of God—hence their clear-eyed criticism of the Greek conceptions which cannot be assimilated by Christianity. On the other hand, it was a humanism truly lived, not detached ideas only, which they brought back from Greece to incorporate into their so essentially Christian spirituality.[48]

Throughout his life Gregory aimed to enlist Greek rhetoric (which involved philosophical concerns) into the service of Christ. To certain modern sensibilities it may seem contradictory, even a pollution of the faith, that Gregory could devote himself so fervently to the Gospel while at the same time bringing it into close contact with classical Greek letters. But this judgment says more about modern developments in Western philosophy, systematic theology, and ecclesiology than it does about the nature of early Christianity. As Lewis Ayres observes, one of the greatest obstacles to understanding pro-Nicene theology is the pervasive and subtle modern strategy of making questionable assumptions about the nature of philosophy and the proper use of Scripture. Accordingly, a pristine "biblical" Christianity is seen as being threatened by self-establishing and self-enclosed philosophical systems, which are liable to corrupt or overwhelm it.[49] Thus it seems implausible in this modern view that Gregory could use elements of philosophical traditions in a selective and adaptive way—again, primarily for the purpose of Christian persuasion and conversion—

---

46. McGuckin, *St. Gregory*, p. 75.
47. Pinault, *Le Platonisme*; Moreschini, "Nuove Considerazione."
48. Bouyer, *Spirituality*, p. 338.
49. Ayres, *Nicaea*, pp. 390–392.

without automatically compromising the apostolic character of his doctrine. However, as several fine scholars have shown, this is exactly what Gregory is doing.[50]

A particular point on which Gregory's use of Platonic tradition has been questioned is the place of the human body in the process of purification. In certain passages he appears to hold a caricatured Platonist view that purification entails the soul's escape from the body, with the result that the body is denigrated and does not retain any place in renewed Christian existence. One text that is often cited in this regard comes from his funeral oration for his brother:[51]

> I believe the words of the wise, that every fair and God-beloved soul, when it is set free from the bonds of the body, departs from here and at once enjoys a sense and a perception of the blessings that await it, to the extent that what darkened it has been purged away, or laid aside (I don't know how else to put it); and it feels a wonderful pleasure and exultation and goes rejoicing to meet its Lord, having escaped, as it were, from the grievous poison of life here and shaken off the fetters that bound it and held down the wings of the mind; and so it enters into the enjoyment of the bliss that is laid up for it, of which even now it has some conception. (7.21)

On the face of it, Gregory seems to be unquestioningly accepting a Platonist view of purification ("the words of the wise" refers to Plotinus)[52] and defining purification literally as the soul's escape from the body, which imprisons and darkens it. Yet here again there is more than meets the eye in Gregory's rhetorical situation and doctrinal agenda. Gregory's brother, Caesarius, served as physician to the imperial court and later as treasurer in Bythinia, and we can assume that there would have been high-ranking officials in the congregation for whom traditional Greek consolation philosophy would have some meaning at a time such as this. Moreover, in a funeral oration Gregory has the dual pastoral task of focusing on the heavenly life of the deceased, for the comfort of the survivors, while also taking seriously the death that has occurred and the

---

50. Especially Pinault and Plagnieux; see also Gregg, *Consolation Philosophy*, pp. 197–198. Yet cf. Moreschini's judgment that Gregory reinterprets Christian doctrine within the parameters of Platonic philosophy, rather than utilizing the latter for the former. "Il Platonismo Cristiano"; "Lumière et Purification" and "Le Platonisme Chrétien" (SC 358, pp. 62–81), esp. pp. 70–71. Likewise, Elm argues that Gregory essentially aims to convert pagans and heretics to a correct, Platonic cosmology, into which Scripture is adapted as part of an ongoing debate between rival Middle and Neoplatonist schemes. "Inscriptions and Conversions," pp. 3–4, 15–16, 20–24.

51. See, e.g., Pinault, *Le Platonisme*, pp. 121–125; Moreschini, SC 358, p. 67, on 7.17, earlier in the same oration.

52. *Enn.* 1.2; 1.6.9; 6.9.9 and passim.

general human mortality that death evokes, in order to support his hearers' grief. Socrates' teaching on purification and the soul's liberation from the bonds of the body is perhaps the most famous example of such consolation literature,[53] and it serves both of these ends well, as can be seen in its frequent use by all three Cappadocians.[54] Moreover, the use of this material by Gregory and other Christian preachers should come as no surprise in light of similar ideas found in Scripture, such as Paul's statement, "My desire is to depart and be with Christ, for that is far better; but to remain in the flesh is more necessary for you" (Phil 1.23b–24), which Basil and Gregory both cite in connection with the Platonic material.[55]

Again reflecting artificial modern divisions—and in this case a wild oversimplification—it has become something of a commonplace to contrast pro-body biblical doctrine with anti-body Greek philosophy. However, Gregory's own view of the body and its relation to the soul is rather more complex than this simple contrast allows. On the most basic level, Gregory, like most early Christians, regards the soul as being closer to God than the body is. This is not because the body is inherently evil or the soul naturally good, but it reflects what most premoderns take to be self-evident: that it is the soul that gives meaning and ultimate value to things, makes choices, and has faith, hope, and the love of God. In this sense the soul is practically synonymous with the willing self or the human subject, whereas the body is a secondary part of that subject and can even appear to be an object. It seems more natural to say that I "have" a body, while I "am" my soul, even though it is equally true that human beings are necessarily composed of both. Thus Gregory regards the human image of God, properly speaking, to be the soul, without implying that souls can exist without bodies or that bodies are evil.

The soul's superiority over the body is for Gregory the result of God's work of creation. God first created the intellectual world of angels, which is naturally more akin to God. He then created a second, material world of earth and sky, which is naturally less similar to God, though also good. Finally, he took a body from the material creation and gave it his own breath, or spirit (namely an

---

53. Gregg, *Consolation Philosophy*, p. 9.

54. In addition to similar themes that continue to recur in Christian funeral homilies. According to Basil's *To Young Men*, Plato and Paul agree that "the body is serviceable only for the pursuit of virtue" (*Adolesc.* 12). Gregory encourages Philagrios to "live for the life to come, making this life a preparation for death, since, as Plato said, the soul is to be released from the body, or the Prison," echoing *Phaed.* 64a (*Ep.* 31.4). See also Gregg, *Consolation Philosophy*, pp. 126, 198–199.

55. Basil refers to the Philippians passage in *Ep.* 29, as well as in *Ep.* 76. Gregory combines it with the preparation theme from *Phaed.* 64a. See also Gregg, *Consolation Philosophy*, p. 199n2.

intelligent soul and the image of God), making human beings to be, as it were, a mixture of opposites:

> another kind of angel, a mingled worshipper, a spectator of the visible creation and an initiate into the intelligible, king of the things on earth yet ruled from above, earthly and heavenly, subject to time yet deathless, visible and knowable, poised halfway between greatness and lowliness. (38.11)[56]

Each order of creation, Gregory notes, is good and glorifies God in its own way. And so human agency, virtue, and freedom belong to the soul in a way that transcends our bodily dimension per se (26.13), making the soul more valuable than the body.

This view is reinforced in several ways by Gregory's understanding of Scripture and human experience. As a matter of discomforting empirical truth, the body shows itself to be less directly controllable than one's intellectual or spiritual existence.[57] In many cases one's body is experienced as an obstacle to the fulfillment of one's will, and so must be guided and governed accordingly. While progress in virtue is possible in the face of physical ailments—and can even be helped by them, Gregory is wont to note (*Carm.* 2.1.14)—the body does not automatically respond to progress in virtue in the same way, even if it does to a certain extent. The most obvious example of this is physical illness, which often comes irrespective of one's moral condition. "For it is clear to me," Gregory writes on his oration *On the Love of the Poor*, "that bodily sickness is involuntary, but [the sickness of the soul] is the result of our deliberate choice" (14.18).[58] In similar ways, bodily existence can be seen as oppressive, at times even more trouble than it is worth. In his autobiographical poems Gregory frequently laments the vicissitudes of corporeal existence.[59] It is in just such a context—the wretched plight of the poor, the homeless, and the lepers of

---

56. Trans. Daley. See also *Ors.* 2.17; 7.23; Richard, *Cosmologie et théologie*. This passage is a good illustration of how Gregory's rhetorical sensibilities interweave with his theological doctrine. In construing mind and body as "opposites," he is playing on the traditional form of antithesis for argumentative effect; he is not suggesting that they are ontological, cosmological, or moral opposites, as in a caricatured Gnostic or Manichean view. See the similar statement by Athanasius that Christ's body is "foreign in essence" to the Word, which is in it (*Ep. Epict.* 8).

57. Assuming the grace of Christ to redeem the soul from sin.

58. Trans. Vinson.

59. See, e.g., *Carm.* 2.1.28, lamenting existence in the flesh and esp. the pain of old age; 2.1.29, on the afflictions of illness (with figurative reference to his rejection at Constantinople); 2.1.50 *Against the Burden of Sickness*. Yet, in Gregory's eyes, these difficulties pale in comparison with the evils of envy and strife that he has experienced at the hands of wicked bishops. See *DVS*; 2.1.13 *On the Bishops*; 2.1.14 *On Himself and Against the Envious*; 2.1.40 *Against the Envious*. Encompassing a whole range of evils is 2.1.45 *Threnody Over the Sufferings of His Soul*.

Caesarea—that Gregory makes some of his most disparaging remarks about the body (14.6–8).[60] He intimates that the body's mortal and corruptible condition, with which we are familiar, is the result of the fall: the "coarser flesh" represented by the coverings of skin that God gave Adam and Eve (38.12; Gen 3.21). Likewise, the risen Christ no longer exists in corruptible "flesh" as we know it;[61] in a mysterious way known only to God, he now possesses "a body of more divine form" (θεοειδέστερον σῶμα), visible and tangible to the disciples when he appeared to them as "God without our thick corporeality" (θεὸς ἔξω παχύτητος, 40.45). In fact Gregory explicitly insists that it is not a Christian ideal to "put off the body" (41.5) and that the risen Christ continues to possess a body, against the view that he no longer does, as Origen was (wrongly) accused of teaching. Yet, in a manner similar to Irenaeus' and Origen's accounts of creation, Gregory reads the resulting corruption of our physicality back into the narrative of God's original design: God created us with spirit and flesh so that our pride over our spiritual greatness might be checked through the suffering that we would endure in the flesh. In light of what was to happen in the fall, God's mercy is shown from the beginning, in creating us as mixed creatures whose very constitution provides for our training and divinization (38.11).[62]

In order to progress toward God, the soul therefore needs the body and makes special use of it. As the recipients of Christ's grace and the gift of the Holy Spirit, Christians live according to the Spirit together with their bodies (41.18); far from being expendable or something to be discarded, the body is to be appreciated as the soul's coworker (14.7) and its kindred (7.21), even in its most recalcitrant and frustrating moments. As an illustration of this balanced view, Gregory criticizes Novatian for uncharitably condemning the physical sin of fornication more harshly than the spiritual sin of covetousness—"as if he himself were not flesh and body!" (39.19). Yet because of its fallen condition, the body also exercises a sort of tyranny over us (45.30). Gregory regularly characterizes Greek religion as being "bodily" (41.1), focused on the passions and worshipping gods that represent the worst of our bodily disorder (27.6). Hence, in order for one to partake of God's new life in Christ, the body must be "risen above" (42.12), "conquered" (43.2), or disciplined in its various organs and sensory functions (44.6). In a climactic conclusion to the Epiphany series, Gregory exhorts, "Let us cleanse every member, brothers and sisters, let us

---

60. See also Ors. 7.17; 12.3; 40.36.
61. See also Or. 18.4.
62. See also Or. 40.7: "To sin is human and belongs to the compound on earth, for composition is the beginning of separation."

purify every sense. Let nothing in us be imperfect or of our first birth. Let us leave nothing unilluminated." He then provides a dense litany of spiritual exegesis enjoining the purification of the five senses and the bodily organs, from the head to the loins, so that all of our earthly members may be offered to God (Col 3.5) and all of our physical desires may become spiritual (40.38–40).

Rather than involving the separation of the soul from the body, then, purification occurs both "in soul and in body" (27.3). Immediately after his account of creation and the fall in *Oration* 38, Gregory argues that in order to save us Christ took on both flesh and an intelligent soul, in order to purify them both (38.13).[63] Moreover, it is the soul that needs purifying most of all, both on account of its natural superiority (37.22)[64] and also because sin began and most properly resides in the soul, giving it an even greater need of healing (*Ep.* 101.52). Thus it is significant that in *Oration* 39 (quoted above), although Gregory speaks initially of purifying the flesh, he goes on to describe the process in terms of the exorcism of unclean spirits from the soul, which will enable Christ to dwell within (39.8–10). The body is therefore very much a part of redeemed human existence, as is evident in Gregory's discussion of the resurrection of the dead. In the passage quoted above from his funeral oration for Caesarius, he beautifully completes the picture:

> Then, a little later, [the soul] receives its kindred flesh, which once shared in its pursuits of things above, from the earth which both gave and had been entrusted with it, and which is in some way known to God, who knit them together and dissolved them, entering with [the flesh] upon the inheritance of the glory in that place. And since, through their close union, [the soul] shared in the hardships of the flesh, so too it bestows upon it a portion of its joys, gathering it up entirely into itself, and becoming one with it in spirit and in mind and in God, the mortal and mutable being swallowed up by life. (7.21)

For both Gregory Nazianzen and Gregory of Nyssa (though less so for Basil),[65] the resurrection of the dead is the most powerful consolation for grief over the loss of a loved one. Through a lifetime of purification, both body and soul come to share in God's glory at the resurrection of the dead.[66]

---

63. See also *Or.* 11.4 (above), where Gregory quotes 2 Cor 7.1 on the purification of body and spirit, and even adds "soul" to Rom 12.1; see also 40.45; *Ep.* 101.51.

64. See also *Ors.* 2.16–22; 32.12.

65. In his consolation literature, Basil mentions the resurrection infrequently. Gregg, *Consolation Philosophy*, pp. 208–209.

66. Thus Plagnieux argues that Gregory's doctrine of purification is his surest defense against the charge of being a Neoplatonist. *Saint Grégoire*, pp. 92–101.

While purification involves real ascetical effort and concrete practices, Gregory is equally concerned to emphasize that the ultimate source of purification is God. As we just saw, it is Christ who effects the purification of Christians (38.13),[67] enlivening all of the virtues that they practice and purifying their bodily senses (45.13–14). God's gift of new life in Jesus Christ is the main subject of the Epiphany series, where Gregory gives so much attention to purification:

> This is our feast, which we celebrate today: the coming of God to the human race, so that we might make our way to him..., putting off the old humanity and putting on the new (Eph 4.22–24). For I must experience the beautiful conversion (ἀντιστροφή): just as pain came out of happiness, so happiness must return from pain. 'Where sin has abounded, grace has abounded all the more' (Rom 5.20). If the taste of the fruit condemned us, how much more have Christ's sufferings justified us. (38.4)[68]

The source of the transformation that one undergoes through purification is the justifying grace of Jesus Christ. Hence Christ is called Sanctification "because he is purity, so that what is pure may be filled with his pureness" (30.20), and the path of purification is above all to follow Jesus, the Master (19.6). Indeed, it is incumbent on us all, Gregory says—and motivating of charity to one's neighbors—to recognize that God is the source of all of our life, and especially of our knowledge of him (14.23).[69] God causes the entire process of purification, through which we are divinized (38.7).[70] This was the mark of Solomon's wisdom: to acknowledge that his understanding is really God's own understanding working in him (20.5).

For Gregory, God is exceedingly generous, far more ready to give than we are to receive (40.27),[71] and we will never be able to give as much as we have received from God (19.8). It is significant that in one of his most important treatments of theological method Gregory ties the requirement of purification directly to God's grace. Those who aspire to teach Christian doctrine, he says, must wait until they have been trained in Christian praxis and become mature in faith; as a reason, he then paraphrases Paul's question that so strongly

---

67. See also Ors. 11.4; 30.6; 39.1; 40.7.
68. Trans. adapt. Daley.
69. See also Or. 41.12 on the Spirit's purifying power, as well as 45.11.
70. See also Or. 20.4, in which the process of purification is represented in Gregory's spiritual exegesis of the story of Zacchaeus, as well as 21.1.
71. See also Or. 40.13.

influenced Augustine's doctrine of grace: "For what do you have of your own that was not given to you and you did not receive? (1 Cor 4.7)" (32.13). In his commentary on two biblical texts relating to God's grace—Jesus' teaching that celibacy can be accepted by "only those to whom it is given" (Mt 10.11) and Paul's statement that God's mercy "depends not on the person who wills or the person who runs, but on God, who shows mercy" (Rom 9.16)—Gregory argues that we must neither imagine, like the Gnostics, that some people are naturally predisposed to receive salvation and practice virtue and others are not, nor that our human successes are due to our own efforts alone. Rather, "it is necessary both that we should be our own masters and also that our salvation should be of God." Since the ability to will comes also from God, Paul rightly attributes the whole process to God. Thus Gregory understands God's grace to be fully productive of salvation and human virtue, so that Christian purification is both the result of human effort and ascetical discipline and at the same time entirely the gift of God. The proper awareness of God's generosity and grace should therefore inspire one to be even more diligent about one's purification, not less (40.34). In the passage from *On the Holy Lights* that we examined above, Gregory exhorts his readers to purify themselves because grace has been given to them (39.8). Although he does not make the same kind of inquiry into the relationship between divine and human agency that so exercised Augustine, Gregory—like most theologians of his day—simply proclaims both that purification involves serious moral effort, and that, in a mysterious way, it is at the same time entirely the result of God's grace in Christ in and beyond that effort (38.4). Readers formed in Augustinian theological traditions must be wary of suspecting here a Pelagian program of virtue leading to faith simply because Gregory does not anticipate later Western conversations.[72]

The grace of purification is seen above all in Christian baptism. The theme of baptismal grace runs throughout *Oration 40 On Baptism* and forms the common thread of Gregory's various attempts to recommend Christian initiation. Baptism is called a gift, he says, because it is given to debtors, in exchange for nothing (40.4).[73] Yet at the same time, he admonishes his hearers to work hard (φιλοπονεῖν) for their purification, and after baptism to preserve the gift they have been given (40.34). For Gregory baptism is the paradigmatic

---

72. Pinault argues that Gregory's emphasis on God's grace very sharply distinguishes his doctrine of purification from that of Plotinus. *Le Platonisme*, p. 147. See also Pelikan's helpful discussion of the different approaches to the doctrine of grace by Eastern and Western theologians, as represented by Maximus Confessor and Augustine. *Spirit of Eastern Christendom*, pp. 182–183.

73. See also *Ors.* 40.24: baptism is "the Grace"; 40.26: people should not be picky about which clergy baptize them, since grace comes from the Holy Spirit and not human social status or a notable, metropolitan church.

enactment and symbol of purification, and all purification is most fundamentally baptismal (8.14).[74] The great contrast between Christian purification and pagan religion, with which he begins the Epiphany sermons, refers specifically to baptism (39.1–6).[75] At the thought that he might fail to confess the Trinity, Gregory responds, "No, I shall not deny you, dear purifying power of baptism!" referring to the Trinitarian confession in the baptismal rite (*Carm.* 1.1.3.47).[76] It is in the oration *On Baptism*, of course, where we find Gregory's most extensive treatment of the effects of the sacrament. Baptism is "a purification of the sins of each person" (40.7) and the concrete means by which God's re-creation of humanity is realized. In the following section he further explains baptism's purifying effect in light of the anthropology discussed above:

> Since we are twofold, I mean composed of soul and body, and our nature is partly visible and partly invisible, our purification is also twofold, "by water and the Spirit" (Jn 3.5). One part is received visibly and corporeally; the other agrees with it incorporeally and invisibly; the one figurative (τυπικός), the other real (ἀληθινός), purifying the depths. Coming to the aid of our first birth, [baptism] makes us new instead of old, like God instead of what we are now, recasting us without fire and re-creating us without breaking us up. For, in a word, the virtue of baptism is to be understood as a covenant with God for a second life and a purer way of life (πολιτεία). (40.8)

At once a physical and a spiritual purification, the bodily cleansing of the water bath corresponds with and typifies the more real, spiritual cleansing that baptism brings about; and the result is nothing less than renewal, divinization, re-creation, and a covenant for a second life. Gregory spends much of *Oration* 40 exhorting his hearers, regardless of age, occupation, or marital status, to offer themselves and/or their children for baptism now rather than later, so that they may enjoy its life-changing benefits and also so that they will not be left unclean at the day of judgment, should they die unexpectedly (40.17–18).

Yet for all the moral and eschatological seriousness of his appeal, Gregory is equally insistent that the purification of baptism is not limited to the rite itself. As we have already seen, he spends considerable effort exhorting people to purify themselves in order to prepare for baptism, and to work hard to

---

74. See *Or.* 40.3–4 for the rich variety of traditional motifs with which Gregory defines baptism. On Gregory's understanding of baptism, see Moreschini, "Il battesimo"; Elm, "Inscriptions and Conversions."

75. See also *Or.* 40.11. Here again Pinault contrasts Gregory's baptismal purification with Platonic katharsis. *Le Platonisme*, pp. 145–148.

76. Trans. adapt. Sykes.

preserve it afterward (40.31). As the paradigmatic act of Christian purification, baptism is the culmination of catechetical preparation and the beginning of a lifelong process of transformation and growth toward God. Gregory had the bittersweet occasion of commenting on this very dynamic in his funeral oration for his sister, Gorgonia, who had postponed her own baptism until her deathbed. Although her baptism was "the blessing of purification and perfection that we have all received," in another respect her entire life was purification, which assured her regeneration by the Spirit in baptism. "In her case almost alone, I will venture to say, that mystery was a seal rather than a gift of grace!" (8.20). He makes a similar observation about his father, who was wondrously baptized and ordained at the same time (18.13). Even though baptism is the definitive act of purification—the "regeneration by water and the Spirit, by which we confess to God the formation and completion of the Christlike person" (18.13)—it is not so much an instantaneous transformation as the crystallizing event for a whole process of purification, and the primary context in which it is to be understood;[77] just as purification is not a state of perfection that can be finally achieved, but an ongoing process of *being* purified.[78] Hence, even as he encourages people to be baptized, Gregory's message is the same for every moment of the Christian life: "always be diligent about your purification" (40.34).

Throughout Gregory's writings—in the *Theological Orations,* the great Epiphany series, and scattered other texts—the first element of Christian doctrine is to be clear about the purification of the theologian. In order to know God at all, one must be profoundly changed. This "first wisdom" Gregory calls "a life worthy of praise and kept pure for God—or being purified—for the One who is all-pure and all-luminous, who demands of us, as his only sacrifice, purification, that is, a contrite heart and the sacrifice of praise (Pss 50.23; 51.29), and a new creation in Christ (2 Cor 5.17), and the new person (Eph 4.24), and the like, as the Scripture loves to call it" (16.2). Yet for Gregory, the requirement of purification determines not only the faith and life of the theologian but also the very nature of Christian doctrine. He frequently contrasts the empty babbling of theological words with doctrine that authentically represents and promotes this new life. The true theologian proves the trustworthiness of his language by his life. Just as the purification symbolized in baptism is an ongoing process, so too Gregory consistently aims to move his hearers toward new life in Christ, in a way that reflects both his vocation as a Christian priest and his advanced training in Hellenistic philosophical rhetoric. This purpose is

---

77. See Elm, "Inscriptions and Conversions," pp. 2, 17–20, 24.
78. Plagnieux, *Saint Grégoire,* pp. 83–84.

especially evident in the ascent of Mount Sinai in *Oration* 28 (28.2–3). The first half of the passage (28.2), with its array of more or less purified characters, is a pointed exhortation for the hearer to consider his or her moral and spiritual condition. The overall rhetorical force of Gregory's doctrine is indicated as well in his allusion to Jesus' parable of the sower in the preceding, introductory section to the oration (28.1). Just as Jesus presents his hearers with different types of soil with which to compare their own lives, so Gregory challenges his readers with the prospect that not all spiritual conditions are capable of ascending to the knowledge of God.[79]

The priority of purification is also represented in the literary structure of several of Gregory's works, and in the telling way in which he characterizes these passages. In the second *Theological Oration,* for example, he marks the transition from his discussion of purification (in 27; 28.2; and further in 28) to his discussion of the knowledge of God and the Trinity (from 28.3 through 31) with the comment: "Now that we have purified the theologian with our doctrine" (28.1).[80] Gregory is saying that he *has* purified the theologian, simply by delivering a propaedeutic address in *Oration* 27 (and 28.2 to come).[81] Again, immediately after his major statement of purification in *Oration* 39 (39.8–10), Gregory shifts to a discussion of the Trinity with a similar phrase: "Now that we have purified the theater by what has been said" (39.11).[82] The formal character of these transitional markers indicates that Gregory does not understand purification in a strict, linear fashion, as a punctiliar state that one must achieve, in chronological order, before practicing theology. Rather, purification is the necessary condition for knowing God which *always* obtains, for every theologian, as he or she grows in holiness in order to know God more fully. It is therefore not surprising that Gregory so strongly opposes the spiritual rigorism of the Novatianists (39.18), who err on precisely this point. By conceiving of purification and holiness in an overly literal way, they ironically miss the more comprehensive and powerful sense of the idea. Just as purification occurs before, in, and after the definitive moment of baptism, so Gregory's doctrine possesses a permanent rhetorical—we might even say existential—character, constantly drawing the reader forward into the transforming knowledge of God.

---

79. Mt 13 and par. See also *Or.* 2.73, where Gregory employs the parable of the sower against excessive haste in the formation of pastors.

80. Ἐπειδὴ ἀνεκαθήραμεν τῷ λόγῳ τὸν θεολόγον. λόγος here refers both to Gregory's teaching, in terms of content, and to the course of his unfolding argument.

81. The phrase also occurs at *Or.* 20.5 to mark the same transition.

82. For further examples, see *Ors.* 6.5–6; 39.2; 40.1.

Contrary to the popular distinction between rhetorical form and substantive content, the rhetorical force of Gregory's doctrine of purification is not merely the superficial embellishment of an otherwise distinct theological system; it is an essential indication of the epistemic nature of that system. Again in the Sinai passage, he writes that his doctrine (λόγος) withdraws from the impure and is engraved on both sides of the stone tablets, "because the law is partly visible and partly hidden." Gregory's doctrine, as with the Gospel itself, is not epistemically neutral: it is not susceptible of being perceived in just any condition, but it possesses a different epistemic status according to the state of the recipient, "the Law of the letter" for the unpurified, and "the Law of the Spirit" for the purified. Here Gregory is making use of Origen's doctrine of the dual nature and function of divine revelation in Scripture, which he understands in terms of Paul's categories of the letter and the spirit in 2 Corinthians 3.[83] In this scheme, the simpler, clearer level of meaning is available to a wide variety of hearers, while the deeper meaning is available only to those who are transformed into the likeness of God through holiness of life.[84] By invoking this image Gregory indicates that his doctrine is continuous with biblical teaching and possesses the same dual character. We should note that this depth of meaning does not correspond with intellectual difficulty in the modern sense. It is characterized by moral-spiritual wisdom, irrespective of one's education, so that on all levels Christianity remains a "simple and uncomplicated religion" (36.2).[85]

Gregory concludes his admonition to purification in the oration *On the Holy Lights* (39.8–10) with this rich statement: "For the same doctrine (λόγος) is *in its own nature* terrible to those who are unworthy, but can be received in loving kindness by those who are thus prepared" (39.10; emphasis added). By its very nature, Christian doctrine adapts itself, as it were, to the recipient's spiritual condition, conveying radically different meanings to different people. Ultimately, this dual function reflects the intrinsically eschatological character of Christian teaching, which prefigures the final judgment of Christ. In the final sections of the Epiphany series, Gregory both promises and warns that God's judgment will be light to the purified—the kingdom of heaven, or "God seen and known"—while it will be darkness, or estrangement from God, for those

---

83. 2 Cor 3.6–8; Rom 2.29; 7.6. See also *Or.* 43.72: "Moses . . . legislated the double Law, the outward Law of the letter as well as an inward Law of the Spirit."

84. Origen's famous discussion of the threefold sense of Scripture (*Princ.* 4.2.2) is a further analysis of his more basic, twofold scheme. Passages on spiritual exegesis make up roughly half of Basil and Gregory's anthology of Origen.

85. ἡ ἁπλῆ καὶ ἄτεχνος εὐσέβεια.

who remain impure (40.45). Purification is therefore not merely an extrinsic injunction meant to prepare the theologian for the knowledge of God, but it represents the internal dynamic of Christian doctrine from beginning to end. As we will see in the chapters that follow, the meaning of Gregory's doctrine of the Trinity is at every point tied up with the reader's involvement in the mysteries that it describes.

Illumination: The Knowledge of the Incomprehensible God

In Gregory's work, the second pole of the internal dynamic of Christian doctrine is the divine illumination of the theologian. For a paradigmatic treatment of illumination we turn again to Gregory's ascent up Mount Sinai in the second *Theological Oration* (28.2–3). After establishing the requirement of purification in the first half of the passage, Gregory turns in the second half, and in the remainder of *Oration* 28, to the knowledge of God per se. On account of its importance, the passage bears quoting in full:

> What happened to me, friends and initiates and fellow lovers of the truth? I was running to comprehend (καταλαμβάνειν) God, and so I went up into the mountain and came through the cloud and entered away from matter and material things, and as far as I could I withdrew within myself. Then when I looked up, I barely saw the back parts of God; and in this I was sheltered by the rock, the Word that was made flesh for us (Ex 33.22–23; Jn 1.14; 1 Cor 10.4). When I looked a little closer I saw, not the first and pure nature (ἡ πρώτη τε καὶ ἀκήρατος φύσις),[86] which is known to itself—to the Trinity, I mean—and that part of it (ὅση) that abides within the first veil and is hidden by the cherubim (Ex 26.31–33; 36.35–36); but only that part of it (ὅση) that is posterior and comes down to us. This is, as far as I know, God's majesty that is manifested among the creatures that he has produced and governs—or as holy David calls it, God's "glory" (Ps 8.2). For these are the back parts of God, which he leaves behind as tokens of himself, like the shady reflections of the sun in the water, which show the sun to our weak eyes because we cannot look at the sun itself; for by its unmixed light it defeats our perception. In this

---

86. Lit. "undefiled nature." I take ἀκήρατος to be a form of κηραίνω (with Wickham), rather than κεράννυμι (Browne and Swallow).

way, then, you shall do theology, even if you are a Moses and "a god to Pharaoh" (Ex 7.1), even if you are caught up like Paul "to the third heaven" and heard "unspeakable words" (2 Cor 12.2–4), even if you are raised above them both and exalted to angelic or archangelic status and rank! For even if something is all heavenly—or even above heaven, much higher in nature than we are, and nearer to God—it is still farther from God and from the complete comprehension (κατάληψις) of him, than it rises above our complex and lowly and earthward-sinking composition. (28.3)

Having made the purifying ascent up the mountain, and concentrating as fully as possible on God alone, Gregory reports what he sees and describes the character of the knowledge of God. This brief but complicated passage is Gregory's most famous statement of the nature of theological vision,[87] and it introduces several major themes in his doctrine of the Trinity, which we will consider in turn. Although it has often been read out of context, it is imperative that we take into account the particularities of Gregory's argument against the Eunomians in *Oration* 28 as well as the wider theological context of his corpus as a whole. As we will see, Gregory means to convey two interrelated points concerning the incomprehensibility of God and the way in which Christians know God.

The most immediate doctrinal context of the above passage (28.3), and of the *Theological Orations* altogether, is Gregory's debate with the Eunomians. A central point of the disagreement is the Eunomians' claim to know the essence of God precisely and completely. Although our knowledge of actual Eunomian theologians and their activities in Constantinople in 380 is minimal, Gregory seems to be responding to the doctrine of Eunomius himself, largely as a kind of ideal opponent whose views allow him to identify the problems in other positions as well.[88] In his *Apology*, written almost two decades before Gregory's arrival in the capital,[89] Eunomius begins his confession of faith by arguing that God, the Father of Jesus Christ, is one, and that God is characterized above all by the fact that he exists apart from any source, either within or exterior to himself. Eunomius therefore describes God as "unbegotten essence" (οὐσία ἀγέννητος).[90] The idea that God the Father is unbegotten essence does not in itself upset Gregory so much as the several qualifications that accompany it. For Eunomius, the fact of God's unbegottenness (τὸ ἀγέννητον)

---

87. Referred to extensively by Plagnieux, McGuckin, and others.
88. For recent summaries of Eunomian doctrine, see p. 21n60.
89. Since 360 or 361. See Vaggione, *Eunomius: The Extant Works*, pp. 8–9.
90. *Apol.* 7.

must be understood not merely "in name," as if it were only a human invention, but as literally depicting the reality of God.[91] What is at stake here for Eunomius is the reliability of our knowledge of God: in order for our knowledge of God to be true, then the names by which we know God must refer to him accurately, as he really is, with the same knowledge that God possesses of himself.[92] To this end, he adopts a Christianized version of the essentialist view of language found in Platonic and Stoic traditions, according to which the names of things are given by God himself and directly reveal the nature of each thing.[93] Yet, in this essentialist framework, Eunomius is not simply saying that God's essence is unbegotten, as one among many predicates that can be accurately attributed to God, but that God's unbegottenness is the primary definition of God's essence, superior to all others.[94] God's unbegottenness, he argues, cannot be understood as the privation of a quality that God previously had (begottenness), since God was never begotten by anything; nor can it be applied only to a part of God, or to something separate or different from God, since God is without parts, simple, uncompounded, and "one and only" unbegotten;[95] therefore, God's essence simply *is* unbegottenness.[96] This insistence on using accurate language is in Eunomius' view crucial for Christian piety: God deserves to be acknowledged exactly as he is, and to do so is to honor God properly. Thus Eunomius believes that he has sufficiently demonstrated to theologians like Basil "that the God of all things is one and that he is unbegotten and incomparable (ἀσύγκριτος)."[97] If we can accept the authenticity of a fragment preserved by Socrates, Eunomius summarizes these views in quite a strong statement:

> God does not know (ἐπίσταται) anything more about his own essence than we do, nor is that essence better known (γιγνωσκομένη) to him and less to us. Rather, whatever we know (εἰδείημεν) about it is exactly what he knows (οἶδεν), and conversely, what he knows is what you will find without change in us.[98]

---

91. *Apol.* 8. οὐκ ὀνόματι μόνον κατ' ἐπίνοιαν ἀνθρωπίνην, . . . δὲ κατ' ἀλήθειαν.
92. See Vaggione, *Eunomius of Cyzicus*, pp. 245–256.
93. Plato, *Crat.* 430a–431e; Albinus, *Epit.* 6; Chrysippus, *Frag.* 895; Norris, *Faith Gives Fullness*, p. 34n167; see also Jean Daniélou, "Eunome l'Arien." Eusebius argued as well for the harmony between Plato's *Cratylus* and Genesis. See *Prep. ev.* 11.6, 9; and Michel René Barnes, *Power of God*, p. 203n132.
94. *Apol.* 7.
95. ἀμερής, ἁπλοῦς, ἀσύνθετος, εἷς καὶ μόνος ἀγέννητος.
96. *Apol.* 8.
97. *Apol.* 11.
98. *Frag.* 2, in Socrates, *HE* 4–7 (Vaggione, *Eunomius: The Extant Works*, p. 178). This statement is corroborated by a similar fragment of Aetius in Epiphanius, *Panar.* 76.4.2. See also Ayres, *Nicaea*, p. 149n49.

Whether the fragment is authentic or not, Eunomius believes that his knowledge of God's essence as unbegottenness is both absolutely accurate and logically comprehensive.

While Gregory is in agreement with several of the minor points of Eunomius' argument—for example, that God the Father has no source, that God deserves the highest regard in all human speech and understanding, and that God is indivisible, simple, and uncompounded—he nevertheless draws radically different conclusions from them.[99] In his view, Eunomius' real error is that he selectively, and with no apparent justification, elevates unbegottenness above all other attributes, to the point of making it the very definition of God's essence and the one quality that encompasses all others and exactly expresses the entirety of what God is, with no remainder.[100] As a result, Eunomius in effect claims to know God's essence completely.

Gregory stages his ascent up Mount Sinai specifically to test the Eunomian claim to know the essence of God completely. The passage begins with Gregory ascending the mountain in earnest hope of meeting with God (28.2), and in the next section he makes his purpose clear: "I was running to comprehend (καταλαμβάνειν) God" (28.3)—not simply to know God, but to know him entirely, as Eunomius claims to do. In the final sentence he reiterates the point, framing the entire passage with this theme: no matter how exalted one might be compared to others, one would still be infinitely far from the "complete comprehension (κατάληψις)" of God. Although it is easily missed in the current English translations,[101] the main topic of the passage is the question of God's comprehensibility. In this regard, Gregory's definitive story of theological vision is in a sense one of failure: he does not comprehend God as he had hoped, but just barely manages to see the "back parts of God." Within this context, Gregory's immediate polemical concern in the passage is to establish the incomprehensibility of God, to show that God cannot be fully known, as Eunomius claims.

---

99. In this he was joined by Basil, who argued against Eunomius' doctrine of ἀγεννησία in *Eun.* 1.

100. For example, in his reply to Basil's *Against Eunomius*, Eunomius refutes Basil's argument that the biblical term "Father" ought to be regarded as a more definitive title for understanding the Father than "unbegotten," partially because Eunomius believes that God (the Father) existed before he begot the Son, and so cannot have been Father as long as he was unbegotten (*Apol. Apol.* I.182.2–6; 192.20–193.1; Vaggione, *Eunomius: The Extant Works*, p. 103). See also *Apol. Apol.* 26, 28 and passim; *Apol. Apol.* 1.5–8; 2.4; with Basil, *Eun.* 1.9–15; 2.4, 9; *Frag.* 2, 11. Vaggione, *Eunomius: The Extant Works*, pp. 170, 178–179.

101. The significance of these statements at the beginning and at the end of the passage is missed in the most recent English translation of Wickham. The rendering of the first sentence, that Gregory was running to "see" God, is esp. misleading for reasons which will become clear below. Browne and Swallow's translation of the first as "lay hold of" and the second as "comprehension" is somewhat better, though the variation of terms weakens the connection between this passage and Gregory's discussion of comprehension later in *Or.* 28.

A major theme of Gregory's work, and another point on which he follows Origen,[102] the incomprehensibility of God dominates the second *Theological Oration* and appears in numerous other passages.[103] Following the introductory sections that we have been examining (28.1–3), Gregory sets the multiple themes of *Oration* 28 within an overarching framework of divine incomprehensibility (28.4, 31). The main argument of the oration, to which he continually returns, is that "the Divine cannot be grasped by human understanding,[104] and the entirety of its greatness can not even be imagined" (28.11).[105] In statements such as these, Gregory uses a variety of forms of λαμβάνειν, made popular through Stoic epistemology, to express the idea of grasping, mastering, or "getting one's head around" something; comprehension is thus a matter of complete and total understanding. His basic argument is that, on account of God's infinite grandeur and magnitude, he cannot be fully known or mastered by any created being. Gregory makes the point especially clearly in his funeral oration for his father:

> Since [God's] every quality is incomprehensible (ἀκατάληπτον) and beyond our conception (ἐπίνοια), how can that which surpasses [our level of existence] be either conceived (νοηθήσεται) or taught? How can the infinite be measured, so that the Divinity should suffer the condition of finite things and be measured by degrees and levels of descent? (18.16)

To imagine that God can be comprehended reflects a serious misunderstanding of the relationship between the nature of God and created existence. For Gregory the incomprehensibility of God is the necessary result of the infinitude of God's being and the finitude of creaturely existence, including human thought. In his discussion of divine incomprehensibility, he is making a very specific point about the greatness, or magnitude, of God compared to the theologian's ability to know him. As the Creator and source of all,[106] God surpasses all things in magnitude and greatness.[107] He is the "supreme na-

---

102. See *Princ.* 1.1.5; 4.4.8; Moreschini, "Influenze di Origene," pp. 45–47; "Nuove Considerazione," pp. 215–216.

103. Among the most explicit statements, see *Ors.* 2.74.77; 14.32; 18.16; 32.14; 30.17; 39.13. Norris goes so far as to say that this idea is the most frequent in the *Theological Orations*. *Faith Gives Fullness*, p. 40 and n182. See also McGuckin, "Perceiving Light," pp. 12–13; "Vision of God," p. 148.

104. τὸ μὴ ληπτὸν εἶναι ἀνθρωπίνῃ διανοίᾳ τὸ θεῖον.

105. See also *Or.* 28.4: "To comprehend (περιλαβεῖν) so great a subject as this with the understanding (διάνοια) is entirely impossible and impracticable, not only for the utterly careless and those who sink to the ground, but even for those who are highly exalted and who love God."

106. *Ors.* 34.8; 28.31; 38.9; 39.12.

107. Origen speaks of God in similar terms of superlative magnitude. See, e.g., *Princ.* 4.1.7.

ture" (ἀνωτάτω φύσις, 31.10), the one who is so great that all other things are small and weak by comparison, unable to approach him (2.5, 74). Yet God is not merely greater than all things by degree, he is *infinitely* great, entirely transcending creation. Gregory makes the point in his early *First Oration on Peace:* "God is the most beautiful and exalted of the things that exist (τῶν ὄντων)—unless one prefers to think of him as transcending being (ὑπὲρ τὴν οὐσίαν), or to place the sum total of existence (τὸ εἶναι) in him, from whom it also flows to others" (6.12). On the one hand, God is known to be supremely great, beautiful, and lofty, yet on the other hand his greatness exceeds even the category of greatness. Hence God is beyond (ὑπέρ) time and space, the universe as a whole, and even all purity and goodness (2.5, 76; 37.2).[108]

In the first Epiphany oration, Gregory describes God's transcendence in a dense combination of biblical and philosophical expressions. God is eternal "Being," as he told Moses ("ὁ ὢν" ἀεί, Ex 3.14),[109] "for he contains and possesses the whole of existence (ὅλον τὸ εἶναι) in himself, without beginning or end, like an endless, boundless ocean of Being (οὐσία),[110] extending beyond every notion of time and nature" (38.7).[111] While God is likened to a vast sea of existence, he is not relatively but absolutely great, and therefore transcends being itself and even the very category of greatness: God is so great that he is utterly beyond quantity (ἄποσον) and absolute (or simple, τὸ ἁπλοῦν, 37.2). Gregory concludes his argument for God's incomprehensibility in *Oration* 28 on just this point: God's nature is not simply "greater" than our ability to understand (νοῦ κρείττων), or even "above all things" (ὑπὲρ ἅπαντα), in the sense of being superior to them on their own terms, but it is "first and unique" (πρώτης καὶ μόνης) in an absolute sense (28.31),[112] because God's existence is of a radically different kind from our own (25.17). Thus God is not only greater than all things but he is also greater even than the idea of greatness, entirely surpassing our ability to understand him or to express him in language (30.17).[113]

Yet paradoxically—as our discussion here already indicates—God's absolute transcendence can only be understood and expressed *through* the categories of greatness, magnitude, and loftiness (37.2). It is crucial to see that for

---

108. See also *Or.* 38.7 (= 45.3); 39.12.
109. Interestingly, Gregory locates this revelation "on the mount," confusing the burning bush episode with the theophany on Mount Sinai.
110. A figure borrowed from Plato, *Symp.* 210d. On the transcendence of being in Platonic tradition, see Plato, *Rep.* 509b; Plotinus, *Enn.* 5.3.13–14, 17; 6.8.21.
111. See also *Or.* 34.8.
112. On God as the "first nature," see also *Ors.* 34.8; 40.7.
113. See also *Ors.* 32.14; 38.18; 42.18; and esp. 31.7–11, 22, 31–33.

Gregory the pure logic of transcendence serves to characterize a real epistemic ascent through created concepts of greatness, which themselves depend on and reflect the nature of the transcendent Creator. Because the knowledge of God represents a positive ascent through a scale of worldly concepts and values, the idea of greatness, rather than simplicity, is Gregory's preferred metaphysical designation for God's transcendence. Simplicity, then, serves as a kind of cipher for ideas like "greater than greatness" and "better than goodness," rather than as a fundamental theological principle which they inadequately and therefore dispensably express.[114] As Gregory notes, simplicity per se is not necessarily divine, and could just as soon be comprehensible as incomprehensible (38.7). Thus, in saying that God transcends all existence and language, he is not suggesting that we would be better off avoiding religious language altogether, but quite the contrary. For Gregory, the limited terms of Christian speech are necessary and truly signify with their actual meanings, even as they transcend themselves in the process. Hence Gregory routinely understands God's transcendent nature chiefly through concepts of magnitude. Speaking of our ability to understand or express God's transcendent nature, he writes in the fourth *Theological Oration,* "No one has yet breathed the *whole* air, nor has any mind *entirely* comprehended, or speech *comprehended,* the being of God" (30.17; emphasis added). Likewise, in his dense treatment of God's transcendence in *Oration* 38, he relies on the same structure of divine greatness: God is like a vast ocean of being compared to a small, single creature; he is the truth itself compared to a mere image, or a brilliant flash of lightning to our weak eyes. Hence—again in quantitative terms—God is comprehended "in part," even though "in part" he remains incomprehensible.[115] In sum, we can be sure that the Divine is infinite (ἄπειρον τὸ θεῖον): not merely simple, but extending without bounds beyond all beginning and end, so vast that the mind becomes dizzy from gazing into the abyss (38.7–8).

It is primarily this creaturely inability to know the full magnitude, or the entirety, of God that Gregory means by God's incomprehensibility. When someone "knows" (γιγνώσκειν) God in a real way—even to the extent of the great biblical figures[116]—he notes that they do not know God completely. Even if one's knowledge is said to be perfect, this simply means that one knows God

---

114. Here, too, Gregory follows Origen's understanding of God's simplicity (see *Princ.* 1.1.6; *Comm. Jn.* 1.119; *Cels.* 7.38), though with even less emphasis, for the reasons mentioned above.

115. The same quantitative terms used in *Or.* 28.3.

116. In *Or.* 28.18–21: Enosh, Enoch, Noah, Abraham, Jacob, Elijah, Manoah, Peter, Isaiah, Ezekiel, Paul, Solomon, and David. See also 14.30; 27.9.

more than others: one's knowledge of God is perfect only in a relative sense, at least in this life (30.17). For Gregory, the witness of the great saints bears this out: the same Paul who was raptured to the third heaven also writes that "we know in part and we prophesy in part," and that all our knowledge of God is but "puzzling reflections in mirrors" (1 Cor 13.9, 12; *Or.* 28.20).[117] Neither Jacob nor any of his descendants could boast of "having comprehended (χωρεῖν) the entire nature or vision of God" (28.18); and the more Solomon entered the depth of divine knowledge, "the more dizzy he became, and he declared the perfection of wisdom to be the discovery of just how far she flies from him" (28.21).[118] From such examples Gregory concludes that God's greatest reward for those who are purified and ascend to divine knowledge is to make them more fully enlightened concerning the Trinity, who is known only in part, and in part always remains the object of our quest (26.19). The greatest theologian, then, "is not the one who has discovered the entirety [of God's being], . . . but the one who has imagined more of it than someone else, and has gathered in him- or herself more of an appearance (ἴνδαλμα), or a faint trace (ἀποσκίασμα), of the truth" (30.17).[119] This fundamentally quantitative sense of the incomprehensibility of God remains programmatic for Gregory, and it must be carefully borne in mind if we are not to miss the overall sense of his theology.

In several places Gregory describes the incomprehensibility of God in more purely ontological terms. After the Sinai passage, he "begins again" by restating his argument about the incomprehensibility of God (28.4) and then sharpens his focus: "Our subject is not only 'the peace of God which passes all understanding (νοῦς)' (Phil 4.7) and comprehension (κατάληψις), nor how great are the things that God has stored up for the righteous in the promises . . . , nor even the exact knowledge (κατανόησις) of creation," all of which we know only in part. "But far above these things, we are talking about the ungraspable and incomprehensible nature that is above them and out of which they come[120]—not, I mean, the fact that it exists, but what it is" (28.5). The subject here is not simply God's works (which are themselves incomprehensible), but the fullness of God's being, the entirety of who or what God is. Gregory is referring not simply to the fact that God exists, which is a relatively minor point that can be demonstrated from a basic analysis of the universe, but to God's

---

117. So the cherubim indicate the primal Being to the diligent only "to a certain extent" (τοσοῦτον, *Or.* 34.13).
118. For more biblical examples, see *Or.* 14.30.
119. See also *Or.* 38.7.
120. ἡ ὑπὲρ ταῦτα καὶ ἐξ ἧς ταῦτα φύσις ἀληπτός τε καὶ ἀπερίληπτος.

very nature or being.[121] Thus none of the biblical figures who knew God more perfectly than others "'stood in the substance' and being (ὑπόστημα[122] καὶ οὐσία) 'of the Lord,' as it is written (Jer 23.18 LXX), or either saw or expounded the nature of God" (28.19). The saints' knowledge of God is not a full perception of God's being or nature.

As this last passage suggests, a particular difficulty arises in the interpretation of statements that express God's incomprehensibility in more universal terms. For example, as he once more "begins again" halfway through *Oration* 28, Gregory declares emphatically, "God—what he is in nature and being—no human being has ever discovered or can discover" (28.17). On the face of it, he seems to be saying that human beings cannot know God's being or nature at all,[123] yet this is not what he means. When Gregory speaks of our inability to know or discover God's nature, he is merely expressing the divine incomprehensibility in slightly different terms. Because we cannot know *all* of God's infinite essence, it can also be said that we are unable to know God's essence at all. Such statements of pure unknowability are rare in Gregory's work; the fact that he is so often taken to mean that humans do not know God's essence at all is an indication of the extent to which the *Theological Orations* have been the exclusive focus of Gregorian scholarship. Even in *Oration* 28, where the idea is most prominent, Gregory carefully qualifies his meaning, arguing that the question of our knowledge of God has to do primarily with our inability to encompass God's full magnitude, which he typically expresses in the language of comprehension. In the statement quoted above—"The Deity is not graspable by the human intellect; neither can the entirety of its magnitude be imagined" (28.11)—the second clause specifies the first, setting the idea of comprehension (or grasping) within the conceptuality of divine magnitude.[124]

---

121. Gregory uses several expressions for the divine nature in *Or.* 28 alone: ἥτις ἐστίν (28.5); τὸ/ὅ τί ποτὲ ἐστί (28.5, 17); and εἶναι θεόν (28.6). It was commonplace for early Christians to acknowledge that many non-Jews and non-Christians knew something of God's existence and attributes, however incomplete or inaccurate that knowledge may have been. See Acts 14.15–17; 17.22–31; 25.19; Rom 1.19–21; Clement of Alexandria, *Strom.* 1.19; 4.5; 5.14; and Origen, *Cels.* 7.41–47 and passim. Various notions of God's existence pervaded the Hellenistic philosophical schools.

122. Gregory takes the rare term ὑπόστημα to mean "substance" (see Lampe, s.v.). While it does not carry this meaning in classical Greek usage (LSJ, s.v.), the term derives from ὑφίστημι and is thus related to ὑπόστασις. However, it is hard to see how it could carry the meaning of the Hebrew text "counsel," which Browne and Swallow prefer.

123. For example, Plagnieux, *Saint Grégoire*, p. 283: Gregory's main argument in *Or.* 28 is "notre ignorance en face de l' 'inconnue' divine." Better assessments can be found in McGuckin, "Perceiving Light," pp. 12–13; Norris, "Theology as Grammar," p. 241.

124. The same pattern appears in *Or.* 20.11: "How do you suppose that you have an exact knowledge of God—what and how great he is?"

And so Gregory concludes *Oration* 28 in these terms, saying that the nature of God's being is "greater than our understanding (νοῦ κρείττων)" (28.31).[125] The same point applies to statements that we cannot "know" God or speak about God at all; for example, in Gregory's reversal of Plato's dictum:[126] "It is impossible to express (φράσαι) God; but to understand (νοῆσαι) him is even more impossible" (28.4).[127] For Gregory God is ineffable not because we cannot say anything about him or express his nature with any certainty, but because we could never possibly express *all* of what God is. Even though much of what is believed and said about God is true, because we cannot express all of God's nature God is in that sense "unspeakable." To conclude from such statements that we do not know or cannot make true statements about God's essence at all greatly exaggerates Gregory's apophaticism and misses the ultimate purpose of his doctrine, which is to show how Christians *do* know God.[128]

Gregory analyzes the epistemological dimension of incomprehensibility primarily in terms of human corporeality. As the Creator of all things, God exceeds the finitude, definition, and form that characterize created existence. For Gregory, as for Origen, all created things exist and have their unique identities precisely by being limited and formed in distinct ways, which makes them in some sense "corporeal" (σωματικός). Human mental activity is also fundamentally corporeal;[129] even though we are a mixture of intelligible and material realities (38.11),[130] the human mind conceives things by means of form and order, within the dimensions of time and space and involving the categories of quality, quantity, and relationship that characterize all creatures.[131] Thus Gregory describes human mental activity as a kind of passion (20.9), and he frequently comments on the bodily "thickness" (παχύτης) of the human condition.[132] Anything that can be understood, and all language, is mentally "embodied," so that we are constitutionally incapable of transcending

---

125. On God's infinitude, see also *Ors.* 38.7–8; 40.41.

126. *Tim.* 28c.

127. See also *Or.* 30.17: God cannot be named or expressed.

128. Cf. Hanson's emphasis on Gregory's "apophatic, agnostic theology." *Search for the Christian Doctrine of God*, p. 708.

129. For Origen, only the divine nature of the Father, Son, and Holy Spirit exists without material substance and without a body (*Princ.* 1.6.4; 2.2.2; 4.3.15). Everything else, including angels and demons, is embodied to some degree (pref. 8).

130. See also *Or.* 28.12. The themes of corporeality and incorporeality are generally absent from the Epiphany sermons; cf. 39.8, 13.

131. Origen, *Princ.* 4.3.15.

132. See *Ors.* 2.17, 74; 22.6; 34.6; 28.7, 12; 29.11, 19; 38.12–13 (= 45.8–9); 45.11–12, 45; *Ep.* 101.49, 56.

the corporeality of our knowing. By contrast, God exceeds these creaturely limitations, transcending space and time (20.9), and is thus incorporeal (ἀσώματον).[133] Again echoing Origen, Gregory notes that the incorporeality of God is universally taught in Christian theological tradition (28.9),[134] a point on which he and Eunomius, in fact, are in full agreement.[135] If God were a body, Gregory reasons, he would be either a member of the universe, or possibly the universe itself, and he would therefore be dominated by it or assimilated into it, rather than the Creator and Lord of it and the true object of creaturely worship (28.7).[136]

Yet even more than Origen,[137] Gregory is aware of the limitations of human language in conceiving of God, no doubt due in large part to the Eunomians' assurance that they know the divine essence. So he comments, "It is like using a small tool for big constructions" (28.21).[138] In his discussion of God's incomprehensibility in the second *Theological Oration*, Gregory turns first to the question of God's corporeality, concluding that "comprehension is a form of circumscription" (28.10).[139] By virtue of our corporeal nature and God's incorporeal boundlessness, God is incomprehensible to us. Even though we naturally long for an unmediated knowledge of God, any attempt to know God apart from created images and concepts runs up against the inherent limitations of human knowing.[140] Several times Gregory muses that the corporeal limits of our knowledge actually serve a good end and were designed by God as a mark of his benevolence, to promote our well-being. God has imposed "the darkness of the body" between himself and human beings, so that we might not lose what was too easily gained, fall from such great knowledge like Lucifer, or lack something to strive after, for which we can later be rewarded (28.12). In a mysterious way, the fact that God "lies hidden in the darkness poured over our eyes" serves both to give us hope for a better life in the midst of our present troubles, and also to check any illusions that we may harbor of being

---

133. See also Or. 30.17.

134. Origen had argued that even though the term ἀσώματον does not appear in Scripture, the idea is present nevertheless, and is an essential part of the Christian doctrine of God. *Princ.* pref. 8–9; 1.1–4 and passim.

135. See Eunomius, *Apol.* 12–22.

136. God would also be composite and subject to disintegration and dissolution (*Or.* 28.7), and could not fill the whole universe at once or function as its mover (28.8).

137. See Richard, *Cosmologie et théologie*, p. 439; Trigg, "Knowing God."

138. Trans. adapt. Wickham. See also 14.32: we are the ones who are spinning and irrational, not the world.

139. See also *Or.* 22.9.

140. See also *Ors.* 2.74; 24.15; 31.7; 39.13; 45.11.

sufficient unto ourselves (17.14).[141] This natural state of our corporeality—which is to say, our creatureliness—is thus both an obstacle and a help to the knowledge of God, and as such it is not conceptually parallel with sin, which unequivocally separates us from God.[142]

In its most immediate, anti-Eunomian context, Gregory's ascent up Mount Sinai in *Oration* 28 makes the negative point that we are unable to comprehend God (28.2–3). Yet in a broader sense—and more central to Gregory's theological interests—it indicates how we can and do know God. Again the choice of terms is significant: although he does not "comprehend" God, Gregory tells us that he does "see" God; he attains a real knowledge of God, even if it is less than full comprehension. Like Moses, Gregory sees the "back parts of God" (Ex 33.23), the posterior fringe of God's being, as God passes by. While he does not see God's nature fully, as God himself does ("that part of [God's nature] that abides within the first veil and is hidden by the Cherubim"),[143] Gregory does see God's nature "to some extent": he sees "that part of it (ὅση) that is posterior and comes down to us" (28.3).[144] Here again Gregory has been misinterpreted in an overly apophatic direction, as if he were saying that he did not see God's nature at all.[145] While he does not see all of God's nature, he does see the part of it that extends toward creation, the "tokens of himself" by which God is known by creatures and which the Bible calls God's "majesty" or "glory." When Gregory refers again to Moses' ascent up Mount Sinai in his final oration, further removed from the Eunomian context, he now describes Moses' ascent purely in terms of a positive revelation, with no mention of God's incomprehensibility: "For in that mount God appears (φαντάζεται) to human beings" (45.11).[146] Alongside his carefully articulated qualifications of our attempts at full comprehension, Gregory is

---

141. Gregory calls this fact of our created existence an "old and fixed ordinance of God" (*Or.* 17.4). See also 24.19; 29.11; 39.8.

142. See *Or.* 2.74.

143. On the first and second veils, which conceal God, see also *Ors.* 6.22 and 38.8: God, i.e., the Trinity, is the Holy of Holies, hidden even from the seraphim.

144. The phrase could also be translated to mean God's nature "*as* it abides within the first veil" and "*as* it reaches us," as Wickham does, in which case the divine nature is still the referent of both statements.

145. The Browne and Swallow translation is particularly misleading on this point, adding a second, created "nature" to the clause—"the first and unmingled nature" as opposed to "that nature which ... reaches to us"—rather than distinguishing two "parts" of God's one nature, as the Greek text reads. No more helpfully, Vladimir Lossky argues that Gregory is unclear about the nature of the vision of God, sometimes denying the possibility of knowing the divine essence and sometimes affirming it. *Vision of God*, pp. 82–84.

146. Cf. the more negative use of Moses in *Or.* 32.16, from the contentious autumn of 379, when caution and theological reserve were very much on Gregory's mind.

even more concerned to stress the real possibility of knowing God, even to the point of exaggeration. Those who are purified, he says, will come to know the Trinity as well as the Father, Son, and Holy Spirit are known by one another (25.17).[147]

Not surprisingly, Gregory gives his clearest statement of the positive knowledge of God in the Epiphany orations. He devotes more attention to the knowledge of God in *Orations* 38–40 compared to *Orations* 27–28, partly because his critique of the Homoians and Eunomians is less urgent, now that he has been installed as archbishop, but also because his main purpose is baptismal catechesis and the distinctiveness of Christianity against unbelief and traditional Greek religion, not dogmatic controversy within the Christian fold. Following the introduction on the difference between Christian and pagan religion, Gregory begins his main doctrinal exposition with an important reflection on the nature and the knowledge of God.

> God always was and is and will be—or better, God always *is*. For "was" and "will be" are divisions of the time we experience, which is a nature that flows away; but God always is and gives himself this name when he identifies himself to Moses on the mountain (Ex 3.14). He contains all of existence (ὅλον τὸ εἶναι) in himself without beginning or end, like an endless, boundless ocean of being. He extends beyond all our notions of time and nature, and is outlined (σκιαγραφούμενος) by the mind alone, but only very dimly and in a limited way—not by things that represent him completely, but by the things that are peripheral to him (οὐκ ἐκ τῶν κατ' αὐτόν, ἀλλ' ἐκ τῶν περὶ αὐτόν), as one representation (φαντασία) is derived from another to form a kind of singular image of the truth (ἕν τι τῆς ἀληθείας ἴνδαλμα): fleeing before it can be mastered, escaping before it can be conceived, shining on our guiding reason (provided we have been purified) as a swift, fleeting flash of lightning shines in our eyes. And he does this, it seems to me, so that to the extent that the Divine can be comprehended (τῷ ληπτῷ) it may draw us to itself—for what is completely incomprehensible (ἄληπτον) is also beyond

---

147. γνώσῃ τοσοῦτον, ὅσον ὑπ' ἀλλήλων γινώσκονται. This common Greek construction has an absurdly hyperbolic effect if taken literally. Gregory does not of course believe that we will share the uncreated magnitude of God's own self-knowledge, except by a very partial participation in it. The same qualified, rhetorical sense can be seen in his famous statement that Christ became human "so that we might become god to the same extent that he became human" (ἵνα γένωμαι τοσοῦτον Θεός, ὅσον ἐκεῖνος ἄνθρωπος, 29.19). See also the end of the passage quoted below (*Or.* 38.7).

hope, beyond attainment; and that to the extent that it is beyond our comprehension (τῷ ἀλήπτῳ) it might stir up our wonder, and through wonder might be yearned for all the more, and through our yearning might purify us, and in purifying us might make us like God; and when we have become this, that he might then associate with us intimately as friends—my words here are rash and daring!—uniting himself with us and making himself known to us as God to gods, perhaps to the same extent that he already knows those who are known by him. (38.7)[148]

Here Gregory describes God as superabundant Being, exceeding the dimensions and the categories of our existence, so that the finite human mind is only barely able to grasp him. And yet despite this fact—Gregory admits the idea seems unbelievable—we can know God, otherwise we would have no hope. Although we cannot entirely comprehend God being (κατ' αὐτόν), nevertheless we do perceive something of the "edge" of God's being, as it were (περὶ αὐτόν), a small extension of it, as we saw above (28.3).[149] Even though the mind, by reason of its natural limitations, knows God through created images and ideas, which are shadows compared to God's supreme reality and which, taken together, produce only an image of God's truth, nevertheless through these images God himself is known to the believer, as the "edge" of God's being, his outer parts, are truly seen. As Gregory writes in *Oration 2*, God has created us "able to touch God, though not to comprehend him" (2.75). Thus God draws us closer to himself by what we know of him, gradually transforming us and uniting himself to us, even as he always exceeds this knowledge in order to attract our longing. As a result, God is known to such an extent that our relationship to him can only be described in incredibly intimate terms.

The positive relationship between the divine nature and the human knowledge of God is evident above all in Gregory's treatment of divine light and illumination. A particularly telling passage comes early in the oration *On Baptism*:

God is light (1 Jn 1.5)—supreme (ἀκρότατον), inaccessible (1 Tim 6.16) and ineffable—which can be neither comprehended with the mind nor uttered in speech, and which illumines every rational na-

---

148. Trans. adapt. Daley.
149. See a similar expression in *Or.* 30.17. This phrase has usually been rendered in ways that undermine the reality of the knowledge of God that Gregory is trying to convey. For Browne and Swallow, God is known "not by His Essentials, but by His Environment"; for Gallay, "non pas d'après ce qui est en Dieu, mais d'après ce qui est autour de lui."

ture. It is among intelligible things what the sun is among sensible things. It appears to us to the extent that we are purified; it is loved to the extent that it appears; and in turn it is conceived to the extent that it is loved. It contemplates and comprehends itself and pours itself out a little bit on those who are external to it. I mean that light that is contemplated in Father, Son, and Holy Spirit, whose richness is their harmony and the one outleaping of their brightness. (40.5)

Gregory's primary concept for God's nature is light, and he frequently refers to the knowledge of God as illumination, or coming to share in the divine light.[150] The supreme light of the Trinity—God's very being, which transcends all comprehension[151]—naturally extends outward toward others as the source of all other light in heaven and earth (45.2):[152] first to the angels, the "secondary splendors" who receive God's "primary splendor," and through them to human beings (39.9).[153] Gregory occasionally compares the light of God to the sun.[154] Like the physical sun, God is dangerously bright to human perception (28.3);[155] just as the sun illuminates the world of sense, so God illuminates human beings, especially the human mind (40.5).[156] While Gregory occasionally speaks of divine illumination as human mental life in general (the soul or reason),[157] illumination more commonly refers to God's gift of the saving knowledge of himself. As the physical sun perfects our bodies, making them

---

150. This concept overlaps with the contemplative language of vision. The standard treatment of Gregory's imagery of light is John Egan's "Knowledge and Vision of God." See also Kertsch, *Bildersprache*; Moreschini, "Luce e purificazione"; and *SC* 358, pp. 63–66. In addition to the Scriptures (see esp. the Johannine literature: Jn 1.4–9; 3.19–21; 8.12; 9.5; and 1 Jn 1.5; see also Hb 1.3), the imagery of light is well established in fourth-century creeds and theological works, including the statement of Nicaea that Christ is "light from light."

151. *Pace* Egan, who argues that for Gregory "light" does not designate God's nature itself, but only God's illuminative causality and human beings' resemblance to him, as in the work of Plotinus ("Knowledge and Vision of God," pp. 134, 141), or "the mutual penetration of the soul and the divine spirit" (p. 159). As *Or.* 40.5 indicates, Gregory does use the imagery of light to refer to God's transcendent nature, not just God's communication of his nature (see also 37.4; 44.3).

152. See also *Ors.* 2.76; 12.4; 17.8; 20.1; 32.15; 21.1–2; 28.31; 31.3; 36.5; 37.4; 39.1, 9; 40.37, 41; 44.3; 45.2; *Carm.* 1.1.32.13–18; 2.1.12.753; 2.1.36.7.

153. See also *Ors.* 38.9; 40.5. On the angels as transmitters of God's primal light, see also 28.31; 44.3; 45.2.

154. A traditional biblical and Greek image: Pss 84.11; 89.36; Mal 4.2; and Mt 17.2 (the Transfiguration); see also Rv 10.1; 12.1; 19.17; Origen, *Comm. Jn.* 13.23. Among the Greeks, see esp. Plato, *Rep.* 6.508, 510a, e; 516c; *Phaed.* 67b; Plotinus, *Enn.* 6.7.16. And see Egan, "Towards a Mysticism of Light," esp. nn10, 28–32; Moreschini, "Luce e purificazione," pp. 545–546; and Pinault, *Le Platonisme*, p. 89.

155. See also *Ors.* 9.2; 17.7; 20.10.

156. See also *Ors.* 21.1; 28.3; 44.3–4; *Carm.* 1.2.10.946–960; Gottwald, *De Gregorio Nazianzeno Platonico*, pp. 40–41, 48; and Kertsch, *Bildersprache*, p. 125 and n3.

157. See *Ors.* 28.17; 39.1; *Carm.* 1.1.4.32–34; 1.1.8.1–3; Egan, "Knowledge and Vision of God," pp. 160–161.

sunlike (ἡλιοειδεῖς), so God perfects our intellectual natures, making them godlike (θεοειδεῖς, 21.1).

For Gregory, divine illumination begins in this life, even though the full vision of the divine light occurs only in the life to come. In his funeral oration for Caesarius, Gregory movingly addresses his dead brother, "You are filled with the light that streams forth from [God]," while those who remain in this world receive only a small stream of light "in this day of mirrors and enigmas (1 Cor 13.12)" (7.17). Gregory regularly cites Paul's statement in 1 Corinthians 13.12 to indicate that we see God only partially during our earthly life, as if the divine light were reflected in a mirror. We do not currently comprehend God's essence, but "what reaches us is a scant emanation, as it were a small beam from a great light" (28.17).[158] In his study of Gregory's imagery of mirror and light, John Egan argues that Gregory clearly distinguishes between the knowledge of God in this life, seen indirectly in the reflections of the inner mirror of the soul, and the complete face-to-face vision of God in the life to come.[159] Yet while the earthly and heavenly visions are distinguished in this way, it is important not to overstate the postponement of full divine knowledge as a radical distinction between two different kinds of knowledge. Central to Gregory's theological vision is the reality of the knowledge of God's nature in this life, and the *continuity* of that knowledge with the eschatological vision, with which it differs only in degree. In *Oration* 40, quoted above, he emphasizes this very point: while God is incomprehensible in his fullness, nevertheless the divine light appears to the purified, "pouring itself out" on them in a partial but real way, so that even now they contemplate the rich brilliance of the Trinity (40.5).[160] In the anti-Eunomian context of *Oration* 28, Gregory naturally emphasizes the incomprehensibility of God; but this is not his usual focus.[161] More typically (as in the Epiphany orations) he celebrates the extraordinary fact that the incomprehensible God has revealed himself through the illumination of his eternal brightness. An important passage on light from *Oration* 32 makes this clear. God "treads on our darkness (γνόφος) and 'makes darkness (σκότος) his hiding place,'" Gregory says—referring to God's presence in the

---

158. See also *Ors.* 11.6; 12.4; 20.1, 12; 24.19; 32.15; 25.16; 26.19; 38.7, 11; 43.82; *Carm.* 1.2.10.946–960; 2.1.1.213; 2.1.87.15f.; 2.2.3.286.

159. Egan, "Knowledge and Vision of God," pp. 1–2, 18 and passim.

160. In his commentary on this passage, Moreschini, e.g., stresses the ontological *difference* between God and creatures (*SC* 358, p. 204n4), adding that, in his use of light imagery, Gregory is aware that it does not contradict "negative theology" ("Luce e purificazione," p. 536)—as if to protect us from the very point that Gregory is making!

161. As noted previously, the argument of *Or.* 28 is rare in Gregory's corpus.

cloud on Mount Sinai in Hebrews 12.18, and in the raging thunderclouds of Psalm 18.11[17.12]—so that we might attain the knowledge of God stably and reliably through purification "and that light might commune with light, drawing it ever upward with desire" (32.15). Even the limitations of our vision, in other words, are meant to promote God's self-revelation, not to isolate him in a cloud of unknowing. As Gregory continues, commenting on 1 Corinthians 13.12, the divine light reveals itself partially now (τὸ μέν), and partially in the life to come (τὸ δέ), to those who "intimately associate" (ὁμιλεῖν) with it while on earth. Even as he notes God's incomprehensibility and the eschatological nature of full vision, in this oration on restraint in theological discourse, the entire passage shines with the real, if partial, knowledge of the divine light that begins in this life.

The positive revelation of God's being is the dominant idea conveyed by the imagery of light throughout Gregory's corpus. It is, he says, the very nature and purpose of the divine light to illuminate Christians partially (τὸ μέτριον) in this life, so that they may "see and experience the brightness of God" more fully in the next (38.11).[162] Even now believers receive a "tiny emanation and, as it were, a small beam from a great light" (28.17). The reality of earthly illumination can be seen in the strong terms that Gregory uses in *Oration* 40 to say that the light of the Trinity "pours itself out (χεῖσθαι) a little bit" on the pure (40.5). The verb here is the same one that he uses to speak of the eternal generation of the Son and the Holy Spirit from God the Father (23.8) and the outpouring of God's goodness in the act of creation (38.9), particularly to the intelligible world (38.10);[163] and here again the continuity of divine knowledge is expressed in terms of differing quantitative measures of the same light (ὅσον, ὀλίγα, 40.5). Though they are comparatively small, the rays of the divine light truly illuminate believers in this life (8.19).[164] At Epiphany in 381 Gregory exhorts the members of his congregation to be purified, so that they may be illuminated by the Trinity, "of which you have now received in part this one ray from the one Divinity" (39.20).[165] In another significant text, he comments that God draws people to himself by an enlightenment that naturally[166] resembles his own

---

162. See also *Ors.* 8.23; 16.9.
163. Though Gregory is wary of the Neoplatonist connotations of the overflowing of the Monad (*Or.* 29.2); cf. Plotinus, *Enn.* 5.1.6; 5.2.1; see also 2.9.3; Plato, *Tim.* 41d (with a different context). Moreschini, *SC* 358, pp. 77–80; and see chap. 4, on the philosophical resonance of 29.2.
164. See also *Ors.* 7.17; 39.1–2; *Carm.* 1.2.10.142; 2.1.1.630–632.
165. See also *Or.* 17.8.
166. συγγενής. Mossay prefers the safer translation "innée en nous" (*SC* 270, p. 111); however, the connotations of kinship and natural origin, together with the context of the divine light in *Or.* 21.1–2, demand a stronger reading. See the similar judgment of Browne and Swallow (*NPNF* II.7, p. 269).

light, because it comes from him and is constituted by our vision of him (21.1). So strong is Gregory's sense of the positive knowledge of God that he occasionally oversteps his own definitions and speaks of our present illumination in extreme terms. As he nears the climactic end of his Epiphany orations, he rouses his hearers, "Let us lay hold of the Divinity! Let us lay hold of the first and brightest Light. Let us walk toward his radiance!" (40.37)—the language being that of full comprehension (λαμβάνειν). Finally, as he commends the confession of the Trinity, he speaks euphorically of being already illuminated by the Three in his contemplation of the One, and of his vision of a single light (μία λαμπάς) in his contemplation of the Three (40.41).[167]

In the Sinai passage of *Oration* 28, Gregory has created his own unique version of the sun analogy to indicate these several points. He likens the back parts of God to the sun's rays refracted into dim shapes of light in water (28.3). The image suggests that God is too immense and powerful to be known in his fullness, but that, nevertheless, he illuminates his creatures with a real, though attenuated, vision of his being. While one might be inclined to read the image along the lines of shadows cast by the sun in silhouette, which would suggest that we do *not* see God's light, but know it only negatively through the shadows that it casts, Gregory is again less apophatic than this. His use of a similar image to refer to the three persons of the Trinity—that of a sunbeam, its reflection off a wall, and refraction in water (31.32)—indicates the continuity between the sun and its image in the water, rather than the discontinuity, indirection, and unknowing of a silhouette. The image of the sun cast in the water conveys the positive light of God's being in an attenuated form that the weak eye can perceive. Except for the diminished power of the light—which speaks against the Eunomian claim to comprehend God—there would be no question that what one is seeing is the same light cast by its source. We see the same emphasis in the passage from *On the Holy Lights* quoted above. Beginning with purification and fear, one is moved by desire for the transcendent God and is raised—even now—to the heights of illumination by the light of divine knowledge (39.8–10). Through this positive image of light and illumination, Gregory closely identifies the believer's knowledge of God with the being of God itself. God's transcendent being overflows, as it were, into our knowledge of him, so that, while God's infinitude is always a limiting factor, the result is a direct and continuous relationship between God's being and the human knowledge of God. Because of this continuity, the question of whether

---

167. See also *Carm.* 2.1.1.194–213.

light is a relative or an absolute term for God in fact breaks down, since the distinction depends on the assumption that what Christians know of God is not (even partially) what God is in himself.[168]

Just as holy baptism is the paradigm of purification, so too is it the preeminent instance of divine illumination. Again in the Epiphany series, the light of the incarnate Christ leads directly to the illumination that Christians receive as they are "signed with the true light" in baptism (39.1–2). Gregory's discussion of the divine light and illumination in *Oration* 40.5, discussed above, is a direct explanation of the knowledge of God conferred in baptism, and this sense can be applied to several other passages in the series as well. Gregory's sense of baptism as the great Christian illumination can be seen in the way he alters the traditional term φωτισμός to φώτισμα ("illumination"), so as to echo βάπτισμα ("baptism").[169] Early in the oration Gregory describes the multifaceted healing and transformation of Christian baptism as the Illumination par excellence:

> Illumination (τὸ φώτισμα) is the splendor of souls, the conversion of life, the conscience's appeal to God. Illumination is help for our weakness, the renunciation of the flesh, the following of the Spirit, communion with the Word, the improvement of the creature, the destruction of sin, participation in light, the dissolution of darkness. It is the carriage that leads to God, dying with Christ, the perfecting of the mind, the bulwark of faith, the key of the kingdom of heaven, a change of life, the removal of slavery, the loosing of chains, the renewal of our complex being. Why should I go into further detail? Illumination is the greatest and most magnificent of the gifts of God. (40.3)

On a more personal note, Gregory vividly describes his own baptism as a divine illumination. In the *Carmen lugubre* he portrays his baptism as a dreamlike appearance of the female figures of Virginity and Simplicity, who "stand within the presence of Christ the Lord" and invite him to merge his flame with theirs, so that they can usher him through the ether "to stand in the radiance of the immortal Trinity.[170]

---

168. Pace Althaus and Egan, who argue that Light is a relative, not an absolute, name for God (based on Or. 30.18). Althaus, *Die Heilslehre*, pp. 159–160 and n62; Egan, "Knowledge and Vision of God," p. 476.

169. Following Clement of Alexandria, *Paed.* 1.6, 26, 29–30. See also the texts attributed to Didymus the Blind: *In Pss.* 20–21 14.7; *In Gen.* 7A.4 (not referring to baptism); *Trin.* 1.15, 18; 2.1, 5, 7, 14; 3.39 (mostly referring to baptism); and Origen, *Fr. in Ps.* 44.11–14, l.28. The term appears frequently in *Or.* 40: 40.3 (5×), 4 (2×), 24, 25; as does the continued use of φωτισμός: 40.1, 3, 5 (3×), 24, 36 (2×), 37 (2×).

170. *Carm.* 2.1.45 *Carmen lugubre*, here ll. 257–263. See also McGuckin, *St. Gregory*, pp. 67–76.

The identification of baptism with both purification and illumination[171] highlights the complex interrelationship between the two poles of Gregory's spiritual dialectic. The concept of purification connotes the removal of impurities that stand in the way of one's life with God, whereas illumination describes the conveyance of the divine light to the believer; and one must be purified in order to be illuminated, as we saw dramatized in the Sinai narrative (28.2–3). Purification leads to illumination (39.8), and God illuminates rational beings to the extent that they are purified, leading them through love to contemplation (40.5). So Christ is called "Light" because he is "the illumination of souls who are purified in world and life" (30.20). In nearly synonymous terms, Gregory speaks of action (or practice, πρᾶξις) as leading to the contemplation (or vision, θεωρία) of God. While action serves Christ in the world through the power of love, contemplation rises above the world to behold God directly (14.4). Gregory exhorts the would-be theologian to ascend to the knowledge of God through virtuous living, to reach the Pure through purification, which he summarizes in the famous statement: "Action is the stepping-stone to contemplation" (20.12).[172] It is the priority of the Spirit, he writes in the *First Oration on Peace*, first to purify oneself "through the philosophy that resides in actions (ἔργα)," and then to receive divine wisdom from the Spirit (6.1). Such expressions might suggest a kind of chronological sequence, with illumination and contemplation coming only after one has been purified through action. Yet, as Thomas Spidlík has shown,[173] for Gregory there is a constant, fluid, and dynamic relationship between action and contemplation, and purification and illumination, so that they are, in effect, two dimensions of a single movement. In his panegyric on Basil, he positively discourages imagining one without the other. "Unreasoning practice and impractical reason (ἄλογος πρᾶξις καὶ λόγος ἄπρακτος)" are equally deficient, and so Basil wisely combined them (43.43), excelling in both life and knowledge (βίος and λόγος, 43.12). Athanasius, too, is an example of one who combined contemplation and action, "using life as a guide to contemplation and contemplation as a seal of life" (21.6).[174]

---

171. See Elm, "Inscriptions and Conversions," pp. 16–18.
172. πρᾶξις γὰρ ἐπίβασις θεωρίας. Or "*praxis* is the patron (πρόξενος) of contemplation" (40.37). The idea of practice leading to contemplation is found also in Origen (e.g., *Comm. Jn.* 2.36.219). See Moreschini, "Influenze di Origene," p. 40.
173. Spidlík, *Grégoire de Nazianze*, p. 113; see also Plagnieux, *Saint Grégoire*, pp. 141–164.
174. In his monastic reforms, Athanasius also reconciled the solitary life of contemplation with the communal life of action (*Or.* 21.19–21). See also 14.4: Christ shows that action is just as important as solitude and contemplation.

Hence, in the first *Theological Oration*, Gregory argues that the knowledge of God requires both contemplation and purification (27.3, quoted above).[175]

Purification, then, is the constant preparation and the active, practical foundation for illumination. The dynamic relationship between the two constitutes the movement of the Christian toward God, with baptism as its defining moment. The fluidity of this spiritual process can be seen in the way in which Gregory frequently shifts back and forth from purification to illumination, and sometimes brings them right together. The final paragraph of *On the Holy Lights* shows this coalescence better than perhaps any other passage:

> Be completely purified and you shall be pure, . . . so that you may stand as perfect lights beside that great Light, and in his presence be initiated into the Mystery of Light (φωταγωφγία),[176] being illuminated by the Trinity more purely and clearly, of which even now you have received in part this one ray from the one Divinity, in Christ Jesus our Lord; to whom be the glory and the might for ever and ever. Amen (39.20)

Throughout the process of purification, the Christian is increasingly illuminated by Christ with the light of the Trinity. With this view of the Christian life now laid before them, Gregory has prepared his hearers for the following oration on baptism itself. The aim of Gregory's doctrine of purification, illumination, and baptism, we might say, is not to produce a tight, self-contained, ascetical system, but rather to exhort his hearers to purify themselves, so that they can receive the divine Light of Christ and bear that light in the world. As we will see below, Gregory's major doctrinal reflections on Jesus Christ, the Holy Spirit, the Trinity, and the pastoral ministry of the Church give concrete expression to this dynamic of spiritual growth.

Conclusion

Gregory's doctrine of purification and illumination defines the basic shape of how God is known and the epistemic structure of all theology. In a paradoxical but highly deliberate way, he has constructed a mystical tension[177] that draws

---

175. Cf. *Or.* 27.8 on faulty Eunomian attempts at λόγος and θεωρία.
176. Gregory again uses a rare term for light, to echo μυσταγωγία. He may have borrowed it from Eusebius, *Comm. Pss.,PG* 23.1228.52; see also Pseudo-Didymus, *Trin.* 2.14.
177. The phrase is Moreschini's; however, his understanding of the nature of this tension, which he contrasts with the supposedly more systematic work of Gregory of Nyssa, differs from that argued here. *SC* 358, p. 69.

the reader into a deeper knowledge of God. Gregory provides what we might call a rhetorical-theological dynamic that reflects the persuasive aims of both the biblical word of God and classical rhetorical dialectic and whose chief purpose is to move the theologian toward the visionary knowledge of God.[178] As Gregory sees it, God reveals himself to our limited understanding, while ever remaining transcendent, so as to create a dynamic of growth that moves us through yearning and wonder to ever greater degrees of purification and illumination. Much more than a rhetorical posture, this transformation is woven into the very fabric of Gregory's doctrine and determines its meaning and scope.

Gregory's treatment of these themes characterizes the nature of theology in another important respect as well. In his debate with the Eunomians in *Oration* 28, he radically qualifies the human ability to know God by reason alone, in order to point the reader to the knowledge that only comes in response to divine revelation. He summarizes the point at the end of his long hymn on creation: "Let faith lead you rather than reason, that is if you have learned the weakness of reason in matters close at hand, and have acquired enough knowledge of reason to know things that are beyond reason!" (28.28).[179] Gregory wants to show not only that God can never be fully known, but also that we are dependent on faith to know God at all. Not to acknowledge the limits of our reason is, he says, to be "ignorant even of your own ignorance" (28.8). Similarly, in the *Second Oration on Peace*, he argues that the source of many difficulties is the failure to recognize what sort of things are within our power and can be investigated by reason alone (things other than God), and which ones are beyond our power and can be known only by faith (22.11). It is inherent in the work of faith to see beyond the limitations of earthly reason in order to discern the mind of God, which is obscure to our unaided natural powers (14.33). To be sure, reason is for Gregory the image of God given in creation and, as the center of the human person, it is the primary faculty by which we know God and manage our complicated lives.[180] Yet all the same, he warns that reason is profoundly limited by human finitude, corrupted by sin and the devil (6.7),[181]

---

178. As Winslow remarks, "Gregory's thought operates more effectively in the realm of dynamic function than in that of static description." *Dynamics of Salvation*, p. 91. See also McGuckin, "Vision of God," p. 148; *St. Gregory*, pp. 58, 65, 74–75, 220 and passim.

179. The seminal insight here again belongs to Origen. In *Cels.* 6.65, he argues that God is unattainable by human reason (λόγος), but that, contrary to Celsus' skepticism, God is indeed attainable by the divine Λόγος and by those to whom he reveals the Father (Mt 11.27). See Lieggi, "Influssi Origeniani."

180. Among numerous such statements, see *Ors.* 15.2; 6.6, 10; 11.6; 14.33; 17.1, 3, 9; 22.7; 24.7; 25.1; 27.5; 32.7, 24, 27; 33.9; 36.8; 37.14, 21; 39.7; 40.5, 37, 45; 42.6; 44.6.

181. See also *Or.* 40.37 on the good light that comes from God versus the wicked appearance of light that comes from the devil.

and useless for knowing God apart from faith (4.44).[182] In an extended section of *Oration* 32 he argues that illumination comes only through faith, referring especially to the teaching of the Scriptures. Those who are intellectually weak are therefore in just as great a position to be saved as the more gifted, through the faith of their minds and the confession of their mouths,[183] for righteousness comes through faith alone (32.23–27).

Regrettably, this important element of Gregory's thought has frequently been misunderstood in modern scholarship. Plagnieux, for example, takes *Oration* 28 as a manifesto on the natural knowledge of God, which exemplifies Gregory's great confidence in the power of reason.[184] Alternatively, R. P. C. Hanson faults Gregory for not properly distinguishing between the natural and revealed knowledge of God.[185] Such assessments might seem to be supported by passages like *Oration* 28.16, where Gregory writes that, even after the fall, our God-given reason leads us to God. Yet this statement refers merely to the knowledge of God's existence, nothing more. Earlier in the oration he argues that it is possible to know that God exists from a basic observation of the universe—not in order to establish a natural proof of the existence of God, but, quite the contrary, to say that since such knowledge tells us nothing about *what* God is, it is relatively useless (28.6). So he concludes with a pointed rhetorical question: "What will you conceive the Deity to be if you rely on the approximations of reason?" (28.7). His answer is that the knowledge of God's being comes only by the Holy Spirit, which searches the depths of God (28.6).[186] A second such text is Gregory's statement that the mind either makes visible things into gods or else it "discovers God through the beauty and order of visible things" (28.13). However, here he is contrasting the idolatry of created things in the history of religion with the way in which we are meant to know God through them.[187] Rather than exalting reason as being capable of knowing God independently, Gregory's point is that apart from faith and grace, reason is profoundly incapable of knowing God with any accuracy or saving benefit. Reason, he says, is "hard to trace out" (28.21), yet "it is faith that fulfills our reason" (29.21).

---

182. In the *Theological Orations* Gregory systematically critiques the Eunomians' pride in their reason, from the opening section onward. See also below, chap. 3.

183. See Rom 10.6–8.

184. Plagnieux, *Saint Grégoire*, pp. 277–287. Thus he coins the term "foi-raison" for what he takes to be Gregory's hybrid concept (pp. 278, 287).

185. Hanson, *Search for the Christian Doctrine of God*, p. 708n119, based on *Or.* 6.32–33.

186. 1 Cor 2.10; see also 28.17.

187. Apparently following Paul's argument in Rom 1.18–23.

Gregory aims to point his readers away from reason alone and toward faith as reason's fulfillment.[188] Despite the expectations of twentieth-century theologians, he is not promoting a theory of the natural knowledge of God any more than he is asserting pure apophaticism. Instead, he is drawing the theologian toward the knowledge of God as God has revealed himself in Jesus Christ by the Holy Spirit in the economy of salvation.[189] When Gregory reports his vision of God on Mount Sinai, he adds an important detail in this regard: he tells us that he was "sheltered by the rock, the Word that was made flesh for us" (28.3). It is through Christ that Gregory is able to see even a glimpse of God's being.[190] Likewise the illumination of which he so often speaks is not a generic kind of divine knowledge, but the supreme Light of the Holy Trinity revealed through the incarnation of Jesus Christ. Gregory's sense of the knowledge of God in Christ is so strong that he again exaggerates his own limiting terms: the purpose of the incarnation is that in the human form of Jesus "the Incomprehensible might be comprehended (ἵνα χωρηθῇ ὁ ἀχώρητος)" (39.13).[191] Gregory makes this statement at the midpoint of the Epiphany series, just as he is turning from the incarnation of Christ to the conferral of divine illumination on Christians in baptism, which further indicates the preparatory nature of this first part of his doctrine. The topics that that we have been examining from *Orations* 27–28, 38–40, and elsewhere represent a kind of propaedeutic orientation to the broad contours of theology, which aims to move the theologian toward the knowledge of God. "In this way you shall do theology" (28.3), Gregory says—knowing by faith the divine light of the incomprehensible God through the economy of salvation.

---

188. On the fulfillment of reason by faith, see Norris, *Faith Gives Fullness*, pp. 126–127, and the title of that volume; "Of Thorns and Roses," pp. 462–464; McGuckin, *St. Gregory*, pp. 57–58, 288, 332.

189. On the nature of the divine economy, see chap. 4.

190. See also *Or.* 32.16.

191. See also *Or.* 37.3.

2

Jesus Christ, the Son of God

Christ is on earth—be exalted!

—Oration 38

When Gregory portrays himself on Mount Sinai beholding the fringe of God's being, at the apex of his account of theological vision in the second *Theological Oration*, he tells us that he was "sheltered by the rock, the Word that was made flesh for us" (28.3). As this image suggests, for Gregory the knowledge of God that takes place through the purification and illumination of the theologian is constantly enabled by the figure of Jesus Christ, the Word made flesh. Christ has of course been the center of the Church's doctrine and devotion since apostolic times, and "Jesus is Lord" (1 Cor 12.3) is possibly the earliest Christian confession. Similarly, in Gregory's doctrinal system, Christ is not simply one member of the Trinity, a figure whose earthly career is accidental to Trinitarian doctrine, strictly speaking, and who could just as well have been God the Father or the Holy Spirit made incarnate; but he is the necessary and permanent focus of the knowledge of God. While there is an obvious and even simplistic sense in which Christ's divinity is implied in a full doctrine of the Trinity (if we could imagine beginning there), for Gregory the confession of Christ's identity as the eternal Son of God is, in a deeper sense, the direct means by which the Trinity is conceived and known in the first place, and, by the presence of the Holy Spirit, Christ remains the centerpiece of that knowledge.

Gregory Nazianzen was one of the chief architects of the language and concepts used in the Christological controversies that occupied the Church, in increasingly scholastic terms, from the fifth to the eighth centuries. Yet, ironically, his doctrine of Christ is not primarily concerned with technical terminology or the precise definition of the composition of Christ's person, as several generations of students have been taught to regard pre-Chalcedonian Christology. In fact, Gregory is quite insistent that technical and terminological questions must be subjugated to the basic faith of which they are but an imperfect expression.[1] In the same way that the doctrine of God and the doctrine of the knowledge of God cannot be separated in Gregory's work, so too the identity of Christ cannot be separated from the human salvation that Christ effects. It would not be an exaggeration to say that Gregory's Christology is essentially a particular expression of his soteriology, so that our understanding of the nature of Christ's person is determined throughout by the nature of Christian salvation, and vice-versa. In this chapter we will examine Gregory's doctrine of Christ in light of his soteriological concerns, in an attempt to uncover the most basic meaning and rationale of his Christology and its place within his doctrine of the Trinity as a whole. The basic contours of Gregory's Christology appear to have been fairly well established by the time he began ordained ministry in 362,[2] even if we allow for some editing of the early writings during his retirement. Yet at the same time, his later engagement with the Eunomians, Antiochenes, and Apollinarians brought many points into greater relief. We will therefore make use of Gregory's corpus as a whole, emphasizing the later works in their controversial context while also drawing on the earlier material.[3]

Christology and Divinization

Gregory understands Christian salvation in terms of the larger idea of θέωσις (*theosis*), or "divinization,"[4] the transforming participation of the human per-

---

1. Among his numerous statements to this effect, see Ors. 16.2; 19.10; 20.8–10; 32.14, 26; 41.7–8; 28.4, 20; 29.8; 31.9–11, 20, 22, 24, 33; 25.2, 18; 37.2, 4; 39.11; 42.16, 18; 43.11, 13, 15, 65, 68–69. Recent discussions of this theme can be found in Norris, "Theology as Grammar"; "Gregory Nazianzen."
2. A point observed by Norris, "Gregory Nazianzen's Doctrine of Jesus Christ," p. 207.
3. The best single treatment of Gregory's Christology is Norris' 1970 Yale dissertation, "Gregory Nazianzen's Doctrine of Jesus Christ," even though its analysis of the differences between Gregory's early and late work and its treatment of Athanasius are now out of date. Other important studies include Althaus, *Die Heilslehre*; Winslow, *Dynamics of Salvation*.
4. The most helpful studies of divinization in Gregory are Russell, *Doctrine of Deification*, pp. 213–225, 341–344, and Winslow, *Dynamics of Salvation*, which have superceded Gross's earlier treatment (*La divinisation*,

son in the being and life of God. Earlier Christian writers—above all Clement, Origen, and Athanasius—had begun to speak of divinization sporadically, with reference to both pagan and Christian religious ideas.[5] Yet it was Gregory who established divinization as the primary concept for salvation in Greek Christian tradition.[6] He coined the term θέωσις, from θεόω, and made the idea central to his work;[7] through the imitation of the Pseudo-Dionysius and Maximus Confessor, his doctrine of *theosis* then become the standard concept for salvation in later Byzantine theology.[8]

In the same way that the imagery of light and illumination serves to indicate the close relationship between the nature of God and the human knowledge of God, the concept of divinization—"becoming godlike," or "becoming divine"—likewise expresses the meaning of human existence as a participation in God's very being. While Gregory typically speaks of divinization as the result of the saving work of Christ, *theosis* is, in a broader sense, a process of growth and transformation that is rooted in creation and has its fulfillment in the age to come. His most comprehensive treatment of *theosis* comes in his account of creation in the Epiphany series. Everything that exists, Gregory writes, is rooted in God's eternal being, goodness (38.7, 9), and light (40.5), which abound to such an extent that they overflow, as it were, into the act of creation. In the beginning God created the "first world" of angels, who are secondary lights next to God's primary light (38.9), followed by the "second world" of material reality (38.10)—both of which are good and glorify God in their respective ways. From the intelligible and material worlds, God then created the human being (ἄνθρωπος) as a composite creature. Taking a body from the material world, God breathed into it an intelligent soul, which is the image of God, and so made the human being as "a kind of second world,[9] ... another angel, a mingled worshipper" to glorify God on earth and to be the fullest representation of God's wisdom and generosity in all of creation (38.11).[10] Here again Gregory inter-

---

pp. 244–250). See also Norris, "Gregory Nazianzen's Doctrine of Jesus Christ," pp. 58–62, 129–148; Moreschini, *Filosofia e letteratura*, pp. 34–36.

5. Although Athanasius is often regarded as the first major theorist of divinization among the Greek fathers, and he does use the term more than earlier writers, it appears almost exclusively in his polemical literature (esp. *Ar.* and *Ep. Serap.* 1); it does not appear in his primarily soteriological and spiritual works, such as the *Festal Letters* and the *Life of Antony*; and it does not hold the fundamental soteriological significance that it does for Gregory. See Russell, *Doctrine of Deification*, p. 167.

6. It would later be taken up by Augustine and other Western theologians as well.

7. Earlier writers, following Clement, had used θεοποιεῖν/θεοποίησις, as well as θεοῦν.

8. Cyril of Alexandria being an exception, who follows Athanasius in using θεοποίησις. Russell, *Doctrine of Deification*, pp. 341–343.

9. δεύτερος κόσμος, the same phrase used above for material creation (38.10).

10. See also *Ors.* 39.13; 40.8.

weaves biblical and philosophical themes for both missionary and pastoral purposes,[11] much as we saw in his treatment of purification and the nature of the human body.[12] He then brings his account of creation to a climax with the divinization of human beings: Poised between heaven and earth, the human being was created to be "a ruler on earth yet ruled from above, earthly and heavenly, temporal and immortal...a living being cared for (οἰκονομεῖν) in this world, then transferred to another; and—the final stage of the mystery—made divine (θεοῦν) by his inclination towards God" (38.11).

As Gregory analyzes it, the very nature of creation, reflecting God's infinite goodness, is designed to provide for the growth of human beings toward God and their final divinization.[13] We have been created, in other words, in a state of dynamic movement toward God, so that the process of divinization is rooted in the structure of our existence.[14]

Gregory then focuses on the end and the ultimate goal of divinization in two important passages in his funeral oration for his brother and his panegyric on Athanasius. As he reflects on the vicissitudes of earthly existence, Gregory laments that "we linger in the tombs [of our bodies] which we carry around because, even though we have become gods (θεοὶ γεγονότες), we die the death of sin like human beings" (7.22).[15] Despite our sin and mortality, it remains our created end to become gods, beginning even in this life. More fulsome is his description of the holy life in the opening of *Oration* 21. Both before and after the fall,[16] the incomprehensible God lifts us up to himself through the illumination of his own light, causing us to ascend beyond the fleshly veil of our earthly existence, "to hold communion with God, to be associated with the purest light, as far as human nature can attain," and so to be divinized through our union with the Holy Trinity (21.1–2).[17] Here *theosis* is closely related to the notions of ascent, illumination, and union as the overall process of coming to

---

11. As Augustine does as well in his treatment of Genesis; see *Conf.* books 10–13.

12. See chapter 1, pp. 75–83. Again we must be wary of overinterpreting the philosophical resonances of Gregory's creation narrative. Cf. Ellverson, *Dual Nature of Man*, which reads his anthropology exclusively through such themes; and Elm, "Inscriptions and Conversions," p. 20, which argues that Gregory's purpose in *Ors.* 38–40 is essentially to promote the mixing of Platonic opposites.

13. Helpfully summarized in Winslow, *Dynamics of Salvation*, pp. 54, 58–60.

14. The process of divinization also distinguishes humankind from the rest of creation (*Carm.* 1.2.2.560–561). See Winslow, *Dynamics of Salvation*, p. 60n4. On Gregory's doctrine of creation, see also Richard, *Cosmologie et théologie*, pp. 68–83.

15. Russell, *Doctrine of Deification*, p. 217. In *Or.* 7.22, our bodies are tombs not because they are evil, but because our souls are dead through sin. See Ps 82.6–7.

16. The phrase "God lifts people up—or lifts them up again—to himself" (21.1) indicates that the enlightenment we receive in redemption is fundamentally the same as the one that God provides apart from sin.

17. On the Platonic resonances of this passage, see McGuckin, "Strategic Adaptation of Deification."

know the Trinity.[18] As if to ward off potential objections, he stresses that divinization does not mean becoming God in the full sense of the word (42.17),[19] but that the difference between the Creator and creation must be maintained as a fundamental tenet of Christian doctrine.[20] Yet for Gregory divinization is much more than simply an analogy for baptism or a metaphor for the ethical imitation of God, as has been suggested.[21] As we noted above with regard to divine illumination, his language of divinization indicates a real and growing participation in God's nature, so that human beings, in a mysterious but real way, become filled with God's being and "divinized" to the extent that they, as creatures, are capable. Gregory's use of *theosis* is so bold, in fact, that more than once he acknowledges that he is making statements that stretch the boundaries of credulity.[22] The definition and goal of our existence, as established in creation, is thus to be increasingly illuminated with the divine light, to partake of God's own being more and more, beginning in this life and continuing in the life to come. *Theosis* thus represents at the same time our original definition, our present nature, and our eschatological destiny.

However, in the current state of human existence, our original nature and our ultimate end have been marred. In the fall of Adam and Eve we separated ourselves from God (39.13),[23] and interrupted the created, eschatological process of divinization. As a result, we have been cut off from the Tree of Life and banished from paradise, and we are no longer growing toward union with God (38.12).[24] At the final judgment Christ will therefore divide those who have remained separated from God from those who are once again growing in the knowledge of God toward union with him (40.45). Within this larger scheme, salvation is the restoration of the process of *theosis* that God established in creation and intends to perfect in the age to come. Gregory uses a wide array of traditional images to describe the salvation that Christ has effected. The early sections of *Oration* 38 provide a rich example: here he describes Christ's re-

18. On *theosis* and illumination, see also *Ors.* 39.10, 17 and passim; 45.5, 28; *Carm.* 1.1.8.70–77.

19. γένεσθαι κυρίως θεός.

20. A premise that underlies much of his argumentation for the divinity of the Son and the Holy Spirit. See chaps. 3 and 4.

21. Russell argues that Gregory's use of *theosis* is purely metaphorical and, in distinction to Athanasius, does not include any sense of realistic participation in the divine being (*Doctrine of Deification*, pp. 213–214, 222–225); however, this judgment divorces Gregory's understanding of *theosis* from the closely related notions of illumination and participation in the Trinity.

22. *Ors.* 14.23; 11.5; 38.7.

23. "My sin and my condemnation were complete in the disobedience of the first creature (ὁ πρωτόπλαστος) and the treachery of the Adversary" (22.13).

24. See also *Ors.* 2.23–24; 36.5; 45.28; *Ep.* 101.51; *Carm.* 1.1.7.55–64; Winslow, *Dynamics of Salvation*, pp. 60–66; and Althaus, *Die Heilslehre*, pp. 79–82.

demptive work in terms of light,[25] the new replacing the old, the Spirit over the letter, the truth in place of shadows, putting off the old humanity and putting on the new, dying in Adam and living in Christ, the healing of our weaknesses, and the re-creation of a decaying world (38.2–4). Yet among this diversity of images, and tying them all together, is the central soteriological idea of *theosis*. Because of the fallen condition of humanity and the interruption of divinization, the determinative factor in our existence is now the incarnation of Jesus Christ, which restores our divinization. The larger scope of *theosis*, from its created origin to its eschatological fulfillment, is now known to us only through the mystery of the Word made flesh.[26] Although divinization is rooted in creation, our knowledge and experience of this transformation occur exclusively through the reformation of *theosis* that Christ effects. For Gregory, the essence and goal of human life, then, is to become divine as a result of Christ's having become human. In *Oration* 7 he reflects on how our created nature has become darkened by sin and mortality. In this fatal condition, there is only one solution: "I must be buried with Christ, arise with Christ, be a joint heir with Christ, become a son of God, be called God himself!" (7.23).[27] It is through Christ alone that we can recover the dynamic nature of our original creation.

The divinization that Christ reinstates is not in the first place a benefit that we receive from him or an effect that he produces, but it is more closely related to his own identity. In his first oration, *On Easter*, Gregory gives a rich, euphoric description of the Christian life, which in several respects outlines the Christological program that he will follow for the rest of his career.[28] Christ renews us with his own Spirit, Gregory proclaims, and clothes us with new humanity, as we figuratively die and rise with him (1.2–4); and so he concludes in a dramatic exhortation, "Let us become like Christ, since Christ has become like us. Let us become gods for his sake, since he became human for ours" (1.5).[29] While it involves real moral effort and the commitment of one's whole life,[30] salvation consists chiefly in the reestablishment of the process of *theosis* in the incarnation

---

25. (Light chasing away darkness, Israel illuminated by the pillar of fire; "the people who sat in the darkness" of ignorance have seen "the great light" of knowledge) (Is 9.2).

26. Note that the full discussion of *theosis* in Ors. 38–40 (above) takes place in the context of a dominical feast celebrating Christ's birth and baptism.

27. See also Or. 14.23.

28. And which, on account of its summary quality, may possibly reflect later editing.

29. A passage that the Edinburgh series mistranslates, changing "become gods" to "become God's," perhaps in defense against the shocking nature of its claims. Winslow, *Dynamics of Salvation*, p. 91; Russell, *Doctrine of Deification*, p. 215n16.

30. On the contribution of asceticism, or "philosophy," to divinization, see Ors. 3.1; 4.71; 21.2; 25.2; *Ep.* 6.3; *Carm.* 1.2.10.630; 1.2.17.1–2 (cf. 1.2.33.88–90). Although Russell argues that Gregory is the first Christian writer to connect ascetical practice with divinization, Origen clearly does so before him. *Doctrine of Deification,*

of the Word of God in Jesus Christ.[31] The soteriological principle of divinization through Christ lies at the heart of Gregory's major doctrinal work in the *Theological Orations*, the Epiphany sermons, and the late Christological epistles. In *Oration* 38 he writes that, after disciplining us through the Law and the prophets, God provided the "stronger remedy" for the ever-worsening disease of sin by sending his Son: "he assumes the poverty of my flesh so that I may assume the richness of his Divinity" (38.13)—a motif which, again, resonates with the image of light and the discussion of the knowledge of God throughout *Orations* 38–40. Divinization is also the central point of Gregory's argument against the Eunomians in the *Theological Orations*. In the thematic opening statement of his discussion of the divinity of Christ on the basis of Scripture (29.17–21), Gregory makes his famous statement that God was born (γέγονε) "so that I might be made God as far as he is made human" (29.19). Likewise, divinization is the focus of his exegetical discussions in *Oration* 30. "What could be greater for the lowliness of a human being," he asks the Eunomians, "than to be intertwined (πλακῆναι) with God and to become God from the mixture" of God with human existence in Christ? (30.3). Because Christ has submitted to human form for our salvation, "God stands in the midst of gods"[32] (30.4); and we are made to share in what is properly Christ's own (the divine nature) through the intermingling of the incarnation, so that finally "God will be all in all" (1 Cor 15.28) when we are completely like God,[33] completely filled with God and him alone (30.6).[34] For Gregory, the purpose and rationale of the incarnation is to bring about our divinization, which has been interrupted by the fall; and conversely, the basis of our divinization is the incarnation of Christ. Yet we are saved and divinized not merely as an extrinsic effect of the incarnation; the human Jesus is himself the first instance and the archetype of our divinization, the one in whose own *theosis* Christians participate and are thus saved. The determining factor in Gregory's doctrine of salvation, then, and the key for understanding the work of Christ, is the identity of Christ—who Christ is in order to restore the divinization of humanity.[35] This means that he does not separate the doctrine of Christ from

---

p. 222; cf. p. 218. Gregory does not believe *theosis* is the privilege of an ascetical elite: see *Or.* 2.22 and the many references to baptismal deification in *Ors.* 31, 38–40, and elsewhere.

31. A helpful discussion of this connection can be found in Harrison, "Some Aspects of St. Gregory the Theologian's Soteriology," p. 11. See also Russell, *Doctrine of Deification*, pp. 220–221.

32. Ps 81.1.

33. See 1 Jn 3.2.

34. Further statements of divinization in Christ can be found at *Ors.* 11.5; 30.21; 25.16; 37.2; 38.3, 7, 11, 16; 39.16; 40.8, 10, 16, 42; *Ep.* 101.46; *Carm.* 1.1.11.9; 1.1.2.47. Several of these passages will be discussed below. The role of the Holy Spirit in divinization will be discussed in chap. 3.

35. So *Or.* 38 begins with a celebration of who Christ is, on account of the salvation that he has brought.

the narrative story of his works of creation, salvation, and consummation, since that narrative forms the basis for understanding Christ's identity.[36] Gregory's Christology and his soteriology are thus inseparably involved with each other, and in a sense amount to the same thing.

The Identity of Christ

Thanks to certain developments in nineteenth- and twentieth-century scholarship, it has become common to evaluate the Christology of early theologians primarily in terms of later categories and conciliar standards. Above all, students of historical theology have been taught to assess Christological doctrines in terms of the combination of the two natures of divinity and humanity in Christ, and the structural elements of Christ's person(s). Yet, despite this anachronistic and overly technical approach, Gregory's substantial Christological reflection proceeds differently, with a scope and meaning that modern categories of analysis have typically missed. Rather than seeking to define Christ's identity in a static or abstract sense, Gregory understands it to be governed by the economy of salvation viewed as a whole, as Frederick Norris has pointed out.[37] He views the identity of Jesus Christ and the salvation that stems from him chiefly through what we could call a narrative, economic framework. While this perspective runs throughout Gregory's corpus, it is especially prominent in the major Christological works written from 379 on.[38] The "economic paradigm" can be seen in four key Christological statements from the *Theological Orations*, *Oration 37*, the Epiphany sermons (*Ors.* 38–40), and the late Christological epistles (*Ep.* 101–102, 202). These texts merit our attention individually, as they will form the basis of our analysis for the rest of the chapter.

For the basic structure of Gregory's Christology we must first look not to his well-known Christological epistles, but to the heart of his work in Constantinople, where his doctrine of Christ assumed its full expression.[39] The first major statement comes near the beginning of Gregory's dispute with the Eunomians over the divinity of Christ as revealed in Scripture. As he prepares

---

36. Winslow calls this the dynamic character of Gregory's Christology. *Dynamics of Salvation*, p. 91; see also Harrison, "Some Aspects of St. Gregory the Theologian's Soteriology," p. 12.
37. Norris, "Gregory Nazianzen's Doctrine of Jesus Christ," p. 167.
38. An outstanding early example is 1.5. A helpful, though ultimately different, analysis of Gregory's "economic paradigm" can be found in Norris, "Gregory Nazianzen's Doctrine of Jesus Christ," pp. 167–201.
39. Although they are often regarded as Gregory's main Christological exposition, *Ep.* 101–102 and 202 are but the final installment of a doctrinal project that was largely complete by the time he left the capital in 381.

to responds to a series of ten contested biblical texts in the fourth *Theological Oration*, he first gives a positive summary of his own doctrine:

> The one whom you now scorn was once above you (ὑπὲρ σέ). The one who is now human was at one time not composite (ἀσύνθετος). What he was, he continued to be; what he was not, he assumed. In the beginning he existed without cause (ἀναιτίως), for what is the cause of God? But later on he was born for a cause (δι' αἰτίαν)— namely that you might be saved (29.19)

In order to understand who Christ is, Gregory argues, we must know the larger story of salvation: In order to save us and to restore the process of divinization that had been broken in the fall, the divine Son of God, who was previously incomposite (ἀσύνθετος) and not mingled with his creation, took upon himself our created, human existence—a form of existence radically different from his own—and became composite (σύνθετος, 29.18). While he remains the divine Son of God—"what he was, he continued to be," he has now become also a human creature—"what he was not, he assumed."[40] This narrative scheme then governs the discussion of individual biblical texts that Gregory gives throughout the fourth *Theological Oration*.

The second passage comes in the opening sections of *Oration* 37. Here Gregory describes Christ as the one who is uncontained but now moves from place to place, the one who exists above and apart from time but has now come to exist under time, the invisible one who has become visible (esp. 37.1–3). "He was in the beginning and was with God and was God (Jn 1.1)," and he has now assumed creaturely existence (37.2).

An even fuller definition comes in *Oration* 38, which is then echoed throughout *Orations* 39–40.[41] The opening sections begin to narrate God's saving work in sending Christ (38.1–4); then, after commenting on the proper observance of a Christian feast (38.5–6), Gregory rehearses the entire economy of God's relationship toward his creatures, beginning with the creation as an expression of God's own being (38.7f.). Within this larger narrative, Gregory turns to the incarnation in the climactic section 13. Here he argues that the incomprehensible and invisible Word of God "took upon himself flesh for the sake of our

---

40. This passage shows several resemblances to Origen's Christology. In his account of the Rule of Faith at the beginning of *On First Principles* Origen comments that, even when Christ was made human, he "remained what he was, namely God" (*Princ.* pref. 4). Origen also writes that, on account of the incarnation, "We call him a sort of composite being" (σύνθετόν τι χρῆμά φαμεν αὐτὸν γεγονέναι, *Cels.* 1.66; see also 3.41).

41. See esp. *Ors.* 39.13; 40.33, 45.

flesh and mingled himself with an intelligent soul for my soul's sake, purifying like by like, and in all ways except sin was made human" (38.13 = 45.9).

Finally, Gregory gives a similar narrative scheme near the beginning of both letters to Cledonius. As he begins the main argument in the body of *Letter* 101, he gives a summary statement (δογματίζειν) of his Christology: before he was a human being, the divine Son of God initially existed "before the ages," apart from the temporal economy of salvation; but finally he assumed human existence and became also a human being for our salvation (*Ep.* 101.13–14).[42] The second letter to Cledonius begins in the same way: the Son of God is eternally begotten of the Father, "and after this" (καὶ μετὰ τοῦτο) was born of the Virgin Mary (*Ep.* 102.4).[43] It is noteworthy that, in setting his Christology in an economic framework, Gregory is adhering to the shape of the biblical narrative as well as the long ecclesiastical tradition expressed in rules of faith, confessional statements, and formal creeds. As we examine each element of Gregory's Christology, we must keep in mind this basic narrative framework.

As the above statements make plain, Gregory means to argue that Christ is the fully divine Son of God who has become also human for our salvation. It is common in modern doctrinal analysis, influenced to no small extent by the parallel, two-nature language of the Chalcedonian Definition, to assess how a particular theologian envisions the combination of divinity and humanity in Christ. Moreover, Gregory's Christology—along with that of Basil and of Gregory of Nyssa—is typically regarded as a vindication of the full humanity of Christ against the doctrine of Apollinarius.[44] However, this approach is only partially helpful in Gregory's case, and can even be positively misleading. In light of the work of salvation mentioned above, the explicit focus of Gregory's Christology is very clearly on the divinity of Christ, within the framework of the divine economy,[45] not on how two natures are equally combined in one person. There are several reasons for this. In his polemical situation, Gregory needs to argue explicitly for Christ's divinity against the denials of the Eunomians and other opponents. Moreover, even the most extreme anti-Nicene theologians in the fourth century—such as Arius, Aetius, and Eunomius—all believe that the Son of God, who is in some sense divine, became flesh for the salvation of the human race; most of the participants in the fourth-century debates, in other

---

42. πρότερον μὲν οὐκ ἄνθρωπον, ἀλλὰ Θεὸν καὶ Υἱὸν μόνον καὶ προαιώνιον, ἀμιγῆ σώματος καὶ τῶν ὅσα σώματος, ἐπὶ τέλει δὲ καὶ ἄνθρωπον, προσληφθέντα ὑπὲρ τῆς σωτηρίας τῆς ἡμετέρας.

43. The same pattern is also followed in the dogmatic poems 1.1.2 *On the Son* and 1.1.10 *On the Incarnation, Against Apollinarius.*

44. See below, n95.

45. See Norris, "Gregory Nazianzen's Doctrine of Jesus Christ," p. 65.

words, envision some kind of incarnation.[46] But there are deeper reasons as well. In focusing on Christ's divinity Gregory is representing what is arguably the soteriological mainstream of the early Church. Since the early apostolic confession "Jesus is Lord" (1 Cor 12.3), the creeds and confessions of the early Church, and the speculations of a wide range of Christian groups, have focused on Christ's heavenly origin and his identity as the divine Savior more than on the fact that he was a human being.[47] In the second century the exaltation of Christ to a divine status at times became so exclusive that later New Testament texts such as 1 John 4.2–3 and postapostolic writers like Ignatius of Antioch and Irenaeus of Lyons were compelled to take up the defense of his full humanity against docetic or "Gnostic" Christologies that deny that Christ was fully human. The theological tradition in which Gregory stands, including Irenaeus, Clement, and Origen, likewise emphasized Christ's divinity as the central, operative fact of his identity. So too at the heart of Gregory's Christology is the confession that Christ is the fully divine Son and Word of God, from which follows a whole range of implications for the human existence of Christ's followers. Gregory makes the point concisely in one of his most important Christological arguments: "If I worshipped a creature, I would not be called a Christian. Why is Christianity precious? Is it not that Christ is God?" (37.17).

The main question in the late-fourth-century debates concerned the exact nature of the divine being who was made flesh in Jesus, and consequently what that nature means for the identity of Christ and the life of his followers.[48] For Gregory, as for other so-called Homoiousians and pro-Nicenes of this time, it is essential to Christian salvation that Christ be fully and completely divine. The terms and imagery used in the passages above are meant to show that Christ is the eternal Word of God who fully shares the brilliant Divinity of the Father, and that the child of Mary is none other than the Creator God in human form.[49] In *Oration* 38 Gregory continues in exhilarated wonder over the mystery of God become human: "O new mixture! O unexpected blending! The One Who Is (Ex 3.14) has come to be (ὁ ὢν γίνεται), the Uncreated One is created, the Uncontained One is contained!... What is this Mystery all around

---

46. Although Gregory mentions Photinus (*Or.* 33.16), there do not appear to be any who imagine that Christ is merely a human being (whether or not adopted to divine sonship) in Gregory's immediate environment in Cappadocia or Constantinople.

47. For a survey of early Christian creeds and confessions, see Kelly, *Early Christian Creeds*.

48. Meanwhile, different construals of his humanity are by no means absent, as we shall see.

49. So Gregory freely uses the divine image of light to describe Christ, as of course the New Testament (esp. Jn 1.4–9; 8.12; 9.5; Hb 1.3) and the creed of Nicaea also do. See *Ors.* 18.28; 39.1; 45.2.

me?" (38.13).[50] In a mysterious and paradoxical way, the created, limited, and even suffering man Jesus is the infinite Creator God, the tangible and visible human form of the invisible, incorporeal Son of God; so that in worshipping and glorifying Christ, Christians are in fact worshipping God himself (38.13).[51]

The operative concept in this narrative framework is that of assumption. Gregory frequently writes that the Word of God "assumed" human existence for our salvation—the Son "took on" human life: was conceived, born, lived, died, rose, ascended, and will come again as a human being—adding it to his own preexistent, divine being. Christ is thus the eternal Son of God dwelling in human form in time and space. By virtue of the great difference between God and the human form which he took on, the resulting shape and character of the Son's assumption of human nature is one of condescension, self-emptying, and self-humbling; it is a downward and lessening movement on God's part, relatively speaking. Rather than remain in the incomprehensibility of his eternal being, the Son of God "condescended to our infirmity" (37.3); he "submitted to a body" (*Carm.* 1.1.2.57) and "assumed the poverty of my flesh" (38.13) in order to save us. In Pauline terms, the Son "emptied himself" and descended to us in order to become comprehensible (37.3), and he became a humble creature out of care for creatures (37.1, 4).[52] Gregory is aware of the temptation to take the language of condescension and self-emptying in an absolute sense, as if in becoming human the Son literally diminished or emptied himself of his divine being in his own proper existence, so that after becoming incarnate he was no longer, or at least not fully, divine. Hence Gregory issues the qualification that when the Son of God deigned to become Son of Man for our sake, he neither changed what he was nor stripped himself of his Divinity in any way, but rather assumed what he was not (39.13; *Carm.* 1.1.2.60–61). When the Son is said to have diminished his glory (37.3), this refers to the fact that in assuming our nature he "bears and endures all things" for our salvation (37.1, 4), so that Christ's condescension is his assumption of our condition (14.15) in order to reveal himself to us in a comprehensible way,

---

50. See also *Or.* 38.2: "The fleshless one is made flesh, the Word becomes material, the invisible is seen, the intangible is touched, the timeless has a beginning, the Son of God becomes Son of Man—'Jesus Christ yesterday and today and the same for all ages (Hb 13.8)!'"

51. For simple statements of Christ's divinity, see also *Ors.* 20.4; 32.18; 23.9; 41.4; 30.1, 4, 7, 12; 31.26, 28, 29, 33; 26.7.

52. Phil 2.5–11; see also Hb 12.2. For an extended discussion of Christ's self-emptying, see Norris, "Gregory Nazianzen's Doctrine of Jesus Christ," chap. 3 and passim; on condescension and self-emptying, see Winslow, *Dynamics of Salvation*, pp. 92–96, 99.

through the assumed humanity.[53] Condescension and self-emptying, then, are relative, not absolute, terms; they describe the shape of Christ's assumption of our nature and the degree to which his glory is visible, relative to our perspective, in the divine economy.[54] For Gregory Christ is thus the eternal Son of God who has taken on human form and dwelled among us.

Although he places great emphasis on Christ's divinity, Gregory typically assumes Christ's humanity and gives it little positive explanation. Despite the fact that his Christology is usually characterized as an anti-Apollinarian defense of the full humanity of Christ, there are very few passages before the end of his career in which Gregory explicitly argues that Christ is fully human; and the strongest example prior to 379, in *Oration* 2.23, may reflect later editing.[55] By the time he arrived in Constantinople in 379, Gregory had become aware of the Christological debate between Diodore and Apollinarius that had come to full force in the late 370s (22.13).[56] As we shall see, he had more in common with Apollinarius than he did with Diodore, even in the so-called anti-Apollinarian epistles. When he finds himself in a dispute with a group of Apollinarians who tried to take possession of his church in Nazianzus in 383, Gregory finally makes an explicit argument for the full humanity of Christ near the end of his career. In his view, the basic Christian confession that the Son of God became human in order to save us implicitly includes the whole of our human condition. When Apollinarius claims that the Word of God takes the place of a human mind in Christ,[57] Gregory's response is simply to point out this obvious aspect of the incarnation. Since we need healing in body, soul, and mind—and especially in our mind, which was the first to sin and is really the source of all our troubles—Christ must have assumed all of these elements in order to save us (*Ep.* 101.50–55). Hence he utters his famous soteriological dictum, "That which has not been assumed has not been healed; but that which is united to God is also being saved" (*Ep.* 101.32).[58] Gregory's defense of the full humanity of Christ against Apollinarius is not a major, formative piece

---

53. See also *Or.* 45.26.
54. On Christ's assumption of human existence, see also *Ors.* 19.13; 34.10; 30.5, 9, 21; 26.7; 37.4; 44.2, 7; 45.13, 26–29.
55. *Pace* Winslow, *Dynamics of Salvation*, p. 79.
56. Another rare reference to the denial that Christ possesses a human mind (along with *Or.* 2.23) in Gregory's work before 383. If Gregory was aware of the Apollinarian problem by 379—either from Damasus' *Illut sane*, which the Antiochene synod of 379 validated, from Melitius, when he appointed Gregory bishop of Constantinople on the synod's behalf, or from his own study of Apollinarius—he pays it little attention until 383.
57. On the rationale of Apollinarius' soteriology, see this book's conclusion.
58. The phrase originally appears in Origen's *Dialog with Heraclides* 7.7–8: "The whole human being would not have been saved if he had not assumed the whole human being."

of his Christology, but merely an application of the position that he had already articulated at great length during his ministry in Constantinople. He frankly finds the whole question ridiculous: "Whoever hopes in a mindless person is mindless himself!" (*Ep.* 101.32). He otherwise considers it obvious that Christ is a complete human being, possessing human choice and self-determination as well as an animal soul and body; to deny as much is an absurd annoyance.

The Unity of Christ

As the statements above indicate, the nature—or better, the dynamic thrust—of the incarnation is for Gregory a unifying one. The whole point of the Son's assumption of human existence is to unite it to himself in order to heal and save it. The unity of Christ is thus the central tenet of Gregory's Christology, and it defines the main point of contention with all three of his Christological opponents: the Eunomians, the Antiochenes, and the Apollinarians. Again each of the four key Christological texts bears on the issue. In *Oration* 29 Gregory continues by saying that the Eunomians oppose Christ's divinity,

> because he took upon himself your thickness,[59] associating with flesh through the intermediary of a [human] mind, and being made a human being who is God on earth (γενόμενος ἄνθρωπος ὁ κάτω θεός),[60] since [human existence] was blended with God and he was born as a single entity (εἷς), because the One who is more powerful prevailed [over his assumed humanity], so that we might be made divine to the same extent that he was made human. (29.19)

Later in the same year, Gregory concludes his Christological statement in *Oration* 37 in just the same way. With apologies for the difficulty of expressing such thoughts, he tries to explain the unity that results from the incarnation:

> What he was he set aside; what he was not he assumed. Not that he became two things, but he deigned to be made one thing out of two (οὐ δύο γενόμενος, ἀλλ' ἓν ἐκ τῶν δύο γενέσθαι ἀνασχόμενος).

---

59. That is, the thick corporeality of human existence.
60. The translation of this phrase by Browne and Swallow—"his inferior nature, the humanity, became God"—is misleading in a dualist direction, suggesting that Christ's humanity somehow independently existed and *then* was divinized. Gallay's French translation reflects the same problem: "l'homme d'ici-bas est devenu Dieu" (*SC* 250, p. 219). Nothing could be farther from Gregory's mind. Wickham's translation ("being made that God on earth, which is Man") avoids this error, while unfortunately (and no doubt inadvertently) suggesting that humanity in general is divine.

For both are God, that which assumed and that which assumed, the two natures meeting in one thing (δύο φύσεις εἰς ἓν συνδραμούσαι). But not two sons: let us not give a false account of the blending (ἡ σύγκρασις). (37.2)[61]

Likewise, in *Oration* 38, from January 381, Gregory goes on to explain that, as a result of the incarnation, the one born of Mary is "God together with what he assumed, one thing made out of two opposites (ἓν ἐκ δύο τῶν ἐναντίων), flesh and Spirit, of which the latter deifies and the former is deified" (38.13). Each of these three passages from 380–381 occurs in an overt, though gradually shifting, context of anti-Eunomian (and probably anti-Antiochene) polemic. The first (29.19) is a direct and heated debate with the Eunomians; the second (37.4) was written after Theodosius had entered his capital and installed Gregory as archbishop; and the third (38.13) comes from Gregory's celebration of the high feast of Epiphany, just after Theodosius had outlawed the Eunomians and various other heretics.

Finally, Gregory makes the same point in the late Christological epistles. Before we turn to the text it is worth noting that these three letters are almost universally regarded as anti-Apollinarian treatises. However, on the central point of Christ's unity, they are in fact more strongly anti-Antiochene than anti-Apollinarian. When Gregory offers his own Christological confession early in *Letter* 101 he mentions only briefly the Apollinarian idea that the Word takes the place of Christ's human mind, and then turns in quite a different direction to focus instead on the unity of Christ. He explains that he prefers the title "our Lord and God" because it conveys the singular identity of Jesus as the eternal Son of God: "For we do not separate the human being from the Divinity, but we teach one and the same (εἷς καὶ ὁ αὐτός) God and Son," who was at first only the eternal Son but later became also a human being; "so that by the same one, who is a complete human being and also God, a complete humanity, which had fallen under sin, might be created anew" (*Ep.* 101.13, 15).[62] Next Gregory gives a list of ten anathemas, seven of which argue for the unity of Christ, probably against Diodore (nos. 1, 3–8). Number 1 defends the title *Theotokos*, which Apollinarius had used to signal his opposition to Diodore's dualist Christology, and which became the famous watchword for unitive Christology in the next century (*Ep.* 101.16a). Number 3 denounces the dualistic idea that God "put on" a previously formed human being, rather than the

---

61. Trans. adapt. Browne and Swallow.
62. Οὐδὲ γὰρ τὸν ἄνθρωπον χωρίζομεν τῆς θεότητος, ἀλλ' ἕνα καὶ τὸν αὐτὸν δογματίζομεν ... Θεὸν καὶ Υἱόν ... ἵν' ὅλῳ ἀνθρώπῳ τῷ αὐτῷ καὶ Θεῷ ὅλος ἄνθρωπος ἀναπλασθῇ πεσὼν ὑπὸ τὴν ἁμαρτίαν.

incarnation's being "the birth of God" (*Ep.* 101.17). Number 4 again asserts the phrase "one and the same" against the doctrine of two sons, with further elucidation of the real union of Christ's two natures (*Ep.* 101.18). Number 5 opposes Diodore's language of grace in favor of the stronger language of union and conjunction (*Ep.* 101.22a). Number 6 defends the singular worship of the crucified Lord (*Ep.* 101.22b). Number 7 opposes the idea of moral development in Christ, since he is fundamentally God (*Ep.* 101.23). And number 8 opposes the idea that Christ no longer possesses his body, using the unitive language of assumption and a hermeneutical practice of single predication (*Ep.* 101.25).[63] If we observe that number 2, against the reputedly Apollinarian idea that Christ's humanity descended from heaven (*Ep.* 101.16b), probably follows number 1 because they both refer to Mary, and that Christ's unity also figures secondarily in numbers 9–10, then we can say that for all intents and purposes Gregory has begun the letter with a strong, lengthy statement of the unity of Christ. The same pattern is repeated in the second letter to Cledonius. Gregory begins his argument with a briefer but even clearer statement of Christ's unity: "We treat the Son of God, who was begotten of the Father and who was later [born] of the Virgin Mary, as a single entity (εἰς ἓν ἄγομεν), and we do not name two sons. Rather we worship one and the same in undivided Divinity and honor" (*Ep.* 102.4).[64] In the late epistles, then, Gregory offers the same doctrine of the unity of Christ that he had developed earlier in a somewhat different context in Constantinople as the central tenet of his Christology, and as a matter of greater significance than the question of whether Christ possesses a human mind.

In the incarnation, Gregory says, the Son of God assumes human existence by "blending" it with his own, so that, in a mysterious way, Christ is born as a single entity (εἷς, ἕν).[65] Because of the divinizing effect of the divine Son on his human form, the single entity of Jesus Christ remains most fundamentally the Son of God: Christ is the human life of God on earth, "God together with what he assumed." Being God already, he remains "one and the same" Son of God, even in his human form. Gregory often cautions against relying too heavily on technical terms, because theology is concerned not with particular terms

---

63. On which more below.

64. In light of his consistent commitment to the unity of Christ, it is unlikely that Gregory is rehearsing a unitive Christology in these letters simply to answer Apollinarian charges that he teaches a doctrine of two sons. Although Gregory of Nyssa answers similar charges in his letter *To Theophilus*, his Christological milieu is rather different from Gregory Nazianzen's, and there is no indication that Gregory Nazianzen actually felt so intimidated by the Apollinarians on doctrinal grounds.

65. Note that Gregory expresses Christ's unity with both masculine and neuter pronouns; he does not make either gender into a technical term.

(ὀνόματα) but with the realities (πράγματα) that they signify (31.20 and passim). When he does use terser or more technical expressions for Christ's unity, they usually serve to express the narrative dynamic of the incarnation that we have been examining. So the Son assumes human form and is born as "a single entity" (εἷς, 29.19); he becomes "one thing" out of the vastly different realities of God and human existence (ἓν ἐκ δύο, 37.2; 38.13; εἰς ἕν, 37.2; *Ep.* 102.4). In a similar vein, Gregory speaks of the Son "mixing" or "blending" human existence with his own. After describing the unity of Christ as "one thing out of two opposites," Gregory pauses in wonder and praise, "O new mingling (μίξις); O wondrous blending (κρᾶσις)!" (38.13). Again, he uses both expressions at once: "The two are one thing through the blending"[66] (*Ep.* 101.28). While these terms would have been familiar to Gregory from Stoic and Platonic texts,[67] he is probably following Apollinarius or Origen in using them to describe the incarnation.[68] The language of blending would later be condemned at Chalcedon, on the prompting of the Antiochenes, for seeming to compromise the transcendence of the Son's divine nature. In Gregory's usage, however, it helpfully conveys both the narrative movement of the incarnation and also the mysterious union between God and humanity in Jesus: first there was the eternal Son of God, and then he took on the full reality of a human being, mixing it with himself to make one incarnate Lord. In Gregory's view, the real danger lies not in compromising the integrity of these two realities, as the Antiochenes would argue, but rather in the opposite direction: the blending should not be misunderstood as being anything *less* than a real union (37.2). If our humanity is not fully united to God in Christ, then he is in fact two different sons and we have not been divinized in the incarnation. In the fifth anathema of *Letter* 101 Gregory seems to be defining his view of the union against that of Diodore (though anonymously, for understandable political reasons): the Son did not merely operate (ἐνεργεῖν) in Christ by grace, as in a prophet, but he was and is joined together with human existence in his essence (κατ' οὐσίαν συνάπτειν[69]) (*Ep.* 101.22).[70] The clearest and most significant technical term that Gregory uses for the unity of Christ is the phrase that

---

66. τὰ γὰρ ἀμφότερα ἓν τῇ συγκράσει. See also *Ors.* 14.7; 27.7; 28.3, 22; 32.9; 38.9.

67. On the philosophical pedigree, see Harrison, "Some Aspects of St. Gregory the Theologian's Soteriology," p. 13, with citations and bibliography.

68. See *Frag.* 10, 93; and possibly a fragment of Origen on Jn 1.23–24 (*GCS* Origenes 4, pp. 498.23–24). See also Daley, "Nature and the Mode of Union," p. 172. On the correspondence of κρᾶσις and περιχώρησις in Gregory's work, see Harrison, "Perichoresis," pp. 55–57.

69. Or brought into contact with it.

70. See also *Or.* 30.21: the Son divinizes human nature not by grace but by the assumption of it. Yet cf. 30.8: Christ is one thing by union, not by nature.

Christ is "one and the same" Son of God both before and in the incarnation.[71] It is in this phrase that we see the main point of each of Gregory's terms for unity: the Son's assumption of human existence into his own being, as a single entity, makes possible the confession of Christians that Christ is the eternal Son of God and the worship of the man Jesus as God.[72] In this unitive scheme, together with certain semi-technical terms, Gregory gives a narrative, economic account of the identity of Christ as the eternal Son of God. The "action," or the result, of the incarnation is to produce a single, unified Lord, the eternal Son of God who has been made human.[73]

In addition to the narrative and technical descriptions of Christ's unity, Gregory gives a basic rule of biblical interpretation that supports his unitive, economic understanding of Christ. Although he rarely explains his theological or exegetical method in such detail, his debate with the Eunomians in Constantinople led him to give a more explicit definition of his method of Christological exegesis. The first of three such statements comes immediately before the Christological passage in *Oration* 29 quoted above (29.19). In order to understand properly the wide variety of statements about Christ in Scripture, Gregory argues, one must observe the following general rule:

> Apply the loftier passages to the Divinity, to the nature that is superior to passivities and the body; and apply the lowlier passages to the composite One (ὁ σύνθετος), to him who for your sake emptied himself and became flesh and (to say it just as well) was made human, and afterwards was also exalted. (29.18)[74]

The key to interpreting the many passages about Christ in Scripture, Gregory says, is to understand that the more exalted and the humbler statements all refer to the same Son of God, though in different ways. In order to answer Eunomian arguments against the full divinity of Christ, he distinguishes purely divine statements about Christ from those that describe him in his

---

71. The phrase appears increasingly in the late Christological epistles, e.g., *Ep.* 101.13, which is echoed in the following sentences. It derives from Irenaeus (*Adv. haer.* 3.16.3), though Gregory probably learned it from Apollinarius: see *KMP* 36; *Frag.* 42, 109.

72. See also *Carm.* 2.1.11.631–651: Christ does not merely "participate in divine qualities," but in him there is a "complete merging of human nature with the whole God" (trans. Norris, "Gregory Nazianzen's Doctrine of Jesus Christ," p .190).

73. In addition to its strong parallels with Apollinarius, Gregory's Christology echoes the more unitive aspects of Origen's doctrine, in which the Word is so united with the created soul (and later body) of Christ that the humanity of Christ is divinized and the incarnate Word functions virtually as a single subject. See esp. *Princ.* 2.6.

74. The hermeneutical rule appears in *Ors.* 29.18; 30.1, 2. See also 34.10.

incarnate state. Grander titles like "God," "Word" (Jn 1.1), and "Christ the power of God and the wisdom of God" (1 Cor 1.24) indicate Christ's identity as the divine Son of God in his eternal relationship with the Father, which Gregory signifies here with the shorthand phrase "the Divinity."[75] Alternately, lowlier expressions like "slave," "he hungered," and "he wept" (Phil 2.7; Mt 4.2; Jn 11.35)—and above all Christ's cross and death—refer to the Son of God as he has assumed human existence in the person of Jesus and is now "composite," a single mixture of God and human existence. Thus when the Word says, in the figure of Wisdom, "The Lord *created* me as a beginning of his ways" (Prv 8.22), this is not a statement about the Son in his preincarnate condition, as if to say without qualification that the Word of the Father is a creature. Rather, the Son as Wisdom is making a proleptic statement about his future incarnation, or composite state, in which he becomes also a creature of God, the human being Jesus. By referring the lesser sayings to the Son in his incarnate form, Gregory is able to counter the claim that such texts prove that the Son is merely a creature and therefore not fully divine. Yet at the same time, when he distinguishes between unqualified and qualified references to Christ, Gregory is saying that both kinds of statements refer to *the same Son of God*. While the lofty sayings refer to the Son without qualification, the lowly ones refer to the same Son with the qualification that he is now the incarnate, human Lord. If they did not refer to the same Son, then the lowly objections could easily be passed off as referring to a different subject and therefore not threatening the Son's divinity. In other words, Gregory's rule of interpretation is as much a definition of the unity and unchanging identity of the Son of God in his eternal and incarnate states as it is a distinction between those states, in keeping with his narrative statements of the divine economy.

Gregory has often been misunderstood on the question of whether there is a fundamental unity or a fundamental duality in Christ. In this passage on Christological exegesis (29.18), he has been taken to be advocating a strong distinction between Christ's divine and human attributes, so that the lofty and lowly statements refer to two distinct subjects.[76] In what was until recently the standard English translation of the *Theological Orations* by Charles Gordon Browne and James Edward Swallow, for example, the phrase in question reads: "the composite condition of him who for your sakes made himself of no reputation."[77] Here the lowly statements refer to the composite (incarnate)

---

75. Gregory gives a longer list of such passages in *Or.* 29.17.
76. See, e.g., Hanson, *Search for the Christian Doctrine of God*, p. 713.
77. Trans. Browne and Swallow.

condition *of* the Son, that is, to Christ's humanity as distinct from his divinity, rather than to the Son himself in human form. However, the Greek text does not support this reading. The parallel dative construction τῷ συνθέτῳ καὶ τῷ διὰ σὲ κενωθέντι makes it clear that ὁ σύνθετος means "the one who is composite" (in parallel with "the one who emptied himself"), that is, the Son of God who is incarnate, rather than "the composite condition" of the Son of God.[78] The correct reading is supported by the second instance of Gregory's hermeneutical rule in the *Theological Orations*. Here the "lowlier and more human" expressions refer to "the New Adam, God made passible in order to defeat sin" (30.1), that is, to the eternal Son of God in his human form as the New Adam. Gregory is not saying that the lofty sayings refer to the Son's divinity and the lowly sayings to his humanity, nor is he distinguishing between Christ's preincarnate and incarnate states, as if the lofty expressions referred to him before the incarnation and the lowly ones referred to him in the incarnation. Statements that refer to Christ's divinity apply *always*, both before and during the incarnation, which is reflected in the very confession that Jesus is the eternal Son of God. To read the exegetical rule in a dualist fashion, so as to predicate the different sayings to two different subjects or two distinct phases of Christ's career, misses Gregory's meaning entirely. At this central point of his career, when he is pressed to give an account of his Christological method, Gregory both assumes and advances a doctrine of the unity and unchanging identity of the Son of God in his eternal and his incarnate states, a position that he has most likely held since the beginning of his career.[79]

Gregory's doctrine of the unity of Christ is so deeply embedded that he appears to have reframed the Eunomians' position in terms of his own, unitive scheme. In his extant works Eunomius argues against the full divinity of Christ on the basis of texts that refer to the *pre*incarnate Son, so that the Son of God is already a creature, apart from the incarnation. There is no indication that Eunomius ever appealed to Jesus' lowly, human status per se, in the way that Gregory portrays it in *Oration* 29.18–19.[80] After listing several biblical texts that Eunomius has cited,[81] Gregory then adds some of his own, sayings that refer not to the Son's preincarnate condition, but specifically to his lowly, human status:

---

78. Wickham's translation avoids this error: "predicate the lowlier [expressions] of the compound, of him who because of you was emptied." See also Bouteneff, "St. Gregory Nazianzen," p. 260.

79. *Pace* Winslow, who views the single subject of Christ as a late development in Gregory's work. *Dynamics of Salvation*, p. 94.

80. However, Eunomius does identify the human soul of Jesus with the preincarnate Logos, as Arius, Eusebius, and Apollinarius did.

81. Jn 20.17; 14.28; Prv 8.22; Acts 2.36; and Jn 10.36.

If you want, list also "slave" and "obedient," "he gave," "he learned" (Phil 2.7, 8; Jn 18.9; Hb 5.8).... And if you want, add those sayings that are even lowlier than these, like the fact that he slept, was hungry, got tired, wept, was in agony, was subjected (Mt 8.24; 4.2; Jn 4.6; 11.35; Lk 22.44; 1 Cor 15.28). Maybe you even reproach him for his cross and death! (29.18)

Gregory is suggesting that if texts like Proverbs 8.22 indicate the Son's created status, how much more do his hunger, tears, and death on the cross? The hidden premise, of course, is that both kinds of statement refer to the same subject, a point that Gregory assumes and which Eunomius seems to have held as well.[82] If Christ were composed of two different subjects, then the humble passages that Gregory raises could simply be attributed to the human Jesus as distinct from the preincarnate Son, and they would not stand as proof against his divinity at all. But, significantly, Gregory does not do this. He extends the Eunomian position to include *all* biblical expressions of Christ's creaturely status—preincarnate and incarnate—to which he replies with a statement of faith: the lowly, crucified Christ "is for us true God and of equal honor with the Father" (29.18). To be sure, Gregory is also making the second point that such texts refer to the Son in a different way—in the incarnation, or "economically" (29.18)—but the ultimate purpose of his method of predication is to confess that the crucified Lord is himself, as a single subject, the eternal Son of God. Rather than avoiding Eunomian objections by separating human from divine referents, his argument runs in the just opposite direction, as the next section shows: that the very one whom the Eunomians scorn is none other than the merciful Lord who was crucified for our salvation (29.19). Gregory thus advances the unity of Christ both in the way he sets up the problem and in the exegetical method that he offers in response.

According to Gregory's rule of interpretation, all of Christ's qualities and actions, whether godly or human, ultimately belong to the same subject, so that Christ is, in his most fundamental identity, the eternal Son of God made flesh. As a dramatic conclusion to this introductory passage on Christological exegesis, he applies this exegetical method in one of the most beautiful passages in early Christian literature. With rhetorical flair and great liturgical sensibility, he recites a litany of seemingly contrary acts of the one incarnate Son of God, paired in matching antitheses:

---

82. Vaggione, *Eunomius of Cyzicus*, p. 109.

> He was begotten (ἐγεννήθη), but he was also born (γεγέννητο)[83] of a woman.... He was wrapped in swaddling bands, but he took off the swaddling bands of the grave by rising again.... He was exiled into Egypt, but he banished the Egyptian idols.... He is baptized as a human being, but he remitted sins as God.... He hungered, but he fed thousands.... He thirsted, but he cried out, "If anyone is thirsty, let him come to me and drink."... He prays, but he hears prayer. He weeps, but he makes weeping to cease. He asks where Lazarus was laid, for he was a human being; but he raises Lazarus, for he was God.... As a sheep he is led to the slaughter, but he is the shepherd of Israel.... He lays down his life, but he has power to take it up again.... He dies, but he gives life, and by death destroys death. He is buried, but he rises again. (29.19–20)[84]

With each of Christ's divine qualities or actions—some extra-incarnate, some incarnate—Gregory pairs a corresponding action that he accomplishes as a human being, so that it is the same Son of God who does them all. In somewhat different terms, he comments that the Son does some things "as God," things that only God can do (whether or not in human form), like rising from the dead, forgiving sins, and destroying death; while others he does "as a human being," such as praying, being hungry, and dying, things which humans do apart from God's saving work, and which characterize the condition that the Son came to heal and save—though it is the same Son of God who is the subject of them all, either apart from or in the incarnation.

Gregory carries out this practice of single-subject predication in a point-by-point discussion of contested biblical passages in *Oration* 30, and in other later works. In *Letter* 101, for example, he argues that Christ is not an independently existing human being whom the Son then "put on," but rather God himself in human form; thus Mary is literally the Mother of God (*Ep.* 101.16–17; anathemas 1, 3). There was not even an instant when the man Jesus existed as a human being before God assumed him; rather, the nativity of Jesus must be seen the other way around, as the human birth of *God* (*Ep.* 101.17). Even though God and humanity remain distinct kinds of reality (ἄλλο καὶ ἄλλο), when the Son took on human existence they became "one thing" (ἕν), and the incarnate Son continues to be a single subject of existence (ἄλλος), as he was before (*Ep.* 101.20–21). Thus Gregory positively opposes the idea that there are

---

83. The majority manuscript reading. Gallay prefers the *lectio difficilior* ἐγεγέννητο. SC 250, p. 218.
84. Gregory's fondness for this construction can be seen in his adaptation of it at least twice more, in *Or.* 38.15–16 and *Carm.* 1.1.2.62–75. See also 4.67; 30.15; 37.5; 40.45; *Ep.* 101.14–15.

two independently existing subjects, or two sons, in Christ, as he takes Diodore to be saying, but only "one and the same Son" (*Ep.* 101.18). Even though Christ is fully human, possessing a human mind, soul, and body, one cannot split him into two beings, divine and human, like two people who coexist (*Ep.* 101.19). Again, Jesus' development must be understood as God's human development (which renders moral progress out of the question), and after the resurrection Christ continues to exist "along with what *he* assumed" (*Ep.* 101.23–25); in both cases the subject of Christ's human existence is God.

References to a single subject of Christ's acts abound in Gregory's work. In his first major Christological statement in Constantinople he insists on the confession that *God* was born and died and rose for us, and he severely criticizes those who avoid such vivid language (22.13). So the one who is uncontained moves from place to place; the one who is above time came under time (37.2); Christ came forth from Mary "as God with that which he had assumed"; and the Son, who is full of Divinity, empties himself and becomes poor in order to make others rich (38.13–14).[85] Since, in this unitive scheme, Christ truly is the Son of God, it also makes sense for Gregory to speak of "Christ" being and doing both divine and human things, even apart from the incarnation. This is actually Gregory's most typical way of speaking throughout his work, beginning with his first Christological statement: "Let us become like Christ, since Christ became like us.... He descended that we might be exalted.... He ascended, so that he might draw us to himself" (1.5). Likewise, it is "Jesus" who created us and became human to save us (14.2; 40.2). Gregory observes this practice even in passages where it would be more natural to say "Son" or "Word," as in a discussion of John 1.1 (e.g., 37.2). He is not suggesting that Christ's human form literally preexisted the incarnation;[86] rather, he is simply appealing to the singular identity of Christ as the eternal Son of God and reflecting the usual practice of the New Testament. Since Christ is the Son of God, it is not merely acceptable but a positive confession of faith to say that *he* created us and *he* became human to save us.[87] In Gregory's work, such statements are a solid theological confession of the unity and identity of Jesus

---

85. See also *Or.* 34.10: all that the Father has belongs also to the Son, except whatever is spoken of him as a human being because of the incarnation; 45.27: the Son is "sent" both eternally from the Father (in the divine generation) and in the economy according to his humanity (in the incarnation).

86. Any more than Apollinarius seems to have done, although he was accused of having claimed as much.

87. Among the many examples, see esp. *Ors.* 2.98; 15.1; 4.19, 37, 67; 5.36; 7.23; 14.4, 15; 8.14; 12.4; 17.12; 19.12–13; 24.2, 10; 32.33; 33.9; 41.4–5; 31.12; 26.6; 37.1–3, 7–8; 38.1; 39.1, 12; 40.2; 43.61, 64; 44.2, 7; 45.1. It is noteworthy that the *Theological Orations* (as well as *Or.* 42) generally lack such references, since Gregory is arguing with greater technical precision. For a lengthier discussion of this practice, see Beeley, "Gregory of Nazianzus on the Unity of Christ."

Christ as "one and the same" Son of God, and are much stronger than the mere cross-predication of attributes, or *communicatio idiomatum*, as Diodore and the Antiochenes practiced it.

It is here that we come to the heart of Gregory's Christology and its most practical significance. For Gregory it is soteriologically essential that "God was conceived and born" (*Carm.* 1.1.10.22), that

> God came to an end as man, to honor me,
> so that by the very things he took on, he might restore,
> and destroy sin's accusation utterly,
> and, by dying, slaughter the slaughterer. (*Carm.* 1.1.10.6–9)[88]

For Gregory, the focus and climax of Christ's saving work is his death on the cross. In observation of its great significance, he frequently speaks of God—a single subject—dying on the cross for our salvation.[89] The soteriological importance of Christ's divine identity is clearest at the greatest point of his suffering. When Jesus cries from the cross, "My God, my God, look upon me, why have you forsaken me?" (Ps 21.1 LXX; cf. Mt 27.46), Gregory argues that this does not indicate that God has abandoned him (in which case there would certainly be two subjects): Christ has not been abandoned either by the Father or by his own Divinity—as if God were afraid of suffering! Rather, he says, this ultimate point of human desolation shows just how authentically the Son has assumed and represented (τυποῦν) our fallen condition, "making our thoughtlessness and waywardness his own" (30.5). Jesus' cry of abandonment, in other words, does not reflect the absence of God in his suffering, but God's inclusion of our abandonment within his saving embrace and his healing *presence* in the midst of our desolation and death. In his life and especially in his death, Gregory writes, Christ bears our entire existence in himself as the incarnate Son of God, so that in his divine being he might burn up sin and death as fire melts wax, and we might participate in his divine life "through the intermingling"[90] (30.6). And, as if to anticipate the later monothelite controversy, he clearly stipulates that, in order to assume our sin and suffering, Jesus possesses both a divine and a human will (30.12).

The strong, even paradoxical, terms that Gregory uses to describe the unity of the incarnation emphasize the reality of Christ's assumption of our human brokenness. Even though the Son remains unconquerable in his own proper

---

88. Trans. Gilbert.
89. Norris, "Gregory Nazianzen's Doctrine of Jesus Christ," p. 134. See also Winslow, *Dynamics of Salvation*, p. 105.
90. ἵνα ... κἀγὼ μεταλάβω τῶν ἐκείνου διὰ τὴν σύγκρασιν.

divine existence,[91] God has fully entered into and "submitted" to human suffering and death (30.2), so that when the devil attacks Jesus, he unwittingly meets with God, and death is defeated by death (39.13). Christ's suffering shows just how great is God's love for us because in him *God* has died in order to forgive our sins (33.14). Gregory firmly states that it is not enough for God to associate himself with human existence without actually becoming human: the Son himself must assume and undergo human suffering and death in order to purify like by like (*Ep.* 101.51). Though he is keenly aware of the paradox involved, he holds the central Christian conviction to be that Christ is "God made passible for our sake against sin" (30.1),[92] so that we are "saved by the sufferings of the impassible one" (30.5).[93] Thus for Gregory the awesome nature of the Christian faith is chiefly "to see God crucified" (43.64). It is with this shocking proclamation that he chooses to end his final oration: "We needed an incarnate God, a God put to death, so that we might live, and we were put to death with him"; and so "God is crucified" (45.28–29). Because it was God who died on the cross—the Son of God made human just for this purpose—his death can be the death of all fallen humanity, and we can be purified and made a new creation by his divine life.[94]

Before we delve more deeply into the spiritual dimension of Gregory's Christology, we should note that the unitive dynamic of his doctrine is almost universally neglected in current Gregorian scholarship. As we have already noted, in nineteenth- and twentieth-century historical theology Gregory's Christology is usually regarded as being primarily anti-Apollinarian and dualist.[95] In several passages in the fourth *Theological Oration*, he appears to say that we should conceive of the human Jesus (or Christ's humanity) as a subject of existence independent of the eternal Son of God. In certain sections he follows the pattern of single-subject predication outlined in *Orations* 29.18 and 30.1, which we have just examined, but in others he seems to practice a kind of double predication, referring certain things to Christ's humanity in a way that

---

91. See *Or.* 26.12: God is supreme in Christ's suffering; 45.13: Christ cannot be sacrificed in his first nature.

92. See also *Ors.* 17.12; 30.1; 26.12; 39.13; 44.4.

93. τὰ τοῦ ἀπαθοῦς πάθεις. See also *Or.* 17.12.

94. See also *Ors.* 15.11; 14.3; 11.7; 18.28; 20.4; 22.13; 21.24; 32.33; 33.14; 31.29; 26.12; 39.13, 17; 44.4; 45.13, 19, 22, 30; *Carm.* 1.1.6.77; 1.2.14.91; 1.2.34.190; 2.1.11.1603; 2.1.13.35; 2.1.60.9.

95. In the standard handbooks, Kelly notes approvingly that for Gregory Christ is "twofold" (διπλοῦς; *Or.* 38.13), though without teaching that there are two Sons (*Early Christian Doctrines*, p. 297). Grillmeier also focuses on Gregory's two-nature language, commenting that his Christological formula "sounds very 'Antiochene'" (*Christ in Christian Tradition* [1975], p. 369). This assessment pervades more recent scholarship on Gregory: see Winslow, *Dynamics of Salvation*, pp. 83–84; Wesche, "Union of God and Man"; Moreschini, SC 358, p. 53f.; Bouteneff, "St. Gregory Nazianzen"; Norris, "Christ/Christology"; "Gregory of Nazianzus"; and Russell, *Doctrine of Deification*, pp. 221, 223.

appears to be independent of his divinity. Some of these passages resolve themselves into the single-subject paradigm,[96] such as *Or.* 30.2, where he considers the interpretation of Proverbs 8.22 and gives the third instance of his hermeneutical rule. He comments that whatever has to do with the fact that Christ is caused, such as the term "created," must refer to his humanity (ἡ ἀνθρωπότης), whereas whatever is simple and uncaused refers to his Divinity (ἡ θεότης). The question is whether Gregory means Christ's human nature per se, as a subject of existence other than the Son of God, or whether he means the Son of God in his human form (as indicated in 29.18 and 30.1). At the end of the section he plainly indicates the latter, saying that Wisdom (the divine subject) is called these things in different respects.[97]

Yet there are other passages that do not resolve themselves so neatly into a unitive scheme, most of them in the fourth *Theological Oration*.[98] For example, he argues that statements about Christ's human acts—such as keeping God's commandments,[99] learning obedience through suffering,[100] and the agony of his passion[101]—refer to "the passible element, not the immutable nature that is far above passion" (30.16). Rather than referring the lowly passages to the Son of God in his human form, Gregory seems to be saying that they do not refer to God at all, but to Jesus' humanity as *distinct* from his divinity, thus explicitly denying the single-subject predication that he has previously outlined. In other passages he describes Christ as being dual or double in various ways. In his reply to Eunomian arguments from John 14.28 and 20.17—"the Father is greater than I" and "I am ascending to my Father and your Father, to my God and your God"—Gregory explains that while the Father is Father of the Word, God is not the God of the Word, "because he was two-fold (διπλοῦς)." What misleads heretics, he says, is a failure to appreciate this duality, and to realize that even though Christ's divine and human titles are "yoked together on account of the mixture (ἡ σύγκρασις)," nevertheless "the natures are distinguished and the names are separated in our thoughts.... Even though the combination of [God and human existence] is a single entity, he is such not in his [divine] nature, but in the union of the two" (30.8).[102] As

---

96. See Norris, "Gregory Nazianzen's Doctrine of Jesus Christ," pp. 172–176.
97. Other seemingly dualist passages that resolve themselves in this way are *Or.* 30.9, 10, 13, 21.
98. *Ors.* 30.2, 5, 8, 12, 15, 16, 21; 38.15 (= 45.27); 43.69; 45.25.
99. Jn 15.10; cf. 10.18; 12.49.
100. Hb 5.8.
101. Hb 5.7; Lk 22.44.
102. Εἰ γὰρ καὶ τὸ συναμφότερον ἕν, ἀλλ' οὐ τῇ φύσει, τῇ δὲ συνόδῳ τούτων. Similar passages can be found at *Or.* 30.5, 12; but cf. *Ep.* 102.28, where Gregory denies that he holds a doctrine of two, opposed natures, which violates the union in Christ.

above, Gregory appears to be saying that the key to understanding Christ's identity is to distinguish his two natures from each other as distinct referents and subjects of existence.[103]

In order to understand these passages, we must first observe that the single-subject paradigm is by far the most prevalent mode of Christological reflection in Gregory's work. Single-subject constructions outweigh dualist passages, in both frequency and importance, in the major and minor orations alike, as well as the dogmatic poems. Second, it is significant that the greatest concentration of apparently dualist exegesis comes in the fourth *Theological Oration*—a fact that urges us to reconsider this oration as a whole. We have examined the introduction to *Oration* 30 above, where Gregory establishes the unitive Christological paradigm together with the practice of single-subject exegesis (29.17–21). If we also examine the conclusion, we find that Gregory again makes a general statement of the principles of Christological exegesis, recapitulating his argument in a lengthy meditation on the names of God and Christ (30.17–21). He first discusses the Son's lofty names, which belong to him "both above us and for us," and then turns to his lowly names, which are "uniquely ours and belong to what he assumed from us" (30.21). This second phrase might again suggest the dualist model: that the lowly names belong to Christ's humanity as opposed to the eternal Son; but here Gregory re-emphasizes the unity of Christ's human existence with his divine sonship. Christ is called "human being," he says, to signify that the incomprehensible One is comprehended "through *his* body," and that he sanctifies humanity "through *himself*": in each case the eternal Son is the subject of Christ's human actions. Gregory also signals the unitive model by returning to his usual practice of using the term "nature" to refer primarily to the divine being,[104] and in the commentary that follows, Christ's divine identity clearly subsumes and defines his incarnate, human status. While he is a complete human being—body, soul, and mind—Christ has united human existence to himself so fully that he is "God made visible to intellectual perception."[105] He is called "Christ" for the same reason: because in becoming human the divine Son anoints his humanity through "his complete presence as the anointer,"[106] as opposed to the anointing of prophets and kings, which takes place merely by divine action (ἐνεργείᾳ)—and which necessarily occurs between two distinct entities. Thus,

---

103. See also *DVS* 651, in addition to *Or.* 38.15: "He was sent, but as a human being; for he was two-fold (διπλοῦς)." However, unlike 30.8, this passage resolves more clearly in the single-subject paradigm.
104. A practice in which he was followed by Cyril of Alexandria. See Beeley, "Cyril of Alexandria."
105. θεὸς ὁρώμενος, διὰ τὸ νοούμενον.
106. παρουσίᾳ δὲ ὅλου τοῦ χρίοντος.

in these final sections, Gregory firmly resolves the oration into the unitive, economic paradigm with which it began.[107]

The overall pattern of Gregory's corpus and the larger argument of *Oration 30* (29.17–30.21) both present a unitive, economic paradigm for understanding the identity of Christ, which suggests that we reexamine the questionable texts in this light. To return to Gregory's most strongly dualist passage (30.16), we need not take him to be saying that Jesus' human and divine acts refer to two different subjects of existence. He is more likely arguing that Christ's human acts refer to "*his* passible element, not *his* immutable nature that is far above passion," a meaning that the Greek text admits;[108] the lowly passages refer to the human existence, or the human form, that the Son has assumed, rather than to his own, divine nature per se, apart from the incarnation. Likewise, Gregory's statements that Christ is "twofold" (διπλοῦς, 30.8; 38.15) need not mean anything other than what he argues in *Oration 29*: that in the economy the Son is now "composite" (σύνθετος), and thus can be said to be and do human things on account of the human form that he has assumed (29.18). On closer examination, each of the apparently dualist texts can be similarly interpreted within the economic paradigm. What appears to be happening in *Oration 30*, with some residual effect afterward, is that Gregory is stretching himself, possibly with the influence of other theologians in Constantinople at the time, in order to make his case for the unitive, economic paradigm as strongly as possible. As he responds to the Eunomian exegesis, he adds the qualification that, precisely because the actions of Jesus are God's *human* actions, they must not be understood as God's divine actions apart from the incarnation. As important as it is to confess that the Son of God died a human death in Jesus Christ, it is equally important not to suggest that he died a *divine* death as well—that in the fullness of his divine being God died on the cross and ceased to be God, in which case the Eunomian position would have very much to recommend it indeed.[109] The single-subject, economic paradigm is not only capable of accommodating such qualifications, but it necessarily includes them, either explicitly or implicitly—whether they be fulsome accounts of Jesus' humanity or statements that he possesses two natures or elements—without subverting the central claim that Christ's identity is determined pri-

---

107. We will consider the last section of the oration (30.21) below.
108. τὸ πάσχον . . ., οὐ τὴν ἄτρεπτον φύσιν καὶ τοῦ πάσχειν ὑψηλοτέραν.
109. Gregory makes just such a qualification in his late *Ep*. 202: that in the incarnation the "only-begotten God" must not be thought to have suffered "in his proper Divinity," in which case the eternal Son would have died in his divinity during his three days in the tomb and needed resurrecting by God the Father. *Ep*. 202.15–16.

marily by his divinity. The economic paradigm is more inclusive in this regard: a unitive understanding of Christ implicitly includes the notion of his composite condition in the economy, whereas a dualist position does not produce a unitive doctrine. Given that the contested passages fit perfectly well within Gregory's unitive structure, it would appear, then, that the confusion stems from a presupposed Christological dualism on the part of the interpreter. If one has a full economic understanding of Christ's unity, as Gregory does, then there is no trouble in saying that certain things belong to Christ's humanity as distinct from his divinity, so long as one assumes that the ultimate subject of Christ's human actions is the eternal Son of God; moreover, it is unnecessary—indeed it would be tiresome—to spell this out every time. Gregory's Christology is therefore dualist only if one assumes that the unitive paradigm is not in force, which very much begs the question. By reading *Oration* 30 superficially and analyzing Gregory's statements in overly ontological and synchronic ways, rather than within the context of the narrative economy of salvation, later readers have unfortunately subjected Gregory to the same misinterpretation that so many have given to the Chalcedonian Definition.[110]

Throughout his corpus, and above all in his mature work after 379, the main force of Gregory's Christology is to express and defend the basic Christian confession that Jesus Christ is himself "one and the same" Son of God, as proclaimed by the apostles, the early rules of faith, and the fourth-century creeds.[111] Gregory's primary Christological concern is to confess the singular identity of Christ as the eternal Son of God made human, and this unitive confession is the root of his opposition to the Eunomians, the Antiochenes, and the Apollinarians alike. What are often distinguished in modern systematic theology as distinct Trinitarian and Christological doctrines are thus for Gregory parts of one and the same idea.

Christological Spirituality

For Gregory, the central principle of Christian salvation is not merely the work of Christ, but his identity as one and the same Son of God made human; and the Son's assumption of fallen human existence is also the basic structural

---

110. The correction of which required several centuries of Christological controversy, in order to return to a more Gregorian and Cyrilline doctrine.

111. Note the single-subject language used in the second article of Nicaea and other creeds: "And [we believe] in one Lord Jesus Christ, the Son of God,... *who* suffered and rose again on the third day...."

principle of Christian spirituality. It is here that the mystery of the unity of Christ is tied up with the mystery of salvation, and Christology and soteriology are, paradigmatically speaking, the same thing.

Although the exact nature of the union of the Son with human existence is ineffable (*Carm.* 1.1.10.26, 50–51), there is nevertheless much that can be said about its structure and unifying principle, as we again see in each of the four key texts examined above (29.19; 37.2; 38.13; *Ep.* 101). First of all, the unifying principle of the incarnation is the divine Son himself—who is begotten Divinity: both the divine nature and hypostatic existence within the eternal Trinity—and his divinizing action on the humanity that he assumed. When the Son assumes human form, Gregory writes, he blends it with his own divine nature and unites it to himself *because he is God*. In other words, the Son is able to assume human existence, blending it with himself, "and he was born as a single entity, because the more powerful part prevailed."[112] It is indicative that Gregory describes the action of the Son on his assumed humanity—sometimes in the same sentence—as both unifying and divinizing. In the incarnation the Son did not become two things (the Son plus a human being), but he became one thing out of the two because "both are God, that which assumed and that which was assumed" (37.2), including Christ's physical body (39.16). That is to say, by assuming human existence the Son divinizes it, and in divinizing it he assumes it into himself, in one and the same divine action. As Gregory writes in the first letter to Cledonius, "Both things are one entity by the mingling, since God has been 'in-humanized' and humanity 'divinized,'[113] or however we should put it" (*Ep.* 101.21).[114] The unity (or unification) of Christ and the redivinization of humanity are thus two aspects of the same reality: the Son's assumption of human existence into his own single being—so that the Savior is "one and the same" Son of God—is what we might call the structural principle of the divinization of humanity, and the divinization of humanity by Christ's divinity represents the character and effect of the incarnation.

Implicit in both the structural and the soteriological aspects of Gregory's Christology is the belief that God and humanity—and indeed all creation—are of radically different orders of existence. In order to understand the identity and the saving purpose of Christ, Gregory argues, it must be borne in mind that we are talking about the union of the Creator with a creature, not the union of two

---

112. γέγονεν εἷς, τοῦ κρείττονος ἐνικήσαντος.

113. τὰ γὰρ ἀμφότερα ἓν τῇ συγκράσει, Θεοῦ μὲν ἐνανθρωπήσαντος, ἀνθρώπου δὲ θεωθέντος.

114. See also *Or.* 30.2: Christ's divinity anoints his humanity; *Ep.* 101.29: when the risen Christ returns, his invisible Divinity will (continue to) predominate over his visible flesh; 101.46: Christ assumed both human flesh and mind so that they could be made holy and "deified by his Divinity."

creatures. This infinite difference in being between God and creation is implied, and sometimes argued, throughout Gregory's theological system, from his doctrine of creation to his understanding of salvation and eschatological fulfillment, and it reflects the biblical narrative as he has learned to read it through Greek Christian tradition.[115] It is the nature of God, compared with the nature of human creatures, that provides the principle of the union of the two in Christ. Because God is infinitely greater than all creatures, he is able to assume human existence into his own nature without contradiction and without threat to himself. In the course of his dispute with the Apollinarians in 383, Gregory has occasion to elaborate on this principle. As he reports in *Letter* 101, the Apollinarians have argued that the Word cannot coexist with a human mind because they would mutually exclude each other: "They say that he did not have room for two complete things" (*Ep.* 101.37).[116] The Word and a human mind would presumably compete with each other, like two similar objects that cannot occupy the same space. But, in Gregory's view, this objection reflects a basic misunderstanding of the "two things" in question, namely thinking that God and a human mind (or any creature) are of the same order of existence, such that they could conflict with each other at all. Even among creatures, he argues, one can find examples of things that occupy or coexist with each other, such as a human soul in a body, or the way that sounds and smells mix with one another in our perception; and of course God fills the universe already without contradiction (*Ep.* 101.36–39). Yet, although these are helpful examples to illustrate the point, for Gregory it is ultimately a question of relative ontology, or relative perfection. Even were one to imagine God and humanity as the same kind of thing—Apollinarius seems to be thinking of them as two instances of mental intelligence—there is still the question of their relative "size."

Here we return to Gregory's fundamental theological category of magnitude: a single beam of light does not threaten the sun in which it exists, nor a drop of water the river. Perfection, Gregory says, is relative: something can be perfect with respect to one thing but imperfect compared to something else. Just as Moses can be a god to Pharaoh but a servant of God,[117] so too the human mind rules and governs the body but is itself governed by God, without contradiction between the two sets of terms. In Gregory's debate with the

---

115. The radical distinction between God and creation had most recently been argued by the Homoiousians; see the conclusion.
116. οὐκ ἐχώρει δύο τέλεια. See also *DVS* 616–618: the Apollinarians argue that Christ lacks a human mind because they fear that it would conflict with the presence of God in him, to which Gregory replies that surely human flesh conflicts with God more than a mind!
117. Ex 7.1; Jo 1.15.

Apollinarians, we see in quantitative terms the same point of disagreement that he had raised with the Eunomians in Constantinople. In that case, the Eunomians (in Gregory's view) object that God cannot submit himself to human suffering and death, that the human condition and God are mutually exclusive. Gregory replies that what the Eunomians despise as unworthy of God in fact reflects God's mercy to stoop down and save us. Based on the same underlying principle that we see in *Letter* 101, Gregory is saying that God is so great as to be able to humble himself to the point of a human death for our salvation, and that the unity of God with our fallen condition not only does not contradict or threaten God, but that it is precisely in God's character to do this.[118] Likewise, he faults Diodore for missing the central significance of the unity of God and humanity in Christ as well. Here again the same principle of the unity of Christ underlies Gregory's opposition to all three opponents, the Eunomians, the Apollinarians, and the Antiochenes.

The perfection of God, which causes the unifying and divinizing work of the incarnation, in turn points us back to Gregory's constant emphasis on the divinity of Christ. For Gregory the focus of the Christian faith is the confession that the crucified Christ is himself the eternal Son of God. Gregory emphasizes the predominance of the divine Son over his assumed humanity in several summary titles: Christ is not the "lordly man,"[119] as the Apollinarians maintained, but "our Lord and God" (*Ep.* 101.12); rather than "a man who is also God," he is the "God-man"[120] (40.33); and Christians do not worship a God-bearing flesh" (or "God-bearing man"), but a "man-bearing God"[121] (*Ep.* 102.18–20).[122] The incarnation, like the divine economy as a whole, is therefore to be seen primarily as the work of God. Contrary to the instincts of certain theologians (both ancient and modern), to emphasize the supremacy of God in Christ's person and saving work does not, for Gregory, denigrate or otherwise overlook the validity and importance of created life, but rather elevates it: the greatest thing that can happen to lowly human beings is to be made God (γενέσθαι θεόν) by the incarnation of the Word (30.3). Hence the ontological possibility of the incarnation, as well as its character and saving

---

118. A similar argument occurs in Gregory Thaumaturgus' *To Theopompus, On the Impassibility and Passibility of God*; on which see this book's conclusion.

119. Or "man of the Lord," ἄνθρωπον κυριακόν.

120. ἄνθρωπος, ὁ αὐτὸς καὶ Θεός, μᾶλλον δὲ Θεὸς ἄνθρωπος.

121. τὸ δεῖν προσκυνεῖν μὴ σάρκα θεοφόρον (or ἄνθρωπον θεοφόρον, *Ep.* 102.18), ἀλλὰ Θεὸν ἀνθρωποφόρον.

122. See also *Or.* 9.6: on the last day Christ will be the final manifestation and revelation of "our great God."

purpose, is the divinization of humanity by God in the person of Christ, so that the incarnation and the process of divinization are in fact the same thing. God and human existence become one in Christ so that God can divinize humanity, and they are one because in Christ God divinizes humanity. As Donald Winslow aptly notes, "The unity of Christ's person, for Gregory, is *theosis*."[123]

God's assumption of human existence in Christ achieves salvation and divinization in such as way as to be determinative for humanity as a whole. In order to save us, Christ has assumed human existence in a way that contains or represents the entirety of the fallen race of Adam. In Paul's terms, Christ is the New Adam and the progenitor of a renewed human race.[124] Much as Irenaeus had done, Gregory follows Paul in seeing Christ as the recapitulation of all of God's generosity toward us, a summary of the race of Adam, and even of "all that is" (38.7).[125] In the incarnation, Gregory writes, Christ bears "all of me in himself, along with all that is mine ... so that I may share in that which is his through the intermingling" (30.6). In an ideal or potential sense, we were all put to death and rose again and were glorified with Christ, so that we might all be purified (45.28). Yet, as Winslow has argued, while the divinization of Christ is in principle the divinization of all humanity, in actual practice it is the divinization of only Christ's human nature.[126] Contrary to the popular modern view that, for Gregory and other Greek fathers, divinization is a kind of automatic, even physical, infusion of God's saving life into the human race,[127] this is not Gregory's view. To be sure, Christ contains the entirety of a renewed humanity, and the sin and mortality of all people are conquered in him, so that he is the first new creature and the head of a new race, yet the exchange does not automatically run in the other direction. By sanctifying human nature in himself, Christ becomes yeast in the whole lump of humanity (30.21) in a potential, ideal sense; the leavening action requires more than the fact of the incarnation itself.

The incarnation is thus not only the paradigm of the divinization of all humanity, but it is also the instrument of the realization of that divinization by

---

123. *Dynamics of Salvation*, p. 87. On the role of *theosis* in Gregory's Christology, see also Norris, "Gregory Nazianzen's Doctrine of Jesus Christ," pp. 128–166.
124. *Ors.* 30.1, 5; 39.13.
125. See also *Or.* 2.23–24.
126. *Dynamics of Salvation*, pp. 88, 92.
127. This view is sometimes ascribed to Harnack, although not entirely fairly: see *History of Dogma*, vol. 3, pp. 163–171; Winslow, *Dynamics of Salvation*, p. 89n1. See also Lampe, *Seal of the Spirit*, p. 150; Norris, "Gregory Nazianzen's Doctrine of Jesus Christ," p. 132n4.

people other than Christ. The Son's descent into the depths of our fallen condition enables us to rise from it.[128] Christ has taken on the poverty of our flesh, Gregory says, so that we might come to possess the richness of his Divinity; "he who is full has emptied himself... so that I might participate in his fullness" (38.13). Gregory makes the point in a powerful series of biblical images in *Oration* 38. By humbling himself in the incarnation, Christ is the Good Shepherd, who sought out the sheep that is lost: he took it upon his shoulders, where he also bore the cross, and raised it to the life on high. He is the woman who lit the candle of his own flesh, swept the house to cleanse the world from sin, and sought out the lost coin, which is the royal image of God that was covered up by passion; when he had found it, he rejoiced with the angels by sharing with them the secret of his Nativity (38.14).[129] Christ's accomplishment of this humiliation and exaltation in himself, as a unified, single divine-human subject, makes possible both the divinization of humanity in his own person as well as the divinization of Christians through participation in his saving life. Gregory often speaks of the process of salvation as "ascending" to God by means of Christ's incarnation. Because he has become incarnate in Jesus, God is accessible to us; and for those who know Christ to be the eternal Son of God, he is "God made visible" (Θεὸς ὁρώμενος), God seen and known for our salvation (30.21).[130] In other words, Christ took on our condition, humbled himself to the point of death, and was exalted so that, through our knowledge of him as the incarnate Lord, our own earthbound existence might be elevated to God. Because Christ's humiliation is the humiliation of *God*, in knowing Christ Christians identify their own humiliation with his and ascend with him to God, being made God to the same extent that he was made human (29.18–19).

In this regard, Christ's divinization becomes our divinization through the *doctrine* of the incarnation. Gregory stresses the role of the saving knowledge of Christ's identity both at the beginning and at the end of the third *Theological Oration*. When he first gives his rule of Christological exegesis, he concludes that by applying the lofty sayings to the Son's divine nature and the lowly

---

128. A principle that Norris calls the "kenosis-theosis" pattern of the incarnation. "Gregory Nazianzen's Doctrine of Jesus Christ," pp. 128–148. See also Winslow, *Dynamics of Salvation*, pp. 95–96, 99.

129. See also *Ors*. 40.45; 45.22.

130. Likewise, the New Covenant manifests God in the Son (31.26, 28); *Or*. 38 celebrates the birth of Jesus, by which God is made manifest (38.3); and in Christ we confess that this human being is in fact God (40.33). Commenting on Lk 2.52, Gregory writes that over the course of his life, Christ's divine character was gradually displayed (43.38). On the Transfiguration, see 40.6.

sayings to his incarnation (οἰκονομία), one may "ascend with him to the Divinity"[131] and move through his visible manifestation to behold spiritual realities (29.18).[132] In other words, the practice of interpreting the biblical witness to Christ moves the believer through Christ's earthly revelation toward the knowledge of his true, divine identity. Gregory concludes his lengthy discussion of Christ in the third and fourth *Theological Orations* with the same spiritual purpose. After rehearsing many of the names of God and Christ, he adds,

> There you have the titles of the Son. Now walk through them—those that are lofty in a godly way (θεϊκῶς) and those that are bodily in a sympathetic way (συμπαθῶς). Or rather, treat them all in a godlike manner, so that you may become God by ascending from below, on account of him who came down from on high for us. (30.21)[133]

Even as we initially identify with Christ's assumed, human qualities because they are our own (συμπαθῶς), the goal of faith is to come to see that these, too, belong to God (θεϊκῶς), so that as a result of Christ's condescension we may ascend to become divine. The nature and purpose of recognizing Christ's identity as God made human—which is to say the nature and purpose of Christological doctrine and biblical piety—is to come to know that Jesus Christ, who is perceptible in bodily form, as a reflection of his sympathy with us, is the divine Son of God, and to see that his human element is also God, having been divinized by union with the Divinity. The doctrine and confession of Christ is thus the primary means of divinization, and our ascent to God through the knowledge of Christ is the ultimate meaning of Gregory's Christology.

As Gregory notes in *Oration* 29, the doctrinal ascent through Christ also represents the interpretation of Scripture "according to the Spirit" (29.18), namely the practice of spiritual exegesis that Gregory initially learned from Origen, following Paul's argument in 2 Corinthians 3.[134] The incarnation

---

131. Or "ascend by means of his Divinity," συνανιέναι θεότητι.

132. Literally "not resting with visible things, but rising up with him to intelligible things," μὴ τοῖς ὁρωμένοις ἐναπομένοις, ἀλλὰ συνεπαίρῃ τοῖς νοουμένοις.

133. See also *Ors.* 2.98; 6.4; 34.7; 37.4. Gregory's exegetical, dogmatic, and spiritual focus on the biblical terms for Christ distinctly follows Origen, for whom reflection on the titles or aspects (ἐπίνοιαι) of Christ is the chief means of spiritual ascent. See *Princ.* 1.2.4; *Comm. Jn.* 1.9.52; 1.20.123, 120; 1.31.217–219. Gregory modifies Origen's scheme by distinguishing more clearly between the eternal and the economic sayings about Christ—which enables him to avoid the suggestion that the preexistent Word or Word-soul of Christ represents a principle of multiplicity compared to the simple unity of God the Father—by speaking more consistently of Christ as a single subject of existence, and above all by focusing more centrally on the cross than Origen does. He also shares Origen's doctrine that the human soul of Christ acts as a mediator between the divine Word and Christ's flesh (*Princ.* 2.6.3).

134. On which see chap. 3.

represents the letter giving way and the Spirit coming to the fore (38.2); thus to fail to recognize that Christ is one and the same Son of God made human—whether on the basis of a Eunomian, Antiochene, or Apollinarian position—is to be tripped up by the literal sense of Scripture and to miss its spiritual meaning. Ascending to God through Christ by the spiritual interpretation of Scripture means, for Gregory, participating in Christ's life, death, and resurrection, which have been given to us as patterns for our imitation (40.30).[135] One of his most common exegetical practices is to speak of participating in Christ through meditating on various aspects of his life and work. In the Epiphany sermons, for example, he invites his hearers to make themselves disciples of Christ by "traveling without fault through all the stages and acts of Christ's career," from his birth and his teaching in the Temple as a child to his trial and crucifixion as an adult (38.18). Having died in Adam, Christians will live in Christ by being born, crucified, buried, and risen with him (38.4). The exhortation rises to a crescendo in the climactic final passage of *On the Theophany*: "Finally, be crucified with him, die with him, be buried with him eagerly, so that you may also rise with him and be glorified with him and reign with him,[136] seeing God as much as possible and being seen by him, who is worshipped and glorified in Trinity" (38.18).[137] Our participation in Christ's life, death, and resurrection is both the definition of the incarnation and the identity of Christ and the substance of Gregory's spirituality, so that this meditative and imitative approach to Scripture is naturally tied together with ascetical practice and the life of Christian worship.[138] Through the spiritual interpretation that results in participation in Christ,[139] the doctrine of Christ becomes the very material of Christian salvation and ascent to God. Even the use of human language to express Christ's identity is for Gregory a participation in Christ's self-emptying and condescension: just as Christ condescended to human flesh in order to be comprehended, so he condescends to endure the finite and imperfect human language by which he is known (37.1–4). The salvation and divinization of Christians thus not only depends on the

---

135. See also *Or.* 32.15: Christ ascribes glory to the Father in all things to give us a model of piety.

136. The rhetorical form of the Greek, which is difficult to capture in English, encourages this participation in a climactic repetition: τέλος συσταυρώθητι, συννεκρώθητι, συντάφηθι προθύμως, ἵνα καὶ συναναστῇς καὶ συνδοξασθῇς καὶ συμβασιλεύσῃς.

137. Among many examples, see *Ors.* 1.2, 4; 14.14, 18, 21; 8.9, 23; 16.11–12; 18.4; 19.1; 24.4; 39.14–16; 45.1, 22–25.

138. See chap. 1.

139. By biblical exegesis and interpretation I do not mean only the literate study of the biblical text, but any act of interpretation that might occur through listening to Scripture read orally, hearing a sermon, viewing Christian images, or recollecting in one's prayers.

doctrine of Christ but it is also the meaning and purpose of that doctrine: "for God rejoices in nothing as much as the correction and salvation of human beings, which is the purpose of every doctrine (λόγος) and every mystery" (39.20).[140] When Gregory claims that he knows Christ's divinity from the Scriptures (29.17), his exegesis reflects much more than merely the letter of the text. Only in the spiritual and soteriological interpretation of Scripture, lived out by Christians in the community of the Church, does the doctrine of Christ have its real meaning. As Louis Bouyer has observed, at the heart of Gregory's meditation on the Gospel is the mystery of Christ in us.[141] The meaning of Gregory's Christology, and Christ's potential divinization of all humanity, is thus realized only by the presence and work of the Holy Spirit.

---

140. Or "every word and sacrament." See also *Or.* 38.16: each of the mysteries of Christ has the same basic meaning and end result (κεφάλαιον ἕν): "my perfection and recreation and return to the first Adam."
141. Bouyer, *Spirituality*, p. 348.

3

The Holy Spirit

From the Spirit comes...our recognition of the honor of the one who recreates us.

—*Oration* 31

"I give myself and my all to the Spirit!" (12.1). So Gregory begins his first episcopal oration in Nazianzus. It has long been recognized that Gregory of Nazianzus distinguished himself among the late-fourth-century fathers for his clear and systematic teaching on the divinity of the Holy Spirit.[1] While his doctrine of Christ was central to the contemporary debates and seminal for several later Christological traditions, it was the Holy Spirit that attracted Gregory's greatest personal attention and professional commitment—along with the doctrine of the Trinity as a whole, which the Spirit completes—to the point that it eventually cost him his position as archbishop of Constantinople and president of the great council of 381.

The Holy Spirit pervades every aspect of Gregory's doctrine—from the purification and illumination of the theologian and the confession of Christ's divinity to the knowledge of the Trinity and the work of pastoral ministry. As he puts it, "Everything we do is spiritual" (11.6). This pervasiveness if not surprising; in an important sense it is precisely the character of the Spirit to be self-effacing, because

---

[1] See, e.g., Swete's assessment in *The Holy Spirit and the Ancient Church*, pp. 245–246.

the Spirit serves primarily to enable the knowledge of God that is focused in Jesus Christ. Gregory devotes fewer passages to the explicit discussion of the Spirit than he does to his ascetical theory, to Christ, or to the Trinity, yet at the same time he is the leading pioneer in the doctrine of the Holy Spirit among his contemporaries, and the Spirit figures centrally in his work. In many respects, it is Gregory's Pneumatology that most distinctively characterizes his theological project. It not will be our purpose here to summarize the entirety of his views on the Holy Spirit; instead we will focus on his central arguments concerning the Spirit and the unique role that it plays in his theological system.

Gregory's doctrine of the Holy Spirit represents fundamentally soteriological concerns in ways that are both similar to and different from his Christology. Even as Christ is himself the salvation and redivinization of humanity, so too the Holy Spirit is "the mystery of new salvation" (14.27). Patristic scholars generally agree that the driving force of the major fourth-century doctrinal developments was a concern to speak adequately of Christian salvation. It has long been the standard view that Athanasius and the three Cappadocians ushered in a new, critical wave of reflection on the Holy Spirit from the 360s to the 380s, which led to the orthodox doctrine of the Trinity, by taking the arguments that they had used for the divinity of the Son and applying them to the Spirit with the same results.[2] Thus Gregory's Pneumatology has been seen as simply the logical extension of the soteriological arguments he makes with regard to Christ—as if he began with Christ and then moved on to the Holy Spirit in the same frame of mind. While it is true enough that his doctrines of Christ and the Spirit are both fundamentally soteriological, the way in which they are so, and the specific rationale and arguments involved in each, differ significantly. By virtue of his identity as God made human, Christ is our salvation in principle; whereas, by virtue of its identity as God dwelling in the Church and within individual Christians, the Holy Spirit is our salvation in actual human lives. Just as Gregory's Christology expresses the particular way in which Christ saves and divinizes human beings, so too his doctrine of the Holy Spirit must be understood in light of the particular contours of his soteriology. Even as Christ remains the focus of the Christian's knowledge of the Trinity, with Gregory's understanding of the Holy Spirit we come in many ways to the heart of his theological endeavor and the immediate rationale of the Trinitarian confession.

Bishops, theologians, and imperial officials around the Mediterranean had spent considerable energy debating the identity of Christ even before the

---

2. See, e.g., Winslow, *Dynamics of Salvation*, pp. 121, 126; Ayres, *Nicaea*, p. 215.

outbreak of the Arian crisis in the 320s. Yet, when Gregory began his ministry in 362, no sustained reflection on the Holy Spirit had appeared that came close to matching the attention given to Christ, or that was even comparable to the earlier work of Irenaeus and Origen. Athanasius and Basil both wrote important works on the Spirit in the next twenty years,[3] which to some extent respond to recent opposition to the Spirit's divinity, but neither developed the full range of doctrinal and practical dimensions of the doctrine of the Spirit that Gregory would show to be fundamental to Christian theology.[4] Despite the fact that the Council of Constantinople refused to confess the Spirit's full divinity and consubstantiality with the Father, as he so strenuously urged it to do, it was Gregory who played the leading role in reestablishing the Spirit's key position in subsequent Christian theology, and who defined what soon became the orthodox doctrine of the Spirit.[5] This fact should not surprise us for such an assiduous disciple of Origen, who gave the Spirit a central place in his theology and spirituality, and who provided Gregory (and Basil) with the main ligaments of his own doctrine. A large part of Gregory's contribution to Christian theology lies here in his Pneumatology, which in the fullest sense includes the ascetical themes that we explored in chapter 1 and the Christological spirituality in chapter 2. As in Gregory's theological system, the doctrine of the Holy Spirit thus functions in this book with a sort of leavening effect, including and decisively altering the character of the other main points, however invisibly. At great personal cost to himself, and with a depth of insight not seen since Origen, Gregory championed the full, substantial divinity of the Holy Spirit, and he clarified the essential role that it plays in Christian doctrine and life.

Gregory's Pneumatology shows a more pronounced development over the course of his career than his doctrine of Christ does. While there are a few statements in the early orations, for all intents and purposes Gregory's public

---

3. Basil, *Eun.* 3; *Spir.*; Athanasius, *Ep. Serap.* We should note also Hilary's fragmentary though important initiatives toward a full doctrine of the Spirit in his *On the Trinity* 8–9, from around 360. Although some have pointed to Athanasius as the first Christian theologian to take on the doctrine of the Spirit in any serious way (e.g., Hanson, *Search for the Christian Doctrine of God*, p. 749), that honor surely belongs to Origen, who laid the groundwork for what became Eastern pro-Nicene Pneumatology through the work of Gregory and, to a lesser extent, Basil and Gregory of Nyssa.

4. For a comparative assessment of these writers on the Holy Spirit, see the conclusion.

5. Gregory's achievement is matched only by that of Augustine in the West. Augustine quoted Gregory's *Or.* 41 *On Pentecost* from Rufinus' Latin translation, though only in his late anti-Pelagian works and not apparently with any substantial effect on his own Pneumatology. See Lienhard, "Augustine of Hippo." On Gregory's theological leadership in relation to Basil, see McGuckin, *St. Gregory*, pp. 204–206 and passim. For the conventional view that Athanasius and Basil are chiefly responsible for orthodox Pneumatology, cf. Haykin, *Spirit of God*; Ayres, *Nicaea*, pp. 211–218.

teaching on the Holy Spirit dates from the time of his episcopal ordination in 372. In his first episcopal orations in Nazianzus, *Orations* 9–12, Gregory launches his Pneumatological program in bold terms. In 380, after a lengthy hiatus brought on by several factors, he returns to the doctrine of the Spirit in *Orations* 21 and 34. The full flowering of his Pneumatology then comes in two orations from the summer of 380: *Oration* 41 *On Pentecost* and especially *Oration* 31, the fifth *Theological Oration*, a piece that H. B. Swete has rightly called "the greatest of all sermons on the doctrine of the Spirit" from the early Church.[6] Yet while the importance of *Oration* 31, and to a lesser extent *Oration* 41, has long been recognized, several key points of Gregory's argument—and, consequently, the full richness of his doctrine—have typically escaped modern commentators. Taking into account the dogmatic poem *On the Spirit* (*Carm.* 1.1.3), which he wrote sometime between 381 and 383 in Cappadocia, we find Gregory occupied in roughly a decade of focused theological work on the Holy Spirit. Since Gregory articulates his Pneumatology in a sophisticated rhetorical mode, especially in *Oration* 31, our study will, again, take special account of both historical and rhetorical context.

The Development of Gregory's Pneumatology: 372–380

Gregory's Pneumatology developed over the course of his career more noticeably than his Christology, which bears witness to the greater degree of controversy within pro-Nicene ranks than was waged over the doctrine of Christ during the same period. When he arrives in Constantinople in 379, Gregory laments the number of different views that he finds on the Holy Spirit: the belief that the Spirit is the uncreated God (Gregory's own view), of equal honor with God (the doctrine of Basil and Gregory of Nyssa up to this time, and that of the council of 381), merely a creature (possibly the view of the Eunomians and Homoians),[7] an energy of God (possibly the view of the Eunomians),[8] or merely a name and not a distinct thing at all (a modalist view; 32.5).[9] As we noted in the introduction, by the early 370s a distinct group can be identified in Asia Minor, apparently composed primarily of Homoiousians, whose members affirm the divinity of the Son but deny the divinity of the Holy Spirit, and

---

6. Swete, *The Holy Spirit in the Ancient Church*, p. 240. See also Haykin, *Spirit of God*, p. 174.
7. A view that can also be found earlier, in Eusebius of Caesarea. See *Eccl. theo.* 1.6.
8. See also the statements of Athanasius, *Ep. Serap.* 1.20; and Basil, *Spir.* 61.
9. The following year, in August 380, he gives a similar list: some consider the Spirit to be an energy of God, God, or a creature, and others prefer not to say, since Scripture is not clear on the matter (*Or.* 31.5).

who seem to have regarded strongly Trinitarian (eventually pro-Nicene) doctrine as modalist—the so-called Pneumatomachians or Macedonians.[10] Gregory has some version of this group in mind (or different versions at different times), along with the Eunomians and Homoians, as he articulates his doctrine of the Spirit over the next decade.[11] Having been deeply formed in the study of the Bible and Origen, Gregory begins his episcopal ministry in this polemical context by committing himself to the fullest possible affirmation of the Spirit's divinity. The attention that he gives to the Spirit in his first episcopal orations in 372 (*Ors.* 9–12) indicates the importance that he believes the doctrine of the Spirit should hold at this point in the Church's life. Although he will initially be drawn into the debates over the divinity of the Son when he arrives in Constantinople, he will also renew his attention to the Spirit there, and ultimately stake his career on defending what he believes to be orthodox Pneumatology.

"Chrism and Spirit on me again!" Gregory exclaims at the beginning of his first episcopal oration (9.1). By referring to his anointing in the ordination rite, he draws attention to the major dogmatic theme to which he is devoting himself, as well as to his new teaching authority as a bishop. Shortly afterward, in his sermon for the martyr festival at the shrine of St. Orestes on his way to be installed as bishop of Sasima,[12] Gregory announces his opposition to "the false christs in our very midst who war against the Spirit" (11.6)[13] This statement is Gregory's first direct reference to the Pneumatomachians; although it is not a technical term for him to the degree that it is for Basil and Gregory of Nyssa,[14] it is descriptive nevertheless and will be useful for our purposes. He is presumably referring to the groups around Eustathius of Sebaste; and since at this time Basil was still allied with Eustathius and was present at the festival, it may also be Gregory's first public challenge to Basil, whose Pneumatology Gregory had already found to be lacking. His appeal to the witness of the martyrs to the true faith (11.5) may be a signal to Basil and others that, whether or not they will

---

10. On the origin and provenance of these terms, see the introduction, p. 29.

11. References occur throughout the 372–381 period. See esp. *Ors.* 12.6; 21.33–34; 34.11; 41.7–8; 31.1–3 and passim; 39.12.

12. The second part of *Or.* 11 (11.4b–7), which was later assembled from different sermons. See McGuckin, *St. Gregory,* p. 193.

13. οἱ ἐν ἡμῖν αὐτοῖς ψευδοψρίστοι καὶ πολεμίοι τοῦ Πνεύματος.

14. Gregory normally uses this language to speak of those who fight *for* the Spirit: either the true believers he has shepherded (*Ors.* 33.13; 42.11), the true pastor (2.87; see also 40.43), or those guided by a true pastor (16.2). The only other passage that refers to Pneumatomachians in negative terms is 25.15, where the confession that the Spirit is "God" is "fought" by some. See also 42.13, on those who "make war" against the Divinity in general, referring to Eunomians, Homoians, and Pneumatomachians alike. For the contemporary usage of the term, see above, p. 29n88.

join the full confession of the Spirit, Gregory can rely on the support of fully Trinitarian monks who were in attendance.[15] Upon his return from a retreat in Pamphylia, Gregory explains that he has been communing with the Spirit like Elijah and John the Baptist, and that he returned to his congregation on account of the bond and the presence of the Spirit between them (10.1, 3). By contrast, Christ is mentioned only twice in this oration, and rather formally, in the introduction and conclusion (10.1, 4).

In 372 Gregory began to work as assistant bishop to his father in Nazianzus, which placed him in the diocese of Cappadocia Secunda, rather than in Cappadocia Prima under the authority of Basil. As he takes up his ministry in his home church, he announces his doctrine with full episcopal *parrhesia*. In the proem of *Oration* 12, his first episcopal oration in Nazianzus, he signals his Trinitarian program in his most moving personal description of the Spirit's work outside of the later poetry.

> "I opened my mouth and drew in the Spirit" (Ps 119/118.131) and I give myself and my all to the Spirit—in practice and word and nonpractice and silence. Only may it hold me and guide my hand and mind and tongue.... I am a divine instrument, a rational instrument, an instrument tuned and struck by that master musician, the Spirit. Yesterday it worked silence in me—my philosophy was not to speak. Today it plays my mind—my speech will be heard and my philosophy will be to speak.... I open and close the door of my mouth to the Mind and the Word and the Spirit, who are together one nature and Divinity. (12.1)

Gregory often speaks passionately of the common life of the Church and the office of pastoral ministry as the work of the Holy Spirit. Having worked throughout the covenants in angels, patriarchs, prophets, and apostles (41.11, 14), the Spirit now enlivens Christian communities and binds them together with one another[16] and with their leaders.[17] The Spirit also calls and anoints priests and bishops to the office of pastoral ministry,[18] and it enables their primary work of teaching—"possessing the one who will breathe on its behalf" (21.7)—even as it gifts all believers with a variety of spiritual gifts (41.12). In the early episcopal orations Gregory defines his friendship with Basil (not too

---

15. McGuckin, *St. Gregory*, p. 196.
16. *Ors.* 34.6; 26.1–2.
17. *Or.* 13.4.
18. Gregory writes he that came to Constantinople because he had been invited and because he followed his conscience and the call of the Spirit (*Or.* 33.13). See also 26.1–2; 42.1, 12; 43.37.

subtly) as being subjugated to the Spirit (10.2–4), and argues that Basil offended the Spirit by appointing Gregory to Sasima, a move which Gregory of Nyssa then had to repair, so as to reconcile them both to the Spirit (11.3).[19] It is significant that before Gregory proclaims the unity of the Trinity, he points first to the Spirit's work of inspiring and guiding his doctrine and practice, a fundamental connection that he will explicate much more fully several years later, in *Oration* 31. Although the ostensible topic of *Oration* 12 is his father and his new episcopal ministry, the real theme is the Spirit and Gregory's authority as its newly appointed interpreter. While his elderly father guided the flock "in the power of the Spirit" and with "spiritual works," he now requires a crutch to prop himself up, just as Moses relied on the help of Aaron (i.e., Gregory), "on whose beard and clothing runs the spiritual and priestly ointment" (12.2). Gregory the Elder still possesses "spiritual strength," despite his old age, and as bishops they have both made "spiritual professions," despite the fact that they are accused of having carnal motives by those who have recently come to wield the worldly power of the episcopate (i.e., Basil) (12.3). Finally, the Spirit has led Gregory to choose a middle course between solitary contemplation and the public service of the Church, since "the reformation of a whole church is preferable to the progress of a single soul" (12.4–5).[20]

Again referring to his consecration, Gregory then makes the first unequivocal declaration in extant patristic literature that the Spirit is "God." In a climactic conclusion, he offers himself to the Spirit, to whom he gave himself when he was anointed as a bishop in the name of the Almighty Father, the Only-Begotten Word, and "the Holy Spirit, who is God (Θεόν)."[21] He then signals the importance of his confession of the Spirit for the full doctrine of the Trinity: "How long should we hide the lamp under the bushel and withhold the complete Divinity from others, when it ought to be put on the lampstand right now to give light to all churches and souls and to the whole fullness of the world, no longer by means of images or intellectual sketches, but by a distinct

---

19. Years later, when he sought to rekindle the support of the late Basil's network in Caesarea, Gregory will glowingly say that Basil's election to the throne was the work of the Spirit, that he was single-mindedly devoted to the things of the Spirit, and that his advocacy for the Spirit's divinity in his writings and in his prudent "economy" of words personally encouraged Gregory's own confession (*Ors.* 43.37, 59, 65, 67–69, 73)!

20. An assertion that highlights Gregory's key position in the development of the Church's reflection on pastoral leadership; on which see chap. 5.

21. See also *Or.* 33.16, from 380: orthodox Christians worship "the Father and the Son and the Holy Spirit, one Divinity: the Father as God, the Son as God, and (don't be angry!) the Holy Spirit as God [or: God the Father, God the Son, God the Holy Spirit], one nature in three distinctive things" (Θεὸν τὸν Πατέρα, Θεὸν τὸν Υἱόν, Θεόν, εἰ μὴ τραχύνῃ, τὸ Πνεῦμα τὸ ἅγιον, μίαν φύσιν ἐν τρισὶν ἰδιότησι). The phrase is repeated almost verbatim in 31.28. On the confession of the Spirit as God, see also 31.3, 5, 10 and passim.

declaration?" (12.6). Gregory adamantly insists it is theologically and pastorally indefensible to deny the full revelation of God in Jesus Christ through the Holy Spirit. As a result, he wants it to be clearly known that, whatever hesitations Basil and others may have, he will champion the divinity of the Holy Spirit and declare its central place in the doctrine of God. In a statement of faith made years later, during his retirement, Gregory specifically identifies his proclamation that the Spirit is God as the one essential point of orthodox doctrine that the Council of Nicaea did not declare, since the question had not yet been mooted. It is this confession that should now define the communion of the catholic Church, he says, especially after the lingering unclarity of the council of 381 (*Ep.* 102.2).

Due to a series of personal, familial, and local tragedies, and his period of retreat in Seleucia, there is a seven-year hiatus in Gregory's work on the Holy Spirit from 372 to 379.[22] In the first few months of his time in the capital, too, Gregory gives little attention to the Spirit, thanks to more pressing needs in the debates over the doctrine of the Son.[23] However, in the spring of 380 he returns to the subject and, over the next few months, offers the most significant body of teaching on the Spirit since Origen. This second phase of Gregory's Pneumatology coincides with the arrival of the Alexandrians, who had apparently been sent with Bishop Peter's blessing to support Gregory's work, as well as to claim their own share in the new theological ascendancy at the heart of the Eastern empire. In his first oration dedicated to the new Egyptian contingent, *In Praise of Athanasius*, Gregory narrates a history of the Arian crisis, in which the wickedness of Arius' denial of the Son's divinity has recently been applied to the Trinity as a whole—referring to the denial of the Spirit's divinity by Eunomians, Homoians, and certain Nicenes. He then praises Athanasius for his virtuous leadership and his orthodoxy (21.13), and for the great distinction of having arrived, near the end of his career, at "the same faith concerning the Holy Spirit that had previously been granted to most of the Fathers concerning the Son," which he then confessed in writing to the Emperor Jovian (21.33).[24] As in his panegyric on Basil, the success of Gregory's persuasive abilities in this oration has tended to exaggerate the real nature of his relationship to Athanasius.[25] His purpose here is multifold: He not only

---

22. He makes only brief references to the Spirit during this time, concerning the Spirit's work in the Church and individual sanctification. See *Ors.* 13.4; 16.1; 17.2, 6; 18.29, 36; 19.2.

23. He does discuss the Trinity as a whole, which of course includes the Holy Spirit. See esp. *Ors.* 20.5–11; 23.6–12.

24. Referring to Athanasius' *Ep. Jov.*

25. On which see this book's conclusion.

means to celebrate the arrival of his new Egyptian contingent, to garner their support for his ministry in the capital, and to signal to multiple opponents that it is his congregation that fulfills the new imperial requirement of adhering to the faith of Peter of Alexandria and Damasus of Rome,[26] but he is above all claiming the legacy of Athanasius for his own ministry in the capital on behalf of the orthodox faith. It is largely Gregory himself who created the narrative that he is the heir to Athanasius' labors in the construction of Nicene orthodoxy. He knows, largely by hearsay, that for many years Athanasius championed the divinity of the Son against the "Arians," and he has some indication that his doctrine of the Spirit comes close to his own. But he knowingly overstates the case that Athanasius confessed a complete faith in the Holy Spirit, just as he did in the case of Basil (43.67–69). In his *Letter to the Emperor Jovian*, Athanasius writes that certain people renew the Arian heresy by "blaspheming against the Holy Spirit, saying that it is a creature and came into being as a thing made by the Son."[27] In response, Athanasius adds the following commentary: "The Synod at Nicea ... wrote ὁμοούσιος, which was peculiar to a genuine and true Son, truly and naturally from the Father. And they did not make the Holy Spirit alien from the Father and the Son, but rather glorified it together with the Father and the Son, in the one faith of the Holy Trinity, because there is in the Holy Trinity also one Divinity."[28] It is significant that Gregory refers to Athanasius' *Letter to Jovian* rather than the *Letters to Serapion*, Athanasius' most extensive treatment of the Spirit, the reason being that in all likelihood he does not know them. Gregory's acquaintence with Athanasius' work is sparse, and what little he knows does not inform his own work to any great extent. Even in the *Letter to Jovian* there are several points of difference: Gregory does not make the characteristically Athanasian argument that the Son is true, proper to, or internal to the Father, or that the Spirit is not "alien" to the Father and the Son (or the Son to the Father); he also calls the Spirit "God" and consubstantial with the Father, which Athanasius does not do.[29] The shift in Trinitarian argumentation toward distinguishing the relational categories of Father and Son from the ontological categories of Creator and creature was by now fairly well established among Nicenes in Asia Minor;[30] so on this point Athanasius merely

---

26. In *Cunctos populos* (*C. Th.* 16.1.2).
27. *Ep. Jov.* 61.1.
28. *Ep. Jov.* 61.4.
29. Gregory is probably not aware of Athanasius' two statements that the Spirit is ὁμοούσιον with the Father in *Ep. Serap.* 1.27 and 3.1; on which, see the conclusion.
30. Particularly in the work of Basil of Ancyra and George of Laodicea, as well as Basil of Caesarea. See the introduction, pp. 21–23, and the conclusion pp. 310–311.

corroborates Gregory's inherited theological agenda. Nevertheless, he vaguely knows that Athanasius has begun to defend the divinity of the Spirit, and he is happy to claim his legacy for his own, fuller doctrinal program.[31] Having established himself as the successor to Athanasius' labors, Gregory continues in the ensuing weeks to discuss the Spirit's divinity to a greater extent than any theologian before him.

In a second oration for his Egyptian supporters, Gregory then confesses the Spirit's divinity in clearer terms and introduces a major point of argument:

> I find two primary differences among things that exist, namely rule and servitude—not the kind that tyranny has cut and poverty has severed among us, but the kind that nature has distinguished, so to speak (for what is First is also above nature). The first of these is creative and originating and unchanging, while the other is created and subject and changing. Or to speak even more plainly, the one is above time and the other is subject to time. The first is called "God" and subsists in Three Greatests, namely the Cause, the Creator (δημιουργός) and the Perfecter—I mean the Father, the Son, and the Holy Spirit.... The other division is with us and is called "creation," though one may be exalted above another according to the proportion of one's nearness to God. (34.8)

In order to clarify his approach, Gregory defines the radical division between God and creatures, or rule and servitude, the sharp ontological divide that admits of no intermediate, third status of being. Basil also contrasts the free and active lordship of the Spirit with the servitude of creatures;[32] however, he does not identify the Spirit's active character as that of "God," as shared by the Father and the Son. In fact, he seems to avoid such a statement intentionally, thus leaving open the rather pressing question of whether the Spirit might be an intermediary divine being that shares in God's lordship, in contrast with ordinary creatures. What is at stake for Gregory here is the clear assertion that the Spirit belongs with the Father and the Son as God, the ruler, and is not merely a creature and a servant of God, there being no third alternative between the two. By speaking in terms of rule and servitude he is also raising a more pointed and far-reaching concern, to which he will return soon: that to regard the Spirit as anything other than God is to deny that, through its

---

31. Athanasius' work also fits Gregory's generous description better than Basil's, considering Basil's refusal to make a stronger confession when Gregory plainly showed him the way.

32. *Ep.* 159.2; *Spir.* 19.50–20.51; see also *Eun.* 2.31; 3.2.

indwelling, the authority of God is present in the believer's life and in the life of the Church.

On the feast of Pentecost, June 9, 380, just a month after taking up the subject in *Oration* 21, Gregory brings his proclamation of the Spirit to its penultimate level. Now he makes explicit the fuller implications of the Creator-creature distinction: "Those who reduce the Holy Spirit to the rank of a creature are blasphemers and wicked servants, and worst of the wicked. For it is the part of wicked servants to despise lordship and to rebel against dominion and to make what is free their fellow servant" (41.6). With hints of Jesus' warning about the unforgivable sin against the Holy Spirit,[33] Gregory urges his hearers to recognize that by regarding the Spirit as anything less than fully divine they are de facto treating it as merely a creature and are blaspheming God (41.5, 7). In one of his most crucial and distinctive insights in the doctrine of the Spirit, he reasons that to deny that the Spirit is God is, in effect, to refuse to acknowledge God's lordship over his creation. Elsewhere he writes that the denial of the Son's divinity reflects a disparagement of God's mercy in sending Jesus (29.19); yet here his argument runs deeper, for he is no longer speaking of the incarnate Christ, whose divine nature is spelled out in Scripture, external to one's immediate experience (important as that is), but of the presence of God in the most intimate respect (which enables the confession of Christ). Later in the oration, he goes on to describe the Spirit in fairly strong terms: as the one by whom the Father is known and the Son glorified, the Spirit exists eternally and is ranked with the Father and Son, representing the glory and perfection of God; it deifies and is not deified; it transcends all created categories, receiving the divine being from God the Father, the First Cause, and sharing everything with the Father and the Son except being unbegotten and begotten (41.9); it is consubstantial with the Father and Son (41.12) and shares with the Son in the work of creation and regeneration, as seen in Scripture (41.14)—all of which he will take up again soon, in *Oration* 31. Having briefly identified this connection between doctrine and personal piety, Gregory has now arrived at the heart of his Pneumatology. At this time he may have also been preparing the *Theological Orations* (41.6), in which he will further expound his doctrine in about two months' time. Here he intends only to make a basic confession of the Spirit's divinity, and to note briefly what the alternative involves spiritually. For the moment he continues the conciliatory policy of consensus building that he has practiced thus far,[34] in an effort to gain the support of the Spirit-Fighters, leading them as brethren, not

---

33. Mt 12.31; Lk 12.10.
34. As recently as *Or.* 23.13. Previously, see *Ors.* 6, 22, and 32.

enemies, from the confession of the Son's divinity to that of the Spirit as well and thus to the full Trinitarian faith. If they will but confess the Trinity to be of one Divinity or nature, then they will have reached the point of acknowledging that the Spirit is God in the fullest sense of the word (41.8).[35]

Judging from the heightened vigor of *Oration* 31, Gregory was unsuccessful in his attempts at reconciliation. The momentous fifth *Theological Oration* contains his fullest Pneumatological exposition, in opposition to both the Pneumatomachians and the Eunomians, and by extension the Homoians associated with Demophilus. Here we see Gregory's doctrine of the Spirit in full bloom, encompassing a broad range of dogmatic, epistemological, and spiritual concerns. His earlier confession that the Spirit belongs with the Father and the Son on the side of the rule of God of course begs the question: if one does not believe that the Spirit is God, which his opponents do not, then one would hardly be inclined to agree that blasphemy has been committed. In its current form, Gregory's argument from the Creator-creature distinction is essentially a dogmatic proclamation coupled with a sophisticated threat. For, as he hinted in *Oration* 41.6, the basic question runs much deeper, and in *Oration* 31 he seeks to address it on this more fundamental level. Before proceeding with his argument, however, he reiterates his basic position in a simple confession at the beginning of the piece: because he has such confidence in "the Divinity of the Spirit, whom we worship," he will begin the work by again applying to the Spirit the same terms of Divinity that he grants to the Father and the Son: "light and light and light, but there is one light and one God" (31.3). A few sections later he returns to this basic conviction: "What, then, is the Spirit God? Of course! Then, is it *homoousion*? Yes, if it is God" (31.10).[36] While he realizes that this is still a radical statement for some, Gregory is convinced that the Spirit must be confessed as "God" and *homoousion* with the Father if one is to avoid blasphemy of the highest order.[37] Yet because the idea has met with such difficulty, he also realizes that he needs to make his argument as persuasively as he can—an argument that he believes is self-evident from the historical faith and common life of the Church—and this is his agenda for the remainder of the oration.

Over the course of *Oration* 31, Gregory patiently and methodically guides his readers toward the heart of his Pneumatology, where it again intersects

---

35. A tactic he had just used in the previous oration (*Or.* 34.9, 14). See also 41.14.

36. See also *Ors.* 25.16; 41.12; 38.16; *Carm.* 1.1.3.3–4.

37. Apollinarius is probably the only other theologian Gregory knew who called the Spirit *homoousion* with the Father. See *KMP* 33, written between 358 and 362; see also the reports of Philostorgius, *HE* 8.11–13; Sozomen, *HE* 6.22.3. The same language appears in Epiphanius' *Panar.* 74.11.2, written probably before 377.

with the doctrine of salvation. While it can be said that all early Christian doctrine arises from the interpretation of Scripture, Gregory's doctrine of the Spirit involves exegetical and hermeneutical issues that are both central and far reaching, to a degree that surpasses even his Christology. In a manner not seen since Origen, Gregory's Pneumatology reflects a fundamental interconnection between dogmatic, epistemological, and hermeneutical concerns, which require the full length of *Oration* 31 to disclose. As Gregory reports it, the debate has come to a head over the question of what the Bible says—or rather, what it does not say—about the Spirit's divinity; this question is the leading problem taken up in the piece.[38] We do not possess enough textual evidence to know whether Gregory's account is accurate, but as he describes the situation, the Pneumatomachians (and possibly also the Eunomians)[39] claim that in declaring the Spirit to be "God" and consubstantial with the Father Gregory has introduced "a strange and unscriptural God" (31.1)[40]—an objection which is summarized in the single term τὸ ἄγραφον ("being unscriptural") (31.21). The point is not lost on him: Gregory realizes that the Bible does not call the Spirit "God" in plain terms, and he certainly believes that the doctrine of the Spirit must be based on Scripture. But in his mind the question is not whether or not one's doctrine is biblical, but *how* it is so, and what exactly this involves hermeneutically, theologically, and ecclesially. He does not mean to address these questions fully, at least not right away; instead he carefully crafts his argument so as to create rhetorical tension and suspense, meeting his opponents' objections first, and only gradually revealing his own doctrine.[41]

Although it is typically overlooked by interpreters (perhaps as an annoying and doctrinally insignificant piece of invective), Gregory briefly indicates the real issue in his initial reply to his opponents:

---

38. On the *stasis* of the oration, in terms of Hermogenean rhetorical theory, see Norris, *Faith Gives Fullness*, p. 184.

39. It is difficult to identify Gregory's interlocutors in each section of *Or.* 31. As Norris puts it, "This oration reeks with the smell of live debate and intolerance, problems not yet clarified, parties not yet solidified." *Faith Gives Fullness*, p. 190. Norris argues that Gregory also has the Eunomians in mind in this passage (p. 203), and scholars generally recognize a predominantly anti-Eunomian agenda throughout the oration. See also Norris, "Gregory Nazianzen's Opponents in Oration 31"; McGuckin, *St. Gregory*, p. 278n269.

40. ξένον θεὸν καὶ ἄγραφον. See also *Or.* 31.3, 21. Haykin argues that this was an important point of the Pneumatomachian position, though his only evidence is Gregory's statement in 31.21, "Time and again you return to the silence of Scripture (τὸ ἄγραφον)," together with 31.1 and 29. *Spirit of God*, p. 175n36.

41. There is some background to this point in Origen. While the Scriptures make it clear that the Holy Spirit should be honored together with the Father and the Son, he says, there is much that they do not tell us, such as whether it is begotten or unbegotten, or whether it is another Son (*Princ.* pref. 4). Among the things that they do not tell us, Gregory argues, is the fact that the Spirit is fully divine.

> Those who are angry with us on the ground that we are bringing in a strange or interpolated God—the Holy Spirit—and who fight very hard for the letter, should know that they are afraid where there is nothing to fear. And I want them to understand clearly that their love for the letter is only a cloak for their impiety, as will be shown later on, when we refute their objections to the best of our ability. (31.3)

More than once Gregory denies his opponents counterargument that the Scriptures do not convey the Spirit's divinity (31.5, 21), but he makes it a point to add an important qualification: the Bible proclaims the Spirit's divinity "according to the Spirit," if not according to the letter (2 Cor 3.6).

Among the many ideas that he drew from Origen, Gregory's Pneumatology strongly reflects the central importance that the letter-spirit dichotomy of 2 Corinthians 3.6 plays in Origen's work—most visibly in *On First Principles* book 4, a text which Gregory is partially responsible for preserving in Greek. Later in the oration, he argues that the biblical witness to the Spirit's divinity has been shown "by the many people who have treated the subject and handled the Holy Scriptures, not with indifference or as a mere pastime, but have gone beneath the letter and looked into the inner meaning, and have been deemed worthy to see the hidden beauty, and have been irradiated by the light of knowledge" (31.21).[42] Gregory is referring here to both traditional and contemporary theologians, specifically Origen and Basil, and possibly Amphilochius of Iconium.[43] By aligning himself with inspired predecessors and esteemed contemporaries, he is establishing his own credentials in a highly controversial context, even more than acknowledging a theological debt.[44]

---

42. See also *Or.* 25.15: the Spirit is God to those who apprehend things spiritually; 33.17: can one be spiritual without the Holy Spirit?

43. It is not clear that Gregory Nazianzen knew much of Gregory of Nyssa's early work on the Trinity, and the latter's work on the Holy Spirit, beginning with the *Against Macedonius*, dates most likely from after the council of 381. In any event, their doctrinal approach is different in several respects (see this book's conclusion). In *Or.* 31.2 Gregory mentions others who have undertaken systematic studies of the Spirit in Scripture. All agree that this includes Basil; other suggestions have included Amphilochius or Gregory of Nyssa (Norris, *Faith Gives Fullness*, p. 185), or Origen (Wickham, *St. Gregory of Nazianzus, On God and Christ*, p. 143n2). In 31.28 Gregory gives a Trinitarian statement in terms that, he says, "one of the inspired men explained not long ago." This source has conventionally been taken to be the creed ascribed to Gregory Thaumaturgus in Gregory of Nyssa's *Life of Gregory Thaumaturgus* (see McGuckin, *St. Gregory*, p. 309); however, this creed is likely the invention of Gregory of Nyssa's apologetic agenda and cannot be accepted as authentic (again, see the conclusion). Abramowski argues that the phrase μικρῷ πρόσθεν in 31.28 refers to a contemporary, most likely Gregory of Nyssa ("Das Bekenntnis," p. 149), which is again unlikely considering the great differences between their texts. Origen and Basil are the likeliest candidates.

44. Though his debt to Origen is enormous, Gregory, like most ancient writers, feels no compulsion to name names or cite chapter and verse for his sources. This passage should not be taken as an exception to the rule.

Gregory notes that he is not the first to argue that the Bible shows the Spirit to be divine, but he also emphasizes that this can only be done by more penetrating exegesis, which goes beneath the mere letter of the text to perceive its inner meaning. Although he fervently disagreed with Basil's position on the Spirit until Basil's death on January 1, 379, and he appears to have been opposed by Gregory of Nyssa at the council the following year,[45] it obviously behooves him to identify himself not only as a traditional theologian but as a well-connected Eastern bishop, which of course he is.

Gregory now means to go farther than Basil did, to consider more deeply what it means to understand the Spirit's divinity "according to the Spirit." In the early sections of the oration he asks how the Spirit can be of the same rank as himself, namely, a creature, if it makes him God and joins him with the Divinity (31.4). His point is that the doctrine of the Spirit's divinity somehow involves the divinizing work of the Spirit; however, at this point he does not elaborate, and abruptly shifts to another subject. It is ironic that even sympathetic commentators have tended to read Gregory's argument in a way that favors the Pneumatomachian position, by expecting that he is going to provide an exposition of the Spirit's divinity directly from the biblical text.[46] But this is exactly what he means not to do. Although he touches on the exegetical question at the beginning of the oration, his appeal to the spirit versus the letter of Scripture also recognizes that in an important sense the text of Scripture does *not* state that the Spirit is God. For reasons that will soon become clear, he does not return to the biblical witness until near the end of the oration; in the meantime, he creates a rhetorical space between the beginning and ending sections in which to develop his central argument. In these brief, early passages Gregory intimates that the confession of the Spirit's divinity has to do with interpreting the deeper meaning of the Bible according to the Spirit—that it is a matter of spiritual exegesis—and that this in turn depends on becoming worthy of divine knowledge (31.12); yet exactly what this means must wait for the opportune time.

Before we proceed, it will be helpful to see the overall structure of *Oration 31* to get a sense of the flow of Gregory's argument. Following the introductory material we have just discussed, Gregory makes his way through a series of descending steps in sections 4–27, in response to his opponents' objections,

---

45. Amphilochius seems to have supported Gregory's doctrine at the council, despite the fact that he had been a disciple of Basil. See Haykin, *Spirit of God*, p. 182, and nn80–83 for further bibliography.

46. For example, Swete, *The Holy Spirit in the Ancient Church*, pp. 243–244.

which clears the way for his own positive doctrine in section 28, just before the end of the oration. The oration can be outlined by section number as follows:

1–4	Introductory problem: the lack of direct biblical proof of the Spirit's divinity (τὸ ἄγραφον); initial reply, with Trinitarian confession
5–6	Survey of current positions
7–20	Reply to logical objections to the Spirit's divinity and the Trinity
21–24	Defense against τὸ ἄγραφον from logic
25–27	Defense against τὸ ἄγραφον from the divine economy
28	Positive argument for the Spirit's divinity: baptismal deification
29–30	The witness of Scripture to the Spirit's divinity
31–33	Conclusion on the limits of theological language and on the guidance of the Holy Spirit

With the same approach that he used for the divinity of the Son in *Orations* 29–30, Gregory first addresses his opponents' more technical, logical objections to the divinity of the Spirit and the full doctrine of the Trinity (31.4–20), and then proceeds to answer their objections from Scripture (31.21–27). There is a good deal of constructive theology in these middle sections, especially Trinitarian logic, which will concern us in the next chapter. Gregory makes an important contribution to Trinitarian terminology by identifying the generation of the Spirit as "proceeding" from the Father (ἐκπορεύεσθαι, Jn 15.26), as distinct from the Son's being "begotten" (γεννητός).[47] But his immediate aim in these sections is negative and defensive: it is not to prove the Spirit's divinity or the doctrine of the Trinity at all—recall his insistence that reason cannot establish the basics of Christian faith (28.28)—but rather to show that it is not logically *im*possible for the Spirit to be God and consubstantial with the Father, even though the Bible does not explicitly say that it is.

Once he has removed these logical and conceptual obstacles, Gregory returns in sections 21–27 to his opponents' primary objection, that the Spirit's divinity is not witnessed in Scripture (τὸ ἄγραφον). He first argues that since there are certain things that are true but are not clearly named in Scripture—such as the fact that the Father is unbegotten, on which everyone in the debate

---

47. See also *Or.* 29.2. He will later use other terms as well: προϊέναι (25.15) and πρόοδος (25.15; 39.12).

agrees—the divinity of the Spirit cannot be denied simply on the basis that it is not explicitly stated. To regard all such things as untrue simply because they are "unbiblical" in this sense is, he believes, an obvious case of enslavement to the letter and a preference for syllables over the actual facts (τὰ πράγματα).[48] Paradoxically, the key to understanding the real meaning (τὰ νοούμενα) of the literal statements of Scripture (τὰ λεγόμενα) is to accept the silence of Scripture on the divinity of the Holy Spirit "according to the letter," and to approach it instead "according to the Spirit" (31.24).

Τάξις Θεολογίας: The Witness of Scripture and the Order of Theology

Before he gives a positive account of his spiritual exegesis, Gregory makes one last defensive argument, this time against his opponents' biblical objections. In what is probably the most famous passage in the oration (31.25–27), Gregory explains the silence of Scripture on the divinity of the Spirit in terms of the history of the covenants and the development of Christian theology. This passage has long been regarded as a major patristic statement of the progress of the divine economy and the positive role of tradition in the development of Christian dogma,[49] as well as the first statement of a Christian doctrine of progressive revelation.[50] Yet in this regard it has often been misunderstood. Gregory is not making a statement of progressive doctrinal development through the history of the Church, as in the nineteenth-century views of Schleiermacher or Newman, so much as developing the eschatological spirituality of Origen in terms of the history of the covenants. For Origen, the Old Testament represents the pattern and shadow of the Gospel; in the New Testament Christ embodies and reveals the Gospel that had been only prefigured before then (thus clarifying the Gospel in the Old Testament as well); and the eschatological age will bring the face-to-face vision of God, which is the

---

48. Gregory borrows from Aristotelian (e.g., *Interp.* 16a–b) and Epicurean sources (e.g., *Ep. Herodot.* 37, 75) to craft what he thinks is an obvious and theologically necessary theory of language. For both Gregory and Basil, human language is a system of conventional signs, which bear complicated and often ambiguous relationships to the things that are signified, rather than indicators of a thing's essence, as the Stoics and Platonists held. See Norris, *Faith Gives Fullness*, p. 192. Although their theories differ in significant respects, Origen is again a major influence here (e.g., *Princ.* 4.2.2).

49. See Plagnieux, *Saint Grégoire*, p. 51f.; Gallay, SC 250, pp. 322–332n4, 326–329n2.

50. See Kelly, *Early Christian Doctrines*, p. 261; Hanson, "Basil's Doctrine of Tradition"; and Winslow, *Dynamics of Salvation*, p. 125n3.

"eternal" or "spiritual Gospel" (Rv 14.6), compared to which the Gospel of the New Testament is itself another shadow and mystery.[51] Gregory encapsulates Origen's doctrine of spiritual progress and eschatological ascent and brings it to bear on the proclamation of the Trinity in his late-fourth-century context. In Gregorian scholarship, this passage is typically regarded as the constructive heart of the oration.[52] Yet, although it is extremely interesting in its own right and does make an approach toward Gregory's positive position, it is important to bear in mind that Gregory's argument here is still primarily defensive and deconstructive. As in the preceding sections, his intention is chiefly to refute his opponents' objection that because Scripture does not plainly declare the Spirit to be God, it therefore cannot be God.

Gregory focuses not on any individual texts that might prove the Spirit's divinity, but rather on the overarching narrative of the covenants and the divine economy as a whole. There are, he says, three great changes, or earthquakes, in human history, which occur with the giving of the Old Covenant and the New Covenant and with the coming eschatological transformation. In each major change God moves his people from one set of beliefs and practices to another and from one degree of divine revelation to another:

> The Old Covenant[53] proclaimed the Father openly and the Son more obscurely. The New manifested the Son and suggested the deity of the Spirit. Now the Spirit itself dwells among us and provides us with a clearer demonstration of itself. For it was not safe to proclaim the Son clearly when the divinity of the Father was not yet acknowledged; or to burden us further (if I can put it somewhat boldly) with the Holy Spirit when the divinity of the Son had not yet been received. (31.26)

Under the Old Covenant God reveals himself to Israel primarily as the all-transcendent Father, while only hinting at the person of the Son, presumably through prophecies of the coming Redeemer. The New Covenant then reveals the Son directly in the person of Jesus, though the revelation of the Holy Spirit is only suggested, presumably by Jesus' promise of the other Comforter and vague

---

51. *Comm. Jn.* 1.6.33–7.40; *Princ.* 3.6.8–9; see also 4.2.2–6. On Gregory's use of Origen in *Or.* 31.25–27, see McGuckin, *St. Gregory*, p. 309; Trigg, "Knowing God." Cf. Epiphanius' theory of gradual revelation, mentioned briefly in *Ancor.* 73.5–6, from the mid-370s: the Bible proclaims one Divinity in Moses, a Dyad in the prophets, and a Triad in the Gospels. Despite the tantalizing parallel, Gregory is probably unaware of Epiphanius' work.

52. Plagnieux focuses on these late sections, though without noting the crucial role of the Holy Spirit (*Saint Grégoire*, esp. pp. 44–49). On the novelty and influence of this passage, see Norris, *Faith Gives Fullness*, pp. 206–207.

53. Or "Testament" (διαθήκη). In these sections Gregory shifts from the sense of covenant relationship to that of a written testament, as he prepares to cite biblical texts in sect. 29.

references to the Spirit in Acts and Paul's letters. But now, in the age of the Church, the eschatological period of salvation history that began with Jesus' ascension to the Father and the giving of the Spirit at Pentecost, the Holy Spirit "dwells among us" and reveals itself to Christians directly. Thus there is a gradual revelation of the Trinity over the course of salvation history, the completion of which comes penultimately in the age of the Church, and only finally in the age to come. In this way, God moves his people from idols to the Law, from the Law to the Gospel, and finally from the earth to a place that can never be destroyed.

The key to interpreting this sequence of events, Gregory argues, is to perceive their character, purpose, and effect. The sequential self-revelation of the Father, Son, and Holy Spirit reflects an increase in the power and intensity of the revelation, so that each successive stage prepares the recipients for the next one, much as one must be purified and transformed into the likeness of God in order to receive greater divine illumination. The Son communicates the Divinity more powerfully than the Father does, and the Spirit again more powerfully than the Son. The history of divine revelation thus brings about the increasing nearness of God to his people. Basing himself on the Gospel of John, and, we may surmise, Acts and Pauline texts like 1 Corinthians 12.3, Gregory comments that the knowledge of God through the Holy Spirit surpasses the disciples' knowledge of God in Jesus before Pentecost, just as their knowledge of God in Jesus exceeded Israel's knowledge of the Father alone; and of course eschatological knowledge, being the fulfillment of the economy of the Spirit, will surpass all three. God the Father, as revealed in the Old Testament, is relatively distant or transcendent (though the relationship is tightly held); the Word made flesh in Jesus represents an experience of God that is more intimate and tangible than the people of Israel had known; and, finally, the Spirit "dwells among" the disciples and the Church, revealing God in a still more intimate way than Jesus did in his earthly mission. Here we should note that Gregory is not saying that the Son and the Spirit are more powerful in themselves—they share the same divine being as the Father—but simply that they convey the Divinity more powerfully to human beings, because the economies of the Son and the Spirit represent God's increasingly nearer presence with the human race. As the Gospel of John indicates,[54] the coming of the Spirit is therefore superior to the coming of Christ (31.27). The greater intensity of the Son and the Spirit is so striking, Gregory believes, that an untimely revelation of either would have been dangerous; taken out of

---

54. Jn 14.12, 26; 16.12.

order, they would be like food beyond our strength or direct sunlight to the naked eye (31.26).[55] In the pedagogical perspective that often characterizes his thought,[56] and which he shares with Irenaeus, Clement of Alexandria, and Origen, Gregory understands God's dealings with his people as consistently reflecting God's beneficence, so that God is constantly adapting his self-revelation to the ability of his people to receive it. In this regard, the knowledge of God in the Holy Spirit correlates with the state of the knower—a theme to which he will turn momentarily.

Gregory's clearest statement of the Spirit's self-revelation comes in his commentary on the giving of the Spirit to the disciples in *Oration* 41. Just as God reveals himself gradually as Father, then as Son, then as Holy Sprit, Gregory says, so too the Spirit came to dwell with the disciples in three stages of increasing intensity, according to their capacity to receive it. At the beginning of the time narrated in the gospels the Spirit worked (ἐνεργεῖν) in the disciples, completing their powers and enabling them to heal the sick and cast out evil spirits.[57] Second, after his passion Jesus then breathed the Spirit onto the disciples, which represents a real divine inspiration.[58] And third, after Jesus' ascension, the Spirit descended on the disciples in the upper room and appeared in fiery tongues.[59] In a striking passage Gregory then distinguishes the event of Pentecost from the first two:

> The first instance manifested the Spirit indistinctly, and the second more distinctly; but this present occasion [Pentecost] did so more perfectly, since the Spirit is no longer present only in energy (ἐνεργείᾳ) as before, but in its very being (οὐσιωδῶς), so to speak, associating with us and dwelling among us. For it was fitting that as the Son had lived among us in bodily form, so too the Spirit should appear in bodily form;[60] and that after Christ had returned to his own place, it should have come down to us. (41.11)

Here Gregory identifies in very strong terms the reality of the Holy Spirit's divine nature and its presence in the Church. Whereas Basil had argued that

---

55. The potential danger of untimely revelation is Gregory's main concern in the similar passage on the progressive revelation of the Spirit's divinity in *Carm.* 1.1.3.17–33. See also *Or.* 45.12, which speaks of the gentle economy of God's healing work in salvation history.
56. Still the best treatment of this subject is Portmann, *Die Göttliche Paidagogia*.
57. Mt 10.1; Mk 3.15; 6.7; and Lk 9.1.
58. Jn 20.22.
59. Acts 2.3.
60. In the tongues of flame.

the activity, or energy, of the Spirit (ἐνέργεια Πνεύματος) is present in the purified soul,[61] Gregory is making the bolder claim that, in the age of the Church, the Holy Spirit now presents itself to believers as being fully divine and consubstantial with the Father—that it is present "in its very Being."[62] He then notes the parallel between the essential presence of the Spirit in the Church and that of Christ in the incarnation. Just as the Son took on bodily existence in order to dwell among us as a human being, so too the Spirit acquires a bodily manifestation, signified by the tongues of flame (though of course not a human incarnation), as it comes to dwell in the Church. And whereas Christ died a human death in order to redeem the world, the Holy Spirit is now "the mystery of new salvation" (14.27); and the divine economy has shifted from the bodily manifestation of Christ to that of the Holy Spirit (41.5). In this progressive "order of theology" (τάξις θεολογίας, 31.27), the direct revelation of the Spirit to the Church represents the apex of the human encounter with God thus far, so that "by gradual additions, and, as David says, by 'ascents' (Ps 83.6 LXX) and advances and progress 'from glory to glory' (2 Cor 3.18), the light of the Trinity shines upon the more illuminated" (31.26).

Gregory brings the entire scheme to bear on the question at hand in what he believes is an original interpretation, which he has not found in the work of other theologians. Among the things that Jesus said the disciples could not bear at the time, but which the Spirit would teach them later when they were capable of receiving it,[63] the greatest of all is the Divinity of the Spirit (31.27). Even according to the letter, he is saying the Bible indicates that the revelation of the Spirit will come to the Church only after Jesus' earthly ministry is complete. Although the Eunomians and Pneumatomachians are right to point out that the deity of the Spirit is absent from the literal text of Scripture, Gregory can cite Christ himself as saying that Scripture (or at least Christ's earthly teaching) does not contain all that God intends to reveal to his people. Rhetorically, Gregory's representation of the Spirit's self-revelation as the apex of the human knowledge of God casts the Pneumatomachian and Eunomian denials of the Spirit's divinity in a rather stark light, for it implicitly convicts them of denying the presence of God in the Church.

---

61. *Spir.* 61. See also Gregory's report that, among Christians, some consider the Spirit to be merely an accident or activity (συμβεβηκός, ἐνέργεια) of God and not a substance (οὐσία) in its own right (*Or.* 31.6).

62. The boldness of Gregory's assertion has continued to confound interpreters. Although Lampe (s.v.), e.g., records "essentially" as the dominant meaning of the word in patristic literature, he hesitates to include this text as an example; instead he defines the word as "genuinely, truly." Basil's reserve lingers on.

63. Jn 14.26; 16.12.

Yet it must be admitted that Gregory's claim in *Oration* 41 that at Pentecost the Spirit came in its own Being (41.11) goes beyond what the text literally says: it is itself a spiritual interpretation based on a *prior* conviction of the Spirit's divinity. Gregory's argument in these sections serves only to show that it is possible, in a biblical framework, for the Spirit to be God, even though Scripture does not explicitly say that it is, and that Scripture points us to the Spirit's essential dwelling with the Church. However, it does not positively demonstrate that this is so. Having dispelled both logical and biblical objections to the Spirit's divinity, Gregory moves finally to the real ground of his doctrine in the sections that follow.

"A Truly Golden and Saving Chain": The Direct Proof of the Spirit's Divinity

Gregory has hinted several times in the course of *Oration* 31 that the proof of the Spirit's divinity—and thus the real basis of his Pneumatology—comes through the Spirit's direct indwelling in the Church. In the opening sections he mentioned that the Spirit makes him God, joins him to the Divinity (31.4), and makes him perfect (31.6). These passages echo similar, brief statements from other orations earlier in the same year. Twice he argues that those who deny the Spirit's divinity are in effect depriving him of his regeneration in baptism, since only God can deify us (33.17; 34.12). And in *Oration* 41, the Spirit is "always being partaken, not partaking; perfecting, not being perfected; sanctifying, not being sanctified; deifying, not being deified" (41.9); and it is "the author of spiritual regeneration (41.14). But it is late in *Oration* 31—after he has taken apart his opponents' arguments bit by bit and just five sections before the conclusion of the entire series—that Gregory comes to the heart of his Pneumatology and the hermeneutical key to his theology as a whole. In sections 28–29 Gregory gives "the more perfect reason" for the Spirit's divinity that he promised in section 12. He repeats his basic confession, that he will worship the Father, the Son, and the Holy Spirit each as God, and then states his position in the form of a rhetorical question:

> If [the Spirit] is not to be adored (προσκυνητόν), how can it deify me by baptism? And if it is adored, how is it not worshiped (σεπτόν)? And if it is worshiped, how is it not God (θεός)? The one is linked to the other, a truly golden and saving chain. (31.28)

The fundamental basis of the doctrine of the Holy Spirit, Gregory says, lies in the Christian life of deification, which begins in baptism. The Spirit is known to be God, and is therefore worshipped and adored, because it deifies Christians. Paradoxically, this means that the Spirit's divinity is recognized only from the Christian's actual experience of the divine life, as it is conveyed through the Holy Spirit in the Church.

The point appears in several other key texts as well. After his installation as archbishop by Theodosius, Gregory returns to this theme in the Epiphany sermons, aware that his candidates had only recently been catechized by the homoian bishop Demophilus. "If I may digress a little, how is [the Spirit] not God," he asks, "by whom you too are made God?" (39.17). Near the end of the oration *On Baptism* he stresses that "if I worshipped a creature or were baptized into a creature I would not be made divine," and that whoever severs the Divinity, denying that the Spirit is God, will not receive the gift and grace of baptism (40.42, 44).[64] And soon after his return to Cappadocia, he again emphasizes this experiential basis in the opening lines of his poem *On the Holy Spirit:* "Sing the praise of the Spirit! ... Let us bow in awe before the mighty Spirit, who is God in heaven, who to me is God, by whom I came to know God, and who in this world makes me God" (*Carm.* 1.1.3.1–4); later in the same poem he adds that whoever wants to understand the divinity of the Spirit must first draw the Spirit into his or her own heart (*Carm.* 1.1.3.13–14). As these texts all indicate, the ground of Gregory's praise of the Spirit and his confession that the Spirit is God lies in his own experience of the Spirit's making him God, so that the Spirit's work in the Christian life is the source of the doctrine of the Spirit.

Elsewhere in *Oration* 31 Gregory seems to argue for the Spirit's divinity on the basis of worship: that because Christians worship the Spirit it must be God. However, the direct proof from baptismal deification is the basis of this argument as well. When he comments that worshipping "in" the Spirit means that the Spirit gives worship to itself,[65] he issues the disclaimer that "the more perfect reason" for the Spirit's divinity is yet to come (31.12). And when he writes "I will not abandon the object of my adoration," in reply to Eunomian and Pneumatomachian arguments for separate numbering of the Father, Son, and Holy Spirit, he indicates that the worship of the Spirit itself requires theological justification, again referring to the argument to come (31.17).[66] The

---

64. On the Spirit's role in baptism, see also *Or.* 14.14.
65. The texts in question are Jn 4.24; Rom 8.25; and 1 Cor 14.15.
66. On the worship of the Spirit, see also *Or.* 31.14.

connection is most apparent in Gregory's next statement in section 28: "From the Spirit comes our regeneration (ἀναγέννησις, Jn 3.3–5), and from our regeneration our recreation (ἀνάπλασις, 2 Cor 5. 17), and from our recreation our acquaintance (ἐπίγνωσις) with the honor of the one who recreates us" (31.28). The Spirit's deifying work of regeneration and re-creation conveys to the Church that it is God and therefore deserving of worship; so that the source of the adoration of the Spirit and the so-called liturgical argument for the Spirit's divinity is again the Spirit's work of divinization.

We have now arrived at the soteriological heart of Gregory's Pneumatology: the knowledge of the Holy Spirit derives directly from the Spirit's saving work of divinization. While commentators have long noted that Gregory's soteriology plays an important role in his Pneumatology, the nature, centrality, and implications of that role have not been fully appreciated. R. P. C. Hanson briefly observes that Gregory makes "the religious experience of the Church and the Christian individual" the necessary context for the interpretation of the Spirit's divinity in Scripture, and he notes that Gregory's doctrine is much more satisfactory in this regard than Basil's appeal merely to extrabiblical tradition and Gregory of Nyssa's lack of any such notion.[67] But it is not clear what Hanson means by religious experience; he makes no mention of baptism or deification, and his earlier remark that Gregory's Trinitarian doctrine does not differ from Basil's in any matter of real importance suggests that he is not aware of the full extent of Gregory's doctrine. Donald Winslow and Frederick Norris bring us closer by pointing to the Spirit's function of divinization and noting that divinization and baptism are crucial to Gregory's argument.[68] For Gregory, the Spirit's dwelling in the Church and in the lives of individual believers is indeed central, not only for the doctrine of the Spirit but also for the theological endeavor as a whole.

Gregory locates the deifying work of the Holy Spirit chiefly in baptism. As we observed in chapters 1 and 2, baptism is the primary and paradigmatic instance of purification and illumination, and of the redivinization that the believer receives through Christ; so too it is the definitive enactment of the divinizing work of the Holy Spirit. Gregory comments in the following section of *Oration* 31 that the Spirit "makes us its temple, it deifies us, it perfects us, so that it both precedes baptism and is sought for after baptism" (31.29). Here again, the divinization that occurs in baptism is symbolic of the Spirit's work before and after the rite: it is the seal of Christian conversion begun before baptism and the beginning of a lifelong process of transformation after it. As

---

67. Hanson, *Search for the Christian Doctrine of God*, pp. 782–783; see also pp. 778–779 on Basil.
68. Norris, *Faith Gives Fullness*, pp. 187, 209; Winslow, *Dynamics of Salvation*, pp. 127–134 and ff.

Winslow observes, each of the many terms and images that Gregory uses to describe baptism refers to the Spirit's work of divinization, and it is this central point that Gregory is most concerned to stress here.[69] Yet, as we have also noted, while baptism is the definitive beginning of the Christian life, absolving one of past sins and giving one the power to resist sin and the devil in the future, and although it is the ultimate divine gift and grace (40.4), it does not function as a purely mechanical act or an irrevocable guarantee of divinization and future salvation, for it produces and requires both real transformation and ongoing moral growth. Hence Gregory emphasizes that the divinization that begins in baptism must always be understood as the real transforming work of the Spirit in a Christian life, without which baptism loses its meaning.

As we have already noted, the divinizing work of the Holy Spirit is both similar to and different from that of Christ. Whereas Jesus' divinization of his own humanity and his defeat of sin and death is the principle of the divinization of others, the presence and work of the Holy Spirit through faith, baptism, and ongoing spiritual growth is the actual realization of Christ's divinization in the Church. This soteriological function of the Spirit is twofold. First, it appropriates in the lives of Christians the divinization that has occurred paradigmatically in Christ, bringing to actuality the salvation that Christ accomplished and made potentially available. Thus when Gregory distinguishes God as Creator and ruler from creatures, which are subject to God, he describes the Trinity as "the Source, Creator and Perfecter (αἴτιος, δημιουργός,[70] τελειοποιός[71]) of all that God does" (34.8). It is the Spirit's character and function to complete, to bring to realization in the Church and the world, the work of God the Father, which has been archetypically accomplished by the Son in the incarnation.[72] Near the end of *Oration* 31, Gregory dwells on the fact that the Spirit fills the universe with the divine Being and accomplishes all the works of God (31.29), above all the divinization of men and women.

The perfecting work of the Spirit has appeared to some interpreters as being oriented essentially toward the individual, as opposed to the Church or the entire human race. Winslow, for example, follows Vladimir Lossky in distinguishing between the work of the Son and that of the Spirit as applying to the universal and the particular, so that while Christ assumed human nature in general, and potentially saved humanity as a whole, the Spirit's work is focused

---

69. Winslow, *Dynamics of Salvation*, pp. 133–134.
70. See also *Or.* 33.17.
71. See also *Or.* 32.6.
72. See also *Or.* 41.9.

on the individual human "person."[73] While this approximates Gregory's view to some extent—Christ certainly assumed human nature in a universal way as the New Adam—it misses the central point of Gregory's Pneumatology and renders it more individualistic than it is.[74] Gregory does not understand the Spirit's work of divinization individualistically, nor is it necessary to hold a modern view of personhood in order to assert that the doctrine of the Spirit is based in Christian experience. This divinizing experience of the Holy Spirit belongs rather to the Church as a whole, more fundamentally than it does to particular individuals, even if one believes that the Church is a group of individuals who will someday give account for themselves to Christ as individuals. As the presence of God in the Christian life and the immediate cause of the knowledge of God in Christ, the Spirit is the means by which the Church, both corporately and as individual believers, comes to share in Christ's saving work.[75]

The work of the Spirit, then, is to bring Christians into participation in Christ, to make Christ's divinization real in them, and so to convey the knowledge of God in Christ. For it is by the Spirit alone that the Father is known and the Son glorified, Gregory notes in his oration *On Pentecost* (41.9). It is thus not accidental or inconsistent that he speaks of baptism primarily in terms of Christ in the Epiphany orations—the first two of which are dedicated to Christological feasts—whereas in the latter sections of *Oration* 31 he speaks of it primarily in terms of the Spirit, since it is Christ's divinization that the Spirit confers in baptism. Likewise, in his first oration *On Easter*, he prays that the risen Christ would renew him by his own Spirit (1.2). For Gregory, the Spirit's role in revealing Christ can be seen clearly in Christ's earthly career: the Spirit deifies Christ's flesh in the incarnation (38.13), and at Christ's baptism it bears witness to his divinity, who is of the same divine nature as The Spirit (39.16). When he returns to the witness of Scripture at the end of *Oration* 31, Gregory emphasizes the Spirit's constant cooperation with Christ in carrying out God's creative and redemptive work (31.29).[76]

The second distinctive aspect of the Spirit's saving work is what we might call quasi-subjective. Unlike the doctrine of the Son, in which Christ's identity

---

73. Winslow, *Dynamics of Salvation*, p. 129 and n3; Lossky, "Redemption and Deification," p. 55. The definition of "person" in this context is Lossky's.

74. Winslow (*Dynamics of Salvation*, p. 131) points to Gregory's use of the first-person singular and describes baptism as "that most 'individual' and 'personal' of Christian rites."

75. In *Ep.* 101.38, e.g., Gregory argues that he (and by implication every Christian) contains "soul, reason, mind, and the Holy Spirit as well."

76. A point made earlier in *Or.* 41: According to Scripture, "the Spirit works together (συνδημιουργεῖ) with the Son in both creation and the resurrection" (41.14), accompanying Christ as his equal (41.11), just as the Son never lacks the Spirit in the eternal divine life (41.9). See also 21.7.

is the basis of his saving work and the central meaning of the Gospel message, the Spirit's identity and saving work are not so purely objective and external to the believer. The Spirit is distinguished chiefly by the fact that it is known here and now in the life of the Church. Although the Spirit always remains primarily the divine Other and an "object" of belief like the Son, because it is God and thus infinitely superior to all created things, nevertheless it is in a sense perceived subjectively—we might say experientially or existentially—in the Christian's own life and in the corporate life of the Church. While it is possible to understand the story of Christ's incarnation and passion without that understanding having any real claim on one's life (the demons' knowledge of Jesus in the synoptic gospels comes to mind), the economy of the Spirit does not admit to the same sort of detachment: to confess the divinity of the Spirit—and at the same time to confess Jesus as Lord[77]—is to acknowledge the ruling presence of God *in one's own life,* because this is precisely "where" the Spirit exists for the theologian. This experiential mode of knowing reflects the way in which the presence and work of the Spirit serve to activate the Gospel narrative in one's life and, in a sense, transposes the external narrative of God's creating, redeeming, and perfecting work into an internal narrative of God's work in oneself and in the contemporary Christian community. Through the Holy Spirit the story of Christ becomes the story of God's revealing himself in one's own new life, just as he revealed himself in the human life of Jesus—though of course Gregory distinguishes between the Son's divinization by nature and our divinization by the divine gift of the Spirit. The confession of the Spirit's divinity—and in many ways the whole enterprise of Christian theology—is thus the result of the Spirit's direct and immediate work in the life of the Church. Despite the common view of the dogmatic textbooks, the Nicene *homoousion* of the Spirit is the conclusion, not the premise, of Gregory's Pneumatology.[78]

The indwelling of the Holy Spirit is thus the epistemic principle of all knowledge of God in Christ. As we noted initially, the doctrine of the Spirit gives rise to the doctrine of the Son, as well as the process of Christian purification and the knowledge of the incomprehensible God altogether. It is therefore appropriate that the chapter on the Spirit stands at the center of this book. In the eternal life of God the being and the mission of the Son and the

---

77. See 1 Cor 12.3.

78. It is a nearly universal error of modern scholarship to regard fourth-century Nicene theology as based on, or essentially consisting in, the consubstantiality of the Trinity. See Michel René Barnes, "De Régnon Reconsidered," p. 56. For an example of this view with respect to Gregory, see Winslow, *Dynamics of Salvation,* pp. 75–76 (on the Son) and 121 (on the Spirit).

Spirit depend on their being generated by the Father and sent by the Father and the Son; whereas from the Christian's point of view it proceeds in reverse, with the Spirit enabling the confession of Christ, who gives access to the Father. While the effect of the Spirit is to divinize Christians, the content and structure of that divinization is to bring about the transforming knowledge of God in Christ, so that the recognition of the Spirit's divinity is the confession that the very means of the knowledge of God in Christ is itself God—that Christians see God from God in God (31.3). Through the particular work of the Spirit, God is the prime agent of the life of faith and the theological enterprise, just as he is the prime agent of creation, salvation, and eschatological consummation. The divinity of the Holy Spirit is therefore the ontic and epistemic basis of the entire doctrine of grace. The key difference between the soteriological dimension of Gregory's Christology and that of his Pneumatology, then, is not between universal and particular salvation, but between the ideal or potential salvation embodied in Christ and the actual salvation that the Holy Spirit realizes in the Christian life. The Spirit's epistemic priority in bringing the new life of Christ into the Church is fundamental to Gregory's doctrine as a whole, for it makes the theologian's experience of the divine life a necessary part of the Trinitarian confession. It is only by the Spirit, who purifies and illuminates the theologian, that God can be understood, interpreted, and heard (2.39).[79] The Spirit's revelation of God in Christ through baptism and the continuing life of the Church represents the order of theology in the deepest sense, the τάξις θεολογίας of all Christian doctrine. To understand and articulate this dynamic movement of spiritual theology is one of Gregory's major contributions to the principles of Trinitarian orthodoxy.

Spiritual Exegesis and the Rhetoric of Piety

The Spirit's divinization of Christians through baptism not only reveals the divinity of the Spirit and the Son, but it is the active ingredient in Gregory's understanding of spiritual exegesis, much as it was for Origen. Consequently, the theological experience of deification is Gregory's chief response to the charge that he has introduced an unscriptural God (τὸ ἄγραφον, 31.29).[80] As

---

79. τὸ Πνεῦμα ᾧ μόνῳ Θεὸς καὶ νοεῖται καὶ ἑρμηνεύεται καὶ ἀκούεται. Gregory invokes the epistemic priority of the Spirit in dramatic terms in the opening of his dogmatic poems (*Carm.* 1.1.1.1–24).

80. "This is what one can say, therefore, on the premise that 'it is not in the Bible' (τὸ ἄργαφον)," referring to the argument for baptismal deification in the preceding section. See *Or.* 43.67 for Gregory's discussion of spiritual exegesis as practiced by Basil.

he continues his efforts to persuade the bishops to confess the Spirit's full divinity, he writes in his farewell address to the council that we will one day be received in the heavenly mansions "not by the prosaic letter, but by the life-giving Spirit" (42.11). Although it has often escaped the notice of Gregorian scholars,[81] the interconnection between divinization, spiritual exegesis, and Christian doctrine represents the heart of Gregory's theological method and is therefore crucial for understanding the meaning and import of his message as a whole. Here again, Gregory proves himself a faithful disciple of Origen, who taught that one can interpret the Scriptures only by the inspiration and sanctification of the Holy Spirit, which also inspired their composition.[82] It is highly significant that Gregory first establishes the basis of his Pneumatology in baptismal deification before he returns to the question of the biblical witness to the Spirit. "*Now*," he says, referring to the initial argument, "a swarm of testimonies will burst upon you, from which it will be shown that the Divinity of the Spirit is very much written in Scripture (ἔγγραφος, the antidote to ἄγραφος), for those who are not exceedingly dull or strangers to the Spirit" (31.29). From the perspective of Church's faith-experience of the Holy Spirit, the Bible does indeed declare the Spirit's divinity—according to the Spirit, that is, not the letter. The exegesis of Scripture according to the Spirit means quite literally to interpret it on the basis of the presence and work of the Holy Spirit in the life of the Church and one's own life of purification and illumination. Now that he has clarified the nature of spiritual exegesis, Gregory gives a resume of biblical texts on the Holy Spirit that Hanson aptly calls "a densely packed and beautifully expressed cento of biblical allusions."[83] He first lists the roles that the Spirit plays in the career of Christ, which display its divine power: at Christ's birth, baptism, temptations, miracles, and ascension. Next he rehearses several titles of dignity, such as "the Spirit of God," "the Spirit of Christ," "the Lord," and "the Spirit of adoption, truth, and wisdom." Finally, he appeals to the Spirit's divine activity of creation, restoration, and regeneration: the Creator Spirit re-creates through baptism and resurrection, and the Spirit deifies Christians before, in, and after baptism. In sum, the Spirit does everything that God does (31.29).[84] The first group of texts seems to address the Pneumatomachian position—the Spirit who is associated so closely in the saving acts of Christ should certainly be regarded as divine, if Christ is—while

---

81. E.g., Plagnieux, *Saint Grégoire*, p. 51n39; Hanson, *Search for the Christian Doctrine of God*, p. 783.
82. Especially in *Princ.* 4.1–3. See also Gregory, *Or.* 14.35: the Scriptures are the instrument of the Spirit.
83. Hanson, "Basil's Doctrine of Tradition," p. 254; Haykin, *Spirit of God*, p. 175n37.
84. Similar lists can be found in *Ors.* 34.13–15 and 41.14.

the second and third groups address both Eunomians and Pneumatomachians.[85] In conclusion to this passage, Gregory offers a similar hermeneutical rule to the one he gave for the interpretation of Christ in *Orations* 29.18 and 30.1–2. Having just commented on the texts that show the Spirit's divinity, he adds that the lowlier expressions, which speak of the Spirit's mission (such a being sent, divided, and a grace),[86] refer to the Spirit's derivation from God the Father as First Cause (31.30).

It is significant that at this point Gregory appeals to the identity of the Spirit's work with the work of God—that is, the doctrine of identical operations among the persons of the Trinity—not as a fundamental argument for the Spirit's divinity but as an element of spiritual exegesis, based on baptismal deification. Despite the common scholarly view that Nicene theologians established the unity of the Trinity on the basis of the common activity of the three persons,[87] or the presence of this argument, for example, in Gregory of Nyssa,[88] Gregory of Nazianzus does not establish his Trinitarian doctrine in this way, because he recognizes that any argument from the identity of activities depends on a prior question—namely, how do we know that God does not do divine things through nondivine or semidivine intermediaries? In his argument for the divinity of the Son and the Spirit, particularly in the *Theological Orations*, Gregory squarely bases his position on the soteriological principles of divinization through the divine economy and the corresponding spiritual exegesis of Scripture. In this respect, it must be admitted that a different understanding of salvation, or even a different baptismal practice, could yield a different doctrinal understanding, for the two go hand in hand.[89] For this reason the argument from identical activities cannot suffice to establish the doctrine of the Trinity without the more primary soteriological approach that it assumes and represents. We might compare Gregory's approach to Ludwig Wittgenstein's argument that learning the language game of naming involves not simply learning what to call specific objects, or "ostensive definition," but more fundamentally learning the human activity of naming, which includes all sorts of mental, bodily, and social practices.[90] For Gregory it is the Christian's actual knowledge of God through the presence of the Holy Spirit within the life

---

85. Norris, *Faith Gives Fullness*, p. 209.
86. Jn 16.7; Hb 2.4; and 1 Cor 12.9, 30.
87. Famously put forth in 1892 by Théodore de Régnon and later taken up by many scholars. See Michel René Barnes, "De Régnon Reconsidered."
88. E.g., Ayres, *Nicaea*, pp. 348–349, 355–358. See further discussion below, p. 309 and n. 221.
89. Norris, *Faith Gives Fullness*, pp. 203, 208. See also Kopecek, *History of Neo-Arianism*, pp. 398–400.
90. Wittgenstein, *Philosophical Investigations*, §§ 1–43 and passim.

of the Church that enables him or her to identify the Spirit as God in the biblical text, and to practice theology at all. The Spirit's divinity, and consequently the knowledge of God in Christ, is thus shown directly in and through the lived process of Christian growth, and it is this fuller sense of knowing that is epistemically foundational. In Gregory's system, the Bible, we might say, necessarily connects with Christian theological experience (without losing its authority or canonical force), just as Christians undergo the sanctification that is attested in Scripture and typified definitively in the person of Christ. By integrating all of these themes, Gregory completes the rhetorical chiasmus that he began with the question of the witness of Scripture (31.1), and the reader's sense of expectation is fulfilled at last.

The soteriological and experiential foundation of Gregory's Pneumatology, now fully revealed at the end of *Oration* 31, sheds considerable light on the invective remarks that he makes in many passages, and on the literary structure of the *Theological Orations* as a unified composition. A typical sentiment is Gregory's quip that whoever does not recognize the Spirit's divinity in the Bible "must be extraordinarily dull and far from the Spirit!" (31.30). Whoever is not laughing at this point must remember that insulting one's opponent or one's audience was an expected component of Greek rhetoric since Homer, and provided an important element of levity and humor, much as violent gestures function in Renaissance and modern comedy. Such remarks appear at the beginning and the end of the fifth *Theological Oration* (31.1–3, 30), forming another *inclusio* around the main argument.[91] In addition to the traditional rhetorical form, in passages such as these Gregory is also pressing his sense of spiritual exegesis to its rhetorical conclusion: those who cannot perceive the divinity of the Spirit in Scripture, he says, are literally "far from the Spirit," in the sense that the shortcomings of their doctrine stem from a resistance to the Spirit's role in their piety. This may be a startling charge in the judgment of a modern historian, who would rightfully question the plausibility of Gregory's claim to know the spiritual state of his enemies. But that would be to read him too straightforwardly, ignoring both the conventions of fourth-century rhetoric as well as the standard mode of biblical prophecy.[92] While he is making a serious criticism of his opponents' spirituality,[93] he is even more pointedly drawing our attention to what he believes is the necessary correlation between

---

91. Gregory aims even more colorful remarks at those who deny the Spirit's divinity in *Or.* 41.6–8.
92. Norris, *Faith Gives Fullness*, p. 109.
93. See *Ors.* 23.12; 34.9: The Spirit will reward those who confess its divinity and punish those who deny it. See also 18.36; 19.2.

one's spiritual state and one's theological confession. Gregory believes with every fiber of his being that it is nothing short of blasphemy to refuse God the honor, worship, and theological confession that he deserves, regardless of whatever protestations of Christian virtue one might make. Nor is he claiming that the Eunomians or Pneumatomachians have no acquaintance with God whatsoever;[94] rather, he is charging them with the impiety of spurning God's gracious gift of himself, and with teaching a doctrine of God to others that denies God's saving work. For this reason, he believes that God's greatest revelation is not the giving of lesser spiritual gifts like healing, prophecy, or even Christian love, but the revelation of the Spirit's divinity, the knowledge of God dwelling among us (31.25–27). His primary concern is how Christians regard God, whether they worship the Spirit as God, or treats it as a fellow creature and servant of God, which is at least a grave insult if not outright idolatry. In one sense, Gregory means his invective quite literally: as Origen had taught already,[95] only a personal acquaintance with the triune God, and the transformation that this entails, can produce orthodox doctrine. In these final sections of *Oration* 31, Gregory has fulfilled his promise to demonstrate why his opponents' "love for the letter" is, in his view, "a cloak for impiety" (31.3). More than any lesser manifestations of the Spirit, what matters most is the basic attitude of reverence and worship in response to the gift of God's grace, without which all manner of Christian practices and virtues cannot make for "lawful striving (2 Tim 4.8)" (41.8).

Looking back on all five *Theological Orations*, the last sections of *Oration* 31 reveal most clearly the hermeneutic of piety that governs the series as a whole, and the approach that Gregory believes is required for all biblical interpretation and Christian doctrine. His accusations that his opponents are impious and far from the Spirit (31.3, 12, 30), subverting the faith and emptying the Christian mystery (31.23), echo similar phrases in the first *Theological Oration* (27.1–3; 28.2), thereby framing the entire series with the theme of spiritual exegesis and divinization.[96] At the conclusion of the series we return, then, to the topic of moral and spiritual preparation, with which it began in *Orations* 27–28. Through his exquisitely designed rhetorical structure, Gregory conveys the message that it is one's impiety above all that leads to doctrinal error and empties the great mystery of the faith (27.2; 31.23). For Gregory, the real threat

---

94. On the Eunomians, see *Or.* 27.2, 5; on the Pneumatomachians, 41.7–8; in general, 6.22; 23.3, 10, 13.

95. For example, Origen, *Princ.* 4.3.14: "But in all our speculations [concerning the Scriptures] let our understanding have sufficient coherence with the rule of piety" (trans. Greer).

96. See also *Or.* 33.17: whoever does not honor the Spirit does not participate in the Spirit.

to orthodox theology is an inattentiveness to the spiritual-theological dynamic of divinization, whereas (to state it positively) theological understanding always involves a growth in righteousness, as one is "made God" through the process of coming to know God. This emphasis on the matters of the Spirit in *Orations* 27–28 and 31 provides the definitive theological and rhetorical framework for understanding the doctrine of Christ presented in the central texts of the series, *Orations* 29–30, just as it is the Spirit's function generally to enable the theological enterprise, which is focused on Christ.

Gregory concludes the series in the same way that he began it—with the foundation of his doctrine now made more fully explicit—by pointing again to the root and goal of theological language in the Christian life in the Spirit. Now that he has labored long and hard in the *Theological Orations* to defend the faith in the Trinity, he takes his leave of the debate in the manner in which he started, ascending beyond all images and shadows and retaining only "the more pious conception (ἔννοια)" of God—that is, the knowledge that can be held only from a position of divinization and worship:

> taking the Holy Spirit as my guide, in its company and in partnership with, it safeguarding to the end the genuine illumination that I have received from it, as I strike out a path through the world and persuade all others to the best of my power to worship Father, Son, and Holy Spirit, the one Divinity and power. (31.33)

For Gregory the substance, the rhetorical force, and the linguistic boundaries of Christian doctrine constantly represent—and promote—the life of God in Jesus Christ that is given to the theologian by the indwelling of the Holy Spirit.

Having discussed and defended the infusion of divine life by the Holy Spirit, Gregory has thus placed the Trinity in full view, arguably for the first time since the debates of the 320s.[97] Given the sort of Pneumatological argumentation we have just examined, it is not surprising that the same theologian who championed the doctrine of the Spirit with such power and insight should also be one who presents the most comprehensive and penetrating doctrine of the Trinity in his age.[98] Gregory summarizes his larger program at the beginning of *Oration* 28, in a passage that he probably wrote later with the

---

97. Allowing for the earlier achievement of Origen, whose work builds on an explicitly Trinitarian program.

98. Note how the two go together textually in the fifth *Theological Oration*, which is, at the same time, a major discussion of the Trinity and one of the most important treatises on the Holy Spirit in Christian tradition.

whole series in mind. As he begins to make his doctrinal argument, he prays for the exposition of the Trinity that he is about to offer: "that the Father may approve of it, the Son may aid it, and the Holy Spirit may inspire it—or rather that it may be enlightened by the single Divinity's single illumination, unified in its distinction and distinct in its conjunction, which is a marvel" (28.1).

4

The Trinity

O Trinity, whose worshipper and undisguised herald I have long been privileged to be!

—*Oration* 23

Gregory Nazianzen stands out among Christian theologians of every generation for the clarity, the power, and the spiritual depth of his teaching on the Trinity. More than any theologian before him, he understands the Trinity to be the content, the structure, and the meaning of the Christian faith. Each of the topics that we have examined thus far—the purification and illumination of the theologian, the spiritual ascent to God through the doctrine of Christ, and the divinizing presence of the Holy Spirit in theology and exegesis—finds its proper place in the doctrine of the Trinity as a whole. The Trinity is the constant focus of Gregory's theological meditations and personal devotion, in both the orations and the poems,[1] and it represents for him the saving confession of all Christians. Yet we could go further and say that for Gregory the doctrine of the Trinity is not only the essential expression of the Christian life; in an important sense it is that life. In the same way that his Christology and Pneumatology reflect a concern for Christian salvation, so too the basic meaning

---

1. For an overview of the Trinity in Gregory's poetry, see Trisoglio, "La poesia della Trinita."

and rationale of his doctrine of the Trinity lies in the eschatological process of divinization, through which God is received and known. Despite the relative neglect of his theology in modern Western scholarship, Gregory has been honored with the title "the Theologian" since the fifth century for his definitive teaching on the Trinity as the basis and the meaning of the Christian life. At the heart of his many achievements, the doctrine of the Trinity is the centerpiece of his theological vision and the driving force of his personal and ecclesiastical life.

From the time of his first three orations, at Easter 362, Gregory defines the Christian faith in explicitly Trinitarian terms. Speaking as a newly ordained presbyter, he warns his hearers to avoid those who would lead them away from the sound faith "in Father, Son, and Holy Spirit, the one Divinity and power" (1.7). As we have already noted, a large part of Gregory's motivation for accepting the priestly office was a desire to lend his support to the cause of the Trinitarian faith in the region, in reaction to the homoian establishment of 359–360 and the schism in his father's church. In his second oration, devoted to the priesthood, he gives his first significant discussion of "the sovereign and blessed Trinity," which is, he says, the supreme subject of all Christian teaching (2.36). Rounding out the Easter series, he declares in his third oration that the basis of the Church's unity is a full Trinitarian confession, which regards the Son and the Spirit as being equal to the Father (3.6). Gregory repeatedly states that the doctrine of the Trinity represents the faith of the apostles and received Christian tradition.[2] In a closely related oration from 364, he makes the telling remark that his basic sense of the Trinity is "stable and unchanging" (6.11)—an observation that proved to be true of his work taken as a whole. While he will certainly elaborate it in greater depth and sophistication over the next twenty-five years, Gregory's "single definition of piety"—the basic confession that he claims for himself and enjoins on others—will continue to be "the worship of Father and Son and Holy Spirit, the one Divinity and power in the three" (22.12).[3]

As we noted in chapter 1, one of the most distinctive aspects of Gregory's doctrine—particularly for the interpreter accustomed to the divisions of modern systematic theology—is the way in which he moves so easily between simple doxology and fine conceptual work. While he may appear to be confusing two distinct types of theological discourse, in his view they belong together as a single, if admittedly complex, doctrinal approach, for reasons that are

---

2. Ors. 3.7; 6.22; 21.35; 34.6; 31.3, 5–6; 39.12; 43.67–68; Ep. 102.1; DVS 157.
3. See also Ors. 15.12; 11.6; 12.6; 13.4; 19.17; 20.5; 32.5, 21; 34.6; 36.10; 25.17–18; 40.41; 42.27.

central to his theological position.[4] Gregory is aware that more technical theological analysis is highly specialized in comparison with everyday Christian language, and therefore out of the reach of most believers; and he even complains about the risk that it poses of dissolving the faith into "sophistics" (25.17). Yet at the same time he is insistent that higher levels of theological understanding build upon the foundation of basic faith and that advanced theological language always serves to articulate that same faith. In his Constantinopolitan oration *On Moderation in Debate*, for example, he encourages the simple not to trouble themselves with the technical details of the contemporary debates, but to "leave sophisticated language to the more advanced." Yet, he continues, the simple and the advanced alike will be saved by the same faith and confession, which is based on the words of Scripture (32.21, 24–25).[5] While it is not strictly necessary for establishing the apostolic faith or promoting growth in divinization, more advanced modes of argument and analysis can be helpful tools for refining one's understanding of the faith, for defending it against philosophically motivated opponents, and for recommending the faith in cultural situations dominated by other worldviews and philosophical systems (as we saw in chaps. 1 and 2). In this chapter we will examine Gregory's comprehensive approach to the Trinity, from the level of simple confession to the refinements of technical argumentation. After identifying the key texts in question and establishing Gregory's methodological approach, we will examine the core of his doctrine, namely the eternal being and generation of the Father, Son, and Holy Spirit, organized around the priority of God the Father as the source and cause of the Trinity; the more refined expressions of that doctrine in public confessional formulas and further conceptual refinements; and finally its ultimate meaning in the theologian's participation in the Trinity. In the end, Gregory's mixture of the basic rule of faith, technical argumentation, and spiritual contemplation shows the Trinity to be as much the object of Christian worship as it is the subject of theological debate.

Gregory's teaching on the Trinity is scattered throughout his orations and poems, from numerous minor statements to lengthy, major discussions, leaving no obvious system with which to orient one's reading beyond the complex rhetorical structure of the works themselves. Not only are there many

---

4. The significance of Gregory's integrative approach has often been missed by modern theologians even among the Eastern Orthodox. Lossky, e.g., faults Gregory's work for being "more like contemplative meditations than doctrinal exposition"—as if they could be so clearly distinguished. *Vision of God*, p. 89. From the Western church, Prestige characterizes Gregory as merely an "inspired popularizer," with the same sort of opposition in mind. *God in Patristic Thought*, p. 234.

5. See also *Ors.* 11.6; 22.12; 33.15; 21.37; 34.6, 9; 31.17; 25.8, 17; 26.19; 42.3; 43.30.

texts to study and catalog, but the rhetorical and polemical contexts of each oration can vary considerably. The most outstanding example in both respects is the famous *Theological Orations*. Although they are often treated as the central reservoir of Gregory's doctrinal exposition, they are chiefly defensive in character, as we have already noted, consisting mainly of negative argumentation in response to Eunomian and Pneumatomachian objections. While they are key witnesses to Gregory's thought on many points, the *Theological Orations* must be interpreted carefully within their rhetorical and polemical contexts and in concert with other texts that indicate Gregory's doctrine in clearer, more positive terms. The typically narrow reading of Gregory in modern scholarship can be attributed in large measure to an overreliance on the *Theological Orations*,[6] and, to a lesser extent, to the fact that three of the four most important texts on the Trinity in Gregory's corpus have only recently been translated into English.[7] Before we examine Gregory's doctrine in detail, it will therefore be helpful first to give an overview of the texts.[8]

Most of Gregory's extensive treatment of the Trinity occurs during his short time in Constantinople from 379 to 381—a fact that indicates just how much the intense demands of his office drew out his best theological work. Among the early orations there are effectively two important passages, both from the initial series of sermons that he gave in order to repair his father's orthodoxy. When Gregory the Elder signed the homoian creed of Rimini-Constantinople, causing a schism with the local monks, Gregory delivered *Orations* 1–3, and later *Oration* 6, in order to signal that the pastoral leadership of Nazianzus, now under his surrogate command, remained firmly based on the Trinitarian faith. Along with terse, formulaic definitions (1.7 and 3.6), Gregory gives a longer, fairly important doctrinal statement in *Oration* 2.36–38, a passage that is remarkably balanced and comprehensive among his early works. In *Oration* 6, the *First Oration on Peace*, Gregory concentrates on lobbying for peace and harmony among the disconnected local groups. In order to strengthen his case, he argues for unity among Christians on the basis of the unity of the Trinity, thus engaging a key point of the monks' own confession and introducing a type of social-Trinitarian argumentation to which he will return twice more.[9] Compared to the compre-

---

6. This holds for the vast majority of twentieth-century scholarship, from Holl's 1904 *Amphilochius* to Markschies' 2000 "Gibt es eine einheitliche 'kappadozische Trinitätstheologie'?"

7. Specifically, *Ors.* 20, 23, and 25 by Vinson; *Or.* 20 by Daley. I consider the fourth text to be the *Theological Orations* as a set.

8. For a more comprehensive narrative of this period, see the introduction. I will focus here only on the texts on the Trinity.

9. In *Ors.* 22 and 23. See also 32.

hensiveness of *Oration* 2.36–38, *Oration* 6 as a whole is heavily colored with the theme of unity, on account of its rhetorical urgency. At the end of the oration Gregory gives a dense and somewhat formal statement of the Trinity, which stands out as the only time that he uses οὐσία language in reference to the Trinity before 379 (6.22).[10] Both texts show a sophistication that might seem to suggest later editing; however, Gregory has at this point been collaborating with Basil for several years, and the passages are not beyond the scope of doctrinal discussion in the early 360s. Between 364 and 379 Gregory makes only brief, minor references to the Trinity, which are largely occupied with the imagery of light and the themes of worship and divine illumination.[11]

The order of Gregory's orations in Constantinople is difficult to establish with any precision. More significant than their order, however, are the polemical situation and rhetorical thrust of each piece, which are on the whole fairly evident. Among the Constantinopolitan orations there are several major texts that figure as primary statements of Gregory's doctrine of the Trinity (namely, 20.5–12; 32.5; 23.6–12; 34.8–15; 41.7–9; several passages in the *Theological Orations* [28.1; the bulk of 29–31]; 25.15–19; certain sections of the Epiphany series [38.7–9, 13–15; 39.11–12; 40.34, 41–45]; and 42.14–18). In between these texts are important, minor statements of a more formulaic nature, which we will consider in due course.

As soon as he arrived in the capital, Gregory set about trying to consolidate the various Trinitarian figures and groups—many of whom were separated by the ongoing Antiochene schism—into a single, allied community,[12] while at the same time taking note of the incumbent homoian presence in the city. In *Oration* 20 he announces his Trinitarian doctrine in a comprehensive, detailed discussion. After giving a formulaic opening confession, which is designed to be easily recognizable and broadly conciliatory (20.5), he quotes and expands on his earlier treatment (2.38) in a passage that ranks among his four most significant doctrinal statements (20.6–12). He then speaks directly to the Antiochene schism in *Oration* 22, the *Second Oration on Peace*. Here he offers two brief definitions of the Trinity and a list of heresies against which the true faith is defined (22.12, 14), and he expresses his fervent hope that the rival

---

10. See also *Or.* 6.4, 11–13.

11. See esp. *Ors.* 7.18; 8.23; 11.6; 12.1, 6; 13.4; 16.9; 17.8; 18.16; 19.17.

12. What these groups seem to have shared in common was a commitment to (or some inclination toward) the full divinity of Christ, and in some cases the divinity of the Spirit, and/or the single Divinity of the Father, Son, and Holy Spirit, and/or the divine unity among the three persons, as well as an opposition to (or a growing disaffection with) the homoian regime of Valens and Bishop Demophilus. The extent to which they identified their faith with Nicaea is much less clear at this point.

factions will find common ground in the confession that he has laid out. Toward the end of 379, as hostilities among Nicene groups were increasing, he delivered another sizable oration on peace, order, and discipline in theological speech (*Or.* 32), in which he gives two further basic statements in a somewhat creedal form (32.5, 21).[13]

In the spring of 380 Gregory's pastoral situation shifted, as tensions with homoian and heterousian groups increased following Theodosius' February decree in support of a strong Trinitarian confession.[14] After the violent disruption of his Easter services and an attempt on his life, Gregory now began to engage the Homoians and Heterousians directly (33.15), while still working for the consolidation of different Trinitarian parties (23.3). In *Oration* 33 he provides another broad, formulaic definition of the Trinity and a list of heresies, against those who deny the divinity of the Son and/or the Spirit (33.16–17). In *Oration* 23, the *Third Oration on Peace*, he then gives the second of his four major doctrinal statements (23.6–12).[15] At this point Gregory combines each of the different challenges that he faces into a unified theological and ecclesiastical project. Reconciling the fractious pro-Nicenes (especially the Antiochenes; 23.3–5), completing the faith of the Pneumatomachians (some of whom were Antiochene-affiliated), and converting or expelling the anti-Nicenes all demanded the clarification, proclamation, and defense of the full doctrine of the Trinity.

With the arrival of his new Egyptian contingent, Gregory increased his attempts to unify the pro-Nicenes. In the course of narrating Athanasius' labors against the Arians, he gives two brief doctrinal statements, with reference to Athanasius' *Letter to Jovian* (21.13; 33), as well as a recognition of the policy on equivocal theological terms adopted at the Synod of Alexandria in 362 (21.35). In the closely related *Oration* 34, also addressed to the Egyptians, he gives another important, comprehensive discussion, which again has each of the respective groups in mind (34.8–15). *Oration* 41 *On Pentecost* then focuses on the conflicts over the divinity of the Holy Spirit in Gregory's own congregation, presenting another dense treatment of the Trinity (41.7–9). *Oration* 41 represents Gregory's final effort to win over his Pneumatomachian colleagues

---

13. Between *Ors.* 22 and 32 Gregory briefly mentions the ancient doctrine of the Trinity in his panegyric on Cyprian (24.13).

14. *Cunctos populos* (*C. Th.* 16.1.2), issued from Thessalonica and addressed to the people of Constantinople, defines the catholic faith as that confessed by Damasus of Rome and Peter of Alexandria, and as "the single Divinity of the Father, the Son, and the Holy Spirit, under the concept of equal majesty and of the Holy Trinity." The decree does not mention Nicaea.

15. Thus *Or.* 23 marks a shift from 6, 22, and 32 toward more directly anti-homoian and anti-heterousian polemic.

by persuasion and brotherly argument; from now on he adopts a more aggressive, polemical approach.

It is at this point that Gregory delivers his famous *Theological Orations*. While they corroborate the doctrine that he advances elsewhere, their unique rhetorical and polemical character has often made it difficult, and in some cases positively misleading, to interpret them apart from other, clearer texts. When read in concert with other orations, they represent the third of his four major works on the Trinity (in 28.1 and most of 29–31). Gregory's fourth and most important major discussion of the Trinity comes in the late summer of 380, in *Oration* 25, his sermon in praise of the Alexandrian theologian Maximus. At the heart of the oration Gregory commissions Maximus to teach the true faith, which he outlines in a brief creedal statement followed by several pages of detailed commentary that ranges from technical matters of Trinitarian logic to the ascetical and rhetorical dimensions of right doctrine (25.15–19), thus matching *Oration* 20 and the *Theological Orations* in breadth of subject matter. In these last two major texts, delivered within a month or two of one another, Gregory has reached the summit of his public teaching on the Trinity.

In December of 380 Gregory's magisterial theological achievement was matched by his elevation to the see of Constantinople. In light of the new ecclesiastical situation, the cause of Nicene unification receded for the time being, only to explode again at the council in the following summer. In his final set of orations in the capital, delivered before the emperor over the winter of 380–381, Gregory reiterates the doctrine that he has proclaimed thus far and continues his attempt to convert the Homoians, many of whom are now in his cathedral congregation. In *Oration* 36 he speaks triumphantly of the restoration of the orthodox faith at the heart of the empire (36.1–2), which he briefly defines here (36.10) and in the following oration, along with an appeal for the reform of unjust Roman marriage laws (37.5, 18, 22). The great triptych of orations from Christmas-Epiphany 380–381 offers a lengthy mystagogical catechesis for the baptismal candidates, which contains a number of important passages on the Trinity (38.7–9, 13–15; 39.11–12; 40.34, 41–45). With the handful of major texts that he has now assembled, Gregory has essentially concluded his constructive theological work in the capital. As we have already examined in detail, he labored assiduously for the adoption of the full Trinitarian faith at the Council of Constantinople the following summer, only to be frustrated by the rapid decomposition of the proceedings. In his final speech to the council, he gives a further exposition of the faith in by now standard terms (42.14–18). Early in his retirement to Cappadocia, Gregory finally writes a versified synopsis of the doctrine that he has established in Constantinople, in the *Poemata Arcana* (esp. *Carm.* 1.1.1–3), and in *Oration* 45 he reprints much of the text that he had delivered in *Oration* 38.

Gregory's many discussions of the Trinity—from the lengthy, major texts to the brief, minor references—exhibit a common structure that can most easily be described as a narrative doctrinal statement involving a subject and a predicate. First he identifies the Father, Son, and Holy Spirit as distinct entities, after which he asserts, as a kind of predicate, their shared divine nature and their unity with one another.[16] In this way Gregory presents his core doctrine, confessing both the distinctions and the unity among the Father, Son, and Holy Spirit on the basis of their relations of origin. As a secondary type of argumentation, he occasionally makes certain conceptual refinements that are implied in or derivative of his core doctrine, usually as a defensive measure against critics,[17] and he offers a number of brief formulas that summarize his core teaching and signal his position within the wider debates.[18] It will be our task in this chapter to examine each of these key elements, in order to discern the overall meaning and purpose of Gregory's doctrine of the Trinity.

Theology of the Divine Economy

Gregory's basic approach to the Trinity can be understood most easily in terms of what he calls "theology" and the divine "economy." As we have seen in the previous two chapters, the central focus of Gregory's Christology and Pneumatology is to perceive, to confess, and as far as possible to understand the implications of the divinity of the Son and the Spirit as the basis and structure of the Christian life. Through faith one comes to recognize that Jesus Christ and the Holy Spirit, who have been met in the economy of salvation, share fully in the Divinity of God the Father. This act of confessing the divinity of the Father, Son, and Holy Spirit in the economy of salvation Gregory typically calls "theology" (θεολογία). The doctrine of the Trinity builds on the "theology" of the Son and the Spirit, not simply in the obvious sense that it combines Father, Son, and Spirit to make a unity of three persons, but in that it expresses the meaning that

---

16. See, e.g., *Or.* 32.5: "We must recognize one God, the Father, without source and unbegotten, and one Son, begotten of the Father, and one Spirit, which takes its existence from the Father and which, while yielding unbegottenness to the Father and begetting to the Son, is however in all other respects equal to them in nature, dignity, glory, and honor."

17. For a clear example of this movement from core doctrine to refined analysis, see *Or.* 25.15–18.

18. The first example being *Or.* 1.7: We must preserve "the sound faith in the Father, the Son, and the Holy Spirit, the one power and Divinity." Gregory repeats the same formulation, with slight variation, in many other passages.

the divine economy has possessed all along. Contrary to the assumptions of much modern patristic scholarship, Gregory's doctrine of the Trinity is not fundamentally about the metaphysics of consubstantiality,[19] nor is it a quasi-mathematical solution to the problem of how three things can be one, as it is often conceived in popular imagination. Rather, it represents the theology of the divine economy in the deepest sense—not as a synthesis of the doctrines of God, Christ, and the Holy Spirit made after they are complete, as it were, but as the fuller clarification, deepening, and extending of the meaning of the divine economy.

Gregory commonly uses the ancient Christian term οἰκονομία and its cognates to speak of God's relations with the created order.[20] As formulated by Irenaeus[21] and especially the Alexandrian tradition,[22] "economy" refers in Gregory's work to God's purposeful governance, administration, and arrangement of the affairs of the created order, both in general and in particular, from creation to the final consummation, as it is definitively represented in the biblical revelation.[23] While this broad, providential sense of divine governance is much more common in Gregory's work, in a few passages οἰκονομία refers specifically to the incarnation, which is God's primary act of governing the affairs of creation, by restoring the process of growth toward *theosis*.[24] (Gregory

---

19. See chap. 3, n79.

20. In ancient Greek οἰκονομία refers to the administration of a household or any purposeful activity, and in Hellenistic rhetorical theory it came to signify the proper arrangement of a discourse. The New Testament writers used οἰκονομία to refer to God's plan of salvation, which has its focus in Jesus Christ (Eph 1.10; 3.9; 1 Tim 1.4), as well as the commission of God's grace given to Paul and his stewardship of the mysteries of God (1 Cor 4.1–2; 9.17; Eph 3.2; and Col 1.25); the bishop's role as God's steward (Ti 1.7); the role of all Christians as stewards of God's grace (1 Pt 4.10); literal household management (Lk 12.42; 16.2–4; Gal 4.2); and the city treasurer (Rom 16.23). On the history of Christian usage of the term, see Michel René Barnes, "Oeconomia"; Grillmeier, *Christ in Christian Tradition*, pp. 118–120; and Lampe (s.v.).

21. Among sporadic instances in other second-century Christian authors (e.g., Ignatius of Antioch, *Ep. Eph.* 18.120; Justin Martyr, *Dial.* 87.5; 120.1), it was Irenaeus who gave the concept of God's economy of salvation a central place in Christian theology (e.g., *Adv. haer.* 1.10.1–3). Although Hippolytus and Tertullian spoke of the divine economy as the relationships between the Father, Son, and Spirit against modalistic conceptions of God (see *Adv. Noet.* 3–14; *Prax.* 2), this intra-Trinitarian meaning did not carry forward into later patristic usage.

22. Clement, *Strom.* 1.11, 19; 6.6; Origen, *Princ.* 3.1.14; 4.2.4, 9; *Cels.* 1.66; 2.9, 26; 4.7; *Comm. Jn.* 10.3; 13.32; *Comm. Mt.* 12.43; Dionysius, in Eusebius, *HE* 7.11.12; Eusebius, *Mart. Palest.* 11; *V. Const.* 1.18; *Ev. theo.* 1.7; *HE* 1.1.7; and Athanasius, *Ar.* 1.59; 2.11; *Ep. Aeg. Lib.* 2; *Ep. Serap.* 2.7. On the influence of Irenaeus, Clement, and Origen on Gregory's understanding of οἰκονομία, see Kovacs, "Divine Pedagogy"; Trigg, "God's Marvelous Oikonomia"; "Knowing God."

23. *Ors.* 2.24, 106; 7.4, 24; 14.9; 17.9 (cf. 38.11); 18.20; 24.13 (cf. 6.8); 32.25, 30; 21.18; 41.5; 30.11, 19; 25.5; 38.11 (= 45.7; cf. 17.9); 39.15; 42.1, 27; 43.25; 45.7, 12, 22, 23; *Ep.* 8.3; 139.1; 101.59; 204.8; 215.1, 2; 221.2; 222.6; 238.1. It is interesting that the term occurs infrequently in the *Theological Orations*; although when it does it is theologically significant, as in Gregory's discussion of the divine names in 30.19.

24. Eleven out of forty-seven total references to God's ordering of created affairs: *Ors.* 19.12; 41.11; 29.18; 30.19; 38.8 (= 45.4); 38.14 (= 45.26); 45.22; *Ep.* 110.59; 202.10. Gregory's usage is roughly reflected in the other two Cappadocians as well: see Basil, *Eun.* 2.3; 3.7; *Spir.* 37; 2.3; *Ep.* 5.2; 81; 101; 188; 193; 210.3; 214.1; 236.7; Gregory of Nyssa, *Eun.* 5, 8; *Ablab.*; and throughout the *Or. cat.* Of the three, Gregory of Nyssa uses the term most frequently.

uses the term just as frequently to refer to the human administration of affairs, primarily various kinds of pastoral and theological administration, which we will discuss in chap. 5.[25]) In the most general terms, then, οἰκονομία denotes God's active, ordering, and purposeful lordship over creation. The concept of the divine economy not only conveys the idea that God's presence in and activity toward creation are deliberate, beneficent, and ordered; it also indicates the divine agency in these acts and events, that they are the works of *God* and can only be properly understood as such. The notion of the divine economy therefore implicitly contains a sense of what Gregory calls "theology," without which it could not be considered God's economy at all.

As important as the divine economy is in Gregory's thought, he devotes even more attention to "theology." Among the three Cappadocians, it is Gregory who makes theology his central concern. Although he refers to the divine economy no more than Basil and Gregory of Nyssa, he speaks of θεολογία and its cognates far more than they do. In the most general sense, "theology" simply means any discussion or teaching about God,[26] and a "theologian" is someone who knows and possibly also teaches about God, in any religious tradition.[27] In a more focused sense, theology is the confession of the divinity of the Son and the Spirit, or of the entire Trinity, as they are revealed in the divine economy.[28] At the beginning of his episcopal career Gregory writes that to confess in clear and certain terms that the Holy Spirit is "God," and thus to proclaim "the complete Divinity" in the Father, Son, and Spirit, is "a most perfect exposition of theology" (12.6).[29] Likewise, when he chides Basil for his insufficient doctrine of the Spirit, he says that, according to the report of his teaching by certain monks, Basil "theologized concerning the Father and the Son, but slurred over the Spirit" (*Ep.* 58.7). Following the preparatory doctrine of pu-

---

25. Forty-two human compared to forty-seven divine references: *Ors.* 2.29, 35, 52; 3.7; 4.18; 6.8; 14.24; 16.18, 19; 18.1, 3, 20, 21, 36; 21.10, 34, 35; 34.3, 4; 41.6; 31.25; 26.11; 39.14; 40.18, 44; 42.13, 14, 24; 43.39, 68 (twice), 69, 81; 44.9; *Ep.* 58.11, 12 (thrice), 14; 79.79; 162.4; *Carm.* 1.1.26.17. Once he even speaks of the economy exercised by animals: 28.23.

26. *Ors.* 2.37; 27.3; 28.1f.; 31.3; 43.66.

27. Thus there are both good and bad theologies and theologians. Among the good: Jeremiah (*Or.* 31.16), Paul (34.15), and even Christ himself (31.8); orthodox teachers of the Church, including Athanasius (21.10), Basil (43.81), and Gregory (20.12; 22.9); or anyone who seeks to know God better (20.5, 12; 27.7; 28.1; 30.17). Among the bad: pagan figures like Orpheus, the poets who depict the Greek pantheon (4.115, 117, 121; 5.31; 31.16; 25.15), Plato (28.4), or other pagan teachers (27.6; 31.5); Gregory's opponents, esp. the Eunomians and Pneumatomachians (23.3; 21.12; 34.12; 28.2, 7; 29.10; 40.42; *Ep.* 102.7); and those who promote themselves to pastoral office without the proper theological and spiritual formation (20.1; 27.4, 9; 2 passim). Gregory occasionally expresses the same idea with the phrases "philosophizing about God" or simply "knowing God."

28. *Ors.* 12.6; 18.17; 23.3, 12; 34.11, 15; 25.17; 43.67–69; *Ep.* 58.7–8, 14.

29. For theology as the confession of the divinity of the Son, see *Or.* 43.69; and for the Spirit, 23.12; 25.15.

rification in the first *Theological Oration,* the entirety of the doctrine of God, the Son, the Holy Spirit, and the Trinity as a whole, which Gregory covers in the last four *Theological Orations,* constitutes "theology" (28.1).[30]

In the most important sense, then, "theology" properly concerns the Trinity. Gregory's most succinct definition of the nature of theology—and possibly the most complete and nuanced definition of the Trinity in all of patristic literature—comes in his opening confessional statement in the fifth *Theological Oration:*

> "There was the true light, which enlightens everyone who comes into the world" (Jn 1.9)—the Father. "There was the true light, which enlightens everyone who comes into the world"—the Son. "There was the true light, which enlightens everyone who comes into the world"—the other Paraclete (Jn 14.16, 26). "Was" and "was" and "was," but one thing was (ἓν ἦν); "light" and "light" and "light," but one light and one God. This is what David imagined long ago when he said, "In your light we shall see light" (Ps 36[35].10). And now we have both seen and proclaimed the concise and simple theology (σύντομος καὶ ἀπέριττος θεολογία) of the Trinity: out of light (the Father) we comprehend light (the Son) in light (the Spirit). (31.3)

As he sets out to defend the divinity of the Holy Spirit, Gregory first proclaims his faith in the Trinity as a whole. In its most basic sense, "theology" is the knowledge of the Divinity of the Father in the person of the divine Son by the indwelling of the Holy Spirit, who is also divine. Similarly, in *Oration* 40 he enjoins the baptismal candidates, "In the Lord's light see light: in the Spirit of God be enlightened by the Son—the threefold and undivided light" (40.34).[31] "Theology" is therefore the knowledge of the Trinity as it is revealed within the divine economy. When one comes to know God, one enters into God's own triune life, knowing the Divinity that comes from the Father in the face of Jesus Christ by the power of the Holy Spirit, who fully share that Divinity, as God come from God in God. In this regard, theology is for Gregory virtually synonymous with contemplation, illumination, and the vision of God,[32] being the knowledge of God in the most comprehensive sense. And as

---

30. "Let us now move on to the discourses on theology (οἱ τῆς θεολογίας λόγοι), invoking as the head of our doctrine (λόγος) the Father and the Son and the Holy Spirit, which are the subject of our doctrine (περὶ ὧν ὁ λόγος)."
31. See also *Or.* 34.13.
32. *Ors.* 7.17; 12.6; 21.10; 28.2; 30.17; 31.33; 26.5; 43.67, 81.

in *Oration* 31.3, this contemplative sense of theology includes the articulation and defense of Trinitarian doctrine against the errors of its detractors, whether in simple or more refined, philosophical terms.[33]

While "theology" refers to the knowledge of God in a wide variety of economic senses, Gregory occasionally distinguishes it from other subjects, most famously the divine economy itself.[34] The passage most often cited to illustrate this distinction comes in *Oration* 38 *On the Theophany*. After briefly discussing God's eternal existence, Gregory stops short in order to return to his main subject, which is the birth of Christ: "This is all I should say about God for now,... for my present subject is not theology but the economy" (38.8 = 45.4). Alongside this text one might place Gregory's discussion of the divine names at the end of the fourth *Theological Oration*. Here he distinguishes between the special names for God's being, such as "the One who is" and "God"; names that are common to the Divinity, i.e., "Father," "Son," and "Holy Spirit"; names that refer to God's power, such as "Almighty" and "Lord Sabaoth"; those which refer to God's economy before the incarnation, such as "God of Abraham, Isaac and Jacob"; and those which refer to God's economy in the incarnation, such as "Christ," "Lamb," and "High Priest" (30.17–21). This scheme could be taken to mean that the noneconomic names represent theology proper, by contrast with the economic names; however, such a distinction is not necessary for the interpretation of the passage.

Although the inclusive, economic sense of theology is overwhelmingly dominant in Gregory's corpus, in both frequency and weight of meaning, it has long been the consensus of Eastern and Western interpreters, on the basis of these few passages, that theology is defined chiefly in contrast with the divine economy. According to the conventional opinion, theology concerns God in himself, God's being and intra-Trinitarian relations, whereas economy refers to God's works in creation. The distinction or division between theology and the economy is ubiquitous in recent patristic scholarship, and has had a devastating effect on the study of Gregory's doctrine of the Trinity. It is indicative of the seminal work of Karl Holl—and consequently much twentieth-century scholarship on Cappadocian Trinitarian theology—that he both misunderstands and criticizes Gregory for his approach to Christian theology. Holl first concludes that Gregory "deduces the threeness of the consubstantial,

---

33. *Ors*. 12.6; 18.17; 23.3, 6–11; 34.11, 15; 27.3, 6; 28.1–3; 31.3, 8, 26–27; 25.8, 17; 43.66–69.

34. In Gregory's orations, theology is distinguished from the general remembrance and praise of God (*Or*. 27.4); the divine economy (38.8 = 45.4); Christian doctrines other than the divinity of the Trinity (26.5); the fleshly witness to Christ in certain evangelists, as opposed to John, who pays more attention to theology (43.69); and possibly, by implication, economic subjects of disputation (27.10; this interpretation is highly debated).

divine hypostases directly from his religious experience (*Erfahrung*)" and "attempts to construct the Trinitarian faith from the experience (*Erlebnis*) of the subject," and then faults him (and Basil) for falling back into the doctrine of Origen[35]—as if Origen and the Cappadocians were German Romantic theologians or Idealist philosophers! In this fragmented perspective, the only alternatives seem to be either Romantic subjectivisim or a bare, logical analysis of technical terms and dogmatic formulas, devoid of theological substance— neither of which reflects Gregory's (or Origen's) work with any accuracy.[36]

This contrastive sense of theology and the divine economy that Gregory and other Greek fathers are supposed to have espoused in fact represents the view of Aristotle more than it does biblical or patristic doctrine. In the *Metaphysics* Aristotle describes the "theological philosophy" as the highest form of speculative thought. This "primary philosophy" concerns "Being as it is" and focuses on the unchanging causes of things, which are "separate" from the objects of direct experience.[37] In the same way, Gregory and other Christian writers are thought to have considered "theology" to be God's nature and Trinitarian relations (or the knowledge of them) apart from the divine economy, so that the relationship between the two is unclear and potentially ambiguous. However, already in Origen Christian "theology" denotes the understanding of God expressed by the Christian Gospel, revealed in the divine economy, and conveyed through the spiritual sense of the Scriptures. Speaking of Jesus' teaching as recorded in the gospels, Origen comments, "He revealed to his true disciples the nature of God and told them about his characteristics. We find traces of these in the Scriptures and make them the starting-points of our theology."[38] For Origen theology arises from and is the ultimate purpose of Christ's revelation in the divine economy, and he is happy to contrast the biblical teaching about God with that of Plato and the Greek poets.[39] To be

---

35. Holl, *Amphilochius*, pp. 164–165.

36. Among recent works, see Gallay's notes to *Ors.* 27–31 and 38–40 in the *Sources Chrétiennes* editions (esp. n2 on 38.8). McGuckin emphasizes the same distinction in Gregory's Constantinopolitan orations (*St. Gregory*, pp. 278, 283, 285–286, 295–297, 333, 337, 339), as does Behr (*Nicene Faith*, pp. 290–293, 347–348). A typical general statement is that of Studer (*Trinity and Incarnation*, p. 2): "The division between the doctrine of God and the doctrine of salvation worked out since the fourth century has proved to be extremely productive. It underlies the patristic syntheses, which then led to the scholastic summas. Accordingly, the modern history of dogma is largely determined by this distinction." See also Michel René Barnes, "Oeconomia," p. 826; cf. Rahner's well-known argument for the unity of the "economic" and the "immanent Trinity" in *The Trinity*.

37. *Metaph.* 6 (1026a7–33); see also 1 (983b29); 3 (1000a9); 10 (1071b27); Daley, *Gregory of Nazianzus*, p. 42.

38. *Cels.* 2.71 (trans. Chadwick), 121. In *Comm. Jn.* 2.34.205, Origen notes that the Son's eternal relation to the Father is revealed by the prophets as well as the apostles. On Origen's use of "theology," see Crouzel, "Θεολογία et mots de même racine chez Origène," pp. 83–90.

39. E.g., *Cels.* 6.18; 7.41.

sure, theology does concern the transcendent life of God, including the eternal relationship between the Father and the Son, but it is always based on God's revelation in the divine economy, and is regarded as the primary content of that revelation. Yet even in Origen a trace of the more abstract sense of theology can be found, since (in certain texts) God the Father stands farther removed from the cosmos and can only be revealed through the mediator-Logos. By insisting that the Word made flesh fully shares the divinity of the Father, and that the Holy Spirit is fully divine and present in the Church "in its substance" (41.11), Gregory and other pro-Nicenes emphasize God's presence and direct revelation in the divine economy more strongly than Origen did, thus showing theology to be even more unambiguously economic.

While Gregory strongly maintains God's transcendence of creation and of all categories of human knowledge,[40] as we have seen, he would be scandalized by the idea of separating the transcendent God from God as he is revealed in the divine economy. For Gregory, the eternal God who is revealed in the economy certainly existed "before" creation, infinitely exceeds creation, and is not himself dependent on creation in any way; nevertheless, the presence and work of God in creation is the presence and work—the economic revelation—*of the eternal God*. Not only is there no sense here that the transcendent God is potentially different from God as he is revealed in the divine economy, but this notion runs directly contrary to the very idea of the divine economy: that God has revealed himself as he really is—that we know the uncreated light of God in Christ through the Holy Spirit, even if in an attenuated form. As in Gregory's distinction between the Son's identity above and in the incarnation (29.18), the latter category includes the former (the incarnate Lord is one and the same Son of God) although the former does not necessarily include the latter (the identity of the eternal Son does not depend on becoming incarnate). In the rare instances when Gregory contrasts theology with the divine economy, he must therefore not be interpreted as saying that in the economy God is someone other than the eternal God; he is simply referring to the eternal God's presence and work in creation as distinct from God's being in eternity, which exists apart from creation as well as within it. Nor should the theology-economy distinction be taken to mean that God in himself, eternal and transcendent of creation, can be known apart from the divine economy; for Gregory there is no such thing as extra-economic theology—except in the sense of bad or false theology. Such an idea not only misrepresents his thought, but it

---

40. *Ors.* 20.8–11; 23.9–11; 34.8, 10; 29–31 passim; 25.15–18; 38.7; 40.42–43; 41.7; 42.15, 17. See also chap. 1.

makes the questionable assumption that any theologian exists outside the divine economy and has direct access to God. The distinction between theology and the divine economy, in other words, is not between two different modes of human knowing; theology and economy are not parallel or rival epistemological categories. The twentieth-century convention of distinguishing between "immanent" and "economic" modes of thinking about God and allowing that they might differ from one another is extremely misleading; it undermines the revelatory character of theology, and thus the very basis of Christian doctrine, in the fathers. Just as Gregory normally assumes Christ's humanity and focuses instead on his divine identity, so too he begins with the divine economy and directs his attention to the identity of the triune God revealed in it.

For Gregory, theology—that is, the doctrine of the Trinity—concerns the being and work of the eternal God, as God has revealed himself to be the meaning of the divine economy within the created order. Far from being a case of two disjointed or contrasting terms, Gregory's basic approach to the Trinity, and to Christian doctrine altogether, can best be defined as "the theology *of* the divine economy." In this regard, his doctrine directly reflects the biblical covenants and the ongoing life of the Church, and it fundamentally resists the idea that Christianity is an abstract, philosophical, or purely speculative metaphysical system. For Gregory the Christian life within the divine economy is thus always theological, and Christian theology is always economic.[41] When Gregory is regarded as "the Theologian" par excellence of the patristic period, his title is best understood in this sense: as the one who most clearly showed the theological meaning of the divine economy, by which God is truly known.

The Monarchy of God the Father

At the heart of Gregory's doctrine of the Trinity—as the theology of the divine economy—lies a central body of ideas that represents the core of his thinking. Stemming from this core doctrine, by implication and by extension, is a wide (and potentially endless) range of conceptual qualifications and refinements, which bear not only the nature of God per se, but also on how the knowledge of God pertains to our understanding of time, space, numbering, linguistic signification, and the limits of human knowing, as well as a number of summary

---

41. On this point, see also McGuckin, "Perceiving Light," p. 13; "Vision of God," pp. 147–148.

statements of a more formulaic nature. While both types of teaching run throughout his work, they are exhibited in the greatest concentration and detail in the Constantinopolitan period. Gregory's core doctrine, along with certain conceptual refinements, can be clearly seen in his most significant single doctrinal statement, *Oration* 25.15–18. At the climax of the oration Gregory gives a lucid, positive exposition of his Trinitarian doctrine in the form of a brief creedal statement, followed by several pages of detailed commentary. The first two sections bear quoting at length.[42] "Define our piety," Gregory tells Maximus, "by teaching the knowledge of:

One God, unbegotten, the Father; and
One begotten Lord, his Son,
    referred to as "God" (θεός) when he is mentioned separately, but "Lord" when he is named together with the Father—the first on account of the [divine] nature, the second on account of the monarchy; and
One Holy Spirit, who proceeds (προελθόν) or goes forth (προϊόν) from the Father, "God" (θεόν) to those who understand things properly—combated by the impious but understood by those who are above them, and even professed by those who are more spiritual;[43]
    Teach also that we must not make the Father subject to [another] source (ὑπὸ ἀρχήν), lest we posit a "first of the First," and thus overturn the [divine] existence;[44] nor should we say that the Son or the Holy Spirit is without source (ἄναρχος), lest we take away the Father's special characteristic (τὸ τοῦ Πατρὸς ἴδιον). For they are not without source—and yet in a sense they are without source, which is a paradox. They are not without source with respect

---

42. I have formatted this passage to highlight the creedal structure of the opening lines and to distinguish the various points of the elucidation that follows. It is difficult to render in English because, in Gregory's highly periodic, Asianic Greek style, the entire section is a long series of dependent clauses following on the opening sentence, "Define our piety, teaching...." Rather than convert them all into finite clauses, as Vinson does, I have tried to preserve more of the Greek syntax for the sake of rhetorical and theological clarity, as in Mossay's French translation.

43. Gregory refers here to the three groups he has recently addressed in his efforts to champion the divinity of the Spirit (*Or.* 41.6; see also 31.5): the Pneumatomachians, those who claim to believe in it but do not confess it publicly (including the late Basil), and those who, like Gregory, openly confess the divinity of the Spirit, and thus the Trinity as a whole.

44. ἵνα μὴ τοῦ πρώτου τι πρῶτον εἰσαγάγωμεν, ἐξ οὗ καὶ τὸ εἶναι πρώτῳ περιτραπήσεται.

to their cause (τῷ αἰτίῳ), for they are from God (ἐκ Θεοῦ) even if they are not subsequent to him in time (μετ' αὐτόν), just as light comes from the sun.[45] But they are without source with respect to time, since they are not subject to time.

And teach that we do not believe in three first principles, lest we espouse the polytheism of the Greeks; nor in a solitary (μία) principle, Jewish in its narrowness and somewhat grudging and ineffectual, either by saying that the Divinity absorbs itself (the view of those who say that the Son issues from the Father only to dissolve back into him again) or by casting down the natures [of the Son and Spirit] and making them foreign to Divinity (the view of our current experts)[46]—as though Divinity feared some rival opposition, or was able to produce nothing higher than creatures!

Teach that the Son is not unbegotten, for the Father is unique (εἷς ὁ Πατήρ); and that the Spirit is not Son, for the Only-Begotten is unique (εἷς ὁ Μονογενής), the result being that they each possess this divine quality of uniqueness (τὸ μοναδικόν), the one sonship (ἡ υἱότης) and the other procession (ἡ πρόοδος), which is different from sonship.

Rather, teach that the Father is truly a father—much more truly even than human fathers are—because he is a father uniquely and distinctively (μόνως, ἰδιοτρόπως), in a way different from corporeal beings; unique (μόνος), being without a mate; of one who is unique (μονοῦ), namely the Only-Begotten; only a father (μόνον), since he was not formerly a son; completely a father (ὅλον) and father of one who is complete (ὅλου), which is not clear with us;[47] and father from the beginning (ἀπ' ἀρχῆς), since he did not become a father at a later point in time (οὐ γὰρ ὕστερον).

Teach that the Son is truly a son, because he is a son alone, of one alone, absolutely, and only (μόνος καὶ μόνου καὶ μόνως καὶ μόνον), since he is not also a father; and completely a son, and of one who is complete, and from the beginning (καὶ ὅλον Υἱὸς καὶ ὅλου καὶ ἀπ' ἀρχῆς), having never come to be a son, since his Divinity

---

45. Gregory holds the ancient view that the sun emits light instantaneously, taking no time.

46. The Homoians, Eunomians, and Pneumatomachians, who claim that the Son and/or the Spirit are subordinate in nature to God the Father.

47. That is, fatherhood and sonship are not as clear among humans because human fathers are also sons, whereas in the Trinity fatherhood and sonship are perfectly clear because they are absolute.

is not due to a change of purpose, nor his divinization to moral progress (προκοπή), otherwise there would be a time when the one was not a father and the other was not a son.

Teach that the Holy Spirit is truly holy, because there is nothing else that is like it or holy in the same way. Its sanctification does not come by way of addition, but it is holiness itself (αὐτοαγιότης), It is neither more or less; it did not begin, nor will it end, in time.

In effect, common to Father, Son, and Holy Spirit is the fact that they were not created, as well as their Divinity. Common to the Son and Holy Spirit is the fact that they come from the Father. Uniquely characteristic (ἴδιον) of the Father is unbegottenness (ἡ ἀγεννησία); of the Son begottenness (ἡ γέννησις); and of the Spirit being sent (ἡ ἔκπεμψις). But if you seek after the manner [of the divine generation], what will you leave to those who are attested in Scripture as alone knowing each other and being known by each other,[48] or even to those of us who will later be illuminated from on high? (25.15–16)

In this dense and carefully wrought passage, Gregory begins his doctrinal exposition with a creedal-type statement of faith in the Father, Son, and Holy Spirit, together with a detailed discussion of the particular characteristics of each. For the last several months he has been concentrating his efforts on asserting the full divinity of the Son and the Spirit and their coequality with God the Father, against homoian, heterousian, and Pneumatomachian detractors, yet when he gives a summary statement of his own doctrinal position he chooses to emphasize not the triune equality, as we might expect (though this is indicated), still less the unity or consubstantiality of the three persons, but rather the unique characteristics of the Father, Son, and Holy Spirit and the interrelations between them.

Gregory conspicuously anchors the identity of each figure—and the divine life altogether—in the unique role of God the Father as source (ἀρχή) and cause (αἰτία) of the Trinity. Although it may seem striking to modern interpreters, he defines the faith in the biblical and traditional pattern of referring to God primarily as "the Father," just as the creed of Nicaea had done.[49] Following the New Testament witness, God is first and foremost the Father of

---

48. See 1 Cor 13.12; Jn 17.3, 20–26.
49. Gregory employs a similar creedal format, also with emphasis on the priority of the Father and the relations of origin, at Ors. 32.5, 21; 39.12; 40.43–45.

Jesus Christ, the Son of God;[50] and yet in virtue of their timeless generation from the Father, the Son and the Spirit fully share the Father's divine nature and are therefore also God.[51] Accordingly, Gregory characterizes the three persons chiefly by their point of origin and their resulting relationships to one another: the one God is the unbegotten Father of Jesus Christ; the Lord Jesus Christ is the Son of God, who is begotten from the Father; and the Holy Spirit proceeds from the Father. Yet in addition to this brief set of terms, and before he has even finished the opening creedal statement, he makes it a point to specify the causal relationships that derive from God the Father. With respect to creation ("when mentioned separately"), the Son is also "God," because he fully possesses the divine nature that he receives from the Father; but in the eternal relations among the three persons of the Trinity ("named together with the Father"), the Father is primarily God, and the Son is "Lord," on account of the monarchy of God the Father—again, as they are typically named in the New Testament. As Gregory elaborates, it is the special property of the Father to be both the source of himself—in the sense that he is self-existent Divinity, being unbegotten, uncaused, and without source[52]—and the source of the Son and the Holy Spirit, and thus the cause and source of the Trinity as a whole. To deny the Father's identity as source of the Trinity—either by positing a source other than the Father or by conceiving of the Son or the Spirit other than as deriving their existence from the Father as their cause—is for Gregory equivalent to denying the existence of God altogether. Hence he argues at length, in a staccato series of key terms, for the uniqueness of the Father, Son, and Holy Spirit: from the opening words of the passage ("one God," "one Lord," "one Holy Spirit") to the monarchy (or singleness of source, μοναρχία); the divine quality of uniqueness (τὸ μοναδικόν) represented by causality, sonship, and procession, or unbegottenness, begottenness, and being sent; absolute fatherhood, sonship, and holiness; and the various forms of "only" or "sole" (μόνος)—all of which derive from the unique identity of the Father (τὸ τοῦ Πατρός ἴδιον) as source and cause. Even the equality mentioned in the opening lines itself depends on the unique identities spelled out below.

---

50. E.g., Rom 1.7; 1 Cor 1.9; 2 Cor 1.2; 13.3; Gal 1.1; Jas 1.1; and 1 Pt 1.3. In the Gospels, the Johannine epistles, and Hebrews, "Son" typically occupies the place of "Lord" in the other books.

51. I use the term "generation" to refer both to the begetting of the Son and the sending forth of the Spirit by God the Father. When I mean to distinguish them, I will speak of the "begetting" of the Son and the "sending forth" or "procession" of the Spirit.

52. "The Father exists unbegottenly (τὸ τὸν Πατέρα εἶναι ἀγεννήτως)" (Or. 20.7), and is not generated, begotten, or derived from any other thing (ἀγέννητος, ἄναρχον, 25.16; 42.15).

The monarchy of God the Father—his unique identity as the "only source" and "sole principle" of the Trinity—lies at the heart of each of Gregory's major doctrinal statements,[53] and it proves to be the fundamental element of his theological system. In his first published discussion of the Trinity, at Easter 362 (2.36–38), he establishes the paradigm that will carry throughout his later work. Taking up the conventional definition of orthodoxy as being opposed to both Arianism and Sabellianism, he argues that what distinguishes the true faith from both errors is the monarchy of the Father. On account of the Father's rank as source of the Son and Spirit (τὸ τῆς ἀρχῆς ἀξίωμα, 2.38), the Son cannot be understood as a creature, as the Arians argue (who are "overly devoted" to the Father), nor can all three be simply different manifestations of only one person, as the Sabellians allege (who are "overly devoted" to the Son). Years later, in his first oration in Constantinople, Gregory quotes and elaborates on this early statement, explaining more fully the fundamental principle of the divine life: that the monarchy and primary causality of the Father is the root of both the oneness of God (εἷς μὲν θεός) and the fact that there are three unique hypostases or persons (αἱ δὲ τρεῖς ὑποστάσεις..., εἴτ' οὖν τρία πρόσωπα, 20.6–7).[54]

The unity or oneness of the Trinity, in other words, is constituted by the Father's begetting of the Son and sending forth of the Spirit. In generating the Son and the Spirit, the Father fully conveys his Divinity to them, causing them to possess the same divine nature, so that all three together are one God. Gregory frequently stipulates that there is one God because the Son and the Spirit "refer back" to the Father as a single cause (ἀνάγεσθαι εἰς ἓν αἴτιον) and the origin of everything that they are and do (20.7).[55] So when the Scriptures speak of the Son and the Spirit as possessing divine qualities or being generated or sent by the Father, they are referring ultimately to the Son's and the Spirit's eternal source in the Father. In the fourth *Theological Oration*, for example, he argues that Jesus' statement that the Father is greater than him (Jn 14.28) refers not so much to the Son's economic inferiority as the incarnate Lord, but to the Father's superiority to the Son as the eternal source of his existence (30.7).[56]

---

53. Among the four crucial texts: *Ors.* 20.6–7; 23.6–8; 25.15–16; and throughout *Ors.* 29–31. See also 2.36–38; 6.22; 41.9f.; 40.43f.; 42.15f.

54. In *Or.* 23, another major text, Gregory again begins with a lengthy argument for the monarchy of the Father against modalist (Marcellan/Photinian) and subordinationist (homoian/heterousian) errors (23.6–8). God is worthy of highest honor, he says, because he (the Father) is the cause and source of the divine issue of the Son and the Spirit (23.6).

55. See also *Ors.* 41.9; 29.3; 30.16; 31.14, 30; 38.15 (= 45.27); 42.15.

56. This point marks an interesting contrast with Augustine, who prefers to interpret such expressions as indicating the Son's lesser status as a human being. See, e.g., *Trin.* 1.15, 18; 6.10.

When he outlines his rule of Christological exegesis in *Oration* 29, Gregory includes John 14.28 among the lowly expressions that refer to the Son's incarnate state (29.18); yet in the lengthier discussion in the following oration he indicates his preference for the interpretation that reflects the eternal monarchy and causality of the Father: "to say that the Father is greater than the Son considered as a human being is true, but trivial" (30.7).[57] Likewise, lowly expressions brought by the Eunomians or Pneumatomachians against the divinity of the Spirit, such as its being given, sent, and a means of intercession, also refer back to the Father as the First Cause and as the source of the Spirit (31.30).[58] Consequently, Gregory famously states that the unity of the Trinity simply *is* the Father, from whom the Son and Spirit come and to whom they are referred (42.15). As the ground of the divine unity, the monarchy of the Father thus serves as Gregory's consistent reply to the charge of tritheism issued by the Eunomians and Homoians.[59] The unity of God lies in the fact that there is only one first principle of God; the real error of polytheism is not that there are more than one divine figure, but that they represent a plurality of principles and are not ordered under any single one in the way that the Son and the Spirit are, by sharing an identical divine nature, which they derive from the Father.

The singular being and work of God, which all three persons are and carry out, constantly originates from the Father and is shared by the Son and the Spirit, because the Father gives it to them and they receive it. For this reason, Gregory repeatedly locates the divine unity not in the common Divinity—as if the Father, Son, and Holy Spirit were one God in virtue of being members of the same class, or because they just happen to share the same nature—but in the monarchy of the Father, by which the Father fully shares his being with the Son and the Spirit. As he argues in his first Constantinopolitan oration, "The unity (τὸ ἕν) of God would, in my view, be preserved if both the Son and the Spirit refer back to one cause (ἓν αἴτιον), without being synthesized or fused with it, and if they share one and the same movement and will of the Divinity" (20.7). They do this simply by virtue of their identity *as* Son and Spirit: the Father, Son, and Spirit "belong (ἔχεσθαι) to each other" as the divine relations (σχέσεις) that they are. So Gregory emphasizes that the Son made all things "from the First Cause" (ἐκ τῆς πρώτης αἰτίας, 37.5), and is the

---

57. Clarifying the Father's eternal causality of the Son is the burden of much of the exegetical argumentation in the fourth *Theological Oration:* see 30.7, 9–12, 15–16, 20.

58. See also *Or.* 41.9: "Everything that pertains to the Spirit refers back to the First Cause [God the Father], just as everything that pertains to the Son." On the term "First Cause," see 31.14, 16, 30; 37.5.

59. *Ors.* 20.6; 23.6–7; 31.30; 25.16, 18; 38.8, 15; 40.41; 42.15.

Source of all things which itself derives from the primary Source (ἡ ἐκ τῆς ἀρχῆς ἀρχή, 38.13).

In addition to being the root of the divine unity, the monarchy of the Father also gives rise to the distinct identities of the three persons of the Trinity. As Gregory continues in *Oration* 20, the Father, Son, and Holy Spirit are preserved as three unique entities because the Father is "the Source who is without source—Source in the sense of cause, fount, and eternal light,"[60] and the Son (like the Spirit) is not uncaused or without source (20.7). In other words, it is the Father's role as the eternal source of the Son and the Spirit, and consequently their respective generations from the Father, which causes all three to be distinct from each other. Hence Gregory gives the well-known definition that the three persons are "relations" (σχέσεις) or "modes of existence" toward one another (τὸ πῶς ἔχειν πρὸς [ἄλληλα], 29.16).[61] What distinguishes the Son and the Spirit from one another (and from the Father) is therefore their unique modes of generation (begetting versus procession) (31.8–9), in contrast with the Augustinian tradition, which locates the difference in the Spirit's dual procession from the Father and the Son.[62] The Father, Son, and Spirit are defined by the way in which they are related to one another as a result of the divine generation, of which the Father is the source; their distinct identities are thus eternally and continually being defined. In order to preserve the three hypostases, it is essential, Gregory says, that we not conceive of them as coalescing or dissolving into one another, or confuse them in any way (συναλειφή, ἀνάλυσις, σύγχυσις), even out of a strong desire to honor the divine unity; otherwise, we will negate the identities of the Father, Son, and Holy Spirit and end up destroying the Trinity as a whole (20.7).[63] The Trinity is thus deserving of honor and worship precisely because of the unique identities of the three persons—the Father because he is the divine source, whose issue

---

60. καὶ ἀνάρχου καὶ ἀρχῆς ἐπινοουμένου καὶ λεγομένου (ἀρχῆς δέ, ὡς αἰτίου καὶ ὡς πηγῆς καὶ ὡς ἀϊδίου φωτός).

61. See also *Or.* 31.9: ἡ πρὸς ἄλληλα σχέσις, 31.14: "It is as if there were a single intermingling of light among three suns that are related to one another" (οἷον ἐν ἡλίοις τρισὶν ἐχομένοις ἀλλήλων, μία τοῦ φωτὸς σύγκρασις). The term is found originally in Origen and Eusebius, and was taken up by George of Laodicea, Basil of Caesarea, and Epiphanius (see this book's conclusion)—though it was Gregory who made it programmatic for Trinitarian doctrine.

62. See Augustine, *Serm.* 71.20.33; *Jo. ev. tr.* 99.8–9; *Trin.* 4.29; 15.29, 47–48. While Augustine emphatically asserts the unity and consubstantiality of the Trinity against Arians/Eunomians and Pneumatomachians, he shares their assumption that the difference between begetting and procession does not suffice to prevent the Spirit from being a second Son, which is the chief objection that Gregory is addressing in *Or.* 31.7–9.

63. See also *Or.* 25.18: "Do not show a perverse reverence for the divine monarchy by contracting or truncating deity, nor feel embarrassed when you are accused of worshipping three gods" (trans. Vinson).

fully share in his nature, and the Son and Spirit because they share the divine nature of the Father, from whom they derive (23.8).

In his debates with Heterousians, Homoians, and Pneumatomachians in Constantinople, Gregory specially emphasizes the divinity of the Son and the Spirit and their coequality with the Father, yet in doing so he appears to have been accused of modalism by some. Hence we should not be surprised by the strong anti-Sabellian element in these same works, which also happens to reflect Gregory's own convictions. As a rule, he announces his opposition to Sabellianism before Arianism throughout his career.[64] The fact that he stresses the uniqueness of the three persons first in sections 15–16 of *Oration* 25 and elsewhere not only shows how fundamental the point is in his doctrine, but it gives an indication of just how deeply rooted anti-Sabellian feeling was among Eastern theologians from Constantinople to Antioch[65] and serves to remind us that Gregory's doctrine is firmly rooted in the depictions of three distinct though interrelated figures in the Bible, the second- and third-century rules of faith, and the numerous creeds and doctrinal definitions of the fourth century Christian East.

In modern patristic studies, the divine monarchy is typically associated with the denial of eternal Trinitarian distinctions by so-called modalists and adoptionists in the second and third centuries. Yet, ironically, this central tenet of Gregory's work, which lies at the heart of fourth-century Trinitarian orthodoxy, remains one of the most confused points among current interpreters.[66] Most of the confusion revolves around a pervasive assumption by modern historians and theologians, quite apart from the textual evidence, that God the Father's superiority to the Son and Spirit as their source and cause conflicts a priori with their unity and equality in being,[67] or else that the divine monarchy and causality is located not in the Father specifically, but in the divine nature irrespective of its origin in the Father.[68] Yet, as we have already seen, for Gregory the monarchy of the Father and the coequality and consubstantiality of the three persons not only belong together, but necessarily do

---

64. *Ors.* 2.36–38; 3.6; 18.16; 20.5–6; 22.12; 33.16; 21.13; 31.30; 36.10; 39.11; 42.16; though cf. 24.13; 23.6; 34.8; 37.22; 43.30 for the inverse order.

65. For a similar example in close proximity to Gregory, see Basil's *Hom 24 Against the Sabellians, Arians, and Anhomoians*, from the early to mid-370s. On Gregory's relationship to Eastern theological tradition, see the conclusion.

66. For an analysis and resolution of the scholarly debate, see Beeley, "Divine Causality."

67. Beginning with Meijering's 1973 "Doctrine of the Will and of the Trinity," esp. pp. 232–234; found also in Norris, *Faith Gives Fullness*, pp. 45, 136–137, 176, 199; Hanson, *Search for the Christian Doctrine of God*, p. 713; Torrance, *The Trinitarian Faith*, pp. 319–322; and Egan, "Primal Cause," p. 28. See also Pannenberg, *Systematic Theology*, vol. 1, pp. 279–280.

68. In the work of Hanson, *Search for the Christian Doctrine of God*, p. 710; Richard Cross, "Divine Monarchy," pp. 114, 116; and Ayres, *Nicaea*, pp. 244–245.

so and in fact amount to the same thing. The priority of the Father within the Trinity does not conflict with the divine unity and equality, but is rather what causes and enables them. The Father, Son, and Holy Spirit are one God, sharing the exact same divine nature, only because the Father conveys that nature to the Son and the Spirit, while the consubstantiality of the Son and the Spirit with the Father is the corollary and the eternal result of the monarchy of the Father. Rather than being opposed, monarchy and consubstantiality therefore belong together in the same concept, and the divine unity has a particular "shape," being structured under the priority of the Father.

To put it more sharply, Gregory is firmly rejecting the notion that the monarchy of the Father in any way conflicts with the equality of the three persons—on the grounds that it is precisely what brings about that equality! The modern objection in fact represents the very argument that the Eunomians brought against Gregory, Basil, and other pro-Nicenes: that the Son and the Spirit cannot be equal in nature with the Father because they are caused by him.[69] Rather than resulting in ontological inequality, Gregory argues, the Father's generation of the Son and the Spirit results in their ontological *equality* and essential identity.[70] Central to his Trinitarian doctrine, in other words, is the insistence that causality and consubstantiality, just as much as causality and personal distinctions, within the Trinity necessarily belong together in the same theological principle. For Gregory, there is no unity and equality in the Trinity—indeed there is no Trinity—if the Father does not convey his Divinity to the Son and the Spirit by generating them; and there is no sense of causality and ordered hierarchy within the Trinity except the one by which the Father produces the Son and the Spirit as full partakers in his Divinity and ontological equals. The monarchy of the Father within the Trinity is thus the sort of causality that produces equality and shared being, rather than inequality; and the equality of the three persons is the sort of equality that derives from and involves a cause, source, and first principle, not the sort that exists apart from any first principle. In the Trinity, then, dependence and equality are mutually involved in each other, however much the idea may run counter to certain ancient or modern sensibilities.[71]

Although some have maintained that the orthodox doctrine of God excludes all causal relations and any sense of superiority within the Trinity—by assuming either that the divine unity is chiefly characterized by divine

---

69. *Ors.* 29.15; 30.7; see also 38.15.
70. *Ors.* 29.15; 40.43; 42.15.
71. The ecclesiological and political implications of this central point are momentous, complex, and often overlooked.

simplicity and therefore admits of no further qualifications, or that the Trinity contains a purely reciprocal *perichoresis* that admits of no hierarchies whatsoever—Gregory emphasizes that the Son and the Spirit are not without source (ἄναρχος, 25.16), and that it dishonors them to imagine that they exist apart from being caused by the Father (23.7). Hence the first characteristic with which he defines the Son and the Spirit (25.15) is the fact that they derive from the Father: "one *begotten* Lord, the Son" and "one Holy Spirit who *proceeds* from the Father"—again, echoing traditional creedal forms. The Father is "truly a Father" in such a way that entirely defines his identity and the identities of the Son and Spirit, making them each unique (μόνως, ὅλον, ἰδιοτρόπως, 25.16). Gregory would therefore reject the suggestion that once the Father has set the Trinity in motion (as if previously), the ordered structure of the relations of origin somehow fades from view, leaving only a purely reciprocal, "perichoretic" exchange of Divinity. As the Father, Son, and Holy Spirit continually pour out and return the divine being, and are in this sense "in" and "with" each other, it is always, in an eternally prior sense, the *Father's* divine being that they share. It can hardly be overemphasized that Gregory is not arguing for the unity or consubstantiality of three divine things in general. Indeed, such an argument would fail to answer his opponents, for the Eunomians are not objecting to the unity or indivisibility of a common divine nature, in the sense of a generic class to which three members belong, but specifically to the idea that the Son *who is begotten from the Father* can receive the Father's divine being (the only divine being) without dividing it (e.g., 31.14).[72] Like some modern interpreters, the Eunomians are thus objecting to the idea that divine relations are both causally ordered and equal at the same time. Gregory's response is therefore to argue not for the unity or consubstantiality of three things in general—as if unity-in-diversity were the problem[73]—but in defense of the intrinsic connection between causality and ontological equality in God.[74]

For Gregory, the unity of the Trinity is not an abstract logical principle or a prior fact of the divine life, but it always refers to—and is—the Father's divine generation of the Son and the Spirit. In the major Trinitarian passages that we have been examining, this monarchical sense of the divine unity is very clear. Only after carefully outlining the monarchy of the Father in *Oration* 25 does

---

72. On the contested interpretation and translation of this passage since the seventh century, see Beeley, "Divine Causality," pp. 200, 210–211, 213, with bibliography.

73. As in the definition Ayres adopts for Gregory and other pro-Nicene theologians. *Nicaea*, p. 236–240 and passim.

74. See *Or.* 30.7: "Being derived from such a cause [as the Father] does not mean being less than the uncaused."

Gregory conclude with the more abstract statement that "unity is worshipped in Trinity and Trinity in unity, both its union and its distinction miraculous" (25.17).[75] Divorced from its doctrinal context, this statement could be interpreted in the quasi-mathematical sense in which the Trinity is often imagined: that the one God (somehow) exists "in" three persons and the three persons are (somehow) united to one another, with no deeper sense of what this means.[76] But for Gregory, this is not a flat, generic statement of divine unity at all, but a shorthand expression for the Father's eternal generation of the Son and the Holy Spirit.

Even more widespread is the related confusion over whether, according to the fathers, personhood or the divine essence per se holds priority in the Trinity, and consequently in Christian ontology, cosmology, and anthropology. Based on a convoluted interpretation of Théodore de Régnon's seminal study of early and medieval Trinitarian theology, twentieth-century theologians developed a caricatured distinction between Greek patristic "personalism," which prioritizes personhood over essence, and Latin scholastic "essentialism," which prioritizes essence over personhood.[77] John Meyendorff argues that Gregory is a paradigmatic example of the Greek view of the priority of the Father, whereby the *hypostasis* of the Father, not the divine nature, is "the origin of hypostatic 'subsistence.' "[78] By artificially separating the categories of *hypostasis* and nature from one another, Meyendorff grossly misrepresents Gregory's doctrine. For Gregory, the first principle of the Trinity is neither "personhood" nor the divine essence per se, but God the Father, who, as unbegotten Divinity, is both *hypostasis and* divine essence.[79]

Consequently, Gregory would also reject any notion of Trinitarian *perichoresis* that conceives of the divine life as being purely reciprocal and not eternally based in the monarchy of the Father—as if, once the Father establishes the consubstantial Trinity, the hierarchical structure of the divine generations gives way to a purely reciprocal exchange of Divinity. Gregory is insistent that

---

75. The same sequence occurs in *Or.* 23.8: because God is made up of a source of divinity and divine issue from that source (the Son and the Spirit), they are *therefore* "one in their separation and separate in their conjunction, even if this is a paradoxical statement, . . . a perfect Trinity of three perfect entities."

76. See, e.g., the entry on the "Trinity" in the *Oxford Dictionary of the Christian Church*, 3rd ed.

77. Régnon, *Études de théologie positive sur la Sainte Trinité*, which builds on the seventeenth-century work of Petau; on Gregory, see vol. 1, p. 405. For an account of the strange reception of Régnon's argument in the twentieth century, see Michel René Barnes, "De Régnon Reconsidered"; Hennessy, "Answer to de Régnon's Accusers."

78. Meyendorff, *Byzantine Theology*, p. 183.

79. See the fine study by Halleux, "Personalisme ou essentialisme trinitaire?" pp. 149–150; and Beeley, "Divine Causality," pp. 213–214.

the three persons do not mingle with one another in such a way that their identities relative to one another change (20.7), and he is equally clear that the Father is always the source of Divinity in the Son and the Spirit. However much one wants to ally him with the tradition of *perichoresis* found in the Pseudo-Cyril and John of Damascus,[80] it must be borne in mind that for Gregory the divine life is eternally rooted and expressed in the monarchy of the Father. Even though the Father, Son, and Holy Spirit continually pour out and return the divine being and so can be said mutually to inhere in one another, it is always, in an eternally prior sense, the *Father's* divine being that they share. The entire process of divine generation and reception is caused by and originates with God the Father.

Because the priority of God the Father is universally taken for granted in his theological milieu, Gregory does not identify it as such in every discussion of the Trinity. While he makes the point explicitly in his most significant expositions and he frequently refers to it in passing, he also refers to it through secondary, derivative concepts, such as the language of consubstantiality. The Nicene term ὁμοούσιος functions mainly as a cypher for the more fundamental concept of the monarchy, and as a public moniker with which to announce his alignment with the emerging pro-Nicene consensus. Even though he points to Paul's interchangeable usage of the terms "Father," "Son," and "Spirit" as proof of their consubstantiality (34.15), for example, he never speaks of the Father as being consubstantial with the Son and the Spirit, or of the "consubstantial Trinity" as a whole.[81] He uses the term only in one direction, to indicate that the Son and the Spirit fully share in the *Father's* divine being. Moreover, the fact that Gregory uses the term so seldom,[82] and often as a response to the arguments of others,[83] further highlights that it is a byproduct rather than a fundamental element of his doctrine.

The consubstantiality of the Son and the Spirit with the Father and the divine unity, as well as the distinct identities of the Father, Son, and Holy

---

80. See Egan, "Primal Cause."

81. The phrase "consubstantial Trinity" is rare among Nicene theologians up to this point. It briefly appears in the literature from the Synod of Alexandria in 362 (Athanasius, *Ep. cath.* 7, also reported in Socrates, *HE* 3.7; but notably not the *Tom.*); in Didymus the Blind (*Comm. Zach.* 3.261.10); and in Epiphanius (*Ancor.* 64.3.1; *Panar.* 57.4.11; 76.45.5; *De fide.* 14.1). Yet for Athanasius *homoousios* very clearly refers to the Son's full possession of, and existence in, the Divinity of God the Father, as conveyed also by the second technical phrase of the Nicene Creed, that the Son is "from the essence of the Father."

82. The term *homoousios* is entirely absent from Gregory's major Trinitarian statement in *Or.* 25.15–18.

83. E.g., *Or.* 31.10: "What, then? Is the Spirit God? Certainly. Is it consubstantial? Yes, if it is God." See also 30.20: Christ's title "Son" indicates both that he is identical with the Father in essence (ταὐτὸν κατ' οὐσίαν) and that he derives from him (κἀκεῖθεν).

Spirit, are thus the eternal corollary and *result* of the Father's divine generation. The monarchy of the Father is the foundational principle of Trinitarian logic and the fundamental dynamic that contains and gives meaning to the grammatical aspects of unity and distinctness. The centrality of the monarchy of the Father in Gregory's doctrine can be seen in the fact that, as a heroically pro-Nicene bishop, he continues to stress that the Father is "greater" than the Son and the Spirit as their cause and source. In his great oration *On Baptism*, in which he gives a summary of the faith to recently homoian catechumens, Gregory goes so far as to say that he would rather simply call the Father "greater," on account of his role as the source of both the equality and the divine being of the Son and the Spirit, except that his detractors wrongly assume that a divine cause produces inferiors rather than equals (40.43). For this reason he is forced several times to explain that just because the Father is greater than the Son as cause does not mean that he is greater in being.[84] For many moderns, just as for the Eunomians of the fourth century, it must be emphasized that in making this qualification, Gregory does not mean to cancel the priority of the Father, but on the contrary to clarify it as the foundation of the unity, the distinctions, and indeed the very being of the Trinity. At the heart of Gregory's doctrine, then, the monarchy of God the Father is the root of both the unity and the distinctions within the Trinity, and is thus the deeper principle of both aspects of the divine life. All conceptualizations of the divine unity ultimately refer to the eternal generations and the sharing of the divine nature by the Father with the Son and the Spirit, and to their reference back to God the Father, as do our ideas about the distinctions among the three persons.

Gregory therefore understands God to be revealed as a kind of dynamic, ordered life that eternally arises from and returns to God the Father. While the exact manner of the divine generations remains a mystery, and the internal order of the Trinity is fully known only to itself,[85] Gregory believes that, through faith within the divine economy, we nevertheless gain a real understanding of the structure and "motion" of God's eternal being. Because the Father generates the Son and Spirit, who share fully in his divine being and yet are distinct from him, God intrinsically possesses a divine generosity and potency that would not be the case otherwise (25.16). By centering his doctrine on the eternal dynamic life of the Trinity, Gregory again follows closely the work of Origen.[86] He

---

84. *Ors.* 29.15; 30.7.
85. *Ors.* 6.22; 20.10–11; 23.11; 29.8; 25.16.
86. For a helpful discussion of Origen's dynamic understanding of the Trinity, versus an "ontological" view, see Crouzel, *Origen*, pp. 187–188. For Gregory—and probably for Origen too—we should amend Crouzel's point to say that ontology, or the divine being, is itself intrinsically dynamic.

contrasts the Trinity with doctrines that leave God either alienated, disconnected, and unlimitedly diffuse, or else constricted and grudging, whether out of envy or fear—the former standing for polytheistic and the latter for Eunomian or homoian positions (23.6, 8; 25.16). In a famous, though often misunderstood, passage at the beginning of the third *Theological Oration*, Gregory gives a summary description of the dynamic life of the Trinity, which constantly arises from and returns to God the Father. Contrary to the anarchy and polyarchy of the Greeks, which tend toward chaos and disorder, Christians recognize the divine monarchy:

> But what is honored among us is monarchy—not a monarchy that is delimited by a single person (πρόσωπον)[87] (for it is possible for the One [τὸ ἕν], being at "discord" with itself, to become a plurality), but one that is held together by an equal dignity of nature, a common accord of will, and an identity of action, and by the convergence to the One of the things that come from it . . .; so that while there is a difference in number, there is no division in essence. Hence from the beginning[88] a Monad, being moved toward a Dyad, stops at a Triad—and this is for us the Father and the Son and the Holy Spirit. The [Father] is the begetter (ὁ γεννήτωρ) and emitter (ὁ προβολεύς), and the others are the offspring (τὸ γέννημα) and the emission (τὸ πρόβλημα). (29.2)

Here again Gregory summarizes his view of the Trinity specifically in terms of the monarchy of the Father—as the divine generativity that eternally stems from the Father and results in the production of the Son and the Spirit, and thus a complete Trinity.[89] The constitution and the unity of the Trinity result

---

87. That is, the solitary Father of the Eunomian scheme.
88. See 1 Jn 1.1; see also Jn 1.1.
89. It has long been recognized that in *Or.* 29.2 Gregory is using terms that have a philosophical resonance, as indicated by his comment "and this is for us," i.e., for Christians, not for the Greeks. Similarities can be found in Plotinus, *Enn.* 3.8.10 (on the flow of power and the return of all things to the One); and 5.1–2 (how duality and multiplicity came into being from the One and exist in or as the One). For recent discussion, see Meijering, "The Doctrine of the Will and of the Trinity," p. 226; Gallay, SC 250, p. 181; Norris, *Faith Gives Fullness*, p. 44; Vaggione, *Eunomius of Cyzicus*, p. 83n92; and Bergjan, *Theodoret von Cyrus*, pp. 73–79. Although it has been fashionable since the nineteenth century to place great stock in the appearance of philosophical material in early Christian theologians—Dräseke based much of his case for Gregory's Plotinian influence on this single passage ("Neuplatonisches," pp. 142–143)—the ideas and terms that Gregory uses here do not figure prominently in other passages and are not fundamental to his doctrine. More to the point, Gregory is again mainly capitalizing on cultural currency for rhetorical effect. Such statements are also traditional within the Christian fold: Athanasius quotes a similar expression by the third-century Dionysius of Alexandria (*Dion.* 17, 19), whom Gregory may have read. In any event, Gregory is not trying to establish a philosophical doctrine of a unified divine Triad. As Pinault comments, even if he is making an allusion to Plotinus, this text does not indicate any serious Neoplatonic influence. *Le Platonisme*, p. 232.

from the Father's generation of the Son and the Spirit and their "convergence" back to the Father, who is "the One" (τὸ ἕν), on account of the divine generativity. In an earlier draft of the same idea, Gregory speaks of the Monad transcending the Dyad and producing the Triad (or Trinity)[90] out of its superabundance (23.8). The perfection of the Trinity, he says, is indicated by the fact that it transcends the duality that is the basis of the created order—"the form and matter of which bodies consist" and the "synthesis of duality." As Trinity, God is therefore abundantly generative and at the same time possessive of order—both of which are principles of life and health.[91] In these statements Gregory is also indicating that the inner generativity of the Trinity, which produces its unity and distinctions, is reflective of the divine nature in its primal mode of existence in the person of the Father: that Christians believe God to be a Father who eternally produces a divine Son and Spirit, which is the essence of the Trinitarian revelation. Despite the sharp distinction between the divine nature and the personhood of the Father, Son, and Holy Spirit that is often assumed to be the conceptual basis of Trinitarian doctrine,[92] for Gregory there is also a strong impetus in the other direction, to stress the interrelationship and the mutual implication between the two categories, which, it must be remembered, do not in fact exist in themselves: There is no such thing as a nonessential divine person or a nonpersonal divine being; rather, the Father, Son, and Holy Spirit—which are always the primary theological categories—are each both *hypostasis* and divine being. As Gregory comments in *Oration* 25, there is a fundamental correspondence between the uniqueness of each of the three persons and the uniqueness of God as a whole (25.16).[93]

More fundamental than the metaphysics of consubstantiality or the logic of unity or personal distinction, the Trinity contains—and is—an eternal movement or dynamic, based on the monarchy of God the Father. In a way similar to his Christology and Pneumatology, then, we find as the root of Gregory's doctrine of the Trinity a kind of *narrative*—that the Father eternally begets the Son and emits the Holy Spirit, by which the divine life is constituted.

---

90. Here we must remember that the Greek term τρίας most simply means a triad. It does not contain the hybrid connotation of both "three" and "one" that the Latin *Trinitas* does.

91. See also *Or.* 20.6. Gregory argues that the order in creation, on several levels, represents the divine being and will. See, e.g., 2.4 on order and rule within the body of the Church; 7.7 on order among the stars; 32.8, 18 on order in heaven and earth and human behavior. He exploits this parallel to great effect in the three orations *On Peace* (6, 22, 23) and in his oration *On Moderation in Debate* (32).

92. On which see Lienhard, "Ousia and Hypostasis." The distinction plays a much greater role in the work of Basil and Gregory of Nyssa; see this book's conclusion.

93. Just as the Father, Son, and Holy Spirit are each unique (εἷς, μόνος), so they each share in the divine quality of uniqueness (τὸ μοναδικόν).

It is precisely God's generativity of his coequal Son and Spirit that makes God worthy of honor (23.6),[94] so that there is a deep correspondence in Gregory's work between the narrative character of the economic revelation of God and the narrative character of the theological meaning of that revelation. The monarchy of God the Father is thus the foundational principle of Trinitarian logic, the fundamental dynamic that gives meaning to the grammatical aspects of unity and distinctness within the Trinity, and also the basic shape of the divine economy, by which the eternal God is known.

Conceiving of the Trinity

As a pastoral theologian, Gregory often worked in an environment of acute doctrinal conflict, and he participated in larger ecclesiastical networks on several levels. The various situations in which he found himself naturally required different rhetorical approaches and doctrinal styles, some of which are more superficial or formulaic in character, while others take up matters of logic and metaphysics in painstaking detail, most often begrudgingly. Gregory's basic doctrine, which we have just examined, is reflected in a variety of other forms, from brief confessional formulae, which serve to indicate his position among theological alliances and ecclesiastical definitions, to detailed points of conceptual and linguistic refinement, which frequently respond to specific arguments of the current debates.

Gregory's most important simple statement of the Trinity appears in his first extant oration. In response to the local schism in Nazianzus, he enjoins his congregation to defend "the sound faith in Father, Son, and Holy Spirit, the one Divinity and power" (1.7). Again, in an early statement in Constantinople, he offers the same basic definition as a rallying point for building a broad Trinitarian consensus: "Will we not hold to a single definition of piety, the worship of Father, Son, and Holy Spirit, the one Divinity and power among the three?" (22.12).[95] In the same way he concludes his complicated *Theological Orations* (31.33),[96]

---

94. "God is the object of proportionately more honor than his creatures are to the extent that it is more in keeping with the greater majesty of the first cause to be the source of divinity rather than of creatures, and to reach the creatures through the medium of divinity rather than the reverse."

95. If *Or.* 20 is dated later, then this statement is Gregory's first in the capital. See also 23.12, where he summarizes the faith in similar terms: "our faith and rebirth in the Father, Son, and Holy Spirit, and in our common name," i.e., the Divinity; and 33.16.

96. Adhering to the "more pious conception (ἔννοια)" of God that rests on few words, guarding the illumination he has received from God and persuading others "to worship Father, Son, and Holy Spirit, the one Divinity and power."

makes his initial confession before the emperor (36.10), and defines the faith with which he baptizes Christians (40.41, 45).[97] This simple confession is notable in several respects. It uses only biblical language and avoids the term οὐσία, which was an infamous point of contention, forbidden under the homoian regimes of Constantius and Valens and still disputed among otherwise like-minded homoousian and homoiousian theologians—the latter being highly concentrated in Gregory's immediate Asian environment and in his sponsoring network around Melitius. Like his Asian contemporaries, Gregory himself prefers to speak of the "Divinity" rather than in terms of "being." Yet, particularly with the further argumentation that usually surrounds it, this statement also indicates Gregory's belief that the Son and the Spirit fully possess the Father's Divinity, and so his opposition to those who maintain that they have a different nature from the Father, however "like" each other they may be said to be.[98] Formally speaking, it names the Father, Son, and Holy Spirit—the three persons met in the divine economy—and then, as a predicate, declares that they each possess and are the one Divinity and power, which is universally associated with God the Father. The statement therefore reflects the same basic shape as the lengthier passages that we discussed above. As a rule, Gregory initially discusses the distinct identities of the Father, Son, and Holy Spirit (part A), after which he turns to their shared Divinity and unity of nature (part B).[99] This brief confession thus serves as a shorthand expression for his fuller doctrine,[100] a point to which we will return momentarily. In terms of its social function, it serves as a memorable and relatively unspecific doctrinal statement, about which strongly Trinitarian groups can agree, as we can see from its frequent appearance in orations where he is attempting to consolidate different theological parties.[101] It

---

97. See also *Ors.* 12.1; 32.21; 36.10; 26.19; 38.8; 40.5; 42.15, 16; and in reverse order (the one Divinity of the Father, Son, and Holy Spirit): 19.17; 21.33; 34.9; 28.3 (see 31.9).

98. As in the currently reigning imperial definition of Rimini/Constantinople 360.

99. See *Or.* 6.22: "worshipping Father, Son, and Holy Spirit (A), knowing the Father in the Son, the Son in the Spirit (B)," after which the pattern repeats twice more. 20.5: "We therefore worship Father, Son, and Holy Spirit, distinguishing their individual characteristics (ἰδιότητας) (A) while uniting their Divinity (B)." 20.6 again takes up the three individualities (A), after which 20.7 addresses the divine unity (B). 23.4: "exalting Father, Son, and Holy Spirit (A), ... uniting and exalting God (B). 26.19: "Holy Triad (A), ... rightly united by us and worshipped (B)." See also the quasi-creedal statements at 32.5, 21; 39.12; 42.15; *Carm.* 1.1.1.25–39 and the following two poems.

100. For which reason it does not appear in *Or.* 25, where Gregory's doctrine is expressed more fully and clearly.

101. E.g., *Ors.* 1.7; 22.12; 32.21; 33.16; 23.12; 21.33; 34.9; 36.10; and, if we grant this function to the *Theological Orations*, 28.31 and 31.33 as well.

is Gregory's most common Trinitarian formula, and fairly unique in patristic sources.[102]

The second brief definition that Gregory gives is to contrast the true faith with the erroneous doctrines of Sabellius and Arius. Again, he makes such a statement mainly to signal his commitments within the emerging pro-Nicene movement, for which it is becoming a traditional moniker;[103] hence, like the previous formula, it appears most frequently in passages where he is attempting to reconcile or to build alliances between different groups.[104] Technically speaking, it defines the faith against the opposite errors of either fusing the three persons of the Trinity into one or else dividing them from one another in being, which are often portrayed as two extremes that must be avoided. In two important passages, for example, Gregory defines them as excessive devotion to the Father or the Son. The "Arians," he says, are such fervent "devotees of the Father" (φιλοπάτορες) that they exalt him above the Son in being; whereas the Sabellians are such strong "devotees of Christ" (φιλοχρίστοι) that they regard him as exactly the same thing as God the Father, only different in manifestation (2.38; 20.6–7). Yet we miss the point of Gregory's rhetoric if we take him to be saying that the Christian faith is literally a mean between two unacceptable extremes; the sarcasm and teasing in these passages should warn us against reading them so straightforwardly. The idea

---

102. Epiphanius uses similar phrasing in the mid-370s: "There is one Divinity and one glory, the Trinity being consubstantial..., a perfect Trinity and one Divinity, one power, one being" (*Panar.* 3.255.21–23, against Marcellans); "There are two perfects, Father and Son, and they are one (ἕν) on account of their equality (ἰσότης), on account of their [one] Divinity and one power and one likeness (ὁμοιότης)" (*Panar.* 3.218.2–3, against Sabellians); see also *Panar.* 3.178.30–31, 201.2–3, against Arians; 3.367.12–13, against Aetius. Epiphanius' prevalent use of *homoousios* and his application of it to the Trinity as a whole, after the manner of Athanasius, is not reflected in Gregory's work, nor are many of his arguments against the heresies, making him unlikely as a source for Gregory. Only slightly later than Gregory Nazianzen, Gregory of Nyssa uses similar language, though less frequently: true faith believes in "one power, one goodness, one life-giving authority, one Divinity, one life" (*Spir.* 115.24–25); see also *Eust.* 5.18–19; 6.9–10; *Ep.* 5.9. Similar phrasing again occurs in a Greek translation of a sermon attributed to Ephraem, whose date is uncertain: "There is one Divinity, one power, one kingdom in three persons or *hypostases*" (*Serm. trans.* 30.5–6; see also *Ad Ioan. mon.* 190.5). No other writer uses the same formula in such a programmatic way as Gregory does. Formulas based on "one Divinity" alone are much more common: see Athanasius, *Ar.* 1.18; 3.6; *Ep. Serap.* 1.14; 3.6; Epiphanius, *Ancor.* 6.9.1; 10.5.4; *Panar.* 3.11.17; Gregory Nazianzen's own *Ors.* 30.12; 31.9; Gregory of Nyssa, *Ablab.* 3.1.57.12; *Ref.* 144.3; and the definition of the catholic faith in Theodosius' decree *Cunctos populos* as belief "in the sole Divinity of the Father and of the Son and of the Holy Spirit, within an equal majesty and an orthodox Trinity." For the connection between this formula and Gregory's Eastern theological heritage, see this book's conclusion.

103. See Athanasius, *Dion.* 9, 12–13, 25, 27; *Tom.* 6; Epiphanius, *Ancor.* 17.6; 116.9; *Panar.* 69.72.4; 72.1.2, 11.5; 78.24.5. Interestingly, the pairing appears only in the title, but not the text of Basil's *Hom.* 24 *Against the Sabellians, Arians, and Anhomoians.*

104. E.g., *Ors.* 2.36; 6.22; 20.5; 22.12; 33.16; 23.6; 21.13; 34.8; 31.9, 12, 30; 36.10; 37.22; 38.15; 39.11; 42.16, 18; 43.30. For other contexts, see 18.16; 24.13.

that Sabellians and Arians "overworship" or "underworship" is of course facetious, as Gregory lets on in *Oration* 22, since it is impossible to worship any person of the Trinity too highly, and not to worship them enough is impious (22.12). His deeper point is that neither Sabellians nor Arians honor or worship the Trinity enough. So Gregory replies to the "Sabellians" (the party of Photinus) that to deny the Son's distinct, eternal generation from the Father is to rob him of his sonship and his divinity, and to the "Arians" (Eunomians and Homoians) he writes that denying the Son's full divinity robs the Father of his fatherhood.[105] Both views fail to honor the Father or the Son as they claim to do, and both undermine the Father's role as cause and source of the Trinity (2.38; 20.6–7). In making this critique, Gregory is taking up the traditional Eusebian and homoian defense of the monarchy of the Father against the Sabellians, while at the same showing that the homoian view of the monarchy is itself insufficient: "to save yourself the trouble of defending the monarchy, you have denied the Divinity!" (31.17). Sabellianism and Arianism are therefore not extreme doctrinal positions, compared to which Nicene orthodoxy is a happy medium, but they are fundamentally insufficient in themselves. For Gregory, only a full doctrine of the Trinity adequately expresses the divine monarchy, the honor and dignity of the three persons, and the existence of God. On the whole, the formulaic opposition to Sabellius and Arius carries little doctrinal or even polemical content for Gregory: he rarely calls the Eunomians "Arians,"[106] and he uses the terms infrequently in his narration of the fourth-century controversies in his oration *In Praise of Athanasius* (21.13, 25).[107] Like the first definition, the dual opposition to Sabellians and Arians thus serves as a formulaic reference to his fuller doctrine of the Trinity, based on the monarchy of the Father.

As a second type of derivative discourse, Gregory takes up several points of conceptual clarification. Whereas the brief doctrinal statements that we have just examined occur at various points within a given oration, he usually offers these technical discussions in a set position within the argument. As a pattern, he initially lays out his basic doctrine, as outlined above, and then turns to more refined matters, often at length. First, as a point of technical commentary, Gregory speaks of the Trinity in terms of oneness and threeness, both in fairly abstract terms and in terms that further specify what is one and what is

---

105. What he calls elsewhere "a perverse reverence for the monarchy" (*Or.* 25.18).
106. In the *Theological Orations*, e.g., *Or.* 31.30 is an oblique reference, and 30.6 and 18 refer only to imaginary Sabellians.
107. As in *Or.* 33, despite its traditional title *Against the Arians and On Himself*: see 33.16.

three. Following the major statement in *Oration* 25.15–16 (quoted above), he offers the summary comment that, in the Trinity, we worship "a Monad in a Triad, and a Triad in a Monad, both its distinction and its union incredible" (25.17).[108] While this phrase may suggest a sort of metaphysical or quasi-mathematical problem of how three things can also be one, Gregory is again taking up traditional phrasing[109] to refer to the dynamic structure discussed above, in which the divine generation is likened to a Monad transcending a Dyad to become a Triad (23.8; 29.2). Abstract statements of one-in-threeness are comparatively rare in Gregory's work, and they often occur in conjunction with the opposition to Sabellianism and Arianism.[110] More frequently, Gregory speaks of oneness and threeness within the Trinity in ways that specify what is one and what is three.

In confessing that the Son and the Spirit are fully divine as a result of their generation from God the Father, Gregory recognizes that he is distinguishing between the divine nature, which all three persons share, and the distinctive characteristics and identities of the three persons, by which they are distinguished from one another. He expresses the singularity and the threeness of God in several different ways. On the oneness of God, he variously states that the three are one God (θεός),[111] one in Divinity (θεότης),[112] a single nature (φύσις)[113] or being (οὐσία),[114] or, again, simply a single thing (Μόνας, ἕν). It is noteworthy that, on the whole, Gregory prefers the biblical terms "God,"[115] "Divinity,"[116] and "nature"[117] over the more controversial term "being." On the threeness of the Trinity, he speaks of three hypostases or subsisting entities (ὑποστάσεις),[118] three persons (πρόσωπα),[119] three unique things or character-

---

108. This passage repeats a statement from *Or.* 6.22 almost verbatim. A related expression is τὸ ἕν/τὰ τρία (see 6.22; 21.13; 31.4, 9, 14, 18, 19, among many others).

109. The Μόνας-Τριάς construction appears most notably in Dionysius of Alexandria, apud Athanasius, *Dion.* 17, 19; Marcellus of Ancyra, apud Eusebius of Caesarea, *Eccl. theo.* 3.4; Athanasius, *Decr.* 26 (more loosely); Eusebius, *Laud. Const.* 6.11; Epiphanius, *Ancor.* 22.7; *Panar.* 2.391; 3.406; Basil, *Eun.* 3.6; *Spir.* 29.72; fragments of Amphilochius; and in the *Trin.* 3.9, attributed to Didymus the Blind.

110. See *Ors.* 18.16; 24.13; 23.8; 28.1; 31.14, *Carm.* 1.1.3.43, 60, 72, 75, 88.

111. *Ors.* 18.16; 20.7.

112. *Ors.* 21.13; 34.15; 31.14, 28; 37.22; 43.30; *Carm.* 1.1.3.74.

113. *Ors.* 33.16; 34.15; 26.19; 42.15.

114. *Ors.* 34.13; 42.16. Gregory declares the identity of being among the Father, Son, and Holy Spirit in 6.13 and 20.7. There is a striking, unique parallel between the phrase "the concord [literally same-mindedness] and identity of being" (τὴν ὁμόνοια ἢ τὴν τῆς οὐσίας ταὐτότητα) in 6.13 and a similar statement in Origen, *Cels* 8.12, a passage that was used in several conciliar statements from the Council of Antioch in 341 forward.

115. Passim.

116. See Col 2.9.

117. See Rom 1.26; 2 Pt 1.4.

118. *Ors.* 20.7; 34.15; 31.28; 42.16.

119. *Ors.* 31.30; 37.22; 42.16.

istics (ἰδιότητες),[120] or, often, simply three things (τρία). This distinction between a single divine nature and three hypostases or persons, usually tightened up to read "one *ousia* and three *hypostases*," is often regarded as the distinctive Cappadocian achievement in Trinitarian doctrine[121]—although the phrase as such appears first in Augustine.[122] Not only is this an overgeneralization about three diverse theologians, but, in Gregory's case especially, it is an overstatement of the role that this secondary formulation plays in his work.

Crucial to our appreciation of the meaning and function of this distinction is to recognize first of all that, as with one-in-three constructions, it serves to express and clarify the dynamic life of the Trinity based on the monarchy of the Father and revealed in the divine economy, as discussed above. Furthermore, the distinct categories of Divinity and hypostasis (and parallels) are linguistic and conceptual tools that are employed in the analysis of Trinitarian doctrine, but they are not by themselves realities. There are no abstract hypostases that exist apart from the divine nature that they share;[123] there are only the Father, Son, and Holy Spirit, who are unoriginate, begotten, and proceeding Divinity. Likewise, the divine nature does not exist apart from the Father, Son, and Holy Spirit, who are the Divinity.[124] Both categories are involved in every aspect of the divine life and exist only in thought, not in reality. Moreover, on account of the movement of the divine life that is recognized in the theologizing of the economy, Gregory frequently makes statements that speak across and even blur the category distinctions. As a result of the divine generations, Christians worship the Father "in the Son" and the Son "in the Holy Spirit" (24.16), and God is glorified "in the Son and the Holy Spirit" (15.12). In their respective modes of generation (begetting versus procession), the Son and the Spirit possess the uniqueness that is characteristic of the divine nature (25.16). So Gregory has no trouble arguing that the Holy Spirit is holy in a sense that is proper to it, even though the Divinity, and thus the Trinity as a whole, is also holy (25.16).[125] Likewise, the Son is, properly speaking, the divine Word on

---

120. *Ors.* 33.16; 21.13; 34.13; 26.19; 42.15; 43.30.
121. See, e.g., Hanson, *Search for the Christian Doctrine of God*, p. 710. For a trenchant critique of this view, see Lienhard, "Ousia and Hypostasis." Recent studies that approach Cappadocian Trinitarian theology from this vantage point include Ritter's "Die Trinitäts-Theologie der drei großen Kappadozier" and Markschies' "Gibt es eine einheitliche 'kappadozische Trinitätstheologie'?"
122. *Trin.* 5.8.10, as well as 7.4.7–8. See also Plagnieux, *Saint Grégoire*, pp. 405–406; Lienhard, "Augustine of Hippo."
123. As in the Romantic personalism of Orthodox theologians like Giannaras, Meyendorff, and Zizioulas.
124. *Ors.* 28.3; 38.8; 39.11–12.
125. See also *Ors.* 41.9; 31.4.

account of his declaratory function with respect to the Father (διὰ τὸ ἐξαγγελτικόν), like a definition compared to the thing defined, because he is the "concise explanation (ἀπόδειξις) of the Father's nature" (30.20),[126] even though God as a whole is also rational and wise.[127] The Son, moreover, is able to take on human flesh and suffering in a way that the Father, as pure Mind, is not, even though the divine nature and the eternal Son himself are incorporeal.[128] Although Basil and especially Gregory of Nyssa place much stock in the firm distinction between the two categories, Gregory Nazianzen uses them more loosely as conceptual tools for discussing the complicated, dynamic reality of the Trinity, the true apprehension of which more fundamentally represents the theology of the divine economy.

These statements of the singularity and threeness of the Trinity are therefore neither the starting point nor a comprehensive summary of Gregory's doctrine. They are discernable by analysis, and they function as shorthand expressions of the more basic narrative, economic doctrine. Above all, Gregory does not regard them as representing an independent metaphysical or logical scheme that the Scriptures and the Church then replicate and make widely accessible. He shows no interest in exploring the metaphysical problems or implications of three things being one, and he does not trouble himself over these distinctions enough to make any significant doctrinal assertions about their character per se.[129]

Thus far we have considered summary definitions and positive conceptual statements of Gregory's doctrine; we must now consider the negative statements that he makes as well. In each the four major texts on the Trinity,[130] Gregory appends several points of conceptual refinement to his doctrinal exposition which, through a process of denial and negation, identify where theo-

---

126. The Son is also called "Wisdom" because he is the knowledge of divine and human realities (*Or.* 30.20). See also 6.4–5, which is followed by a lengthy meditation on cosmic and social order.

127. A similar mutual implication between the categories can be seen in Gregory's statements that the Father, Son, and Spirit are distinctions "with respect to the [divine] being" (περὶ οὐσίαν, *Or.* 41.9; also περὶ τὴν φύσιν, 42.15; cf. 29.12; *Carm.* 1.1.2.34–35), and in his variable usage of τὸ ἕν to refer either to God the Father or to the Trinity or the divine unity as a whole (cf. 33.16 with 20.6 and 31.14). See also 28.3; 31.16, 29; 38.8; 39.11–12.

128. *Carm.* 1.1.1.28–29; 1.1.2.36–38.

129. In fact he refuses to do so: the Trinity's internal ordering is known only to itself, "and to those purified souls to whom the Trinity may make revelation either now or in the future" (*Or.* 23.11; see also 6.22).

130. The relevant sections are *Ors.* 20.8–11; 23.9–11; selections from 29.3–16 and 31.4–20; 31.33 (the logical-linguistic sections of the *Theological Orations* on the Son and the Spirit, and the concluding section of the series); and 25.16–17. See also 34.10; 38.7; 39.12; 40.42; 42.15, 17; and *Carm.* 1.1.1–3, in other significant Trinitarian passages. The negative material in *Or.* 34.10 is omitted in *Or.* 41, the similar oration that follows it chronologically.

logical language leaves off and loses its creaturely connotations, on account of the incomparable difference between God and creation.[131] For example, he argues against the idea that the divine generation is corporeal or passionate, like human generation, saying instead that it is spiritual, incorporeal, and free from passion.[132] On a number of points where an overly literal use of certain categories would violate other beliefs held about God, he issues qualifications of an apophatic nature: the Trinity is beyond time,[133] free from the capriciousness of human willing[134] and from the creaturely genesis from non-being into being.[135] Although some have seen in Gregory a strong apophaticism,[136] these qualifications chiefly serve to indicate where the God who is being described in *positive* doctrinal language transcends that language. Similar to the constructions examined above, they serve as further clarifications of Gregory's basic doctrine, but not as foundational points themselves. The high concentration of these arguments in polemical texts indicates their disputational function; the greatest example being the *Theological Orations*, which, as we have noted, are almost entirely defensive in character. As Gregory states at the conclusion of one such passage, "I am satisfied with the declaration that he is Son and that he is from Father, and that the one is Father and the other Son; and I refuse to engage in meaningless speculation beyond this point" (20.10). Even at its most technical, apologetic level, Gregory reminds us that his doctrine must always retain its basic, soteriological meaning.

The final and most significant point of Trinitarian conceptuality concerns the nature of the eschatological vision of God. Here again we come to a point of scholarly debate. Certain interpreters have argued that Gregory contradicts himself in saying both (a) that Christians know God in Jesus Christ through the Holy Spirit, with their sight focused primarily on God the Father, and (b) that Christians also know God as Father, Son, and Holy Spirit, with the Trinity as a whole as the object of vision. The modern Orthodox writer Vladimir Lossky, for example, argues that Gregory's understanding of the vision of God is both unclear and a radical departure from mainstream Trinitarian orthodoxy,[137] a

---

131. *Ors.* 20.8; 23.9; 28; 29.4; 25.17; *Carm.* 1.1.1.1–6.
132. *Ors.* 20.8–9; 23.9–11; 29.4; 31.7; *Carm.* 1.1.2.13–17.
133. *Ors.* 20.9; 23.8; 29.3, 5, 13; 31.4; 25.16; 39.12; *Carm.* 1.1.2.18–27. We may note here Origen's seminal doctrine of the eternal generation of the Son from the Father. As if anticipating later Nicene arguments, he emphasizes several times that "there was no time when [the Son] was not" (οὐκ ἦν ὅτι οὐκ ἦν) generated by the Father (*Princ.* 1.2.9; 4.4.1; *Comm. Rom.* 1.5; 1.8). Crouzel, *Origen*, p. 187.
134. *Ors.* 20.9; 29.6–8.
135. *Or.* 29.5, 9.
136. See chap. 1, pp. 98–102.
137. Lossky, *Vision of God*, p. 69.

judgment with which Rowan Williams agrees.[138] In Lossky's view, not only does Gregory contradict himself as to whether the vision of God is even possible, but he also makes a decisive shift from the earlier, "relational" doctrine of Origen and Athanasius (a) toward a more purely "objective" understanding of the Trinity (b). Whereas earlier writers had taught that Christians participate in the Trinity by sharing in the Son's relation to the Father, becoming "sons [and daughters] in the Son," Gregory conceives of the Trinity as an object of vision separate from and outside of the Christian's experience. Moreover, this objectification of the Trinity is seen to be a Christianized version of the vision of the single divine substance of pagan Greek mysticism. Thus Williams believes that in Gregory's hands the doctrine of the Trinity is in danger of being severed from its vital connection with the doctrine of salvation and "reverting to the simple human subject-divine object antithesis which earlier Christian writers had sought so hard to modify."[139]

At a basic level, this sort of analysis resembles the claim that the priority of God the Father and the ontological equality of the Trinity are mutually contradictory, which we discussed above, and it too is common in modern interpretation. To oversimplify for the sake of argument, we could describe two basic models or "grammars" of Trinitarian doctrine. According to the first grammar, Christians come to know God the Father in Jesus Christ by the inspiration of the Holy Spirit, as sons and daughters of God and brothers and sisters of Christ, being included within the intra-Trinitarian relations. According to the second grammar, Christians come to know the Trinity, or the divine nature, which exists equally in the three persons, as a single object of vision, in the way that a subject knows an external object. The first grammar is inclusive of the believer, can appear subordinationist, and is often used to characterize pre-Nicene doctrine. The second grammar is exclusive of the believer, is properly unitive, consubstantial, and Trinitarian, and describes Nicene doctrine. In this scheme, Lossky and Williams are saying, in effect, that Gregory is making a major shift from the first to the second grammar. However, this kind of differentiation artificially separates what in Gregory's doctrine is a single theological principle, and it misrepresents both pre-Nicene and Nicene theology as well. As with the criticisms addressed above, Lossky's argument shares an underlying commonality with the Eunomian position: his claim that the vision of God the Father in Jesus Christ by the inspiration of the Spirit conflicts with the vision of the whole Trinity is strikingly similar to the Eunomians' objection that the monarchy of the Father

---

138. Rowan Williams, *The Wound of Knowledge*, p. 67.
139. Ibid.

conflicts with the triune equality. Again, this is just the reverse of Gregory's view, which holds the two grammars together in one. Gregory's achievement is precisely to preserve the Origenist, "relational" structure of the divine life and the soteriological force of Trinitarian doctrine by clarifying its theological meaning more fully than Origen, Athanasius, or Basil did,[140] while also maintaining a more consistent focus on the divine economy, centered on the cross of Christ, than we find in Origen or Eusebius of Caesarea. If we keep in mind the full economic-theological significance of the monarchy of the Father, then the apparent contradiction between these two grammars becomes implausible. For Gregory, the eternal life of the Trinity, which Christians come to know in the divine economy, is already structured both hierarchically and equally, just as the economic knowledge of God is that of the eternal, coequal Trinity. Gregory's doctrine of the Trinity is thus neither subjective nor objective, but both—or quasi-subjective and quasi-objective—being inclusive and exclusive of the believer at the same time. The theology of the divine economy does not remove one out of, or set one above, the divine economy, making the inclusive model exclusive, but it leads one *deeper into it,* revealing its true meaning in the combination of the two grammars.

The combination of these apparently separate models of Trinitarian doctrine is evident throughout Gregory's work. In an early oration, for example, he writes that Christ is worshipped by those who regard the Son and Spirit to be equal to the Father and who uphold the complete faith in the Trinity (3.6). Again, in the final sentence of *Oration* 38, he writes that to participate in Christ, traveling spiritually through his life, death, and resurrection, is to see and to be seen by God, who is worshipped and glorified in the Trinity (38.18).[141] Being focused on Christ and being focused on the Trinity as a whole are not only compatible, but they necessarily belong together. Speaking of the Spirit's role in the Trinity, Gregory begins his poem *On the Spirit,* "Let us bow in awe before the mighty Spirit, who is God in heaven, who to me is God, by whom I came to know God, and who in this world makes me God" (*Carm.* 1.1.3.3–4). In this invitation to praise, there is no conflict or contradiction between the Spirit's status as the eternal God known by Gregory (like an object) and its role as the one who enables Gregory to know God in Christ (like a quasi-subject). Commenting on biblical statements that Christians pray in the Spirit and the Spirit intercedes with God on their behalf,[142] Gregory writes that this should be

---

140. McGuckin gives brief indications in this direction. *St. Gregory,* p. 296n335. See also his rebuttal to Lossky in "Vision of God," pp. 145–146.

141. See also *Or.* 23.13–14.

142. See Jn 4.24; 1 Cor 14.15; and Rom 8.26.

understood as referring to the Spirit praying to itself, since the worship of one member of the Trinity is in effect the worship of all three (31.12), *because* the Father communicates his nature to the Son and the Spirit—again, the monarchy of the Father is the deeper principle.[143]

Gregory's clearest statement of the unified sense of theology comes in his treatment of the vision of the divine light. The eschatological illumination of the being, character, and magnitude[144] of the Trinity will come, he says, "in Christ our Lord himself" (20.12); and Christ initiates Christians into the enlightenment of the whole Trinity (39.20).[145] In his key doctrinal statement near the beginning of the fifth *Theological Oration,* based on Psalm 35.9 ("In your light we shall see light"), he writes first that the three lights of the Father, Son, and Holy Spirit are a single light and one God, and then adds that, according to the "theology of the Trinity," the one divine light of the Trinity is seen specifically in the Son: "out of light (the Father) we comprehend light (the Son) in light (the Spirit)" (31.3).[146]

For Gregory, the knowledge of God in Christ by the gift of the Holy Spirit is the same knowledge that Christians have of the Trinity as a whole. What we have been calling a combination of two models or grammars of the Trinity is simply the basic meaning of the theology of the divine economy. If one believes that the Son and Spirit are truly divine, then the quasi-objective dimension of Trinitarian doctrine (the vision of the Trinity as a whole) is already implied in that confession, even as the quasi-subjective dimension reflects the epistemic structure of the vision of God. On account of the monarchy of the Father, which both orders the Trinity as a causal hierarchy and provides for the equality of all three members in being, Christians are drawn into the life of God both inclusively and exclusively through the divine economy, whose fundamental meaning is theological. As a final point of conceptual clarification, then, we may observe that Gregory's doctrine is both Christocentric and focused on the entire Trinity at the same time, and that to regard these two conceptualities as divergent theological positions is to miss the point of both.

---

143. See also *Or.* 34.6: the grace of the Spirit causes believers to honor all three persons of the Trinity equally. Gregory combines both ideas in 29.21: being reconciled by Christ and illuminated by the Spirit constitute "the more complete revelation" of the Trinity.

144. ἥτις ἐστὶ καὶ οἵα καὶ ὅση.

145. Both of these statements are concluding passages in their orations. See also *Or.* 33.17: the faithful will come to a greater knowledge of the Trinity, which is the bliss of heaven, "in Christ our God."

146. In *Or.* 40.34 Gregory gives the same interpretation of Ps 35.10, and then continues in a Christocentric direction, encouraging his hearers to receive the Word and the healing powers of Christ. Earlier statements can be found in 6.22; 14.9. See also *Or.* 20.7: the eternal light of the Trinity is, again, primarily the Father's.

For Gregory, Christians meet God through the incarnation of Jesus Christ by the inspiration of the Holy Spirit, and in doing so they come to know the one light of the eternal Trinity.

Participation in the Trinity

We began this chapter by noting that at every point Gregory's doctrine of the Trinity expresses the faith of the Church and the basic shape of Christian existence. Just as his Christology and Pneumatology find their meaning in the divinization of the believer, so too his Trinitarian doctrine, centered in the monarchy of God the Father, represents and aims to promote this same process of divinization. We can now say more specifically that, as the theology of the divine economy, the doctrine of the Trinity arises from and includes the economic situation of the theologian. Together with the language of divinization and illumination, Gregory describes the economic nature of theology in terms of "participation" in the Trinity. At the end of one of his most important passages on the Trinity, in the *Third Oration on Peace*, he writes:

> [The Trinity] does not admit into its presence anything of equal honor, since something that is created and servile and participating (μετέχων) and circumscribed cannot attain to its uncreated and sovereign and participated (μεταληπτή) and unbounded nature. For some things are far from it in every respect, while others to some extent draw near to it, and will continue to do so. They draw near not by nature, but by participation (μετάληψις) and precisely when, by serving the Trinity properly, they rise above servitude (Jn 15.15)— unless freedom and dominion consist of this very thing: acquiring a proper knowledge of sovereignty without confounding things that are distinct because of a poverty of mind! If servitude is so great (Mk 9.35), how great must be the sovereignty of those whom one serves? And if knowledge is blessedness, how great must be that which is known? (23.11)

At the conclusion of a detailed and technical discussion of the Trinity, Gregory emphasizes that the purpose and import of Trinitarian doctrine is to draw near to the Trinity and to participate in it. While God infinitely transcends the created order and is unapproachable by creatures in their natural state, God has also condescended to reveal himself in the divine economy in order to be approached by those who serve him and are purified accordingly. This economic knowledge of the Trinity takes place not by comprehension, which is impossible in light of God's infinite magnitude, but by participation, a form of knowledge that comes by faith and service to God. Paradoxically, the freedom of Christian servitude lies in acknowledging the merciful sovereignty of the Trinity that one has met in the divine economy. By confessing that in Christ the Son of God has become human for our salvation, and by accepting the divinizing presence of God in the Holy Spirit, as the revelation of the eternal life of God, one comes to know God not as an object to be mastered, but as the Lord of one's life and of all creation. In the same way that the doctrine of Christ is the means by which one participates in Christ, and the confession of the Spirit's divinity reflects the divinization that one has received from it, so too the doctrine of the Trinity is for Gregory the primary representation of Christian service and the means by which one knows God; and conversely this lived participation is the real meaning of the doctrine of the Trinity.

Gregory emphasizes this basic sense of the Trinity in the passage that immediately follows the one above. Speaking of participation through servitude, he writes,

> *This* is what our great mystery intends (βούλεσθαι)[147] for us. This is our faith and rebirth in the Father, Son, and Holy Spirit, and in our common name:[148] our rejection of godlessness and our confession of Divinity. In fact, this *is* our common name! And so, to dishonor or separate any one of the three is to dishonor our confession—that is, our rebirth, our Divinity, our divinization, our hope. (23.12)

Throughout Gregory's work, the purpose and meaning of the doctrine of the Trinity is to represent and to promote the participation of Christians in the Divinity of God the Father through the Son in the Holy Spirit. Thus the knowledge of the Trinity *is* the faith, rebirth, deification, and hope of Christians. In his farewell address to the council of 381 Gregory says that the best summary of his doctrine is the congregation he has shepherded for the last two years, whose members worship the Trinity with great devotion and are "ruled by each other, by us, and by the Trinity" (42.15).[149] In their lives and their belief, the orthodox faithful of Constantinople themselves represent Gregory's doctrine as well as he could by teaching it point by point. By their true con-

---

147. Vinson translates "means," and Mossay "veut dire." See also *Or.* 2.23, where Gregory discusses the "intention" of the Law, the prophets, and the incarnation in causing the healing ministry of the Church.

148. ἡ θεότης, the Divinity. See also *Ors.* 40.45; 29.13; cf. 31.19; 29.16.

149. Echoing Paul's statement that the Corinthians themselves are the "letter of Christ,... written with the Spirit of the living God... on the tablets of human hearts," which certifies his apostleship (2 Cor 3.1–3).

fession they are governed by the Trinity, which is the source of their solidarity with one another and with Gregory, their leader. Again in *Oration 23*, he states that all of his work on the Trinity is designed "to teach, not to engage in polemic, like the fishermen's Gospel not Aristotelian philosophy, spiritually not maliciously, as befits the Church rather than the marketplace,"[150] so that it makes his hearers both more orthodox and more charitable toward one another (23.12–13).

The connection between conversion of life and participation in the Trinity, which mirrors the dynamic of purification and illumination, is equally prominent in Gregory's other two orations *On Peace*, where he seeks to address the discord among Christians in Constantinople. He concludes the first with a statement to this effect: the Trinity is "the truth that we received from our fathers, reverencing Father and Son and Holy Spirit; knowing the Father in the Son, the Son in the Holy Spirit, in which names we have been baptized, in which we believe, and under which we have been enlisted" (6.22). In the *Second Oration on Peace,* he encourages the discordant Christians in the capital to find harmony with one another by recognizing the internal harmony of the Trinity. All forms of peace and concord derive from the peace of the Trinity, he says, "whose unity of nature and internal peace are its most salient characteristic." Through the peaceable angels, the peace of the Trinity is reflected in the beautiful harmony of the virtues in the human soul and in the marriage of form and function in the healthy members of the body (22.14).[151] Through faith in the Trinity, the unity of God's own eternal being will be realized in all of creation.[152] Likewise, in his most important discussion of the Trinity (25.15–19), Gregory writes that his doctrine is a definition of Christian piety (εὐσέβεια) that includes the entirety of Christian thought and practice. In the middle of this passage he tells Maximus, "First get to *be* one of the things that we have talked about, or someone like them, and then you will come to know them to the same extent that they are known by one another" (25.17). In this regard, the doctrine of the Trinity can only be understood by participating in the Trinity. As he puts it in the final section of *Oration* 20, another major text on the Trinity: "Ascend by the way you live: by purification obtain what is pure. Do you want to be a theologian someday, worthy of the Divinity? Keep the com-

---

150. Similar statements can be found in *Ors.* 41.10 and 40.44.
151. A similar argument occurs in *Or.* 6.12–15.
152. Thus Gregory loosely offers a kind of Nicene social Trinitarianism, though without making the implausible parallel between divine and human persons that has found its way into modern theology.

mandments" (20.12). Here Gregory speaks of the transformation and divinization of the believer that comes through the confession—the theologizing—of Christ, the Holy Spirit, and the entire Trinity within the divine economy, and which is encapsulated in the hermeneutic of piety that governs the literary text of the *Theological Orations*, *Oration* 20, and other works.[153] Before, during, and after his major treatments of Trinitarian doctrine, Gregory emphasizes that the knowledge of the Trinity comes only through purification, illumination, divinization, and participation, by which Christians are "restored" by the Trinity and cling to it as their salvation (42.16, 18).[154]

In his oration *On Baptism*, Gregory defines Christian illumination and divinization in terms that clearly express his Trinitarian theology of the divine economy. The illumination of baptism, he says, is essentially God's contemplation and comprehension of himself, "pouring himself out on what is external to him" as the Spirit enables one to know God in Jesus Christ; and it is at the same time the contemplation of the Father, Son, and Holy Spirit as a whole, "whose riches is their unity of nature and the single outleaping of their brightness" (40.5). The doctrine of the Trinity thus signifies God's own self-knowledge and divine life operating in the believer (20.5; 28.31).[155] As Gregory goes on to argue, it is only the full Trinitarian confession that makes baptism a saving gift and grace of God (40.44).[156] The greatest illumination of baptism, then, is to come to be "with" the Trinity (40.16),[157] and the life of baptismal deification is a participation in the divine life of the Trinity from within.[158] As he states at the end of *Oration 39 On the Holy Lights*, in preparation for the following day's baptisms, the purpose of all Christian doctrine is the "correction and salvation of human beings" through the illumination of the Trinity (39.20).[159] Although the vision of the Trinity will not be complete until the world to come, nevertheless through faith it begins now, in baptism and in the Christian life of ongoing discipleship and deification. Following his Trinitarian exposition in *Oration* 20, Gregory writes, "You have grasped something; now

---

153. See *Ors.* 27; 28.1–3; 31.28–29 and passim, and above, pp. 180–185.
154. See also *Ors.* 33.15; 40.16–17.
155. See also *Or.* 28.3: the divine nature is fully known only to the Trinity itself.
156. See also *Or.* 42.16: it is in the Trinity that baptism has its perfection.
157. μετὰ τῆς Τριάδος γενέσθαι.
158. See also *Or.* 40.41, where Gregory's summary of the Trinity redounds with piety and personal devotion.
159. See also *Or.* 33.15: Christians become gods through the adoration of the Trinity; 40.41: Gregory baptizes and makes people grow with the Trinity, giving it to them to share and defend as an "illumination by the splendor of the Three"; and *Carm.* 1.1.3.47–53, on baptism's cleansing power through the Trinity.

pray to grasp the rest. Love what abides within you, and let the rest await you in the treasury above" (20.12). The kingdom of heaven that Christians hope to attain in the resurrection, when they will know as they are known, is the knowledge of God and "the full illumination of the Holy Trinity." The beginning of that knowledge is given already in this life, even as it is being constantly drawn forward in wonder and desire for God (38.7).[160]

With great spiritual insight, Gregory Nazianzen shows that the Trinity is both the beginning and the end of the Christian life, leading from basic confession and purification to ever-higher levels of participation in God. As he repeatedly insists, Trinitarian doctrine, or Christian language about God, conveys the knowledge of God in Christ and the Holy Spirit; and yet, on the other hand, by its very nature our limited human speech inevitably falls short of its goal. Only when one fully comes to participate in the Trinity can the doctrine of the Trinity be said to have accomplished its purpose, for it is in the actual knowledge of God that its meaning lies. This soteriological meaning is thus inherent in Gregory's doctrine, not merely a secondary application of it, so that to understand the Trinity is to come to know God in Christ by the Holy Spirit, and to have one's life reshaped accordingly. It is not accidental that in Gregory's work the practices of Christian discipleship, divinization, participation, and Trinitarian doctrine are all of a piece. His doctrine of the Trinity not only originates and culminates in a soteriological imperative,[161] but it is soteriological through and through—from its epistemic character as the theology of the divine economy; through the central idea of the monarchy of God the Father, which generates the Son and the Spirit as both distinct from and equal to the Father; to the literary form and conceptual qualifications of Trinitarian statements; to the participatory character of the whole enterprise. When the economic-theological nature of Gregory's doctrine is appreciated, it becomes evident just how seamlessly his Christology, Pneumatology, and Trinitarian theology weave together. Just as the doctrine of Christ amounts to confessing that Jesus is "one and the same" eternal Son of God made flesh, so too the doctrine of the Trinity amounts to recognizing that the Father, Son, and Holy Spirit as revealed in the economy possess "one and the same divine movement and purpose" in eternity (20.7).[162] In each case the theological confession acknowledges the divine identity of the entities in question. The theology of the

---

160. See also *Ors.* 23.12; 30.6; 39.9; 40.5–6; *Carm.* 2.1.45.261–263 *Carmen lugubre*; 2.1.1.194f. *De rebus suis*.
161. See McGuckin, "Perceiving Light," pp. 18–19, 32.
162. See also *Or.* 23.11: their nature is "eternally the same."

divine economy is not a fixed moment in the development of Christian doctrine, after which one dispenses with its economic nature and proceeds in a purely abstract or "immanent" fashion, as if Christian metaphysics stood on its own, apart from its economic context. Rather, in Gregory's view, the doctrine of the Trinity—which is theology in the fullest sense—is fundamentally confessional and doxological, representing the lived communion that Christians have with God through the covenants and the ministry of the Church.

5

Pastoral Ministry

In one thing does the work of a priest lie, and only one: the purification of souls through his life and doctrine.

—*De seipso et de episcopis*

Among his many achievements, Gregory Nazianzen is one of the foremost pastoral theologians of the early Church. Although it is a well-known patristic resource, Gregory's teaching on pastoral ministry is usually studied independent of his teaching on Christ, the Holy Spirit, and the Trinity. From this vantage point, the ministry of the Church, like the purification and illumination of the theologian, is seen to be extrinsic to his Trinitarian doctrine and his other, properly theological concerns. Yet such a view could hardly be farther from Gregory's mind. Since the doctrine of the Trinity—and all Christian theology—takes place within the divine economy in the age of the Church, it involves the Church's pastoral and teaching ministry in an integral way. The transformation of individuals and human society through the participatory knowledge of the Trinity comes about decisively through the ministry of the Church, and so the content of Christian teaching and the practice of Christian leadership reflect the Trinity in central ways. In this chapter we will examine both the pastoral dimension of Gregory's Trinitarian doctrine and the Trinitarian shape of pastoral ministry.[1]

In a fortuitous combination of personal commitments and historical circumstances, the subject of pastoral ministry—and especially the place of the Trinity in it—imposed itself on Gregory at the time of his ordination to the priesthood in 362, and it remained a central concern throughout his career. Gregory's reflections on the priesthood are intimately tied up with his own struggles as a Church leader, and with his work of theological and personal self-definition that lasted until the very end of his life. As he labored to articulate the doctrine of the Trinity in a coherent form between 362 and 381, and again with a flourish of literary activity during his retirement from 381 to 390, he was aiming specifically to clarify the definition and place of the Trinity in the Church's teaching and pastoral ministry. The events of these years—including the local schism in Nazianzus in 361–362, his presbyteral and episcopal ministry in Nazianzus, the Maximus affair in 380, and his struggle at the council of 381—all served to solidify his views in this regard. Time and again, Gregory was faced with the task of defending and teaching the doctrine of the Trinity as a pastor and priest of the Church. As a result, he gives as much attention in his work to Church office as he does to the Trinity per se.[2] In this final chapter we therefore come full circle: having begun with the transformation of the theologian by God, we end with the concrete ecclesiastical means by which this transformation occurs.[3]

The extant collection of Gregory's forty-four orations begins with three orations (1–3) on Christian leadership and the doctrine of the Trinity from the year 362, to which we could add *Oration 6* on the same subject, delivered two years later. If we couple these early works with his many poetic verses on the episcopate and numerous other references to the ministry throughout his career, then the administration of the Trinity by the pastoral leaders of the Church makes up the predominant context and is arguably the overarching

---

1. On Gregory's pastoral theology, see most recently Louth, "St. Gregory Nazianzen on Bishops"; Sterk, *Renouncing the World*, pp. 119–140; Elm, "Diagnostic Gaze"; Daley, "Saint Gregory of Nazianzus as Pastor and Theologian"; Rapp, *Holy Bishops*, esp. pp. 40–45, 121–134; and Gautier, *La retraite*.

2. Bernardi, SC 247, p. 39.

3. The same movement outlined in *Or.* 2.99: one must first study (σχολάζειν) the wisdom of God that is hidden in a mystery, and then speak about it (λαλεῖν) to others. An interesting parallel occurs in the basic framework of Augustine's *On Christian Teaching*, which moves from the discovery (*inveniendo*) to the delivery (*proferendo*) of Christian truth; see *Doctr.* pref.

subject of Gregory's work as a whole.[4] His most developed single treatment of the ministry is the long *Oration 2 On the Priesthood*,[5] which he first delivered in 362 and doubtless expanded during his retirement. Up to this time, explicit reflection on Christian leadership consisted of scattered remarks in the New Testament and a handful of early Church orders, biblical commentaries, and letters.[6] In *Oration 2* Gregory brings the full weight of his piety and education to bear in giving an extended account of the nature of the priesthood. Although he addresses the delicate situation of the local schism and his own flight from the pastoral office, he uses the occasion to offer a much more comprehensive reflection on the priesthood—the first of its kind in Christian literature—which ranges from the personal qualifications and training needed for the ministry to the doctrinal substance and the practical technique of pastoral care.[7] He draws deeply from his study of the Scriptures and early Christian literature, especially Clement and Origen, as well as from the tradition of Greek philosophical rhetoric in which he and Basil had been educated.[8] *Oration 2* was not only the first theological treatise on pastoral ministry in Christian tradition, but it was also the most influential. Within a generation it contributed to Ambrose's idea of clerical decorum and provided the blueprint for John Chrysostom's famous six books *On the Priesthood*. It also exercised a strong influence, through Rufinus' Latin translation, on Gregory the Great's *Pastoral Rule* near the end of the sixth century, and possibly on Augustine's *On Christian Teaching*—the two most influential Western treatises on the ministry—thus making Gregory's work the fountainhead of pastoral reflection in both Eastern and Western Christendom.

Gregory's attention to pastoral ministry continued throughout his career in several different settings: in his early episcopal orations, where he again reflects on his own ministry (*Ors.* 9–12); in his orations in praise of his father, Cyprian of Antioch, Athanasius, and Basil (*Ors.* 18, 24, 21, and 43), which give us more of an indication of Gregory's ideal of the Christian bishop than

---

4. The idea of administering the Trinity is admittedly bold, but, as we shall see, Gregory believes that pastoral leaders—and in fact all Christians—directly participate in the economy of God's saving grace.

5. The work was also entitled an *Apology* (in different variations) in the manuscript tradition. Bernardi, SC 247, p. 84.

6. For a helpful survey of the literature, see Rapp, *Holy Bishops*, pp. 24–41.

7. McLynn notes that Gregory's *Or.* 2 is addressed not so much to the people of Nazianzus as to a "confused Christian society... in ecclesiastical conflict." "Self-Made Holy Man," pp. 468–469.

8. Elm stresses the novelty of Gregory's theory, which proposes an alternative to the previous credentials of "noble birth and free status" ("Diagnostic Gaze," pp. 84–85). While it may have been innovative in his immediate context, the main elements of Gregory's theory were also deeply traditional.

they do of their ostensive subjects;[9] in the three orations on peace, which argue for the sort of pastoral and theological leadership that will unify the current factions within the Church (*Ors.* 6, 22, and 23); in his farewell oration to the council (*Or.* 42); and in several autobiographical poems written during his retirement that focus directly on the character and role of bishops—above all the *De vita sua* and *De seipso et de episcopis* (*Carm.* 2.1.11; 2.1.12). We also have an important reflection on the ministry of all the baptized, in the oration *On the Love of the Poor* (*Or.* 14). Taken together—although *Oration* 2 alone would suffice in this regard—Gregory's writings on pastoral leadership are considerably more thorough and insightful than either Basil's or Gregory of Nyssa's.[10] In the twentieth century—a time when few scholars read beyond the *Theological Orations* in Gregory's corpus and familiarity with the conventions of ancient rhetoric declined among the educated population in general—Gregory came to be stereotyped as an almost pathologically individualistic figure,[11] a far cry from ecclesiastical greatness and, by some accounts, an outright failure compared with the illustrious Basil.[12] Although his stature as a pastoral theologian lags behind that of other Church fathers in modern scholarship and in Western ecclesiastical usage (which followed Augustine and Gregory the Great), Gregory was deeply committed to the ministry of the Church, and he was enormously effective (if deliberately complicated) as an ecclesiastical leader. The quality of his work and the extent of its influence make Gregory the premier patristic teacher on pastoral ministry, equaled only by Augustine in the Latin West.

Gregory's practical recommendations for the exercise of ministry and his descriptions of the character of good and bad bishops have attracted the attention of several scholars,[13] and it was these elements in particular that John Chrysostom and Gregory the Great chose to focus on. Yet for Gregory pastoral ministry is not so much a matter of technique or moral stature (though it includes these), as it is a deeply theological activity. He defines the nature of the priesthood primarily in terms of the divine economy of salvation, and he

---

9. The range of scholarly opinion on this point is broad. Norris argues that Gregory's portrait of Basil is fairly accurate, although he believes that *Or.* 21 shows little knowledge of Athanasius. "Your Honor, My Reputation," pp. 140–159. Elm, on the other hand, regards the portrait of Basil in *Or.* 43 as a complete fabrication. "Programmatic Life," p. 423. As Sterk notes, it was chiefly Gregory's portrait of Athanasius that influenced later Byzantine depictions of him. *Renouncing the World*, p. 129. On Gregory's use of Athanasius as a pastoral exemplar, see Pouchet, "Athanase d'Alexandrie," which concludes that Gregory essentially projects onto Athanasius his own ideals of a bishop in the new Theodosian age (p. 357).

10. Sterk, *Renouncing the World*, pp. 119–140 (here, p. 119).

11. E.g., Bouyer, *Spirituality*, p. 341; Otis, "The Throne and the Mountain."

12. E.g., Rousseau, *Basil*, pp. 65, 87; Gallay, *La vie*, pp. 705–706.

13. Most recently, Elm, "Diagnostic Gaze." See also Sterk, *Renouncing the World*, pp. 119–141; Rapp, *Holy Bishops*, pp. 42–45; and Daley, "Saint Gregory of Nazianzus as Pastor and Theologian."

identifies its main character to be the administration of the Holy Trinity. Nearly two decades before his discussion of the gradual revelation of the Trinity in the fifth *Theological Oration,* Gregory's first reflection on the scope of the divine economy focuses on the pastoral ministry of the Church:

> *This* is what the Law, our schoolmaster (Gal 3.24), intends for us.[14] This is what the Prophets intend, who come between the Law and Christ. This is what Christ intends, who fulfills and is the end of the spiritual Law (see Hb 12.2). This is the intention of the emptied Divinity (Phil 2.7). This is the intention of the flesh taken on (Hb 2.14). This is the intention of the new mixture, God and humanity, one thing out of the two and both present in the one.... This is why... the economy, out of philanthropy toward the one who fell through disobedience, became a new mystery.

He then continues with a litany of Christ's saving deeds, from his conception to his resurrection, in a series of rhetorical antitheses similar to *Oration* 29. 19–20.[15] Finally, he explains,

> All of these were a kind of training (παιδαγωγία) from God for us, and a healing (ἰατρεία) of our weakness, restoring the old Adam to the place from which he fell and conducting him to the tree of life, from which the tree of knowledge estranged him because it was partaken of unseasonably and improperly.... Of *this* healing we who are set over others are the ministers and fellow-laborers (cf. 1 Cor 4.1; 3.9). (2.23–26)

In this long and tightly wrought passage, Gregory describes the basic continuity that exists between the economy of salvation recorded in the Scriptures and the work of the Christian priest in the contemporary Church. He argues that the whole of God's saving work—from the Law and the prophets to Christ's incarnation, passion, and resurrection—"intends" the pastoral ministry of the Church. Standing between Christ's first and second coming, pastoral ministry is both the direct consequence and the intended goal of God's saving work throughout history, even as it prepares creation for the last judgment and the life to come. Just as the New Covenant fulfills and is the end of the Old Covenant, so the life of the contemporary Church, guided by its pastors, fulfills and is the end of both. Now that Christ has returned to the

---

14. On the similar notion of the "intention" of Trinitarian doctrine, see chap. 4, pp. 229–230, on *Or.* 23.12.
15. See chap. 2, pp. 135–136.

Father, Gregory writes in his first oration, he has given us another shepherd and another temple like himself in the person of the Christian priest (1.6). Hence the priest is a steward, or administrator (οἰκονόμος), of the Word, sharing in the stewardship of the divine economy (οἰκονομία) (3.7),[16] and it is God's own correction and loving-kindness (θεία νουθεσία καὶ φιλανθρωπία) that the priest exercises (16.13). As he laments the abuses of episcopal leadership in the late *De seipso et de episcopis,* Gregory notes by contrast the nature of an authentic pastorate, which conveys only divine healing: "How great a salvation we possess from God, which extends through practically the whole universe" (*Carm.* 2.1.12.355–356).[17] The idea is similar to his argument in the fifth *Theological Oration,* where the revelation of the Holy Spirit in the age of the Church surpasses the previous revelations of the Father or the Son (31.25–27): in both cases the Church's knowledge of the Trinity is the apex of the biblical covenants thus far.

This deep continuum of divine grace illuminates Gregory's conception of both the history of salvation and the Church's ongoing pastoral ministry. He characterizes God's saving work in the biblical covenants as the same divine training, or education (παιδαγωγία), and healing (ἰατρεία) that a Christian pastor would administer in the fourth century (2.25). At the same time, he is also saying that the biblical covenants establish and include the present-day ministry of the Church, so that covenantal salvation is the basic form and content of priestly work. The Old Covenant and the New Covenant are thus not merely the foundation of the Church's life and the reservoir of its collective memory, but they are active and present in its ongoing healing and growth toward God. For Gregory, the character of the covenants and of the Church's ministry is one and the same: "Of this healing we, who are set over others, are the ministers and fellow-laborers" (2.26). Consequently, the interpretation of the Bible—of the Old and New Testaments, or Covenants—is the lifeblood of the Church, since in Scripture Christians come to know Jesus Christ, the image of God the Father, as he is worshipped and obeyed in the teaching and the mysteries of the Church by the power of the Holy Spirit. Thus Gregory exhorts clergy to remember above all that they administer the same healing love of men and women (φιλανθρωπία) that God has extended in the covenants, and that they are direct participants in Christ's redemption of Adam.

---

16. See also *Ors.* 18.1; 40.44; 42.24.
17. See also *Or.* 12.4.

The Art of Arts and the Science of Sciences

Gregory understands the work of pastoral ministry, in the most general sense, as an exercise of leadership that is both a service (λειτουργία) carried out in great humility and self-sacrifice, and a form of command (ἡγεμονία, 2.4) that bears real authority (προστασία), responsibility, and the power of spiritual governance (ἐπιστατεῖν, 2.78) within the Christian community. Literally speaking, of course, pastors are shepherds of sheep (1.6);[18] they seek to ensure the well-being of their flocks, who in turn depend on them for nourishment and protection. At the heart of pastoral work for Gregory is the moral and spiritual guidance of men and women (ἄνθρωπον ἄγειν, 2.16), the leadership of souls (ψυχῶν ἡγεμονία, 2.78), which he describes in a broad range of terms. The same principles of leadership apply to both bishops and presbyters, for their work is essentially the same, even as bishops bear a supervisory authority. As an indication of the central work of spiritual guidance, Gregory typically refers to both presbyters and bishops with the traditional term "priest," especially in *Oration* 2.[19] Bishops and presbyters share in the priesthood and in the "presidency" (προεδρία) over the local Christian community (2.111). For Gregory the leadership of the Church (at its best) reflects God's providential ordering of all things. As in the cosmos and in the divine economy, there is a certain order in the constitution of the Church, according to which some members are gifted and well disposed to lead and others to follow, all for the good of the whole body (2.3).[20] As the power differential between shepherds and sheep indicates, the priest is a spiritual ruler of those who are ruled (2.3)[21] and thus occupies a high and noble office (7.3).[22] Gregory stresses that this order of pastoral guidance should be preserved and not upset (19.10),[23] since "the rule of many is the rule of none" (32.4). Although the leadership of priests and bishops is seen as primary and decisive for the overall health of the body, it is not exclusive: its primary function, in fact, is to enable and promote the ministry of all baptized (16.13); and through it all, it is Christ who ultimately leads and guides his

---

18. See also *Ors.* 9.4; 12.2; 13.4.
19. In the poems, however, Gregory speaks to bishops more specifically. Overall he refers to "bishops" and "priests" roughly the same amount (just under 100 times each), and to "presbyters" about half as much.
20. See also Gregory's lengthy meditation on ecclesiastical leadership and cosmic and social order in *Or.* 32.
21. See also *Ors.* 21.7; 32.10–13.
22. See also *Ors.* 18.37; 36.3; *Carm.* 2.1.12.18.
23. See also *Or.* 1.7.

Church (18.4).[24] We have already seen the strong and even pioneering ways in which Gregory speaks of the leadership exercised by women like his mother, Nonna, and his sister, Gorgonia.[25] It should be noted at the outset that, despite his high view of priestly authority and effectiveness, Gregory does not envision the kind of strict, exclusive clerical mediation found in the Pseudo-Dionysius' *Ecclesiastical Hierarchy*.[26]

Gregory draws on Scripture, Christian tradition, and Greek professional categories of philosophy, rhetoric, and medicine in order to describe the nature and work of pastoral ministry. He calls it a τέχνη, a distinctive art or craft with its own method and sense of expertise, a science or profession based on a discreet body of knowledge (ἐπιστήμη).[27] Yet among all the arts and sciences priestly ministry is preeminent: the spiritual guidance of men and women is, in Gregory's famous phrase, "the art of arts and the science of sciences" (2.16).[28] As he prepares to undertake the responsibilities of his own episcopal ministry, he describes the work of a bishop as "the service and ministry of the Spirit, the strengthening of the people, the governance of souls, teaching through word, deed, and example 'with the weapons of righteousness' (2 Cor 6.7)"; it leads people from the world to God, "consumes the body, dedicates them to the Spirit, turns away from the darkness, glories in the light, drives away predators, draws together the fold, guards against precipices and desert solitudes, and helps it to reach the mountains and high places" (9.3). A decade later, Gregory looks back on his work in Constantinople with this summary reflection:

> In one thing does the work of a priest lie, and only one: the purification of souls through his life and his doctrine. He should raise them towards the heights with inspired movements; he should be serene, high-minded, reflecting like a mirror only the godly and

---

24. For a discussion the several terms for leadership used in *Ors.* 1–3, see Bernardi, SC 247, pp. 45–48.

25. It was Nonna, Gregory says (*Or.* 18.6–7), who was the true spiritual leader (ἀρχηγός) in the family, even though his father was the bishop. Since all priests and bishops in Gregory's time were men, I will use masculine pronouns to refer to them, for the sake of historical accuracy; when speaking of the ministry of all the baptized in Gregory's time, and of both lay and ordained leaders in our own, I will refer to both men and women.

26. On the similarity of ordained and non-ordained Christian leadership and priesthood in Origen, see McGuckin, "Origen's Doctrine of the Priesthood."

27. In ancient Greek ἐπιστήμη refers most generally to a practical or professional skill and the understanding that accompanies it, as well as to knowledge in general. Plato and Aristotle further developed the latter meaning into scientific knowledge, as opposed to opinion (δόξα). ἐπιστήμη is coupled with ἐμπειρία and τέχνη in Plato, *Rep.* 422c and *Ion* 536c, and in Aristotle, *Metaph.* 981a2 (LSJ, s.v.), an association which Gregory continues.

28. τέχνη τεχνῶν καὶ ἐπιστήμη ἐπιστημῶν. See also *Or.* 36.12: true faith is the "first of all the sciences." Gregory the Great will take up this pithy definition in his own *Pastoral Rule*.

unspotted images that have been formed inside him; he should send
up pure offerings for his children, until the day when he perfects
them into an offering. Other matters should be left to those who are
capable of dealing with them. In this way we could have a secure life.
(*Carm.* 2.1.12.751–760)²⁹

Central to Gregory's many writings on the subject is a concern to clarify the essentials of ecclesiastical leadership, both for those who aspire to be Christian leaders at any time, and especially for clergy in times like his own, when faithful leadership seems to be so compromised. Everything that the priest does should be devoted to purifying his flock and leading it to God, and Gregory is deeply critical of those who forsake this basic responsibility for any other motive.

In order to highlight the unique character and the superiority of the pastoral art—to clarify his pastoral "technology"—Gregory employs the conventional metaphor of a physician, long familiar in biblical parlance and Hellenistic rhetorical and medical theory. In what would become the dominant metaphor for pastoral ministry in later Christian tradition, he describes the treatment of souls (ἰατρεία) by comparing it with the treatment of bodies (θεραπεία). The immediate focus and the material (ὕλη) of the pastoral science, he argues, is the human soul (2.16); through the treatment of souls (θεραπεία ψυχῶν) the priest grafts people into the olive tree of Israel, much as Gregory's father had been drawn into the Church through the influence of Nonna (7.3). Although medical treatment is difficult, Gregory says, pastoral treatment is even more so, on account of the worth of its subject, the kind of work that it involves, and the final aim of its efforts. Whereas the medical art strives to prevent physical disease and decay, the body is fated to die regardless, and cannot escape the limitations of its mortality, no matter how successful the physician (2.16).³⁰ Pastoral treatment, on the other hand, strives to heal the soul, which is divine and shares more closely in the dignity of heaven (2.17). Because the soul is immortal, the pastoral science promises an eternal result that the most successful medical treatment can never attain. Yet even while the priest focuses on the healing of souls, Gregory makes it clear that pastoral care is not unconcerned with the body, for the soul's growth closely involves that of the body and is meant to benefit the body permanently. Drawing its "lower nature" to itself, the leading power (ἡγεμονικόν) of the soul frees the body from its

---

29. For other definitions, see *Ors.* 2.22; 7.3; 9.5–6; 19.9; 43.66.
30. See also *Ors.* 2.27; 14.18, 37.

grossness, redeems it, and makes it able to partake in the resurrection of the dead, so that "the soul may be to the body what God is to the soul, leading on the matter that serves it, and uniting it, as its fellow-servant, to God" (2.17–18).[31] In terms of its subject, the human soul and body, the pastoral science demonstrates its superiority, since in the end it ensures the well-being of the body more effectively than physical medicine.

In terms of its scope and method, medical treatment deals mainly with surface phenomena and rarely explores the real source of one's problems, whereas the treatment of souls focuses on the "hidden man of the heart" (1 Pt 3.4) in order to address the deeper causes of our malaise (2.21).[32] While the physician seeks to cure physical ailments by examining several different factors and symptoms, it is even more difficult to cure the internal malignancies of "our habits, passions, lives, and wills" (2.18), for they are both harder to diagnose and more resistant in their treatment. Gregory shares the lament of many clergy before and since that pastoral treatment and Christian growth are greatly obstructed by human cleverness (σύνεσις), selfishness (τὸ φίλαυτον), and a general disinclination to submit to pastoral guidance. Like an armed defense, people self-destructively resist their spiritual physicians with the very zeal with which they should welcome their treatment (2.19). People tend either to hide their sin and make excuses for it, Gregory observes, or they parade it openly and shamelessly (2.20). As if this was not enough, the priest faces a daunting inner adversary, the devil, who causes us to destroy ourselves, "hands us over to the death of sin," and makes us treat our true benefactors like enemies (2.20–21). The madness (παραπληξία) of this disordered state of mind (πάθος) thus makes the pastor's job especially challenging (2.20), so that leading other people is not only exceedingly important, but is more difficult than being obedient to a superior (2.10).[33]

In order to cure souls and lead people to God, then, the priest must apply God's healing grace to people in a wide variety of conditions; and it is in this complex adaptation that much of the skill and method (λόγος) of pastoral work lies. In the traditions of Christian theology and Greek philosophical rhetoric in which Gregory was steeped, it had long been observed that anyone who hopes to guide others in moral or religious development must account for their different situations and needs, and respond accordingly.[34] Gregory considers the

---

31. On Gregory's Christian use of soul-body language, see chap. 1, pp. 79–83.
32. See also *Or.* 37.22.
33. See also *Or.* 13.4.
34. See, e.g., 1 Cor 9.19–23; Clement of Alexandria, *Strom.* 7. In earlier Greek tradition, see esp. Gorgias, *Pal.* 22; Plato, *Phaedr.* 277b–c.

problem with great sensitivity and sophistication in *Oration* 2. Those whose souls the pastor seeks to heal often differ widely in a variety of natural and environmental factors, including sex, age, affluence, mood, health, power, knowledge, virtue, fortune, marital status, religious vocation, competence in prayer, place of residence, craftiness, and occupation (2.28–29). Yet even more challenging, he says, are people's psychological and moral qualities, the desires and appetites that make up our personalities, which differ even more greatly than the former categories. The management and ordering (ἡ οἰκονομία) of each of these conditions, Gregory admits, is not at all easy (2.29). As many pastors have no doubt seen for themselves, the most difficult traits of all are excessive piety (εὐσέβεια), which ironically makes people resistant to new teaching,[35] insolent opposition,[36] and fickle eclecticism[37] (2.39–42).[38] Finally, encompassing each of the other factors, the pastor must account for different stages of Christian growth. Here Gregory again shows himself to be a disciple of Origen, whose entire theological system was organized according to the spiritual development of the saints. Origen saw a scheme of spiritual progress in the whole of Scripture—particularly the three books of Solomon[39]—that could be summarized using the images of milk and solid food found in Paul and Hebrews.[40] Hence some Christians are babes and require the milk of the most simple and elementary doctrines; if they were taught beyond their level, they would be overwhelmed with food they could not digest, and would possibly even lose their original strength. Yet the more mature require "the wisdom that is spoken among the perfect (1 Cor 2.6) and the higher and more solid food," since they have learned to discern the truth from falsehood; simple doctrine would annoy them and fail to strengthen them in Christ (2.45).[41]

Among this great complexity of human situations and spiritual needs, Gregory argues, it is crucial that the pastor accurately discern each person's condition and administer the appropriate treatment, just as a physician diagnoses a bodily sickness in order to prescribe the right cure. For unlike virtue and vice, which are always respectively beneficial and harmful, the various medicines (φαρμακεῖαι) of pastoral treatment are not either wholesome or

---

35. See Rom 10.2.
36. See Ps 72(73).8; Mt 7.6; and 2 Tim 3.8.
37. See Eph 4.14.
38. See also *Ors.* 6.2; 19.6–7.
39. See esp. Origen, *Comm. Cant.*
40. See Rom 14.2; 1 Cor 3.1–3; Hb 5.12–14; Origen, *Orat.* 27.5–6; *Comm. Cant.* Prol., 1.4; *Cels.* 3.53; see also *Ors.* 2.66; 4.18.
41. See Phil 4.13; Col 2.19.

dangerous in every case, and a particular therapy can be healing in one situation but harmful in another (2.33). Some people therefore require direct and frank instruction, while others need to be taught by example; some need to be encouraged, but others must be restrained; and so on (2.30–32). Moreover, the priest must administer each treatment with a sense of the proper timing: it is not enough to apply the right therapy to the right condition if it is done at the wrong time, which can cause injury (2.31). Gregory makes the Homeric observation that human beings are "the most variable and manifold of creatures" (2.16), and so the priest must be like a skilled musician, playing his congregation like a many-stringed instrument (2.39), or like an animal tamer who trains a monster made up of numerous wild animals (2.44). In other words, the Christian leader (ὁ ἐπιστάτης, ὁ προστάτης) must possess the essential quality of adaptability. He must be both "simple (ἁπλοῦς) in his uprightness in all respects, and as far as possible manifold and varied (παντοδαπὸς καὶ ποικίλος) in his knowledge," in order to apply a suitable treatment in each case (2.44).

The Christian priest thus embodies a paradox of stability and flexibility, of simplicity and multiplicity, in order best to guide the moral and spiritual development of his flock. So Gregory praises Athanasius for embodying this quality, in terms that reveal Gregory's own ideal: "Some he praised, yet others he rebuked (with moderation). With some he stirred up their indolence; with others he calmed their hotheadedness. With some he took care to keep them from falling, but with others he devised a way for them to recover from a fall. He was simple (ἁπλοῦς) in disposition, yet manifold (πολυειδής) in his administration.... He truly combined in himself all of the names that the sons of Greece gave to their different gods.... O, how many names does this man's many-sided virtue afford me when I want to name them!" (21.36). Athanasius' adaptability was so exceptional that he united a whole array of virtues and episcopal practices in a perfect combination of simplicity and multiplicity.[42] Likewise, Basil fulfilled Paul's description of pastoral adaptability, pleasing others by becoming all things to all people (1 Cor 9.22, 43.64). Gregory praises his father for the same reason: Gregory the Elder showed his great power to cleanse others (18.15) by knowing the right time to use the rod and the staff (though of course he relied most on the staff), showing compassion toward sinners and sympathy for the strong in their faith, rebuking pride but encouraging the lowly (18.22–23).[43] As each of these examples demonstrates,

---

42. On Athanasius' simplicity, see also *Or.* 21.33.
43. See also *Or.* 18.13.

Christian priests administer God's economy of salvation by exercising the superior craft of pastoral ministry, adapting themselves to the particularities of each recipient's situation, and applying the appropriate treatment for the eternal health of the whole person.[44]

Pastoral Experience and Priestly Virtue

At the same time that Gregory describes pastoral ministry as a professional skill based on a discrete body of knowledge, he is equally concerned that it not be imagined as an abstract theory or an airtight system of rules that one can first learn, say, from a textbook and then simply apply in practice. Rather, like the medical profession, pastoral work is rooted in human experience. After describing the method of pastoral adaptability that we have just examined, Gregory makes the following qualification: "Now to set before you the distinction between all these things and to give you a perfectly exact view of them, so that you can have a complete comprehension of our therapy, is quite impossible, even for someone who is highly qualified in care (ἐπιμελεία) and cleverness (σύνεσις). But actual experience and practice are required to form a medical system and a medical man"[45] (2.33). In the same way that the knowledge of God depends on and consists in a thorough transformation of the whole person by God, so too, Gregory insists, pastoral ministry is rooted in the priest's own experience of God's redeeming work. His point is not that pastoral ministry has no foundation in a coherent body of doctrine or lacks any concrete standards of procedure, but rather that the administration of the divine economy requires a deep, experiential knowledge of the things one is administering and the people whom one serves. Time and again Gregory argues that it is impossible to convey to others a good that one does not possess oneself, even as one cannot minister to those whom one has not diagnosed in their concrete reality. In his indictment of pastoral abuses in Constantinople, he focuses on this very point. While some would claim that grace alone is sufficient to make a good bishop, regardless of his training, reputation, or character, he replies that an untrained and inexperienced priest will only cheapen Christian doctrine and risk making it no longer recognizable.[46] He asks, who would think of teaching flute playing or dancing without having

---

44. On pastoral adaptation, see also *Ors.* 9.5–6; 13.4; 27.3, 5–6; 37.1 (on Jesus' own adaptability).
45. ἐπὶ δὲ τῆς πείρας αὐτῆς καὶ τῶν πραγμάτων τῷ θεραπευτῇ λόγῳ καὶ ἀνδρὶ καταφαίνεται.
46. See also *Or.* 27.3.

mastered these arts oneself (2.50)? Or who would presume to captain a ship without having first handled the oar, manned the helm, and had some experience of wind and sea (43.26)?[47] As in any other profession, the priest must have an actual experience of his craft in order to practice it well; otherwise, Gregory says, the flock will be superior to the shepherd (*Carm.* 2.1.12.541–574). As Gregory the Elder demonstrates, experience (ἐμπειρία) is the basis of pastoral wisdom (16.20).[48]

Yet the experience needed to master the science of pastoral care is not simply the previous exercise of priestly tasks, in a purely external sense; it is most fundamentally the pastor's inner character of virtue and holiness. As in the purification of the theologian, the virtue that is prerequisite to pastoral ministry is a prominent theme in Gregory's reflection on the priesthood. Near the beginning of *Oration* 2, he writes, "Those whom God appoints to lead his people must be distinguished above all by their virtue" (2.3). In order to care for one's sheep with a pastoral method (λόγος ποιμαντικῆς) that is worthy of Christ, the true Shepherd, a good priest must "walk in the King's Highway (Nm 20.17)" by living a life of Christian virtue (2.34).[49] In his oration *On Moderation in Debate*, Gregory confronts the aspiring pastor with this central question:

> Do you think talking about God is important? It is more important to purify yourself for God.... Do you think teaching is important? It is safer to be a disciple.... Why do you make yourself a shepherd when you are a sheep?... If you are an adult in Christ and your "faculties have been trained" (Hb 5.14) and the light of your knowledge is bright, then utter the wisdom of God that is spoken among the perfect and is secret and hidden (1 Cor 2.6–7) whenever you receive it and it has been entrusted to you. (32.12–13)

As Gregory frequently reiterates, only those who have been purified are in a position to purify others.[50]

The personal character of the priest is one of the major themes of Gregory's late poem *De seipso et de episcopis*. Speaking to bishops who are unworthy of the office, he admonishes, "It would be better for you to be completely

---

47. Gregory continues in this passage with metaphors of the military, medicine, and painting.
48. See also *Ors.* 6.19; 26.1.
49. So Christ is called "Shepherd" (Jn 10.11, 14; Hb 13.30; and 1 Pt 5.4) because he employs the "principles of pastoral science" (λόγοι ποιμαντικῆς ἐπιστήμης) to gather us into the heavenly sheepfold (*Or.* 30.21).
50. *Ors.* 6.1–2; 7.3; 8.5 (on Gregory the Elder); 15.12 (on Eleazar); 20.1–4; 39.14; *Carm.* 2.1.12.475–574.

purified;...whereas you purify others while you yourself are filthy" (*Carm.* 2.1.12.476–478). It is not enough simply to avoid vice; a priest must excel in virtue, never resting on the laurels of his progress but focusing on how much he still has to grow (2.14).[51] Purity of heart not only enables one to understand the depths of Scripture (2.48) and to know God at all, but it is the necessary foundation for the safe exercise of religious power and authority. For only a virtuous priest, Gregory says, can lead others by persuasion; every other form of influence amounts to the tyranny of the world (2.15).[52] For reasons of kindness as well as effectiveness, he insists that the rulers of the Church must lead others by goodwill and persuasion based on their exemplary character, never by force or compulsion. Although he possesses great authority within the community, in practice the priest should lead not by the power of his office, but by the magnetic quality of his instruction (12.5).[53] While he is deeply committed to the institutions and offices of the visible Church, Gregory, like Origen before him, insists that the authority of all the Church's ministries must be based in the charisma of holiness, or else it will be both a fraud and menace to Christian people.[54] To endeavor to guide others without first attaining this prerequisite virtue is exploitive, foolish, and rash, and can be disastrous for everyone involved (2.47).[55] Priestly virtue is thus the single most important element of pastoral ministry, above education, eloquence, and social status. Gregory's emphasis on the virtue of the priesthood strongly influenced later traditions of pastoral reflection.

As with purification in general, Gregory is clear where the source of priestly virtue lies. The holiness and the diagnostic insight on which the priest depends come directly from the Holy Spirit, who confers the grace of Christ for pastoral work. This is the first aspect of his own ministry that Gregory mentions in his collected orations; as he begins his ordained ministry on the Easter feast (1.1), he prays that the risen Christ would renew him by his Spirit, so that he can be a good example and teacher for Christ's people (1.2). The entire process of pastoral development—from elementary purification to the inspired

---

51. See Phil 3.7.

52. See Jesus' warning against adopting the tyranny of the Gentiles in Church leadership (Mk 10.42–45 and par.).

53. οὐκ ἀρχή, ἀλλὰ παιδαγωγία. See also *Or.* 6.20; *Carm.* 2.1.12.775. Rapp calls the prerequisite of virtue for all pastoral functions the "dialectic of episcopal leadership" in late antiquity. *Holy Bishops*, p. 41.

54. Gregory thus belies the distinction between institutional and charismatic or prophetic authority that has often been invoked since the seminal works of Holl, *Enthusiasmus und Bussgewalt*, and Campenhausen, *Ecclesiastical Authority*.

55. See also *Or.* 2.91.

study of Scripture to the work of guiding God's people—represents what Gregory calls "the order of the Spirit (ἀκολουθία πνευματική)" (6.1).[56] In *Oration* 2 he describes the Spirit's effect on Christian leaders in similar terms: only by the Spirit are they able "to perceive, to expound, or to embrace the truth in regard to God, for only by purity can one grasp the one who is pure" (2.39). As with the purification of all Christians, pastors must surrender to the Spirit (9.2) and be enabled by the Spirit to speak of the things of the Spirit (19.2). In the ordination rite the priest or bishop is also anointed with the oil of chrism— literally, "made a christ"—and is "entrusted with the Spirit" to lead and guide God's people (6.9). So Gregory refers to his own sacramental anointing at his ordination to the priesthood (1.2)[57] and (with not a little exasperation) to the episcopate: "chrism and Spirit on me again!" (9.1). Yet, just as baptism is the paradigmatic, but not the exclusive, enactment of purification, the priest's anointing by the Spirit at his ordination is an essential empowerment for ministry that is part of a much longer, ongoing process of formation and surrender to the Spirit, without which the pastor's authority is undermined.[58] The spiritual authority of the priest or bishop is therefore based on his own purification and illumination, in all their practical and contemplative dimensions, which also come from the Spirit,[59] and episcopal ministry is fundamentally a "spiritual profession" (12.3). It was the Holy Spirit, Gregory says, that led him to combine monastic study and priestly service; he now dedicates himself completely to the Spirit, so he can become "an instrument of God, an instrument of the Word (ὄργανον λογικόν) tuned and plucked by the Spirit" (12.1), and he in turn can play his congregation like a musician (2.39).[60]

---

56. See also *Or.* 18.15, where Gregory applies the same phrase to his father's preparation for the episcopate.

57. "A mystery anointed me." We should probably include *Or.* 6.9 as a similar reference: [In the voice of God] "I shall add to their number the most venerable of shepherds, even if, for spiritual reasons, he postpones the assumption of his pastoral duties." The identity of the shepherd has been debated (see Calvet-Sebasti, SC 405, pp. 16–18, 142–143n1), but it should probably be understood as Gregory himself: a consecrated priest who wisely postpones his pastoral duties, but will in due time take up his staff and shepherd the flock—referring to his expected succession of his elderly father as bishop of Nazianzus, and possibly to his future ministry in Constantinople, if the passage was added later.

58. As can be seen in Gregory's many passages directed against bad bishops, on which see below. Gregory does not seem to have held the belief that the conferral of the Spirit at ordination stems from the physical apostolic succession of the ordaining bishop.

59. Thus Gregory's work does not show the kind of distinction that Rapp observes between "spiritual authority," which comes from the Spirit, and "ascetic authority," which comes from one's own efforts. See *Holy Bishops*, esp. chaps. 3 and 4, though the complex interrelationship between the two is noted on pp. 100–101.

60. See also *Ors.* 12 (on Gregory); 13.4 (on Eulalius); 18.1, 3, 36, 40 (on Gregory the Elder); 21.7, 9; 33.13; 42.12; 43.37.

Just as Moses is the chief exemplar of the knowledge of God (28.2–3), so he appears regularly in Gregory's work as a model of the initiated hierophant who is qualified to teach others about God (2.92).[61] Moses, in fact, becomes the premier biblical model of episcopal leadership in early Christian literature,[62] thanks again in large part to Gregory's influence.[63] In Gregory's panegyric Athanasius also exemplifies the bishop whose virtue provided the ground for his ministry according to the order of the Spirit. Unlike illegitimate intruders, who "paid nothing in advance for the priesthood ... and purify others before being purified themselves" (21.9), Athanasius entered holy orders by way of the requisite virtue, which God instilled in him as "a foundation for great deeds" (21.7). He abounded with private and public virtue: in fasting, prayer, vigils, psalmody, care for the poor, courage in the face of rulers, condescension to the lowly, guidance of the simple, legislation and support of monks and virgins, protection of orphans, and treatment of the sick (21.10, 35–36), so that his life and his teaching were in perfect harmony (21.30, 37). Basil, too, exhibits the virtue that should precede ordination: out of his love for men and women (φιλανθρωπία) and his saving plan (οἰκονομία), God revealed Basil's virtue and enlisted him in presbyterate. Unlike the many who want to lead after becoming wise in an instant, God conferred on Basil the honor of ordination "according to the order and law of spiritual ascent" (43.25), which brought about a true development of virtue.[64]

In *Oration* 2 Gregory draws special attention to the example of the apostle Paul. While both Peter and Paul received the skill and grace for ministry (2.51),[65] Paul stands out among all the disciples, lawgivers, and prophets as the one who demonstrates in word and deed the great importance of the care of souls (2.52). Not only did Paul suffer numerous external hardships in his

---

61. See esp. *Ors.* 20.2; 32.16–18. Gregory looks to other biblical figures as well, esp. Aaron, Jacob, Manoah, Isaiah, Jeremiah, Peter, and Paul. See 1.1; 7.3; 9.1; 18.14; 21.3; 26.4. Rapp argues that Moses is also the preeminent model of the leader who combines spiritual, ascetical, and pragmatic authority for a variety of patristic writers. See *Holy Bishops*, pp. 20, 125–136; see also Sterk, "On Basil, Moses, and the Model Bishop." It happens that most of the authors Rapp cites were probably inspired by Gregory's work on Moses, including Basil of Caesarea, Gregory of Nyssa, John Chrysostom, Palladius, and John of Damascus—Eusebius of Caesarea being an interesting exception before Gregory, who associates Moses not with the model bishop but the Emperor Constantine (see *V. Const.* 1.20.2; 38.2–5; 44.1).

62. Rapp, *Holy Bishops*, pp. 20, 125–136. See also Sterk, "On Basil, Moses, and the Model Bishop."

63. See chap. 1, p. 65n6.

64. See also *Or.* 43.26: "We manufacture holy people in a single day, and we invite them to be wise (σοφούς) who have never been instructed (σοφίζεσθαι)"; 43.34–38. The entire oration aims to praise Basil's virtue. Gregory also praises the virtue of his father (7.3; 12.2; 18); Eulalius (13.4); Cyprian of Carthage (24); and Melitius of Antioch (*DVS* 1512–1524).

65. Possibly referring to their respective vocations as apostles to the Jews and the Gentiles (Gal 2.8–9); Browne and Swallow, *NPNF* 2.7, p. 215nζ.

care for the churches (2.53), but he masterfully combined kindness and strictness in a ministry that was both simple and manifold. So he instructed "slaves and masters (Eph 6.5–9), rulers and ruled (Rom 8.1–3), husbands and wives (Eph 5.22, 25), parents and children (Eph 6.1–4), marriage and celibacy (1 Cor 7), self-discipline and indulgence (Rom 14.3, 6), wisdom and ignorance (1 Cor 1.27; 3.18), circumcision and uncircumcision (Rom 2.25, 29), Christ and the world, the flesh and the spirit (Gal 5.16)" (2.54). The consummate pastor, Paul administers the appropriate treatment to each type of person—accompanying, checking, excommunicating, grieving, rejoicing—always according to the needs of each, in the best interest of his spiritual children (cf. 1 Cor 10.33) (2.55). Above all, Paul's ministry was defined by the cross of Christ, and he lived always "for Christ and his preaching" (2.56). Paul's exemplary ministry thus fulfills the requirements of faith, grace, and adaptive priestly skill (2.21), providing a perfect model for the contemporary pastor.[66] As a result of Gregory's reflections in these passages of *Oration 2*, Paul became the chief exemplar for John Chrysostom and many subsequent pastoral theologians.[67]

In addition to these positive examples, Gregory devotes considerable attention to the abuses of the ministry and to castigating bad bishops, especially following his disillusionment with the state of the Church in the capital.[68] Such problems seem to have been fairly common in Cappadocia in the late fourth century; complaints about clerical incompetence and misbehavior, as well as local violence and the needed reform of marriage regulations, can be found in the correspondence of Basil and Amphilochius as well.[69] In a letter to the bishops of Italy and Gaul, Melitius complains about rampant pastoral abuse in terms so similar to Gregory's that he may have been informed by a reading of Gregory's *Oration 2*.[70] Yet it was Gregory's profound disillusionment in the summer of 381 that brought out some of his most prophetic work on this common theme. In his panegyric on Basil he laments, "At this moment the holiest office of all is in danger of being the most ridiculous among us; for promotion depends not on virtue but on vice, and the thrones go not to the most worthy but to the most powerful" (43.26). Gregory is referring specifically to his successor to the throne of Constantinople, the theologically inept but

---

66. See also *Or*. 21.1, 7.
67. John Chrystostom, *Sacerd*. 3.7; 4.6–8; 6.9.
68. Major passages occur in *Ors*. 20, 32, 21, 42, and 43, as well as *Carm*. 2.1.12 *De seipso et de episcopis*; *Carm*. 2.1.11 *De vita sua*; and several other poems from his retirement, as well as the section on wicked shepherds in *Or*. 2, which Gregory probably added after he left Constantinople.
69. Basil, *Ep*. 188, 199, and 217 to Amphilochius. Van Dam, *Becoming Christian*, pp. 53–54.
70. Pseudo-Basil, *Ep*. 92.

well-connected senator Nectarius, but also to the more general problem of clergy who approach Church leadership from the system of social patronage that was central to the standard careers in municipal and imperial service. Like his great Western counterpart, Augustine of Hippo, Gregory appreciated the obvious advantages that a good education and an acquaintance with the systems of power could contribute to one's ministry—especially if one hoped to capture the hearts and minds of the ruling elite in the capital of the Eastern empire. Yet throughout his career he detested the intrusion of worldly ambition and the direct carryover of traditional patronage into the leadership of the Church, which, as we have seen, should be based primarily on spiritual virtue.[71] Although it is usually assumed that Gregory regarded Nectarius with pleasant respect (again due to a limited reading of Gregory's texts), John McGuckin has demonstrated what a profound disgust Gregory felt for his successor.[72] In Gregory's mind Nectarius represented the very worst of spiritual inexperience in a Christian leader, and one whose authority was based entirely on political and ecclesiastical connections. In his retirement, it was the memory of Nectarius, more than anyone else, that galled him to no end.

Oration 2 contains twelve sections of admonitions from the Old Testament prophets against pastoral abuses (2.57–68), followed by two from the New Testament (2.69–70) and another eight on the troubles of the current episcopate (2.79–86), much of which was likely added during Gregory's retirement from the debacle of Constantinople.[73] His complaints are several. To begin with, many ordinands ignore the need to study the Scriptures, pray the Psalms, and undertake philosophic ascesis before presuming to lead others (2.49). Even though it is obvious that other arts, like dancing and flute playing, require training and discipline in order to attain a level of mastery, some clergy think that divine wisdom can be acquired simply by wanting to be wise (2.50).[74] There is partisan fighting and a general lack of holiness among Church leaders, and social networks have taken precedence over personal virtue in the selection of priests, with no order to be found anywhere (2.79–82). Wicked leaders have taken to quarreling over just about anything, all under the pretext of faith and without any fixed rules, so that Christians have again become a

---

71. See Rapp's penetrating argument that spiritual authority is the real basis of the ascetical and pragmatic authority of Christian bishops in late antiquity. *Holy Bishops*, pp. 16–18 and passim.

72. McGuckin has convincingly reconstructed the situation, reinterpreting the epistolary record and decoding anonymous references in *De vita sua*, *De rebus suis*, and *De seipso et de episcopis*. See "Autobiography as Apologia"; *St. Gregory*, pp. 374–384. See also McLynn, "Voice of Conscience."

73. See also *Or.* 1.1.

74. See also *Or.* 43.26.

spectacle at public festivities and in the theater (2.83–85). This state of affairs brings him to tears (2.51). Gregory's ire was certainly piqued in the wake of the events of 381, yet we can see the same concerns evident in the period before 379 as well. He praises his father, for example, for protecting the priesthood from unholy candidates during the current disorder (18.15, 22).[75] In his disgust at the theological cowardice of the bishops at the Council of Constantinople, he comments, "We are on a knife-edge: either our holy and venerable dogma can be saved, or it will cease to exist, torn apart by strife.... An incompetent priest—and how much more an incompetent bishop!—is an outrage to the mystery" (*DVS* 1645–1653).[76] Those who abuse pastoral office are not the only ones subjected to the high standard of priestly virtue; Gregory believes that all pastoral leaders will be called to give account for the work they have done (2.113). He is acutely aware of his own unworthiness, and he fears the great responsibilities involved (2.10).

Excursus: On the Love of the Poor

Before we move to the heart of Gregory's pastoral theology, it will be valuable to examine a particular example of the ministry of all Christians, in the care for the poor, the sick, and the homeless. In his efforts to address the social crisis that arose from the famine in the area of Caesarea in the late 360s,[77] Gregory composed a lengthy oration *On the Love of the Poor* (*Or.* 14), in which he gives a fulsome account of the theological basis of this ministry;[78] similar themes are echoed elsewhere, including *Oration* 16 and the panegyrics on Basil and Athanasius (*Ors.* 21, 43). Gregory worked closely with Basil and Gregory of Nyssa, whose own sermons on the love of the poor share many themes with Gregory's.[79] By comparison, Gregory's oration is at once the richest in classical

---

75. Plus whatever material on bad bishops existed in the original version of *Or.* 2; see also 19.2. Post-379, see 21.9; 32.17; 42.24; and the passages in *DVS* (esp. ll. 1545–1571, 1645–1653, 1713–1718) and *De seipso et de episcopis* (ll. 35–48 and 331–454) on the behavior of the bishops at the council.

76. Trans. adapt. White.

77. On the nature of the crisis in Caesarea, see Brown, *Poverty and Leadership*, pp. 39–40.

78. On Gregory's *Or.* 14, see Daley, "Building a New City"; Holman, *The Hungry Are Dying*, esp. pp. 140–148; and Finn, *Almsgiving in the Later Roman Empire*. In a more cynical vein, Peter Brown argues that episcopal care for the poor at this time was esp. effective as a method for maintaining the aristocratic power base and general social order. *Power and Persuasion*, pp. 71–117. On the dating of *Or.* 14, see Holman, *The Hungry Are Dying*, pp. 144–148.

79. In light of direct verbal parallels between them, and the fact that Gregory's oration is more elaborate, Heck argues that Gregory Nazianzen drew on Gregory of Nyssa's second homily as a source. *Gregorii Nysseni*, pp. 121–124; Daley, "Building a New City," p. 454. Holman, on the other hand, argues that Gregory of Nyssa relied on Gregory Nazianzen's work. *The Hungry Are Dying*, pp. 143n30, 145.

rhetorical form and literary allusions, and also the most theological in its approach.[80] In concert with the doctrinal program that we have seen thus far, this work stands out for the way it treats the love of the poor as a theological response to the divine economy of salvation. For Gregory, caring for the poor is a basic expression of the knowledge of God in Christ through the Holy Spirit. In *Oration* 14, he depicts the love of the poor as a concrete, universal example of the impact of the divine economy on the world at large, based on the preaching of the Gospel and the sacramental life of the Church.

Poverty, Gregory argues, is not simply the problem of the materially poor, but a basic fact of the human condition. He encourages his better-off hearers to recognize that those who are materially poor are in fact a symbol of all people. The poor remind those who are not poor of their own weakness, and discourage them from becoming attached to their more comfortable, but unreliable, circumstances (14.12). For it is the natural state of every person to be poor, he says, and all people are subject to the same weakness that the poor represent in a visible way. It is this universal human need that the Christian Gospel aims to meet, "for we are all poor where divine grace is concerned" (14.1). Gregory makes the same point in his catechetical instruction in *Oration* 40: if a poor person approaches, Christians must recall how rich they have been made in Christ, and honor the bread and cup of the Eucharist, with which they have been fed, by feeding the poor (40.34). Because poverty is a universal experience, in this symbolic sense, human compassion is a natural virtue and not unique to the Christian revelation (14.14). On this basis, Gregory makes a classical appeal to the enlightened self-interest of his hearers, arguing that, despite what they may think, their own welfare and happiness depend on their care for their less fortunate neighbors (14.8, 10).[81] By having mercy on the poor in their midst, Gregory's hearers will purify themselves in virtue, since Christ heals those who are likewise compassionate (14.37);[82] they will, moreover, protect themselves from general human cruelty, which their disregard for the poor fosters. Those who care for the poor will therefore gain their lives by their charity (14.22) and save their souls by their benefactions (14.27).

---

80. Compared with Basil's more civic approach and Gregory of Nyssa's more cosmological view. Holman aptly calls the work "a vivid appeal to biblical virtue and divine justice"; *The Hungry Are Dying*, pp. 142–143; Daley, "Building a New City," p. 456.

81. Ancient Greeks and Romans had long admired and depended on self-interested and conspicuous public generosity—the εὐεργεσία (desire to do good) and φιλοτιμία (love of public honor)—of the wealthy. As Brown comments, "Centuries before Saint Paul had declared ... that 'God loves the cheerful giver,' the *hilaron dotēn* (2 Cor 9.7), Greeks and Romans had professed to admire and to depend upon the interventions of 'cheerful givers.'" See *Poverty and Leadership*, p. 3.

82. See also *Or.* 40.34.

From this relatively tame starting point, Gregory turns to the deeper cause of the Christian concern for the poor, which lies in the nature and work of God. The loving concern for the poor is an imitation of the quality of care and compassion that God showed his creatures in creation, and a reversal of the subsequent history of sin. "Shame on you for clinging to what belongs to another," Gregory admonishes. "Imitate God's even-handedness, and no one will be poor.... May we not be so addicted to luxury as actually to scorn the compassion of a God who condemns this behavior" (14.24). In contrast with the human "law of the tyrant" (14.26), the "first law" of the Creator is to make equal provision for all. In creation God gave plenty of land, waters, forests, air, and all the necessities of life (14.25), so that, prior to when they fell into sin, Adam and Eve lived richly in humanity's ancient freedom and equality. In this state, "freedom and wealth meant simply keeping the commandment; while true poverty and slavery came from its transgression" (14.25–26). In their current sinfulness, however, human beings hoard the resources that God gave them and refuse to have compassion toward those who do not have enough. Indeed, oppositions of poverty versus wealth and freedom versus slavery are the very "companions of evil" (14.25), and belong to the human history of sin (14.26). Yet despite our misuse of our resources, Gregory maintains, the generosity that God showed in creation has continued throughout the long history of divine gift-giving: from the unwritten law of nature and the Law and the prophets to the incarnation of Christ, "apostles, evangelists, teachers, pastors" (Eph 4.11), and countless gifts of the Holy Spirit for healing and ministry.[83] So, he concludes, "In nothing does the affinity of human beings with God lie so much as in doing good" (14.27).[84] The greatest of all Christian virtues and the surest road to salvation is the care for the poor, who are most in need of Christian charity (14.1–5; 22). However much we give to each other, God's generosity will always exceed ours, and the love of the poor will remain a key means by which Christians can imitate the nature of their Creator.

More specifically still, Gregory powerfully defines the love of the poor as a direct participation in Christ's cruciform ministry, and even an act of care for Christ himself. The very name and identity of a Christian, Gregory argues, is determined by the one who gently "bore our weaknesses" (Is 53.7; Mt 8.17), who humbled himself to assume our nature and "became poor for our sakes" (Phil 2.8; 2 Cor 8.9), who suffered pain and was bruised (Is 53.5; 2 Cor 8.9), "so

---

83. See Hb 2.4.
84. See also *Or.* 19.11.

that we might become rich in divinity" (14.15). In the incarnation, God identified with human poverty and need in order to redeem and elevate us, and so following Jesus' command to "take up your cross" (Mk 8.34) means above all to imitate his divine generosity by loving the poor as he did (14.18). Through faith and baptism, Christians who are materially better off must therefore realize that they are united with the poor in the body of Christ (14.8). By helping the poor, they show compassion toward their fellow members and pay reverence to Christ himself (14.37). Hence Gregory concludes, "Let us take care of Christ while there is still time. Let us heal Christ, let us feed Christ, let us clothe Christ, let us welcome Christ, let us honor Christ" through the love of the poor (14.40). Gregory's oration stands out among the other Cappadocians' by the degree to which it links the love of the poor with Christ and the doctrine of the incarnation.[85]

For the same reasons, we find Gregory praising the love of the poor among other Christian virtues in his panegyrics, and regularly listing it among the practices of the authentic Christian philosopher.[86] He writes that Basil's parents excelled in generosity to the poor (43.9) and that Basil himself cared extensively for the poor and the sick (43.34, 61). He provided relief in time of famine (43.35); led the way in showing philanthropy toward the poor and sick in Caesarea (43.63), a ministry in which Gregory's own *Oration* 14 played a key part; and was personally devoted to poverty as a form of carrying Christ's cross (43.60). Gregory also praises his father's care for the poor when he was bishop of Nazianzus (18.20–21), as well as Athanasius' patronage of the needy, his protection of widows, his fatherliness toward orphans, his love of the poor, and his treatment of the sick (21.10).

At the strongest rhetorical moment of *Oration* 14, Gregory appeals to the prospect of Christ's impending final judgment. He pointedly reminds his hearers that whether or not they care for the suffering Christ now, "while there is still time," will decide whether they will continue with Christ in the life to come or suffer the condemnation of divine judgment. The mark of true wisdom will be to share this eschatological perspective. Recognizing that our present human existence is filled with "inconstant breezes" and "deceitful dreams," the wise place no confidence in their wisdom, wealth, strength, or any worldly good, but place their treasure instead in the life to come (14.19–21). The only cause for Christian boasting, Gregory says, is "that one knows God

---

85. Holman, *The Hungry Are Dying*, p. 142. See also *Carm.* 2.1.12.460–461.
86. See above, chap. 1, pp. 72–75, and Daley, "Building a New City," p. 439.

(Jer 9.24) and seeks him, grieves along with those who suffer, and lays up something that will serve one well in the age to come" (14.20).[87] In a moving passage Gregory situates the love of the poor in this eschatological pilgrimage:

> Who is wise and understands these things (Hos 14.10)? Who will pass beyond the things that are passing away? Who will throw in his lot with the things that abide? Who will come to recognize that the things now present are passing away, and that the things we hope for stand firm? Who will distinguish between what is and what only seems to be, and pursue the one and let go of the other?... Who will purchase the world to come at the cost of present things? Or the wealth that cannot be destroyed with the kind that is always in flux (Mt 6.20)? Or what is unseen with what is seen?... Let us seek our rest in the world to come, and cast away our excess possessions in this world. Let us only hold on to the portion of them that serves a good end. Let us gain our souls by acts of mercy; let us share what we have with the poor, in order that we may be rich in the things of the world to come. (14.21–22)

The more one comes to believe in the reality of Christ's heavenly kingdom and the lower value of all things earthly, the more one is willing to relinquish one's possessions in order to care for the needy. As in Gregory's thought as a whole, it is this theological vision of the life of God in Christ within the divine economy that gives one a proper understanding of the world as it really is, reorients one's deepest values and motivations, and causes one to make God's kingdom more fully present by responding to the needs of the poor.

The Training of Holy Scripture

The high standard of priestly virtue that Gregory maintains and the many examples that he gives of pastoral abuse and failure raise the question of how this spiritual condition can be achieved, and whether it is really attainable at all. Are Gregory's claims to inspiration by the Holy Spirit compatible with the moral and spiritual rigor of his requirements for ministry? He addresses this question directly as he faces the difficult problem of his own unworthiness for the office to which he has been ordained. In order to clarify the means of priestly purification, he first reasserts the unbendable requirement of con-

---

87. See also Or. 19.11.

version and holiness, playing on the biblical language of sacrifice, and then finally turns the question on himself:

> No one is worthy of the mightiness of God and the sacrifice and priesthood who has not first presented himself to God as a living, holy sacrifice and shown the reasonable, well-pleasing worship (Rom 12.1), and sacrificed to God the sacrifice of praise and the contrite spirit (Ps 50.14), which is the only sacrifice required of us by the Giver of all. How could I dare to offer him the external sacrifice, the antitype of the great mysteries, or clothe myself with the garb and name of priest [before all of my members and senses] had become instruments of righteousness (Rom 6.13) and all mortality had been put off and swallowed up by life (2 Cor 5.4) and had yielded to the Spirit? (2.95)

In order to offer to God the sacrifice of priestly ministry, which is represented most visibly in the eucharistic offering ("the external sacrifice"), the priest must have offered the "interior" sacrifice of himself in penitence, praise, and a life purified of earthly defilement. In the face of this high standard, Gregory professes his own weakness. In an intentional dramatization, he uses his own flight from the priestly office as an example, saying that he did not believe he had undergone the proper formation. Yet, as his performance illustrates, even in his own case he is not recommending a spontaneous change of character or a program of self-help. He comes to the point in the following section:

> Who is the one whose heart has never been made to burn (Lk 24.32) as the Scriptures have been opened to him, with the pure words of God that have been tried in a furnace (Ps 12.7)? Who has not, by a triple inscription (Ps 22.20 LXX) of them on the breadth of his heart, attained the mind of Christ (1 Cor 2.16), nor been admitted to the treasures that remain hidden to most people, secret and dark, to gaze on the riches within (Is 45.3) and to become able to enrich others, comparing spiritual things with spiritual things (1 Cor 2.13)? (2.96)

Rather than a self-motivated program of moral improvement, the priest's purification, self-offering, and yielding to the Spirit are for Gregory the direct result of the study of the Scriptures. It was for this very reason, to pray and study the Bible, that Gregory left Nazianzus to visit Basil between Epiphany and Easter 362. He reiterates the point in *De seipso et de episcopis:* one must first learn the Law and then teach it (*Carm.* 2.1.12.552–553), which the Spirit reveals to the good shepherd in the deeper meaning of the Scriptures (ll. 608–609). In another oration, he writes that his counselors in all matters are his reason and

God's ordinances (36.8). While Gregory's idea of a righteous priesthood may seem rigorist and unattainable, it is really quite the opposite: not because his standard is lower than it appears, but because he believes that the power of Scripture to sanctify its reader is so effective. Consequently, he distances himself from rigorism of the Novationists (33.16; 39.18–19), and, for all his criticism of bad bishops, he cautions people against judging their clergy unworthy, because pastors still need healing themselves (40.26).[88] As Brian Daley has argued, it is the teaching of Scripture that must now define public virtue and civility in Roman society at large as far as Gregory and his fellow bishops are concerned.[89]

Here again Gregory holds a view of biblical study that is deeply informed by the work of Origen. As we have seen, the spiritual exegesis of the Bible purifies the theologian and illuminates him or her with the theological confession of the Trinity. Likewise, it also forms the character of the Christian priest, inflaming his heart and giving him the mind of Christ as a clear means of grace. The pastor's formation in virtue and knowledge, by the power of the Holy Spirit, takes place primarily through the means of Holy Scripture. Just as Gregory's doctrine of the Trinity within the divine economy naturally includes the pastoral ministry of the Church, it is fitting that the pastor's ministry of the divine economy, rooted in his own knowledge of God and of the needs of others, should arise out of the study of Scripture. As Gregory summarizes, "Of this healing we who are set over others are the ministers and fellow-laborers" (2.26)—that is, of God's saving work that is definitively recorded and spiritually available in the Bible.

Gregory illustrates his ideal of scriptural preparation in the figure of Basil, who underwent this very form of preparation. While many advance themselves into holy office unprepared, Gregory writes, Basil "trained himself in the divine words" while he ordered his flesh into submission to his spirit (43.26). Basil shows clearly how the study of Scripture is both the primary means of the Spirit's divinizing work and the efficient cause of pastoral effectiveness:

> Who more than he cleansed himself by the Spirit and prepared himself to be worthy to discuss divine things? Who was more enlightened by the light of knowledge and penetrated into the depths of the Spirit and with God beheld the things of God?... To search all things, even the deep things of God, is witnessed by the Spirit (1 Cor

---

88. See also *Or.* 17.15: only God is perfect.
89. Daley, "Building a New City," p. 459.

2.10)—not because it is ignorant of them, but because it delights in the contemplation of them. Now all the things of the Spirit had been investigated by him, and from them he instructed us in every aspect of character (ἦθος), taught us loftiness of expression (ὑψηγορία), deterred us from things present, and refashioned us toward things to come. (43.65)

It was chiefly through the study of Scripture that the Holy Spirit purified Basil and incorporated him in God's own self-contemplation, and thus gave him the ability to practice the sort of adaptive priestly *techne* that Gregory describes as worthy of Christ, the Good Shepherd.

As we can see in this description of Basil, the sort of biblical study that prepares one for the priesthood is for Gregory a Trinitarian enterprise, as the Spirit purifies one to know God and minister Christ to others. He resolves his own discussion in *Oration* 2 in similar terms: "Who has never contemplated with a worthy contemplation the fair beauty of the Lord and visited his temple (Hos 26.4)—or rather, become the temple of God (2 Cor 6.16) and the habitation of Christ in the Spirit (Eph 2.22)?" (2.97). As for Origen,[90] the fruitful study of the Bible does not merely yield information about events of the past, or even about God's will in the present, but brings one into direct contact with God, as God's own Spirit comes to dwell within and gives the knowledge of the Father through the study of the written word. The spiritual exegesis of Scripture, studied, prayed, and preached, is thus both the instrument of union with the Trinity and the immediate source of the pastor's work. In the following passages Gregory defines spiritual exegesis in classically Origenist terms— distinguishing between figures and the truth, "escaping from the oldness of the letter and serving the newness of the Spirit (Rom 7.6; cf. 2 Cor 3.6)," and passing from the Law to grace (2.97); he recommends in particular the contemplation of the names and powers of Christ (2.98),[91] which Origen outlined in his seminal *Commentary on the Gospel of John* and which, as we saw in chapter 2, is the climax of Gregory's spiritual exegesis in the fourth *Theological Oration* (30.17–21).

In negative terms, to seek or accept priestly office without having undergone this biblical transformation is, Gregory says, "the extremest of dangers" and "of all things most to be feared" (2.99). Yet on the positive side, he is saying that the divine economy revealed in Scripture provides Christians with

---

90. E.g., *Princ.* 1.8; 4.2.
91. αἱ τοῦ Χριστοῦ προσηγορίαι καὶ δυνάμεις.

a reliable means with which to acquire the virtue and skill necessary for priestly office. While he highly values his own classical education (4.100) and he believes that traditional Greek παιδεία is useful for pastoral formation and should not be disparaged (provided it is guided by Christian belief and virtue) (43.11), he prizes the Bible far above Homer, Plato, and the tragedians, and he believes that pagan letters are far outweighed by the Christian παίδευσις that comes primarily through the study of the Scriptures.[92] The main prerequisite for pastoral ministry, then, is the transforming knowledge of God in Christ that is mediated by the spiritual study of Scripture.

As a personal addendum, Gregory discusses the role that biblical study played in his own acceptance of the priestly office. The Scriptures are in fact the main reason that he gives for his return to Nazianzus to accept church leadership with his father, making them a kind of instrumental cause of his entire ministry. While he was also motivated by his longing for the people of Nazianzus and his duty to care for his elderly parents (2.102–103), Gregory took up his pastoral duties primarily because he "remembered the days of old (Ps 143.5) and, turning to one of the ancient histories, drew counsel there for myself as to my present conduct" (2.104). Speaking of the place of Scripture in his own ministry, he then elaborates on his understanding of spiritual exegesis. The events told in Scripture, he says, are recorded for a purpose. They are not merely "words and deeds gathered together for the entertainment of those who listen to them ... for the sole purpose of giving pleasure," as the Greeks prefer (2.104); rather, Christians "extend the accuracy of the Spirit to the merest jot and tittle (Matt 5.18)" of the text. They believe that even the smallest details provide instruction for our own lives in similar circumstances, and that the examples found in Scripture are "rules and models for our warning and imitation" (2.105). The Holy Spirit has thus crafted the whole of Scripture for the purpose of edifying God's people, and especially the ministers and leaders of the Church.

Specifically, Gregory relates how the story of Jonah, the famous prophet who fled from God's call, motivated him to accept his own divinely appointed office. For four sections (2.106–109) he begins to give a detailed interpretation of the narrative, then stops himself short and returns to his own case. He tells us he has learned how to read Jonah from "a man wise in such matters,"

---

92. McLynn aptly comments on this passage, "Gregory is not making a generalized plea for Christian humanism" ("Gregory Nazianzen's Basil," p. 180), despite the common view that he is. The unqualified praise of Greek letters is extremely rare in Gregory's corpus, and typically reflects strong apologetic or missionary motives, as in *Or.* 43.

whom most of the scholia identify as Origen, although we have no evidence of homilies or commentaries by him on that Old Testament book.[93] The point that Gregory derives from the story is that, while Jonah might have received God's indulgence for his reluctance to prophesy to the Ninevites, how can Gregory presume to excuse his sheer disobedience? (2.110). However high the standard of priestly righteousness and virtue might be, who would dare to make it an excuse for blatant disobedience? (2.111). Such an offense, he says, would be simply "uneducated" (ἀπαίδευτος, 2.112). Jonah therefore provides a sort of anti-type for Gregory's own case: a biblical example that should not be followed! This line of reasoning leads Gregory to reflect that other biblical figures who willingly accepted the call to leadership, like Aaron and Isaiah, were praised for their eagerness, while those who initially disparaged it, like Moses and Jeremiah, were likewise accepted by God (2.114). Through such examples the Spirit worked its magic on Gregory and relaxed his soul, so that he would return and declare that "the testimonies of God, to which I had entrusted my whole life, were my counselors" (Ps 119.24; *Or.* 2.115).[94]

The Administration of the Holy Trinity

For Gregory, the grace of the divine economy that the priest administers is the same biblical doctrine, which is summed up in the theology of the Trinity. By the inspiration of the Spirit, Gregory says, a bishop "teaches and speaks the things of the Spirit" (19.2). In *Oration* 2 he writes that the first of all pastoral duties is "the administration (οἰκονομεῖν) of the word" (2.35), and it is through the work of teaching and preaching especially that the pastor participates in and extends the divine economy.[95] Even as Christian bishops in the late fourth century increasingly came to function as civil magistrates, they continued to be defined primarily as preachers and teachers in Christian liturgical assemblies.[96] As he takes up the priestly office in 362, Gregory tells the church of Nazianzus that Christ has given them a pastor who will guide them by his teaching, and whose sermons (λόγοι) the Spirit will engrave deeply in their

---

93. In the absence of a text, Duval speculates that Jerome's typological exegesis in his *Commentary on Jonah* was influenced by Origen's own lost commentary on the book. See *Comm. Jon.*, SC 323, pp. 103–104, 111–113.
94. For a similar statement, see also *Or.* 36.8.
95. See also *Or.* 34.2: Gregory is the distributor (χορηγός) of the nourishing food of right faith (ὀρθῶς πιστεύειν); 42.13: bishops are stewards of souls and dispensers of the word (ψυχῶν οἰκονόμοι καὶ τοῦ λόγου ταμίαι).
96. Daley, "Building a New City," pp. 438–439.

hearts, "not with ink, but with grace" (1.6).[97] Because God is made known to us through his Word (6.5), the Spirit inspires Gregory to speak words about God,[98] and sometimes also to be silent (12.1).[99] Gregory has a special occasion to reflect on the centrality of Christian doctrine for the life of the Church in his farewell address to the council of 381. By contrast with the bishops of the council, whom Gregory believes have compromised the true faith for the sake of political expediency, through the faithful bishop God "cultivates the whole world with the fair seeds and doctrines of piety" (42.4), much as through his own words Gregory helped to produce the true doctrine of those bishops who remained sound (42.12). Looking back on his ministry there, he later remarks, "I watered this parched flock with my teachings (λόγοι) and sowed the faith that is rooted in God" (*Carm.* 2.1.12.116–117).[100] For, he says, "Nothing is more magnificent to God than pure doctrine (λόγος) and a soul perfected in the decrees (δόγματα) of the truth" (42.8). For Gregory, the "leaders and teachers of the people, who bestow the Spirit" must be primarily men who "pour forth the word of salvation from their high thrones" (*DVS* 1546–1549).[101]

For those accustomed to thinking that the priesthood is defined chiefly by the celebration of the Eucharist, it may come as a surprise that Gregory's reflections on pastoral ministry, like those of other major patristic witnesses,[102] focus almost entirely on the ministry of the word. To be sure, the worship of Gregory's church centers on the weekly Eucharist, and we have seen the even greater extent to which he speaks of the sacrament of baptism. In a handful of passages he refers to the priest's regular eucharistic celebration,[103] he mentions the reserved sacrament (8.18), and he refers to the holy table and vessels;[104] these practices, however, are noted in passing, and Gregory does not explicitly draw on them to any significant extent in his pastoral theology. Some scholars

---

97. 2 Cor 3.2–3, the key biblical text for Origenist spiritual exegesis.
98. See also *Or.* 18.3.
99. See also *Or.* 19.1.
100. See also *Or.* 26.5: the many doctrines (λόγοι) that Gregory has lavished on his flock.
101. οἱ γὰρ πρόεδροι καὶ λαοῦ διδάσκαλοι, / οἱ Πνεύματος δοτῆρες, ὧν σωτήριος / Θρόνων ἀπ' ἄκρων ἐξερεύγεται λόγος (trans. White).
102. Including John Chrysostom's *On the Priesthood* and Gregory the Great's *Pastoral Rule*. It would not be a stretch to add Augustine's *On Christian Teaching* as well.
103. Gregory's references to the Eucharist often involve the rich and multivalent use of the term "sacrifice," which makes them hard to discern from other meanings. See esp. *Ors.* 2.95–96, quoted above; perhaps 17.20, the "spiritual sacrifice" (1 Pet 2.5) that assuages God's anger; 36.2, the mystic rites forbidden to public view; 42.24, holy priests offer pure sacrifices; and cf. 18.39: Gregory the Elder provided the needed sacrifices through the misfortunes of his son!
104. *Ors.* 3.4; 18.22; 25.2; 40.31.

have speculated that this omission reflects a more immediate concern with pastoral abuses and the lack of true spiritual authority, compared to which outward sacramental acts pale in comparison.[105] However, such views probably reflect an anachronistic understanding of the nature of the sacraments and of the relationship between word and table. Gregory takes it for granted that pastors are engaged in eucharistic ministry, and he seems to have a much broader understanding of a sacramental rite, or "mystery" (μυστήριον), than the modern Western division between word and sacrament allows. In his view, the entire liturgy is a "mystery," including celebrations of the martyrs and a wide variety of religious festivals;[106] yet he also calls the Eucharist "the mystery of divinization" in a special sense (25.2). Moreover, Gregory does not distinguish the liturgy of the table from the liturgy of the word as "the sacrament" properly speaking; for him the priest's work of preaching and teaching is an integral part of the mystery. The names of God, Christ, and the Holy Spirit, which he lists at the end of the fourth *Theological Oration*, are in this sense "mysteries" (μυστήρια, 30.16), and so, by extension, is the work of biblical interpretation as a whole. The combination of word and table in a single sacramental rite can be seen in a brief but moving letter that Gregory writes to his cousin, Bishop Amphilochius of Iconium. Having just recovered from an illness and still feeling fragile, Gregory asks Amphilochius to intercede for his sins. Since "the tongue of a priest that is theologizing (φιλοσοφεῖν) the Lord lifts up the sick," Gregory now asks him to do the even greater work of loosing his sins "when you undertake the sacrifice of the Resurrection," that is, celebrate the Eucharist (*Ep.* 171.1). In his letters Amphilochius' teaching has formed Gregory's soul in knowledge (*Ep.* 171.2), and so Gregory now asks him to continue to pray for him "when you call down the Word with your word," probably referring to the sermon, "and when you sever the masterly Body and Blood in a bloodless cutting, using your voice as the sword," referring now to the eucharistic prayer (*Ep.* 171.3). Thus Gregory interweaves the priest's work of theological confession, teaching, prayer, and eucharistic sacrifice in a single act of ministry; and it is in this combined work that Amphilochius' prayers will be specially heard. We may note as well that Gregory's silence on the details of the rite of the Eucharist also reflects the continuing *disciplina arcani* (36.2) to which Basil refers as well.[107]

---

105. Bernardi, "Saint Grégoire de Nazianze," p. 356; Sterk, *Renouncing the World*, p. 138 and n99. See also Greer, "Who Seeks for a Spring in the Mud?"

106. *Ors.* 15.5; 14.12.

107. *Spir.* 66.

Within an assumed eucharistic context, then, the administration of the word in preaching, teaching, and personal counseling is for Gregory the heart of pastoral ministry. Speaking as the recently appointed pro-Nicene bishop of Constantinople, and as one who is laboring mightily for the catholic unity of the Church, he goes so far as to say that it is not the external credentials of office that give a bishop "the true right of succession," even in an apostolic see, but the truth of his faith and doctrine (εὐσέβεια) that he believes "in an apostolic and spiritual manner" (21.8).[108] (It is often surprising to modern students that none of the great fathers regarded the external formality of direct descendance from the apostles through the laying on of hands in ordination as establishing a bishop's authority or "apostolic succession.")[109] Consequently, Gregory devotes considerable attention in his panegyrics on Athanasius and Basil to the two bishops' work of Christian teaching.[110] As Gregory portrays him, Athanasius is the ally of the Word who breathes on behalf of the Spirit (21.7). With persuasive words he reconciled enemies and set free the oppressed (21.31), and his most important achievement as a bishop, in Gregory's view, was his teaching on the Trinity (21.11). Likewise, Basil is "a voice of God enveloping the universe," famous for his eloquence and the power of his teaching (43.65). It was "by his word and paranesis" that Basil brought relief to the poor and hungry from those who had more than enough to share (43.35). And his preparation for ministry through the study of Scripture bore particular fruit in his teaching ministry; for "it requires no small amount of the Spirit to give to each his share of the word in due season (Lk 12.42) and to dispense (οἰκονομεῖν) the truth of our doctrines judiciously" (2.35).

Among the many subjects that one might teach—and recapitulating them all—the chief aim of pastoral ministry is the administration of the doctrine of the Trinity. Gregory summarizes the topics that the pastor must cover in his "distribution of the word," in a list that echoes Origen's *On First Principles*.

> Our doctrines include the things that have been philosophized about the worlds (or the world), matter, the soul, the intellect and the in-

---

108. Speaking in this case of Athanasius, who suffered several exiles and replacements in the throne of St. Mark, but whom Gregory recognizes for his orthodoxy above all.

109. This applies also to Irenaeus, who famously lists the succession of presbyter-bishops as they have descended from the apostles, not as a proof of the authority or validity of their office per se, but as evidence against Gnostic claims to secret traditions that the apostolic faith—which is the only basis of episcopal authority—has been publicly taught since apostolic times (*Adv. haer.* 3.2–3). See the helpful discussion in Behr, *Way to Nicea*, pp. 41–43.

110. If this theme seems underemphasized in *Or.* 18 (though see 18.16, 37), we may recall that Gregory had already learned the hard way that his father was theologically unskilled.

tellectual natures (both the better and the worse), providence, which binds together and guides all things, inasmuch as they also seem to move according to some *logos*, and yet in opposition to the *logos* here below (the human one).

Again, one must take up subjects that concern our original composition and final renewal, as well as the types of the truth and the covenants and the first and second appearance of Christ, his incarnation, passion and death (ἀνάλυσις), his resurrection, the end, judgment and recompense (both the very sorrowful and the very glorious), and—above all—the things that pertain to the most fundamental (ἀρχικός) and blessed Trinity. (2.35–36)[111]

On the first group of topics, Gregory says, one is free to "philosophize," but the key biblical doctrines of the faith listed in the second paragraph must not be altered. Among them, the doctrine of the Trinity—for Gregory, "theology" proper—holds the place of honor. He then gives a brief, formulaic summary of the Trinitarian faith: "both the Unity of God (ὁ εἷν θεός)[112] must be preserved and the three hypostases confessed, each with its own unique property (ἰδιότης)" (2.38). Moreover, Gregory's lengthy analysis of pastoral adaptability and the requirement of virtue, which we examined above, refers specifically to the challenge of teaching the Trinity; and he focuses on the Trinity in each of his four early orations on the ministry.[113] Gregory's entire career is, in a very real sense, his own attempt to complete the pastoral doctrine of the Trinity that he initially sets out in these texts. Thus in 380 he commissions Maximus to teach the Trinitarian faith (25.15–19), and he enjoins his own flock to "keep the confession of Father, Son, and Holy Spirit firm and intact," making sure that their doctrine and conduct are in accord with each other (36.10). At his departure from the council in 381 he proclaims that the stewardship of souls and the dispensation of the word consists mainly in the doctrine of the Trinity (42.13–18).[114]

---

111. See also *Or.* 27.9. Gregory's theological poems, the *Poemata Arcana* (*Carm.* 1.1.1–5, 7–9), likewise proceed through a similar list of topics on God, the Son, the Holy Spirit, the universe, providence, rational beings, the soul, the Old Testament and the New Testament, and the coming of Christ, the first of which is entitled *On First Principles*, after Origen's great work.

112. Literally "the God who is one," or "the fact that God is one."

113. *Ors.* 1.7; 2.36–40; 3.6; 6.11–15, 22. In the early episcopal orations, see 11.6; 12.1, 6.

114. See also *Or.* 32.23, the confession of the Trinity is the greatest gift of all; 33.15, the Homoians may have the churches, but we have the faith (in the Trinity); 42.8, the doctrine of the Trinity is the greatest of all things to God; *Carm.* 2.1.12.116–118, Gregory waters his flock with doctrine and lights the lamp of the Trinity.

In his panegyric, Gregory focuses on Athanasius' long work on behalf of the Trinity, summarizing his doctrine in another simple formula: "He happily preserved the Unity, which belongs to Divinity, and piously taught the Three, which belong to uniqueness (ἰδιότης), neither confounding [the Three] into the Unity, nor dividing [the Unity] among the Three" (21.13).[115] The bulk of Oration 21 is in fact a history of the Arian movement and Athanasius' response to it (21.13–37)[116]: Athanasius "cleansed the temple" with words (Jn 2.15) by speaking boldly of the Trinity to the ecumenical Church (21.32), which was his greatest achievement as a bishop (21.36). If Athanasius is an example of the pastoral administration of the Trinity, Basil is even more so. Gregory extols Basil's preaching, his public controversy, and especially his written works. His doctrine has been dispersed throughout the world, like that of David and the apostles; his treatises are the delight of all sorts of people, and they surpass those of all previous writers in their biblical interpretation (43.66).[117] Although Gregory mentions only two of Athanasius' written works, he gives a comprehensive list of Basil's *Hexaemeron*, the polemical works (*Against Eunomius*), *On the Holy Spirit*, the exegetical writings (the homilies on the Psalms, among others), the panegyrics on the martyrs, and the moral and practical discourses (*Corpus asceticum*, 43.67).[118] But the most noteworthy of all, he says, are Basil's labors and writings on behalf of the Trinity, "the only true devotion and saving doctrine" (43.30). In his preaching and liturgical presidency Basil "revealed to us the Holy Trinity" (43.72), and as a theologian he ably represented the Cappadocians—who, Gregory is careful to note, are specially distinguished "for their unshakeable faith (πίστις) and for their sincere loyalty (πιστόν) to the Trinity," which is their unity, their strength, and the real power of their ministry (43.33). Gregory also notes that Basil's *Against Eunomius* is "a treatise of pious doctrine" (43.43), and his *On the Holy Spirit* represents Basil's "theology" (43.67–68).

In his praise for Basil's boldness and courage in defending the faith in the Trinity against "imperial soul-destroying doctrines" (43.46),[119] Gregory paints what became the most memorable picture of Basil's ministry, his examination by the Eastern *praefectus arbi* Modestus, whom Valens had appointed to scru-

---

115. As we noted above, Gregory retroactively assigns Athanasius his own complete doctrine of God, including the divinity and consubstantiality of the Holy Spirit (*Or.* 21.33).

116. See also *Or.* 25.11.

117. Placing Basil over Origen is of course a hyperbole, which further indicates Gregory's apologetic motives in this piece.

118. Gregory omits only Basil's letters, *To Young Men*, and the *Philocalia*.

119. See also *Or.* 43.34.

tinize Basil's doctrine and possibly remove him from his see.[120] Although Modestus "roared like a lion" and wielded his authority, Basil replied in strong terms, that no matter what the emperor demands, he will not worship a creature (43.48). Modestus then boiled over with rage and threatened Basil with the imperial wrath, but Basil pronounced himself untouchable, saying that he fears neither banishment nor torture nor death, because he has been hastening to God for a long time anyway (43.49). At this point Modestus exclaimed in amazement, "No one has ever spoken to Modestus in this way and with such boldness!" to which Basil simply replied, "Then perhaps you have never met a bishop." He explains that bishops are gentle and modest people—except when it comes to defending the things of God, in which case they are exceedingly bold and fearless of any worldly authority (43.50). Gregory writes that Basil would have willingly suffered expulsion from his throne and even exile and death to defend "orthodox doctrine, and the conjunction and co-divinity of the Holy Trinity" (43.68). As a further example, he notes that when Basil was banished for defending the truth, his simple response was to tell a servant to bring along his writing tablet so he could compose his treatise on the Holy Spirit. In this book, he says, Basil exercised a prudent "economy" of words by not proclaiming the Spirit's divinity in uncertain terms when the political situation was against it, even though he did of course acknowledge that the Spirit is God (43.68–69). Although he is veiling his real feelings about Basil's confession for apologetic reasons, Gregory's portrayals of Athanasius and Basil amply show how central he considers the Trinity to be for pastoral work.[121]

Having solidly established the ministry of the word—and above all the administration of the Trinity—as the core of pastoral ministry, Gregory shows himself to be, in the truest sense of the word, a pastoral theologian par excellence. For Gregory, the doctrine of the Trinity represents the very meaning of the Christian life, and so it is also the essence and the unifying element of pastoral ministry. To find one's life in anything other than the Trinity, conceived in this way, is for Gregory a serious inner malady; so that spiritual health can be restored only by reestablishing one's growth toward union with God in Christ by the power of the Holy Spirit. He ties together the different elements of pastoral ministry in an elegant summary remark on Basil: "His beauty was virtue; his greatness was theology; his course was the perpetual

---

120. Modestus had also exiled Eunomius in 369–370. Bernardi, SC 384, p. 226n2.
121. Gregory also speaks of the administration of the Trinity in the ministries of Eulalius (13.4), Gregory the Elder (18.16, 37), and Cyprian of Antioch (22.13).

motion that carries him by ascents even to God; and his power was the dissemination and distribution of the word" (43.66). The ministry of Christian pastors and priests is founded upon and fulfilled in theological doctrine, which they administer by adapting themselves to the variable and unpredictable circumstances of human life. The pastoral administration of Trinitarian doctrine is thus the intended consummation of the divine economy until Christ returns. Hence Gregory beautifully defines the priesthood in Trinitarian terms:

> The scope of our therapy is to provide the soul with wings, to rescue it from the world and give it to God—to watch over that which is in his image if it abides, to take it by the hand if it is in danger, or to restore it if it is ruined—to make Christ to dwell in the heart by the Spirit, and in short to deify and bestow heavenly bliss upon those who have pledged their allegiance to heaven.[122] (2.22)

---

122. τὸν τῆς ἄνω συντάξεως, possibly a reference to the renunciation of Satan and adhesion to Christ in the baptismal rite. See Bernardi, SC 247, p. 120n1.

Conclusion

Gregory among the Fathers

Now that we have brought Gregory's theological system into full view, we can highlight the distinctive character of his work in relation to his key predecessors and contemporaries and note his seminal position in later Christian tradition. Although a surprising number of major patristic figures still lack comprehensive doctrinal studies,[1] a distinctive picture of Gregory's place among the fathers can nevertheless be discerned in its basic outlines. References to comparisons made earlier can be found in the general index.

Origen

In this book's introduction we traced Gregory's deep formation in Origenist Christianity, and we have noted his debt to Origen on numerous specific points in each chapter.[2] In reading Gregory Nazianzen, one gets the palpable sense of someone steeped in the Christian mysteries through biblical study, prayer, and ascetical discipline, who speaks of the Trinity directly out of that experience,

---

1. Including Origen, Athanasius (whose critical edition is finally under way again), Didymus the Blind, Epiphanius, Gregory of Nyssa, and to a lesser extent Basil of Caesarea.

2. See also below, on Gregory's relationship to Origen's disciple Gregory Thaumaturgus. References to Origen's works can be found in the notes to each chapter. On Origen's influence on Gregory, see Moreschini, "Influenze di Origene"; *Filosofia e letteratura*, pp. 97–116; "Nuove Consideratione"; and Trigg, "Knowing God."

and who endeavors to engage the best of pagan Greek learning in his efforts to transform his culture with the Christian Gospel. In this regard Gregory proves to be a true disciple of Origen. Through his combination of biblical piety, spiritual exegesis, and Greek philosophical and rhetorical training, Gregory imbued his work with a spiritual and kerygmatic quality that reflects Origen's influence at a deep level. Not surprisingly for one who studied in Origen's Caesarea and who collected the *Philocalia*, Origen's influence on Gregory can be felt in nearly every area of his thought. He based the structure of his *Theological Orations* and *Carmina Arcana*, as well as his summary lists of theological topics (see *Ors.* 2.35–36; 27.9), on the model of Origen's *On First Principles*. Even more pervasively, he reflects the Trinitarian structure of Origen's spiritual and theological program, and he closely follows Origen's theory and practice of spiritual exegesis—both of which he also develops in original ways. Gregory's doctrine of the knowledge of God shows the hand of Origen in several places: on the fundamental correspondence between one's spiritual growth, understanding of Scripture, and knowledge of God; the relationship between the purification and illumination of the theologian; and the moral and ascetical practice of Christian "philosophy," with its emphasis on biblical study and prayer, the practice of a moderate form of asceticism, and a mixed commitment to solitary contemplation and service to the Church and community. Likewise, Gregory's cosmology and anthropology are heavily influenced by Origen, on the corporeality of all created things compared to the incorporeality of the Trinity, the incomprehensibility of God, and the positive divine illumination revealed through Christ. Again, Gregory reflects Origen's idea that God is knowable not by human reason alone, but only by faith, which fulfills reason, and he shares Origen's basic sense of the stages of spiritual growth.

In his soteriology and Christology, Gregory borrows and expands on Origen's doctrine of divinization, and he shares Origen's basic sense of the incarnation of the divine Word of God. Like Origen, he focuses predominantly on the divinity of Christ, and he capitalizes on Origen's construction of the Word's union with Christ's humanity through the intermediary of Christ's human soul, and the consequent singularity of Christ, even as he makes important clarifications and corrections.[3] While he gives greater emphasis to the cross than Origen does, Gregory shares and expands on Origen's basic idea of the Christian's ascent to God through the meditation on, and therefore the doctrine of, Christ's divine-human identity. Origen also provides the root for Gregory's

---

3. On this point see below on Gregory Thaumaturgus and Apollinarius.

doctrine of the Holy Spirit, especially in its divinizing work of sanctification. Again, it is on the basis of Origen's work that Gregory develops the spiritual character of all theology and the continuum among biblical interpretation, personal sanctity, and the knowledge of God—what we have called Gregory's hermeneutic of piety and the theology of the divine economy. Likewise, Gregory follows Origen's acknowledgment of the unclarity of Scripture on the divinity of the Holy Spirit, and he expands Origen's eschatological spirituality in his distinctive treatment of the gradual revelation of the Trinity through the history of the covenants. Origen's influence on the fourth-century debates over the divinity of Christ and the Holy Spirit is abundant. As he follows Origen's Trinitarian program with unusual faithfulness, Gregory expands his understanding of theology and the divine economy. He upholds and vindicates his "relational"[4] doctrine as the most faithful version of Trinitarian theology within the emerging Nicene consensus; he develops Origen's dynamic understanding of the Trinity in both its eternal relations and its involvement in the divine economy; and he maintains Origen's central belief that the Son and Spirit are at the same time derivative of and equal to God the Father. Finally, Gregory's pastoral theology builds on the above points and follows Origen most especially in upholding a charismatic theory of the priesthood. For Gregory as for Origen, the Christian priest must be purified in order to purify others, and he administers Christian doctrine according to the spiritual growth of the recipient, based on the spiritual interpretation of Scripture.

In sum, Gregory produced the most penetrating synthesis of Christian theology and spirituality since Origen, which he expressed with his uniquely powerful literary and rhetorical abilities, while being at the same time the most doctrinally orthodox theologian of his age—much as Origen was in his time. Gregory's achievement, like that of other pro-Nicene theologians, is in no small measure the completion, refinement, and adaptation of Origen's basic system in a new cultural, intellectual, and ecclesial environment.[5] In the spirit of his Alexandrian master, it is the *combination* of dogmatic accuracy and spiritual power that so distinguishes Gregory's work and that has caused it to play such a normative role in the following centuries. Gregory is in many respects the most faithful disciple Origen had among the Nicene fathers of the fourth century, and possibly the later patristic period as a whole.

---

4. This phrase comes from Lossky's argument *against* Gregory. For a response to Lossky, and to the similar critique by Holl, see chap. 4, pp. 199–200, 225–226.

5. As Markschies observes, pro-Nicene doctrine represents "a structure of thinking about the Trinity which is fundamentally based on Origen's thinking." "Trinitarianism," p. 207.

Gregory Thaumaturgus

An important link between Origen and Gregory's fourth-century situation, as well as an independent source in his own right, is Origen's disciple Gregory Thaumaturgus (the "Wonder Worker"). Gregory Thaumaturgus became bishop of Neocaesarea and eventually the patron saint of Cappadocian Christianity; among his most notable accomplishments was the conversion of Macrina the Elder, grandmother of Basil and Gregory of Nyssa. Although his literary remains are scarce, Gregory Thaumaturgus seems to have been a significant influence on Gregory Nazianzen,[6] a possibility that is reenforced by an interesting set of connections between the two in the manuscript tradition.[7] We may first note that his ascetical doctrine resembles Gregory Nazianzen's in several ways. On a broad level, he carries forward Origen's view that the purification of the mind is necessary in order to approach God. Purification and assent, moreover, are accomplished chiefly through piety (εὐσέβεια), which is the mother of the virtues,[8] and piety consists largely in practicing a life of Christian "philosophy," which involves both right faith and Christian practices. Like Origen, Gregory Thaumaturgus also speaks of a strong desire for contemplative quiet (ἡσυχία)[9] while at the same time appreciating the importance of personal relationships in the philosophic life.[10] Each of these points resonates with the work of Gregory Nazianzen. As a point of contrast, the *Address of Thanksgiving to Origen* shows a higher regard for Greek philosophy than Gregory Nazianzen holds (and possibly Origen as well), which makes the questions surrounding its authorship all the more weighty.[11]

---

6. I follow Abramowski ("Das Bekenntnis") in regarding the creed attributed to him as an invention, or at least a heavy-handed adaptation, by Gregory of Nyssa, whose *Life of Gregory Thaumaturgus* gives no indication of a knowledge of his original works. See Bernardi, *Le prédication*, p. 310; Van Dam, "Hagiography and History," p. 281; and Slusser, FC 98, p. 14.

7. If we may assume that it is authentic (the title is also questionable), Gregory Thaumaturgus' *To Philagrius: On Consubstantiality* was attributed to Gregory Nazianzen (as *Ep.* 243 *To Evagrius*) and to Gregory of Nyssa (as *Ep.* 26 *To Evagrius*). Gregory's best attested work, the *Metaphrase on the Ecclesiastes of Solomon*, is included in several manuscripts of Gregory Nazianzen's works, usually next to *To Philagrius/Ep.* 243, as are the spurious *Glossary on Ezekiel* and *To Tatian: On the Soul*. The *Letter of Origen to Gregory* appears in Basil and Gregory Nazianzen's anthology of Origen's writings, the *Philocalia*; however, neither identifies the recipient with Gregory Thaumaturgus, and this identification is generally considered uncertain. For discussion and further bibliography, see Slusser, FC 98, pp. 22, 29–30, 33–35.

8. *Addr.* 12.149; 14.165.

9. *Metaphr.* 10.993C; *Addr.* 16.185.

10. *Metaphr.* 10.997CD–1000A; *Addr.* 1.3–4; 6.81–92; 16.189, 196.

11. For a recent affirmation of the ascription to Gregory Thaumaturgus, see Trigg, "God's Marvelous *Oikonomia*," pp. 38–39.

A more significant area of influence, however, can be found in the Christology presented in the treatise *To Theopompus: On the Impassibility and Passibility of God*.[12] In answer to the query of a certain Theopompus about the impassibility of God, Gregory gives an explanation of God's impassible passion in the incarnation that may have been an impetus for several key elements of Gregory Nazianzen's Christology. The treatise argues that while God remains impassible and by nature cannot suffer[13]—being free, above all things, and not under the necessity of any other thing[14]—nevertheless God does indeed suffer in the incarnation, despite Theopompus' traditional objection to divine suffering. Gregory explains that in Christ God suffers our passion (on the cross above all) in such a way as to preserve his divine impassibility and to defeat our suffering and death. Gregory explains this in highly unitive images and terms that prefigure Gregory Nazianzen's own view: in the incarnation the divine Son actually "enters into relationship with [our] passions;" he "entered into the passions" and "took upon himself" and "participated in" our passions, in order to defeat them with his own impassibility.[15] So God became "mixed" with our condition, the "mingling" being not merely an apparent one, but an actual "fusion."[16] This is possible, Gregory continues, because, even though God's impassible nature and human suffering are incompatible opposites, God's nature is so powerful that it can truly subsume creaturely passion into itself in such a way that transforms passion while remaining unalterably divine—a phenomenon that can even be observed in material examples, such as light that penetrates and eliminates darkness, or asbestos that conquers fire.[17] Nevertheless, Gregory issues the qualification that God remains the same in the incarnation,[18] so that his self-emptying is not absolute; God emptied himself of his dominion, he says, but not of his divine nature.[19] At the same time, Gregory speaks consistently of God and Christ as a single subject of incarnate, divine existence, much like his namesake from Nazianzus (though less like Origen): "He who is life and is superior to death can [for that reason]

---

12. The text is known only in Syriac translation. Its authorship is generally accepted (Crouzel, "La passion de l'impassible"), though cf. Abramowski, "Die Schrift Gregors des Lehrers 'Ad Theopompum,'" which disputes the authorship but not the third-century provenance. Slusser, FC 98, pp. 27–28. In either case, the text can be regarded as a source for Gregory Nazianzen, under the name of Gregory Thaumaturgus, who was believed to be its author by fourth-century Apollinarians as well.
13. *Theo.* 5.
14. *Theo.* 2.
15. *Theo.* 6.
16. *Theo.* 12.
17. *Theo.* 6, 12.
18. *Theo.* 6.
19. *Theo.* 12.

enter death";[20] the crucifixion is "God's death"[21] and the "passion of God."[22] The point of God's impassible passion, Gregory insists, is not that God is changed but that *we* are.[23] Thanks to its reception by Gregory Nazianzen, this move toward unitive constructions, while preserving the distinctness of the divine nature, is arguably the most noteworthy, and the most crucial, advancement on Origen's Christology in several centuries of later patristic tradition.

Against Theopompus' objections, Gregory Thaumaturgus argues further that God's condescension to take on our suffering does not contradict the impassibility of the divine nature but in fact perfectly reflects it. It is positively fitting, he says, for God to show his mercy and effective power through humility and self-abasement.[24] Turning the objection on its head, he argues that the real denial of God's power and mercy would be to imagine that God *cannot* suffer human passion. For God to be unable to take on our suffering would be the real constraint and external necessity that Theopompus fears,[25] and to deny God's impassible passion is to imagine a god who begrudgingly refuses to come to our help, not the true God of our salvation. It would be better, Gregory says, for God to *have* passion than to show the vainglory of being too proud to help us—which is itself a form of passion anyway![26] So Jesus came and suffered among us in order to conquer our passion, even while "he remained what he is,"[27] like a doctor who endures hardships to heal his patients,[28] or a king who puts up with the foul conditions of a prison to deliver the sentence of death to the prisoners (the passions).[29] In his "impassible passion" God ceases to be remote from us.[30] On the model of Jesus' divine passion, then, helping others

---

20. *Theo.* 12.
21. *Theo.* 8.
22. *Theo.* 6.
23. *Theo.* 16.
24. *Theo.* 6. See Origen's statements that God's glory is most clearly reflected in the passion of Jesus, following Jesus' statements in Jn 13–14 (*Comm. Jn.* 32.259), and that the Son reveals the fullness of his divinity by emptying himself of his glory (*Princ.* 1.2.8; see also *Cels.* 7.17). Nevertheless, such statements are rare, and Origen does not pursue the more unitive doctrine that both Gregorys will; cf., e.g., *Comm. Jn.* 32.322: the glory of Christ's death "does not belong to the only-begotten Word, Wisdom, and Truth, which, by nature, cannot die, or to any of the other diviner aspects of Jesus. It belongs rather to the man who was the Son of Man" (trans. Trigg).
25. *Theo.* 10.
26. *Theo.* 12.
27. *Theo.* 17.
28. *Theo.* 6.
29. *Theo.* 8.
30. *Theo.* 10, 14–16.

is the height of virtue and the real fruit of Christian philosophy.[31] This powerful, unitive vision of God's impassible passion in Christ, together with certain elements of Apollinarius' work, will be replicated in large measure by Gregory Nazianzen.[32]

Athanasius and Didymus

Gregory's relationship to the great Athanasius is a matter of no little confusion in modern theology and Church history. Students of early Christianity have long assumed that all three Cappadocians were influenced by Athanasius and the direct heirs of his theological agenda in completing the establishment of Nicene orthodoxy.[33] Yet Gregory never met or corresponded with Athanasius, and he does not appear to have had any firsthand acquaintance with Athanasius' work, except possibly his brief synodical letter to the emperor Jovian. Although there are certain resemblances between them on a broad, impressionistic level,[34] there are several major elements of Athanasius' work that Gregory does not seem to know at all, and it is difficult to locate even basic points of similarity that Gregory would not also share with more immediate figures like Apollinarius, Basil, or Melitius.[35]

One reason for assuming a direct influence has been the fact that Gregory delivered a famous panegyric in praise of Athanasius (Or. 21)—an oration that was the first piece of hagiographic literature on the Alexandrian bishop and the model of many to follow.[36] While Gregory makes considerable claims to

---

31. *Theo.* 16.

32. It was Apollinarians who first adopted Gregory Thaumaturgus as a patron in the late fourth century—although it was a rather one-sided adoption, Christologically speaking. Gregory Nazianzen's Christology is a more faithful representation of the doctrine that we have examined here. Although he does not speak of Christ's passion as defeating passion in quite the same terms as his predecessor, that should be seen as a minor difference. With regard to Gregory Nazianzen's Trinitarian logic and metaphysics, I do not find any signs of borrowing from *To Philagrius*.

33. In 1912 Swete argued that Athanasius' influence on the whole of Nicene Pneumatology was nothing less than immense, so that once the *Letters to Serapion* appeared, the defeat of all forms of Pneumatomachianism was virtually assured (*The Holy Spirit in the Ancient Church*, p. 220). Haykin likewise regards Athanasius' Pneumatology as "the framework within which the Church's later doctrine of the Spirit was to take shape" and the foundation on which Cappadocians built (*Spirit of God*, p. 7). See also Szymusiak, "Grégoire le Théologien, disciple d'Athanase." Hanson was right to question the direct influence of Athanasius on the Cappadocians, although he argues that they nevertheless learned a great deal from him (presumably indirectly) (*Search for the Christian Doctrine of God* pp. 678–679).

34. I borrow the idea of impressionistic parallels from Lienhard, "Augustine of Hippo."

35. Athanasius' influence on the latter two being uncertain at this point as well.

36. See Sterk, *Renouncing the World*, p. 129.

the legacy of Athanasius in this oration, the piece in fact shows little if any direct knowledge of Athanasius' work. Gregory's main purpose in delivering it in the spring of 380 was to secure support for his own ministry in the capital from the newly arrived Egyptian contingent. To this end, he gives an elegy in praise of Athanasius' virtue as a Christian ascetic and bishop. Yet, as we saw in chapter 5, his description of Athanasius' ascetical and practical virtues (his "lesser" qualities, 21.11) is more a projection of Gregory's own ideals and need not reflect any detailed acquaintance with Athanasius' life. In order to portray Athanasius' cardinal virtue of theological teaching and ecclesiastical leadership (21.11), he then spends the bulk of the oration narrating a history of the fourth-century controversy and Athanasius' role in it. Here, too, Gregory's version shows no awareness of Athanasius' extensive works against the "Arians" and on the councils—such as the *Orations Against the Arians, On the Decrees of Nicaea,* and *On the Councils of Ariminum and Seleucia*—nor of the bulk of Athanasius' ecclesiastical activity. Although Gregory identifies the controversy as stemming from the "madness" of Arius and identifies the orthodox position with the Council of Nicaea, as Athanasius frequently does, these motifs circulated broadly in pro-Nicene circles in Constantinople and Asia Minor by this time, and need not reflect a direct borrowing from Athanasius. Moreover, Gregory is the first writer to say that Athanasius played a crucial role at Nicaea (21.14), a role that Athanasius, for all his grandiosity, never claims for himself.[37]

Gregory's initial concern is to give an account of the shady role played by three famous Cappadocians: his namesake Gregory, the intruding bishop of Alexandria in 338–339, whom Gregory says some have still not forgiven (21.15); Philagrius, prefect in Egypt in 335–337 and 338–340 (21.28–29); and, most extensively, the notorious George, usurping bishop of Alexandria from 357 until his murder by a mob in 361 (21.16–19, 26–27). Gregory's fawning account of Philagrius corresponds neither with Athanasius' recorded dislike of him,[38] nor with the record of Philagrius' death several years before, in 358.[39] These sections obviously seek to rehabilitate the reputation of Cappadocian leadership and to distance Gregory from this unsavory legacy, in order that, as the pro-Nicene bishop in the capital, he can now be identified instead with the sort of heroic leadership that Athanasius embodied. Gregory's attention to

---

37. Noted by Bardy, "Athanase," col. 1318, in conjunction with the work of Cavallera. Mossay, SC 270, p. 138n1.

38. Athanasius, *Hist. Ar.* 7.5; 9.3; 12.1.

39. According to Libanius, *Ep.* 372.2; Mossay, SC 270, p. 170n1.

certain local details reinforces the Asianic provenance of the piece, such as the "violent commotion" of monastics who reacted against the homoian status quo and are now causing others to break away from the Nicene faith (21.25)—a probable reference to the Cappadocian schism of 362, which caused Gregory and his father several years of trouble. Unlike Athanasius' detailed account in *On the Councils of Ariminum and Seleucia*, the only post-Nicene council that Gregory mentions is the meeting held in Seleucia in 359, which he knows plenty well from his own immediate environment—he refers to it in local terms as the home of St. Thekla (21.22), where he has most likely just spent his long retreat—and which has been a major source of difficulties for pro-Nicenes throughout the Eastern Church since its ratification at Constantinople in 360. Moreover, Gregory discusses the council in connection with the leadership of George of Cappadocia (21.21-22), rather than Acacius, Eudoxius, and their associates, as Athanasius does,[40] and he makes no mention of Ariminum. It is within this distinctly Eastern perspective, then, that Gregory portrays Athanasius as a pillar of the Church (21.26), who labored and sacrificed mightily on behalf of the orthodox faith and restored the true doctrine of the Trinity—"the brilliant light of the one Divinity"—to its lamp stand (21.31).

The narrative ends with Athanasius' triumphal return from exile in 362, at the death of Constantius (21.27-29), and his theological endeavors through the following year.[41] Gregory speaks vaguely of Athanasius' broad, reconciling effect as an authoritative teacher through his letters and personal visitations (21.31),[42] yet he refers specifically to only one document, the *Letter to the Emperor Jovian*, which Athanasius wrote in 363 from Antioch and which may well be the only text by Athanasius that Gregory knew,[43] along with possibly the *Life of Antony* (21.5).[44] Having formerly suffered for his views (21.35), Gregory says, Athanasius now became the first to declare in writing "the one Divinity and essence of the three,"[45] and therefore to confess the same faith in the Holy Spirit that earlier fathers had confessed of the Son (21.33). Yet even though

---

40. See *Syn.* 1, 9. Athanasius does include George in the list of attendees in *Syn.* 9, but he is not a major player. Gregory writes that the council's confession that the Son is "like the Father according to the Scripture" is deceptive and inadequate (*Or.* 21.22), and he comments as well on its pretense in condemning heretics (21.23); this hardly requires an Athanasian source, though, as these are obvious Nicene views.

41. Gregory refers only to Athanasius' third (*Or.* 21.20, 27-29) and fourth (21.32-33) exiles, omitting his first, second, and fifth.

42. "Legislating for the whole world" (νομοθετεῖ τῇ οἰκουμένῃ).

43. Its Antiochene provenance may account for Gregory's possession of the text.

44. Cf. the more extensive, though still incomplete, list of works by Basil that Gregory lists in his memorial oration (*Or.* 43.67).

45. τῶν τριῶν μίαν θεότητα καὶ οὐσίαν. Cf. *Ep. Jov.* 4: τὸ καὶ μίαν εἶναι ἐν τῇ ἁγίᾳ Τριάδι θεότητα, and Athanasius' defense of the Nicene ὁμοούσιον at *Ep. Jov.* 1, 4. A similar statement appears at *Ep. Serap.* 1.2.

Gregory amplifies Athanasius' statement concerning the Holy Spirit[46] and depicts the letter as achieving a wide consensus in both East and West, these claims do not reflect a detailed engagement with the text of the letter. The fact that the *Letter to Jovian* is far from Athanasius' first written statement of these views further indicates Gregory's lack of acquaintance with the bulk of his work.

Gregory also refers to Athanasius' work of reconciling the different Trinitarian terms used by Easterners and Westerners (Italians). He reports that Athanasius met with both groups and, after ascertaining that they meant the same thing by their different terms, "bound them together in unity of action" (21.35), referring most likely to the Synod of Alexandria in 362. Yet, if we follow Gregory's account closely, he does not seem to know the two documents that Athanasius produced in conjunction with the council, the *Catholic Epistle* and the lengthier *Tome to the Antiochenes*. While the *Tome* responds to the differing views that the Trinity is composed of either three hypostases or one *hypostasis*,[47] Gregory speaks of the variant terms "three hypostases" or "three persons." Whereas Athanasius chiefly addresses the division between the Melitians and Paulinians in Antioch, Gregory speaks of differences in terminology between ("we") Easterners and the Italians.[48] The *Catholic Epistle* also contains nothing that would have necessarily influenced Gregory. Its confession of "the one Divinity of the Holy Trinity," its denial that the Son and Spirit are creatures, and its statement that the Son is consubstantial and the Spirit is conglorified with the Father repeat what Gregory has already reported from the *Letter to Jovian*; and he never uses the letter's expression "consubstantial Trinity."[49] In light of these differences of detail, Gregory seems to be basing his report of the Alexandrian settlement of 362 not on an actual acquaintance with the texts of the synod, but on indirect hearsay from pro-Nicene circles in Antioch, Cappadocia, or Constantinople, or possibly from the report of Maximus or other Egyptians who had recently arrived in the capital. The fact that

---

46. Athanasius denies that the Holy Spirit is a creature or alienated from the Father and the Son (*Ep. Jov.* 1, 4); it is Gregory who absorbs these statements within his own full confession of the Spirit's divinity. See chap. 3.

47. *Tom.* 5–6.

48. There are several other points of dissimilarity with Athanasius' *Tome*: e.g., Gregory never refers to the "Arian heresy" (ἡ Ἀρειανὴ αἵρεσις), which Athanasius identifies as the chief foe that must be anathematized in order to achieve Nicene consensus (*Tom.* 3); he does not warn against adherence to the statement of the Council of Serdica (*Tom.* 5); he never speaks of the Holy Spirit as inseparable from the essence of Christ (*Tom.* 3) or of the Nicene phrase "from the essence of the Father" (ἐκ τῆς οὐσίας τοῦ Πατρός, *Tom.* 6, 11); he does not apply the same list of heretics that Athanasius does (*Tom.* 3); and the technical vocabulary in general does not match Gregory's own (see esp. *Tom.* 5).

49. ὁμοούσιος ἡ Τριάς, *Ep. cath.* 7. See also 1 and 5 in the same source.

Gregory's work in Constantinople resembles the agenda of 362 in several ways—especially his broad-minded approach to Trinitarian consolidation and his attempts to reconcile the rival Antiochenes—is due to motivations independent of Athanasius and the Alexandrian meeting.

There are further resemblances between Gregory's Christology and Pneumatology and some of Athanasius' later writings, yet again a direct influence seems unlikely. Athanasius' *Tome* contains a Christological exposition that resonates with some of Gregory's ideas—an insistence that the Word did not dwell in Jesus as in a prophet, but was himself made flesh from Mary's womb, for example, so that Christ is fully divine without there being two sons.[50] But the points of difference are even more telling: Gregory never uses the characteristically Athanasian phrase the Savior's "economy according to the flesh" or argues that Christ did not possess a soulless (ἄψυχον) body but suffered "in the flesh."[51] On balance, the works of Gregory Thaumaturgus and Apollinarius are stronger candidates for actual Christological influence than Athanasius'. Likewise, Athanasius' *Letters to Serapion Concerning the Holy Spirit* do not appear to be the source of Gregory's doctrine of the Spirit that they are often claimed to be. The two bishops' arguments for the Spirit's divinity are rather different in both character and purpose. The most pronounced difference is that Gregory does not argue for the Spirit's divinity in connection with that of the Son.[52] He does not accuse his opponents of inventing "tropes," as Athanasius does, nor does he accuse them of being innovators who use terms that are contrary to Scripture.[53] In fact, in Gregory's case the charge is just the reverse: it is Gregory who is being accused of innovating his doctrine on the basis of unscriptural ideas. Nor does he discuss the Spirit's divinity in Amos 4.13 or 1 Timothy 5.21,[54] which were the primary texts of Athanasius'

---

50. *Tom.* 7, 10.

51. *Tom.* 7. Other dissimilarities exist with the Christological arguments of the *Ep. Epict.* and the *Ep. Max.*, such as the notion of the human body's one-way communion and union with the Word (*Ep. Epict.* 9), that God was crucified "in the body" (*Ep. Epict.* 10; see *Ep. Max.* 2–3), and that the Word went about on earth "in the body" (*Ep. Max.* 3).

52. Gregory does not speak of the "the Spirit of the Son" (*Ep. Serap.* 1.2; 4.4); he never argues that the Spirit is one with the Son in the same way that the Son is one with the Father (*Ep. Serap.* 1.2; 3.1), or that the Spirit is "internal" to the Word (*Ep. Serap.* 1.14; 3.5), proper to the Son (*Ep. Serap.* 1.25, 27; see 3.3; 4.3–4), and the image of the Son (*Ep. Serap.* 1.20). Moreover, he never argues that the Spirit as anointer is the breath of the Son (*Ep. Serap.* 3.2) or that to receive the Spirit is to receive Christ (*Ep. Serap.* 1.19), and he never says that arguments for the divinity of the Son are transferable to the Holy Spirit (*Ep. Serap.* 3.2)—this last statement being a source for common modern assumptions about the development of fourth-century Pneumatology as a whole.

53. *Ep. Serap.* 1.7; see also 1.1, 17.

54. Gregory's brief reference to Amos 4.13 in *Or.* 30.11 is in an unrelated discussion of the Son's cooperation with the Father.

concern.⁵⁵ Even more striking, Athanasius repudiates the idea that the Trinity went from being a Monad to a Dyad to a Triad, which is exactly the language Gregory uses to express the eternal generation of the Trinity in *Orations* 23.8 and 29.3.⁵⁶ Last, the fact that Gregory identifies the *Letter to Jovian* as the place where Athanasius first publishes his full confession of the Trinity, even though it is plainly declared in the *Letters to Serapion*, further indicates that Gregory does not know these texts.⁵⁷ The handful of thematic similarities that exist between Gregory and Athanasius on the Holy Spirit, such as arguments from divinization and baptismal practice, can more easily be explained as stemming from Gregory's own biblical reasoning as an Origenist Trinitarian theologian in concert with other, more immediate sources. On a broader level, we can observe finally that Gregory's use of the creed of Nicaea is markedly different from Athanasius'—he makes little substantive use of the language of consubstantiality, and he never refers to the phrase "from the essence of the Father," both of which were central points of argument and became watchwords for Athanasius' construction of the Nicene faith—as are their respective styles of Christological exegesis.⁵⁸ Even Gregory's emphasis on the distinction between the Creator and creation, which Athanasius held to be so central from his early *On the Incarnation* onward, can be seen emerging in Asian Trinitarian circles, for example in the work of Basil of Ancyra and George of Laodicea, independent of Athanasius, the networks of Alexandria and Rome, and the Antiochene Paulinians.⁵⁹

The more closely we compare the two men's work, the less similar they appear to be in any detail. Judging from Gregory's substantial level of involvement with the work of Origen, Basil, and Apollinarius—taking up char-

---

55. See *Ep. Serap.* 1.3, 10 and passim.

56. Athanasius, *Ep. Serap.* 1.29; 3.7. That Gregory does not avoid such language may be a further indication that he does not know *On the Councils of Ariminum and Seleucia*, in which Athanasius excerpts Arius' statement to this effect in the *Thalia* (*Syn.* 15).

57. Athanasius, see esp. *Ep. Serap.* 1.2, 16, 30; 3.6; 4.7. Unlike Gregory, he does not say unequivocally that the Spirit is God; he rarely states the Spirit's consubstantiality with the Father (*Ep. Serap.* 1.27; 3.1; *Ar.* 1.9; but not in *Tom.* or *Ep. Jov.*), compared to his extensive discussions of the consubstantiality of the Son; and he does not distinguish between the Son's generation (γέννεσθαι) and the Spirit's procession (ἐκπόρευσθαι) as Gregory does. On Gregory's own advancements in the doctrine of the Spirit, see chap. 3.

58. Despite their superficial similarities (see, e.g., Behr, *Nicene Faith*, pp. 209–215, 349–357), Athanasius' exegesis of biblical statements about Christ according to their different "characters" (πρόσωπα, *Decr.* 14.1) is different in several important respects. In Athanasius, see *Decr.* 14.1–3; *Ar.* 2.51, 60; 3.29–30, 55 and passim. See Beeley, "Cyril of Alexandria."

59. The independence of the Asianic tradition from Athanasius can be seen in his own rather distant regard for them in *On the Councils of Ariminum and Seleucia*.

acteristic phrases and points of argument, even if he does not cite them by name—it is unlikely that he had more than a slight acquaintance with Athanasius' texts. The vague similarities between them have been long overemphasized. Much more important is the fact that Gregory *portrays* himself as carrying forward Athanasius' legacy, as the bold champion of the Nicene faith in the Trinity (21.33) in the new imperial capital, the great reconciler of East and West (21.34), and a broker of peace between the rival factions in Antioch. Gregory was well under way in his attempt to fulfill each of these commitments as bishop of Constantinople several months before the arrival of the Egyptians and the delivery of *Oration* 21—much as he had been doing since the beginning of his ministry in 362, when he labored to make peace among disconnected Trinitarian groups in his home church of Nazianzus before the Synod of Alexandria made such reconciliation a formal program the following autumn. As in the case of his relationship with Basil, Gregory's rhetorical effectiveness has again misled unsuspecting readers. Outside of *Oration* 21, he mentions Athanasius only once, in a parenthetical reference in another rehearsal of the fourth-century debates oriented toward his Egyptian audience (25.11). We must remember that Athanasius, like Gregory, worked hard to establish himself as a theologian of international significance, and that our view of his pervasive influence is the retrospective result of that self-construction. By and large, the churches in Constantinople, Asia Minor, Italy, and Egypt operated independently and separate from one other,[60] which explains why orchestrating the alliances between them proved to be such hard work during the period of pro-Nicene consolidation in the 370s and 380s. In this respect Gregory and Athanasius should be seen as primarily local theologians (in Athanasius' case, "local" includes Rome), even if their effect grew to be more ecumenical over time, as they intended. In a sense, Gregory's relationship with Athanasius was exactly what he claimed it to be: he is the rightful successor of Athanasius in helping to establishing the true faith in the Trinity in Constantinople and Antioch, and by extension the rest of the empire—not by way of direct theological pedigree, but as a major Trinitarian theologian in his own right.

For similar reasons, we can conclude that Gregory was not influenced by Athanasius' younger Alexandrian colleague Didymus the Blind either. Although he studied for a year in Alexandria when Didymus may have worked as

---

60. The relative independence of pro-Nicene theologians is helpfully brought out in Ayres' *Nicaea*.

head of the city's catechetical school, the scant evidence that we possess shows no material derivation on Gregory's part. (The possibility that Didymus was influenced by Gregory is another matter.) While both writers practice an Origenist type of spiritual exegesis, and both emphasize the importance of Jesus' human soul as a mediator between the divine Word and Jesus' flesh in the incarnation, these similarities can be more easily explained by their common debt to Origen. Didymus' only surviving dogmatic work, *On the Holy Spirit*,[61] draws heavily from Athanasius' *Letters to Serapion*.[62] While it is more Origenist in character than Athanasius' work,[63] it shows the same general range of dissimilarities with Gregory's doctrine that we saw above,[64] despite the fact that Didymus affirms that the Spirit is "God" (*Deus*),[65] as Gregory does. Didymus' recently discovered *Commentary on Zachariah* comes from the late 380s and generally follows the Nicene doctrine established at Constantinople and in the theological work of Gregory Nazianzen and Gregory of Nyssa.[66] Athanasius and Didymus thus represent a distinct, Alexandrian tradition of Nicene theology that does not appear to have directly impacted Gregory's work in Cappadocia and Constantinople much at all.[67]

---

61. Extant only in Jerome's Latin translation, made after 385 (*SC* 386). The Greek treatise was available to Ambrose in Italy in 380, when he composed his own work *On the Holy Spirit*, or spring 381, at the very latest, when he presented the work to Emperor Gratian.

62. For example, the interpretation of Amos 4.13 (*Spir.* 65–73); the question of the Spirit's relation to angels, stemming from 1 Tim 5.21 (*Spir.* 25–26); a discussion of the different senses of the word "spirit" (*Spir.* 237–253)—and esp. an Athanasian-type discussion of unity of operation within the Trinity (*Spir.* 85–86 and passim) and of the Spirit's correlation with the Son in the same way that the Son correlates with the Father (*Spir.* 164–166 and passim).

63. In its emphasis on the Spirit's communication of divine gifts and spiritual wisdom through the participation of creatures (*Spir.* 35–59).

64. See Doutreleau's comment regarding all three Cappadocians (*SC* 386, p. 122).

65. *Spir.* 131, 224.

66. *Comm. Zach.* (Hill, p. 21).

67. An assessment of Athanasius' indirect influence on Gregory must await further study of the circulation and readership of Athanasius' works between Constantinople and Antioch in the 360s and 370s. A preliminary guess would be that Athanasius' influence was felt first in the vicinity of Antioch, where some of his works clearly circulated. An Antiochene distribution is suggested by the appearance in Epiphanius of certain characteristically Athanasian phrases that do not appear in Gregory Nazianzen: e.g., "The Trinity is consubstantial" (ὁμοούσιος ἡ Τριάς, *Ep. cath.* 7; see *Syn.* 51.3) in *Anchor.* 64.3; *Panar.* 76.45.5; *De fide* 14.1; that the Holy Trinity is "one Divinity and one principle" (ἀρχή, *Tom.* 5) in *Panar.* 69.29.3; see also Gregory of Nyssa, *Eun.* 1.1.531; "Ariomaniac" (Ἀρειομανίτης, *Ar.* 1.4; 2.17; *Dion. tit.*; 27.3; *Ep. Serap.* 1.32; 2.3; *Hist Ar.* 39.2; *Syn.* 13.2; 41.1; *Tom.* 5; *Ep. Jov.* 3) in *Anchor.* 13.7; 116.8, 10; *Panar.* 69.11.2; 73.1.3; that the Son "makes [his human] body his own" (ἰδιοποιεῖσθαι, *Inc.* 8.3; *Ar.* 3.38; *Ep. Epict.* 6.9) in *Panar.* 77.8.3; and that Christ "suffered in the flesh" (*Ar.* 3.55, 58; *Tom.* 7; *Ep. Epict.* 2) in *Panar.* 69.24.6; 77.18.5, 12; *De fide* 17.1–2—a phrase that admittedly occurs in 1 pt. 4.1 and which is noticeably absent in Gregory Nazianzen, yet is emphasized by Athanasius.

Apollinarius

Apollinarius of Laodicea was one of the leading lights—until he became one of the most controversial figures—among Eastern Trinitarian theologians in the 360s and 370s.[68] As we noted in chapter 2, Gregory Nazianzen took over a substantial, and heretofore unrecognized, amount of basic theological material from Apollinarius—or, at the very least, he shared his theological commitments to an extraordinary degree. On several points of Christology, Pneumatology, and Trinitarian theology, Gregory adopted a striking number of Apollinarius' views, and Apollinarius is probably the immediate source of many ideas that have otherwise been thought to come from Athanasius. The prospect that Gregory may have used a significant amount of Apollinarian doctrine of course raises a retrospective problem of heresiology. Surely Gregory the Theologian could not have been in league with one of the great Christological heretics? As is well known, Gregory did oppose Apollinarius in rather strong terms toward the end of his career, but the situation is much more complicated than we are led to believe by the textbook view that Cappadocian Christology is essentially an orthodox response to Apollinarianism.[69] Such judgments go hand in hand with the view that Gregory's Christology is primarily dualistic, meaning that he emphasizes the dual character, or the two natures, of Christ against the Apollinarian denial of Christ's full humanity. But we must resist the temptation to foreclose on such questions of historical theology out of a desire simply to vindicate the judgments of later theologians and to adhere to a superficial ecclesiastical correctness.

The most conspicuous points of similarity between the two theologians in fact occur in the area of their Christology, where Gregory shares many of Apollinarius' central concerns, sometimes even verbally echoing them. As a staunch Nicene theologian and former associate of Athanasius, whom Basil himself consulted for guidance on how to appropriate the newly ascendant language of consubstantiality, Apollinarius' primary theological commitment is that Jesus Christ is fully and personally divine, and that he is able to save and is worthy to receive worship because he is, in the most fundamental sense,

---

68. In their statements against Apollinarius, Basil and Damasus both refer to him as "one of their own." Basil, *Ep.* 92; Damasus, *Il. sane* (Field, p. 83). Apollinarius' major extant work, the *Detailed Confession of Faith*, dates from 358 to 362, or possibly 363. See Spoerl, "Apollinarius on the Holy Spirit."

69. See esp. Kelly, *Early Christian Doctrines*, pp. 295–301; Grillmeier, *Christ in Christian Tradition* (1975), pp. 366–377; *Jesus der Christus* (1979), pp. 435–447.

the eternal Son of God who has become human. This confession entails the dual belief that Christ is fully divine and that, as the Son of God, he is a different person or *hypostasis* from God the Father.[70] It also entails maintaining an ongoing distinction between human and divine properties in the incarnation, such that human properties cannot be predicated of the Divinity; as well as the union of the two, such that Christ's human body cannot be conceived as existing independently, apart from the incarnate form of the Word made flesh.[71] Apollinarius insists, in other words, that we must neither confuse nor separate Christ's humanity and divinity, nor imagine that they become altered in the incarnation.[72]

With these qualifications in mind, Christ's identity as the eternal Son of God is Apollinarius' fundamental theological conviction. Using a phrase probably borrowed from Irenaeus, he argues that Christ is "one and the same" (εἷς καὶ ὁ αὐτός) both before and after the incarnation.[73] Even though God and human flesh remain distinct, in Christ the creature has come to be "in unity (ἐν ἑνότητι) with the uncreated,"[74] and two distinct things are one (ἑνοῦν) through the union (ἕνωσις) of the flesh with Divinity.[75] Thus even though Christ was not named "Jesus" before his birth from Mary, his human body is inseparable from the divine Son whose body it is, because it is "conjoined into unity with God."[76] In Stoic and Neoplatonic terms, Apollinarius writes that in Christ God and human existence are "mixed" or "mingled,"[77] so that he is a "compound unity in human form."[78] Only if Christ is conceived as a real unity of God and human flesh can he be worshipped as one God, rather than as God plus a human creature, which would be idolatrous.[79] To put it in slightly different terms, Christ's fundamental identity must be that of *God*, who has become flesh for our salvation, not God plus a distinct human being, or a human being who has been joined to God—a position that he takes to be integral to the modalism of Marcellus and Photinus,[80] and later Diodore. For Apollinarius this means that

---

70. *KMP* 1, 6, 12. A good portion of the *Detailed Confession of Faith*, which begins with an anti-Arian statement of faith, is aimed at countering what Apollinarius perceives to be Marcellus' denial of the distinction between the Father and the Son.

71. *KMP* 3; *De unione* 11.
72. *De unione* 8; *Frag.* 127–128.
73. *KMP* 36; see also *Frag.* 42.
74. *De unione* 5.
75. *De unione* 11.
76. πρὸς ἑνότητα θεῷ συνῆπται. *De unione* 2; see also 9.
77. *Frag.* 10, 93.
78. *Ep. Dion.* 1.9.
79. *KMP* 1, 9; see also 28, 31; *Frag.* 9, 85.
80. See also *KMP* 28, 30.

in the union of the incarnation, God predominates over Christ's human flesh; God acts in Christ as a single, divine agent,[81] and the flesh is, by comparison, a passive instrument of the divine activity.[82] In keeping with this highly theological and unitive view, Apollinarius argues that Christ therefore has only one nature,[83] not meaning that he is made up only of Divinity, as the Son exists apart from the incarnation, but that in the incarnation the primary identity of the Word made flesh is divine. Finally, this conception of Christ correlates with an exegetical practice of referring all of Christ's qualities and acts to the single subject of the divine Son of God:[84] "Both what is corporeal and what is divine are spoken of the whole [Christ]," by acknowledging the distinctive characteristics (τὰ ἴδια) and preserving the union (ἡ ἕνωσις).[85] From this brief list of key points it will be readily apparent that Gregory shares a good deal of Apollinarius' Christological vision, which in turn refracts some of the seminal insights of Gregory Thaumaturgus, whom the Apollinarians claimed as a patron.[86]

The part of Apollinarius' thought with which Gregory most strongly disagrees—and the idea for which he eventually became infamous as a Christological heretic—is a set of assumptions concerning the structure and composition of Christ's person. According to Apollinarius, the Word of God took on human flesh (or flesh and a soul) without a human mind.[87] This Christological structure is developed in conjunction with a set of assumptions about the structure of human beings, the nature of human sin, and the kind of salvation that Christ has accomplished. For Apollinarius, a human being is by definition an incarnate mind, a union of mind and flesh.[88] In order for God truly to empty himself and become human—for Christ to be Emmanuel, God who has actually come to visit us, not simply God enlightening an independently existing

---

81. *De unione* 7, 9; *Frag.* 38, 108–109, 127.
82. *Frag.* 117.
83. *KMP* 9, 31.
84. *KMP* 8; *De unione* 7–10, with exegetical examples.
85. *De unione* 17.
86. For a more detailed exposition of Gregory's Christology, with references, see chap. 2.
87. Apollinarius sometimes speaks in terms of a two-part anthropology (flesh and soul), so that Christ is the Word made flesh, without a human soul or spirit (*KMP* 2, 11, 28, 30; *De unione* 12; *Frag.* 19, 22, 28, 41, 72, 129). In certain *Fragments* we also find a three-part anthropology: the Word took on a human soul and flesh, without a human mind (see *Frag.* 22, 25, 89, 91). Whether this difference reflects a substantive change of anthropological model or simply the further clarification of the same basic view is unclear. The fact that, at a relatively early point in Apollinarius' career, his associates signed the Alexandrian *Tome* of 362, which denounces the view that Christ is ἄψυχος (Athanasius, *Tom.* 7), supports the latter view.
88. Or a mind plus soul and flesh. ἄνθρωπος νοῦς ἔνσαρκος ὤν. *Frag.* 69; see also 70–72. It would be worth exploring to what extent Apollinarius' anthropology reflects Origen's idea that human beings are rational beings incarnated in human bodies—minus the now-scandalous theory of their preexistence.

human being (which would not be unique to Christ)[89]—the Word itself must be the mind that has become incarnate in Jesus. In this way alone can there be a true incarnation of the Word.[90] Christ therefore contains only one (divine) essence, nature, will, and activity.[91] Moreover, even if it were structurally possible for a human and a divine mind to be united in Christ, the presence of both would violate Christ's self-determination (αὐτεξούσιος) as a human being and effectively destroy him,[92] because they are mutually exclusive if joined together in the same person. In Apollinarius' view it is therefore constitutionally necessary that the Word occupy the place of Christ's human mind, and it is impossible for him to possess both a divine and a human mind. Although in one sense this makes Christ very different from us—he is not a complete human being,[93] but instead came "in human likeness"[94]—in another sense Christ is like us, even "a human being," in the most important sense, by being composed of the same three parts that we all are: intellect, soul, and flesh.[95] The fact that the Word is the sole activating principle in Christ—that he is "God in his own spirit"[96]—serves a number of purposes for Apollinarius. First, it easily explains the divine aspects of Jesus' life, such as his virgin birth, his miracles, and his resurrection, which are seen as simply the direct, natural acts of the Word in human form.[97] It also ensures that when we worship Christ we are worshipping God alone, not God plus a complete human being, which would be idolatry.[98] This structure also supports an exegetical practice of single-subject predication for all biblical statements about Christ. Apollinarius uses the analogy of an ordinary human soul and body, which combine to form one entity, as an illustration both of the predominance of the Word over Christ's flesh and, more

---

89. *Frag.* 70.
90. *Frag.* 74: "If together with God, who is intellect, there was also a human intellect in Christ, then the work of the incarnation is not accomplished in him"; see also 70–71.
91. *Frag.* 108, 117; see also 109.
92. *Frag.* 87; see also 42.
93. *Frag.* 9, 42.
94. Rom 8.3; Phil 2.7. See *Frag.* 45: "He is not a human being but is like a human being, since he is not consubstantial with humanity in his highest part"; see also 69.
95. *Frag.* 91: "If we are made up of three parts [human mind, soul, and flesh], while he is made up of four [divine mind, plus a human mind, soul, and flesh], then he is not a human being but a man-God" (οὐκ ἄνθρωπος ἀλλὰ ἀνθρωπόθεος). Apollinarius also observes that, just as we are both consubstantial with irrational animals (in the flesh) and not consubstantial with them (being rational creatures), so too is Christ consubstantial with us (in the flesh) and not consubstantial with us (with a divine rather than a human Logos) (*Frag.* 126).
96. *Frag.* 38.
97. At Jesus' conception in the Virgin, the Word spiritually performed the function of the life-giving substance, taking the place of the male seed, which thus became Jesus' divine mind (*De unione* 13; see also 1).
98. *Frag.* 9, 85; or that we worship the Trinity, not the Trinity plus the man Jesus: *KMP* 31.

literally, of the structure of Christ's person, in which the Word takes the place of a human mind but is united with the flesh in a single person.[99]

Apollinarius likewise understands sin and salvation in terms of this anthropological structure. In our fallen condition sinful flesh wields dominance over the unsinful mind or spirit and wars against it, so that sin is by definition the dominance of the passions and desires of the flesh over the control of the mind.[100] We are powerless to save ourselves in that our minds are incapable of controlling and purifying our flesh, which is the seat of sin. God therefore saves us by providing a powerful, divine intellect in Christ, which "moves and energizes" the flesh from without, and thus destroys sin in it.[101] Apollinarius writes, "What was needed was unchangeable Intellect that did not fall under the domination of the flesh."[102] Through the death of Christ, the divine Word conquered sin and death in Christ's assumed flesh, and the power of Christ's divinity restored "the original human beauty."[103] We are in turn saved, or divinized, chiefly by a kind of imitation of Christ: "the self-moved intellect in us shares in the destruction of sin insofar as it assimilates itself to Christ."[104] Just as Christ conquered sin and death in the flesh, we, through faith,[105] conquer sin in our own flesh by means of the mind.[106] It is therefore essential both that the Word assumed human flesh from Mary (in order to defeat sin and suffering where they reside) and that the power of the Word is in no way involved in or threatened by the suffering of the flesh.[107]

Gregory takes issue with these views at virtually every point. While he also operates with a three-part anthropology, he believes that Apollinarius has made a serious mistake in his assessment of how the Word became incarnate. On a

---

99. *De unione* 5; *Frag.* 129; see also 123.

100. Apollinarius is no doubt basing himself on a certain reading of Paul's argument in Rom 7—that the law of sin in his members (or in his flesh, v. 18) is at war with the spiritual law of his mind, his "inmost self," where he "delights in the law of God" (7.22–23)—combined with other NT passages that speak of the opposition between the flesh and the spirit, esp. Rom 8.1–17; 1 Cor 15.35–58; Gal 5.16–26; 6.8, 21; and 1 Jn 2.15–16.

101. *Frag.* 74.
102. *Frag.* 76.
103. *KMP* 2.
104. *Frag.* 74; see also *KMP* 31.
105. *KMP* 2.

106. We may note that Apollinarius' is therefore, in principle at least, a highly ascetical soteriology, defined by the domination of the flesh by the spirit. Again the Pauline resonances are clear.

107. Although "the Divinity took up the flesh's capacity for suffering" (*KMP* 2; see 29), the Divinity remains without change and God's power in the Word suffered no limitation in the incarnation: "whatever sufferings might come to the flesh, the Power of God had its own proper freedom from them" (*KMP* 11; see *De unione* 6, 8), and "his mind is untrammeled by the sufferings of spirit and flesh (*KMP* 30; see also *Frag.* 93, 117). On this point Apollinarius and Diodore are ironically closer to one another than either is to Gregory, who prefers a more radically theopaschite approach to the identity and work of Christ.

basic theological level, he refuses to liken the presence of the Word in Christ to that of a human mind; rather, the Word is the Creator God and cannot be imagined merely as a creaturely intelligence. The presence of a human mind, moreover, does not prevent the Word from being the primary activating principle in Christ (*Ep.* 101.36–45). For Gregory, Christ is still "one and the same" Son of God, even as a complete human being who possesses a human mind. He argues that Apollinarius has confused the radically different realities of God and human creatures. A human mind is superior to the flesh, in its own creaturely sphere, while at the same time being inferior to God, much as Moses was a lord to Pharaoh while being a servant of the Lord God. Moreover, the Word is no less capable of uniting itself with a complete human being, or assuming a complete human form of existence, than it is able to unite itself with a human flesh and soul. Christ's human knowledge and acts continue to be fundamentally the eternal Son's human knowledge and acts and are no less properly the Son's for their being also human. For Gregory, the presence of a human mind, and thus a willing human subject, does not mean that the incarnation of the Word has been compromised, any more than the presence of a human body does. Likewise, Christians still worship only the Son of God in Christ, even as he is also a complete human being; again, the Word's union with a complete human form does not render worship idolatrous any more than its union with a human body. In the end, Apollinarius' argument that Christ does not possess a human mind seems to Gregory frankly absurd.

Gregory's more basic point of disagreement, then, is soteriological. He believes that Apollinarius has lost sight of the true nature of sin and the basic purpose of the incarnation. He argues that the root of our sin lies not in the flesh (even though the flesh does war against the spirit), but in our mind. The healing and purifying effects of the Word are needed most of all in the human mind, which was "the first to sin" (*Ep.* 101.52). Apollinarius' exclusion of the human mind therefore undermines what Gregory takes to be the most important aim and character of the incarnation. So Christ assumed flesh for the sake of flesh, soul for the sake of soul, and mind for the sake of mind (*Ep.* 101.51)[108]—a complete human existence in order to heal us from sin in our totality.

With this one major correction, Gregory has taken over and improved on many of Apollinarius' most basic convictions as a Nicene theologian, as well

---

108. See also *Or.* 38.13.

as the bulk of his technical Christological vocabulary. He hardly mentions Apollinarius or his doctrine until 382 or 383, and when he does he gives no evidence of disagreeing with most of his system, despite his prior condemnation by Damasus and the Western councils and his being anathematized at the Council of Constantinople in 381.[109] On the whole, Gregory shares with Apollinarius a deeply Trinitarian theology that is defined primarily against the Sabellianism of Marcellus and Photinus, who were reputed to have merged the three hypostases into one divine person and to have held a dualistic Christology,[110] and also against "Arian" subordinationism[111]—in other words, a typically Eastern Trinitarian doctrine of the family to which Gregory belongs.[112] Like Gregory, Apollinarius holds—even more clearly than Basil—that the distinct *prosopa* or *hypostases* of the Father, Son, and Holy Spirit are one in essence, Divinity, and eternity,[113] and he declares that not only the Son but also the Holy Spirit is *homoousion* with God the Father.[114] Apollinarius likewise has a robust sense of the monarchy of the Father much like Gregory's,[115] and he, too, discusses the divinity of the Spirit chiefly from the standpoint of the sanctification of believers in baptism.[116] The point is not that Gregory is an Apollinarian, or even a reformer of Apollinarius' doctrine, but that Apollinarius is a sort of incomplete Gregorian. Gregory may have adopted Apollinarian ideas not only because they represented some of his own basic convictions, but also because Apollinarius' work resonated with the basic impulses of Gregory Thaumaturgus. In *Letters* 101–102 Gregory is clearly beating Apollinarius at his own game. Whereas Apollinarius has been characterized as holding an overly unitive view of Christ, in Gregory's view it is not unitive

---

109. Basil, too, hesitated to disparage Apollinarius' work, even when Eustathius accused him of Sabellianism on account of his association with Apollinarius. See Basil, *Ep.* 129, 131, 223, 224, 226; Behr, *Nicene Faith*, pp. 322–323.

110. On which see esp. Spoerl, "A Study of the Κατὰ Μέρος Πίστις," pp. 135–137 and passim; "Apollinarian Christology."

111. The *Detailed Confession of Faith* witnesses both, even before Apollinarius has come in contact with Diodore's teaching.

112. Despite the appearances of his early support for Nicaea, his association with Athanasius (former associate of Marcellus), and his possible recognition of Paulinus (whom Basil accused of Sabellianism) as bishop of Antioch, Apollinarius himself initially wrote most strongly against Marcellus and adopted the view that Christ lacks a human mind, just as Eusebius had. On Gregory's Eastern provenance, see below.

113. *KMP* 10; see also 14, 25, 33. Although he does use the term "*hypostasis*" in the *Detailed Confession*, he speaks of the Father, Son, and Holy Spirit as three πρόσωπα and he does not quite state that they are "three hypostases" (at least in his extant works), on account of the contested nature of the Origenist-Eusebian formula.

114. *KMP* 33. See also the reports of Philostorgius, *HE* 8.11–13; Sozomen, *HE* 6.22.3.

115. *KMP* 14–15: it is the *Father's* divinity that the Son and the Spirit are given to share, and "Divinity is the characteristic property of the Father"; *KMP* 18–19: the unity of the Trinity is the Father's rule as single ἀρχή.

116. See esp. *KMP* 8–9.

enough, for it shies away from including a human mind in the incarnation, and it removes Christ's human suffering from the divine life in a way that is soteriologically untenable. As I have suggested above, Gregory seems, on balance, to consider Diodore and his emerging Antiochene Christology a much greater problem than Apollinarius.

Gregory's vehement opposition to Apollinarius late in his career stems not so much from Apollinarius' Christological errors as from the attempt by a group of Apollinarians to seize Gregory's church in Nazianzus. The textbook caricature of Cappadocian Christology as being primarily anti-Apollinarian is mistaken. Although it may be tempting to regard Gregory's heavily anti-Antiochene position in *Letters* 101–102 as an answer to Apollinarius, as if to prove Gregory's orthodoxy on the most central points of Apollinarius' doctrine, this would be an overestimation of the extent to which Gregory actually felt threatened by Apollinarius as a theologian or a churchman: he knows very well that the Apollinarians have no place in the Theodosian settlement. Rather, these letters represent a fuller statement of Gregory's own position, which happens to be more strongly opposed to Diodore than Apollinarius, even as he makes sure, all the same, to settle his differences with Apollinarius while he is at it.

Basil of Caesarea

We have already traced the outlines of Gregory's complicated personal relationship with Basil—from their close friendship as schoolmates, their theological collaboration in the 360s, and Gregory's support of Basil's career in the Caesarean church, to their eventual falling-out in the mid-370s over the doctrine of the Holy Spirit and, especially, Basil's handling of Gregory's episcopal appointment to Sasima—and we have identified several points of theological similarity and difference between them. Here we can offer a more summary comparison of the distinctive aims and characteristics of both men's approach to Christian doctrine.[117] It is becoming more apparent to patristic scholars that the relationship between Gregory's and Basil's doctrines is more complicated than has previously been assumed. A comprehensive assessment will require greater detail than we can afford here, but the following observations can be offered toward that new work.

---

117. On Basil's Trinitarian theology, see Sesboüé, *Saint Basile et la Trinité*; Hildebrand, *Trinitarian Theology*.

There are several points of obvious similarity between the two men's work, which stem largely from their early collaboration, their common debt to Origen, and their opposition to Eunomius. As noted above, Basil's *Against Eunomius* and Gregory's *Theological Orations* follow the same basic outline, based loosely on Origen's *On First Principles*: beginning with the doctrine of God and questions of theological method, followed by the divinity of the Son and the divine status of the Holy Spirit.[118] The correspondence between their work is greatest on several points found in book 1 of Basil's *Against Eunomius* and Gregory's first two *Theological Orations* (*Ors.* 28–29), and on certain principles of Trinitarian logic. Against Eunomius, Basil and Gregory both make use of Origen's doctrine of the incomprehensibility of God,[119] and both appeal to the incomprehensibility of creation as evidence that we cannot expect to comprehend God.[120] Both hold that the members of the Trinity, however, do possess such knowledge of one another.[121] Not surprisingly, they also share a common denial of Eunomius' argument that unbegottenness defines the essence of God,[122] that the Son's generation makes him later than the Father in time,[123] and that the Son's and the Spirit's divinity makes the divine nature subject to enumeration.[124] Central to both men's work against Eunomius is also a refined exposition of the nature of theological language, particularly the denial of a simple correspondence between terms and the realities that they describe,[125] along with the affirmation that (mainly biblical) terms do convey positive knowledge of God, leading the believer bit by bit toward a fuller (though never complete) knowledge of God's being.[126] As a related matter, both are also critical of the proposition that philosophical reasoning can take the place of biblical faith.[127]

In terms of the logic and structure of the Trinity, Basil, like Gregory, has a strong sense of the internal ordering (τάξις) of the Trinity, which is rooted in

---

118. The last point being less clear in Basil than in Gregory.

119. *Eun.* 1.12–14. However, Basil understands comprehension along more Stoic lines, having to do with pure certainty, and less quantitatively than Gregory.

120. *Eun.* 1.12; though Gregory takes the theme much farther, in both substance and poetic beauty (in *Or.* 28.22–31), than Basil's singular focus on the incomprehensibility of the element of earth.

121. Cf. *Eun.* 1.14 and *Or.* 28.3.

122. *Eun.* 1.4. See also the distinction between knowing that God is and knowing what God is (or God's essence), *Eun.* 1.12, and both men's attention to the question of the temporality of the Son's generation from the Father, which is admittedly more extensive in Basil: *Eun.* 2.12 and passim.

123. *Eun.* 2.12; *Spir.* 6

124. *Spir.* 17–18.

125. Worked out esp. in *Eun.* 1; see also *Spir.* 2 and passim.

126. *Eun.* 1.10.

127. *Spir.* 2–4

the monarchy of God the Father.[128] For both writers, God the Father is greater than the Son and the Spirit as their cause, but not greater in nature or being.[129] Beyond the collaboration of Basil and Gregory and their common reading of Origen, however, we should note that this set of ideas reflects the sort of Trinitarian doctrine that was emerging more broadly in the ecclesiastical network in Asia Minor with which both men were associated—that of Melitius of Antioch and the groups around Basil of Ancyra and George of Laodicea,[130] as opposed to the community of Paulinus in Antioch, which was affiliated with Athanasius and which Melitians such as Basil accused of Sabellianism.[131] Reflective of the same tradition, both Basil and Gregory also hold a relatively nontechnical understanding of divine consubstantiality—it simply means that whatever the Father is in terms of divinity, the Son is also—and they make only infrequent reference to the Nicene ὁμοούσιον, in sharp contrast with the work of Athanasius, as noted above.[132] Both Cappadocians also repudiate the idea of the divine being as a generic class or nature to which different members belong.[133] In their work on the Holy Spirit, Basil and Gregory appeal to the practice of Trinitarian baptism,[134] the divinizing work of the Holy Spirit,[135] and the distinction between being a creaturely servant and the Creator Lord[136] in order to establish the Spirit's divine status.[137]

The chief similarity between Basil's and Gregory's work is that each builds his doctrine of the Trinity on a fundamentally Origenist epistemology. For both writers, God the Father is known through the Son in the Holy Spirit—as illustrated by Psalm 35.10, "In your light we shall see light"[138]—so that the divine generations are themselves regarded as being (or as inconceivable apart from being) revelatory functions in the divine economy.[139] This tight connection between the economic knowledge of God and our beliefs about

---

128. On τάξις, *Eun.* 1.20; on monarchy, *Eun.* 1.25; 2.12; 3.1; *Spir.* 8, 16–18.
129. *Eun.* 1.20, 25; 3.1.
130. On Basil of Ancyra and George, see below. Basil of Caesarea was probably also influenced by Apollinarius; see Spoerl, "A Study of the Κατὰ Μέρος Πίστις," p. 375.
131. See Basil's *Hom.* 24 *Against the Sabellians, Arians, and Anomoians*, from 372.
132. Gregory of Nyssa is less like his Cappadocian colleagues and more like Athanasius in this regard.
133. *Ep.* 52.1–2.
134. *Spir.* 10, 27.
135. *Eun.* 3.5; *Spir.* 19.
136. *Spir.* 19–20.
137. See below on their pronounced differences on the same subject.
138. *Eun.* 2.16. See also Origen, *Cels.* 6.5, excerpted in Basil and Gregory's anthology, *Philoc.* 15.7.
139. For example, Basil, *Eun.* 1.17: by denying the Son shares a communion in essence with the Father, Eunomius thereby removes "the upward path to knowledge" (τῆς γνώσεως ἄνοδον) from the Son to the Father. The Son's divinity is therefore seen as being necessary to, or implied in, his revelatory capacity.

God's eternal life—intimated by Basil but expressed more fully by Gregory—arguably represents the greatest clarification and vindication of Origen's work by the Nicene period.

It has long been assumed that the three Cappadocian fathers worked closely together on essentially the same theological endeavor, showing only slight differences of character or emphasis. In this view, Basil is sometimes regarded as the major doctrinal innovator and the teacher of the two Gregorys, so that we would expect to find the main points of Gregory Nazianzen's theology already expressed, in some form, by Basil. Ironically, this view of a harmonious, common Cappadocian project, like the assumption that the Cappadocians carried on Athanasius' work, stems to a large extent from the success of Gregory Nazianzen's rhetoric, as we have already seen. Gregory's memorial *Oration 43 In Praise of Basil* has often been read superficially and rather selectively, discounting the epistolary evidence for a relationship of rather a different sort. From this standpoint, Gregory appears to be no more than an eloquent articulator of a borrowed doctrinal achievement. Now that scholars have again begun to read the literature more completely, such a view is no longer tenable. Even acknowledging their common education in Cappadocian Caesarea and Athens, and their early collaboration as laymen and young clergymen in Pontus and Cappadocia, much of the similarity between Basil and Gregory stems from their joint study of the Bible and Origen within communities that we can call Asian-Trinitarian from an early point in their theological development. Given the multiple reasons that led Basil and Gregory to begin their careers with certain shared assumptions about Christian doctrine and practice, it is therefore all the more remarkable that they came to be such different theologians.

On a basic point of theological method, for example, Basil distinguishes the divine economy from the knowledge of theology in a way that is very different from Gregory's approach.[140] In his argument for the divinity of Christ against Eunomius, Basil gives an interpretation of Acts 2.36 ("God has made him both Lord and Christ") that is based on seeing the economy and theology as different, even contrasting, kinds of knowledge. In this passage, Basil says, the apostle does not mean to indicate "the *hypostasis* of the Only-begotten, which exists before the ages, ... the very essence of the Word of God, which 'existed in the beginning with God' (Jn 1.2)," but rather "the one who 'emptied himself in the form of a slave' (Phil 2.7)." The nature of the difference, Basil

---

140. On Basil's understanding of theology and economy, see Behr, *Nicene Faith*, pp. 290–293; Ayres, *Nicaea*, p. 220.

explains, is that Peter is not giving us a teaching "in the manner of theology," but he is explaining "the principles of the economy."[141] So Peter's statement refers not to the eternal Word, but "to his humanity (ἀνθρώπινον) and to what is visible to all."[142] On the question of whether the Eunomians can know God's essence, as they claim to do, Basil argues that great biblical figures such as Paul do not even know the rationale of God's economy, let alone God's essence, which would be theology.[143] Similarly, the synoptic evangelists "bypassed theology" and began instead with Jesus' earthly origins (the economy), whereas John began with theology, in describing the Word's eternal life with God. Now, Basil suggests, Christians no longer know Christ according to the flesh, as Paul says (1 Cor 5.16), but theologically.[144] Basil thus imagines theology as being a different kind of knowledge than that of the divine economy— even suggesting that theology only takes place after the economy is complete—so that we know *either* the economy or the content of theology. This strong distinction between theology and the divine economy is strikingly different from Gregory's work, which sees theology as *the meaning of* the divine economy, and knowable only through the economy.[145]

Although Basil does not dwell on the distinction between theology and the economy at great length, it represents a point of method that holds fairly consistently throughout his work and affects a number of other matters. Most obviously, it accompanies a stronger sense of Christological dualism. As the above passage on Acts 2.38 shows, what Gregory calls the lowly passages of Scripture (29.18) Basil refers simply to Christ's humanity, or to the economy, rather than to the *one who* became flesh in the economy (the eternal Word).[146] Basil's Christology on the whole tends toward the dualistic direction that Gregory so fervently avoids, and Basil lacks the fundamental sense of the unity of Christ, on which so much of Gregory's theological and spiritual system depends.[147] On this central point, Basil seems to be reflecting a key Christological element from the Antiochene network of Melitius, in which Diodore was already emerging as the central intellectual force. His Christology therefore tends toward the Antiochene direction of Diodore, whereas Gregory

---

141. οὐχὶ θεολογίας ἡμῖν παραδίδωσι τρόπον, ἀλλὰ τοὺς τῆς οἰκονομίας λόγους παραδηλοῖ.
142. *Eun.* 2.3.
143. See Rom 11.33; *Eun.* 1.12.
144. *Eun.* 2.15. See also *Ep.* 236; *Spir.* 5.12, on the interchangeability of prepositions used for the Father, Son, and Holy Spirit with respect to "theology."
145. See chap. 4. Also, for Basil, see *Eun.* 2.15.
146. The quotation of Phil 2.7 above notwithstanding, Basil's explanation that follows indicates his real meaning.
147. Though there is a hint of the Gregorian idea of God's impassible suffering in *Spir.* 8.

capitalizes on the unitive view seen in Gregory Thaumaturgus—and which Cyril would to some extent reassert as enduring Christological orthodoxy. Likewise, Basil's famous treatment, in *On the Holy Spirit*, of the different prepositions used for the Father, Son, and Holy Spirit, as found in the two doxologies that he uses and in Scripture generally, again distinguishes between uses that are proper to theology and (by implication) those that refer to the economy.[148] In one sense Basil appears to be making a distinction similar to Gregory's rule of partitive exegesis in *Oration* 29.18; the direction of his argument, though, is in fact to *downplay* the theological significance of the prepositions "to the Father, through the Son, in the Holy Spirit." In order to advance the divinity and coequality of the Holy Spirit, Basil insists that these prepositions indicate only the economic activity of the Trinity toward us,[149] whereas Gregory takes them (and similar expression) as being a crucially *theological* revelation of the eternal life of God.[150]

Also fundamental to Basil's approach (beyond the coincidence of terminology) is his "economy" over the confession of the divinity of the Holy Spirit, for which he was so severely criticized by Gregory. For many years students of the Cappadocians have read Gregory's statements in *Letter* 58 at face value, so that when Gregory tells Basil that he explained Basil's reticence to confess the Spirit as God as a gesture of "economy" for political reasons, he is thought to be making a sincere excuse for his friend, rather than sending him the piece of biting sarcasm that the letter in fact is. *Oration* 41 *On Pentecost* has likewise been interpreted as reinforcing this reading. As Gregory is making his final attempt to woo the Nicene Spirit-Fighters toward making a full Trinitarian confession, he makes the irenic proposal that those who believe that the Spirit is God but choose to withhold their public confession in certain situations, as an act of "economy," are acting prudently (41.5). But here again the rhetorical situation is easily overlooked: Gregory's words are a concession made provisionally in order to lubricate his efforts to persuade the Pneumatomachians, not a permanent statement of approval of Basil's or anyone else's confessional reticence. (Gregory is the last person in the fourth century, perhaps other than Athanasius, whom one can imagine agreeing to such a proposal!) His real feelings are clear in the several angry letters that he exchanged with Basil over the matter, and in his panegyric on Athanasius, delivered in 380,

---

148. *Spir.* 5.11; see also 18.45; 18.47; 20.51. The contrastive sense of "theology" and "economy" in *On the Holy Spirit* is picked up in Pruche's note on the last passage (*SC* 17 bis, p. 427n2).

149. Basil's discussion of prepositions occupies a lengthy section of the beginning and the end of the work (*Spir.* 2–8, 25–29), thus framing the entire discussion.

150. On this centrally important point of Gregory's doctrine, see chap. 4.

after Basil's death. There Gregory writes caustically that to keep one's piety within one's bosom, without going so far as to make a public confession, is like having a stillborn child. While kindling a few sparks may seem to avoid certain present difficulties, those who speak the truth boldly (like Gregory) refuse to "economize" (οἰκονομεῖν) their doctrine out of the fear of lesser minds; to shy away from a truthful proclamation makes one not wise but a bad steward (οἰκονόμος, 21.34). Gregory was scandalized to no end by Basil's waffling stance on the Holy Spirit, and his experience of the fence-sitting at the council of 381 only confirmed his fears in this regard.

We have noted above some of the major similarities between Basil's and Gregory's work on the Holy Spirit, including Basil's appeal to the Spirit's divinizing work and the definitive practice of baptism into the threefold name. In light of these similarities, scholars have long been inclined to assume—for the sake of preserving the harmony between two venerable fathers of the Church, if nothing else—that their doctrines of the Spirit are for all intents and purposes the same, or nearly so. Yet if we look more deeply to determine exactly what Basil means by the Spirit's divinity, we find that there are greater points of difference than simply whether or not one employs the words "God" and "consubstantial." Basil associates the Spirit chiefly with the work of sanctification and the inculcation of Christian virtue.[151] Although he argues that the Spirit must not be conceived as a creaturely servant, but as sharing in the kingship of the Creator-Lord,[152] the Spirit does not in fact fully share with the Father and the Son in the creation of all things, but merely perfects them.[153] The Father is the first cause of all things (ἡ προκαταρκτικὴ αἰτία), by willing their existence; the Son is the creative (δημιουργική) cause that brings them into being; and the Spirit is the perfecting (τελειωτική) cause of rational beings; so that their respective roles in creation are distinguished both in terms of function (willing, creating, perfecting) and scope (the Father and Son create all things; the Spirit perfects rational beings). In the Hexaemeron Basil describes the Spirit's function in creation as that of a binding and harmonizing element[154] (similar to the Stoic conception of πνεῦμα),[155] which works to bring about the harmony of the heavens and the holiness of angels and humans. The

---

151. Beginning with Eun. 3.1: the Holy Spirit is sanctification itself, by nature and not by participation, as is the case with creatures.

152. Spir. 51.

153. Here Basil reflects Origen's cosmology to a great extent. See Princ. 1.3.5.

154. Hex. 1.3–4; 2.2, 6; 3.5, 9.

155. On the Stoic influence on Basil's Pneumatology, see Luckman, "Pneumatology and Asceticism."

Spirit thus perfects the rational beings and harmonizes the nonrational beings that the Father and the Son have already made, without sharing in the basic act of creation itself.[156] So God's act of breathing his Spirit into Adam at creation (Gn 2.7) refers for Basil to the giving of grace of holiness to human beings *after* they became lost through the fall.[157]

If we examine the Spirit's role in baptism, we find again a more limited conception than Gregory's. According to Basil, the Spirit comes in baptism to those who through ascetical discipline have already been made worthy to receive it,[158] and it operates primarily through the distribution of gifts.[159] This view stands in contrast with Gregory's doctrine that the Spirit *enables* the candidate's preparatory purification and, at Pentecost and through baptism, dwells in the Church in its very being (οὐσιωδῶς).[160] Likewise, Basil conceives of the Spirit's work of divinization mainly in terms of the ethical perfection of Christians,[161] rather than as their actual participation in the Trinity through the Spirit (which includes growth in virtue), which is so central to Gregory's theological and spiritual project. Even Basil's doctrine that the Spirit is "glorified with" the Father and the Son is not simply a prudent "economy" of words in problematic contexts; since Basil argues that even creatures are said in Scripture to be glorified,[162] the argument from conglorification begs the question. A final point of contrast over the doctrine of the Spirit is their difference of approach to the witness of Scripture. Basil believes that Eunomius and the Pneumatomachians can be directly answered by proofs of the Spirit's dignity from Scripture,[163] because the names of the Spirit (both from Scripture and from unwritten tradition) signify the Spirit's supreme nature.[164] As we have seen, Gregory regards such biblical argumentation both polemically improbable and dogmatically impossible. In the summer of 380, five years after Basil's

---

156. *Spir.* 16.38; cf. Gregory, *Or.* 38.9. Gregory also speaks of the Spirit as "Perfecter," but his use of terms for the Spirit in Trinitarian formulae is more varied, indicating a fuller appreciation of the Spirit's divine nature.

157. *Spir.* 16.39.

158. *Spir.* 10 and 15.

159. *Spir.* 9.23; 16.40; 24.25; 26.21.

160. See chap. 3

161. Meredith, "Pneumatology of the Cappadocian Fathers."

162. *Spir.* 24.55.

163. *Spir.* 21.

164. *Eun.* 3.3–4; *Spir.* 9. Basil appeals to extra-Scriptural traditions and practices throughout *On the Holy Spirit*, but his understanding of the nature of biblical testimony in relation to such practices is markedly different from Gregory's. Basil's discussion of Amos 4.13 in *Eun.* 3.7 is a response to Eunomius' interpretation of the text, and does not indicate a clear influence from Athanasius.

On the Holy Spirit, Pneumatomachians in Constantinople were right to have spotted the insufficiencies of an exegetical approach like Basil's. As we have seen in Gregory's case, this difference of approach over the witness of Scripture is indicative of a host of other basic issues, most especially the way in which the task of theology is understood to be related to the divine economy.

Despite a moderate degree of similarity, then, we are dealing with two rather different doctrines of the Holy Spirit. Basil's refusal to confess clearly the Spirit's divinity corresponds with several key points that belie the apparent similarity on the superficial level of terminology alone. His statements of the Spirit's "natural divinity"[165] and its "intimacy" and "natural communion" with the Father and the Son[166] are easily overinterpreted if they are read apart from a close engagement with the surrounding arguments. While Basil could be seen as working toward a doctrine of communion and inseparable operation among the Father, Son, and Holy Spirit, the fact that he does not show a fuller development of this idea compared with Gregory or even Athanasius is less a reflection of an unfinished journey that was later completed by others than of different paths taken at several important junctures. It is no accident that Basil calls the Spirit "*a* living essence and the Mistress of sanctification,"[167] and that much of his argument for the unity of the Trinity in *On the Holy Spirit* concerns the Father and Son, as the Spirit fades into the background.[168] Basil and Gregory both hold that the divine unity is located in the monarchy of God the Father[169]—a point on which most Eusebian and homoian theologians would also agree—but Basil does not see how this involves the Holy Spirit to anything near the extent that Gregory does.

In light of these several key points, it must be conceded that, by comparison with the public teaching and the urgent pleas of his friend and interlocutor through the early 370s, Basil's understanding of the Spirit's divinity is not, in the end, all that different from the doctrine of an anti-Nicene figure like Eusebius of Caesarea. Thus Basil can say that the Spirit is "united *to* the Divinity,"[170] rather than being the Divinity itself that proceeds from God the

---

165. τὸ οὖν θεῖον τῇ φύσει (*Spir.* 23.54), Basil's strongest statement of the Spirit's divinity in *On the Holy Spirit*.
166. τὸ κοινὸν τῆς φύσεως,...ἡ πρὸς Πατέρα καὶ Υἱὸν οἰκείωσις (*Spir.* 18.45), κοινωνία (18.46), see also 9.22; 19.48; 24.56: φύσει ἐστὶν ἀγαθόν, ὡς ἀγαθὸς ὁ Πατὴρ καὶ ἀγαθὸς ὁ Υἱός.
167. τὸ Πνεῦμα οὐσία ζῶσα, ἁγιασμοῦ κυρία. *Spir.* 18.46.
168. E.g., *Spir.* 18.45. An approach likely supported by Origen's similar reticence.
169. *Spir.* 18.45.
170. συναναληφθὲν τῇ Θεότητι. *Spir.* 24.55.

Father. Many readers have effectively assumed that Basil holds a full doctrine of the Spirit, and have then come to find it expressed in *On the Holy Spirit* and other texts. But this is to give Basil the benefit of *Gregory's* theology, and to overlook the meaning of his work within the theological context of his recent Eustathian associations and his widening pro-Nicene relationships in the early 370s. By 375, when he wrote *On the Holy Spirit*, Basil had been working for several years to bolster the Nicene presence in the Eastern Church through his contacts in the East, his requests for support and intervention from Damasus and the Italian bishops, and his ongoing correspondence with Gregory, who had been urging him to accept a fuller doctrine of the Spirit since at least 372. The suggestion that, by the spring of 381, the pro-Nicene conversation had developed to a point that the council's confession of conglorification alone would signal to everyone involved the Spirit's full divinity, coequality, and identity in being with God the Father[171] is again overly hopeful. It ignores the reality of the debates that were actually taking place with Eunomians, Homoians, and Pneumatomachians, the stronger doctrinal terms presented by Damasus and the Western councils and ratified at Antioch in 379, and especially the strong doctrine of the Spirit and the Trinity being advanced by Gregory at the heart of the pro-Nicene community in Constantinople—as well as Apollinarius, we must remember, to whom most in the network of Melitius, which dominated the council, were by now virulently opposed.[172] Modern depictions of the harmony of Basil's and Gregory's Pneumatologies therefore beg the question in several respects.

With regard to the doctrine of the Trinity as a whole, Basil tends toward the language of divine being (οὐσία, τὸ εἶναι),[173] whereas Gregory prefers to speak in biblical terms of the divine nature (φύσις) and Divinity (θεότης) that the Father shares with the Son and the Holy Spirit. On the surface, Basil's choice of terminology is a sign of his emerging pro-Nicene commitments, in contrast with the prohibition of *ousia* language by the Council of Constantinople in 360. Yet in another sense, Basil's understanding of divine *ousia* highlights, by contrast, Gregory's deeper regard for the unity and monarchy of the Trinity. Basil defines the concepts of *ousia* and *hypostasis* as representing the common and the particular—as in the difference between a living creature of any sort

---

171. E.g., Meredith, "Pneumatology of the Cappadocian Fathers." See also Ayres, *Nicaea*, pp. 257–258.

172. Meredith points out that in some ways even Basil's *Eun.* 3—and we may add some of the letters cited above—is stronger than the later *Spir.* "Pneumatology of the Cappadocian Fathers," p. 198.

173. Hildebrand, *Trinitarian Theology*, p. 45.

compared with a particular human being.[174] In this conception Basil adopts a predominantly Stoic ontology in order to understand Trinitarian metaphysics.[175] On one level this distinction seems obvious, in the sense that the divine being (οὐσία), as a noun, is certainly used to describe the Father, Son, and Holy Spirit, whereas "Father," "Son," and "Holy Spirit" (or Peter, James, and John) are more specific nouns, which apply only to each of the respective persons, not to all three together.[176] Yet while this conceptual definition can serve as a helpful step toward giving "a sound account of our faith," as Basil hopes,[177] Gregory succeeds more fully in the same task by providing a more properly Christian metaphysic in his understanding of the divine monarchy, in which the Son and Spirit are determined by, reflective of, and refer back to the Father's divine being,[178] rather than all three simply being different types of divine being (although in a derivative sense they are this also).[179] The relative absence of this technical distinction in Gregory's work, in preference for more immediate terms and for the idea of Trinitarian "relations," avoids the fallacy of imagining that there are any such things as hypostases or the divine nature in themselves[180]—a problem that will plague the post-Chalcedonian Christological debates in the coming centuries, through the reception of Gregory of Nyssa's redaction of Basil's work and similar metaphysical constructions made later.[181] Even as both men regard the Father and the Son as unbegotten Divinity and begotten Divinity,[182] Gregory has a more robust sense of the monarchy of

---

174. *Ep.* 214.4. Basil also describes the commonality between the Father and Son as the "principle" of the essence, or of Divinity (ὁ τῆς οὐσίας λόγος ... ὁ λόγος τῆς θεότητος), which they share (*Eun.* 1.19; *Ep.* 236.6). And in another passage, the divine represents the common (τὸ κοινόν), while the unique characteristics belonging to the Father or the Son are particulars (τὸ ἴδιον, *Eun.* 2.28). Recent discussions of Basil's distinction between *ousia* and *hypostasis* can be found in Behr, *Nicene Faith*, pp. 293–299; Hildebrand, *Trinitarian Theology*, pp. 91–92. This distinction goes a long way toward providing the textbook idea of the "Cappadocian solution" to the Trinity.

175. Hübner identified the characteristically Stoic resonance of Basil's ontology, in contrast with the Aristotelian metaphysic brought to bear by Gregory of Nyssa in his Pseudo-Basil, *Ep.* 38 ("Gregor von Nyssa als Verfasser").

176. Basil notes the grammatical difference at *Spir.* 17.41.

177. *Ep.* 236.6.

178. On which see chap. 4.

179. As Basil and Gregory both recognized, the Trinity is even less like three members of a common species or class, as they are conceived in an Aristotelian metaphysic such as Gregory of Nyssa's (Pseudo-Basil, *Ep.* 38).

180. See chap. 4.

181. On which see below.

182. Here again, a significant difference appears over the identity of the Holy Spirit: for Basil, the particular characteristic of the Holy Spirit, as a divine *hypostasis*, is "sanctifying power," compared with fatherhood and sonship for the other two (*Ep.* 214.4; 236.6). To some degree Gregory accepts Basil's Origenist argument about the Spirit's nature as sanctification (see *Or.* 31.4), but he goes on to locate the Spirit's eternal identity more solidly in its eternal generation, or its "procession," from the Father (31.8).

God the Father and the causal relationships that constitute the eternal life of the Trinity than Basil's predominantly Stoic ontology allows.[183] Basil also uses "*hypostasis*" in a more technical sense than Gregory does. Gregory is happy to speak of hypostases occasionally, though he typically refers to them simply as "the Three," or by their proper names, "Father, Son, and Holy Spirit"; again, he seems to want to avoid falling into the trap of substituting an alternative metaphysic for the biblical doctrine of the Trinity.[184]

Tying together these several differences—over the relationship between theology and the economy, the unity of Christ, the Spirit's full presence in creation and divinization, and the monarchy within the Trinity—is a different overall sense of the reality of the knowledge of God. In *Against Eunomius* Basil argues that humans have direct knowledge of God's energies alone, not (even partially) of God's essence.[185] By comparison with Gregory's vivid mysticism of the divine light, Basil's is, in the end, a less fully participatory doctrine than Gregory's. Whereas Gregory joyously proclaims Christ to be the illumination of believers, the more they are purified and ascend to the divine Light, for Basil Christ's identity as Light also signifies the *inaccessibility* of the glory in the Divinity.[186] In sum, Gregory has a stronger doctrine of revelation and a greater sense of theological unities.[187]

Gregory of Nyssa

Gregory Nazianzen and Gregory of Nyssa, the third "Cappadocian father," had much less personal and ecclesiastical interaction than did Gregory Nazianzen and Basil (although both chafed under Basil's episcopal authority), and their

---

183. This limitation can be seen as well in Basil's argument that, in this vertical ontological scheme, things are *homoousios* with their own works, as a potter with his pot, or a shipbuilder with his ship, as well as the idea that Peter and Paul are *homoousioi* because they share a common nature. See *Eun.* 2.4. Basil's construction at times rules out the possibility of a consubstantial relationship among three things of the same ontological status, as in the Trinity. See, in comparison, the contradictory statements in *Eun.* 2.19 and 2.32.

184. In his analysis of Basil's conception of the divine plurality, Hildebrand notes that, during the first stage of his career, before he has settled on the "hypostasis," Basil has no term for what sort of subject possesses the distinctive characteristic (ἰδίωμα) of fatherhood or sonship, or what is the Father or the Son (*Trinitarian Theology*, pp. 66–67). In Gregory's case we can say that such a term is unnecessary in the first place, except perhaps as a stylistic convenience.

185. *Eun* 1.6–7; see also 14; cf. 1.10, where Basil discusses theological language that positively describes God.

186. *Eun.* 1.6.

187. Gregory's theological and spiritual superiority to Basil is also observed by Holl, *Amphilochius*, pp. 159, 163, 167.

work shows even less in common. While Gregory of Nyssa drew heavily from both Basil and Gregory Nazianzen, his work is on the whole much closer to Basil's than it is to the other Gregory's. Having been tutored in rhetoric by his older brother, Gregory of Nyssa later worked intensively to defend the legacy of Basil's work against Eunomius, and he wrote *On the Creation of the Human Being* with the explicit intention of completing Basil's *Hexaemeron*. Gregory of Nyssa also seems to have been more closely associated with the Melitian network in Antioch than Basil—he was present at the synod of 379, he delivered Melitius' funeral oration, and he was listed as an arbiter of Theodosian orthodoxy along with Diodore—which further distinguishes his efforts from those of Gregory Nazianzen, who worked, as we have seen, more independent of, and often against, the emerging Antiochene tradition around Melitius' protégé, Diodore. Although he has been the subject of much scholarly interest since the mid-twentieth century, Gregory of Nyssa's doctrine of the Trinity is still surprisingly understudied.[188]

There are several obvious points of commonality between these two theologians who, in their different ways, aligned themselves with the faith of Nicaea—similarities that largely follow the lines that we have examined above in connection with Basil, with some notable exceptions in the doctrine of the Holy Spirit; we will therefore focus here on the features that distinguish each man's work. Being the youngest of the three Cappadocians, Gregory of Nyssa wrote a number of key treatises on the Holy Spirit and the Trinity over a three- to five-year period, probably beginning not long before the council of 381. Considering their later date, and the likelihood that Gregory knew at least some of Gregory Nazianzen's work, it is not surprising that he shows a much stronger sense of the divinity of the Holy Spirit and the unity, equality, and consubstantiality of the Trinity than Basil does. He is absolutely clear, for example, that the Spirit exists and "works" in the fullest sense, along with the Father and the Son, "in every thing and notion—both encosmic and supercosmic, those in time and before the ages,"[189] beyond simply the harmonization of the Son's creation and the sanctification of rational beings, as we saw in Basil. He also argues for the Spirit's vivication and sanctification of Chris-

---

188. The great works on Gregory of Nyssa in the twentieth century by Balthasar, Daniélou, and others served to fill out the remainder of Gregory's thought after the more narrowly focused *dogmengeschichtliche* studies of Harnack, Loofs, Seeberg, and Holl on Gregory's Christology and Trinitarian doctrine. What is needed most at this time is a reappraisal of his Trinitarian doctrine that includes his ascetical theology and anthropology. Several helpful recent works have appeared by Turcescu, Barnes, and Potier.

189. *Spir.* 100.14–16.

tians in baptism, although in ways that resemble Basil more than Gregory Nazianzen.[190] Again like Basil, Gregory of Nyssa places unfailing confidence in his ability to prove the divinity of the Holy Spirit directly from the witness of Scripture,[191] even when he is faced with the same sort of Pneumatomachian objections that Gregory Nazianzen dealt with in *Oration* 31 (that the Scriptures do not plainly call the Spirit either "God" or "Divinity").[192] In stark contrast with Gregory Nazianzen (and apparently with no better results), Gregory of Nyssa refuses to believe that a biblical proof cannot be mounted, which points to significant differences in their approaches to biblical hermeneutics and Pneumatological doctrine. More pronounced is the way in which, in his treatises against the Macedonians, Gregory of Nyssa seeks to prove the Spirit's divinity in a much less convincing manner than Gregory Nazianzen or even Basil. Occasionally he simply asserts the common divine nature among the Trinity and then concludes that the Spirit must therefore be divine[193]—an argument which not very subtly begs the question. We find little of Gregory Nazianzen's central argument for the Spirit's divinity from the divinization of Christians. In fact, Gregory of Nyssa seldom speaks of divinization, and when he does it typically concerns transformation in virtue as distinguished from a noetic participation in the divine light.[194] Gregory of Nyssa also employs arguments for the Spirit's divinity that are not found anywhere in Gregory Nazianzen: for example, the idea that the Spirit's anointing in baptism signifies its nature as "kingship," which proves its shared divinity with the Father and Son, who are each King; and the idea that the inseparability of the oil of anointing from the body that it anoints (in Jesus' baptism) signifies the Spirit's inseparability from the Son.[195] With Gregory of Nyssa we therefore have a doctrine of the Spirit that asserts the divinity of the Spirit more strongly than Basil, and is thus closer to Gregory Nazianzen, but which is less adept at doing so and does not reflect the heart of the older Gregory's argumentation and spiritual infrastructure. Being more firmly allied with the emerging Antiochene school under Diodore than Basil was, Gregory of Nyssa is even further from Gregory Nazianzen in his Christology. The

---

190. The Spirit deserves worship because it vivifies in baptism: Basil's "liturgical argument." See, e.g., *Spir.* 105–109.
191. *Eust.* 6; *Spir.* 90, 92.
192. *Deit. Fil. et Spir.* 573c.
193. *Spir.* 94–96; see also *Eust.* 13–14.
194. See Laird, *Gregory of Nyssa and the Grasp of Faith*, pp. 187, 201.
195. *Spir.* 102–103.

Antiochene character of his work can be seen both in his more dualistic understanding of Christ's person[196] and in the theory of Christ's atonement and deception of the devil.[197] Being naturally oriented against Apollinarius, as an Antiochene theologian, it is Gregory of Nyssa who was chiefly responsible for the modern view that the Christology of all three Cappadocians is predominantly anti-Apollinarian.[198]

Turning to Gregory of Nyssa's doctrine of the Trinity as a whole, we find several major differences from Gregory Nazianzen's. The most substantial—and a matter of far-reaching significance for the unfolding of Nicene Christology in the post-Chalcedonian period—is his definition of *ousia* and *hypostasis*, which follows on and expands that of his older brother. In a concentrated set of works on the Trinity, written from around the time of Basil's death in 379 to about 383—roughly the same period as Gregory Nazianzen's major work—Gregory defines several points of Trinitarian logic and metaphysics. In the *Letter to His Brother Peter*[199] and related works, he defines *ousia* (essence or substance)[200] and *physis* (nature)[201] as a common reality or form that is shared by unique (ἰδίως)[202] *hypostases*, which are themselves particular instantiations of the common essence that are specifically defined or circumscribed (πραγ ματός τινος περιγραφή) and are differentiated from one another by their particular properties (τὰ ἰδιάζουσα).[203] Drawing heavily on a Neoplatonic combination of Platonic forms with Aristotelian metaphysics of the universal and the particular,[204] in a way distinct from Basil's more heavily Stoic approach, Gregory employs this set of concepts as a tool with which to analyze the way that language and being work both in the realm of common speech and in the usage of Scripture. As an example, he argues that the term "human being" (ἄνθρωπος) properly signifies the common essence that all people share, or "the whole of humanity" (τὸν καθόλον ἄνθρωπον), of which individual human beings (like the apostles Peter and John) are particular instances.[205] The

---

196. Especially evident in the *Antirrheticus* against Apollinarius.
197. See *Or. cat.* 24–26. The similarities with Nestorius and Theodore of Mopsuestia are significant.
198. On Gregory Nazianzen's substantial use of Apollinarius and his opposition to Diodore, see above.
199. Pseudo-Basil, *Ep.* 38. Fedwick has argued that this letter serves as Gregory's commentary on Basil's treatment of *ousia* and *hypostasis*. See "A Commentary of Gregory of Nyssa," p. 32n9; see also Behr, *Nicene Faith*, p. 415n30. This letter may be Gregory's first treatise on Trinitarian doctrine.
200. *Ep. Pet.* 1: τὸ κοινὸν τῆς οὐσίας.
201. *Ep. Pet.* 2: τὴν κοινὴν φύσιν.
202. *Ep. Pet.* 3.
203. *Ep. Pet.* 2. On Gregory's concept of individuality as a complex of particular properties, see Turcescu, *Gregory of Nyssa* pp. 100–101.
204. See Turcescu, *Gregory of Nyssa and the Concept of Divine Persons*, pp. 63, 97.
205. *Ep.* 38, 325b and passim.

relationship between an *ousia* and a *hypostasis* is thus the same as that between a form (or species, εἶδος) and an individual thing that represents that form (ἄτομον).[206] For two or more things to be consubstantial with one another, then, means that they are instances of the same common nature.[207] Furthermore, a *hypostasis* has "no communion" with its common nature, meaning that the individual entity qua individual entity is not the same thing as the common essence that all entities of the same kind share with one another; although he concedes that a *hypostasis* does "contain the common property in some ways."[208]

Gregory of Nyssa conceives of *ousia*, moreover, as being superior to and more real than individual hypostases. The divine essence is thus "a single existing essence," to which the Father, Son, and Holy Spirit each belong, or which they each possess.[209] In order to defend himself against the charge of tritheism, Gregory employs this scheme by means of a comparison between the Father, Son, and Holy Spirit, who share a single divine nature, and the plurality of human beings, who share a single human nature. He then argues that the essence of humanity is more real than individual human beings, so that the conventional practice of calling individuals "human beings" is illegitimate[210] according to "the precise rule of the science of language."[211] When Scripture refers to individual human beings, it does so as a kind of incorrect babbling for infants (much like an anthropomorphic description of God), which is designed to lead us on to a more mature and accurate view of the common essence that is being designated, "the perfect [object] that is contemplated in the [common] nature of the things."[212] The one God is therefore known in the three persons or hypostases through this sort of inferential contemplation (θεωρεῖται) of imperfect expressions.[213] Consequently, an essence, or common nature, is further removed from our knowing than the particular instances of it are. The essence of a thing can be conceived only indefinitely, and it cannot be properly signified; whereas a *hypostasis* is delimited and so is able to present the essence in a knowable way.[214] The Father,

---

206. *Comm. Not.* 31.
207. *Ep. Pet.* 328a.
208. *Ep. Pet.* 325c–328a. On the sharp division between *ousia* and *hypostasis*, see also *Comm. Not.* 19.
209. μιᾶς τοιγαροῦν ὑπαρχούσης τῆς οὐσίας, ἧς ἐστι πατὴρ καὶ υἱὸς καὶ ἅγιον πνεῦμα. *Comm. Not.* 22.13–14.
210. *Comm. Not.* 25, 30.
211. ὁ ἀκριβὴς κανὼν τῆς λογικῆς ἐπιστήμης. *Comm. Not.* 32.7.
212. τὸ τέλειον καὶ ἐν τῇ φύσει τῶν πραγμάτων θεωρούμενον. *Comm. Not.* 28.4.
213. *Comm. Not.* 33.3–5.
214. *Ep. Pet.* 3.

Son, and Holy Spirit, *qua* hypostases, are thus specially able to reveal the divine essence, which is incomprehensible.

From the perspective of Gregory Nazianzen's doctrine (as well as Basil's), there are several major problems with this scheme. The first is that it suggests that the divine nature is a generic substance that the Father, Son, and Holy Spirit all possess, or a class to which they all belong. In Gregory of Nyssa, the monarchy of the Father is thus much less clear than in Gregory Nazianzen or even in Basil. Although he occasionally asserts the monarchy,[215] his Neoplatonic idealism yields a theory of divine substance that mitigates against what in Gregory Nazianzen is a more biblical doctrine of the Trinity.[216] Gregory of Nyssa reduces the problematic rigidity of these designations to some extent through the image of a rainbow, in which it is impossible to see where one color (or *hypostasis*) leaves off and another begins, just as the Father, Son, and Holy Spirit are inseparably related in the divine essence, so that the common essence and the particular hypostatic identity of each of the three shine out together.[217] But such passages are the exception. Gregory of Nyssa goes much farther than Basil's largely grammatical recognition of the communion of nature between the Father, Son, and Holy Spirit, to say that that divine essence is a formal reality that is more real than the instantiations of it—a dogmatically Platonist idea that has little appeal to either Basil or Gregory Nazianzen. Gregory of Nyssa's definition of the hypostases of the Father, Son, and Holy Spirit as being constitutionally revelatory of the unknowable divine essence also departs from Basil and Gregory Nazianzen: for Basil the incomprehensible essence is known positively through traits that belong *to the essence* and which all three persons share, whereas for Gregory Nazianzen the Father, Son, and Holy Spirit are not in themselves any more or less comprehensible than the divine being (or the Divinity) in general, because they *are* the Divinity. In this and other respects, Gregory of Nyssa is more apophatic than Basil, and thus even more so than Gregory Nazianzen's positive doctrine of divine illumination and revelation.[218] Gregory of Nyssa's argument for divine unknow-

---

215. E.g., *Comm. Not.* 25.

216. In making this statement, I do not mean to invoke the caricatured, global distinction that took root in high Protestant thought between all "good" biblical doctrine and all "bad" philosophy (on which see the helpful cautions of Ayres, *Nicaea*, pp. 388–392). While it is appropriate—and long overdue—that we eradicate the idea that Christianity and ancient philosophy are absolutely incompatible, nevertheless there are cases, such as this one, in which one can still differentiate biblical Christianity (which is not necessarily completely pure of philosophical ideas) from philosophically inspired schemes that contrast with it.

217. *Ep. Pet.* 5.

218. A difference which comes out in the two Gregorys' different approaches to Moses' encounter with God on Mount Sinai; cf. *V. Mos.* and *Or.* 28.3.

ability in his defense of the divinity of the Holy Spirit against the Macedonians is an especially stark contrast.[219] This strange divergence seems to correlate with Gregory of Nyssa's argument that the "Divinity" is not in fact the divine nature and his denial that the divine nature can be signified at all.[220] On the matter of "incorrect" statements about human and other individualities, Gregory Nazianzen has an almost allergic reaction to this sort of scientific linguistics; for him it betrays a woodenly philosophical approach to language, which, as a highly trained rhetorician, he knows is much more complicated and less patient of analytic purification that Gregory of Nyssa thinks it is. In this respect Gregory and Basil are much closer to each other than either is to Gregory of Nyssa. Finally, as we observed in chapter 4, Gregory of Nyssa's strong reliance on the identical operations of the Father, Son, and Holy Spirit in his argument for the unity of the Trinity[221] differs markedly from Gregory Nazianzen's recognition that such an approach only begs the question.[222] These metaphysical and linguistic aspects of Gregory of Nyssa's work are very far from Gregory Nazianzen's. In Gregory of Nyssa's hands, Basil's definitions of *ousia* and *hypostasis* assume the approximate form that will be taken up, in highly problematic ways, in the later Christological debates, and that will require an eventual readjustment in the direction of Gregory Nazianzen's doctrine.

The Homoiousians and Eastern Theological Tradition

Gregory Nazianzen's doctrine reflects several distinct characteristics of the Trinitarian theological tradition of east-central Asia Minor—a regional character symbolized by the location of Nazianzus directly on the road between

---

219. *Spir.* 114. Gregory to some extent compensates for this negative epistemology by a positive regard for the luminosity and illumination that comes from the grace of the Holy Spirit and the light of the Christian Gospel (see *Comm. Cant.* 5; 2.10). However, he carefully limits such illumination to the realm of faith as distinct from knowing. While faith is enlightened, the mind moves toward darkness and unknowing (see *V. Mos*; *Hom. Cant.* 6 and 11). An exceptional combination of both comes in *Comm. Cant.* 11, where the dark cloud shines with brilliant light, and we have the mysticism of darkness and light together. See Laird, *Gregory of Nyssa and the Grasp of Faith*, pp. 190–91, 201, 204. Gregory of Nyssa thus ends his career with an intimation toward the idea of revelatory illumination with which Gregory Nazianzen begins.

220. *Comm. Not.* 14.7–8. See also *Deit. Fil. et Spir.* 573d; *Eun.* 2.256.28–257.1; *Eust.* 14.

221. E.g., *Eust* 7.

222. As did Basil of Ancyra: the Son's sharing with the Father in the work of creation does not demonstrate his divinity or likeness in being any more than the fact that a priest uses tongs to lift coal from an altar proves that the tongs cannot have been created by him. *Letter* of the Council of Ancyra in 358, in Epiphanius, *Panar.* 73.4.7.

Constantinople and Antioch. It was this loosely defined "homoiousian" network sponsored by Melitius of Antioch that had entered into communion with Damasus of Rome and that Gregory represented in Constantinople at the height of his career, as the bishop charged with building a consensus among disparate Trinitarian groups in the imperial capital. Gregory's doctrine of the Trinity, with its basis in the monarchy of God the Father, its predominantly anti-Sabellian undercurrent, and its characteristically Eastern phrasing, reflects a long history of Eastern theological tradition and creedal definition. When Gregory and Basil began their ministries in the early 360s, they were most closely associated with the homoiousian network that had recently been led by Basil of Ancyra, George of Laodicea, and others. Following the Homoiousians, Gregory and Basil of Caesarea went on to define their doctrine largely in opposition to the radical subordinationism of the Heterousians, and to understand the entire homoian regime and eventually all anti-Nicene theology through that lens. More fully than Basil, Gregory spent his career fulfilling and completing the theological approach of Homoiousians like Melitius and Basil of Ancyra.

Several important common elements with Gregory's work can be perceived in the homoiousian Council of Ancyra in 358. The council emphasizes the terms "Father," "Son," and "Holy Spirit" over "Creator" and "creature" for understanding the nature of the persons of the Trinity, and its main argument is that the divine relations that they signify are to be understood as like each other in being, rather than unlike, as the Heterousians claimed, and not merely like each other in power.[223] Speaking for the council, Basil of Ancyra argues that the Father's begetting of the Son makes them alike, rather than different.[224] Moreover, the Father's begetting of the Son indicates a different relationship than God's creation of creatures,[225] so that the fact that the Father generates the Son but is not himself generated does not betoken a difference of nature such as exists between the Creator and creatures.[226] (Thus they make the same firm distinction between begetting and creating found in Nicaea and the work of Alexander and Athanasius.) The letter goes on to describe the Father's generation of the Son in such a way that marks it as highly transcendent: it is beyond time,[227]

---

223. Basil of Ancyra, *Ep. syn.*, in Epiphanius, *Panar.* 73.3 and passim.
224. Epiphanius, *Panar.* 73.7.8.
225. The terms found in Prv 8.22 and 25. Epiphanius, *Panar.* 73.11.1.
226. Epiphanius, *Panar.* 73.20.1: the substance of Basil of Caesarea's argument against the Eunomians in *Eun.* 1, which carries throughout Gregory's work.
227. Epiphanius, *Panar.* 73.11.6-7.

ineffable,[228] entirely unique,[229] beyond all creaturely passion,[230] and incorporeal.[231] Within the Origenist framework that informs Eastern theology (including Gregory's), the incorporeality of the Trinity compared to the corporeality of creaturely existence marks its transcendence in very strong terms.[232] Also like the Eastern tradition that precedes it, the council's statement emphasizes the monarchy of God the Father, as Gregory will: the Father is cause (αἴτιον) of the Son, giving him an essence like his own;[233] the Father is the only first principle (ἀρχή), which rules out the possibility of there being three gods;[234] and the fact that the Son is "God" (Jn 1.1) and "in the form of God" (Phil 2.6) rather than "the God" (Jn 1.1) indicates his derivation from the Father.[235] George of Laodicea's statement that Easterners confess "one Divinity, which encompasses all things through the Son in the Holy Spirit" likewise expresses the principle that the unity of God consists in the fact that the Son and the Spirit share in the one Divinity of God the Father, and the corollary belief that they are like the Father in being rather than unlike him, again very similar to Gregory's own doctrine. The Homoiousians' central argument that the Son and Spirit are like the Father not only in activity and power,[236] but in Divinity, incorporeality, and therefore being,[237] is possibly being echoed in Gregory's key Trinitarian formula, "the one Divinity *and* power of the Father, Son, and Holy Spirit."

An even more striking similarity with Gregory's doctrine comes in the council's argument concerning theological method. In the synodical letter, Basil of Ancyra addresses those who object that the Father's generation of the Son in being must involve passion, division, or emission.[238] He replies that such persons unreasonably rely on human reason rather than accepting the faith that alone brings salvation,[239] whereas a true understanding of Christ's

---

228. "The ineffable fact that [the Son is begotten] from [the Father] without passion" (τὴν ἀπόρρητον ἐξ αὐτοῦ ἀπαθῶς). Epiphanius, *Panar.* 73.9.6.
229. The Father's "proper and unique generation" (ἡ ἰδίως καὶ μονογενῶς γεννητική) of the Son. Epiphanius, *Panar.* 73.5.3.
230. Epiphanius, *Panar.* 73.3.5, 6.1, etc.
231. A proper understanding of the biblical terms recognizes "the existence of an incorporeal Son from an incorporeal Father." Epiphanius, *Panar.* 73.3.5; see also 3.6–8 and passim.
232. See Epiphanius, *Panar.* 73.9.4: "the Son is like the Father in Divinity, incorporeality, and activity."
233. Epiphanius, *Panar.* 73.3.3.
234. Epiphanius, *Panar.* 73.16.3 (the subsequent letter of George of Laodicea).
235. Epiphanius, *Panar.* 73.9.5.
236. Epiphanius, *Panar.* 73.11.2–3.
237. Epiphanius, *Panar.* 73.9.4 and passim.
238. Epiphanius, *Panar.* 73.6.1–6.
239. Epiphanius, *Panar.* 73.6.1, 4.

divine sonship prevents "the mystery being emptied" by the suspicions of clever arguments.[240] These two motifs—the appeal to faith over reason as being more truly reasonable, and the description of Heterousians as emptying the mystery of the faith through clever argumentation—supply Gregory's two main statements of theological method in the *Theological Orations*. As we have seen, he discusses the limitation of human reason and the superiority of faith at length in *Oration* 28 (with a reverberation in 29.21), and he uses Basil of Ancyra's phrase "the mystery is emptied"—uniquely among extant fourth-century literature[241]—to describe the doctrine of the Homoians, Heterousians, and Pneumatomachians. A second major parallel with this passage is the deep connection that is asserted between the Son's divine generation and being (Trinitarian doctrine) and the "mystery" of his saving work on the cross (soteriology and Christology). Basil argues that those who deny the Son's divine generation and his essential likeness to the Father are implicitly denying the mystery of Christ crucified. In the same theopaschite terms that are so central to Gregory's Christology, Basil says that they cannot account for "how God is crucified," which is the foolishness of the Gospel that is wiser than human beings.[242] The Homoiousians' basic soteriological insistence that the Trinity must share a common Divinity in terms of being as the necessary corollary of God's suffering on the cross in Jesus Christ resembles Gregory's approach to a very great extent. There are several intriguing minor parallels as well: the anti-Sabellian statements that the Father and Son are not "the same entity" (ταὐτός)[243] but "different entities" (ἕτερος) match in reverse Gregory's famous dictum that the Father, Son, and Holy Spirit are three distinct entities (ἄλλος καὶ ἄλλος καὶ ἄλλος)[244]; and in an extremely tantalizing parallel, George argues that the phrase "Father and Son" signifies a "relation" to one another, rather than the difference between the Creator and a creature.[245]

---

240. ἵνα μὴ διὰ τὰ ἐκ λογισμῶν ὑποτευόμενα κενωθῇ <τὸ μυστήριον>. Epiphanius, *Panar.* 73.6.6.

241. The verbal combination of 1 Cor 1.17 and 2.1 into the phrase "the mystery is emptied" (κενωθῇ [τὸ μυστήριον], Epiphanius, *Panar.* 73.6.5, 73.6.6) is a unique parallel between the council's letter and Gregory's *Ors.* 29.21 and 31.23.

242. Πῶς ὁ θεὸς σταυροῦται. See 1 Cor. 1.25. Epiphanius, *Panar.* 73.6.2. The argument includes the standard anti-Sabellian premise that God the Father cannot be said to suffer (73.6.7), which makes the Son's suffering both as "God" and as a distinct entity necessary.

243. For the sake of clarity, I have altered Basil's ταὐτόν to ταὐτός, allowing for the neuter subject τὸ ὅμοιον in place of ὁ Πατήρ or ὁ Υἱός; however, since Gregory does not observe a strict masculine-versus-neuter technical distinction among Trinitarian and Christological pronouns, the parallel holds either way.

244. Epiphanius, *Panar.* 73.8.8; cf. Gregory, *Ep.* 101.20–21.

245. Epiphanius, *Panar.* 73.19.3. The terminology originally stems from Origen, *Comm. Rom.* 146.l.10, 14; *Comm. Jn.* 2.34.205; *Comm. Mt.* 17.33.17, 37; and was taken up by Eusebius, *Eccl. theo.* 1.9.4; 1.10.3; see also

The main force of the homoiousian position, then, is to argue for the singleness of Divinity among the Father, Son, and Holy Spirit in terms of their being, against claims that they are similar only in power or activity, while also maintaining their fundamental distinctness from one another. This second point leads the Homoiousians at Ancyra in 358 to resist the Nicene language of consubstantiality because they take it to mean that the Father and the Son are exactly the same thing.[246] This resistance is not so much a conflation of the categories of hypostases and divine being, which the Cappadocians are alleged to have properly distinguished for posterity, as it is a keen focus on the constantly hypostatic nature of the Divinity that has much in common with Gregory's doctrine. By claming that the Son is "like" but not "the same as" the Father in being, the Homoiousians are not saying that the Son's divinity is of a different genetic sort from God the Father's—that he is not innately all-powerful, all-good, infinite, or the Creator God, for example—as the Heterousians were thought to believe; nor do they allow for any division of the divine nature in the Father's generation of the Son and the Spirit and his unique conferral of his Divinity on them, as later pro-Nicenes themselves were accused of holding.[247] Rather, they are simply voicing an awareness that the divine being of the Son exists in a different way than it does in the Father, as being begotten from the Father. For the Homoiousians, the differences between the Father, Son, and Spirit are structural or relational, as in the difference between θεός and ὁ θεός, not a difference in degree of Divinity or divine being. The Father and Son cannot be said to be exactly the same in being because the divine being does not in fact exist apart from being either (to use Gregory's terms) unbegotten, begotten, or proceeding Divinity.[248] While the doctrine of the Homoiousians is certainly not without its flaws from Gregory's

---

Basil, *Eun.* 1.5, 20; 2.22; *Spir.* 6.14.8 (λέγειν τοῦ Πατρὸς τὸν Υἱόν, οὐ μόνον τῷ σὺν ἀλλήλοις νοεῖσθαι κατὰ τὴν σχέσιν, ἀλλ' ὅτι ἐκεῖνα λέγεται τῷ χρόνῳ δευτέρα). Epiphanius makes a loosely related argument against the Anomoians, that "the Son's share in the perfect name [of God] reflects the true relation (σχέσις) of the Son to the eternal, uncreated Father" (*Panar.* 73.23.3). But cf. the alternative statement by the Council of Ancyra that Wisdom teaches "its relation (σχέσις) to created things" (*Panar.* 73.7.2), as well as Epiphanius' own use of the term to refer to Christ's divine and human elements (*Panar.* 69.74.7).

246. Epiphanius, *Panar.* 73.11.10: the Son is neither ὁμοούσιος nor ταὐτοούσιος with the Father. By 363 Melitius folds Nicaea into the homoiousian program, arguing that the second key phrase, "from the being of the Father," and thereby *homoousios* as well, in fact means that the Son is *like* the Father in being. *Ep. Jov.* in Socrates, *HE* 3.25.

247. See, e.g., Gregory's *Or.* 31.14.

248. They would therefore resist the artificial division of being and *hypostasis* that we saw above in Gregory of Nyssa.

standpoint,[249] failing to give an adequate account of the divinity of the Son or the Spirit is not one of them.

At this point we may observe that a full doctrine of the Trinity can be expressed in either a homoiousian or a homoousian thought system—both of which are defined against homoianism—and that, as should be obvious by now, a Nicene construction does not require any fewer qualifications and conceptual gymnastics than a homoiousian one does. It makes just as much sense to say that the Father, Son, and Holy Spirit are not the same in being (for anti-Sabellian reasons) as it does to say that they are (for anti-Arian reasons). The Nicene terminology of consubstantiality, in other words, is not a metaphysical panacea for straightening out errors in Trinitarian doctrine. It is therefore no accident that pro-Nicenes like Damasus, Gregory Nazianzen, and Gregory of Nyssa took the Homoiousians as their allies. Gregory will of course alter the traditional Eastern phrasing by employing Nicene terms (though not nearly to the extent that Athanasius did), but on balance this is a minor change, and should not be regarded as a substantive correction.

Like the Homoiousians represented at Ancyra in 358, Gregory's doctrine distinctly echoes the Eastern creedal tradition stemming from the Dedication Council of Antioch in 341, at which George of Laodicea was present and which made a passing acknowledgment of Nicaea. Gregory's emphasis on the singularity and completeness of each of the three persons in *Oration* 25 and in the *Theological Orations*[250] strongly echoes the anti-Marcellan terms of the Origenist Dedication Creed[251] and is unique in its density and multiplicity of forms among contemporary pro-Nicene theologians.[252] The language of singularity recurs in later conciliar statements as well, including those from

---

249. In addition to reconciling their doctrine with Nicene language, Gregory will also correct certain statements that seem to limit Christ's experience of human existence and sinfulness—though nothing like to the degree of the Apollinarians. See Epiphanius, *Panar.* 73.9.5–7.

250. In the various forms of ὅλος, εἷς and μόνος; on *Or.* 25.15–16, see chap. 4, pp. 202–206. This emphasis recurs in Gregory's discussion of the divine names at the end of *Or.* 30, where he argues that the Son is called Only-begotten (μονογενής) "not only because he is unique and uniquely comes from one unique, but because he does so in a unique manner, unlike bodies" (μόνος ἐκ μόνου καὶ μόνον, ἀλλ' ὅτι καὶ μονοτρόπως, οὐχ ὡς τὰ σώματα, 30.20).

251. Hahn § 154, l. 6: And we believe in "one Lord Jesus Christ his only-begotten Son, God, through whom all things [are made], who was begotten from the Father before the ages, God from God, whole from whole, sole from sole (ὅλον ἐξ ὅλου, μόνον ἐκ μόνου), perfect from perfect, King from King, Lord from Lord, ... exact image (ἀπαράλλακτον εἰκόνα) of the Divinity and the being and will and power and glory of the Father."

252. The concentration of and μόνος, μόνου, μόνον, and μόνως in Gregory's discussion of the Father and the Son (25.16) is unparalleled, with near exceptions only in Pseudo-Didymus, *Trin.* 1.15.96, and Pseudo-Cyril, *De sanct. Trin.*, PG 77.1136.44, both of which are dependent on Gregory. Gregory's point that each person thus possesses the divine quality of uniqueness (τὸ μοναδικόν, a rare term) can be compared to Basil's argument in *Spir.* 18.45 (also rare) that singular units dwell together in the Trinity.

Antioch 344 (the Macrostich Creed),[253] Ancyra 358,[254] Sirmium 359 (the Dated Creed), Niké 359,[255] and Constantinople 360.[256] Although Athanasius reports each of these statements,[257] he never takes up their terms in his own doctrine, as Gregory does. Also unlike Athanasius, Gregory is happy to call the Son the "exact image" of the Father (38.13 = 45.9), along with the Dedication Creed and the strong image Christology of Eusebius of Caesarea.[258] Likewise, Gregory's statement that, being unique and complete, "the Father is truly a Father," "the Son is truly a Son," and "the Holy Spirit is truly holy" also reflects the Dedication Creed.[259] These phrases originally come from the arch-Eusebian Asterius.[260] Eusebius of Caesarea then defends them against Marcellus' attack on Asterius, arguing that they are not innovations by Asterius but represent the doctrine of Origen and several earlier bishops and synods,[261] and he includes them in his anti-Marcellan commentary on the Caesarean creed that he presented to Constantine and the Council of Nicaea.[262] Although Athanasius occasionally uses similar terms and engages the traditional Eusebian language,[263] Gregory adopts it much more directly and wholeheartedly. His argument that

---

253. Hahn § 159.8, l. 14 (the Only-begotten is genuinely begotten μόνον γὰρ καὶ μόνως). This council more closely followed the dominant Antiochene group that produced the fourth creed from the Dedication Council of 341, as distinct from the bishops who produced the second creed (Dedication Creed) (Hahn § 154).

254. The Father's unique generation of the Son; see pp. 310–311.

255. Hahn § 163, ll. 1 (God the Father is μόνον θεόν), 6 (the Son is μόνον ἐκ μόνου τοῦ Πατρός); § pp. 310–311. 164, ll. 1, 5–6 (using the same terms).

256. Hahn § 167, l. 4: μόνον ἐκ μόνου τοῦ Πατρός. These terms do not appear, however, in the Eastern statement of Serdica 343 (issued from Philippopolis) or in the statements of Sirmium 351 or 357. See the same language in Acacius' argument against Marcellus (Epiphanius, Panar. 72.7.1) and Epiphanius against Aetius (Panar. 76.37.10).

257. See Syn. 23, 8, and 30 (twice), respectively.

258. Athanasius avoids the term by the time of On the Councils of Ariminum and Seleucia in order to distinguish his theology from the Eusebians, even though he had used it willingly in his earlier writings (Gent. 41, 46, 47; Ar. 1.26; 2.33; 3.5, 11). See Hanson, Search for the Christian Doctrine of God, p. 288. See also the rare witnesses in Basil, Hom. 41 C. Sabell. et Ar. 4 (PG 21.608.4); Gregory of Nyssa, Eun. 3.6.11.

259. In its argument that Mt 28.19 teaches baptism into "a Father who is truly a Father, a Son who is truly a Son, and a Holy Spirit who is truly a Holy Spirit" (Hahn § 154 l. 24–26). The same argument from Mt 28.19 occurs in Amphilochius' synod in Iconium in 376.

260. Marcellus, Frag. 65 (Klostermann).

261. Eusebius, Marcell. 1.1.15.

262. "Believing that each of these is and exists, the Father truly a Father, the Son truly a Son, and the Holy Spirit truly Holy Spirit" (Ep. Caes. 5.2–3; in Athanasius, Decr. 33.5.2–3); see also Marcell. 1.1.15. Epiphanius uses similar language against Sabellians at Panar. 62.4.5.

263. Athanasius argues that "God is properly and alone truly Father of his Son" (τὸν Θεὸν κυρίως καὶ μόνον ἀληθῶς ὄντα Πατέρα τοῦ ἑαυτοῦ Υἱοῦ, Ar. 1.23) and that the Nicene phrase "from the essence of the Father" indicates "the true genuineness of the Son towards the Father" (τὸ γνήσιον ἀληθῶς Υἱοῦ Πρὸς τὸν Πατέρα γνωρίζεται, Syn. 36.2). He also tries to correct the Eusebians on their own terms, arguing that if they really meant that the Father is truly a Father and the Son a genuine Son they would embrace the Nicene confession (Syn 39.6; see also Tom. 5).

the Son and the Spirit are not subsequent to the Father in time (25.15–16) again resembles the Dedication Creed.[264] Even as he opposes Constantius' homoian program, Gregory retains key markers of the Eastern theological tradition and creedal language, again along the lines of Basil of Ancyra, George of Laodicea, and Melitius of Antioch. By contrast, Gregory's doctrine is remarkably dissimilar to Athanasius' statements from Alexandria 362: he never settles for the mere confession that the Son and the Spirit are not creatures; he places little emphasis of the Spirit's inseparability from Christ as proof of its divinity (though he certainly believes this); he never calls the Trinity as a whole *homoousios*—a statement that no good Easterner would want to make, except perhaps as a cipher for the monarchy of the Father, because of its connotations of either generic commonality or the division of the divine essence; and he does not look to Nicaea as the unique litmus text of orthodoxy, although he certainly adheres to it and eventually uses it as a positive rallying point.[265]

Gregory is in many respects a strongly Trinitarian theologian from the old homoiousian stream of Asia Minor. He is more strongly opposed to Sabellianism than to Arianism—even though he is opposed to both, and is most immediately occupied with the heterousian problem—and virtually uninfluenced by Athanasius. He went on to become the most illustrious figure and the greatest theological mind to be affiliated with this group, refining and fulfilling its commitments into a comprehensive Trinitarian program. Gregory claims the heritage of moderate Eastern theology represented at the Dedication Council of Antioch in 341, purifies it of the intervening distortions under Constantius and Valens, and draws out of it a full Trinitarian doctrine that accords with the language of Nicaea. In this respect Gregory is far more a reformed Eusebian—or to be even more accurate, a vindicated Origenist—than he is representative of Athanasius and the West.[266] His definitive achievement as an Eastern theologian has far-reaching implications for our understanding the nature of fourth-century theology. At the very least, it can no longer simply be assumed that the Athanasian paradigm is the only viable standard for determining Trinitarian orthodoxy.[267]

---

264. There is "no time, occasion, or age before the Son was begotten" (Hahn § 154 l. 32); and of course Origen's doctrine of the eternal generation of the Son (see *Princ.* 1.2.2–4, 9).

265. Gregory's first mention of Nicaea is in 374 (*Or.* 18.12).

266. Athanasius draws on Origen as well, of course, but not nearly to the extent that Gregory does. The doctrinal elements that emerged from Athanasius' collaboration with Marcellus, in particular, served to distance him from Origenist Trinitarian tradition.

267. Michel René Barnes tentatively but insightfully comments, "Athanasius' role as the examplar of the orthodox trinitarian theology has been overstated by scholars." "One Nature, One Power," p. 220.

Damasus and the West

While he is very much an Eastern theologian, Gregory bears a significant relationship to the West as well, at a crucial point in the consolidation of the catholic faith. As we have noted, in 379 the Council of Antioch ratified a dossier of conciliar statements sent from Damasus, signaling a basic level of doctrinal agreement with the Western bishops. This agreement formed the basis of the establishment of communion and Church order with regard to both the Antiochene schism and the promotion of the Nicene faith in general. When the council selected Gregory to represent its interests in Constantinople, he was commissioned primarily as an authoritative teacher to establish doctrinal orthodoxy as the basis for catholic communion and order in the East. Gregory's doctrine shows a general accord with the Western statements, and on one matter possibly a significant influence. His confession of "the Father, Son, and Holy Spirit, the one Divinity and power" broadly agrees with Damasus' summary of the Nicene faith as belief "that the Father, Son, and Holy Spirit are of one Divinity, one virtue, one form, one substance."[268] The *Ea gratia* in particular gives a clear indication of the monarchy of the Father: the Word possesses "the Father's nature and the fullness of the Divinity ... from God,"[269] and the Word is the splendor of the eternal light of the Father and the Father's true image.[270] The document also speaks in strong terms of the Holy Spirit's divinity: "Let us also confess that the Holy Spirit is not created, but is of one majesty, of one being, of one virtue with God the Father and our Lord Jesus Christ," because "it is connected with them in activity and in the forgiveness of sins."[271] On these individual points and in their overall theological style, the Western documents show a strong resemblance with the doctrine of Athanasius. Gregory does not follow Damasus in adopting opposition to Arius and adherence to Nicaea—in which, Damasus writes, "Easterners and Westerners

---

268. Ut patrem filium spiritumque sanctum unius deitatis, unius uirtutis, unius figurae, unius ... substantiae; *Conf. quid.* 21–23. The *Ea gratia*, which may have been sent separately to Melitius before the council of 379, reads, "The Trinity is of one virtue, one majesty, one Divinity, one substance, so that it is an inseparable power (potestas)." *Ea grat.* (Field, pp. 49–50).

269. *Ea grat.* (Field, pp. 54–57).

270. *Ea grat.* (Field, pp. 58–60).

271. Spiritum quoque sanctum increatum autem unius maiestatis, unius usiae, unius uirtutis cum deo patre et domino nostro Jesu Christo fateamur; *Ea grat* (Field, pp. 63–65, 68–69). Damasus' terms here thus reflect the language of Athanasius' three *Ep. Serap.* See also *Non nobis* (Field, pp. 108–110): the Holy Spirit is "perfect in all things—in virtue, in honor, in majesty, in deity—let us worship it together with the Father and the Son."

exult"—as a litmus test and a key marker of doctrinal orthodoxy,[272] nor does he make the argument that the Word of God is not imperfect like a spoken human word.[273] Nevertheless, it is easy to see why a group of bishops engaged in such an alliance would have chosen Gregory to represent them.

The most striking similarity, however, is with the doctrine of Christ found in the *Illut sane*. This document defines the Westerners' opposition to Apollinarians, who have recently been condemned at a council that included Damasus and Peter of Alexandria.[274] It marvels at "those from among us" who hold a pious faith in the Trinity, yet are ignorant of "the sacrament of our salvation." It then faults the Apollinarians chiefly for believing that Christ assumed human existence without a human mind,[275] and that Christ's humanity is therefore imperfect. In reply, the text argues for Christ's full humanity in ways that closely resemble Gregory's argument in *Letter* 101. If only an imperfect human being was assumed, it says, then "our salvation is imperfect, because the whole human being was not saved"; yet since the whole human person has perished, the whole needs saving.[276] Moreover, because it was the human mind above all that sinned in the fall and is "the sum of original sin and the whole damnation," Christ needed to save our mind most of all, which sinned before the rest. Although the terms are different, and Gregory does not cite the biblical texts that Damasus refers to, the Christological arguments are similar to a remarkable degree. We may conclude that Gregory ably represented the doctrinal concerns of the Western *Exemplum synodi* sent by the somewhat domineering Damasus,[277] and that he possibly drew support from the Westerners in his late reply to Apollinarius.

---

272. Against Arius: *Conf. quid.* (Field, pp. 18); pro-Nicaea: *Conf. quid.* (Field, pp. 18–20, 37–38); *Non nobis* (Field, pp. 106–107), "we retain the Council of Nicaea's inviolable faith in all respects." Damasus' use of these motifs follows the recommendations of Athanasius and the Council of Alexandria in 362 (*Tom.* 3), which are also echoed in the letters of Basil (*Ep.* 243; 263) and Melitius (Pseudo-Basil, *Ep.* 92) written to the Western bishops.

273. *Ea grat.* (Field, pp. 52–53); *Non nobis* (Field, pp. 110–113)—an argument that Gregory of Nyssa takes up: see *Or. cat.* 1.

274. Damasus' *Letter to the Eastern Bishops* (Theodoret, *HE* 5.10) reports the condemnation of Apollinarius and his disciple Timothy by a Western council.

275. Sine sensu hominem suscepisse; *Il. sane* (Field, p. 83).

276. This passage echoes the much older statement of Origen (*Heracl.* 7.7–8). See also Damasus' *Letter to the Eastern Bishops*: "If anyone says that Christ had less of humanity or Divinity, he is full of devil's spirits and proclaims himself a child of hell" (Theodoret, *HE* 5.10).

277. Hanson, *Search for the Christian Doctrine of God*, pp. 798–801, and Simonetti's comment, "Authoritarian and superficial, he was convinced that he knew the affairs of the East well and that he had the authority to bring about their solution" (*La crisi Ariana*, p. 430; trans. Hanson p. 800).

Gregory the Theologian

Gregory of Nazianzus not only offered the most powerful and comprehensive Trinitarian doctrine of his generation, but, as the later fathers soon recognized, he stands out as the preeminent theologian of the fourth century, second only to Origen among the great fathers who came before him. Far from being an ecclesiastical failure or a mere borrower of other people's ideas, Gregory proved to be the one who most deeply understands, prays, and articulates the Christian faith in the Holy Trinity, which is "theology" in the fullest sense.[278] He is far more theologically consistent than is often supposed, and he is at once a deeply traditional and a remarkably original theologian, who made perceptive and influential strides in Christology, Pneumatology, and Trinitarian doctrine, as well as ascetical and pastoral theology.

Gregory is also a quintessentially Cappadocian theologian. He drew significantly on Gregory Thaumaturgus, the Origenist patron saint of Cappadocia, representing his doctrine more faithfully than the Apollinarians did. He was the most highly educated and theologically gifted bishop in Constantinople in 379, even though some ridiculed his provincial accent. During his retirement he remained involved in Cappadocian ecclesiastical and literary affairs and continued to exert his influence through the established networks of patronage. Yet above all Gregory adopted and perfected the fully Trinitarian and unitive Christological impulses of Eastern theological tradition. He updated Origen on several important points; corrected the incipient Christological dualism emanating from Melitius' protégé, Diodore; combated the errors of Apollinarius; and avoided the Marcellan overtones of Paulinus and the earlier Athanasian project. He admirably fulfilled the charge of Antioch 379, backed by the Western councils of the 370s, to build a Trinitarian consensus in the capital, which he did from a classically Eastern theological point of view while representing Western interests as well. As a magisterial pastor, teacher, and literary theologian, Gregory managed to construct a core of Trinitarian doctrine and ecclesial consensus in the capital of the Eastern empire largely independent of the emperor, in the face of Antiochene factionalism, and despite the insinuations of the Alexandrians—a doctrinal program superior to that of the council of 381, which he then validated after the fact, when the

---

278. Moreover, the relationship between influence and originality has been greatly confused in the nineteenth and twentieth centuries. If evidence of borrowing or (as Eliot put it) stealing from other writers constitutes a lack of originality, then Plato, Shakespeare, Goethe, and Freud are deeply unoriginal thinkers.

council had chosen a different course. He also offered the most sensible proposal for ending the Antiochene schism, following the succession plan of Melitius and Paulinus, which was later recognized and supported by the West against the *ambitio* of the second-generation Melitians and the intruding Alexandrians. In each of these ways Gregory exercised a kind of theological leadership remarkably similar to Athanasius' a generation before, stronger in theological acumen if gentler in method and weaker in ecclesio-political stamina.

By comparison, Gregory constructed a more unitive theology than Athanasius, Basil, or Gregory of Nyssa managed to do (as well as Augustine or Leo, who became the dominant Christological models in the West), being closer instead to Origen and Cyril of Alexandria. Gregory's doctrine contains the main elements of the Christological orthodoxy that will be championed by Cyril of Alexandria in the next century and further worked out over the remainder of the patristic period. In his strong sense of divine illumination, his biblical understanding of the theology of the divine economy, his anchoring of the Trinity in the monarchy of God the Father, his highly unitive Christology, and his robust, epistemically inclusive Pneumatology, the strength of Gregory's work lies in what we might call its "doctrinal inclusivity." His work consistently seeks to include in God's being and saving work the full range of human existence, our sin and death, and above all the work of theology—things which at different points invariably seem counterintuitive to other theologians—as the determining factor of their true meaning. At the root of this interconnected theological vision is the eternal life of the Trinity, in which the monarchy of God the Father determines and makes possible the divine unity and distinctions—all of which is known through the dynamic, narrative theological principle that Gregory learned from the Bible and Origen. In concert with this inclusiveness, Gregory's work belies the firm distinction between confessional, doxological, contemplative theology and speculative, technical, systematic theology that modern interpreters have tried to force on him. In his rhetoric, too, Gregory's work incorporates the positions of his opponents, including their existential faith-stance and Christian practice, which are, for him basic elements of Trinitarian doctrine and not secondary to it. This spiritual-theological continuum among ascetical formation, biblical reading, dogmatic confession, worship, and pastoral ministry is the deepest current running through Gregory's doctrine and devotion.

It is therefore not at all surprising that Gregory came to be the veritable father of later Eastern Christianity, both Chalcedonian and non-Chalcedonian alike. Not only did his sermons become the chief model of Byzantine oratory, but his doctrine of Christian salvation, summarized in the idea of divinization (θέωσις), became the dominant soteriological concept for 1,000 years of Byzantine theology,[279] and, through Cyril of Alexandria and John of Damascus especially, it wielded great influence in the West as well.[280] After Origen, Gregory Nazianzen was the premier "spiritual theologian" in Greek patristic tradition. His impact on his contemporaries alone was considerable: in addition to Basil, Gregory of Nyssa, and Amphilochius, we can name Jerome[281] and Evagrius[282] among those who learned from him. In the following generation, he strongly influenced John Chrysostom; to mention just two points of contact, John's treatise *On the Incomprehensible Nature of God* rehearses much of Gregory's *Oration* 28, and his ideal of the priesthood comes directly from Gregory's *Oration* 2 and other texts.

In the late 390s Rufinus of Aquileia translated nine of Gregory's homilies into Latin, making them available to many Western readers to come.[283] Augustine lays high praise on Gregory, saying that his doctrine is widely regarded as a standard of the Christian faith.[284] Although Augustine's use of Gregory's work has long been a matter of speculation,[285] his actual debt seems to have been rather minimal, and to have come late in the formation of his thought.[286] In three works against Julian of Eclanum, he quotes three of Gregory's homilies, from Rufinus' translation, to justify his teaching on original sin and predestination.[287] Augustine's appeal to Gregory serves mainly to prove that his own doctrine has the authority of the catholic Church in both East and West; he does not cite him as an authority on other doctrinal matters, as can be seen in the significant differences between the two on major points of Christology, Pneumatology, and Trinitarian doctrine. Gregory's influence was strongly felt, however, by Gregory the Great, who encountered Gregory's work in Rufinus' Latin translation during his stay in Constantinople as papal

---

279. Although he takes up Athanasius' preferred term θεοποίησις, Cyril of Alexandria's doctrine of Christ largely follows Gregory's. After Cyril, the Pseudo-Dionysius adopts Gregory's invented term θέωσις, followed by Maximus Confessor and John Damascene, at which point it was firmly established in Byzantine usage. See Russell, *Doctrine of Deification*, pp. 341–343, and chap. 2, pp. 116–118.

280. On the correspondence between the doctrines of divinization in Gregory Palamas and Thomas Aquinas, both of whom reflect Gregorian influence, see A. N. Williams, *Ground of Union*.

281. See Jerome, *Ep.* 52; *Vir. illus.* 117; Lim, *Public Disputation*, p. 160n47.

282. See McGuckin, *St. Gregory*, pp. 96, 276–278, 350.

283. *Ors.* 2, 6, 16–17, 41, 26–27, 38, 39.

284. *C. Julian* 1.5.15–16 (*PL* 44.649).

285. See, e.g., Hill's introduction to Augustine's *The Trinity*, p. 45.

286. On Gregory's influence on Augustine, see Lienhard, "Augustine of Hippo," with bibliography. Augustine's direct citations of Gregory's works come mainly from his late, anti-Pelagian treatises.

287. *Ors.* 2, 38, 41, cited in *Contra Julianum*, *De dono perseverantiae*, and *Opus imperfectum contra Julianum*.

emissary. The direct influence of *Oration* 2 on Pope Gregory's *Pastoral Rule* has already been noted. Gregory can therefore claim to have had a major impact on two of the four traditional doctors of the Latin Church, Jerome and Gregory the Great, and possibly three, depending on how much Ambrose borrowed from his work on the Holy Spirit and the Trinity.

In the fifth century Cyril of Alexandria drew heavily on Gregory for his own Christology, Pneumatology, and doctrine of the Trinity, in some ways even more than he did on his fellow Alexandrian Athanasius.[288] We have already noted Gregory's title "the Theologian," given by the Council of Chalcedon in 451 in recognition of his seminal teaching on the Trinity. At the beginning of the sixth century, the Pseudo-Dionysius learned much from Gregory as well, including his vision of Moses' ascent up Mount Sinai in the *Mystical Theology* and the nine hierarchies of angels and much of Gregory's doctrine of the priesthood in the *Celestial* and *Ecclesiastical Hierarchies*. By the seventh century Gregory had acquired a kind of canonical status among the Greek fathers. His works began to accumulate scholia in the fifth century; in the sixth he had his first extant commentator, the Pseudo-Nonnus; and in the seventh he was the subject of a biography by Gregory the Presbyter. Gregory's works were further translated into Latin, Syriac, and Armenian. When certain monks used him to defend their extreme Origenism, Maximus Confessor was forced to negotiate difficulties in Gregory's text, and in doing so he shows the nearly scriptural status that Gregory had come to acquire among the Byzantines.[289] Toward the end of the patristic period, following three centuries of Christological debates since the Council of Chalcedon, John of Damascus definitively synthesized the received tradition largely by reinterpreting it in terms of the doctrine of Gregory, who appears to have been his favorite theologian. In the eleventh century, Gregory was likewise the primary patristic influence on Simeon the New Theologian, so named in order to compare him to Gregory. Together with this monumental theological legacy, Gregory went on to become the chief model of Byzantine letters, earning him the reputation for being superior to Demosthenes, Plato, and the other orators and prose stylists of classical Athens.[290] His most pervasive influence, however, came through the regular reading of his orations in the liturgies of the

---

288. Holl calls Gregory a prototype of later "Alexandrian" Christology, but because of his suspicions of Gregory's epistemology he maintains Gregory's difference from Cyril in terms of Cyril's greater "realism." See *Amphilochius*, pp. 195–196, and chap. 4, pp. 199–200; and Beeley, "Cyril of Alexandria."

289. Above all in his lengthy *Ambigua*, which are largely devoted to resolving puzzles in Gregory's text. See Louth, "The Cappodocians."

290. As described, e.g., by Michael Psellos in the tenth century. See Daley, *Gregory of Nazianzus*, pp. 26–27. Still helpful on Gregory's influence is Rousse, "Saint Grégoire de Nazianze," cols. 960–969.

Eastern churches and in his extensive quotation in the hymnody of the Byzantine rite.[291]

For Gregory the Theologian, the doctrine of the Trinity, which is "theology" in its fullest sense, represents and always seeks to promote the knowledge of God in the divine economy of Jesus Christ and the Holy Spirit within the life of the Church. As the fathers of Chalcedon, the early Byzantines, and many others have recognized, Gregory is the one who consistently understands the meaning of all of existence in terms of the brilliant Light of the eternal Trinity, and who most adeptly articulates the orthodox faith. Each of the major topics that we have examined—from the purification and illumination of the theologian and the pastoral ministry of the Church to Gregory's distinct teaching on Christ, the Holy Spirit, and the Trinity as a whole—helps to constitute the definition of Christian theology. Through his life's work as a pastoral, polemical, and literary theologian, Gregory contributed enormously to the construction of an explicit and unified Christian focus on the Trinity—the only theologian in Greek tradition comparable to Origen in terms of comprehensiveness, theological and exegetical acuity, and depth of vision. For Gregory, as for no one else before him, God *is* the Trinity: the unbegotten Father, source of the divine light, who eternally generates his equally brilliant Son and sends forth his equally brilliant Spirit, in whom and by whom God is known in the divine economy—all three being equally the object of devotion, the focus of theological reflection, and the subject of many a poem. Among his theological, ecclesiastical, and literary accomplishments, Gregory's greatest achievement and the just cause of his renown was to show with practical and theoretical skill that the divine light of God, Father, Son, and Holy Spirit, is the very meaning of the Christian life and indeed of all creaturely existence.

---

291. See Harrison, "Illumined from All Sides by the Trinity."

Bibliography

The most extensive bibliography for Gregory Nazianzen from 1925 to 1993 can be found in Francesco Trisoglio, "San Gregorio di Nazianzo, scrittore e teologo in quaranta anni di recerche (1925–1965)," *Rivista di storia e letteratura religiosa* 8 (1972); and "San Gregorio Nazianzeno, 1966–1993," *Lustrum* 38 (1996): pp. 7–361. A searchable database of editions, translations, and general bibliography is currently maintained by the Centre d'Études sur Grégoire de Nazianze of the Université Catholique de Louvain at http://nazianzos.fltr.ucl.ac.be. Available English translations for ancient sources have been listed where possible.

GREGORY OF NAZIANZUS: TEXTS AND TRANSLATIONS

Orations

Ors. 1–3   Ed. Jean Bernardi, *SC* 247; trans. Charles Gordon Browne and James Edward Swallow, *NPNF* 2.7. 203–229.

Ors. 4–5   Ed. Jean Bernardi, *SC* 309; trans. C. W. King, *Julian the Emperor, Containing Gregory Nazianzen's Two Invectives and Libanius' Monody with Julian's Extant Theosophical Works*, pp. 1–121 (London: George Bell and Sons, 1888).

Ors. 6–12	Ed. Marie-Ange Calvet-Sebasti, *SC* 405; *Ors.* 6, 9–11 trans. Martha Vinson, *FC* 107, pp. 3–35; *Or.* 8 trans. Brian E. Daley, *Gregory of Nazianzus*, pp. 63–75 (Early Church Fathers; London: Routledge, 2006); *Ors.* 7–8, 12 trans. Charles Gordon Browne and James Edward Swallow, *NPNF* 2.7.227–247.
Ors. 13–19	Ed. Armand Benjamin Caillau, *PG* 35; *Ors.* 13–15, 17, 19 trans. Martha Vinson, *FC* 107, pp. 36–106; *Or.* 14 trans. Brian E. Daley, *Gregory of Nazianzus*, pp. 75–97 (Early Church Fathers; London: Routledge, 2006); *Ors.* 16, 18 trans. Charles Gordon Browne and James Edward Swallow, *NPNF* 2.7.247–269.
Ors. 20–23	Ed. Justin Mossay and Guy Lafontaine, *SC* 270; *Ors.* 20, 22–23 trans. Martha Vinson, *FC* 107, pp. 107–141; *Or.* 20 trans. Brian E. Daley, *Gregory of Nazianzus*, pp. 98–105 (Early Church Fathers; London: Routledge, 2006); *Or.* 21 trans. Charles Gordon Browne and James Edward Swallow, *NPNF* 2.7.269–284.
Ors. 24–26	Ed. Justin Mossay and Guy Lafontaine, *SC* 284; trans. Martha Vinson, *FC* 107, pp. 142–190; *Or.* 26 trans. Brian E. Daley, *Gregory of Nazianzus*, pp. 105–117 (Early Church Fathers; London: Routledge, 2006).
Ors. 27–31	*Theological Orations.* Ed. Paul Gallay, *SC* 250; trans. Charles Gordon Browne and James Edward Swallow, *NPNF* 2.7.284–328, and repr. with notes in Edward R. Hardy, ed., *Christology of the Later Fathers*, pp. 128–214 (Library of Christian Classics 3; Philadelphia: Westminster, 1954); trans. Frederick Williams (*Or.* 27) and Lionel Wickham (*Ors.* 28–31) in Frederick W. Norris, *Faith Gives Fullness to Reasoning: The Five Theological Orations of Gregory Nazianzen* (Supplements to Vigiliae Christianae 13; Leiden: Brill, 1991), and repr. with notes in *St. Gregory of Nazianzus, On God and Christ: The Five Theological Orations and Two Letters to Cledonius* (Popular Patristic Series; Crestwood, N.Y.: St. Vladimir's Seminary Press, 2002).
Ors. 32–37	Ed. Claudio Moreschini, *SC* 318; *Ors.* 32, 35–36 trans. Martha Vinson, *FC* 107, pp. 191–229; *Ors.* 33–34, 37 trans. Charles Gordon Browne and James Edward Swallow, *NPNF* 2.7.328–345.
Ors. 38–41	Ed. Claudio Moreschini, *SC* 358; trans. Charles Gordon Browne and James Edward Swallow, *NPNF* 2.7.345–385; *Ors.* 38–39

trans. Brian E. Daley, *Gregory of Nazianzus*, pp. 117–138 (Early Church Fathers; London: Routledge, 2006).

Ors. 42–43   Ed. Jean Bernardi, *SC* 384; *Or.* 42 trans. Brian E. Daley, *Gregory of Nazianzus*, pp. 138–154 (Early Church Fathers; London: Routledge, 2006); Ors. 42–43 trans. Charles Gordon Browne and James Edward Swallow, *NPNF* 2.7.385–422.

Ors. 44–45   Ed. Armand Benjamin Caillau, *PG* 36; *Or.* 44 trans. Martha Vinson, *FC* 107, pp. 230–238; trans. Brian E. Daley, *Gregory of Nazianzus*, pp. 154–161 (Early Church Fathers; London: Routledge, 2006); *Or.* 45 trans. Charles Gordon Browne and James Edward Swallow, *NPNF* 2.7.422–434.

Letters

Ep. 1–249   Ed. Paul Gallay, *Saint Grégoire de Nazianze, Lettres* (2 vols., Collection des Universités de France; Paris: Les Belles Lettres, 1964/1967), with *Ep.* 101–102, 202 repr. in *SC* 208; *Ep.* 1–2, 4–9, 12–13, 16–19, 21–22, 25–29, 37, 39–55, 58–60, 62–66, 77, 88, 91, 93, 101–102, 104–106, 115, 121–124, 126, 131, 135, 139–146, 151–154, 157, 163, 171, 183–186, 202 trans. Charles Gordon Browne and James Edward Swallow, *NPNF* 2.7. 437–482, with trans. of *Ep.* 101–102, 202 repr. with notes in Edward R. Hardy, ed., *Christology of the Later Fathers*, pp. 215–232 (Library of Christian Classics 3; Philadelphia: Westminster, 1954).

Poems

Carm.   Ed. Armand Benjamin Caillau, *PG* 37–38.

Carm. 1.1.1 *On First Principles;* 1.1.2 *On the Son;* 1.1.3 *On the Spirit;* 1.1.4 *On the Universe;* 1.1.5 *On Providence;* 1.1.7 *On Rational Natures;* 1.1.8 *On the Soul;* 1.1.9 *On the Testaments and the Coming of Christ* (the *Poemata Arcana*). Ed. and intro. C. Moreschini, trans. and comm. D. A. Sykes, *St. Gregory of Nazianzus, Poemata Arcana* (Oxford Theological Monographs; Oxford: Clarendon, 1997).

Carm. 1.1.1–12, 37; 1.2.1, 8.11–18; 2.1.6, 21, 39, 45, 78; *Epitaph* 119 on Basil. *PG* 37.397–474, 520–578, 649–667, 752–786, 1023–1024, 1329–1336, 1353–1378, 1425–1426; 38.72. Trans. Peter Gilbert, *On God and Man: The Theological Poetry of St. Gregory of Nazianzus* (Popular Patristic Series; Crestwood, N.Y.: St. Vladimir's Seminary Press, 2001).

>   *Carm.* 2.1.1 *De rebus suis;* 2.1.11 *De vita sua;* 2.1.12 *De seipso et de episcopis.* PG 37.969–1017, 1029–1227; trans. Denis Mollaise Meehan, *Saint Gregory of Nazianzus, Three Poems,* FC 75.
>
>   *Carm.* 2.1.11 *De vita sua;* 2.1.19 *Querela de suis calamitatibus;* 2.1.34 *In silentium jejunii;* 2.1.39 *In suos versus;* 2.1.92 *Epitaph sui ipsius et compendium ipsius vitae.* Ed. and trans. Carolinne White, *Gregory of Nazianzus, Autobiographical Poems* (Cambridge Medieval Classics 6; Cambridge: Cambridge University Press, 1996).
>
>   *Carm.* 2.1.1.194–204, 210–212, 452–456 *De rebus suis;* 2.1.45.191–204, 229–269 *De animae suae calamitatibus carmen lugubre.* PG 37.985–986, 1003–1004, 1367; trans. John A. McGuckin, *St. Gregory of Nazianzus: An Intellectual Biography,* pp. 66–69 (Crestwood, N.Y.: St. Vladimir's Seminary Press, 2001).

Epitaphs

Epit. *Epitaphs.* PG 38.11–80; trans. W. R. Paton, *The Greek Anthology,* bk. 8, LCL 2.401–505.

Testament

Test. *Examplum Testamenti.* PG 37.

OTHER ANCIENT SOURCES

Albinus

Epit. *Epitome.* Ed. Pierre Louis, *Albinus, Épitomé* (Nouvelle Collection des Textes et Documents; Paris: Belles Lettres, 1945).

Ambrose of Milan

Ep.   *Letters.* Bks. 1–6 ed. O. Faller, *CSEL* 82.1; bks. 7–10 and *Epistulae extra collectionem* ed. M. Zelzer, *CSEL* 82.2–3; trans. H. de Romestin, *NPNF* 2.10.411–473; trans. M. M. Beyenka, FC 26.
Spir. *On the Holy Spirit.* Ed. O. Faller, *CSEL* 79; trans. R. J. Deferrari, FC 40.35–213.

Ammianus Marcellinus

Amm. Marc. *Ammiani Marcellini.* Ed. C. Clark, *Ammiani Marcellini Rerum gestarum libri qui supersunt* (Berlin: Weidmann, 1910–1915); trans. John C. Rolfe, LCL (3 vols.).

Amphilochius of Iconium

Ep. syn.   Synodical Letter (of the Synod of Iconium 376). Ed. Cornelis Datema, *Opera*, CCG 3.219–221.

Apollinarius of Laodicea

Anac.   Recapitulation (ἀνακεφαλαίωσις). Ed. Hans Lietzmann, *Apollinaris von Laodicea und seine Schule*, pp. 242–246 (Tübingen: Mohr, 1904).
De unione   On the Union of the Body with the Divinity in Christ. Ed. Hans Lietzmann, *Apollinaris von Laodicea und seine Schule*, pp. 185–193 (Tübingen: Mohr, 1904).
Ep. Diocaes.   Letter to Diocaesarea. Ed. Hans Lietzmann, *Apollinaris von Laodicea und seine Schule*, pp. 255–256 (Tübingen: Mohr, 1904).
Ep. Dion.   Letter to Dionysius. Ed. Hans Lietzmann, *Apollinaris von Laodicea und seine Schule*, pp. 256–262 (Tübingen: Mohr, 1904).
De fide et inc. On the Faith and the Incarnation. Ed. Hans Lietzmann, *Apollinaris von Laodicea und seine Schule*, pp. 194–203 (Tübingen: Mohr, 1904).
Frag.   Fragments. Ed. Hans Lietzmann, *Apollinaris von Laodicea und seine Schule*, pp. 204–242 (Tübingen: Mohr, 1904).
KMP   Detailed Confession of Faith (ἡ κατὰ μέρος πίστις). Ed. Hans Lietzmann, *Apollinaris von Laodicea und seine Schule*, pp. 167–185 (Tübingen: Mohr, 1904).
V. Greg. Thaum. Life of Gregory Thaumaturgus. PG 46.893–958.

Aristotle

Interp.   On Interpretation. Trans. Harold P. Cooke, *LCL*.
Metaph.   Metaphysics. Trans. Hugh Tredennick, *LCL* 287.
Rhet.   Rhetoric. Ed. Rudolfus Kassel (Berlin: De Gruyter, 1976); trans. George A. Kennedy, *On Rhetoric: A Theory of Civic Discourse* (Oxford: Oxford University Press, 1991).

Athanasius of Alexandria

Ar.   Orations Against the Arians. Ed. W. Bright, *The Orations of St. Athanasius Against the Arians according to the Benedictine Text* (Oxford: Clarendon, 1884); trans. John Henry Newman and Archibald Robertson, *NPNF* 2.4.303–447.

Decr.	*On the Decrees of Nicaea.* Ed. Opitz, *Athanasius Werke* 2.1.1–45 (Berlin: De Gruyter, 1940); trans. John Henry Newman and Archibald Robertson, *NPNF* 2.4.150–172.
Dion.	*On the Sayings of Dionysius.* Ed. Opitz, *Athanasius Werke* 2.1.46–67 (Berlin: De Gruyter, 1940); trans. A. Robinson, *NPNF* 2.4173–187.
Ep. Aeg. Lib.	*Letter to the Bishops of Egypt and Libya.* PG 25.537–594; trans. M. Atkinson and A. Robertson, *NPNF* 2.4.222–235.
Ep. cath.	*Catholic Epistle* (of the Synod of Alexandria, 362). Ed. Martin Tetz, "Ein enzyklisches Schreiben der Synode von Alexandrian (362)," *ZNTW* 79 (1988): pp. 262–81, text at 271–73.
Ep. Epict.	*Letter to Epictetus.* PG 26.1049–1070; trans. Archibald Robertson, *NPNF* 4.570–574.
Ep. Jov.	*Letter to the Emperor Jovian.* PG 26.813–820; trans. Archibald Robertson, *NPNF* 4.567–568.
Ep. Serap.	*Letters to Serapion Concerning the Holy Spirit.* PG 26.529–676; trans. C. R. B. Shapland, *The Letters of Saint Athanasius Concerning the Holy Spirit* (London: Epworth, 1951).
Gent.	*Against the Nations.* Ed. Pierre Thomas Camelot, SC 18 bis; trans. R. W. Thompson, *Contra gentes et de incarnatione*, pp. 135–277 (Oxford: Clarendon, 1971); trans. E. P. Meijering, *Athanasius: Contra gentes* (Philosophia Patrum 7; Leiden, Netherlands: Brill, 1984).
Hist Ar.	*History of the Arians.* Ed. Opitz, *Athanasius Werke* 2.1.183–230 (Berlin: De Gruyter, 1940); trans. M. Atkinson, *NPNF* 2.4.266–302.
Inc.	*On the Incarnation.* Ed. Charles Kannengiesser, SC 199; trans. R. W. Thompson, *Contra gentes et de incarnatione*, pp. 135–277 (Oxford: Clarendon, 1971); trans. Archibald Robertson, *NPNF* 2.4.36–67.
Syn.	*On the Councils of Ariminum and Seleucia.* Ed. Opitz, *Athanasius Werke* 2.1.231–278 (Berlin: De Gruyter, 1940); ET: John Henry Newman and Archibald Robertson, *NPNF* 2.4.448–480.
Tom.	*Tome to the Antiochenes.* PG 26.796; trans. H. Ellershaw, *NPNF* 2.4.481–486.
V. Ant.	*Life of Antony.* Ed. G. J. M. Bartelink, SC 400; trans. Robert C. Gregg, *The Life of Antony and the Letter to Marcellinus* (Classics of Western Spirituality; New York: Paulist, 1980).

Augustine of Hippo

C. Julian	*Against Julian of Eclanum.* Ed. N. Cipriani, *Polemica con Giuliano I,* pp. 399–981 (Opera Omnia 18; Rome: Citta Nuova, 1985); trans. Matthew A. Schumacher, FC 35.
Doctr.	*On Christian Teaching.* Ed. W. M. Green, *CSEL* 32; trans. Edmund Hill, *Teaching Christianity: De Doctrina Christiana* (Works of Saint Augustine 1.11; Hyde Park, N.Y.: New City, 1996).
Jo. ev. tr	*Tractates on the Gospel of John.* Ed. R. Willems, *CCSL* 36; trans. John Rettig, FC 78, 79, 88, 90, 92.
Serm. 71	*Sermon 71.* PL 38.444–467; trans. Edmund Hill, *Sermons 51–94* (Hyde Park, N.Y.: New City, 1992).
Trin.	*On the Trinity.* Ed. J. Mountain, *CCL* 50, 50A; trans. Edmund Hill, *The Trinity* (Works of Saint Augustine 1.5; Hyde Park, N.Y.: New City, 1991).

Basil of Ancyra

Ep. syn.	*Synodical Letter* from the Synod of Ancyra 358. Ed. Karl Holl, *Panarion* 73.2.1–11.10, *GCS* 3.

Basil of Caesarea

Adolesc.	*To Young Men.* Ed. and trans. Roy J. Deferrari, *LCL* 4.
Ep.	*Letters.* Ed. Yves Courtonne, *Saint Basile: Lettres* (3 vols., Collection Guillaume Budé; Paris: Les Belles Lettres, 1957–1966); trans. Roy Deferrari, *Saint Basil: The Letters* (4 vols.), *LCL*.
Eun.	*Against Eunomius.* Ed. Bernard Sesboüé, Georges-Matthieu de Durand, and Louis Doutreleau, *SC* 299, 305.
Hex.	*Hexaemeron.* Ed. Emmanuel Amand de Mendieta and Stig Y. Rudberg, *GCS* N.F. 2; trans. Blomfield Jackson, *NPNF* 2.8. 51–107.
Hom.	*Sermons.* PG 31.163–618.
Spir.	*On the Holy Spirit.* Ed. B. Pruche, *SC* 17 bis; trans. Blomfield Jackson, *NPNF* 2.8.1–50; rev. David Anderson, *On the Holy Spirit* (Popular Patristic Series; Crestwood, N.Y.: St. Vladimir's Seminary Press, 1980).

Chrysippus

Frag.	*Fragments.* Ed. H. von Arnim, *Stoicorum Veterum Fragmenta* (Leipzig: Teubner, 1903–1924).

Church Councils

EOM   *Ecclesiae Occidentalis Monumenta Iuris Antiquissima.* Ed. C. H. Turner (vol. 1; Oxford: Clarendon, 1899).

Hahn   *Bibliothek der Symbole und Glaubensregeln der alten Kirche.* Ed. A. Hahn, rev. G. L. Hahn (Hildesheim: Georg Olms, 1962).

Mansi   *Sacrorum Conciliorum Nova et Amplissima Collectio.* Ed. J. D. Mansi (rev. ed.; Paris: H. Welter, 1901–1927).

Clement of Alexandria

Paed.   *The Tutor.* Ed. Otto Stählin, *GCS* 12.87–340; trans. Henri–Irénée Marrou, *SC* 70, 108, 158; trans. Simon P. Wood, *FC* 23.

Protr.   *Exhortation.* Ed. M. Marcovich and J. C. M. van Winden, *Clementis Alexndrini Paedagogus* (Supplements to Vigiliae Christianae 61; Leiden: Brill, 2002); trans. G. W. Butterworth, *LCL* 92.2–263.

Strom.   *Miscellanies.* Ed. Otto Stählen and Ludwig Früchtel, *GCS* 15, 17; trans. W. L. Alexander, *ANF* 2.299–568; bks. 1–3 trans. John Ferguson, *FC* 85.

Damasus

Conf. quid.   *Confidemus quidem.* Ed. and trans. Lester L. Field, Jr., *On the Communion of Damasus and Melitius: Fourth-Century Synodal Formulae in the* Codex Veronensis LX, pp. 10–15 (Studies and Texts 145; Toronto: Pontifical Institute of Mediaeval Studies, 2004).

Ea grat.   *Ea gratia.* Ed. and trans. Lester L. Field, Jr., *On the Communion of Damasus and Melitius: Fourth-Century Synodal Formulae in the* Codex Veronensis LX, pp. 14–17 (Studies and Texts 145; Toronto: Pontifical Institute of Mediaeval Studies, 2004).

Ep.   *Letters.* Ed. and trans. Glen Louis Thompson, *The Earliest Papal Correspondence*, pp. 278–372 (diss., Columbia University, 1990).

Il. sane   *Illut sane.* Ed. and trans. Lester L. Field, Jr., *On the Communion of Damasus and Melitius: Fourth-Century Synodal Formulae in the* Codex Veronensis LX, pp. 16–19 (Studies and Texts 145; Toronto: Pontifical Institute of Mediaeval Studies, 2004).

Non nobis   *Non nobis*. Ed. and trans. Lester L. Field, Jr., *On the Communion of Damasus and Melitius: Fourth-Century Synodal Formulae in the* Codex Veronensis LX, pp. 18–21 (Studies and Texts 145; Toronto: Pontifical Institute of Mediaeval Studies, 2004).
Tom. Dam.   *Tomus Damasi*. Ed. M. Dossetti, *Il simbolo di Nicea e di Costantinopoli: Edizione critica*, pp. 94–111 (Rome: Herder, 1967).

Didymus the Blind

Comm. Zach.   *Commentary on Zachariah*. Ed. Louis Doutreleau, SC 83, 84, 85; trans. Robert Hill, FC 111.
Spir.   *On the Holy Spirit*. Ed. Louis Doutreleau, SC 386.

Ephraem Syrius

Ad Ioan. mon.   *To John the Monk: That He Should Avoid the Madness and Blasphemy of Nestorius*. Ed. K. G. Phrantzoles, Ὁσίου Ἐφραίμ τοῦ Σύρου ἔργα, pp. 173–195 (3 vols.; Thessalonica, Greece: To Perivoli tis Panagias, 1990).
Serm. Mon. Aeg.   *Sermon to the Monks of Egypt*. Ed. K. G. Phrantzoles, σίου Ἐφραίμ τοῦ Σύρου ἔργα, pp. 36–294 (3 vols.; Thessalonica, Greece: To Perivoli tis Panagias, 1990).
Serm. Trans.   *Sermon on the Transfiguration of the Lord*. Ed. K. G. Phrantzoles, Ὁσίου Ἐφραίμ τοῦ Σύρου ἔργα, pp. 13–30 (3 vols.; Thessalonica, Greece: To Perivoli tis Panagias, 1990).

Epicurus

Ep.   *Letters*. Ed. Hermann Usener, *Epicurea* (Leipzig, Germany: Teubner, 1887); trans. Eugene O'Connor, *The Essential Epicurus: Letters, Principal Doctrines, Vatican Sayings, and Fragments* (Great Books in Philosophy; Buffalo, N.Y.: Prometheus, 1993).

Epiphanius of Salamis

Ancor.   *Ancoratus*. Ed. Karl Holl, GCS 25.
Fid.   *Exposition of the Faith*. Ed. Karl Holl, GCS 3.496–526.
Panar.   *Panarion*. Ed. Karl Holl, GCS 25, 31, 37; trans. Frank Williams, *The Panarion of Epiphanius of Salamis* (2 vols.; Leiden: Brill, 1987).
Rescr.   *Rescript to Acasius and Paul*. Ed. Karl Holl, GCS 1.155.

Eunomius of Cyzicus

Apol.	Apology. Ed. and trans. Richard Paul Vaggione, *Eunomius: The Extant Works*, pp. 43–75 (Oxford Early Christian Texts; Oxford: Clarendon, 1987).
Apol. Apol.	Apology for the Apology. Ed. and trans. Richard Paul Vaggione, *Eunomius: The Extant Works*, pp. 99–127 (Oxford Early Christian Texts; Oxford: Clarendon, 1987).
Frag.	Fragments. Ed and trans. Richard Paul Vaggione, *Eunomius: The Extant Works*, pp. 176–179 (Oxford Early Christian Texts; Oxford: Clarendon, 1987).

Eusebius of Caesarea

Comm. Pss.	Commentary on the Psalms. *PG* 23; 24.9–76.
Dem. ev.	Proof of the Gospel. Ed. I. A. Heikel, *GCS* 6; trans. W. J. Ferrar, *The Proof of the Gospel: Being the* Demonstratio evangelica *of Eusebius of Caesarea* (2 vols., Translations of Christian Literature Series 1; London: SPCK, 1920).
Eccl. theo.	Ecclesiastical Theology. Ed. Erich Klostermann, *GCS* 4b.60–182.
Ep. Caes.	Letter to the People of Caesarea. In Athanasius, *Decr.* 33.
HE	Ecclesiastical History. Ed. E. Schwartz, *SC* 31, 41, 51, 73; trans. Paul L. Maier, *The Church History: A New Translation with Commentary* (Grand Rapids, Mich.: Kregel, 1999).
Laud. Const.	In Praise of Constantine. Ed. I. A. Heikel, *GCS* 7.193–259; trans. E. C. Richardson, *NPNF* 2.1.581–610.
Marcell.	Against Marcellus. Ed. Erich Klostermann and Günter Christian Hansen, *GCS* 4b.1–58.
Mart. Palest.	The Martyrs of Palestine. Ed. E. Schwartz, *GCS* 9.2.907950; trans. H. J. Lawlor and J. E. L. Oulton, *Eusebius, The Ecclesiastical History and the Martyrs of Palestine* (2 vols.; London: SPCK, 1928).
Prep. ev.	Preparation for the Gospel. Ed. E. des Places, J. Sirinelli, G. Schroeder, G. Favrelle, and O. Zink, *SC* 206, 215, 228, 262, 266, 292, 307, 338, 369; trans. Edwin Hamilton Gifford, *Eusebii Pamphili Evangelicae Praeparationes* (4 vols.; Oxford: Clarendon, 1903).
V. Const.	Life of Constantine. Ed. Friedhelm Winkelman, rev. ed. *GCS* 1.1; trans. Averil Cameron and Stuart G. Hall, *Eusebius, Life of Constantine* (Oxford: Oxford University Press, 1999).

Gorgias

Pal. *Defence of Palamides.* Ed. F. Blass, *Antiphontis orationes et fragmenta: adiunctis Gorgiae, Antisthenis, Alcidamantis declamationibus* (Leipzig, Germany: Teubner, 1871).

Gregory of Nyssa

Ablab. — *To Ablabius: That We Should Not Say That There Are Three Gods.* Ed. F. Mueller, *Gregorii Nysseni Opera* 3.1. 37–57; trans. Cyril. C. Richardson, in Edward Hardy, ed., *Christology of the Later Fathers*, pp. 256–257 (Library of Christian Classics 3; London: SPCK, 1954).

Ad Theoph. — *To Theophilus Against the Apollinarians.* Ed. E, Bellini, *Apollinare, Epifanio, Gregorio di Nazianzo, Gregorio di Nissa e altri su Cristo: Il grande dibattito nel quarto secolo*, pp. 321–483 (Milan: Jaca, 1978).

Antirrh. — *Antirrheticus (Refutation) Against Apollinarius.* Ed. F. Mueller, *Gregorii Nysseni Opera* 3.1.127–233.

Comm. Cant. — *Commentary on the Song of Songs. Gregorii Nysseni Opera* 6. Trans. Casimir McCambley, *Gregory of Nyssa: Commentary on the Song of Songs* (Brookline, Mass.: Hellenic College Press, 1987).

Comm. Not. — *To the Greeks, From Common Notions.* Ed. F. Mueller, *Gregorii Nysseni Opera* 3.1.17–33; trans. Daniel Stramara, *GOTR* 41 (1996): pp. 381–391.

De opif. hom. — *On the Creation of the Human Being.* Ed. W. Jaeger, GNO; trans. H. A. Wilson, *NPNF* 5.387–427.

Deit. Fil. et Spir. — *On the Divinity of the Son and the Holy Spirit.* PG 46. 553–576.

Ep. — *Letters.* Ed. P. Maraval. SC 363; trans. W. Moore and H. A. Wilson, *NPNF* II.5.

Ep. Pet. — *Letter to His Brother Peter.* (Pseudo-Basil, *Ep.* 38.)

Eun. — *Against Eunomius.* Ed. Werner Jaeger, *Gregorii Nysseni Opera* (vols. 1–2; Leiden: Brill, 1952–); trans. H. C. Ogle, H. A. Wilson, and M. Day, *NPNF* 2.5.33–248.

Eust. — *To Eustathius, On the Holy Trinity.* Ed. F. Mueller, *Gregorii Nysseni Opera* 3.1.1–16; trans. H. A. Wilson, *NPNF* 2.5.326–330.

Or. cat.	Catechetical Oration. Ed. E. Mühlenberg, Gregorii Nysseni Opera (vols. 3–4; Leiden: Brill, 1952–), and repr. in SC 453; trans. Cyril Richardson, in Edward Hardy, ed., Christology of the Later Fathers, pp. 268–325 (Library of Christian Classics 3; Philadelphia: Westminster, 1954).
Orat. Dom.	On the Lord's Prayer. Ed. J. F. Callahan, Gregorii Nysseni Opera vol. 7.2; trans. H. C. Graef, ACW 18.
Pent.	On the Holy Spirit, or On Pentecost. PG 46.696–701.
Ref.	Refutation of Eunomius' Confession. Gregorii Nysseni Opera 1.2; trans. H. C. Ogle and H. A. Wilson, NPNF 2.5. 101–134.
Spir.	On the Holy Spirit Against Macedonius. Ed. F. Mueller, Gregorii Nysseni Opera 3.1.87–115; trans. H. A. Wilson, NPNF 2.5.315–325.
Steph.	Encomium on Saint Stephen. Ed. Otto Lendle, Gregorius Nyssenius Encomium in Sanctum Stephanum protomartyrem (Leiden: Brill, 1968).
V. Macr.	The Life of Macrina. Ed. Werner Jaeger, Gregorii Nysseni Opera vol. 8.1; trans. Kevin Corrigan, Gregory of Nyssa, The Life of Saint Macrina (Toronto: Peregrina, 1987).
V. Mos.	The Life of Moses. Ed. Jean Danielou, SC 1 bis; trans. Abraham J. Malherbe and Everett Ferguson, Gregory of Nyssa. The Life of Moses (Classics of Western Spirituality; New York: Paulist, 1978).

Gregory Thaumaturgus

Addr.	Address of Thanksgiving to Origen. Ed. Henri Crouzel, SC 148; trans. Michael Slusser, FC 98.91–126.
Metaphr.	Metaphrase on the Ecclesiastes of Solomon. PG 10.987–1018; trans. Michael Slusser, FC 98.127–146.
Theo.	To Theopompus, On the Impassibility and Passibility of God. Ed. Paul de Lagarde, Analecta Syriaca 46–64; trans. Michael Slusser, FC 98.152–173.

Gregory the Great

Reg. past.	Pastoral Rule. Ed. Floribert Rommel, SC 381, 382; trans. James Barmby, NPNF 2.12.1b–72b.

Gregory the Presbyter

V. Greg. Naz.   *Life of Gregory of Nazianzus.* PG 35.

Hilary of Poitiers

Trin.   On the Trinity. Ed. P. Smulders, SC 443, 448, 462; trans. Stephen McKenna, FC 25.

Ignatius of Antioch

Ep.   Letters. Ed. Pierre Thomas Camelot, SC 10 bis; trans. William Schoedel (Hermeneia Commentary Series; Philadelphia: Fortress, 1985).

Irenaeus of Lyons

Adv. haer.   Against the Heresies. Ed. A. Rousseau, L. Doutreleau, B. Hemmerdinger, and C. Mercier, SC 100, 152, 153, 210, 211, 263, 264, 293, 294; trans. A. Roberts and W. H. Rambaut, ANF 1.315–578.

Jerome

Comm. Jon.   Commentary on Jonah. Ed. Yves-Marie Duval, SC 323.
Ep.   Letters. Ed. I. Hilberg, CSEL 54–56; trans. F. A. Wright, LCL 262.
Lib. Pamm.   To Pammachius, Against Bishop John of Jerusalem and Rufinus the Defender of Origen. Ed. J.-L. Feiertag, CCL 79A.
Vir. illus.   On Famous Men. Ed. E. C. Richardson, *Hieronymus liber De viris inlustribus* (Leipzig, Germany: J. C. Hinrichs, 1896); trans. Thomas Halton, FC 100.

John Chrysostom

Incompr.   On the Incomprehensible Nature of God. Ed. Anne-Marie Malingrey, SC 28 bis; trans. Paul W. Harkins, FC 78.
Sacerd.   On the Priesthood. Ed. Anne-Marie Malingrey, SC 272; trans. Graham Neville, *Saint John Chrosostom, Six Books on the Priesthood* (Popular Patristic Series; Crestwood, N.Y.: St. Vladimir's Seminary Press, 1964).

Julian the Emperor

Ep.   Letters. Ed. Joseph Bidez, *Oevres completes* (3rd ed., 2 vols.; Paris: Belles Lettres, 1972).

Justin Martyr

Dial. *Dialog with Trypho.* Ed. Miroslav Mackovich, *Dialogus cum Tryphone* (Berlin: De Gruyter, 1997); trans. Thomas B. Falls and Thomas P. Halton, *FC* 3.

Libanius

Or. *Orations.* Ed. Richard Forster, *Libanii Opera* (Hildesheim, Germany: Olms, 1985–1998); trans. D. A. Russell, *Imaginary Speeches: A Selection of Declamations* (London: Duckworth, 1996).

Origen

Cels. *Against Celsus.* Ed. M. Borret, *SC* 132, 136, 147, 150, 227; trans. Henry Chadwick, *Origen: Contra Celsum* (Cambridge: Cambridge University Press, 1965).

Comm. Cant. *Commentary on the Song of Songs.* Ed. L. Brésard, *SC* 375–376; trans. R. P. Lawson, *ACW* 26.

Comm. Jn. *Commentary on the Gospel of John* (lib. 1–2, 4–6, 10, 13). Ed. C. Blanc, *SC* 120, 157, 222, 290, 385; trans. Ronald E. Heine, *FC* 80, 89; bk. 32.318–367 trans. Joseph Trigg, *Origen*, pp. 233–240 (Early Church Fathers; London: Routledge, 1998).

Comm. Mt. *Commentary on the Gospel of Matthew.* Ed. E. Klostermann, *GCS* 40.1–40.2; bks. 1–2, 10–14 trans. John Patrick, *ANF* 10.413.512.

Comm. Rom. *Commentary on Romans.* Ed. Theresia Heither, *Commentarii in Epistulam ad Romanos* (Freiburg: Herder, 1990–1994); trans. Thomas Schenk, *FC* 103–104.

Fr. in Ps. *Fragmenta in Psalmos.* Ed. Jean Baptiste Pittra, *Analecta Sacra*, pp. 2.444f., 3.1f. (Paris: A. Jouby et Roger, 1876–1884).

Heracl. *Dialog with Heraclides.* Ed. Jean Scherer, *SC* 67; ET: Robert J. Daly, *ACW* 54.

Hom. Ex. *Homilies on Exodus.* Ed. M. Borret, *SC* 321; trans. Ronald Heine, *FC* 71.

Hom. Jer. *Homilies on Jeremiah.* Ed. Pierre Nautin, *SC* 232, 238; trans. John Clark Smith, *FC* 97.

Hom. Num. *Homilies on Numbers.* Ed. Louis Doutreleau. *SC* 415, 442, 461.

Hom. Ps. 36 *Homily on Psalm 36.* Ed. H. Crouzel and L. Brésard, *SC* 411.

Orat.	On Prayer. Ed. P. Koetschau, GCS 3.297–403; trans. Rowan A. Greer, Origen: An Exhortation to Martyrdom, Prayer, First Principles; Book IV, Prologue to the Commentary on the Song of Songs, Homily XXVII on Numbers, pp. 81–170 (Classics of Western Spirituality; New York: Paulist, 1979).
Philoc.	Philocalia of the Works of Origen by Basil and Gregory Nazianzen. Chaps. 1–20 ed. Marguerite Harl, SC 302; chaps. 21–27 ed. Éric Junod, SC 226; trans. George Lewis, The Philocalia of Origen (Edinburgh: T. and T. Clark, 1911).
Princ.	On First Principles. Ed. H. Crouzel and M. Simonetti, SC 252, 253, 268, 269, 312; trans. Henry Butterworth, Origen: On First Principles (Gloucester, Mass.: Peter Smith, 1973); bk. 4 trans. Rowan A. Greer, Origen: An Exhortation to Martyrdom, Prayer, First Principles; Book IV, Prologue to the Commentary on the Song of Songs, Homily XXVII on Numbers, pp. 171–216 (Classics of Western Spirituality; New York: Paulist, 1979).

Philostorgius

HE Ecclesiastical History. Ed. Joseph Bidez and F. Winkelmann, GCS; trans. E. Walford, The Ecclesiastical History of Sozomen and Philostorgius (London: Henry G. Bonn, 1855).

Plato

Crat.	Cratylus. Ed. and trans. H. N. Fowler, LCL 167.
Ion	Ion. Trans. W. R. M. Lamb, LCL 164.
Phaed.	Phaedo. Trans. Harold North Fowler, LCL 36.
Phaedr.	Phaedrus. Trans. Harold North Fowler, LCL 36.
Rep.	Republic. Trans. Paul Shorey, LCL 237, 276.
Symp.	Symposium. Trans. W. R. M. Lamb, LCL 166.
Tim.	Timaeus. Trans. R. G. Bury, LCL 234.

Plotinus

Enn. Enneads. Ed. Paul Henry and Hans-Rudolf Schwyzer, Plotini Opera (Oxford: Clarendon, 1964–); trans. A. H. Armstrong, LCL 440–445, 468.

Pseudo-Cyril of Alexandria

De sanct. Trin. On the Holy Trinity. PG 77.

Pseudo-Didymus the Blind

In Gen.	On Genesis. PG 39.1111–1115.
In Pss.	On the Psalms. PG 39.1155–1616.
Trin.	On the Trinity. PG 39.269–992.

Pseudo–Dionysius

De caelesti   *Celestial Hierarchy.* Ed. Beate Regina Suchla, *Corpus Dionysiacum* (Patristische Texte und Studien 33, 36; Berlin: De Gruyter, 1990); ET: Colm Lubheid and Paul Rorem, *The Complete Works*, pp. 143–191 (Classics of Western Spirituality; New York: Paulist, 1987).

De myst.   *Mystical Theology.* Ed. Beate Regina Suchla, *Corpus Dionysiacum* (Patristische Texte und Studien 33, 36; Berlin: De Gruyter, 1990); ET: Colm Lubheid and Paul Rorem, *The Complete Works*, pp. 133–141 (Classics of Western Spirituality; New York: Paulist, 1987).

Rufinus of Aquileia

HE	*Ecclesiastical History.* Ed. M. Simonetti, *CCL* 20.
Or. Greg. Naz.	*Orationum Gregorii Nazianzeni novem interpretatio.* Ed. Augustus Engelbrecht, *CSEL* 46.

Socrates

HE   *Ecclesiastical History.* PG 67.33–841; trans. A. C. Zenos, *NPNF* 2.2.1–178.

Sozomen

HE   *Ecclesiastical History.* Ed. Joseph Bidez, *SC* 306, 418, 495; trans. Chester D. Hartranft, *NPNF* 2.2.179–427.

Tertullian

Prax.   *Against Praxeas.* Ed. and trans. Ernest Evans, *Tertullian's Treatise Against Praxeas* (London: SPCK, 1948).

Themistius

Or.   *Orations.* Ed. G. Downey, *Themistii Orationes* (Leipzig, Germany: Teubner, 1965–1974); trans. Robert J. Penella, *The Private Orations of Themistius* (Berkeley: University of California Press, 2000).

Theodoret

HE   *Ecclesiastical History*. Ed. F. Scheidweiler, *GCS* 44; trans. Blomfield Jackson, *NPNF* 2.3.33–159.

Theodosian Code

C. Th.   *Theodosian Code*. Ed. Paul Krüger, Theodore Mommsen, and Paul Meyer, *Theodosiani Libri XVI cum Constitutionibus sirmondianis* (3rd ed., 3 vols.; Hildesheim, Germany: Weidmann, 2002–2005); trans. Clyde Pharr, *The Theodosian Code and Novels* (New York: Greenwood, 1969).

MODERN STUDIES

Abramowski, Luise. "Das Bekenntnis des Gregor Thaumaturgus bei Gregor von Nyssa und das Problem seiner Echtheit." *Zeitschrift für Kirchengeschichte* 87 (1976): pp. 145–166.

———. "Die Schrift Gregors des Lehrers 'Ad Theopompum' und Philoxenus von Mabbug." *Zeitschrift für Kirchengeschichte* 89 (1978): pp. 273–290.

Althaus, Heinz. *Die Heilslehre des heiligen Gregor von Nazianz*. Münsterische Beiträge zur Theologie 34. Münster, Germany: Verlag Aschendorff, 1972.

Asmus, J. R. "Gregorius von Nazianz und sein Verhältnis zum Kynismus." *Theologische Studien und Kritiken* 67 (1894): pp. 314–339.

Ayres, Lewis. *Nicaea and Its Legacy: An Approach to Fourth-Century Trinitarian Theology*. Oxford: Oxford University Press, 2004.

Bardy, Gustave. *Saint Athanase*. 3rd ed. Paris: Victor Lecoffre, 1925.

Barnes, Michel René. "De Régnon Reconsidered." *Augustinian Studies* 26 (1995): pp. 51–79.

———. "The Fourth Century as Trinitarian Canon." In *Christian Origins: Theology, Rhetoric and Community*, ed. Lewis Ayres and Gareth Jones, pp. 47–67. London: Routledge, 1998.

———. "*Oeconomia*." In *Encyclopedia of Early Christianity*, ed. Everett Ferguson, pp. 825–826. 2nd ed. Grand Rapids, Mich.: Garland, 1997.

———. "One Nature, One Power: Consensus Doctrine in Pro-Nicene Polemic." *Studia Patristica* 29 (1997): pp. 205–223.

———. *The Power of God: Δύναμις in Gregory of Nyssa's Trinitarian Theology*. Washington, D.C.: Catholic University of America Press, 2001.

Barnes, T. D. "The Collapse of the Homoeans in the East." *Studia Patristica* 29 (1997): pp. 3–16.

Baronius, Joseph. *Dissertationes theologicae: De traditionibus; de S. Petri & R. Pontificis Primatu; De Sanctorum cultu & invocatione; Acta de Sanctorum; Reliquiarum & Imaginum cultu. Contra Jacobi Piccinini pro novatoribus apologiam*. Naples: Felicis Mosca, 1725.

Beeley, Christopher A. "Cyril of Alexandria and Gregory Nazianzen: Tradition and Complexity in Patristic Christology," *Journal of Early Christian Studies*, 17(2009): pp. 381–419.

———. "Divine Causality and the Monarchy of God the Father in Gregory of Nazianzus." *Harvard Theological Review* 100 (2007): pp. 199–214.

———. "Gregory of Nazianzus on the Unity of Christ." In *In the Shadow of the Incarnation: Essays on Jesus Christ in the Early Church in Honor of Brian E. Daley, S.J.*, ed. Peter W. Martens, pp. 97–120. Notre Dame, Ind.: University of Notre Dame Press.

———. "The Holy Spirit in Gregory Nazianzen: The Pneumatology of Oration 31." In *God in Early Christian Thought: Essays in Honor of Lloyd Patterson*, ed. Andrew McGowan, pp. 151–62. Supplements to Vigiliae Christianae 94. Leiden: Brill.

Behr, John. *The Nicene Faith*. Formation of Christian Theology 2. Crestwood, N.Y.: St. Vladimir's Seminary Press, 2004.

———. *The Way to Nicea*. Formation of Christian Theology 1. Crestwood, N.Y.: St. Vladimir's Seminary Press, 2001.

Benoît, Alphonse. *Saint Grégoire de Nazianze: Sa vie, ses oeuvres et son époque*. Marseilles/Paris: 1876. Repr., New York: G. Olms, 1973.

Bergjan, Silke-Petra. *Theodoret von Cyrus und der Neunizänismus: Aspekte der altkirchlichen Trinitätslehre*. Berlin: De Gruyter, 1994.

Bernardi, Jean. *La prédication des pères cappadociens: Le prédicateur et son auditoire*. Publications de la Faculté des Lettres et Sciences Humaines de l'Université de Montpellier 30. Paris: Presses Universitaires de France, 1968.

———. *Grégoire de Nazianze: Le théologien et son temps, 330–390*. Initiations aux Pères de l'Église. Paris: Cerf, 1995.

———. "Saint Grégoire de Nazianze, observateur du milieu ecclésiastique et théoricien de la fonction sacerdotale." In *Migne et le renouveau des études patristiques*, ed. A. Mandouze and J. Fouilheron. Théologie historique 66. Paris: Beauchesne, 1985.

Böhringer, Georg Friedrich. *Die drei Kapadozier oder die trinitarische Epigonen*. 2 vols. Stuttgart: Meyer & Zeller, 1875.

Bouteneff, Peter. "St. Gregory Nazianzen and Two-Nature Christology." *St. Vladimir's Theological Quarterly* 38 (1994): pp. 255–270.

Bouyer, Louis. *The Spirituality of the New Testament and the Fathers*. Trans. Mary P. Ryan. London: Burns and Oates, 1963.

Bowerstock, G. W. *Greek Sophists in the Roman Empire*. Oxford: Clarendon, 1969.

Brown, Peter. *Poverty and Leadership in the Later Roman Empire*. Menahem Sterm Jerusalem Lectures. Hanover, N.H.: University Press of New England, 2002.

———. *Power and Persuasion in Late Antiquity: Towards a Christian Empire*. The Curti Lectures 1988. Madison: University of Wisconsin Press, 1992.

Burns, J. Patout. *The Development of Augustine's Doctrine of Operative Grace*. Paris: Études Augustiniennes, 1980.

Cameron, Averil. *Christianity and the Rhetoric of Empire*. Berkeley and Los Angeles: University of California Press, 1991.

Campenhausen, Hans von. *Ecclesiastical Authority and Spiritual Power in the Church of the First Three Centuries.* Trans. J. A. Baker. Stanford, Calif.: Stanford University Press, 1969.

Cross, F. L., and E. A. Livingstone. *Oxford Dictionary of the Christian Church.* 3rd ed. Oxford: Oxford University Press, 1997.

Cross, Richard. "Divine Monarchy in Gregory of Nazianzus." *Journal of Early Christian Studies* 14 (2006): pp. 105–116.

Crouzel, Henri. "Θεολογία et mots de même racine chez Origène." In *Lebendige Überlieferung. Prozessse der Annäherung und Auslegung,* ed. Nabil el-Khoury, Henri Crouzel, and Rudolf Reinhardt, pp. 365–383. Festschrift for Hermann-Josef Vogt. Beirut: Rückert, 1992.

———. "La passion de l'impassible: Un essai apologétique et polémique du IIIe siècle." In *L'homme devant Dieu: Mélanges offerts au Père Henri de Lubac,* vol. 1, pp. 269–279. Paris: Aubier, 1963.

———. *Origen.* Trans. A. S. Worrall. Edinburgh: T. and T. Clark, 1989.

Daley, Brian E. "Building a New City: The Cappadocian Fathers and the Rhetoric of Philanthropy." 1998 NAPS Presidential Address. *Journal of Early Christian Studies* 7 (1999): pp. 431–461.

———. *Gregory of Nazianzus.* Early Church Fathers. London: Routledge, 2006.

———. "Nature and the Mode of Union: Late Patristic Models for the Personal Unity of Christ." In *The Incarnation: An Interdisciplinary Symposium on the Incarnation of the Son of God,* ed. Stephen T. Davis, Daniel Kendall, and Gerald O'Collins. Oxford: Oxford University Press, 2002: pp. 164–196.

———. "'One Thing and Another': The Persons in God and the Person of Christ in Patristic Theology." *Pro Ecclesia* 15 (2006): pp. 17–46.

———. "Saint Gregory of Nazianzus as Pastor and Theologian." In *Loving God with Our Minds: The Pastor as Theologian; Essays in Honor of Wallace M. Alston,* ed. Michael Welker and Cynthia A. Jarvis, pp. 106–119. Grand Rapids, Mich.: Eerdmans, 2004.

———. "Systematic Theology in Homeric Dress: Poemata arcana." In *Re-Reading Gregory of Nazianzus: Essays on History, Theology, and Culture,* ed. Christopher A. Beeley, pp. 3–12. CUA Studies in Early Christianity. Washington, DC: The Catholic University of America Press, 2012.

Daniélou, Jean. "Eunome l'Arien et l'exégèse néoplatonicienne du *Cratyle.*" *Revue des Études Grecques* 69 (1956), pp. 412–432.

Demoen, Kristoffel. *Pagan and Biblical Exempla in Gregory Nazianzen: A Study in Rhetoric and Hermeneutics.* Turnhout, Belgium: Brepols, 1996.

Dossetti, Guiseppe. *Il símbolo di Nicea e di Costantinopoli: Edizione critica.* Rome: Herder, 1967.

Dräseke, Johannes. "Neuplatonisches in des Gregorios von Nazianz Trinitätslehre." *Byzantinisches Zeitschrift* 15 (1906): pp. 141–160.

Edwards, Mark Julian. *Origen Against Plato.* Ashgate Studies in Philosophy & Theology in Antiquity. Aldershot: Ashgate, 2002.

Egan, John P. "The Knowledge and Vision of God according to Gregory Nazianzen: A Study of the Images of Mirror and Light." Diss., Institut Catholique de Paris, 1971.

———. "Primal Cause and Trinitarian Perichoresis in Gregory Nazianzen's *Oration* 31.14." *Studia Patristica* 27 (1993): pp. 21–28.

———. "Toward Trinitarian *Perichoresis*: Saint Gregory the Theologian, *Oration* 31.14." *Greek Orthodox Theological Review* 39 (1994): pp. 83–93.

———. "Towards a Mysticism of Light in Gregory Nazianzen's Oration 32.15." *Studia Patristica* 18 (1989): pp. 8–13.

———. "αἴτιος/'Author', αἰτία/'Cause' and ἀρχή/'Origin': Synonyms in Selected Texts of Gregory Nazianzen." *Studia Patristica* 32 (1997): pp. 102–107.

Ellverson, Anna-Stina. *The Dual Nature of Man: A Study in the Theological Anthropology of Gregory of Nazianzus*. Studia Doctrinae Christianae Upsaliensia 21. Uppsala: Almkvist and Wiksell, 1981.

Elm, Susanna. "The Diagnostic Gaze: Gregory of Nazianzus' Theory of Orthodox Priesthood in his Oration 6 'De Pace' and 2 'Apologia de Fuga sua.'" In *Orthodoxie, christianisme, histoire*, ed. Susanna Elm, Éric Rebillard, and Antonella Romano, pp. 83–100. Rome: École Française de Rome, 2000.

———. "Gregory's Women: Creating a Philosopher's Family." In *Gregory of Nazianzus: Images and Reflections*, ed. Jøstein Bortnes and Tomas Hägg, pp. 171–191. Copenhagen: Museum Tusculanum, 2006.

———. "Inscriptions and Conversions: Gregory of Nazianzus on Baptism (*Or.* 38–40)." In *Conversion in Late Antiquity and the Early Middle Ages: Seeing and Believing*, ed. Anthony Grafton and Kenneth Mills, pp. 1–35. Rochester, N.Y.: University of Rochester Press, 2003.

———. "Inventing the 'Father of the Church': Gregory of Nazianzus' 'Farewell to the Bishops' (*Or.* 42) in Its Historical Context." In *Vita Religiosa im Mittelalter*, ed. Franz Felten and Norbert Jaspert, pp. 3–20. Berlin: Dunker und Humblot, 1999.

———. "Orthodoxy and the Philosophical Life: Julian and Gregory of Nazianzus." *Studia Patristica* 37 (2001): pp. 69–85.

———. "A Programmatic Life: Gregory of Nazianzus' Orations 42 and 43 and the Constantinopolitan Ethics." *Arethusa* 33 (2000): pp. 411–427.

———. *Virgins of God: The Making of Asceticism in Late Antiquity*. Oxford: Clarendon, 1994.

Fedwick, Paul Jonathan. "A Commentary of Gregory of Nyssa on the 38th Letter of Basil of Caesarea." *Orientalia Christiana Periodica* 44 (1978): pp. 31–51.

Field, Lester L., Jr. *On the Communion of Damasus and Melitius: Fourth-Century Synodal Formulae in the Codex Veronensis LX, with Critical Edition and Translation*. Studies and Texts 145. Toronto: Pontifical Institute of Mediaeval Studies, 2004.

Finn, Richard. *Almsgiving in the Later Roman Empire: Christian Promotion and Practice (313–450)*. Oxford: Oxford University Press, 2006.

Fleury, Eugene. *Héllenisme et Christianisme: Saint Grégoire de Nazianze et son temps*. 2nd ed. Études de théologie historique. Paris: Beauchesne, 1930.

Friend, W. H. C. *The Rise of Christianity*. Philadelphia: Fortress, 1984.

Gallay, Paul. *La vie de Saint Grégoire de Nazianze*. Lyons, France: Emmanuel Vitte, 1943.

Gautier, Francis. *La retraite et le sacerdoce chez Grégoire de Nazianze*. Turnhout, Belgium: Brepols, 2002.

Gómez-Villegas, Nicanor. *Gregorio de Nazianzo in Constantinopla: Ortodoxia, heterodoxia y régimen Teodosiano in una capital Cristiana*. Nueva Roma 11. Madrid: Consejo Superior de Investigaciones Científicas, 2000.

Gottwald, Ricardus. *De Gregorio Nazianzeno Platonico*. Bratislava: H. Fleischmann, 1906.

Greer, Rowan A. *Broken Lights and Mended Lives: Theology and Common Life in the Early Church*. University Park: Pennsylvania State University Press, 1986.

———. "Who Seeks for a Spring in the Mud? Reflections on the Ordained Ministry in the Fourth Century." In *Theological Education and Moral Formation*, ed. Richard John Neuhaus, pp. 22–55. Grand Rapids, Mich.: Eerdmans, 1992.

Gregg, Robert C., ed. *Arianism: Historical and Theological Reassessments; Papers from the Oxford Conference on Patristic Studies, September 5–10, 1983*. Patristic Monograph Series 11. Cambridge, Mass.: Philadelphia Patristic Foundation, 1985.

———. *Consolation Philosophy: Greek and Christian Paideia in Basil and the Two Gregories*. Patristic Monograph Series 3. Cambridge, Mass.: Philadelphia Patristic Foundation, 1975.

Grillmeier, Aloys. *Christ in Christian Tradition: From the Apostolic Age to Chalcedon (451)*. Trans. J. S. Bowden. New York: Sheed and Ward, 1965. Rev. ed.: London: Mowbrays; Atlanta: John Knox, 1975. Rev. German ed.: *Jesus der Christus im Glauben der Kirche*. Freiburg, Germany: Herder, 1979.

Gross, Jules. *La divinisation du chreÇtien d'apre's les pegres Grecs: Contribution historique a' la doctrine de la gràce*. Paris: J. Gabalda, 1938.

Guignet, Marcel. *Saint Grégoire de Nazianze et la rhétorique*. Paris: A. Picard, 1911.

Hadot, Pierre. *Philosophy as a Way of Life: Spiritual Exercises from Socrates to Foucault*. Trans. Michael Chase. Oxford, U.K.: Blackwell, 1995.

———. *What Is Ancient Philosophy?* Trans. Michael Chase. Cambridge, Mass.: Harvard University Press, 2002.

Hahn, Johannes. *Der Philosoph und die Gesellschaft: Selbstverständnis, öffentliches Auftreten und populäre Erwartungen in der hohen Kaiserzeit*. Heidelberger althistorische Beiträge und epigraphische Studien 7. Stuttgart: F. Steiner, 1989.

Halleux, André de. "'Hypostase' et 'personne' dans la formation du dogme trinitaire (ca 375–381)." *Revue d'histoire ecclésiastique* 79 (1984): pp. 313–369, 625–670.

———. "Personalisme ou essentialisme trinitaire chez les Pères cappadociens?" *Revue théologique de Louvain* 17 (1986): pp. 129–155.

Hanson, R. P. C. "Basil's Doctrine of Tradition in Relation to the Holy Spirit." *Vigiliae Christianae* 22 (1968): pp. 241–255.

———. *The Search for the Christian Doctrine of God: The Arian Controversy, 318–381*. Edinburgh: T. and T. Clark, 1988.

Harnack, Adolf von. *History of Dogma*. Trans. Neil Buchanan. 3rd ed. 7 vols. Gloucester, Mass.: Peter Smith, 1976.

Harrison, Verna. "Greek Patristic Foundations of Trinitarian Anthropology." *Pro Ecclesia* 14 (2005): pp. 399–412.

———. "Illumined from All Sides by the Trinity: A Neglected Theme in Gregory Nazianzen's Trinitarian Theology." Paper in progress.

———. "Perichoresis in the Greek Fathers." *St. Vladimir's Theological Quarterly* 35 (1991): pp. 53–65.

———. "Poverty, Social Involvement, and Life in Christ according to Saint Gregory the Theologian." *Greek Orthodox Theological Review* 2 (1994): pp. 151–164.

———. "Some Aspects of St. Gregory the Theologian's Soteriology." *Greek Orthodox Theological Review* 34 (1989): pp. 11–18.

———. "Theosis as Salvation: An Orthodox Perspective." *Pro Ecclesia* 6 (1997): pp. 429–443.

Hartmann, Christoph. "Gregory of Nazianzus." In *Dictionary of Early Christian Literature*, ed. Siegmar Döpp and Wilhelm Geerlings, trans. Matthew O'Connell, pp. 259–263. New York: Crossroad, 2000.

Hauschild, W. D. "Das trinitarische Dogma von 381 als Ergebnis verbindlicher Konsensusbildung." In *Glaubensbekenntnis und Kirchengemeinschaft: Das Modell des Konzils von Konstantinopel (381)*, ed. K. Lehmann and W. Pannenberg. Dialog des Kirchen 1. Freiburg: Herder, 1982.

Haykin, Michael A. G. *The Spirit of God: The Exegesis of 1 and 2 Corinthians in the Pneumatomachian Controversy of the Fourth Century*. Supplements to Vigiliae Christianae 27. Leiden: Brill, 1994

Heck, Adrianus van. *Gregorii Nysseni de Pauperibus Amandis Orationes Duo*. Leiden: Brill, 1964.

Hennessy, Kristin. "An Answer to de Régnon's Accusers: Why We Should Not Speak of 'His' Paradigm." In *The God of Nicaea: Disputed Questions in Patristic Trinitarianism*, ed. Sarah Coakley. Special Issue. *Harvard Theological Review* 100 (2007): pp. 179–198.

Hildebrand, Stephan M. *The Trinitarian Theology of Basil of Caesarea: A Synthesis of Greek Thought and Biblical Truth*. Washington, D.C.: Catholic University of America Press, 2007.

Holman, Susan. *The Hungry Are Dying: Beggars and Bishops in Roman Cappadocia*. Oxford: Oxford University Press, 2001.

Holl, Karl. *Enthusiasmus und Bussgewalt beim griechischen Mönchtum: Eine Studie zu Symeon dem Neuen Theologen*. Leipzig: J. C. Hinrich, 1898.

———. *Amphilochius von Ikonium in seinem Verhältnis zu den grossen Kappadoziern*. Tübingen, Germany: Mohr, 1904.

———. *Enthusiasmus und Bussgewalt*.

Honoré, Tony. *Law in the Crisis of Empire, 379–455 AD: The Theodosian Dynasty and Its Quaestors with a Palingenesia of Laws of the Dynasty*. Oxford: Clarendon, 1998.

Hübner, Reinhard M. "Gregor von Nyssa als Verfasser der sog. Ep. 38 des Basilius. Zum unterschiedlichen Verständnis der οὐσία bei den kappadozischen Brüdern." In *Epektasis: Mélanges patristiques offerts à Jean Danlélou*, ed. J. Fontaine and C. Kannengiesser, pp. 462–490. Paris: Beauchesne, 1972.

Humfress, Caroline. "Roman Law, Forensic Argument and the Formation of Christian Orthodoxy (III–VI Centuries)." In *Orthodoxie, christianisme, histoire*, ed. Susanna Elm, Éric Rebillard, and Antonella Romano, pp. 1–26. Rome: École Française de Rome, 2000.

Huxley, George. "Saint Basil the Great and Anisa." *Analecta Bollandiana* 107 (1989): pp. 30–32.

Kelly, J. N. D. *Early Christian Creeds*. 3rd ed. New York: Longman, 1972.

———. *Early Christian Doctrines*. 5th ed. San Francisco: HarperSanFrancisco, 1978.

Kennedy, George A. *The Art of Persuasion in Greece*. Princeton, N.J.: Princeton University Press, 1963.

———. *Greek Rhetoric under Christian Emperors*. Princeton, N.J.: Princeton University Press, 1983.

———. *A New History of Classical Rhetoric*. Princeton, N.J.: Princeton University Press, 1994.

Kertsch, Manfred. *Blidersprache bei Gregor von Nazianz: Ein Beitrag zur spätantiken Rhetorik und Popularphilosophie*. Grazer Theologische Studien. Graz: Johannes B. Bauer, 1978.

———. "Gregor von Nazianz' Stellung zu qewriva und pra'xi aus der Sicht seiner Reden." *Byzantion* 44 (1974): pp. 282–289.

Kopecek, Thomas A. "The Cappadocian Fathers and Civic Patriotism." *Church History* 43 (1974): pp. 293–303.

———. *A History of Neo-Arianism*. 2 vols. Patristic Monograph Series 8. Cambridge, Mass.: Philadelphia Patristic Foundation, 1979.

———. "The Social Class of the Cappadocian Fathers." *Church History* 42 (1973): pp. 453–466.

Kovacs, Judith. "Divine Pedagogy and the Gnostic Teacher according to Clement of Alexandria." *Journal of Early Christian Studies* 9 (2001): pp. 3–26.

Kustas, George. *Studies in Byzantine Rhetoric*. Analekta Vlatadon 17. Thessaloniki, Greece: Patriarchikon Hidryma Paterikon, 1973.

Lafontaine, G., J. Mossay, and M. Sicherl. "Vers une édition critique." *Revue d'histoire ecclésiastique* 40 (1979): pp. 626–640.

Laird, Martin. *Gregory of Nyssa and the Grasp of Faith: Union, Knowledge, and Divine Presence*. Oxford Early Christian Studies. Oxford: Oxford University Press, 2004.

Lampe, G. W. H. *The Seal of the Spirit: A Study in the Doctrine of Baptism and Confirmation in the New Testament and the Fathers*. London: Longmans, 1951.

Lieggi, Jean-Paul. "Influssi origeniani sulla teoria dell'ineffabilità di Dio in Gregorio di Nazianzo." In *Origeniana Octava: Origen and the Alexandrian Tradition*. Vol. II, *The Alexandrian School after Origen*, ed. L. Perrone, pp. 1103–114. Leuven, Belgium: Leuven University Press, 2003.

Lienhard, Joseph T. "Augustine of Hippo, Basil of Caesarea, and Gregory Nazianzen." In *Orthodox Readings of Augustine: Proceedings from the Orthodox Readings of Augustine Conference at Fordham University, 15–16 June 2007*, ed. George Demacopoulos and Aristotle Papanikolaou, pp. 81–100. Crestwood, N.Y.: St. Vladimir's Seminary Press, 2008.

———. *Contra Marcellum: Marcellus of Ancyra and Fourth-Century Theology.* Washington, D.C.: Catholic University of America, 1999

———. "Ousia and Hypostasis: The Cappadocian Settlement and the Theology of 'One Hypostasis.'" In *The Trinity: An Interdisciplinary Symposium on the Doctrine of the Trinity,* ed. S. T. Davis et al., pp. 99–121. Oxford: Oxford University Press, 2000.

Lim, Richard. *Public Disputation and Social Order in Late Antiquity.* Transformation of the Classical Heritage 23. Berkeley and Los Angeles: University of California Press, 1995.

Lossky, Vladimir. *The Mystical Theology of the Eastern Church.* Translated by members of the Society of Saint Alban and Saint Sergius. Crestwood, N.Y.: St. Vladimir's Seminary Press, 1976.

———. "Redemption and Deification." *Sobornost* 12 (1947): pp. 47–56.

———. *The Vision of God.* Trans. Ashleigh Moorhouse. Pref. John Meyendorff. Library of Orthodox Theology 2. London: Faith Press, 1964.

Louth, Andrew. "St. Gregory Nazianzen on Bishops and the Episcopate." In *Vescovi e pastore in epoca Teodosiana,* pp. 281–285. Studia Ephemeridis Augustinianum 58. Rome: Institutum Patristicum Augustinianum, 1997.

———. "The Cappadocians." In *The Cambridge History of Early Christian Literature,* ed. Frances Young, Lewis Ayres, and Andrew Louth, pp. 289–301. Cambridge: Cambridge University Press, 2004.

Luckman, Harriet Ann. "Pneumatology and Asceticism in Basil of Caesarea: Roots and Influence to 381." Diss., Marquette University, 2001.

Malingrey, Anne-Marie. *La littérature grecque chrétienne.* Initiations aux Pères de l'Église. Paris: Cerf, 1996.

———. *"Philosophia": Étude d'un groupe de mots dans la littérature grecque, des présocratiques au IVe siècle après J.C.* Études et commentaires 40. Paris: C. Klincksieck, 1961.

Markschies, Christoph. "Gibt es eine einheitliche 'kappadozische Trinitätstheologie'?" In *Alta Trinità Beata: Gesammelte Studien zur altkirchlichen Trinitätstheologie,* pp. 196–237. Tübingen: Mohr, 2000.

———. "Trinitarianism." In *The Westminster Handbook to Origen,* ed. John Anthony McGuckin, pp. 207–209. Louisville, Ky.: Westminster John Knox, 2004.

Matthews, John. *Laying Down the Law: A Study of the Theodosian Code.* New Haven, Conn.: Yale University Press, 2000.

May, Gerhard. "Die Datierung der Rede 'In suam Ordinationem' des Gregorys von Nyssa und die Verhandlungen mit den Pneumatomachen auf dem Konzil von Konstantinopel 381." *Vigiliae Christianae* 23 (1969): pp. 38–57.

McGuckin, John A. "Autobiography as Apologia in St. Gregory Nazianzen." *Studia Patristica* 37 (1999): pp. 160–177.

———. "Gregory: The Rhetorician as Poet." In *Gregory of Nazianzus: Images and Reflections,* ed. Jøstein Bortnes and Tomas Hägg, pp. 193–212. Copenhagen: Museum Tusculanum, 2006.

———. "Origen's Doctrine of the Priesthood." *Clergy Review* 70 (1985): pp. 277–286, 318–325.

———. "Patterns of Biblical Exegesis in the Cappadocian Fathers: Basil the Great, Gregory the Theologian, and Gregory of Nyssa." In *Orthodox and Wesleyan Scriptural Understanding and Practice*, ed. S. T. Kimborough, pp. 37–54. Crestwood, N.Y.: St. Vladimir's Seminary Press, 2006

———. "Perceiving Light from Light in Light: The Trinitarian Theology of Saint Gregory the Theologian." *Greek Orthodox Theological Review* 39 (1994): pp. 7–32.

———. *St. Gregory of Nazianzus: An Intellectual Biography*. Crestwood, N.Y.: St. Vladimir's Seminary Press, 2001.

———. "The Strategic Adaptation of Deification in the Cappadocians." In *Partakers of the Divine Nature: The History and Development of Deification in the Christian Traditions*, ed. Michael J. Christensen and Jeffery A. Wittung. Madison, N.J.: Fairleigh Dickinson University Press, 2007.

———. "The Vision of God in St. Gregory Nazianzen." *Studia Patristica* 32 (1998): pp. 145–152.

McLynn, Neil. "Among the Hellenists: Gregory and the Sophists." In *Gregory of Nazianzus: Images and Reflections*, ed. Jøstein Bortnes and Tomas Hägg, pp. 213–238. Copenhagen: Museum Tusculanum, 2006.

———. "Gregory Nazianzen's Basil: The Literary Construction of a Christian Friendship." *Studia Patristica* 37 (2001): pp. 178–193.

———. "A Self-Made Holy Man: The Case of Gregory Nazianzen." *Journal of Early Christian Studies* 6 (1998): pp. 463–483.

———. "The Voice of Conscience: Gregory Nazianzen in Retirement." In *Vescove e Pastori in epica teodosiana*, vol. 2, pp. 299–308. Studia Ephemeridis Augustinianum 58. Rome: Institutum Patristicum Augustinianum, 1997.

Meijering, E. P. "The Doctrine of the Will and of the Trinity in the Orations of Gregory of Nazianzus." *Nederlands theolgisch tijdschrift* 27 (1973): pp. 224–234.

Menestrina, Giovanni, and Claudio Moreschini. *Gregorio Nazianzeno teologo e scrittore*. Pubblicazioni dell'Istitute di Scienze Religiose in Trento 17. Bologna, Italy: EDP, 1992.

Meredith, Anthony. *The Cappadocians*. Crestwood, N.Y.: St. Vladimir's Seminary Press, 1995.

———. "The Pneumatology of the Cappadocian Fathers and the Creed of Constantinople." *Irish Theological Quarterly* 48 (1981): pp. 196–212.

Meyendorff, John. *Byzantine Theology: Historical Trends and Doctrinal Themes*. New York: Fordham University Press, 1974.

Moreschini, Claudio. *Filosofia e letteratura in Gregorio di Nazianzo*. Collana Platonismo e filosofia patristica. Studi e testi 12. Milan, Italy: Vite e Pensiero, 1997.

———. "Il battesimo come fondamento dell'istruzione del Cristiano in Gregorio Nazianzeno." In *Sacerdozio battesimale e formazione teologica nella catechesi e nella testimonianza di vita dei Padri*, ed. Sergio Felici. Biblioteca di Scienze Religiose 99. Rome: Las, 1992.

———. "Il Platonismo Cristiano di Gregorio di Nazianzo." *Annali della Scuola Normale Superiore di Pise* 3rd series 4/4 (1974): pp. 1347–1392.
———. "Influenze di Origene su Gregorio Nazianzeno." *Atti e memorie dell'Accademia Toscana di Scienze e Lettere "La Colombaria"* 44 = n.s. 30 (1979): pp. 35–57.
———. "Luce e purificazione nella dottrina di Gregorio Nazianzeno." *Augustinianum* 13 (1973): pp. 534–549.
Mortley, Raoul. *From Word to Silence, Pt. 2: The Way of Negation, Christian and Greek*. Bonn: Hanstein, 1986.
Mossay, Justin, ed. "La Noël et l'Épiphanie en Cappadoce au IVe siècle." In *Noël, Épiphanie, retour du Christ: Semaine liturgique de l'Institut Saint-Serge*, ed. Bernard Botte, A.-M. Dubarle, and Klaus Hruby. Lex Orandi 40. Paris: Cerf, 1967.
———. *Les fêtes de Noël et de l'Épiphanie d'après les sources littéraires cappadociennes du IVe siècle*. Textes et études liturgiques 3. Louvain: Abbaye du Mont César, 1965.
Nautin, Pierre. "La date du 'De Viris Illustribus' de Jérôme, de la mort de Cyrile de Jérusalem et de celle de Grégoire de Nazianze." *Revue d'histoire ecclésiastique* 56 (1961): pp. 33–35.
Noret, Jacques. "Grégoire de Nazianze, l'auteur le plus cité après la Bible, dans la littérature ecclésiastique byzantine." In *Symposium Nazianzenum (Louvain-la-Neuve, 25–28 août, 1981): Actes du Colloque International*, ed. Justin Mossay, pp. 259–266. Studien zur Geschichte und Kultur des Altertums, NF 2. Paderborn: Schöningh, 1983.
Norris, Frederick W. "The Authenticity of Gregory Nazianzen's Five Theological Orations." *Vigiliae Christianae* 39 (1985): pp. 331–339.
———. "Christ/Christology" and "Gregory of Nazianzus." In *Encyclopedia of Early Christianity*, 2nd ed., ed. Everett Ferguson, pp. 242–251, 491–495. New York: Garland, 1998.
———. *Faith Gives Fullness to Reasoning: The Five Theological Orations of Gregory Nazianzen*. Trans. Lionel Wickham and Frederick Williams. Intro. and commentary by Frederick W. Norris. Supplements to Vigiliae Christianae 13. Leiden: Brill, 1991.
———. "Gregory Nazianzen: Constructing and Constructed by Scripture." In *The Bible in Late Antiquity*, ed. Paul Blowers, pp. 149–162. Notre Dame, Ind.: University of Notre Dame Press, 1997.
———. "Gregory Nazianzen's Doctrine of Jesus Christ." Diss., Yale University, 1970.
———. "Gregory Nazianzen's Opponents in Oration 31." In *Arianism: Historical and Theological Reassessments*, ed. Robert Gregg, pp. 321–326. Patristic Monograph Series 11. Cambridge, Mass.: Philadelphia Patristic Foundation, 1985.
———. "Gregory the Theologian and Other Religions." *Greek Orthodox Theological Review* 39 (1994): pp. 131–140.
———. "Of Thorns and Roses: The Logic of Belief in Gregory Nazianzen." *Church History* 53 (1984): pp. 455–464.
———. "The Tetragrammaton in Gregory Nazianzen, Or. 30.17." *Vigiliae Christianae* 41 (1989): pp. 339–444.

———. "The Theologian and Technical Rhetoric: Gregory of Nazianzus and Hermogenes of Tarsus." In *Nova and Vetera: Patristic Studies in Honor of Thomas Halton*, ed. John Petruccione, pp. 84–95. Washington, D.C.: Catholic University of America Press, 1998.

———. "Theology as Grammar: Gregory Nazianzen and Ludwig Wittgenstein." In *Arianism after Arius*, ed. Michel Barnes and Daniel H. Williams, pp. 237–249. Edinburgh: T. and T. Clark, 1993.

———. "Your Honor, My Reputation: St. Gregory of Nazianzus's Funeral Oration on St. Basil the Great." In *Greek Biography and Panegyric in Late Antiquity*, ed. Tomas Hääg and Philip Rousseau. Berkeley and Los Angeles: University of California Press, 2000.

Otis, Brooks. "Cappadocian Thought as a Coherent System." *Dumbarton Oaks Papers* 12 (1958): pp. 95–124.

———. "The Throne and the Mountain: An Essay on St. Gregory of Nazianzus." *Classical Journal* 56 (1961): pp. 146–165.

Pannenberg: 3 vols.

Pannenberg, Wolfhart. *Systematic Theology*. Trans. Geoffrey Bromiley. Grand Rapids, Mich.: Eerdmans, 1991–1998.

Parvis, Sara. *Marcellus of Ancyra and the Lost Years of the Arian Controversy, 325–45*. Oxford: Oxford University Press, 2006.

Pelikan, Jaroslav. *Christianity and Classical Culture: The Metamorphosis of Natural Theology in the Christian Encounter with Hellenism*. Gifford Lectures at Aberdeen 1992–1993. New Haven, Conn.: Yale University Press, 1993.

———. *The Christian Tradition: A History of the Development of Doctrine*. Vol. 2, *The Spirit of Eastern Christendom (600–1700)*. Chicago: University of Chicago Press, 1977.

Pinault, Henri. *Le Platonisme de Saint Grégoire de Nazianze: Essai sur les relations du Christianisme et de l'Hellénisme dans son oeuvre théologique*. La Roche-sur-Yon, France: G. Romain, 1925.

Plagnieux, Jean. "Saint Grégoire de Nazianze." In *Théologie de la vie monastique: Études sur la tradition patristique*, pp. 115–130. Paris: Aubier, 1961.

———. *Saint Grégoire de Nazianze théologien*. Paris: Éditions Franciscaines, 1951.

Portmann, Franz Xaver. *Die Göttliche Paidagogia bei Gregor von Nazianz*. Kirchengeschichtliche Quellen und Studien 3. St. Ottilien: Eos Verlag, 1954.

Pouchet, Jean-Robert. "Athanase d'Alexandrie, modèle de l'évêque, selon Grégoire de Nazianze, Discours 21," pp. 347–357.

Pouchet... in *Vescovi e pastori* [see under Andrew Louth]

Prestige, G. L. *God in Patristic Thought*. London: SPCK, 1952.

Pseudo-Basil of Caesarea, *Against Eunomius* books 4 and 5. Ed. J. Garnier and P. Maran. PG 29.

Quasten, Johannes. *Patrology*. Vol. 3, *The Golden Age of Greek Patristic Literature*. Westminster, Md.: Christian Classics, 1950.

Rahner, Karl. *The Trinity*. Trans. Joseph Donceel. New York: Crossroad Herder, 1999.

Rapp, Claudia. *Holy Bishops in Late Antiquity: The Nature of Christian Leadership in an Age of Transition.* Transformation of the Classical Heritage 37. Berkeley and Los Angeles: University of California Press, 2005.

Régnon, Théodore de. *Études de théologie positive sur la Sainte Trinité.* Paris: Victor Retaux, 1892.

Richard, Anne. *Cosmologie et théologie chez Grégoire de Nazianze.* Paris: Institut d'Études Augustiniennes, 2003.

Ritter, Adolph Martin. *Das Konzil von Konstantinopel und sein Symbol: Studien zur Gechichte und Theologie des II. Ökumenischen Konzils.* Göttingen: Vandenhoeck and Ruprecht, 1965.

———. "Die Trinitäts-Theologie der drei großen Kappadozier." In *Handbuch der Dogmen und Theologiegeschichte,* ed. Carl Andresen, pp. 198–206. Göttingen: 1982.

Roll, Susan K. *Toward the Origins of Christmas.* Kampen: Kok Pharos, 1995.

Rousse, Jacques. "Saint Grégoire de Nazianze." In *Dictionnaire de spiritualité,* ed. Marcel Viller, F. Cavallera, J. de Guibert, et al., cols. 960–969. 17 vols. Paris: Beauchesne, 1937–1995.

Rousseau, Philip. *Basil of Caesarea.* Berkeley and Los Angeles: University of California Press, 1994.

Ruether, Rosemary Radford. *Gregory of Nazianzus: Rhetor and Philosopher.* Oxford: Clarendon, 1969.

Russell, Norman. *The Doctrine of Deification in the Greek Patristic Tradition.* Oxford: Oxford University Press, 2004.

Scholz, Sebastian. *Transmigration und Translation: Studien zum Bistumswechsel der Bischöfe von der Spätantike bis zum Hohen Mittelalter.* Kölner historische Abhandlungen 37 Köln: Böhlau, 1992.

Schwartz, Eduard. *Gesammelte Schriften.* Berlin: De Gruyter, 1938–1963.

Sesboüé, Bernard. *Saint Basile et la Trinité, une acte théologique au IVe siècle: Le rôle de Basile de Césarée dans l'élaboration de la doctrine et du langage trinitaires.* Paris: Desclée, 1998.

Simonetti, Manlio. *La crisi Ariana nel IV secolo.* Studia Ephemeridis Augustinianum 36. Rome: Augustinianum, 1975.

———. *Studi sull'Arianesimo.* Rome: Studium, 1965.

Sinko, Tadeusz. *De traditione orationum Gregorii Nazianzeni: I; De traditione directa.* Meletemata Patristica 2. Krakow: 1917.

———. *De traditione orationum Gregorii Nazianzeni: II; De traditione indirecta.* Meletemata Patristica 3. Krakow: 1923.

Snee, Rochelle. "Gregory Nazianzen's Anastasia Church: Arianism, the Goths, and Hagiography." *Dumbarton Oaks Papers* 52 (1998): pp. 157–186.

Spidlík, Thomas. *Grégoire de Nazianze: Introduction à l'étude de sa doctrine spirituelle.* Orientalia Christiana Analecta 189. Rome: Pont. Institutum Studiorum Orientalium, 1971.

———. "La *theoria* et la *praxis* chez Grégoire de Nazianze." *Studia Patristica* 14 (1976): pp. 358–364.

Spoerl, K.M. "A Study of the Κατα Μέρος Πίστις by Apollinarius of Laodicea." Diss: University of Toronto, 1991.

Spoerl, Kelley McCarthy. "Apollinarian Christology and the Anti-Marcellan Tradition." *Journal of Theological Studies* n.s. 48 (1994): pp. 545–568.

———. "Apollinarius on the Holy Spirit." *Studia Patristica* 37 (2001): pp. 571–592.

Staats, Reinhart. *Das Glaubensbekenntnis von Nizäa-Konstantinopel: Historische und theologische Grundlagen*. Darmstadt: Wissenschaftliche Buchgesellschaft, 1996.

Sterk, Andrea. "On Basil, Moses, and the Model Bishop: The Cappadocian Legacy of Leadership." *Church History* 67 (1998): pp. 227–253.

———. *Renouncing the World Yet Leading the Church: The Monk-Bishop in Late Antiquity*. Cambridge, Mass.: Harvard University Press, 2004.

Studer, Basil. *Trinity and Incarnation: The Faith of the Early Church*. Ed. Andrew Louth. Trans. Matthias Westerhoff. Collegeville, Minn.: Liturgical, 1993.

Swete, H. B. *The Holy Spirit in the Ancient Church: A Study of Christian Teaching in the Age of the Fathers*. London: Macmillan, 1912.

Szymusiak, J. *Éléments de théologie de l'homme selon Saint Grégoire de Nazianze*. PhD diss., Pontificia Università Gregoriana, 1963.

———. "Grégoire le théologien, disciple d'Athanase." *PTAA*: pp. 359–363.

Talley, Thomas. *The Origins of the Liturgical Year*. 2nd ed. Collegeville, Minn.: Liturgical, 1991.

Tillemont, Louis Sébastien Le Nain de. *Mémoires pour servir à l'histoire ecclesiastique des six premiers siècles, justifiez par les citations des auteurs originaux; avec une chronologie, ou l'on fait un abregé de l'histoire eccesiastique & profane; & des notes pour éclaircir les difficultez des faits de la chronologie*. 6 vols. Brussels: E. H. Fricx.

Torrance, T. F. *The Trinitarian Faith: The Evangelical Theology of the Ancient Catholic Church*. Edinburgh: T. and T. Clark, 1988.

Trigg, Joseph W. "God's Marvelous *Oikonomia* and 'The Angel of Great Counsel': Christ and the Angelic Hierarchy in Origen's Thought." *Journal of Theological Studies* n.s. 42 (1991): pp. 35–51.

———. "Knowing God in the *Theological Orations* of Gregory of Nazianzus: The Heritage of Origen." In *God in Early Christian Thought: Essays in Honor of Lloyd Patterson*, ed. Andrew McGowan. Leiden: Brill, forthcoming.

———. *Origen*. Early Church Fathers. London: Routledge, 1998.

Trisoglio, Francesco. *Gregorio di Nazianzo*. Rome: Tiellemedia, 1999.

———. *Gregorio di Nazianzo: Il teologo*. Studia patristica Mediolanensia 20. Milan, Italy: Vita e Pensiero, 1996.

———. "La poesia della Trinita nell' opera letteraria di S. Gregorio di Nazianzo." In *Forma Futuri: Studi in onore del cardinale Michele Pellegrino*, pp. 712–740. Turin: Bottega d'Erasmo, 1975.

Turcescu, Lucian. *Gregory of Nyssa and the Concept of Divine Persons*. Oxford: Oxford University Press, 2005.

———. "'Person' versus 'Individual,' and Other Modern Misreadings of Gregory of Nyssa." *Modern Theology* 18 (2000): pp. 527–539.

354 BIBLIOGRAPHY

Vaggione, Richard Paul. *Eunomius of Cyzicus and the Nicene Revolution.* Oxford Early Christian Studies. Oxford: Oxford University Press, 2000.

Van Dam, Raymond. *Becoming Christian: The Conversion of the Roman Cappadocia.* Philadelphia: University of Pennsylvania Press, 2003.

———. *Families and Friends in Late Roman Cappadocia.* Philadelphia: University of Pennsylvania Press, 2003.

———. "Hagiography and History: The Life of Gregory Thaumaturgus." *Classical Antiquity* 1 (1982): pp. 272–308.

———. *Kingdom of Snow: Roman Rule and Greek Culture in Cappadocia.* Philadelphia: University of Pennsylvania Press, 2002.

———. "Self-Representation in the Will of Gregory of Nazianzus." *Journal of Theological Studies* n.s. 46 (1995): pp. 118–148.

Vinzent, Markus. *Pseudo-Athanasius, Contra Arianos IV: Eine Schrift gegen Asterius von Kappadokien, Eusebius von Cäsarea, Markell von Ankyra und Photin von Sirmium.* Supplements to Vigiliae Christianae 36. Leiden: Brill, 1996.

Weiss, Hugo. *Die grossen Kappadocier: Basilius, Gregor von Nazianz und Gregor von Nyssa als Exegeten. Ein Beitrag zur Geschichte der Exegese.* Braunsberg: A. Martens, 1872.

Wesche, Kenneth P. "The Union of God and Man in Jesus Christ." *St. Vladimir's Theological Quarterly* 38 (1984): pp. 83–98.

Williams, A. N. *The Ground of Union: Deification in Aquinas and Palamas.* New York: Oxford University Press, 1999.

Williams, Rowan. *On Christian Theology.* Challenges in Contemporary Theology. Oxford: Blackwell, 2000.

———. *Why Study the Past: The Quest for the Historical Church.* Sarum Theological Lectures. Grand Rapids, Mich.: Eerdmans, 2005

———. *The Wound of Knowledge: Christian Spirituality from the New Testament to St. John of the Cross.* Rev. ed. London: Darton, Longman and Todd, 1990.

Winslow, Donald F. *The Dynamics of Salvation: A Study in Gregory of Nazianzus.* Patristic Monograph Series 7. Cambridge, Mass.: Philadelphia Patristic Foundation, 1979.

Wittgenstein, Ludwig. *Philosophical Investigations.* Trans. G. E. M. Anscombe. 3rd ed. New York: MacMillan, 1958.

Index of Theological Topics in Gregory's Works

Because Gregory's corpus is relatively unsystematic (in a literary sense), with passages on the same topic often scattered across his orations, poems, and letters, few modern students have ventured far beyond the *Theological Orations* (*Ors.* 27–31) and the late Christological epistles (*Ep.* 101–102, 202) into what are often more significant texts. In order to facilitate further research into Gregory's theology, this index lists key passages by topic, as they are found in each chapter of this book. This is not an exhaustive list; further references can be found in the chapter footnotes and, no doubt, from further research. Passages in the *Orations* are listed by number only according to John McGuckin's chronology. Passages from *Oration* 38 that are repeated verbatim in *Oration* 45 (38.7–13 = 45.3–9; 38.14–15 = 45.26–27) are normally listed only under *Oration* 38.

Chapter 1: God and the Theologian

Purification　　　　　　　　2.71; 6.5; 20.1–4, 12; 32.12–13; 23.11; 27.3–4, 6–7; 28.1–4; 25.17; 38.1, 4–7, 13; 39.1–10, 14; 40.31, 391–40, 45; *Carm.* 1.1.1.1–24

Philosophy (Christian Practice)	2.7, 103; 7.1–15; 14.4; 27.7; 25–26; 44.9
Purification and the Body	7.21, 24; 14.6–8, 18; 41.1, 5; 27.3; 38.11–13; 39.19; 40.38–40; 45.13–14; *Ep.* 101.51–522
Purification and Baptism	8.14, 20; 18.13; 39.1–6; 40.3–4, 7–8, 11–40; *Carm.* 1.1.3.47
Incomprehensibility of God	14.30, 32; 17.4; 18.16; 28.3–5, 11, 18–21, 31 and passim; 30.17; 38.7; 39.13
Divine Magnitude and Transcendence	2.5, 74–76; 6.12; 20.11; 34.8; 28.11, 31; 30.17; 31.7–11, 22, 31–33; 25.17; 26.19; 37.2; 38.7–8; 39.12; 40.41
Corporeal Epistemology	2.17, 74; 17.14; 20.9–10; 22.6, 9; 24.15; 34.6; 28.3, 7–12, 21; 29.11, 19; 31.7; 38.12–13; 39.13; 45.11–12, 45; *Ep.* 101.49, 56
Divine Light and Illumination	2.75–76; 7.17; 8.19; 20.1, 12; 32.15; 21.1; 28.3, 17, 31; 31.3, 32; 37.4; 38.7, 11; 39.1–2, 8–10, 20; 40.3, 4–5, 32, 37, 41; 44.3; 45.2; *Carm.* 1.2.10.142; 2.1.1.194–213, 630–650
Illumination and Baptism	39.1–2; 40.1–5, 24–25, 36–37; *Carm.* 2.1.45.257–263
Purification and Illumination	14.4; 20.12; 21.6; 27.3; 28.2–3; 30.20; 39.8, 20; 40.5, 37; 43.12, 43
Reason and Faith	4.44; 6.6–7, 10; 14.33; 22.7, 11; 32.7, 23–27; 27.5; 28; 29.21; 39.7, 13; 40.5, 37, 45

Chapter 2: Jesus Christ, the Son of God

Linguistic Terms versus Meaning	16.2; 19.10; 20.8–10; 32.14, 26; 41.7–8; 28.4, 20; 29.8; 31.9–11, 20, 22, 24, 33; 25.2, 18; 37.2, 4; 39.11; 42.16, 18; 43.11, 13, 15, 65, 68–69
Creation	21.1–2; 38.7, 9–11; 39.13; 40.5, 8; *Carm.* 1.2.2.560–561
Fall	38.12; 39.13; 40.45
Divinization	1.5; 7.22, 23; 14.23; 11.5; 29.19; 30.3, 4, 6, 21; 25.16; 37.2; 38.2–4, 7, 11, 16; 39.1; 40.8, 10, 16, 42; *Ep.* 101.46; *Carm.* 1.1.11.9; 1.1.2.47

INDEX OF THEOLOGICAL TOPICS IN GREGORY'S WORKS 357

Economic Paradigm of Christology	1.5; 29.18–30.21; 37.2; 38.1–13; 39.13; 40.33; 45; *Ep.* 101.13–14; 102.4; *Carm.* 1.1.2; 1.1.10
Divinity of Christ	20.4; 32.18; 23.9; 29.18–21; 30.1, 4, 7, 12; 31.26, 28–29, 33; 26.7; 37.17; 38.2, 13; 41.4
Humanity of Christ	2.23; 29.18–21; 30.1, 5; 39.13; *Ep.* 101.32, 46–53
Christ's Assumption of Human Existence	14.15; 19.13; 34.10; 29.19; 30.5, 9, 31; 26.7; 37.1, 3–4; 38.13–15; 39.19; 44.2, 7; 45.13, 26–29, 60–61; *Ep.* 101.12–15
Unity of Christ	29.19; 37.2, 4; 38.13; *Ep.* 101.13–31; 102.4
Unity of Christ: Technical Terms	14.7; 32.9; 27.7; 28.3, 22; 29.19; 31.20; 37.2; 38.9, 13; *Ep.* 101.22, 28; 102.4; *Carm.* 2.1.11.631–651
Christological Hermeneutic	29.17–18; 30.1, 2; 34.10
Single-Subject Predication of Christ	1.5; 2.98; 14.2, 4, 15; 22.13; 32.33; 29.18–30.21; 37.1–3, 5, 7–8; 38.1, 13–16; 39.1, 12; 40.2, 45; 45.1; *Ep.* 101.14–25; *Carm.* 1.1.2.62–75
Divine Passibility and the Cross	17.12; 33.14; 30.1, 2, 5, 6; 26.12; 39.13; 43.64; 44.4, 44; 45.28–29; *Ep.* 101.51; *Carm.* 1.1.10.6–9
Seemingly Dualist Passages	30.2, 5, 8–10, 12–13, 15–16, 21; 38.13, 15; 43.69; 45.25; *Ep.* 102.24–28; 202.15–16; *DVS* 618, 642, 651
God Predominates in Christ	9.6; 10.4; 30.2, 3; 37.2; 39.16; 40.33; *Ep.* 101.12, 21–46; 102.18–20
Divinization of All Humanity in Christ	2.23–24; 30.1, 5, 6, 21; 38.7, 13, 19; 39.13; 40.45; 45.22, 28
Divinization through the Doctrine of Christ	14.14, 18, 21; 24.4; 29.18; 30.21; 31.26, 28; 37.1–4; 38.3–4, 16, 18; 39.14–16, 20; 40.6, 30; 43.38; 45.1, 22–25

Chapter 3: The Holy Spirit

Early Pneumatology	14.14, 27; 9.11; 10.1, 3; 11.5, 6; 12; 13.4; 16.1; 17.2, 6; 18.29, 36; 19.2
Mature Pneumatology	33.16; 21.13, 33; 23.13; 34.8, 9, 14; 41.5–8, 14; 31 [see outline on p. 168]; 38.16
The Holy Spirit and the Life of the Church	1.7; 6.1; 10.2–4; 11.3; 13.4; 16.1; 17.2; 18.29; 33.13; 21.7, 9, 24, 33; 34.6; 41.14; 26.1, 2; 42.1, 6, 12; 43.37; 45.1
Spiritual Exegesis	33.17; 31.3, 5, 21, 24–27, 29; 25.15; 42.11; 45.12; *Carm.* 1.1.3.17–33
The Holy Spirit in Scripture	34.13–15; 41.12–15; 31.1, 3, 5, 21–27, 29
Gradual Revelation of the Holy Spirit	41.5, 11; 31.25–27
Baptismal Divinization	14.14; 32.6; 33.17; 34.8, 12; 41.9, 14; 31.4, 6, 12, 28–29; 39.17; 40.42, 44; *Carm.* 1.1.3.1–4; 1.1.3.13–14
Liturgical Argument	31.12, 14, 17, 28
The Holy Spirit Reveals Christ	1.2; 2.39; 41.9, 14; 31.3, 29; 38.13; 39.16; *Carm.* 1.1.1.1–24
Hermeneutic of Piety	18.36; 19.2; 23.12; 34.9; 41.6–8; 27.1–3; 28.1–2; 31.1–3, 12, 23, 30, 33
Opponents of the Holy Spirit	11.6; 12.6; 21.33–34; 34.11; 41.7–8; 31.1–3, 5 and passim; 25.5; 39.12; 42.13

Chapter 4: The Trinity

Key Texts on the Trinity	2.36–38; 6.4, 11–13, 22; 20.5–12; 32.5; 23.6–12; 34.8–15; 41.7–9; 28.1; 29–31; 25.15–19; 38.7–9, 13–15; 39.11–12; 40.34, 41–45; 42.14–18; *Carm.* 1.1.1–3
Apostolic Faith in the Trinity	3.7; 6.22; 21.35; 34.6; 31.3, 5–6; 39.12; 43.67–68; *Ep.* 102.1
Trinity as Basic Christian Confession	11.6; 12.6; 20.5; 32.5, 21, 24–25; 34.6, 9; 25.8; 40.41; 42.3, 27
Divine Economy: General	2.24, 106; 7.4, 24; 14.9; 32.25, 30; 21.18; 41.5; 30.11, 19; 25.5; 38.11; 39.15; 42.1, 27; 45.7, 12, 22–23; *Ep.* 101.59

Divine Economy: Incarnation	41.11; 29.18; 30.19; 38.8, 14; 45.22; *Ep.* 110.59; 202.10
Human Economy	2.29, 35, 52; 6.8; 14.24; 18.1, 3, 20, 21, 36; 21.10, 34, 35; 34.3, 40; 41.6; 31.25; 39.14; 40.18, 44; 42.13, 14, 24; *Ep.* 58.11, 12, 14
Theology: Doctrine of God	2.37; 20.1, 5, 12; 23.3; 21.10, 12; 34.12, 15; 27.3, 4, 6, 7, 9; 28.1, 2, 4, 7; 29.10; 30.17; 31.3, 5, 8, 16; 25.15; 40.42; *Ep.* 102.7
Theology: Confession of Divinity	12.6; 18.17; 23.3, 12; 34.11, 15; 28.1; 31.3; 25.15, 17; 40.34; 43.67–69; *Ep.* 58.7–8, 14
Monarchy of God the Father	2.38; 6.22; 20.6–7; 32.5; 23.6, 7–8; 34.10; 41.9; 29.2; 30.2; 31.14, 33; 25.15, 16; 37.5; 38.13; 42.8, 15; 45.27
Trinitarian "Relations"	20.7; 29.16; 31.9, 14
Against Sabellians and Arians	2.36; 6.22; 18.16; 20.5–6; 22.12; 23.6; 21.13; 34.8; 31.9, 12, 30; 36.10; 38.15; 39.11; 42.16, 18
Against Tritheism	20.6; 23.6–7; 31.30; 25.16, 18; 38.8, 15; 40.41; 42.15
Brief Trinitarian Formulas	1.7; 22.12; 23.12; 21.33; 28.31; 31.33; 36.10; 38.8; 40.5, 41, 45; 42.15, 16
Oneness and Threeness	6.22; 20.7; 23.8; 21.13; 34.13, 15; 28.1; 29.2; 31.4, 9, 14, 18, 19, 28, 30; 37.22; 42.15, 16; *Carm.* 1.1.3.43, 60, 72, 75, 88
Oneness of God	20.7; 21.13; 34.13, 15; 31.14, 28; 42.15, 16; *Carm.* 1.1.3.74
Negative Conceptual Qualifications	20.8–11; 23.9–11; 29.3–16; 31.4–20, 31; 25.16–17; 39.12; *Carm.* 1.1.1.1–6; 1.1.2.13–27
Christocentric and Trinocentric	3.6; 20.12; 33.17; 23.13–14; 34.6; 29.21; 31.3, 12; 38.18; 39.20; *Carm.* 1.1.3.3–4
Participation in the Trinity	6.12–15, 22; 20.12; 22.14; 33.15; 23.11, 12; 25.17; 40.5, 16–17; 42.15, 16, 18

Chapter 5: Pastoral Ministry

Pastoral Ministry and the Divine Economy	1.6; 2.23–26; 3.7; 12.4; 16.13; 18.1; 23.12; 31.25–27; 40.44; 42.24; *Carm.* 2.1.12.355–356
Basic Terms for Christian Leadership	1.6, 7; 2.3–4, 16, 22; 7.3; 9.3–6; 12.2; 13.4; 16.13; 18.4, 37; 19.9–10; 32.4, 10–13; 21.7; 36.3; 43.66; *Carm.* 2.1.12.751–760

360 INDEX OF THEOLOGICAL TOPICS IN GREGORY'S WORKS

The Cure of Souls	2.10, 16–22, 27; 7.3; 14.6, 18, 37; 9.3, 5–6; 13.4; 19.9; 37.22; 43.66; *Carm.* 1.1.8.1–3; 1.2.14.75–76; 2.1.1.229–223; 2.1.12.751–760
Adaptive Pastoral Treatment	2.16, 28–33, 36, 39–45; 6.2; 9.5–6; 13.4; 18.13, 15, 22–23; 19.6–7; 21.33, 36; 27.3, 5–6; 37.1; 43.64
Priestly Experience and Virtue	2.3, 14–15, 33–34, 47–48, 91; 15.12; 6.1–2, 19; 7.3; 8.5; 12.5l; 16.20; 20.1–4; 32.13; 27.3; 26.1; 39.14; *Carm.* 2.1.12.475–574
Empowered by the Spirit	1.1–2; 2.39; 6.1, 9; 9.1–2; 12.1, 3; 13.4; 18.1, 3, 5, 36, 40; 19.2; 21.7, 9; 33.13; 42.12; 43.37
Positive Examples: Moses, Peter, Paul, Athanasius, Basil, etc.	1.1; 2.21, 51–56, 92; 7.3; 9.1; 12.2; 13.4; 18.14; 20.2; 32.16–18; 21.1, 3, 7, 9–10, 30, 35–37; 28.2–3; 26.4; 43.25–26, 34–38
Negative Examples	1.1; 2.10, 49–51, 57–70, 79–86; 18.15, 22; 19.2; 20; 21.9; 32.17; 42.24; 43.26; *Carm.* 2.1.11–12
The Love of the Poor	14; 18.20–21; 19.11; 21.10; 40.34; 43.9, 34–35, 60–61, 63; *Carm.* 2.1.12.460–461
Biblical Formation for Pastoral Ministry	2.26, 95–97, 102–115; 33.16; 36.8; 39.18–19; 43.26, 65; *Carm.* 2.1.12.552–553; 2.1.12.608–609
The Distribution of the Word	1.6; 2.35; 6.5; 12.1; 18.3; 19.1–2; 21.7, 11–25, 31; 34.2; 26.5; 36.2; 42.4, 8, 12–13; 43.35, 65; *Carm.* 2.1.12.116–17; *Ep.* 171.3
Eucharistic Celebration	2.95–96; 3.4; 15.5; 17.20; 18.22, 39; 30.16; 25.2; 36.2; 40.31; 42.24; *Ep.* 171
The Administration of the Trinity	1.7; 2.22, 35–40; 3.6; 6.11–15, 22; 11.6; 12.1, 6; 13.4; 18.16, 37; 22.13; 32.23; 33.15; 21.13–37; 27.9; 25.11, 15–19; 36.10; 42.8, 13–18; 43.30, 33–34, 43, 46, 66–68, 72; *Carm.* 1.1.1–5; 1.1.7–9; 2.1.12.116–118

Index of Citations to the Works of Gregory Nazianzen

Orations

1–3   61 n.221, 190, 236–237
1   59
1.1   249, 251 n.61, 253 n.73
1.2–4   120
1.2   150 n.137, 178, 249–250
1.4   150 n.137
1.5   120, 122 n.36, 137
1.6   240–241, 264
1.7   190, 194 n.18, 217, 218 n.101, 241 n.23, 267 n.113
2   12, 196 n.27, 321 n.283, 321 n.287
2.3   241, 248
2.4   216 n.91, 241
2.5   95
2.7   74 n.29
2.10   244, 254
2.14–15   69 n.18
2.14   249
2.15   249
2.16–22   83 n.66
2.16   241–243, 246
2.17–21   244
2.17   81 n.58, 99 n.134, 243
2.21   252
2.22   121 n.30, 243 n.29, 270
2.23–26   239
2.23–24   119 n.24, 147 n.123
2.23   127, 229 n.147
2.24   195 n.23
2.25–26   240
2.26   260
2.27   243 n.30
2.28–29   245
2.29   196 n.25
2.30–33   245–246
2.33   247
2.35–36   266–267
2.34   248
2.35–36   272
2.35   196 n.25, 263, 266
2.36–40   267 n.113
2.36–38   190–191, **206**, 209 n.64
2.36   188, 219 n.104
2.37   196 n.26
2.38   219–220, 267
2.39–42   245
2.39   75 n.37, 180, 246, 250
2.44   246
2.45   245
2.47   249
2.48   249

362 INDEX OF CITATIONS TO THE WORKS OF GREGORY NAZIANZEN

2.49–50   253
2.50   248
2.51–52   251
2.51   254
2.52   196 n.25
2.53–56   252
2.57–70   253
2.71   75 n.37
2.73   88 n.81
2.74   94 n.103, 95, 99 n.132, 100 n.140, 101 n.142
2.75   103
2.76   95, 104 n.152
2.77   94 n.103
2.78   241
2.79–86   253
2.83–85   254
2.87   12 n.31, 157 n.14
2.91   249 n.55
2.92   65 n.6, 251
2.95–96   259, 264 n.103
2.97   261
2.98   137 n.87, 149 n.133
2.99   236 n.3, 260
2.102–109   264
2.103   74 n.27
2.106   195 n.23
2.110–115   263
2.111   241
2.113   254
3   12
3.1   120 n.30
3.4   264 n.104
3.6   188, 190, 209 n.64, 226, 267 n.113
3.7   12, 188 n.2, 196 n.25, 240
4–5   12, 61 n.221, 72, 76 n.42
4.11   69 n.15
4.18   196 n.25
4.19   137 n.87
4.37   137 n.87
4.44   111–112
4.67   136 n.84, 137 n.87
4.71   120 n.30
4.92   12 n.31
4.100   264
4.113   73

4.115   196 n.27
4.117   196 n.27
4.121   196 n.27
5.31   196 n.27
5.36   137 n.87
5.39   12 n.33
6   13, 163 n.34, 190–191, 216 n.91, 236–238, 321
6.1–2   248 n.50
6.1   69 n.15, 109, 250
6.2   245 n.38
6.4–5   223 n.126
6.4   149 n.133, 191 n.10
6.5–6   88 n.84
6.5   264
6.6   72 n.21, 111 n.180
6.7   111
6.8   195 n.23, 196 n.25
6.9   250
6.10   111 n.180
6.11–15   267 n.113
6.11–13   191 n.10
6.11   188
6.12–15   230 n.151
6.12   95
6.13   221 n.114
6.19   248 n.48
6.20   249 n.53
6.22   13, 101 n.143, 184 n.94, 188 n.2, 191, 206 n.53, 214 n.85, 218 n.99, 219 n.104, 221 n.108, 223 n.129, 227 n.146, 230
6.32–33   112 n.185
7   7, 61 n.221
7.1   74 n.27
7.3   241, 243, 248 n.50, 251 nn.61,64
7.4   6, 195 n.23
7.6   7
7.7   216 n.91
7.9   72
7.15   74 n.27
7.17   69 n.15, 82 n.60, 105, 106 n.164, 197 n.32
7.18   191 n.11
7.21   79, 82–83
7.22   118

7.23   81 n.56, 120, 137 n.87
7.24   195 n.23
8   7, 61 n.221
8.5   248 n.50
8.9   150 n.137
8.14   85–86, 137 n.87
8.18   264
8.19   106
8.20   87
8.23   106 n.162, 150 n.137, 191 n.11
9–12   15, **157–160**, 237
9   61 n.221
9.1–2   69 n.15
9.1   65 n.4, 157, 250, 251 n.61
9.2   104 n.155, 250
9.3   242
9.4   241 n.18
9.5–6   243 n.29, 247 n.44
9.6   146 n.122
10.1   74 n.27, 158
10.2–4   158–159
10.3   158
10.4   158
11.3   159
11.4–5   72 n.21
11.4   75–76, 83 n.63, 84 n.67
11.5   119 n.22, 121 n.34, 157
11.6   15, 105 n.158, 111 n.180, 153, 157, 188 n.3, 189 n.5, 191 n.11, 267 n.113
11.7   139 n.95
12   61 n.221, 250 n.60
12.1–3   15
12.1   153, 158, 191 n.11, 218 n.97, 250, 264, 267 n.113
12.2   241 n.18, 251 n.64
12.3   82 n.60, 159, 250
12.4   15, 74 n.31, 104 n.152, 105 n.158, 137 n.87, 159, 240 n.17
12.5   159, 249
12.6   157 n.11, 159–160, 188 n.3, 191 n.11, 196, 197 n.32, 198 n.33, 267 n.113
13   15, 61 n.218
13.4   15, 158 n.17, 160 n.22, 188 n.3, 191 n.11, 241 n.18, 244 n.33, 247 n.44, 250 n.60, 251 n.64, 269 n.121
14   14, 238, **254–258**
14.2   137
14.3   139 n.94
14.4   74 n.31, 109, 137 n.87
14.6–8   81–82
14.7   82, 131 n.66
14.9   195 n.23, 227 n.146
14.12   265 n.106
14.14   150 n.137, 175 n.64
14.15   126, 137 n.87
14.18   81, 150 n.137, 243 n.30
14.21   150 n.138
14.23   84, 119 n.22, 120 n.27
14.24   196 n.25
14.27   154, 173
14.30   96 n.116, 97 n.118
14.32   94 n.103, 100 n.138
14.33   111
14.37   72 n.21, 243 n.30
15   13
15.1   69 n.15, 137 n.87
15.2   111 n.180
15.5   265 n.106
15.11   139 n.94
15.12   188 n.3, 222, 248 n.50
16–17   16, 321 n.283
16.1   160 n.22
16.2   71, 87, 116 n.1, 157 n.14
16.9   106 n.162, 191 n.11
16.11–12   150 n.137
16.13   240–241
16.18–19   196 n.25
16.20   248
17.1   111 n.180
17.2   160 n.22
17.3   111 n.180
17.4   101 n.141
17.6   160 n.22
17.7   104 n.155
17.8   104 n.152, 106 n.165, 191 n.11
17.9   111 n.180, 195 n.23
17.12   75 n.35, 137 n.87, 139 nn. 92–93

364   INDEX OF CITATIONS TO THE WORKS OF GREGORY NAZIANZEN

17.14   101
17.15   260 n.88
17.20   264 n.103
18   61 n.221, 237, 251 n.64
18.1   196 n.25, 240 n.16, 250 n.60
18.3   75 n.35, 196 n.25, 250 n.60, 264 n.98
18.4   82 n.61, 150 n.137, 242
18.5–43   5 n.6
18.5   6
18.6–7   5, 242 n.25
18.11   6
18.12   316 n.265
18.13   87, 246 n.43
18.14   65 n.4, 251 n.61
18.15   246, 250 n.56, 254
18.16   94, 94 n.103, 191 n.11, 209 n.64, 219 n.104, 221 nn.110–111, 266 n.110, 269 n.121
18.17   196 n.28, 198 n.33
18.20–21   196 n.25, 257
18.20   195 n.23
18.22–23   246
18.22   254, 264 n.104
18.28   125 n.49, 139 n.94
18.29   160 n.22
18.31   8–9
18.35, 37   16
18.36   160 n.22, 183 n.93, 196 n.25, 250 n.60
18.37   241 n.22, 266 n.110, 269 n.121
18.39   264 n.103
18.40   250 n.60
19.1   150 n.137, 264 n.98
19.2   160 n.22, 250, 254 n.75, 263
19.6–7   245 n.38
19.6   69, 84
19.8   84
19.9   243 n.29
19.10   116 n.1, 241
19.11   256 n.84, 258 n.87
19.12–13   137 n.87
19.12   183 n.93, 195 n.24
19.13   127 n.54
19.17   188 n.3, 191 n.11, 218 n.97

20   35, 191, 217 n.95, 231, 252 n.68
20.1–4   35, 64–65, 69 n.15, 248 n.50
20.1   104 n.152, 105 n.158, 196 n.27
20.2   65 n.4, 251 n.61
20.4   68, 75 n.35, 84 n.70, 126 n.51, 139 n.94
20.5–12   35, 191
20.5–6   209 n.64
20.5   84, 88 n.81, 188 n.3, 196 n.27, 219 n.104, 231
20.6–7   206, 218 n.99, 219–220
20.6   207 n.59, 216 n.91, 223 n.127
20.7   205 n.52, 207–208, 213, 221 n.111, 221 nn.114,118, 227 n.146, 232
20.8–11   200 n.40, 223 n.130
20.8–10   116 n.1
20.8–9   224 n.133
20.8   224 n.131
20.9   99–100, 224 nn.132,134
20.10–11   214 n.85
20.10   104 n.155
20.11   98 n.124
20.12   70–71, 75 n.35, 105 n.158, 109, 196 n.27, 227, 230–232
21   8, 37, 50, 237, 252 n.68, **277–281**
21.1–2   104 n.152, 118
21.1   84 n.70, 104–105, 106–107, 252 n.66
21.2   120 n.30
21.3   251 n.61
21.6   109
21.7   158, 241 n.21, 250 n.60, 251–252, 266
21.8   266
21.9   250 n.60, 251, 254 n.75
21.10   196 n.25, 196 n.27, 197 n.32, 251, 257
21.11   266
21.12   196 n.27
21.13–37   38, 268
21.13   160, 192, 209 n.64, 219 n.104, 220, 221 nn.108,112
21.18   195 n.23
21.19–21   109 n.174
21.23   222 n.120

INDEX OF CITATIONS TO THE WORKS OF GREGORY NAZIANZEN 365

21.24 139 n.93
21.25 220
21.30 251
21.31 266
21.33–34 157 n.11
21.33 160, 192, 218 nn.97, 101, 246 n.42
21.34 196 n.25, 298
21.35–37 251
21.35 188 n.2, 192, 196 n.25
21.36 246
21.37 189 n.5
22 35, 163 n.34, 191–192, 216 n.91, 238
22.1–2 35
22.6 99 n.132
22.7 111 n.180
22.8 35
22.9 100 n.139, 196 n.27
22.11 111
22.12 35, 188, 189 n.5, 191, 209 n.64, 217, 218 n.101, 219 n.104, 220
22.13 35, 119 n.23, 127, 137, 139 n.94, 269 n.121
22.14 191, 230
22.15–16 35
23 35 n.112, 37, 192, 216 n.91, 238
23.1–3 37
23.3–5 192
23.3 184 n.94, 192, 196 nn.27–28, 198 n.33
23.6–12 191–192
23.6–11 198 n.33
23.6–8 206 nn.53–54
23.6–7 207 n.59
23.6 209 n.64, 215, 217, 219 n.104
23.7–13 37
23.7 211
23.8 106, 208–209, 212 n.75, 215–216, 221, 224 n.132, 282
23.9–11 200 n.40, 223 n.130, 224 n.130
23.9 126 n.51, 224 n.131
23.10 184 n.94
23.11–13 **228–230**
23.11 69 n.14, 214 n.85, 223 n.129, 232 n.162

23.12 183 n.93, 196 nn.28–29, 217 n.95, 218 n.101, 232 n.160, 239 n.14
23.13–14 226 n.141
23.13 163 n.34, 184 n.94
24 36, 237, 251 n.64
24.2 137 n.87
24.4 150 n.137
24.7 111 n.180
24.10 137 n.87
24.13 192 n.13, 195 n.23, 209 n.64, 219 n.104, 221 n.110
24.15 100 n.140
24.16 222
24.19 101 n.141, 105 n.158
25–26 **73–74**
25 40, 193
25.1 40 n.130, 111 n.180
25.2–3 40, 73
25.2 116 n.1, 120 n.30, 264 n.104, 265
25.4–7 72–73
25.5 157 n.14, 195 n.23
25.8 189 n.5, 198 n.33
25.11 268 n.116
25.13–19 73
25.15–19 191, 193, 230, 267
25.15–18 40, 194 n.17, 200 n.40, 213 n.82
25.15–16 **202–205**, 206 n.53, 211, 314 n.250, 316
25.15 166 n.42, 168 n.47, 196 nn.27,29
25.16–17 223 n.130
25.16 105 n.158, 121 n.32, 164 n.36, 205 n.52, 207 n.59, 214–216, 222, 224 n.132, 315 n.252
25.17–18 188 n.3
25.17 68–69, 95, 102, 189, 196 n.28, 198 n.33, 212, 221, 224 n.131
25.18 116 n.1, 207 n.59, 208 n.63, 220 n.105
26 41, 321 n.283
26.1, 3 41
26.1–2 158 nn.16,18
26.1 248 n.48

26.4–6   41
26.4   251 n.61
26.5   197 n.32, 198 n.34, 264 n.98
26.6   137 n.87
26.7   126 n.51, 127 n.54
26.9–13   41, 73–74
26.11   196 n.25
26.12   139 nn.91–92,94
26.13   81
26.14–19   41
26.19   97, 105 n.158, 189 n.5,
    218 nn.97,99, 221 n.113,
    222 n.120
27–31 (*Theological Orations*)
    3, **39–40**, 88, **183–186**, 190,
    193, 196–197, 218 n.101,
    231, 272, 293
27–28   65, 102
27   88, 231 n.153, 321 n.283
27.1–3   184
27.3   **67–68**, 73, 75 n.35, 83,
    109–110, 196 n.26, 198 n.33, 247
    nn.44,46
27.4   71, 196 n.27, 198 n.34
27.5–6   247 n.44
27.5   111 n.180, 184 n.94
27.6–7   77
27.6   82, 196 n.27, 198 n.33
27.7   71, 74 n.27, 131 n.66, 196 n.27
27.8   110 n.175, 111
27.9   267 n.111, 272
27.9   96 n.116, 196 n.27
27.10   198 n.34
28   224 n.131
28.1–3   198 n.33, 231 n.153
28.1   88, 186, 191, 193, 196
    nn.26–27, 197
28.2–3   65, 87–88, 101, 109, 251
28.2   **66–67**, 184, 196 n.27, 197 n.32
28.3   **90–93**, 96 n.115, 103–104,
    107, 113, 115, 131 n.66, 218 n.97,
    222 n.124, 223 n.127, 231 n.155,
    293 n.121, 308 n.218
28.4   94, 94 n.105, 97, 99, 116 n.1,
    196 n.27
28.5   97, 98 n.121

28.6   98 n.121, 112
28.7   99 n.132, 100, 112, 196 n.27
28.8   100 n.136
28.9   100
28.10   100
28.11   94
28.12   99 nn.130,132, 100
28.13   112
28.16   112
28.17   98, 104 n.157, 105–106,
    112 n.186
28.18–21   96 n.116
28.18   97
28.19   98
28.20   97, 116 n.1
28.21   97, 100
28.22–31   293 n.120
28.22   131 n.66
28.23   196 n.25
28.28   111, 168
28.31   94–95, 99, 104 nn.152–154,
    218 n.101, 231
29–31   200 n.40, 206 n.53
29.2   106 n.163, 168 n.47, **215–216**,
    220 n.105, 221
29.3–16   223 n.130
29.3   206 n.55, 224 n.132, 282
29.4   224 nn.131–132
29.5   224 n.132,135
29.6–8   224 n.134
29.8   116 n.1, 214 n.85
29.9   224 n.135
29.10   196 n.27
29.11   99 n.132, 101 n.141
29.12   223 n.127
29.13   224 n.132, 229 n.148
29.15   210 nn.69–70, 214 n.84
29.16   206, 229 n.148
29.17–21   121
29.17   133 n.71, 151
29.18   123, **132–135**, 139–140, 142,
    148–149, 182, 195 n.24,
    200, 207, 296–297
29.19–20   136, 239
29.19   99 n.132, 102 n.147, 121, 123,
    128, 129, 131–132, 144, 148, 163

INDEX OF CITATIONS TO THE WORKS OF GREGORY NAZIANZEN 367

29.21   112, 227 n.143, 312 n.241
30   121, 136, **140–142**
30.1   126 n.51, 132 n.74, 139–140, 147 n.124, 182
30.2   132 n.74, 138–140, 144 n.114, 182
30.3   121, 146
30.4   121, 126 n.51
30.5   127 n.54, 138,-139, 140 nn.98, 102, 147 n.124
30.6   84 n.67, 121, 138, 147, 232 n.160
30.7   126 n.51, 206–207, 210 n.69, 211 n.74, 214 n.84
30.8   140, 142
30.9–12   207 n.57
30.9   127 n.54, 140 n.97
30.10   140 n.97
30.11   195 n.23
30.12   126 n.51, 138, 140 nn.98, 102, 219 n.102
30.13   140 n.97
30.15   136 n.84, 140 n.98, 207 n.57
30.16   140, 142, 206 n.55, 207 n.57, 265
30.17–21   141, 198, 260
30.17   94 n.103, 95–97, 99 n.127, 100 n.133, 103 n.149, 196 n.27, 197 n.32
30.19   195 nn.23–24
30.20   75 n.35, 84, 109, 131, 207 n.57, 223, 313 n.247
30.21   121 n.34, 127 n.54, 131 n.70, 140 nn.97–98, 147–149, 248 n.49
31   **164–165, 167–168**
31.1–3   157 n.11, 183
31.1   65 n.4, 134, 165, 183
31.2   166 n.43
31.3   104 n.152, 159 n.21, 164, **165–166**, 180, 184, 188 n.2, 196 n.26, **197–198**, 227
31.4–20   223 n.130
31.4   167, 174, 221 n.108, 222 n.125, 224 n.132, 302 n.182
31.5   156 n.9, 159 n.21, 166, 188 n.2, 196 n.27, 202 n.43

31.6   173 n.61, 174, 188 n.2
31.7–11   95 n.113
31.7   100 n.140, 224 n.131
31.8–9   208
31.8   196 n.27, 198 n.33, 302 n.182
31.9–11   116 n.1
31.9   218 n.97, 219 nn.102,104, 221 n.108
31.10   94–95, 159 n.21, 164
31.12   137 n.87, 167, 174–175, 184, 219 n.104
31.14   175 n.66, 206 n.55, 207 n.58, 208 n.61, 211, 221 nn.108, 110, 112, 223 n.127, 313 n.247
31.16   196 n.27, 207 n.58, 223 n.127
31.17   175, 189 n.5, 220
31.18–19   221 n.108
31.19   229 n.148
31.20   116 n.1
31.21   165–166
31.22   95 n.113, 116 n.1
31.23   184, 312 n.241
31.24   116 n.1, 169
31.25–27   **169–173**, 184, 240
31.25   196 n.25
31.26–27   198 n.33
31.26   126 n.51, 148
31.28–29   126 n.51, **174–177**, 231 n.153
31.28   148, 159 n.21, 166 n.43, 221 nn.112,118
31.29   139 n.94, 165 n.40, 178, **180–181**, 223 n.127
31.30   182–184, 206 n.55, 207, 209 n.64, 219 n.104, 220 n.106, 221 n.119
31.31–33   95 n.113
31.32   107
31.33   116 n.1, 126 n.51, **185**, 197 n.32, 217, 218 n.101, 223 n.130
32   36, 163 n.22, 192, 216 n.91, 241 n.20, 252 n.68
32.4   241
32.5   36, 188 n.3, 191–192, 204 n.49, 218 n.99

32.6   177 n.71
32.7   111 n.180
32.9   131 n.66
32.10–13   241 n.21
32.11–13   36
32.12–13   248
32.12   69, 83 n.66
32.13   84–85
32.14   94 n.103, 95 n.113, 116 n.1
32.15–17   36
32.15   104 n.152, 105 n.158, 106, 150 n.135, 194 n.16
32.16–18   251 n.61
32.16   65 n.4, 101 n.146, 113 n.190
32.17   254 n.75
32.18   126 n.51
32.21   36, 188 n.3, 189, 192, 204 n.49, 218 nn.97, 99, 101
32.23–27   112
32.23   267 n.114
32.24–25   189
32.24   111 n.180
32.25   195 n.23
32.26   116 n.1
32.27   111 n.180
32.30   195 n.23
32.33   65 n.4, 137 n.87, 139 n.94
33   37, 192, 220 n.107
33.1–5   37
33.6–12   37
33.9   111 n.180, 137 n.87
33.13   33 n.108, 157 n.14, 158 n.18, 250 n.60
33.14   139
33.15   189 n.5, 231 n.154, 231 n.159, 267 n.114
33.16–17   37, 192
33.16   124 n.46, 159 n.21, 192, 209 n.64, 217 n.95, 218 n.101, 219 n.104, 220 n.107, 221 n.113, 222 n.120, 223 n.127, 260
33.17   166 n.42, 174, 177 n.70, 184 n.96, 227 n.145
34   37, 50, 192
34.2   263 n.95
34.3–4   196 n.25

34.6   99 n.132, 158 n.16, 188 nn.2–3, 189 n.5, 227 n.143
34.7   149 n.133
34.8–15   37, 191–192
34.8   94 n.106, 95 nn.111–113, 162, 177, 200 n.40, 209 n.64, 219 n.104
34.9   164 n.35, 183 n.93, 189 n.5, 218 nn.97, 101
34.10   127 n.54, 132 n.74, 137 n.85, 200 n.40, 223 n.130
34.11   157 n.11, 196 n.28, 198 n.33
34.12   174, 196 n.27
34.13–15   181 n.84
34.13   97 n.117, 197 n.31, 221 n.114, 222 n.120
34.14   164 n.35
34.15   196 nn.27–28, 198 n.33, 213, 221 n.112, 113, 118
36   42, 193
36.1–2   193
36.2   89, 264 n.103, 265
36.3   241 n.22
36.5   104 n.152, 119 n.24
36.8   111 n.180, 260, 263 n.94
36.10   69 n.15, 188 n.3, 193, 218, 219 n.104, 267
36.12   242 n.28
37   42–43, 193
37.1–4   150
37.1–3   123, 126, 137 n.88
37.1   247 n.44
37.2   95, 116 n.1, 121 n.30, 128–129, 131, 137, 144
37.3   65 n.4, 113 n.191
37.4   104 nn.151–153, 116 n.1, 126, 127 n.54, 129, 149 n.133
37.5   136 n.84, 193, 207
37.7–8   137 n.87
37.9–11, 17   74
37.14   74 n.27, 111 n.180
37.17   125
37.18   193
37.21   111 n.180
37.22   83, 193, 209 n.64, 219 n.104, 221 nn.112, 119, 244

INDEX OF CITATIONS TO THE WORKS OF GREGORY NAZIANZEN 369

37.23 34 n.111
38–40 (*Epiphany Series*) **43**, 102, 121, 193
38 59, 69, 321 n.283, 321 n.287
38.1 137 n.87
38.1–4 123
38.1, 4–6 65
38.2–4 120
38.2 125 n.50, 149–150
38.3 121 n.34, 148 n.131
38.4–5 76
38.4 84–85, 150
38.5–6 123
38.7–11 **117–118**
38.7–9 191, 193
38.7–8 96, 99 n.125
38.7 69 n.15, 84, 95–97, **102–103**, 105 n.158, 119 n.22, 121 n.34, 123, 147, 200 n.40, 223 n.130, 232
38.8 101 n.143, 195 n.24, 198, 207 n.59, 218 n.97, 222 n.124, 223 n.127
38.9 94 n.106, 104 n.153, 106, 131 n.66, 299 n.156
38.10 106
38.11 80–82, 99, 105 n.158, 106, 121 n.34, 195 n.23
38.12–13 99 n.132
38.12 82, 119
38.13–15 191, 193
38.13–14 137
38.13 83–84, 121, 124, 126, 129, 131, 144, 148, 178, 207–208, 290 n.108, 315
38.14 148, 195 n.24
38.15–16 136 n.84
38.15 140 n.98, 141 n.103, 142, 206 n.55, 207 n.59, 210 n.69, 219 n.104
38.16 43 n.137, 121 n.35, 151 n.141, 164 n.36
38.18 95 n.113, 150, 226
39 69, 321 n.283
39.1–7 76
39.1–6 86
39.1–2 106 n.164, 108

39.1 43 n.137, 76–77, 84 n.67, 104 nn.156,161, 125 n.49, 137 n.87
39.2 88 n.82
39.7 111 n.180
39.8–10 **69–71**, 83, 89, 107
39.8 85, 99 n.130, 101 n.141, 109
39.9 65 n.4, 75 n.35, 104, 232 n.160
39.10 119 n.18
39.11–12 191, 193, 222 n.124, 223 n.127
39.11 71 n.18, 88, 116 n.1, 209 n.64, 219 n.104
39.12 94 n.106, 95 n.108, 137 n.87, 157 n.11, 168 n.47, 188 n.2, 204 n.49, 218 n.99, 223 n.130, 224 n.132
39.13 94 n.103, 99 n.130, 100 n.140, 113, 117 n.10, 118, 123 n.42, 126, 139, 147 n.125
39.14–16 150 n.137
39.14 69 n.15, 196 n.25, 248 n.50
39.15 195 n.23
39.16 121 n.33, 144, 178
39.17–19 76 n.43
39.18–19 260
39.17 119 n.18, 139 n.94, 175
39.18 88
39.19 82
39.20 106, 110, 151, 227, 231
40 108 n.169
40.1 88 n.82
40.2 137 n.87
40.3–4 75 n.35, 86 n.74
40.3 108
40.4 85, 177
40.5–6 232 n.160
40.5 **103–106**, 108–109, 111 n.180, **117**, 218 n.97, 231
40.6 148
40.7–8 82 n.62, 84 n.67, 86
40.7 95 n.112
40.8 117 n.10, 121 n.34
40.10 121 n.34
40.11–40 75 n.35
40.11 86 n.75
40.13 84 n.71

40.16–17   231 n.154
40.16   121 n.34, 231
40.17–18   86
40.18   196 n.25
40.20   137
40.24, 26   85 n.73
40.26   260
40.27   84
40.30   150
40.31   71–72, 86–87, 264 n.104
40.33   123 n.41, 146, 148 n.130
40.34   85, 87, 191, 193, 197,
       227 n.146, 255
40.36   82 n.60
40.37   104 n.152, 107, 109 n.172,
       111 nn.180–181
40.38–40   82–83
40.39–40   72 n.21
40.41–45   191, 193
40.41   99 n.125, 104 n.153, 107,
       188 n.3, 207 n.59, 218,
       231 nn.158–159
40.42–43   200 n.40
40.42   121 n.34, 175, 196 n.27,
       223 n.130
40.43–45   204 n.49
40.43   157 n.14, 206 n.53, 210 n.70,
       214
40.44   175, 196 n.25, 230 n.150, 231,
       240 n.16
40.45   65 n.4, 82, 83 n.63, 89–90, 111
       n.180, 119, 123 n.41,
       136 n. 84, 148 n.129, 218, 229
       n.148
41   38, 58, 155 n.5, 192, 223 n.130, 321,
       321 n.287
41.1   82
41.4–5   137 n.87
41.4   126 n.51
41.5   82, 163, 173, 195 n.23, 297
41.6–8   183 n.91
41.6   163–164, 196 n.25
41.7–9   191–192
41.7–8   116 n.1, 157 n.11, 184 n.94
41.7   163, 200 n.40
41.8   164, 184

41.9   163, 174, 177 n.72, 178,
       206 nn.53,55, 207 n.58,
       222 n.125, 223 n.127
41.10   230 n.150
41.11   158, **172–173**, 174, 178 n.76,
       195 n.24, 200
41.12   84 n.69, 158, 163, 164 n.36
41.14   158, 163, 164 n.35, 174,
       178 n.76, 181 n.84
41.18   82
42   **54–58**, 238
42.1–3   57
42.1   158 n.18, 195 n.23
42.3   189 n.5
42.6   57, 111 n.180, 202 n.43
42   252 n.68
42.4   264
42.8   264, 267 n.114
42.9–12   57
42.11   157 n.11, 181
42.12   82, 158 n.18, 250 n.60, 264
42.13–18   267
42.13   157 n.14, 196 n.25, 263 n.95
42.14–18   55, 58, 191, 193
42.14   196 n.25
42.15   200 n.40, 205 n.52, 206
       nn.53,55, 207, 210 n.70, 218
       nn.97,99, 221 n.113, 222 n.120,
       223 nn.127,130, 229
42.16   116 n.1, 209 n.64, 218 n.97, 219
       n.104, 221 nn.114, 118, 119, 231
42.17   119, 200 n.40, 223 n.130
42.18   48 n.160, 95 n.113, 116 n.1, 219
       n.104, 231
42.19   34 n.111
42.20–22   57
42.22   55 n.190
42.24   57, 196 n.25, 240 n.16,
       254 n.75, 264 n.103
42.25   58 n.200
42.26–27   56–58
42.27   188 n.3, 195 n.23
43   **54–56**, 237, 252 n.68, 295
43.2   33 n.107, 34 n.110, 74 n.27, 82
43.9   72 n.21, 257
43.11   116 n.1, 264

INDEX OF CITATIONS TO THE WORKS OF GREGORY NAZIANZEN 371

43.12   109
43.13-14   7
43.13   116 n.1
43.15   116 n.1
43.16–22   56
43.19–20   72
43.25   195 n.23, 251
43.26   250, 251 n.64, 252, 253 n.74, 260
43.30   189 n.5, 209 n.64, 219 n.104, 221 n.112, 222 n.120, 268
43.31–32   13
43.33   268
43.34–38   251 n.64
43.34–35   257
43.34   268 n.119
43.35   255
43.37   158 n.18, 159 n.19, 250 n.60
43.38   148 n.130
43.39   196 n.25
43.43   109, 268
43.46   268
43.48–50   269
43.49–50   13 n.35
43.59   159 n.19
43.60   257
43.61   137 n.87, 257
43.63   14, 246, 257
43.64   137 n.87, 139
43.65   116 n.1, 159 n.19, 260–261, 266
43.66–69   198 n.33, 268–269
43.66   196 n.26, 243 n.29, 270
43.67–69   159 n.19, 161, 196 n.28
43.67–68   188 n.2
43.67   180 n.80, 197 n.32
43.68–69   58 n.201, 116 n.1, 196 n.25
43.69   140 n.94, 196 n.29, 198 n.34
43.72   89 n.83, 268
43.73   159 n.19
43.81   196 nn.25,27, 197 n.32
43.82   105 n.158
44   59
44.2   127 n.54, 137 n.87
44.3   104 nn.151–153,158
44.4   104 n.156, 139 nn.92, 94

44.6   82, 111 n.180
44.7   127 n.54, 137 n.87
44.8   69
44.9   72 n.21, 74 n.27, 123
45   59
45.1   137 n.87, 150 n.137
45.2   104, 125 n.49
45.3   69 n.15, 95
45.4   195 n.24, 198
45.5   119 n.18
45.7   195 n.23, 195 n.23
45.8–9   99 n.132
44.9   196 n.25, 315
45.11–12   99 n.132
45.11   65 n.4, 69 n.15, 84 n.69, 100 n.140, 101
45.12   172 n.55, 195 n.23
45.13–14   84
45.13   127 n.54, 139 nn.94,96
45.19   139 n.94
45.22–25   150 n.137
45.22   139 n.94, 148 n.129, 195 nn.23–24
45.23   195 n.23
45.25   140 n.98
45.26–29   127 n.54
45.26   126 n.52, 195 n.24
45.27   137 n.85, 140 n.98, 206 n.55
45.28–29   139
45.28   147
45.30   82, 139 n.94
45.28   119 n.17, 119 n.23
45.45   99 n.132

Poems

1.1.1–5, 7–9 (*Poemata Arcana*)   3–4, 55, 193–194, 267 n.111, 272
1.1.1–3   223 n.130
1.1.1.1–24   65, 180
1.1.1.1–6   224 n.131
1.1.1.8b-15   69 n.15
1.1.1.11–13   65 n.4
1.1.1.25–39   218 n.99

1.1.1.28–29   223 n.128
1.1.2   124 n.43, 218 n.99
1.1.2.13–17   224 n.131
1.1.2.18–27   224 n.132
1.1.2.34–35   223 n.127
1.1.2.36–38   223 n.128
1.1.2.47   121 n.34
1.1.2.57   126
1.1.2.60–61   126
1.1.2.62–75   136 n.84
1.1.3   218 n.99
1.1.3.1–4   175
1.1.3.3–4   164 n.36, 226
1.1.3.13–14   175
1.1.3.17–33   172 n.55
1.1.3.43   221 n.110
1.1.3.47–53   231 n.159
1.1.3.47   86
1.1.3.60, 72   221 n.110
1.1.3.74   221 n.112
1.1.3.75, 78   221 n.110
1.1.4.32–34   104 n.157
1.1.6.77   139 n.94
1.1.7.55–64   119 n.24
1.1.8.1–3   104 n.157
1.1.8.70–77   119 n.18
1.1.10   124 n.43
1.1.10.6–9   138
1.1.10.22   138
1.1.10.26   144
1.1.10.50–51   144
1.1.11.9   121 n.34
1.1.26.17   196 n.25
1.1.32.13–18   104 n.152
1.2.1.189–526   74
1.2.2.560–561   118 n.14
1.2.10.142   106 n.164
630   120 n.30
946–960   104 n.156, 105 n.158
972f   69 n.15
1.2.14.91   139 n.94
1.2.17.1–2   120 n.30
1.2.33.88–90   120 n.30
1.2.34.190   139 n.94
2.1.1 (*De rebus suis*)
195–212   9 n.22, 107 n.167

96–97   8
194f   232 n.160
202   9 n.24
213   105 n.158
307–321   8
630–632   106 n.164
2.1.11 (*De vita sua*)   **54**, 61 n.221, 238,
252 n.68

51–551   56
64   6
68–92   6
72–82   33 n.108
95–100   6
112–113   8
121–209   8 n.16
64   8
157   188 n.2
198   8
229–232   9
239   10, 61 n.219
261   72 n.23
276   9 n.18
270   72
300–311   74 n.31
321–324   72
337   11
345   11
512f   61 n.219
574–578   57
576   51 n.171
592–599   57
596   33 n.108
607–631   33
616–618   145n.116
631–651   132 n.72
651   141 n.103
665   36 n.119
753   104 n.152
728–1112   40 n.131
758   73 n.26
810–814   37
887–902   41
905–912   41
1030   78 n.26
1100   41
1127–1128   57

1140   57
1180   50 n.166
1218–1224   72 n.21
1311–1312   30, 41
1325–1391   42
1414   57
1424   57
1434   57
1441–1484   57
1466–1474   37
1506–1918   44 n.140
1506   46
1506–1508   57
1512–1524   251 n.64
1513   45 nn.145,148
1522–1523   49 n.163
1525–1534   46
1525   45 n.148
1545–1571   254 n.75
1546–1549   264
1546–1547   46
1560–1561   57
1566–1569   46
1576–1577   47
1578   46
1583–1588   47
1591–1679   47
1591–1595   57
1603   139 n.94
1645–1653   254
1645–1647   57
1680–1702   47
1704–1743   48
1703–1709   49, 53
1712–1718   49, 254 n.75
1724–1732   49
1736–1741   49 n.163
1737–1738   49
1738–1739   48
1745   50
1750–1754   49
1755   53
1756   49
1760   49
1766   49
1774–1776   49

1777   50
1781–1795   50
1798–1808   50
1800–1811   50 n.169
1800   48 n.159
1810–1817   51
1827–1855   51, 55
1845   57 n.198
1866–1867   57
1879–1904   51
1919–1920   62
2.1.12 (*De seipso et de episcopis*)   **54**, 238, 252 n.68
18   241 n.22
35–48   254 n.75
77–78   33 n.107
103   36 n.119
116–118   264, 267 n.114
125–134   50
331–454   254 n.75
355–356   240
460–461   257 n.85
475–574   248 n.50
476–478   249
541–574   248
552–553   259
608–609   259
751–760   242–243
775   249 n.53
2.1.13–14   81 n.59
2.1.13.35   139 n.94
2.1.14   81
2.1.15.11   36 n.119
2.1.19.61–74   33 n.109
2.1.19.101–102 59 n.209
2.1.28–29   81 n.59
2.1.30.125   36 n.119
2.1.33.12   36 n.119
2.1.36.7   104 n.152
2.1.39   56 n.197
2.1.40   81 n.59
2.1.45   81 n.59
2.1.50   81 n.59
2.1.45 (*Carmen lugubre*)   16
191–269   9 nn.22–23
257–263   108 n.170

261–263   232 n.160
2.1.60.9   139 n.94
2.1.87.15f   105 n.158
2.2.3.286   105 n.158
2.2.66–102   16 n.48

Letters

6   7
6.3   120 n.30
7   12
8.3   195 n.23
8.4   13
10   7
11   13
16–19   13
19   7
30   7
50.8   61 n.219
52–53   61
58   15, 297
58.7   196
58.8   196 n.28
58.11–12   196 n.25
58.14   196 nn.25,28
77   36
79.9   196 n.25
87.5   51 n.170
101–102, 202 (*Christological Epistles*)
    59–60
101   144, 318
101.12   146
101.13–14   124
101.13, 15   129
101.13   132 n.71
101.14–15   136 n.84
101.16–17   136
101.16   129
101.17   130
101.18–19   137
101.18   130

101.20–21   136, 312 n.242
101.21   144
101.22   130–131
101.23–25   137
101.23   129
101.25   129
101.28   131
101.29   144 n.114
101.32   127–128
101.36–45   290
101.36–39   145
101.37   145
101.38   178 n.75
101.46   121 n.34, 144 n.114
101.49   99 n.132
101.50–55   127
101.51–52   83, 290
101.51   119 n.24, 139
101.56   99 n.132
101.59   195 n.23
102.1   188 n.2
102.2   160
102.4   124, 129, 131
102.7   196 n.27
102.18–20   146
102.28   140 n.98
110.59   195 n.24
115   59 n.209
119   74 n.27
121   59 n.209
130–133   59
135–136   59
138   59 n.209
139.1   195 n.23
162.4   196 n.25
171   265
202.10   195 n.24
202.15–16   142 n.109
204.8   195 n.23
215.1–2   195 n.23
221.2, 6   195 n.23
238.1   195 n.23

General Index

Aaron, 66, 159, 251 n.61, 263
Abramowski, Luise, 166 n.43, 274 n.6, 275 n.12
Acacius of Beroea, 47 n.155
Acacius of Caesarea in Cappadocia, 18, 21, 23, 279, 315 n.256
Acholius of Thessalonica, 30 n.92, 32 n.103, 47 n.154, 48 n.159, 50 n.166
Adam, 82, 119–120, 147, 150–151, 241, 256, 299
adoptionism. *See under* Christ
Aetius, 21–23, 92 n.98, 124, 219 n.102, 315 n.256
ἀγέννητος/ἀγεννησία (unbegotten/ness), of God, 21, 23, **91–93**, 204, 293
αἰτία/αἴτιος (cause). *See* Trinity: monarchy of God the Father
Alexander of Alexandria, 17–18, 310
Alexander of Constantinople, 42
Alexandria/Alexandrians/ Egyptians, 37–38, 40–42, 45 n.145, 46–47, 50–51,
 53, 73, 160–161, 192–193, 278, 282–283, 319–320
 ecclesiastical status of, 43–44, 52–54
 theological tradition of, 68, 78, 195, 284
Althaus, Heinz, viii n.4, 108 n.168, 116 n.3, 119 n.24
Alypius, husband of Gorgonia, 14
almsgiving. *See* poor: care for the
Ambrose of Milan, 32 n.103, 237, 284 n.61, 322
Ammianus Marcellinus, 12 n.32
Amphilochius the Elder, Gregory's uncle, 7
Amphilochius of Iconium, Gregory's cousin, 7, 27, 30 n.90, 45, 54, 166–167, 252, 265, 321
Anastasia, Church of the, 34, 36, 39, 41, 50, 57–59, 69
 hostility against, 36–37
angels, 80–81, 91, 99 n.129, 101 n. 143, 104, 117, 148, 158, 230, 298–299, 322
Annisa, Basil's family estate, 10 n.26

Anomoian(s). *See* Heterousians
Anthimus of Tyana, 14
anthropology. See body, creatureliness, soul, *sunthetos*/composition
Antioch/Antiochenes, 19, 21, 33 n.107, 46–50, 131, 138, 282, 296, 304–306
  ecclesiastical status of, 54
  Gregory's Christological opposition to, 60, 116, 128–129, 143, 146, 150
  Gregory's associations with, 16, 41, 43, 57
  schism in, 26–29, 31–33, 35, 45–51, 191–192, 280–283, 317, 319–320
  See also Council of Antioch 372; Diodore; Melitius of Antioch; Paulinus of Antioch
Apollinarius of Laodicea/Apollinarians, 27 n. 77, 29, 32–35, 45 n.145, 52, 59–60, 116, 127–129, 131–132, 137 n.86, 139, 143, 145–146, 150, 301, 309, 314 n.249, 318–319
  Basil of Caesarea and, 285, 291 n.107, 294 n.130
  Christological dispute with Diodore and Antiochenes, 33–35, 127, 286, 292
  Christology of, 285–289
  Gregory's Christology and, 281–282, **285–292**
  called the Spirit *homoousion*, 164 n.37
apophaticism, 98–102, 107, 113, 224, 308
  See also Trinity: technical clarification: negative
apostolic succession, 250 n.58, 266
ἀρχή (first principle, source). *See* Trinity: monarchy of God the Father
Aristotle, 68 n.11, 72, 169 n.48, 199, 242 n.27, 230, 302 n.175, 306

Arius/Arians, 18–21, 24, 26–27, 42–43, 45 n.148, 52, 60, 124, 134 n.81, 161, 192, 219 n.102, 278, 317
  Gregory's opposition to, 37, 206, 209, **219–220**, 291, 314, 316
  Semiarians, 22 n.64, 52
asceticism/ascetical theology, 150, 153, 155, 268, 271, 299, 320.
  See also philosophy
ascent to God, 66–67, 88, 90–91, 93, 96–97, 101, 109, 118
  through Christ, 148–150
  by the Holy Spirit, 185
  in the Trinity, 173, 187
  See also illumination; Moses; participation, *thoria*; *theosis*
Asian/Eastern churches and theological tradition, 10 n.27, 17–20, 22–27, 31, 44–47, 52–53, 218, 279, 282–283, 285, 294–295, **309–317**, 319–320. *See also* Basil of Ancyra; George of Laodicea; Eusebian theology; Homoiousians/ Melitius of Antioch
  pro-Nicene movement in Asia Minor, 11, 25–27, 29, 31, 158, 278
Asmus, J. R., 72 n.22
Asterius the Sophist, 17, 315
Athanasius, 10 n.27, 17–28, 29 n.88, 32 n.103, 42, 46, 52–53, 62 n.223, 81 n.56, 154, 215 n.89, 219 nn.102–103, 221 n.109, 291 n.110, 297, 299 n.164, 300, 310, 317, 322
  on divinization, 117, 119 n.21
  doubtful influence on Gregory, 8, 27, **277–283**, 285, 315–316
  Gregory claims legacy of, 160–162, 277–279, 283
  Gregory's panegyric for, 37–38, 118, 160–161, 220, 237, 251, 254, 257, 266, 268, **277–280**, 297

on the Holy Spirit, 154–156, 160–162
model of pastoral leadership, 246,
    251, 266, 268
on the monarchy of God the Father,
    213 n.81
on *oikonomia*, 195 n.22
as "theologian," 196 n.27
on the Trinity, compared with
    Gregory, 225–226, 294–295,
    314–316, 319–320
Augustine, compared with Gregory on:
the value of *paideia* for pastoral
    ministry, 253
Christological exegesis, 206 n.56
divinization, 117 n.6
De doctrina Christiana, 236 n.3, 237,
    264 n.102
doctrine of grace, 85
the Holy Spirit, 155 n.5; 208
minimal debt to Gregory, 321
pastoral ministry, 237–238
use of philosophy, 118 n.11
the Trinity, 222
Ayres, Lewis, viii n.7, 10 n.27, 19 n.54,
    21 nn.59–60, 24 n.71, 44
    n.143, 78, 92 n.98, 154 n.2,
    182 n.88, 209 n.68, 211 n.73,
    283 n.60, 295 n.140, 308
    n.216

Balthasar, Hans Urs von, 304 n.188
baptism, 70–72, 76–77, 119, 257, 264
    and illumination, **108–110**, 231
    and purification, **85–87**
    baptismal grace, 85–87
    Gregory administers, 36, 43, 71–72,
        193, 197, 218
    of Christ, 43, 76–77, 120 n.26, 136
    Holy Spirit and, 86, 174–178, 180,
        291, 294, 298–299, 305
    and the Trinity, 231
    See also catechesis; sacraments
Bardy, Gustave, 278 n.37
Barnes, Michel René, 21 n.59, 92 n.93,
    179 n.78, 182 n. 87, 195 n.20,
    199 n.36, 212 n.77, 316 n.267

Barnes, T. D., 30 n.91
Baronius, Joseph, 9 n.21
Basil of Ancyra, 18, 21–25, 29, 45,
    161 n.30, 282, 294, 309 n.222,
    310–312, 316
Basil of Caesarea, vii–viii, 7, 23, 25,
    28–33, 45, 80, 92–93, 199,
    219 n.103, 252, 265, 274, 310,
    318 n.272
    and Apollinarius, 285, 291, 294
        n.130
    and Gregory Nazianzen: doctrinal
        comparison, 10n.28, 74, 199,
        277, 282–283, **292–303**,
        320-32—on:
    ascetical theology, 74–75
    Christology, 124, 296–297
    Holy Spirit, 58, 294, 297–301
    language theory, 169 n.48, 293
    literary structure, 39, 293
    love of the poor, 254–255
    oikonomia/divine economy, 195
        n.24, 295–297
    pastoral theology, 238
    resurrection of the dead, 83
    against Sabellianism, 209 n.65
    theologia/theology, 196,
        295–297
    the Trinity, 208 n.61, 221 n.109,
        223, 226, 258, 293–295,
        301–303, 314 n.252
    and Gregory Nazianzen: personal
        relationship
    as students, 7, 9, 56, 72, 295
    collaboration in 360s, 10–14,
        259, 295
    collected letters, 61
    rupture of friendship in 370s,
        14–15, 30, 55
    Gregory's panegyric on, 55–56,
        109, 160–161, 237, 252, 254,
        257, 266, 268–269, 279 n.44,
        295
    and Gregory of Nyssa: doctrinal
        comparison, 303–306,
        308–309

Basil of Caesarea, (*Continued*)
  on the Holy Spirit, 29–30, 53, 58, 154–162, 172–173, 176
    Gregory Nazianzen's disagreement over the divinity of the Holy Spirit, 15, 157–160, 167, 196, 297–298 (*see also under oikonomia*)
  model of pastoral leadership, 246, 251, 260–261, 266, 268
  ordained Gregory bishop of Sasima, 6, 14, 16
  as "theologian," 196 n.27
  See also Annisa; language theory; *oikonomia*; Origen: *Philokalia*; poor, care for the; Trinity: hypostasis
Beeley, Christopher A., 137 n.87, 141 n.104, 209 n.66, 211 n.72, 212 n.79, 282 n.58, 322 n.288
Behr, John, 10 n.27, 21 nn.59–60, 27 n.77, 43 n.139, 199 n.36, 266 n.109, 282 n.58, 291 n.109, 295 n.140, 306 n.199
Benoît, Alphonse, 9 n.21
Bernardi, Jean, viii n.4, 4 n.3, 35 n.112, 36 n.116, 39, 41 n.134, 55, 60 n.214, 236 n.2, 237 n.5, 242 n.24, 265 n.105, 269 n.120, 270 n.122, 274 n.6
Bergjan, Silke-Petra, 215 n.89
Bible
  basis for Christian doctrine, 4, 20, 22, 24, 49, 65–67, 70–71, 75–80, 89, 95, 97–98, 110–112, 124, 189, 199, 201, 204, 218, 221, 271–273, 293, 303, 308, 320
  Gregory's study of, 6–7, 16, 74, 157, 237, 242, 271–272, 320
  hermeneutic of piety, 184–185, 231
  spiritual exegesis, 84 n.70, 120, 199
    Christology and, 149–51
    the Holy Spirit and, 83, 165–169, 180 n.80, 180–185, 249, 259–262, 272
  study of, as Christian practice, 74
  sustained exegesis of, in *Or.* 37, 43
  See also apostolic succession; Christ: Christological exegesis; Holy Spirit: biblical witness to; pastoral leadership: biblical study; Paul, apostle; Peter, apostle; revelation; spiritual exegesis
Böhringer, Georg Friedrich, viii n.2
body, human/corporeality, 128, 230, 311
  and the knowledge of God, 99–101
  creation of material reality and human body, 117–118
  pastoral care and, 243–244
  purification and, 79–83, 118
  See also Christ; resurrection; God: incorporeality of; soul
Bouteneff, Peter, 134 n.78, 139 n.94
Bouyer, Louis, 64 n.1, 74 n.28, 78, 151, 238 n.11
Brown, Peter, 254 nn.77–78, 255 n.81
Browne, Charles Gordon and James Edward Swallow, English translation by, 90 n.86, 92 n.102, 98 n.122, 101 n.145, 106 n.166, 120 n.29, 128 n.60, 129 n.61, 133, 251 n.65
Byzantine theology, 117

Caesarius, Gregory's brother, 6–7, 14, 79, 105, 118
Caillau, Armand Benjamin, 4 n. 2
Calvet-Sebasti, Marie-Ange, 250 n.57
Campenhausen, Hans von, 249 n.54
Cappadocian Fathers, identified as a group, viii, 8, 154, 198–199, 222, 277, 285, 292, 295, 303, 306, 313
catechesis, 43, 70, 87, 102, 175, 193, 255
cause/causality (αἰτία, αἴτιος, αἴτιον). *See* Trinity: monarchy of God the Father

Christ/Christology/incarnation, **115–151**, 256, 267, 272
  adoptionist Christology, 18, 27 n.77
  assumption of human existence, 126–127, 130–132, 138, 141, 147, 178
  Christocentrism and Trinocentrism, 227, 232
  Christological exegesis and single-subject predication, 122–123, 130, **132–137**, 139–141, 148–151, 163, 206–207, 282, 287–288 (*see also* unity of Christ)
  Chrstological spirituality, **143–151**
  Christology as means of divinization, 149–151, 272
  communicatio idiomatum, 138
  cross and passion of, 133, 135, 138–140, 142, 146, 148, 150, 172, 179, 226, 239, 252, 256–257, 267, 272, 275–277, 289, 312
  divinity/divine nature of, 10 n.27, 39, 115, **121–128**, 129, 132–133, 138, 140, 146, 151, 163–164, 168, 181, 192, 194, 196–197, 227, 229, 231, 286–289, 293
    in the fourth-century debates, 17–27, 31–33
    predominates over Christ's humanity, 128, 141–143, **144–147**, 287–288
    single-nature language, 141, 287–288
    compared to the Holy Spirit's, 153–154, 281
    See also under God; Trinity
  dualistic Christology, 40, **139–143** (*see also sunthetos/* composition)
  two natures of Christ, 130
  two sons, question of, 18, 27, 130, 131, 136–137, 281
  modern confusion over, 133–143
  economic paradigm/narrative framework of Christology, **122–124**, 131–133, 142–143
  identity of, **120–132**
  "exact image" (ἀπαράλλακτος εἰκών), 18, 314–315
  the Good Shepherd, 241–242, 248–249, 261
  humanity of, 127–128, 142 (*see also* will of, human)
    Christ's human soul or mind, question of, 18, 27, 32–34, 127–129, 145–146, 287–290, 318
    Christ assumed both flesh and soul/mind, 83, 123, 126–129, 137, 141, 281, 318
    soul as mediator, 284
  mixture/blending/intermingling (κρᾶσις, μίξις, πλακῆναι), 121, 125, 130–131, 138, 140, 144, 147, 239, 275, 286
  mystery of the incarnation/unity of Christ, 125, 130–131, 144, 239
  names/titles of, 129, 132–133, 140–141, 146, 149, 213 n.83, 261, 265, 303
  the New Adam, 134, 147, 178
  "one and the same" God and Son, 129–130 132, 137–138, 143–144, 150, 286, 290
  pastoral ministry and, 249–250, 252, 256–257, 263–266, 270
  post-Chalcedonian Christology and debates, 116, 129, 138, 143 n.109, 302, 306, 309, 322
  self-emptying and condescension of, **126–127**, 132, 148, 150, 275–276
  as theologian, 196 n.27
  transcendence of, 123–124, 131
  unity/union of, **128–143**, 144, 272, 286–287, 296–297, 320
    essential union (κατ' οὐσίαν συνάπτειν), 131–132

Christ/Christology/incarnation, (*Continued*)
   single entity (ἕν, εἷς), 130–132
   single subject of existence, **135–138**
   made out of two opposites, 129, 131–132
   See also Christological exegesis; divinity of Christ; dualistic Christology;
  will of
   divine, 138
   human, 127–128, 138
  Word of God
   Christ as the eternal Word made flesh, 90, 113, 115, 120–121, 123, 125, 133, 140, 171, 200, 272, 286–290, 295–296, 318
   declaratory function of, 222–223, 264
   See also pastoral leadership: ministry of the word; Trinity
   worship of, 126, 130, 132, 150, 286, 288
   See also Apollinarius; baptism; Diodore of Tarsus; passibility, divine; soteriology; *sunthetos*/composite; poor, care for
Church, 151, 163, 241, 249
  age of the, 171–173
  Chalcedonian/non-Chalcedonian Eastern churches, 320
  communion/catholicity of Eastern and Western churches, 28, 31–3, 57, 160, 280, 283, 310 (*see also* unity of)
  conflict between Eastern and Western churches, 46–47, 50–52, 57, 283
  Eastern, 4, 46–47, 50, 52–53, 58, 167, 301, **309–317**
  in Gaul, 31, 252
  unity of, 36, 190–192, 217–218, 230, 266, 268, 322
  Western, 46–47, 50, 52, **317–318**, 320–321

  See also Alexandria; *Anastasia*, Antioch; Asian/Eastern churches; Constantinople; councils and creeds; Holy Apostles; Holy Spirit; mission and evangelism; pastoral leadership; Rome
Cledonius, Gregory's presbyter, 58–59, 124, 130, 144
Clement of Alexandria and Gregory Nazianzen on:
  baptism as φώτισμα, 108 n.169
  Christ's divinity, 125
  divine pedagogy, 172
  divinization, 117
  the knowledge of God, 68
  oikonomia, 195 n.22,
  pagan knowledge of God, 98 n.121
  pastoral ministry, 237
  pastoral adaptability, 244 n.34
  philosophy, 72
  Plato, 78
Constans, emperor, 18
Constantine, emperor, 18, 30, 42, 251 n.61, 315
Constantinople
  ecclesiastical status of, 30, 42–45, 52–54
  Trinitarian/pro-Nicene community in, **34–54**, 58, 67, 122, 132, 142, 156–157, 160, 191, 209, 229–230, 266, 278, 280, 283–284, 301, 310, 317
  divisions among, 34–36, 191–193, 230, 252–254
  See also Anastasia; councils and creeds; Gregory of Nazianzus: ordination and ministry; Nectarius
Constantius, emperor, 11, 17–22, 24–25 218, 279, 315–316
contemplation. *See* θεωρία/*theoria*
councils and creeds of the Church, 124–125
  Alexandria 362, 22 n.65, 26–27, 192, 213 n.81, 280–281, 316

GENERAL INDEX

Ancyra 358, 21–22, 309–315
Antioch 264 and 268, 18
Antioch 341, "Dedication Council/ Creed," 18–19, 21–22, 31, 221 n.114, 314–316
Antioch 344, 19, 315
Antioch 372, 32
Antioch 379, 31–33, 44, 45–47, 49–50, 301, 304, 317, 319
Aquileia 381, 31 n.97, 45 n.149, 47 n.153
Ariminum/Niké-Seleucia 359, 20, 23–24, 44, 278–279, 315
Chalcedon 451, vii, 52, 116, 124, 131, 143, 322–323 (*see also under* Christ)
Constantinople 336, 22
Constantinople 360, 6, 11, 23–25, 188, 190, 218 n.98, 279, 315
Constantinople 381, 4, 30, 31 n.97, 33 n.106, **44–54**, 58, 60 n.213, 291, 304, 319
  canons, 52
  creed, compared with Nicaea, 52–53
  insufficient doctrine of the Holy Spirit, 49, 53, 155, 301
Constantinople 382, 31 n.97, 33 n.106, 44 n.144, 59, 62 n.223
Dated Creed of 358–359, 20, 22, 315
Iconium 376, 30, 315 n.259
Macrostich Creed of Antioch 344, 19, 21
Nicaea 325, ix, 4, 10 n.27, 17–20, 44, 160–161, 278
  canon 15, 50–51
  creed, ix, 10 n.27, 24–25, 27, 52–53, 104 n.150, 143 n.111, 191 n.12, 192 n.14 204, 213, 224 n.133, 280 n.48, 282, 291 n.112, 294, 310, 313, 316, 317
  faith/doctrine of, 25–26, 32, 38, 49, 52–53, 179, 220, 225, 277, 279, 283, 314
  Gregory first mentions in 374, 16, 316 n.265

  pre-Nicene doctrine, 225
  See also Pro-Nicene movement
Niké 359, 315
Serdica 343, 19, 22, 50 n.169, 280 n.48, 315 n.256
Sirmium 351, 19, 22, 315 n.256
Sirmium 357, 20, 315 n.256
Sirmium 359, 315
Rome/Italy 370s, 31–33, 46, 62 n.223, 282, 291, 301, 317–319 (*see also* Damasus)
Rome 382, 28 n.84, 47 nn.153,155
covenant(s), 148 n.131, 158, 201, 233, 239–240, 267, 273
baptism as, 86
history of, 169–173
creation, creatureliness, 80–82, 99–101, 103, **117–118**, 123, 126, 145, 195–196, 200, 207–208, 256, 267, 298, 311
Creator-creature distinction, 22, 24, 94, 99–101, 119, 125–126, 144–145, 161–164, 224, 228, 282, 290, 294, 312
  versus Father-Son relationship, 22–24, 162, 310
Cross, Richard, 209 n.68
Crouzel, Henri, 199 n.38, 214 n.86, 224 n.133, 275 n.12
Cynics/Cynic philosophy, 73, 77
Cyprian of Antioch, 36, 237
Cyril of Alexandria, 117 n.8, 141 n.104, 320–322
  pseudo-Cyril, 213, 314 n.252
Cyril of Jerusalem, 20, 24

Daley, Brian E., 4 nn. 1,3, 13 n.34, 34, n.110, 51 n.170, 58 n.202, 59 n.208, 70 n.17, 72 n.22, 73 n.25, 74 nn.27,29, 77 n.45, 81 n.56, 84 n.68, 103 n.148, 131 n.68, 190 n.7, 199 n.37, 236 n.1, 238 n.13, 254 nn.78–79, 255 n.80, 257 n.86, 260, 263 n.96, 322 n.290

Damasus of Rome, 10 n.27, 28, 31–33, 36, 46–47, 50 n.169, 54, 127 n.56, 161, 192 n.14, 285, 291, 301, 310, 314, **317–318**. See also Church in the West; councils in Rome 370s
Daniélou, Jean, 92 n.93, 304 n.188
Demoen, Kristoffel, 65 n.4
Demophilus of Constantinople, 26, 37, 39, 41–43, 45, 164, 175, 191 n.12
Demosthenes, 322
Devil, 111, 139, 177, 244, 306, 318 n.276
Dianus of Cappadocian Caesarea, 18
Didymus the Blind, 8, 29n.88, 108 n.169, 110 n.176, 213 n.81, 221 n.109, 283–284, 314 n.252
Diodore of Tarsus, 32–34, 46–47, 51, 53–54, 138, 296, 304–305
  Gregory's opposition to, 51 n.169, 57, 60, 129–131, 137, 146, 286, 291–292, 319
  Christological dispute with Apollinarius, 33–35, 127, 286, 292
  Christological language of grace, 130–131
Dionysius of Alexandria, 195 n.22, 215 n.89, 221 n.109, 321 n.279
Dionysius the Areopagite, Pseudo-, 65 n.5, 117, 242, 322
disciplina arcani, 265
divinization. See θεωρία/*theoria*
docetism, 125
Dorotheus of Antioch, 26
Dräseke, Johannes, 75 n.34, 215 n.89

Eastern churches. See Asian churches
economy. See οἰκονομία/*oikonomia*
Edwards, Mark J., 72 n.24
Egan, John, 104–105, 108 n.168, 209 n.67, 213 n.80
Egyptians. See Alexandrians
ἐκ τῆς οὐσίας τοῦ Πατρός ("from the essence of the Father"), 10n.27, 17, 24–26, 52, 213 n.81, 280 n.48; 282

Eleusis of Cyzicus, 24, 48
Ellverson, Anna-Stina, viii n.4, 118 n.12
Elm, Susanna, viii n.6, 7 n.9, 54–55, 68 n.11, 72 n.22, 74 n.31, 79 n.50, 86 n.74, 87 n.77, 109 n.171, 118 n.12, 236 n.1, 237 n.8, 238 nn.9, 13
ἐνεργεῖν/-εία/*energeia* (energy, operation, activity)
  the Son did not merely operate in Christ as in a prophet, 131, 141
  knowledge of God's energies alone versus God's essence, according to Basil, 303
  Spirit not merely an, 156–157
  Spirit's operation in the disciples, versus essential presence after Pentecost, 172–173
Ephraem the Syrian, 219 n.102
Epicurus/Epicureans, 169 n.48
Epiphanius, 22 n.64, 29n.89, 92 n.98, 164 n.37, 170 n.51, 219 nn.102–103, 221 n.109, 284 n.67, 313 n.245, 315 nn.256, 262
epistemology. See *under* God; theology
eschatology, 83, 98–90, 105–06, 117–120, 169–171, 188, 195, 224–228, 231–232, 257–258, 267. See also judgment
Eucharist, 255, 259, 264–266
Eudoxius of Antioch/Constantinople, 21–23, 26–27, 279
Eulalius of Doara, 15
Eulalius of Nazianzus, Gregory's cousin, 60–61
Eulogius of Edessa, 32
Eunomius of Cyzicus/Eunomians, 11, **21–24**, 26, 30–31, 43, 52, 60, **91–93**, 100, 156, 225–226, 295–296, 299. See also Heterousians
  Gregory's opposition to, 10, 39, 57, 67, 69, 100–102, 105, 107, 111, 116, 121–124, 128–129, 132–135, 140, 142–143, 146,

150, 157, 160, 164–165, 173 175,
  182–184, 190, 203–204,
  206, 215, 220, 293, 301
Euphemius, Gregory's cousin, 14
Eusebian theology, 17–23, 28, 46, 220,
  300
Eusebius of Caesarea in Cappadocia,
  Basil's predecessor, 12–13, 21
Eusebius of Caesarea in Palestine,
  theologian and
  church historian, 17–18, 21, 28,
  72, 92 n.93, 110 n.176, 134 n.80,
  156 n.7, 195 n.22, 208 n.56, 221
  n.109, 226, 251 n.61, 291 n.112,
  300, 312 n.245, 315–316
Eusebius of Nicomedia/Constantinople,
  17–18
Eusebius of Samosata, 31–33, 37
Eustathius of Antioch/Eustathians,
  26–28, 35
Eustathius of Sebaste, 21, 23–24, 28–30,
  32 n.103, 38–39, 56, 157
Eustathius, Gregory's monastic
  associate, 60
Euzoius of Antioch, 26, 29
Eudoxius/Eudoxians, 52
Evagrius of Pontus, 38 n.121, 39 n.124,
  40, 321

faith, 80, 84–85, 137, 139, 146, 149, 168,
  177, 180–181, 184, 187–189,
  194, 197, 214, 229–231, 252,
  257, 268, 274, 293
  and reason, 111–113, 272, 311–312
  See also councils and creeds; pro-
   Nicene movement; theology
Fall, the, 82–83, **118–121**, 123, 147–148,
  256, 289, 299, 318
Fedwick, Paul Jonathan, 306 n.199
Field Jr., Lester L., 28 nn.84, 87, 31
  nn.97–98, 32 nn.100, 103, 33
  nn.105–106, 47 nn.153, 155,
  50 n.169
Finn, Richard, 254 n.78
Flavian of Antioch, 46–48, 51, 54, 57
Friend, W. H. C., 12 n.32

Gallay, Paul, viii n.5, 4 n.3, 5 n.4, 9 n.21,
  35 n.112, 41 n.134, 56 n.195, 59
  n.205, 103 n.149, 128 n.60,
  136 n.83, 169 n.49, 199 n.36,
  215 n.89, 238 n.12
Gautier, Francis, 12 n.30, 72 n.22, 74
  n.31, 236 n.1
George of Cappadocia, bp. Alexandria
  357–361, 278–279
George of Laodicea, 18, 21–23, 29, 161
  n.30, 208 n.61, 282, 294,
  310–311, 314, 316
Giannaras/Yannaras, Christos, 222
  n.123
Gilbert, Peter, 138 n.88
Gnostics, Gnosticism, 81 n.56, 85, 125,
  266 n.109
God
  divine nature, 90–91, **94–99**, 103
   (*see also under* Christ; Holy
   Spirit; Trinity)
  existence of, 97–99, 112
  incomprehensibility of, 39–40,
   93–101, 106, 113, 118, 123, 126,
   141, 179, 228–229, 272, 293,
   307–308, 321
  incorporeality of, 99–101, 224, 272,
   311
  knowledge of, **101–113**, 115–118, 293,
   303, 308–309 (*see also* body;
   illumination; purification;
   theology; *theoria*; *theosis*)
  magnitude/transcendence of,
   94–106, 145–146, 200
  as light, 103–09, 113, 117, 208, 227,
   303, 323
  compared to the sun, 67–68, 90,
   104–105, 107–108, 145,
   171–172, 203, 208 n.61
  names/titles of, 92, 93 n.100, 99
   n.127, 102, 108 n.168, 141,
   149, 195 n.23, 198, 217 n.95,
   229n148, 230, 265, 303
  See also Christ; grace; Holy Spirit;
   ousia; Trinity; union
   with God

384 GENERAL INDEX

Gómez-Villegas, Nicanor, 4 n.3
Gorgonia, Gregory's sister, 6–7, 14
Gospel, the, 42, 59, 69, 72, 75, 78, 89, 151, 169–171, 179, 199, 230, 255, 272, 312. *See also* Bible; faith
Gottwald, Richard, 66 n.7, 75 n.34, 104 n.156
grace of God, **84–87**, 255
  and human effort, 85–87, 247
  conferred through baptism, 85–87, 177
  the Holy Spirit as basis of, 180
  pastoral ministry and, 239–240, 244, 247, 249–250, 260, 264
  for purification and illumination, 84–87
  Gregory's and Augustine's doctrines compared, 84–85
  See also Diodore
Gratian, emperor, 30, 284 n.61
Greek culture/*paideia*
  Gregory's positive use of Greek *paideia*, 7–8, 13, 61–62, 78–79, 118, 215 n.89, 262, 272
  Gregory's opposition to Greek religion, 69, 71–73, 76–77, 82, 102, 196 n.27, 215, 262
Greer, Rowan A., viii n.8, 184 n.95, 265 n.105
Gregg, Robert, viii n.4, 79–80, 83 n.65
Gregory, deacon of Gregory Nazianzen, 61
Gregory, bp. Alexandria 338–339, 278
Gregory of Nazianzus, **4–62, 319–23**
  assassination attempt against, 37, 57
  authority as bishop and theologian, 36, 38, 55–56, 157–160, 166–167
  baptism of, 8–9
  corpus, shape and character of, 3–4, 54, 56–58, 60–62, 64–65, 122, 156, 188–194
  editorial work during retirement, 60, 67 n.9, 116, 120 n.28, 127, 185, 191, 237, 253

legacy of, 321–323
"middle path" between solitude and public service, 9, 11–12, 15, 42, 73–75, 159, 250
ordination as priest, 6, 11, 25, 56, 116, 188, 236, 250, 262
ordination and ministry as bishop, 6, 14, 56, 157–159, 250
  appointment and questioned legitimacy as bishop of Constantinople, 33, 41–42, 45–46, 48, 50–51, 56, 153, 158 n.18, 175, 193, 317
  pastoral leadership of, 11–13, 34, 54, 56–57, 59, 62, 66–67, 87, 118, 157–160, 190, 192, 217, 236, 242, 249–250, 258–259, 262–264, 266, 320, 323
"the Theologian," 188, 196 n.27, 201, 319–323
will and testament of, 58, 60 n.215
See also mission; philosophy; rhetoric; *Theological Orations*; theology; Trinity; pastoral leadership
Gregory the Elder of Nazianzus, 5–7, 11–12, 14, 16, 32, 87, 159, 243, 250 n.57, 251 n.64, 262, 264
  and the homoian creed of Constantinople 360, 6, 11, 188, 190
  and Gregory's ordination to Sasima, 14, 16
  model of pastoral leadership, 246, 248, 254, 257, 269 n.121
Gregory the Great, 237–238, 242 n.28, 264 n.102, 321–322
Gregory of Nyssa, viii, 27, 31–32, 45, 49 n.165, 53–54, 60 n.214, 154, 274, 284, 314, 318 n.273
  Basil of Caesarea and, 303–306
  Creed of Gregory Thaumaturgus and, 274 n.7
  Gregory Nazianzen and, doctrinal comparison, 110 n.177, **303–309**, 320–321—on:

against the Apollinarians, 124,
130 n.64, 306
Christology, 305–306, 315 n.258
the Holy Spirit and the
Pneumatomachoi, 29 nn.
88–89, 53, 156, 166 n.43, 176,
304–305, 308–309
Moses, 65 n.5, 251 n.61
Origen, 75
oikonomia, 195 n.24
orations on the love of the poor,
254–255
pastoral ministry, 238
the resurrection, 83
theologia, 196
the Trinity, 219 n.102, 223, 302,
306–309
Gregory Nazianzen and, personal
relationship, 13, 30, 40, 49,
159, 167, 182, 254
Gregory Palamas, 32 n.278
Gregory the Presbyter, 9 n.21, 322
Gregory Thaumaturgus, 287
Apollinarians' adoption of, 275 n.12,
277 n.32
founder of Cappadocian Christianity,
5, 273
Gregory Nazianzen's use of, 146
n.118, 166 n.43, 273–277, 281,
291–292, 297, 319
Grillmeier, Alois, 139 n.95, 195 n.20,
285 n.69

Hadot, Pierre, 77 n.45
Halleux, André de, 212 n.79
Hanson, R. P. C., 5 n.4, 8 n.14, 9 n.21,
10 n.27, 19 n.54, 21 n.61, 22
n.65, 31 n.97, 44 n.140,
47 n.153, 48 n.157, 51 n.174, 52
nn.175, 178–179, 53 n.180, 99
n.128, 112, 133 n.76, 155 n.3,
169 n.50, 176, 181, 209
nn.67–68, 222 n.121, 277 n.33,
315 n.258, 318 n.277
Harnack, Adolf von, 147 n.127, 304
n.188

Harrison, Verna (Sr. Nonna), viii n.6,
121 n.31, 131 nn.67–68,
323 n.291
Hartmann, Christoph, 61 n.219
Hauschild, W. D., 44 n.140
Haykin, Michael A. G., 155 n.5, 156 n.6,
165 n.40, 167 n.45, 277 n.33
Helladius of Caesarea, Basil's
successor, 32, 54
Hennessy, Kristin, 212 n.77
Hermogenes, rhetor, 165 n.38
Heterousian/Heterousians, 10 n.27,
21–24, 26, 31, 38–39, 192, 204,
206 n.54, 209, 310–313, 315.
See also Aetius; Eunomius
Hilary of Poitiers, 155 n.3
Hildebrand, Stephan, 292 n.115, 301
n.171, 302 n.172, 303 n.182
Himerius, rhetor, 9
Hippolytus, 195 n.21
Holl, Karl, viii n.2, 10 n.28, 190 n.6,
198–199, 249 n.54, 273 n.4,
303 n.187, 304 n.188, 322
n.288
Holman, Susan, 14 n.37, 16 n.46, 254
nn.78–79, 255 n.80, 257 n.85
Holy Apostles, Church of the, 41–42, 58
Holy Spirit, 15, 38, **153–186**, 320
biblical witness to, 165–169, 178,
180–183, 299, 305 (*see also*
Bible: spiritual exegesis)
bodily manifestation of at Pentecost,
172–173
Council of Constantinople 381 on, 53
different views of in Gregory's
milieu, 156–157
divinity of, 10 n.27, 15, 38–39, 49,
155–169, 173, 181, 192, 194,
196–197, 204, 227, 229, 231,
293–294, 317–318
compared to the Son's, 153–154,
281
confessed as "God" and/or
homoousion, 29, 53, 155, 157,
163–165, 175, 268 n.115, 282
n.57, 284, 291, 298, 305

Holy Spirit (*Continued*)
  in fourth-century debates, 26,
    29–30, 32
  dwells in the Church, 158, 163,
    171–174, 178–180, 182–183
  "essentially" (οὐσιωδῶς), 172–174,
    200
  Gregory's distinctive doctrine of,
    153–155
  development of, 155–167
  as holiness itself, 204, 222
  names/titles of, 181–182, 265, 299,
    303
  pastoral ministry and, 15, 157–159,
    242, 249–251, 256, 258–261,
    263–266, 270
  order of the, 250–251
  as Perfecter, 162, 177, 299 n.156
  procession of: ἔκπεμψις,
    ἐκπορεύεσθαι, πρόβλημα,
    πρόοδος, προϊέναι,
    προέρχεσθαι, 168, 202, 204,
    215 (*see also* Trinity: generation
    of the Spirit)
  revelation of, 171–174, 184
  gifts of, 108, 158–159, 184, 256, 284
    n.63, 299
  theological method and, 159, 163, 165,
    174–175, 181–186, 232, 311–312
  means of the knowledge of God in
    Christ, 112, 115, 151, 154, 231
  epistemic principle/quasi-
    subjective work of, 178–180,
    183
  unforgivable sin against, 163
  works with the Son in creation and
    regeneration, 120, 163,
    178–179
  worship/prayer by and to, 164,
    174–175, 184–185, 226–227
  See also Athanasius; baptism; Basil of
    Caesarea; Bible: hermeneutic
    of piety, spiritual exegesis;
    Gregory of Nyssa; Origen;
    Pneumatomachians; salva-
    tion; theology; *theoria*

Homer, 183, 246, 262
ὅμοιος/homoian/Homoian, **20–31**, 35,
  38–39, 41, 43, 57, 67, 102,
  156–157, 160, 164, 175,
  191–193, 203–204, 206, 209,
  214–215, 218, 220, 267 n.114,
  300–301, 310, 312, 314–315.
  See also creed of
  Constantinople 360
ὅμοιος κατ' οὐσίαν ("like in essence"),
  10 n.27, 21–25, 31, 310–312.
  See also homoiousian
ὁμοιούσιος/homoiousian/
  Homoiousian (like in essence),
  10 n.27, 20, **22–29**, 32–34,
  45, 67, 125, 156, 218, 310–317
ὁμοούσιος/homoousian/Homoousian
  (of the same essence,
  consubstantial), 10n.27, 17,
  20, 24–26, 29, 31, 48 n.162,
  49 n.161, 52–53, 161, 179, 195,
  209–214, 216, 218, 225, 282,
  285, 288 n.94, 291, 294, 298,
  304, 313–314
"consubstantial Trinity," 62 n.223,
  213, 280, 284 n.67, 316
Honoré, Tony, 30 n.92
Hübner, Reinhard M., 302 n.175
Huxley, George, 10 n.23
ὑπόστασις/hypostasis. *See under* Trinity
Hypsistarii, religious sect, 6

Ignatius of Antioch, 125, 195 n.21
illumination, 70–71, 83, **90–113**,
  117–119, 153, 235, 260, 272,
  303, 308, 320, 323
  Christ and, 108–110, 113, 115
  dialectical relationship with
    purification, 64–65, 71, 109–11,
    230
  the Holy Spirit and, 153, 171, 173,
    176, 180, 185–186
  the Trinity and, 187, 191, 197, 204,
    227–228, 231–232
  See also baptism; knowledge of God;
    purification; *theosis*

Irenaeus, 82, 125, 132 n.71, 147, 155, 172, 195, 266 n. 109

Jerome, 7 n.11, 28, 38 n.121, 39 n.124, 40, 45, 263 n.93, 284 n.61, 321
John Chrysostom, vii, 237–238, 251–252, 264 n.102, 321
John of Damascus, 213, 251 n.61, 321–323
Jonah, 51, 262–263
Jovian, emperor, 13, 25, 27, 160–161, 279–280
judgment, final, 86, 89–90, 119, 239, 257, 267. *See also* eschatology
Julian, emperor, 6, 10 n.31, 25, 62, 77
  opposition to Christianity, 11–13, 62
  student with Gregory in Athens, 9
Julius of Rome, 18
Justin Martyr, 195 n.21

Kelly, J. N. D., 44 n.140, 52 n.178, 53 n.180, 125 n.47, 139 n.95, 169 n.50, 285 n.69
Kertsch, Manfred, 104 nn.150, 156
Kopecek, Thomas A., 182 n.89
Kovacs, Judith, 68 n.10, 195 n.22

Laird, Martin, 305 n.194, 309 n.219
Lampe, G. W. H., 147 n.126, 173 n.62, 195 n.20
language/language theory, 63, 95–96, 100, 169, 224
  Basil on, 293
  Christological, 116, 126, 130–131
  Eunomius on, 91–92
  Gregory of Nyssa on Trinitarian, 306–309
  See also spiritual exegesis; theology
Libanius, 9 n.24
Liberius of Rome, 28
Lienhard, Joseph, 17 nn.49–50, 155 n.5, 216 n.92, 222 nn.121–122, 277 n.34, 321 n.286
light. *See under* illumination; God; Origen; Trinity

Lim, Richard, 67 n.9, 68 n.11, 321 n.281
liturgy. *See* sacraments
Loofs, Friedrich, 304 n.188
Lossky, Vladimir, 101 n.145, 177–178, 189 n.4, 224–225, 273 n.4
Louth, Andrew, viii n.3, 236 n.1, 322 n.289
Lucifer of Cagliari, 27
Luckman, Harriet Ann, 298 n.155

Macedonius of Constantinople, 21, 24, 29 n.89
Macedonians. *See under* Pneumatomachians
Macrina, Basil's sister, 7, 31 n.97, 56, 74
Malingrey, Anne-Marie, 72
Mamas, Cappadocian martyr, 59
Manicheans, 30, 81 n.56
Marcellus of Ancyra/Marcellans, 17–19, 22, 27 n. 77, 28, 46, 52, 206 n. 54, 219 n.102, 221 n.109, 286, 291, 314–315, 316 n.266, 319
Markschies, Christoph, viii n.7, 10 n.28, 56, 190 n.6, 222 n.121, 273 n.5
Marmarius of Marcianopolis, 54
Marriage
  Gregory's critique of Roman divorce laws, 42, 191
  Gregory's positive view of, 71, 74, 245
  reform of Cappadocian marriage regulations, 252
martyrs, 265, 268. *See also* Mamas
Mary, the Virgin, 26–27, 124–125, 129–130, 136–137, 286
  as *Theotokos*/Mother of God, 129, 136
  Apollinarius on, 286, 289
  Athanasius on, 281
Matthews, John, 12 n.32
Maximus the Cynic, 37, 39 n.124, **40–41**, 45, 47 n.154, 52, 57, 68, 73, 193, 201, 230, 236, 267, 280
Maximus Confessor, 85 n.72, 117, 321–322
May, Gerhard, 52 n.179

McGuckin, John, viii n.6, 4 n.2, 9
    nn.21–22, 14 n.40, 15 n.41, 3
    nn.107, 109, 34, n.110,
    35 nn.112, 114, 38 n.121,
    39 nn.123–125, 41 n.132, 42
    n.136, 47 n.153, 48 nn.157, 161,
    49 n.165, 51 n.172, 55 n.191,
    57 n.199, 59 n.206, 60 n.215,
    61 nn.220, 222, 61, 67 n.9, 74
    n.29, 78, 91 n.87, 94 n.103, 98
    n.123, 108 n.170, 111 n.178, 113
    n.188, 118 n.15, 155 n.5, 157 n.12,
    158 n.15, 165 n.39, 170 n.51, 201
    n.41, 226 n.140, 232 n.161, 242
    n.26, 253, 321 n.282
McLynn, Neil, viii n.6, 10 n.25, 12 n.30,
    54 nn.186–188, 56 nn. 194,
    197, 59 nn.205–206, 60
    n.214, 61 nn.216–217, 221, 237
    n.7, 253 n.72, 262 n.92
Meijering, E. P., 209 n.67, 215 n.89
Melitius of Antioch/Melitians, 24,
    26–33, 44–49, 60, 127 n.56,
    218, 251–252, 277, 280, 294,
    296, 304, 310, 313 n.246,
    316–320
Meredith, Anthony, 53 n.183, 299 n.161,
    301 nn.171–172
Meyendorff, John, 212, 222 n.123
mission and evangelism, 4, 35, 76–79,
    118, 215 n.89, 262 n.92
modalism, 18, 22, 29, 49, 156–157, 206
    n.54, 209. *See also*
    Sabellianism
Modestus, Valens' prefect, 13 n.35, 25
    n.73, 268–269
monarchy of God the Father. *See under*
    Trinity
monasticism. *See under* philosophy
Moreschini, Claudio, viii n. 6, 4 n. 1, 7
    n.10, 65 n.5, 66 n.7, 68 n.10,
    72 n.24, 75–76, 78–79, 86
    n.74, 94 n.102, 104 nn.150,
    105 n.160, 106 n.163, 109
    n.172, 110 n.177, 117 n.4, 139
    n.95, 156, 271 n.2

Moses, 95, 145, 159, 170 n.51, 290,
    308 n.218. *See also* Mount
    Sinai
    example of theological vision, 35–36,
        65–67, 70, 89–91, 101–02,
        322
    example of pastoral leadership,
        36, 251, 263
    Gregory's seminal treatment of, 35,
        65 n.7, 251 n.61
Mossay, Justin, 39 n.122, 41 n.133, 43
    n.137, 106 n.166, 229 n.147,
    278 nn.37, 39
μυστήριον (mystery)
    Christian faith and life, 9 n.18, 90,
        118, 120, 125, 144, 151, 154,
        173, 184, 195 n.20, 229, 254,
        271, 312
    hidden knowledge, 70, 82, 100, 170,
        214, 236 n.3
    sacrament/liturgy, 37, 76–77, 87, 110,
        151, 250 n.57, 265
    See also Christ: mystery of the
        incarnation

nature, divine. *See under* God; Christ;
    Holy Spirit; Trinity
Nautin, Pierre, 61 n.219
Nectarius of Constantinople, 45 n.145,
    46 n.152, 47 n.156, 48 n.161,
    51–54, 57–60, 253
Neoplatonists/Neoplatonism, 72, 77,
    83 n.66, 286, 306, 308.
    See also Plotinus
Newman, John Henry, 170
Nicaea, Council of. *See under* councils
Nicobulus, Gregory's nephew, 60
Nonna, Gregory's mother, 5–7, 16,
    242–243
Nonnus, Pseudo-, 322
Noret, Jacques, viii n. 1
Norris, Frederick, vii nn.4, 4 n.3, 5
    n.4, 6, 8 n.12, 9 n.24, 39
    nn.122–123, 64 n.2, 66 n.6,
    67 n.9, 68 n.11, 75 n.34, 76
    n.40, 92 n.93, 94 n.103, 98

n.123, 113 n.188, 116 nn.1–4,
122, 124 n.45, 126 n.52,
132 n.72, 138 n.89, 139 n.95,
140 n.96, 147 nn.123,127,
148 n.128, 165 nn.38–39,
166 n.43, 169 n.48, 170 n.52,
176, 182 nn.85, 89, 183
n.92, 209 n.67, 215 n.89,
238 n.9
Novatian/Novatianists, 60, 82, 88, 260

οἰκονομία/*oikonomia* (economy)
  administration of the word, 263,
    266
  divine economy, 113, 118, 122, 141,
    170–171, 182, **194–196**, 214,
    217–218, 222–223, 226, 228,
    232–233, 238–239, 273,
    294–295
  of the Holy Spirit, 171–173
  incarnation of Christ, 135, 137 n.84,
    149, 195–196, 198, 281
    (*see also* Christ/incarnation)
  insufficient or summary teaching,
    37, 58
  Basil's "reserve" on the Holy Spirit,
    15, 53, 58, 173 n.62, 297–298
  pastoral adaptation, 245 (*see also
    under* pastoral leadership)
  See also under Basil; Clement of
    Alexandria; Gregory of Nyssa;
    theology
Optimus of Pisidian Antioch, 54
Origen, 117, 287 n.88, 291 n.113, 298
    n.153, 312 n.245, 314–315
  and the fourth-century debates, 19, 23
  influence on/compared with Gregory
    Nazianzen, 7, 10, 16, 78, 157,
    271–273, 282, 293, 316, 319,
    321, 323—on:
  authority as teacher, 66 n.6, 249
  Christ/Christology, 82, 123 n.40,
    125, 127 n.58, 132 n.73, 149,
    276
  doctrinal topics, 266
  eschatological spirituality, 169–170

the Holy Spirit, 155, 160, 165–166,
    273, 302 n.182 (*see also* Bible:
    spiritual exegesis)
incomprehensibility of God, 94,
    99–100, 293
Jonah, 263
light, divine, 104 n.154
magnitude of God, 94
Moses, 65 n.5
oikonomia/economy, 195 n. 22, 295
pastoral ministry, 237, 242 n.26
pagan knowledge of God, 98 n.121
pedagogy, divine, 172
philosophy/Christian *praxis*, 7, 72,
    74–75
Plato, 78
Poemata Arcana, structure of, 3–4,
    55
praxis and *theoria*, 109 n.172
reason, limits of, 111 n.179
simplicity, divine, 96 n.114
Spirit's inspiration of Scripture,
    180–181
spiritual conditions for the
    knowledge of God, 68, 184
spiritual exegesis, 67, 89, 149,
    166, 260–261, 263, 272, 284
stages of spiritual progress, 67 n.9,
    245
Theological Orations, structure of,
    3–4, 39, 272, 293
theological topics, 267
theologia/theology, 199–200
theosis/divinization, 120 n.30
the Trinity, 185 n.97, 199,
    225–226, 294
  dynamic Trinity, 214–215
  epistemology, 294
  eternal generation of the Son,
    224 n.133, 316 n.264
  identity of being in the Trinity,
    221 n.114
  relations, Trinitarian, 208 n.61
Philokalia, compiled by Gregory and
    Basil, 10, 89 n.84, 274 n.7,
    294 n.138

Otis, Brooks, 74 n.30, 238 n.11
οὐσία/*ousia* (being, essence) of God, 17–20, 23–29, 31–32, 43 n.139, 53, 94–98, 100–107, 113, 115, 117, 164, 173 n.61, 189, 191, 198–199, 218, 221–222, 301, 311, 313
  See also under Christ; God; Holy Spirit; Trinity

παρρησία/*parrhesia* (frank speech), 13 n.35, 73, 158
participation/μετάληψις
  in Christ, 121, 148–150, 178, 229, 256
  in the divine economy, 263
  in God, 116–119, 229, 303, 305
  in the Holy Spirit, 174, 229, 299
  in the Trinity, 189, 225, **228–233**, 235, 237 n.4, 299
Pannenberg, Wolfhart, 209 n.67
Parvis, Sara, 17 n.50
passibility/passion, divine, 74, 134, 136, **137–139**, 140, 142, 224, 275–277, 312
  "impassible passion" of Christ, 139, 275–276, 296 n.147
  See also Christ: cross and passion
pastoral ministry and leadership, 54, 56–57, 66, 68, 70–71, 75, 196, 233, **235–270**, 273, 320, 323
  adaptability, 245–247, 252, 267, 270
  administration of the Trinity, 266–270
  authority and power of, 241–243, 249–250, 266, 269
  "the art of arts and science of sciences," 242
  bad bishops/pastoral abuses, 196 n.27, 248–249, 252–254
  biblical study as preparation for, 239–240, 253, 258–263, 266
  cure of souls/medical analogy, 239, 242–247, 251–252, 269–270
  defined, 241–243
  divine economy and, 238–240, 247, 251, 255, 260–262

  ministry of the word, 263–270
  order of the Spirit, 250–251
  rhetoric and, 242, 249
  and social class/patronage, 68, 73, 85 n.73, 217, 249, 252–253, 319
  τέχνη/skill, 238, 242–243, 261
  virtue and holiness, priestly, 247–254, 258–260, 267, 269
  See also under apostolic succession; Athanasius; Basil; Christ; grace; Gregory of Nazianzus; Gregory the Elder of Nazianzus; Paul; sacraments; Trinity
Paul, apostle, 36, 65 n.5, 69, 80 n.54, 84–85, 89, 91, 96–97, 105, 112 n.187, 126, 147, 149, 171, 195 n.20, 216, 229 n.149, 245–246, 251 n.61, 255 n.80, 289 nn.100,106, 296
  pastoral ministry, example of, 251–252
  as "theologian," 196 n.27
Paul of Samosata, 18, 27
Paulinus of Antioch/Paulinians, 26–28, 32 n.103, 46–47, 280, 282, 294, 319–320
Pelagianism, 85, 155 n.5
Pelagius of Laodicea, 32, 53
Pelikan, Jaroslav, 72 n.22, 85 n.72
Peter of Alexandria, 30 n.103, 36–38, 41, 160–161, 192 n.14, 251 n.61, 318
Peter, apostle, 96 n.116, 251, 296, 302, 306
Phiagrius, Egyptian prefect, 278
Philokalia. See under Origen
philosophy, 77
  as Christian *praxis*/asceticism, 7, 40–41, **71–75**, 120 n.30, 158, 253, 272, 274
  See also asceticism; Gregory of Nazianzus: "middle path"; prayer; poor, care for the; *praxis*; virginity
  of consolation, 79–80

Gregory's opposition to Greek
philosophy, 72–73, 308–309
(*see also under* Greek culture)
"philosophizing about God." *See
under* theology
See also Aristotle; rhetoric; Plato;
Plotinus; Pre-Socratic
philosophers; Socrates; Stoics
Philostorgius, 23 n.70, 164 n.37, 291
n.114
Photinus/Photinians, 19, 27 n.77, 30,
43, 52, 124 n.47, 206 n.54,
220, 286, 291
Pinault, Henri, 66 n.7, 72 nn.22, 24,
75–79, 85 n.72, 86 n.75, 104
n.154, 215 n.89
φύσις/*physis* (nature), of God. *See under*
Christ; Holy Spirit; God;
Trinity
Plagnieux, Jean, 64, 66 n.7, 68
nn.11–12, 71 n.20, 75–79, 83
n.66, 87 n.78, 91 n.87, 98
n.123, 109 n.173, 112, 169
n.49, 170 n.52, 181 n.81,
222 n.122
Plato, 68, 71–72, 95 n.110, 131, 199,
242 n.27, 244 n.34, 262, 319
n.278, 322
as bad theologian, 196 n.27
on light, divine, 104 n.154
Gregory's disputed use of, **75–85**,
92, 99
Plotinus, 71 n.20, 75–76, 85 n.72,
95 n.110, 104 n.151, 106 n.163,
215 n.89
Πνευματομάχοι/Pneumatomachians
(Spirit-Fighters), **29–30**, 32,
44, 49, 52–53, 60, 156–157,
299, 301
called "Macedonians," 29, 43 n.139,
45 n.145, 48, 50, 60
Gregory of Nyssa's work against,
305, 309
Gregory's opposition to, 15 n.42,
38–39, 67 n.9, 156–157,
163–167, 173, 175, 181–184,
190, 192, 202 n.43, 203–204,
206, 209, 297, 312
Gregory's varying use of the term,
29 n.88; 157 n.14
poor, care for the, 6, 58, 60 n.215, 71–
72, 81, 238, 251, **254–258**, 266
"Basiliad" project, 13–14
Christ and, 256–258
Portmann, Franz Xaver, 172 n.56
Pouchet, Jean-Robert, 238 n.9
prayer, 71–73, 245, 251, 253, 265, 271
πρᾶξις/*praxis*, 70–75, 84, 109–10, 158.
See also asceticism; philosophy
and *theoria*/vision, 73, 109–110
Pre-Socratic philosophers, 72
Prestige, G. L., 189 n.4
Prohaeresius, rhetor, 9
Pro-Nicene movement, 4–5, 25–27, 30,
34, 37, 41, 57, 69, 125, 160,
182, 214, 273, 283 n.60, 285,
290, 314–315. *See also*
Alexandria; Antioch; Asian/
Eastern churches;
Constantinople; Council of
Nicaea; Rome
defined, ix, 10 n. 27
Pruche, Benoît, 297 n.148
Psellos, Michael, 322 n.290
purification, 35, 57, 63–64, **65–90**,
102–03, 106, 108–10, 115,
118, 196–197, 235, 248–251,
259–260, 272, 274, 323
baptism and, 85–87
biblical basis of, 75–79
dialectical relationship with
illumination, 64–65, 109–111,
230
God as source of, 84–85
the Holy Spirit enables, 153, 171, 176,
179–180
the Trinity and, 187, 228, 230–231

Rahner, Karl, 199 n.36
Rapp, Claudia, 236 n.1, 237 n.6, 238
n.13, 249 n.53, 250 n.59,
251 nn.61–62, 253 n.71

Régnon, Théodore de, 182 n.87, 212
relations (σχέσεις). *See under* Trinity
resurrection. *See also Anastasia*
  of Christ, 137, 150, 187, 226, 239, 265, 267, 288
  of the dead, 59, 79, 83, 83, 178 n.76, 232, 244
  of the orthodox faith in Constantinople, 34, 57
revelation, divine, 101, 105–06, 111, 126, 160, 170–174, 195–196, 199–201, 228–229, 239, 255, 294, 303, 308
rhetoric, in Gregory's work, 3–4, 66–68, 74, 76, 78, 87–90, 111, 135, 150 n.136, 165–167, 183–185, 189, 191, 193, 217, 219, 224, 239, 255, 257, 272, 295, 320–321
  Gregory as teacher of, 9–10, 72
  Greek philosophical, 4, 8–9, 88, 236
  See also under pastoral ministry
Richard, Anne, 81 n.56, 100 n.137, 118 n.14
Ritter, Adolph Martin, 44 n.140, 48 n.157, 50 n.169, 52 nn.178–179, 222 n.121
Roll, Susan K., 43 n.137
Rome and Italy, Church in, 31–33, 50 n.169, 252, 280, 283, 301. *See also* Church: Western
  ecclesiastical status of, 42, 44, 50, 52, 54
Rousse, Jacques, 322 n.290
Rousseau, Philip, 10 n.27, 30 n.91, 238 n.12
Ruether, Rosemary Radford, viii n.4
Rufinus of Aquileia, 44, 50 n.169, 155 n.5, 237, 321–322
Russell, Norman, 116 n.4, 117 nn.5, 8, 118 n.15, 119 n.21, 120 nn.29–30, 121 n.31, 139 n.95, 321 n.279

Sabellius/Sabellianism, 18–19, 27, 29, 52, 219 n.102
  Gregory's opposition to, 206, 209, **219–220**, 291, 294, 310, 312, 314–315
sacraments/sacramental theology, 63, 123, 135, 151, 255, 264
  ordination, 250
  See also baptism; *disciplina arcani*; Eucharist; Gregory of Nazianzus: ordination; Christ, worship of
salvation/soteriology, 256, 289–290. *See also theosis*
  Gregory's understanding of, 116–120
  Christology and, **116–122**, 123–124, 137–138, 143–144, 154
  the Holy Spirit and, 154, 164–165, 180–183
  the Trinity and, 187–188, 224–226, 228–232
  "That which has not been assumed has not been healed," 127
Scholz, Sebastian, 51 n.169
Schwartz, Eduard, 19 n.53, 31 n.98
Second Sophistic, 7
Seeberg, Reinhold, 304 n.188
Sesboüé, Bernard, 292 n.117
Silvanus of Tarsus, 28
Simeon the New Theologian, vii, 322
Simonetti, Manlio, 22 n.65, 31 n.97, 44 n.140, 318 n.277
simplicity
  ascetical, 73, 108
  divine, 92–93, 95–96, 140
  of faith or confession, 36–37, 89, 126 n.51, 164, 188, 197–198, 210–211, 217–220, 245, 251
  pastoral, 246, 252
sin, 71, 77, 82–84, 111, 118–120, 138, 177, 244, 256, 289–290
  Augustine on original sin, 321
Sinai, Mount, 35, 65–66 88–91, 93, 95 n.109, 107, 115, 322. *See also* Moses
Sinko, Tadeusz, 35 n.112, 39

GENERAL INDEX 393

Simeon the New Theologian, vii
Slusser, Michael, 274 nn.6–7,
　　275 n.12
Snee, Rochelle, 58 n.204
Socrates, ecclesiastical historian, 9 n.23,
　　29 n.89, 30 n.92, 33 n.108,
　　42 n.135, 43 n.139, 44–48,
　　52 n.175, 58 n.204, 60 n.210,
　　92, 213 n.81
Socrates, philosopher, 75, 80
Solomon, 69, 84, 96–97, 245
soul, human, 117, 267
　　first to sin/most in need of healing,
　　　　83, 127, 290, 318
　　superiority to the body, 80–83,
　　　　145–146, 243–244
　　pastoral care focused on, 243–244
Sozomen, ecclesiastical historian,
　　9 n.23, 14 n.38, 21 n.59,
　　30 n.92, 42 n.135, 44–49,
　　51 n.173, 52 nn.175, 179,
　　58 n.204, 164 n.37, 291
　　n.114
Spidlík, Thomas, viii n.4, 109
spirituality. *See* asceticism; Bible:
　　spiritual exegesis; Christ; Holy
　　Spirit; illumination, *praxis*,
　　purification, *theosis*, *theoria*
spiritual exegesis. *See under* Bible;
　　Origen
Spoerl, Kelley McCarthy, 27 n.77, 291
　　n.110, 294 n.130
Staats, Reinhart, 44 n.140
Sterk, Andrea, 236 n.1, 238 nn.9–10, 13,
　　251 nn.61–62, 265 n.105,
　　277 n.36
Stoics/Stoicism, 77, 92, 94, 131, 286,
　　302–303, 306
suffering, divine. *See* passibility
σύνθετος/*sunthetos* (composite), 100
　　n.36
　　nature of human beings, 82 n.62,
　　　　91, 117
　　Christ as, 123, 132, 134, 142–143
Swallow, James Edward, *See under*
　　Charles Gordon Browne

Swete, H. B., 153 n.1, 156, 167 n.46,
　　277 n.33
Sykes, D. A., 4 n 1, 76 n.40, 86 n.76
Szymusiak, J., 277 n.33

Talley, Thomas, 43 n.137
Terennius of Scythis, 54
Tertullian, 195 n.21
Thekla, 279
Themistius, 30 n.94
Theodore of Mopsuestia, 306 n.197
Theodore of Tyana, 36
Theodoret, 31 n.97, 33 n.106, 44–46, 48
　　n.157, 52 n.175, 53 n.184,
　　62 n.223, 318 nn.274,276
Theodotus of Nicopolis, 29
Theodosia, Gregory's cousin, 7, 34
Theodosius, emperor, 30–31, 34 n.111,
　　36, 41–45, 48–51, 53, 57–60,
　　175, 193, 218, 268, 304
　　imperial edicts under, 30–31,
　　　　60 n.207, 129
　　Cunctos populos (*C. Th.* 16.1.2;
　　　　Feb 27, 380), 36, 38, 161 n.26,
　　　　192 n.14
　　Nullis haereticis (*C. Th.* 16.5.6;
　　　　Jan 10, 381), 34 n.111, 43
　　Episcopis tradi (*C. Th.* 16.1.3; July
　　　　30, 381), 53–54
Theological Orations (*Ors.* 27–31)
　　audience and context of, 39–40,
　　　　67–69, 124
　　character of, 39–40, 137 n.88, 185
　　　　n.98, 190, 193, 195 n.23,
　　　　224, 231
　　English translation of. *See* Charles
　　　　Gordon Browne, Lionel
　　　　Wickham
　　literary structure of, 217
　　Ors. 27–28, 64–65, 88
　　Or. 28, 94, 98–99
　　Or. 30, 123, 139–143, 148
　　Or. 31, 164–165 167–168, 183–185,
　　　　272, 293
　　manuscript tradition of, 39–40
　　preparation of, 163

θεολογία/*theologia* (theology), **194–201**, 319, 323
  meaning confession of divinity, 194, 196–199
  and the divine economy in modern thought, 198–200
  Gregory's doctrinal inclusivity, 320
  order of (τάξις θεολογίας), 173, 180
  method/epistemic structure of, 39, 63–64, 68, 84, 87–90, 91–93, 95–96, 102–03, 110–111, 115–116, 148–151, 154, 165, 188–189, 201, 227, 232
  concerning the Trinity above all, 197–198, 201, 206, 231–233, 267
  "philosophizing about God," 67–68, 196 n. 27, 265
  See also Bible: spiritual exegesis; illumination; language theory; Moses; purification; Trinity: theology of the divine economy
theopaschite language. *See* passibility, divine
Θεοτόκος/*Theotokos*. *See* Mary
θέωσις/*theosis* (divinization), 77, 82, 84, **116–122**, 146–151, 195, 272, 305
  definition of, 117–120
  of Christ, 120–121, 129–131, 144, 147–148, 177–179
  Gregory's seminal doctrine of, 116–117, 320–321
  by the Holy Spirit, 174–180, 184–185, 294, 298
  pastoral ministry and, 235–238, 235–236, 270
  the Trinity and, 188, 228–231
  See also ascent to God; Holy Spirit; illumination; participation; *theoria*
θεωρία/*theoria* (contemplation/vision of God), 69–71, 77, 101, 105–110, 113, 169–170, 189, 197, 224–227, 231

God's self-contemplation, 104, 231 n.155, 261
  by the Holy Spirit, 163, 167, 174–180, 187, 294, 298–299,
  praxis and, 73, 109–10
  See also illumination; participation; *theosis*
Thespesius, rhetor, 7
Thomas Aquinas, 321 n.278
time, God's transcendence of, 95, 100, 102,162, 201, 203–205, 224, 293, 310–311, 316
  Christ's existence beyond and within, 123–124, 126, 137
Timothy of Alexandria, 53, 57
Torrance, T. F., 209 n.67
translation of bishops. *See* Council of Nicaea, canon 15
Trigg, Joseph, 7 n.10, 65 n.5, 66 n.6, 68 n.10, 170 n.51, 195 n.22, 271 n.2, 274 n.11, 276 n.24
the Trinity/Trinitarian faith and doctrine, **187–324**
  Christocentrism and, 227
  basic confessions of, 158, 187–189, 228, 232
  one Divinity of, 10 n.27, 23, 26, 32, 36, 186, 188, 192 n.14, 203–204, **217–218**, 220–222, 311
  shared divine nature of, 194, 202–203, 205–211, 221, 302, 306–309
  See also monarchy of God the Father; unity of
  class, not members of a, 207, 211, 294, 302 n.179
  conceptual refinement of, 188–189, 194, 202
  consubstantiality of. *See* homoousios
  defined succinctly, 197
  distinctions among the Father, Son, and Spirit, 194, 204–207, **208–209**, 210–214, 216, 320
  versus the shared divine nature, 221–223
  See also hypostasis

dynamic "movement" of, 214–216, 221–223, 320
generation of the Son and Spirit from God the Father, 137 n.85, 189, 194, 202–208, 210–216, 220–222, 224, 282, 294, 310–313 (*see also* monarchy of God the Father)
"Trinitarian," meaning of, ix, 10 n.27
formulaic expressions of, 189, 194, 201, **217–220**, 311
in either homoousian or homoiousian scheme, 314
identical operations of, 182–183, 300, 309
ἰδιότητες (unique characteristics), 222, 267–268
inclusivity and exclusivity of, 225–227
grammars/models of, 224–228
Gregory's distinctive teaching on, 187–188
Gregory's dream vision of, 8
Gregory's major texts on, **189–194**
ὑπόστασις/*hypostasis* (subsistent entity), 17, 23–24, 26, 28, 206, 208, 216, 221–222, 267, 280, 285, 291, 301–303, 313
or *prosopon*, 206, 280, 291
versus *ousia*, defined by Basil of Caesarea, as general and particular, 301–302
versus *ousia*, defined by Gregory of Nyssa, 306–309
light of, 197, 323
modes of existence, 208
Monad, Dyad, Triad, 106 n.163, 170 n.51, 215–216, 221, 282
monarchy of God the Father/source (ἀρχή) and cause (αἰτία) of the Trinity, 23, 26, 125, 189, **201–217**, 220, 222, 226, 232, 291, 293–294, 300, 302–303, 308, 310–311, 317, 320
and consubstantiality/equality, 209–211

narrative basis and shape of, 194, 216–217, 223, 320
oneness and threeness of, 220–223
pastoral ministry and, 235–236, **263–270**
perichoresis in, 211–213
personalism versus essentialism in, 212–213
πρόσωπα/*prosopa* (persons), 206, 221–222, 280, 291
relations (σχέσεις), Father, Son, and Holy Spirit as, 207–208, 302–303, 312
singularity/uniqueness (τὸ μοναδικόν) of, 203, 205, 216, 222, 314–315
social Trinitarianism, 190, 230 n.152
technical clarification of, 214, **220–228**
negative, 223–224 (*see also* apophaticism)
positive, 220–223
theology of the divine economy, 194–201, 222–223, 226–228, 231–233, 272, 295–296, 303, 320, 323
tritheism, accusation of, 207, 307
unity of, 194, **206–208**, 209–216, 230, 267–268, 291, 301–302, 304, 320
worship of, 188–189, 208
See also under Athanasius; Augustine; baptism; Basil; Gregory of Nyssa; *homoousios*; illumination; Origen; *ousia*; participation; pastoral leadership; purification; salvation; theology; *theosis*
Trisoglio, Francesco, viii n.6, 187 n.1
Turcescu, Lucian, 306 n.202

Vaggione, Richard, 21 n.59, 91 n.89, 92 n.92, 93 n.100, 135 n.82, 215 n.89

Valens, Emperor, 5 n.5, 13–14, 25–26, 29–30, 191 n. 12, 218, 268–269, 316
Valentinian, emperor, 25 n.72
Van Dam, Raymond, 5 n.5, 10 n.31, 25 n.73, 30 nn.92–94, 34 nn.110–111, 42 n.135, 55 n.193, 58 n.202, 252 n. 69, 274 n.6
Vinson, Martha, 81 n.58, 190 n.7, 208 n.63, 229 n.147
Vinzent, Markus, 17 n.50
virginity, 42, 74, 108, 251. *See also* Mary
Vitalis, 28–29

Weiss, Hugo, viii n.2
Wesche, Kenneth P., 139 n.94

Wickham, Lionel, 60 n.211, 90 n.86, 93 n.101, 100 n.138, 101 n.144, 128 n.60, 134 n.78, 166 n.43
Williams, A. N., 321 n.280
Williams, Rowan, 64 n.2, 225
Winslow, Donald, viii n.4, 64 n.2, 68 n.12, 74 n.30, 111 n.178, 116 nn.3–4, 118 nn.13–14, 119 n.24, 120 n.29, 122 n.36, 126 n.52, 127 n.55, 134 n.79, 138 n.89, 139 n.95, 147–148, 154 n.2, 169 n.50, 176–179
Wittgenstein, Ludwig, 64 n.2, 182

Zeno of Tyre, 32
Zizioulas, John, 222 n.123

Index to Biblical Citations

Genesis 92n.93

3.21   82
7.2, 8   76n.39

Exodus 66

3.14   102, 125
7.1   91, 145n.117
26.31-33   90
33.22-23   90
33.23   101
36.35-36   90

Leviticus

7.19-21   76n.39
11-15   76n.39

Numbers

18-19   76n.39

Deuteronomy

6.7   71n.19
12.15, 22   76n.39
14-15   76n.39

Job

1.8   71n.19
16.17   76n.39
33.3   76n.39
39.5-12   74

Psalms

1.2   71n.19
8.2   90
12.7   259
18.11(17.12)   106
22.1(21.2)   138
24(23).4   76n.39
34.1(33.2)   71n.19

36.9(35.10)   197, 227
49(50).23   71n.20, 87
51.12(50.14)   259
51(50)   76n.39
51.17(50.19)   71n.20
55.17(54.18)   71n.19
72(73).8   245n.36
73(72).1   76n.39
82(81).1   121n.32
84.5(83.6)   173
85.11(84.12)   104n.154
89.36   104n.154
119(118).24   263
119.131   158

Proverbs

8.22   133, 134n.81, 135, 140, 310n.225
8.25   310n.225

Isaiah

1.16   75
6.5   76n.39
35.8   76n.39
45.3   259
53.5   256
53.7   256

Jeremiah

9.24   258
23.18 LXX   98

Ezekiel

39.24   76n.39

Hosea

14.10   258
26.4   261

Amos

4.13   281, 281n.54, 284n.62

Malachi

4.2   104n.154

Matthew

4.2   133, 135
5.8   75
5.18   262
6.20   258
7.6   245n.36
8.17   256
8.24   135
10.1   172n.57
10.11   85
12.31   163n.33
12.43-45   71
13   88n.79
17.2   104n.154
19.1-12   42
23.26   76n.39
27.46   138

Mark

3.15   172n.57
6.7   172n.57
8.34   257
9.35   228
10.42-45   249n.52

Luke

2.52	148n.130
9.1	172n.57
11.24-26	71
12.10	163n.33
12.42	195n.20, 266
16.2-4	195n.20
19.1-10	71
19.9	71
22.44	135, 140n.101
24.32	259

John 171

1.1	123, 133, 215n.88, 311
1.2	295
1.4-9	104n.150
1.9	77, 197
1.14	90
1.15	145n.117
1.23-24	131n.68
3.3-5	176
3.5	86
3.19-21	104n.150
4.6	135
4.24	175n.65, 226n.142
8.12	104n.150
9.5	104n.150
10.11, 14	248n.49
10.18	140n.99
10.36	134n.81
11.35	133, 135
12.49	140n.99
14.12, 26	171n.54
14.16, 26	197
14.26	173n.63
14.28	134n.81, 140, 206, 207
15.10	140n.99
15.15	228
15.26	168
16.7	182n.86
16.12	171n.54, 173n.63
17.3, 20-26	204n.48
18.9	135
20.17	134n.81, 140
20.22	172n.58

Acts of the Apostles 171

2.3	172n.59
2.36	134n.81
2.38	296
14.15-17	98n.121
15.9	76n.39
17.22-31	98n.121
25.19	98n.121

Romans

1.7	205n.50
1.18-23	112n.187
1.19-21	98n.121
1.26	221n.117
7.6	261
2.25, 29	252
2.29	89n.83
5.20	84
6.13	259
7.6	89n.83
8.1-3	252
8.3	288n.94
8.25	175n.65
8.26	226n.142
9.16	85
10.6-8	112n.183

10.2   245n.35
11.13   296n.143
12.1   76, 83n.63, 259
12.5-6   36n.117
14.2   245n.40
14.3, 6   252
16.23   195n.20

12.13   115
13.9, 12 97
13.12   105, 106, 204n.48
14.15   175n.65, 226n.142
15.24-28 17
15.28   121, 135
28.17   112n.186

1 Corinthians

1.9   205n.50
1.17   312n.241
1.24   133
1.27   252
2.1   312n.241
2.6-7   248
2.6   245
2.10   112n.186, 260-61
2.13   259
2.16   259
3.1-3   245n.40
3.4-9, 22 36
3.9   239
3.18   252
4.1-2   195n.20
4.1   239
4.7   85
5.16   296
7   252
8.1   69
9.17   195n.20
9.19-23   244
9.22   246
10.4   90
10.33   252
12   36n.117
12.3   125, 171, 179n.77
12.9, 30 182n.86

2 Corinthians

1-3   66n.7
1.2   205n.50
3   89, 149
3.1-3   229n.149
3.2-3   264
3.6-8   89n.83
3.6   166, 261
3.18   173
5.4   259
5.17   87, 176
6.7   242
6.16   261
7.1   75, 76n.39, 83n.63
8.9   256
12.2-4   91
13.3   205n.50

Galatians

1.1   205n.50
3.24   239
4.2   195n.20
5.16   252

Ephesians

1.10   195n.20
2.22   261

INDEX TO BIBLICAL CITATIONS   401

3.2	195n.20
3.9	195n.20
4.4, 15-16	36n.117
4.14	245n.37
4.22-24	84
4.24	87
5.22, 25	252
6.1-4	252
6.5-9	252

Philippians

1.23b-24	80, 80n.55
2.5-11	126n.52
2.6	311
2.7, 8	135
2.7	133, 239, 288n.94, 295, 296n.146
2.8	256
2.15	vi
3.7	249n.51
3.21	71
4.7	97
4.13	245n.41

Colossians

1.25	195n.20
2.9	221n.116
2.19	245n.41
3.5	71, 83

1 Timothy

1.4	195n.20
5.21	281, 284n.62
6.16	103

2 Timothy

2.21	76n.39
3.8	245n.36
4.8	184

Titus

1.7	195n.20
2.1	67

Hebrews

1.3	104n.150
2.4	182n.86
2.14	239
5.7	140n.101
5.8	135, 140n.100
5.12-14	245n.40
5.14	248
9.14	76n.39
12.2	126n.52, 239
12.18	106
13.30	248n.49

James

1.1	205n.50

1 Peter

1.3	205n.50
3.4	244

4.10	195n.20	1.15	103
5.4	248n.49	3.2	121n.33
		3.2-3	75
		4.2-3	125

2 Peter

1.4	221n.117

Revelation

1 John

		10.1	104n.154
		12.1	104n.154
1.1	215n.88	14.6	170
1.5	104n.150	19.7	104n.154

Printed in Great Britain
by Amazon